Strategic Information Management

Strategic Information Management

Challenges and strategies in managing information systems

Third edition

Robert D. Galliers and Dorothy E. Leidner

ELSEVIER
BUTTERWORTH
HEINEMANN

AMSTERDAM BOSTON HEIDELBERG LONDON NEW YORK OXFORD
PARIS SAN DIEGO SAN FRANCISCO SINGAPORE SYDNEY TOKYO

Elsevier Butterworth-Heinemann
Linacre House, Jordan Hill, Oxford OX2 8DP
200 Wheeler Road, Burlington, MA 01803

First published 1994
Second edition 1999
Third edition 2003
Reprinted 2003, 2004

British Library Cataloguing in Publication Data
A catalogue record for this book is available from the British Library

Library of Congress Cataloging in Publication Data
A catalogue record for this book is available from the Library of Congress

ISBN 0 7506 5619 0

For information on all Butterworth-Heinemann publications visit our
web site at www.bh.com

Composition by Genesis Typesetting Limited, Rochester, Kent
Printed and bound in Great Britain by Biddles Ltd, *www.biddles.co.uk*

Contents

Contributors*

B. S. H. Baker, Virgin Direct, UK (formerly Research Fellow in Business Innovation and Information Systems Strategies, Warwick Business School, Coventry, UK)

I. Benbasat, University of British Columbia, Vancouver, British Columbia, Canada

R. I. Benjamin, Robert Benjamin Consultants, Rochester, New York and School of Information Studies, Syracuse University, New York, USA

G. Bowles, Storage Dimensions, Milpitas, California, USA

T. H. Clark, Hong Kong University of Science and Technology, Hong Kong, China

M. J. Earl, London Business School, UK (formerly with Oxford Institute of Information Management, Templeton College, Oxford University, UK)

O. A. El Sawy, University of Southern California, Los Angeles, California, USA

R. D. Galliers, London School of Economics, London, UK and Bentley College, Waltham, Massachusetts, USA (formerly with Warwick Business School, Coventry, UK)

T. Goles, University of Houston, Houston, Texas, USA

R. Hirschheim, University of Houston, Houston, Texas, USA

G. P. Huber, University of Texas at Austin, Texas, USA

Z. Irani, Brunel University, Uxbridge, UK

J. Karimi, University of Colorado, Denver, Colorado, USA

B. R. Konsynski, Emory University, Atlanta, Georgia, USA (formerly with Harvard Business School, Boston, Massachusetts, USA)

R. Lambert, Cranfield School of Management, Bedford, UK

A. L. Lederer, University of Kentucky, Lexington, Kentucky, USA (formerly with Oakland University, Rochester, Michigan, USA)

H. G. Lee, Hong Kong University of Science and Technology, Hong Kong, China

---

* Where a contributor's institution has changed since publication of their article, both their current and former affiliations are listed.

D. E. Leidner, Baylor University, Waco, Texas, USA (formerly with INSEAD, Fontainebleau, France)

S. Lester, Lloyd's Register, London and Oxford Institute of Information Management, Templeton College, Oxford University, UK

P. E. D. Love, Australian Agile Construction Initiative, Australia

M. L. Markus, Bentley College, Waltham, Massachusetts, USA (formerly with Claremont Graduate School, Claremont, California, USA)

P. C. Palvia, University of Memphis, Tennessee, USA

S. C. Palvia, Long Island University, New York, USA

B. T. Pentland, Michigan State University, Michigan, USA

J. Peppard, Cranfield School of Management, Bedford, UK

K. G. van der Poel, Tilburg University, Tilburg, The Netherlands

M. E. Porter, Harvard Business School, Boston, Massachusetts, USA

B. H. Reich, Simon Fraser University, Vancouver, British Columbia, Canada

P. M. A. Ribbers, Tilburg University, Tilburg, The Netherlands

R. Sabherwal, University of Missouri, St Louis, Missouri, USA

V. Sethi, College of Business Administration, University of Oklahoma, Norman, Oklahoma, USA

M. T. Smits, Tilburg University, Tilburg, The Netherlands.

E. K. Somogyi, The Farrindon Partnership, London, UK (formerly with PA Computers & Telecommunications)

A. R. Sutherland, Ess Consulting, Perth, Western Australia (formerly with Corporate Systems Planning)

L. P. Willcocks, Warwick Business School, Coventry, UK (formerly with Oxford Institute of Information Management, Templeton College, Oxford University, UK and Erasmus University, Rotterdam, The Netherlands)

Preface

As with the first and second editions, this third edition of *Strategic Information Management: Challenges and strategies in managing information systems* aims to present the many complex and inter-related issues associated with the management of information systems, with a likely audience of MBA or other Master's level students and senior undergraduate students taking a course in strategic information management or something similar. Students embarking on research in this area should find the book of particular help in providing a rich source of material reflecting recent thinking on many of the key issues facing executives in information systems management. And like the first two editions, this third does not aspire to familiarize the reader with the underlying technology components of information systems nor enlighten the reader on expected trends in emerging technologies. While the second edition was a large departure from the first in the organization and readings, the third edition follows the same framework presented in the second edition while updating the chapters as much as possible. We will briefly recapture the organizing framework for those not familiar with the second edition.

The concept of 'strategic information management' conveys manifold images, such as the strategic use of information systems, strategic information systems planning, strategic information systems . . . Our conceptualization of the term, and hence of the scope of the book, is presented in Figure 0.1.

The inner circle of the figure depicts the information systems (IS) strategy. Whether explicitly articulated, or not[1] as appears to be frequently the case (Reich and Benbasat, 1996), without an IS strategy, the achievements of the IS in any given organization are likely to be more a result of hap and circumstance than a carefully guided intentional objective. Three of the dimensions of IS strategy proferred in Galliers (1991), drawing from Earl (1989), form the major topics of the readings in the first section of the book – information, information technology (IT), and information management strategy, and the related change management strategy.

[1] See also Ciborra *et al.* (2000).

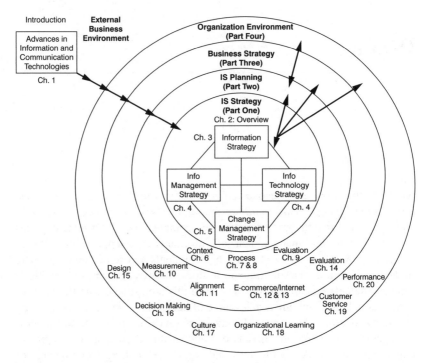

Figure 0.1 *Conceptualizing strategic information management*

The second circle in Figure 0.1, encompassing that of the IS strategy, depicting IS Planning, forms the basis of the second section of the book. While the literature often associates Strategic IS Planning with IS strategy, we consider the topics as two: the plan produces the strategy. Included under the umbrella of IS planning are considerations of the IS planning environment, of the major issues of importance to IS planners, of the principal approaches used in developing IS plans, and of the evaluation of the success of IS.

The third circle in Figure 0.1 naturally forms the third section of the book, which considers the link between an organization's IS strategy (the inner circle) and the organization's business strategy. Because of the common substitution of IS planning for IS strategy in the literature, it was difficult to find articles that dealt explicitly with an IS strategy component as conceptualized in our figure. The topics forming this third section include two readings on IS-Business alignment, two readings concerned with eBusiness Strategies, and one reading concerned with the evaluation of IT proposals. Four of these chapters are new to this edition.

The outermost circle depicts the fourth and final section of the book, which offers some readings that examine the organizational outcomes of IS. The articles in this section deal less with IS strategy as the underlying basis but with IS and their impact on the organization. The reason behind the inclusion of this fourth section is that, ultimately, the aim of introducing IS into organizations is to have positive results on the organization. These articles consider the relationships of IT to organizational structure, organizational design, organizational culture, organizational communication and decision making, organizational learning, customer relationships, and organizational performance. Two new chapters in Part Four are included in this edition.

The specific readings included in each section will be briefly summarized in the section introductions and hence will not be introduced here. Some of the articles included are marked by an academic quality. It might be helpful to suggest students prepare an analysis of the article using the following basic questions: (1) The research question: what is the major question and why is it important? (2) The assumptions: what are some of the primary assumptions guiding the study and are these valid in today's context? (3) The method: what method was used to investigate the questions (interviews, surveys, experiments, other) and how might the method have influenced, for better or worse, the results? (4) The results: what were the major findings, what was new, interesting, or unexpected in the findings and what are the implications of the findings for today's IT manager?

Following each article, we offer some questions that could serve as points of departure for classroom discussion. We recommend additional readings relevant to the chapters in the section introductions. What we have attempted to achieve is to cover some of the more important aspects of each topic, while at the same time providing references to other important work.

The subject of strategic information management is diverse and complex. It is not simply concerned with technological issues – far from it in fact. The subject domain incorporates aspects of strategic management, globalization, the management of change and human/cultural issues which may not at first sight have been considered as being directly relevant in the world of information technology. Experience, often gained as a result of very expensive mistakes (for example, the London Stock Exchange's ill-fated Taurus System), informs us that without due consideration to the kind of issues introduced in this book, these mistakes are likely to continue.

In selecting readings for this edition with the objective of covering the topics introduced in Figure 0.1, we noticed that the majority of new work dealt with topics covered in the third and fourth sections. We were unable to find many new ideas about IS strategy *per se* or about IS planning *per se*.[2] However, we found many new ideas concerning the IS–Business Strategy relationship as well as the relationship of IS to organizational outcomes.

---

[2] A Special Issue of the *Journal of Strategic Information Systems* is planned, designed to fill this gap.

We attempted to include as many new readings of high calibre without unduly increasing the page length. We were particularly happy to note the new articles on alignment. In the second edition, we had observed much talk about alignment but little research on the nature of the link. This gap has been filled with fascinating work by Reich and Benbasat (Chapter 10) and by Sabherwal, Hirschheim, and Goles (Chapter 11).

We hope the third edition has built upon the framework offered in the second and introduces some additional current thinking to help you consider some of the many ways that IS can contribute to organizations.

Bob Galliers and Dorothy Leidner

References

Ciborra, C. U. and Associates (2000). *From Control to Drift: The Dynamics of Corporate Information Infrastructures*, Oxford University Press, Oxford.

Earl, M. J. (1989). *Management Strategies for Information Technology*, Prentice Hall, London.

Galliers, R. D. (1991). Strategic information systems planning: myths, reality, and guidelines for successful implementation. *European Journal of Information Systems*, **1**(1), 55–64.

Reich, B. H. and Benbasat, I. (1996). Measuring the linkage between business and information technology objectives, *MIS Quarterly*, **20**(1), 55–81.

Introduction: The Emergence of Information Technology as a Strategic Issue

Although information systems of some form or another have been around since the beginning of time, information technology (IT) is a relative newcomer to the scene. The facilities provided by such technology have had a major impact on individuals, organizations and society. There are few companies that can afford the luxury of ignoring IT and few individuals who would prefer to be without it . . . despite its occasional frustrations and the fears it sometimes invokes.

An organization may regard IT as a 'necessary evil', something that is needed in order to stay in business, while others may see it as a major source of strategic opportunity, seeking proactively to identify how IT-based information systems can help them gain a competitive edge. Regardless of the stance taken, once an organization embarks on an investment of this kind there is little opportunity for turning back.

As IT has become more powerful and relatively cheaper, its use has spread throughout organizations at a rapid rate. Different levels in the management hierarchy are now using IT where once its sole domain was at the operational level. The aim now is not only to improve efficiency but also to improve business effectiveness and to manage organizations more strategically. As the managerial tasks become more complex, so the nature of the required information systems (IS) changes – from structured, routinized support to *ad hoc*, unstructured, complex enquiries at the highest levels of management.

IT, however, not only has the potential to change the way an organization works but also the very nature of its business (see, for example, Galliers and Baets, 1998). Through the use of IT to support the introduction of electronic markets, buying and selling can be carried out in a fraction of the time, disrupting the conventional marketing and distribution channels (Malone *et al.*, 1989; Holland, 1998). Electronic data interchange (EDI) not only speeds up transactions but allows subscribers to be confident in the accuracy of information being received from suppliers/buyers and to reap the benefits of cost reductions through automated reordering processes. On a more strategic level, information may be passed from an organization to its suppliers or customers in order to gain or provide a better service (Cash, 1985). Providing a better service to its customers than its competitors may provide the differentiation required to stay ahead of the competition in the short term. Continual improvements to the service may enable the organization to gain a longer-term advantage and remain ahead.

The rapid change in IT causes an already uncertain business environment to be even more unpredictable. Organizations' ability to identify the relevant information needed to make important decisions is crucial, since the access to data used to generate information for decision making is no longer restricted by the manual systems of the organization. IT can record, synthesize, analyse and disseminate information quicker than at any other time in history. Data can be collected from different parts of the company and its external environment and brought together to provide relevant, timely, concise and precise information at all levels of the organization to help it become more efficient, effective and competitive.

Information can now be delivered to the right people at the right time, thus enabling well-informed decisions to be made. Previously, due to the limited information-gathering capability of organizations, decision makers could seldom rely on up-to-date information but instead made important decisions based on past results and their own experiene. This no longer needs to be the case. With the right technology in place to collect the necessary data automatically, up-to-date information can be accessed whenever the need arises. This is the informating quality of IT about which Zuboff (1988) writes so eloquently.

With the use of IT, as with most things, comes the possibility of abuse. Data integrity and security is of prime importance to ensure validity and privacy of the information being held. Managing the information involves identifying *what* should be kept, *how* it should be organized, *where* it should be held and *who* should have access to it. The quality of this management will dictate the quality of the decisions being taken and ultimately the organization's survival.

With the growth in the usage of IT to support information provision within organizations, the political nature of information has come into sharper focus. Gatekeepers of information are powerful people; they can decide when and if to convey vital information, and to whom. They are likely to be either highly respected, or despised for the power that they have at their fingertips.

Such gatekeepers have traditionally been middle managers in organizations. Their role has been to facilitate the flow of information between higher and lower levels of management. With the introduction of IT such information can now be readily accessed by those who need it (if the right IT infrastructure is in place) at any time. It is not surprising then that there is resistance to the introduction of IT when it has the potential of changing the balance of power within organizations. Unless the loss in power, through the freeing up of information, is substituted by something of equal or more value to the individuals concerned then IT implementations may well be subject to considerable obstruction.

Developments in IT have caused revolutionary changes not only for individual organizations but for society in general. In order to understand the situation we now find ourselves in with respect to IT, it is as well to reflect on their developments. This is the subject matter of Chapter 1. Written by Somogyi and Galliers, it describes how the role of IT has changed in business and how organizations have reacted to this change. They attempt, retrospectively, to identify major transition points in organizations' usage of IT in order to provide a chronicle of events, placing today's developments in a historical context. The chapter charts the evolution of the technology itself, the types of application used by organizations, the role of the DP/IS function and the change in the methods of system development. Such histories are not merely academic exercises, they can serve as a foundation for future progress, allowing organizations to avoid past mistakes and to build on their successes. A postscript has been added in order to bring the original article up to date, listing a number of key applications that have appeared over the past decade or so.

References

Cash, J. I. (1985) Interorganizational systems: an information society opportunity or threat. *The Information Society*, **3**(3), 199–228.

Galliers, R. D. and Baets, W. R. J. (1998) *Information Technology and Organizational Transformation: Information for the 21st Century Organization*, Wiley, Chichester.

Holland, C. (ed.) (1998) Special edition on electronic commerce. *Journal of Strategic Information Systems*, **7**(3), September.

Malone, T. W., Yates, J. and Benjamin, R. I. (1989) The logic of electronic markets. *Harvard Business Review*, May–June, 166–172.

Zuboff, S. (1988) *In the Age of the Smart Machine: The Future of Work and Power*, Butterworth-Heinemann, Oxford.

1 Developments in the Application of Information Technology in Business

Information technology in business: from data processing to strategic information systems

E. K. Somogyi and R. D. Galliers

Introduction

Computers have been used commercially for over three decades now, in business administration and for providing information. The original intentions, the focus of attention in (what was originally called) data processing and the nature of the data processing effort itself have changed considerably over this period. The very expression describing the activity has changed from the original 'data processing', through 'management information' to the more appropriate 'information processing'.

A great deal of effort has gone into the development of computer-based information systems since computers were first put to work automating clerical functions in commercial organizations. Although it is well known now that supporting businesses with formalized systems is not a task to be taken lightly, the realization of how best to achieve this aim was gradual. The change in views and approaches and the shift in the focus of attention have been caused partly by the rapid advancement in the relevant technology. But the changed attitudes that we experience today have also been caused by the good and bad experiences associated with using the technology of the day. In recent years two other factors have contributed to the general change in attitudes. As more coherent information was made available through the use of computers, the general level of awareness of information needs grew. At the same time the general economic trends, especially the rise in labour cost, combined with the favourable price trends of computer-related technology, appeared to have offered definite advantages in using computers and automated systems. Nevertheless this assumed potential of the technology has not always been realized.

This chapter attempts to put into perspective the various developments (how the technology itself changed, how we have gone about developing information systems, how we have organized information systems support services, how the role of systems has changed, etc.), and to identify trends and key turning points in the brief history of computing. Most importantly, it aims to clarify what has really happened, so that one is in a better position to understand this seemingly complex world of information technology and the developments in its application, and to see how it relates to our working lives. One word of warning, though. In trying to interpret events, it is possible that we might give the misleading impression that things developed smoothly. They most often did not. The trends we now perceive were most probably imperceptible to those involved at the time. To them the various developments might have appeared mostly as unconnected events which merely added to the complexity of information systems.

The early days of data processing

Little if any commercial applications of computers existed in the early 1950s when computers first became available. The computer was hailed as a mammoth calculating machine, relevant to scientists and code-breakers. It was not until the second and third generation of computers appeared on the market that commercial computing and data processing emerged on a large scale. Early commercial computers were used mainly to automate the routine clerical work of large administrative departments. It was the economies of large-scale administrative processing that first attracted the attention of the system developers. The cost of early computers, and later the high cost of systems development, made any other type of application economically impossible or very difficult to justify.

These first systems were batch systems using fairly limited input and output media, such as punched cards, paper-tape and printers. Using computers in this way was in itself a major achievement. The transfer of processing from unit record equipment such as cards allowed continuous batch-production runs on these expensive machines. This was sufficient economic justification and made the proposition of having a computer in the first place very viable indeed. Typical of the systems developed in this era were payroll and general ledger systems, which were essentially integrated versions of well-defined clerical processes.

Selecting applications on such economical principles had side-effects on the systems and the resulting application portfolio. Systems were developed with little regard to other, possibly related, systems and the systems portfolio of most companies became fragmented. There was usually a fair amount of duplication present in the various systems, mainly caused by the duplication of interrelated data. Conventional methods that evolved on the basis of practical experience with developing computing systems did not ease this situation. These early methods concentrated on making the computer work, rather than on rationalizing the processes they automated.

A parallel but separate development was the increasing use of operational research (OR) and management science (MS) techniques in industry and commerce. Although the theoretical work on techniques such as linear and non-linear programming, queueing theory, statistical inventory control, PERT-CPM, statistical decision theory, and so on, was well established prior to 1960, surveys indicated a burgeoning of OR and MS activity in industry in the United States and Europe during the 1960s. The surge in industrial and academic work in OR and MS was not unrelated to the presence and availability of ever more powerful and reliable computers.

In general terms, the OR and MS academics and practitioners of the 1960s were technically competent, enthusiastic and confident that their discipline would transform management from an art to a science. Another general remark that can fairly be made about this group, with the wisdom of hindsight, is that they were naive with respect to the behavioural and organizational aspects of their work. This fact unfortunately saw many enthusiastic and well-intentioned endeavours fail quite spectacularly, setting OR and MS into unfortunate disrepute which in many cases prohibited necessary reflection and reform of the discipline (Galliers and Marshall, 1985).

Data processing people, at the same time, started developing their own theoretical base for the work they were doing, showing signs that a new profession was in the making. The different activities that made up the process of system development gained recognition and, as a result, systems analysis emerged as a key activity, different from O&M and separate from programming. Up to this point, data processing people possessed essentially two kinds of specialist knowledge, that of computer hardware and programming. From this point onwards, a separate professional – the systems analyst – appeared, bringing together some of the OR, MS and O&M activities hitherto performed in isolation from system development.

However, the main focus of interest was making those operations which were closely associated with the computer as efficient as possible. Two important developments resulted. First, programming (i.e. communicating to the machine the instructions that it needed to perform) had to be made less cumbersome. A new generation of programming languages emerged, with outstanding examples such as COBOL and FORTRAN. Second, as jobs for the machine became plentiful, development of special operating software became necessary, which made it possible to utilize computing power better.

Concepts such as multi-programming, time-sharing and time-slicing started to emerge and the idea of a complex large operating system, such as the IBM 360 OS, was born.

New facilities made the use of computers easier, attracting further applications which in turn required more and more processing power, and this vicious circle became visible for the first time. The pattern was documented, in a lighthearted manner, by Grosch's law (1953). In simple terms it states that the power of a computer installation is proportional to the square of its cost. While this was offered as a not-too-serious explanation for the rising cost of computerization, it was quickly accepted as a general rule, fairly representing the realities of the time.

The first sign of maturity

Computers quickly became pervasive. As a result of improvements in system software and hardware, commercial systems became efficient and reliable, which in turn made them more widespread. By the late 1960s most large corporations had acquired big mainframe computers. The era was characterized by the idea that 'large was beautiful'. Most of these companies had large centralized installations operating remotely from their users and the business.

Three separate areas of concern emerged. First, business started examining seriously the merits of introducing computerized systems. Systems developed in this period were effective, given the objectives of automating clerical labour. But the reduction in the number of moderately paid clerks was more than offset by the new, highly-paid class of data processing professionals and the high cost of the necessary hardware. In addition, a previously unexpected cost factor, that of maintenance, started eating away larger and larger portions of the data processing budget. The remote 'ivory tower' approach of the large data processing departments made it increasingly difficult for them to develop systems that appealed to the various users. User dissatisfaction increased to frustration point as a result of inflexible systems, overly formal arrangements, the very long time required for processing changes and new requests, and the apparent inability of the departments to satisfy user needs.

Second, some unexpected side-effects occurred when these computer systems took over from the previous manual operations: substantial organizational and job changes became necessary. It was becoming clear that data processing systems had the potential of changing organizations. Yet, the hit and miss methods of system development concentrated solely on making the computers work. This laborious process was performed on the basis of ill-defined specifications, often the result of a well-meaning technologist interpreting the unproven ideas of a remote user manager. No wonder that most systems were not the best! But even when the specification was reasonable, the resulting system was often technically too cumbersome, full of errors and difficult to work with.

Third, it became clear that the majority of systems, by now classed as 'transaction processing' systems, had major limitations. Partly, the centralized, remote, batch processing systems did not fit many real-life business situations. These systems processed and presented historical rather than current information. Partly, data was fragmented across these systems, and appeared often in duplicated, yet incompatible format.

It was therefore necessary to re-think the fundamentals of providing computer support. New theoretical foundations were laid for system development. The early trial-and-error methods of developing systems were replaced by more formalized and analytical methodologies, which emphasized the need for engineering the technology to pre-defined requirements. 'Software engineering' emerged as a new discipline and the search for requirement specification methods began.

Technological development also helped a great deal in clarifying both the theoretical and practical way forward. From the mid-1960s a new class of computer – the mini – was being developed and by the early 1970s it emerged as a rival to the mainframe. The mini was equipped for 'real' work, having arrived at the office from the process control environment of the shopfloor. These small versatile machines quickly gained acceptance, not least for their ability to provide an on-line service. By this time the commercial transaction processing systems became widespread, efficient and reliable. It was therefore a natural next step to make them more readily available to users, and often the mini was an effective way of achieving this aim. As well as flexibility, minis also represented much cheaper and more convenient computing power: machine costs were a magnitude under the mainframe's; the physical size was much less; the environmental requirements (air conditioning, dust control, etc.) were less stringent; and operations required less professional staff. The mini opened up the possibility of using computing power in smaller companies. This, in turn, meant that the demand grew for more and better systems and, through these, for better methods and a more systematic approach to system development.

Practical solutions to practical problems

A parallel but separate area of development was that of project management. Those who followed the philosophy that 'large is beautiful' did not only think in terms of large machines. They aspired to large systems, which meant large software and very large software projects. Retrospectively it seems that those who commissioned such projects had little understanding of the work involved. These large projects suffered from two problems, namely, false assumptions about development and inadequate organization of the human resources. Development was based on the idea that the initial technical specification, developed in isolation from the users, was infallible. In addition, 'large is beautiful' had an effect on the structure of early data processing departments. The highly functional approach of the centralized data processing departments meant that the various disciplines were compartmentalized. Armies of programmers existed in isolation from systems analysts and operators with, very often physical, brick walls dividing them from each other and their users. Managing the various steps of development in virtual isolation from each other, as one would manage a factory or production line (without of course the appropriate tools!) proved to be unsatisfactory. The initial idea of managing large computer projects using mass production principles missed the very point that no two systems are the same and no two analysts or programmers do exactly the same work. Production line management methods in the systems field backfired and the large projects grew manifold during development, eating up budgets and timescales at an alarming rate.

The idea that the control of system development could and should be based on principles different from those of mass production and of continuous process management dawned on the profession relatively late. By the late 1960s the problem of large computing projects reached epidemic proportions. Books, such as Brooks's *The Mythical Man-Month* (1972), likening system development to the prehistoric fight of dinosaurs in the tar-pit, appeared on the book-shelves. Massive computer projects, costing several times the original budget and taking much longer than the original estimates indicated, hit the headlines in the popular press.

Salvation was seen in the introduction of management methods that would allow reasoned control over system development activities in terms of controlling the intermediate and final products of the activity, rather than the activity itself. Methods of project management and principles of project control were transplanted to data processing from complex engineering environments and from the discipline developed by the US space programme.

Dealing with things that are large and complex produced some interesting and far-reaching side-effects. Solutions to the problems associated with the (then fashionable) large computer programs were discovered through finding the reasons for their apparent unmaintainability. Program maintenance was difficult because it was hard to understand what the code was supposed to do in the first place. This, in turn, was largely caused by three problems. First, most large programs had no apparent control structure; they were genuine monoliths. The code appeared to be carved from one piece. Second, the logic that was being executed by the program was often jumping in an unpredictable way across different parts of the monolithic code. This 'spaghetti logic' was the result of the liberal use of the 'GO TO' statement. Third, if documentation existed at all for the program, it was likely to be out of date, not accurately representing what the program was doing. So, it was difficult to know where to start with any modification, and any interference with the code created unforeseen side-effects. All this presented a level of complexity that made program maintenance problematic.

As a result of realizing the causes of the maintenance problem, theoreticians started work on concepts and methods that would help to reduce program complexity. They argued that the human mind is very limited when dealing with highly complex things, be they computer systems or anything else. Humans can deal with complexity only when it is broken down into 'manageable' chunks or modules, which in turn can be interrelated through some structure. The uncontrolled use of the 'GO TO' statement was also attacked, and the concept of 'GO TO-less' programming emerged. Later, specific languages were developed on the basis of this concept; PASCAL is the best known example of such a language.

From the 1970s onwards modularity and structure in programming became important and the process by which program modules and structures could be designed to simplify complexity attracted increased interest. The rules which govern the program design process, the structures, the parts and their documentation became a major preoccupation of both practitioners and academics. The concept of structuring was born and structured methods emerged to take the place of traditional methods of development. Structuring and modularity have since remained a major intellectual drive in both the theoretical and practical work associated with computer systems.

It was also realized that the principles of structuring were applicable outside the field of programming. One effect of structuring was the realization that not only systems but projects and project teams can be structured to bring together – not divide – complex, distinct disciplines associated with the development of systems. From the early 1970s, IBM pioneered the idea of structured project teams with integrated administrative support using structured methods for programming (Baker, 1972), which proved to be one of the first successful ploys for developing large systems.

From processes to data

Most early development methods concentrated on perfecting the processes that were performed by the machine, putting less emphasis on data and giving little, if any, thought to the users of the system. However, as more and more routine company operations became supported by computer systems, the need for a more coherent and flexible approach arose. Management need for cross-relating and cross-referencing data, which arises from basic operational processes, in order to produce coherent information and exercise better control, meant that the cumbersome, stand-alone and largely centralized systems operating in remote batch mode were no longer acceptable. By the end of the 1960s the focus of attention shifted from collecting and processing the 'raw material' of management information, to the raw material itself: data. It was discovered that interrelated operations cannot be effectively controlled without maintaining a clear set of basic data, preferably in a way that would allow data to be independent of their applications. It was therefore important to de-couple data from the basic processes. The basic data could then be used for information and control purposes in new kinds of systems. The drive for data independence brought about major advances in thinking about systems and in the practical methods of describing, analysing and storing data. Independent data management systems became available by the late 1960s.

The need for accurate information also highlighted a new requirement. Accurate information needs to be precise, timely and available. During the 1970s most companies changed to on-line processing to provide better access to data. Many companies also distributed a large proportion of their central computer operations in order to collect, process and provide access to data at the most appropriate points and locations. As a result, the nature of both the systems and the systems effort changed considerably. By the end of the 1970s the relevance of data clearly emerged, being viewed as *the* fundamental resource of information, deserving treatment that is similar to any other major resource of a business.

There were some, by now seemingly natural side-effects of this new direction. Several approaches and methods were developed to deal with the specific and intrinsic characteristics of data. The first of these was the discovery that complex data can be understood better by discovering their apparent structure. It also became obvious that separate 'systems' were needed for organizing and storing data. As a result, databases and database management systems (DBMS) started to appear. The intellectual drive was associated with the problem of how best to represent data structures in a practically usable way. A hierarchical representation was the first practical solution. IBM's IMS was one of the first DBMSs adopting this approach. Suggestions for a network-type representation of data structures, using the idea of entity-attribute relationships, were also adopted, resulting in the CODASYL standard. At the same time, Codd started his theoretical work on representing complex data relationships and simplifying the resulting structure through a method called 'normalization'.

Codd's fundamental theory (1970) was quickly adopted by academics. Later it also became the basis of practical methods for simplifying data structures. Normalization became the norm (no pun intended) in better data processing departments and whole methodologies grew up advocating data as the main analytical starting point for developing computerized information systems. The drawbacks of hierarchical and network-type databases (such as the inevitable duplication of data, complexity, rigidity, difficulty in modification, large overheads in operation, dependence on the application, etc.) were by then obvious. Codd's research finally opened up the possibility of separating the storage and retrieval of data from their use. This effort culminated in the development of a new kind of database: the relational database.

Design was also emerging as a new discipline. First, it was realized that programs, their modules and structure should be designed before being coded. Later, when data emerged as an important subject in its own right, it also became obvious that system and data design were activities separate from requirements analysis and program design. These new concepts had crystallized towards the end of the 1970s. Sophisticated, new types of software began to appear on the market, giving a helping hand with organizing the mass of complex data on which information systems were feeding. Databases, data dictionaries and database management systems became plentiful, all promising salvation to the overburdened systems professional. New specializations split the data processing discipline: the database designer, data analyst, data administrator joined the ranks of the systems analyst and systems designer. At the other end of the scale, the programming profession was split by language specialization as well as by the programmer's conceptual 'distance' from the machine. As operating software became increasingly complex, a new breed – the systems programmer – appeared, emphasizing the difference between dealing with the workings of the machine and writing code for 'applications'.

Towards management information systems

The advent of databases and more sophisticated and powerful mainframe computers gave rise to the idea of developing corporate databases (containing all the pertinent data a company possessed), in order to supply management with information about the business. These database-related developments also required data processing professionals who specialized in organizing and managing data. The logical and almost clinical analysis these specialists performed highlighted not only the structures of data but also the many inconsistencies which often exist in organizations. Data structures reflect the interpretation and association of data in a company, which in turn reflect interrelationships in the organization. Some data processing professionals engaged in data analysis work began to develop their own view of how organizations and their management would be transformed on the basis of the analysis. They also developed some visionary notions about themselves. They thought that they would decide (or help to decide) what data an organization should have in order to function efficiently, and who would need access to which piece of data and in what form.

The idea of a corporate database that is accurate and up to date with all the pertinent data from the production systems, is attractive. All we need to do – so the argument goes – is aggregate the data, transform them in certain ways and offer them to management. In this way a powerful information resource is on tap for senior management. Well, what is wrong with this idea?

Several practical matters presented difficulties to the naive data processing visionary who believed in a totally integrated management information system (MIS) resting on a corporate database. One problem is the sheer technical difficulty of deciding what should be stored in the corporate database and then building it satisfactorily before an organizational change, brought about by internal politics or external market forces or both, makes the database design and the accompanying reports inappropriate. In large organizations it may take tens of person-years and several elapsed years to arrive at a partially integrated MIS. It is almost certain that the requirements of the management reports would change over that period. It is also very likely that changes would be necessary in some of the transaction processing systems and also in the database design. Furthermore, assuming an efficient and well-integrated set of transaction processing systems, the only reports that these systems can generate without a significant quantum of effort are historical reports containing aggregated data, showing variances – 'exception reports' (e.g. purchase orders for items over a certain value outstanding for more than a predefined number of days) and the like. Reports that would assist management in non-routine decision making and control would, by their nature, require particular views of the data internal to the organization that could not be specified in advance. Management would also require market data, i.e. data external to the organization's transaction processing systems. Thus, if we are to approach the notion that seems to lie behind the term MIS and supply managers with information that is useful in business control, problem solving and decision making, we need to think carefully about the nature of the information systems we provide.

It is worth noting that well-organized and well-managed businesses always had 'systems' (albeit wholly or partly manual) for business control. In this sense management information systems always existed, and the notion of having such systems in an automated form was quite natural, given the advances of computing technology that were taking place at the time. However, the unrealistic expectations attached to the computer, fuelled by the overly enthusiastic approaches displayed by the data processing profession, made several, less competently run, companies believe that shortcomings in management, planning, organization and control could be overcome by the installation of a computerized MIS. Much of the later disappointment could have been prevented had these companies realized that technology can only solve technical and not management problems. Nevertheless, the notion that information provision to management, with or without databases, was an important part of the computing activity, was reflected by the fact that deliberate attempts were made to develop MISs in greater and greater numbers. Indicative of this drive towards supporting management rather than clerical operations is the name change that occurred around this time: most data processing departments became Management Services departments. The notion was that they would provide, via corporate databases, not only automated clerical processing but also, by aggregating and transforming such data, the information that management needed to run the business.

That the data processing profession during the 1970s developed useful and powerful data analysis and data management techniques, and learned a great deal about data management, is without doubt. But the notion that, through their data management, data aggregation and reporting activities, they provided management with information to assist managerial decision making had not been thought through. As Keen and Scott Morton (1978) point out, the MIS activity was not really a focus on management information but on information management. We could go further: the MIS activity of the era was concerned with *data* management, with little real thought being given to meeting management information needs.

In the late 1970s Keen and Scott Morton were able to write without fear of severe criticism that

> ... management information system is a prime example of a 'content-free' expression. It means different things to different people, and there is no generally accepted definition by those working in the field. As a practical matter MIS implies computers, and the phrase 'computer-based information systems' has been used by some researchers as being more precise.

Sprague and Carlson (1982) attempted to give meaning to the term MIS by noting that when it is used in practice, one can assume that what is being referred to is a computer system with the following characteristics:

- an information focus, aimed at middle managers
- structured information flows
- integration of data processing jobs by business function (production MIS, personnel MIS, etc.), and
- an inquiry and report generation facility (usually with a database).

They go on to note that

> ... the MIS era contributed a new level of information to serve management needs, but was still very much oriented towards, and built upon, information flows and data files.

The idea of integrated MISs seems to have presented an unrealistic goal. The dynamic nature of organizations and the market environment in which they exist forces more realistic and modest goals on the data processing professional. Keeping the transaction processing systems maintained, sensibly integrated and in line with organizational realities, is a more worthwhile job than freezing the company's data in an overwhelming database.

The era also saw data processing professionals and the management science and business modelling fraternities move away from each other into their own specialities, to the detriment of a balanced progress in developing effective and useful systems.

The emergence of information technology

Back in the 1950s Jack Kilby and Robert Noyce noticed the semi-conducting characteristics of silicon. This discovery, and developments in integrated circuitry, led to large-scale miniaturization in electronics. By 1971 micro-processors using 'silicon chips' were available on the market (Williams and Welch, 1985). In 1978 they hit the headlines – commentators predicting unprecedented changes to business and personal life as a result. A new, post-industrial revolution was promised to be in the making (Tofler, 1980).

The impact of the very small and very cheap, reliable computers – micros – which resulted from building computers with chips, quickly became visible. By the early 1980s computing power and facilities suddenly became available and possible in areas hitherto untouched by computers. The market was flooded with 'small business systems', 'personal computers', 'intelligent work stations' and the like, promising the naive and the uninitiated instant computer power and instant solution to problems.

As a result, three separate changes occurred. First, users, especially those who had suffered unworkable systems and waited for years to receive systems to their requirements, started bypassing data processing departments and buying their own computers. They might not have achieved the best results but increased familiarity with the small machines started to change attitudes of both users and management.

Second, the economics of systems changed. The low cost of the small machines highlighted the enormous cost of human effort required to develop and maintain large computer systems. Reduction, at any cost, of the professional system development and maintenance effort was now a prime target in the profession, as (for the first time) hardware costs could be shown to be well below those of professional personnel.

Third, it became obvious that small dispersed machines were unlikely to be useful without interconnecting them – bringing telecommunications into the limelight. And many office activities, hitherto supported by 'office machinery' were seen for the first time as part of the process started by large computers – that is, automating the office. Office automation emerged, not least as a result of the realization by office machine manufacturers, who now entered the computing arena, that the 'chip' could be used in their machines. As a consequence, hitherto separate technologies – that of telephony, tele-communication, office equipment and computing – started to converge. This development pointed to the reality that voice, images and data are simply different representations of information and that the technologies that deal with these different representations are all part of a new complex technology: information technology.

The resulting development became diverse and complex: systems developers had to give way to the pressure exercised by the now not so naive user for more involvement in the development of systems. *End-user computing* emerged as a result, promoting the idea that systems are the property of users and not the technical department. In parallel, the realization occurred that useful systems can only be produced if those who will use them take an active part in their development. Integrating the user became a useful obsession, helping the development of new kinds of systems.

It also became clear that a substantial reduction in the specialist manual activity of system development is necessary if the new family of computers, and the newly-discovered information technology, are to be genuinely useful. Suddenly, there were several alternatives available. Ready-made application systems emerged in large numbers for small and large machines, and *packages* became a fashionable business to be in. *Tools for system development*, targeting directly the end user and supporting end-user computing, were developed in the form of special, high-level facilities for interrogating databases and formatting reports. Ultra high-level languages emerged carrying the name 'fourth generation languages' (4GLs) to support both professional and amateur efforts at system development.

For the first time in the history of computing, serious effort was made to support with automation the manifold and often cumbersome activities of system development. Automated programming support environments, systems for building systems, analysis and programming workbenches appeared on the market, many backing the specialist methodologies which, by now, became well formulated, each with its own cult following.

New approaches to system development

In addition, new discoveries were made about the nature of systems and system development. From the late 1960s it was realized that the development of a system and its operations can be viewed as a cycle of defined stages. The 'life-cycle' view of systems emerged and this formed the basis of many methods and methodologies for system development. It became clear only later that, while the view of a life-cycle was the correct one, a *linear* view of the life-cycle was counter-productive. The linear view was developed at the time when demand for large-scale systems first erupted and most practitioners were engaged mainly in development. The first saturation point brought about the shock realization that these systems needed far more attention during their operational life than was originally envisaged. As the maintenance load on data processing departments increased from a modest 20 to 60, 70 and 80 per cent during the 1970s, many academics and practitioners started looking for the reasons behind this (for many, undesirable and unexplained) phenomenon.

It was discovered that perhaps three different causes can explain the large increase in maintenance. First, the linear view of the life-cycle can be misleading. Systems developed in a linear fashion were built on the premise that successive deductions would be made during the development process, each such deductive step supplying a more detailed specification to the next one. As no recursive action was allowed, the misconceptions, errors and omissions left in by an earlier step would result in an ever-increasing number of errors and faults being built into the final system. This, and the chronic lack of quality control over the development process, delivered final systems which were far from perfect. As a result, faults were being discovered which needed to be dealt with during the operational part of the life-cycle, thereby increasing unnecessarily the maintenance load. It was discovered that early faults left in a system increase the number of successive faults in an exponential way, resulting in hundredfold increases in effort when dealing with these faults in the final system.

Second, there are problems associated with specifications. The linear lifecycle view also assumed that a system could be safely built for a long life, once a specification had been correctly developed, as adjustments were unlikely to be required provided the specification was followed attentively. This view had negated the possibility that systems might have a changing effect on their environment, which, in turn, would raise the requirement for re-tuning and readjusting them. The followers of this approach had also overlooked the fact that real business, which these systems were supposed to serve, never remains constant. It changes, thereby changing the original requirements. This, in turn, would require readjusting or even scrapping the system. Furthermore, the idea that users could specify precisely their requirements seems to have been largely a fallacy, negating the basis on which quite a few systems had been built.

Third, maintenance tends to increase as the number of systems grows. It is misleading to assume that percentage increase in the maintenance load is in itself a sign of failure, mismanagement or bad practice. Progressing from the state of having no computer system to the point of saturation means that, even in a slowly changing environment and with precision development methods, there would be an ever-decreasing percentage of work on new development and a slow but steady increase in the activities dealing with systems already built.

Nevertheless, the documented backlog of system requests grew alarmingly, estimated by the beginning of the 1980s at two to five years' worth of work in major data processing departments. This backlog evolved to be a mixture of requests for genuine maintenance, i.e. fixing errors, adjustments and enhancements to existing systems, and requirements for new systems. It was also realized that behind this 'visible' backlog, there was an ever-increasing 'invisible', undocumented backlog of requirements estimated at several times the visible one. The invisible backlog consisted largely of genuine requests that disillusioned users were no longer interested in entering into the queue.

As a response to these problems, several new developments occurred. Quality assurance, quality control and quality management of system development emerged, advocating regular and special tests and checks to be made on the system through its development. Walk-throughs and inspections were inserted into analysis, design and programming activities to catch 'bugs' as early (and as cheaply) as possible.

The notion that systems should be made to appeal to their users in every stage of development and in their final form encouraged the development of 'user friendly' systems, in the hope that early usability would reduce the requests for subsequent maintenance. Serious attempts were made to encourage an iterative form of development with high user involvement in the early stages, so that specifications would become as precise as possible. The idea of building a prototype for a requirement before the final system is built and asking users to experiment with the prototype before finalizing specifications helped the system development process considerably.

By now, the wide-ranging organizational effects of computer systems became clearly visible. Methods for including organizational considerations in system design started to emerge. A group of far-sighted researchers, Land and Mumford in the UK, Agarin in the USA, Bjorn-Andersen in Denmark, Ciborra in Italy and others, put forward far-reaching ideas about letting systems evolve within the organizational environment, thereby challenging the hitherto 'engineering-type' view of system development. For the first time since the history of computing began, it was pointed out that computerized information systems were, so to speak, one side of a two-sided coin, the other side being the human organization where these systems perform. Unless the two are developed in unison, in conjunction with each other, the end result is likely to be disruptive and difficult to handle.

Despite these new discoveries, official circles throughout the world had successively failed to support developments in anything but technology itself and the highly technical, engineering-type approaches (Land, 1983). It seems as though the major official projects were mounted to support successive problem areas one phase behind the time! For example, before micros became widespread, it was assumed that the only possible bottleneck in using computers would be the relatively low number of available professional programmers. Serious estimates were made that if the demand for new systems should increase at the rate shown towards the end of the 1970s, this could only be met by an ever-increasing army of professional programmers. As a result, studies were commissioned to find methods for increasing the programming population several-fold over a short period of time.* Wrong assumptions tend to lead to wrong conclusions, resulting in misguided action and investment, and this seems to be hitting computing at regular intervals. Far too much attention is paid in the major development programmes of the 1980s to technology and far too little attention is paid to the *application* of the technology.

New types of systems

The 1980s have brought about yet another series of changes. It has become clear that sophisticated hardware and software together can be targeted in different ways towards different types of application areas. New generic types of systems emerged on the side of data processing systems and MISs. Partly, it was realized that the high intelligence content of certain systems can be usefully deployed. Ideas originally put forward by the artificial intelligence (AI) community, which first emerged in the late 1950s as a separate discipline, now became realizable. Systems housing complex rules have emerged as 'rule-based' systems. The expressions 'expert systems' and 'intelligent knowledge-based systems' (IKBS) became fashionable to denote systems which imitate the rules and procedures followed by some particular expertise. Partly, it was assumed that computers would have a major role in supporting decision-making processes at the highest levels of companies and the concept of decision support systems (DSS) evolved. When remembering the arguments about management information systems, many academics and professionals have posed the question whether 'decision support system' was a new buzz-word with no content or whether it reflected a new breed of systems. Subsequent research showed that the computerized system is only a small part of the arrangement that needs to be put in place for supporting top-level decision makers.

* This approach is reminiscent of the famous calculation in the 1920s predicting the maximum number of motor cars ever to be needed on earth. The number was put at around 4 million on the basis that not more than that number of people would be found to act as chauffeurs for those who could afford to purchase the vehicles. It had never occurred to the researchers in this case that the end user, the motor car owner, might be seated behind the wheel, thereby reducing the need for career chauffeurs; or that technological progress and social and economic change might reduce the need for specialist knowledge, or that the price might also change the economic justification – all factors which affect the demand for motor cars.

Manufacturers got busy in the meantime providing advanced facilities that were made available by combining office systems, computers and networks, and by employing the facilities provided by keypads, television and telecommunications. Electronic mail systems appeared, teleconferencing and videotex facilities shifted long-distance contact from the telephone, and – besides the processing of data – voice, text and image processing moved to the forefront. The emphasis shifted from the provision of data to the provision of information and to speeding up information flows.

Important new roles for information systems

The major task for many information systems (IS) departments in the early 1980s is making information available. The problems of interconnecting and exchanging information in many different forms and at many different places turned the general interest towards telecommunications. This interest is likely to intensify as more and more people gain access to, or are provided with, computer power and technologically pre-processed information.

As a result of recent technological improvements and changes in attitudes, the role of both data processing professionals and users changed rapidly. More systems were being developed by the users themselves or in close cooperation with the users. Data processing professionals started assuming the role of advisers, supporters and helpers. Systems were being more closely controlled by their users than was the practice previously. A new concept – the information centre – emerged, which aimed at supporting end-user computing and providing information and advice for users, at the same time also looking after the major databases and production systems in the background.

The most important result of using computer technology, however, was the growing realization that technology itself cannot solve problems and that the introduction of technology results in change. The impact of technological change depends on why and how technology is used. As management now had a definite choice in the use of technology, the technological choices could be evaluated within the context of business and organizational choices, using a planned approach. For this reason more and more companies started adopting a planned approach to their information systems. 'System strategy' and 'strategic system planning' became familiar expressions and major methods have been developed to help such activities.

It has been realized also that applying information technology outside its traditional domain of backroom effectiveness and efficiency, i.e. moving systems out of the back room and into the 'sharp end' of the business, would create, in many cases, distinct competitive advantage to the enterprise. This should be so, because information technology can affect the competitive forces that shape an industry by

- building barriers against new entrants
- changing the basis of competition
- changing the balance of power in supplier relationships
- tying in customers
- switching costs, and
- creating new products and services.

By the mid-1980s this new strategic role of information systems emerged. From the USA came news of systems that helped companies to achieve unprecedented results in their markets. These systems were instrumental in changing the nature of the business, the competition and the company's competitive position. The role of information systems in business emerged as a strategic one and IS professionals were elevated in status accordingly. At the same time the large stock of old systems became an ever-increasing burden on companies wanting to move forward with the technology.

More and more researchers and practitioners were pointing towards the need for linking systems with the business, connecting business strategy with information system strategy. The demand grew for methods, approaches and methodologies that would provide an orderly process to strategic business and system planning. Ideas about analysing user and business needs and the competitive impact of systems and technologies are plentiful. Whether they can deliver in line with the expectations will be judged in the future.

Summary

The role of computerized information systems and their importance in companies have undergone substantial transition since the 1950s. Over the same period both the technology and the way it was viewed, managed and employed changed considerably. The position and status of those responsible for applying the technology in various organizations have become more prominent, relevant and powerful, having moved from data processing, through management services, to information processing. At the same time, hitherto separate technologies converged into information technology.

As technology moved from its original fragmented and inflexible form to being integrated and interconnected, the management of its use in terms of both operations and system development changed in emphasis and nature. Computer operations moved from a highly regulated, centralized and remote mode to becoming more *ad hoc* and available as and when required. The systems effort itself progressed from concentrating on the programming process, through discovering the life-cycle of systems and the relevance of data, to more planned and participative approaches. The focus of attention changed from the technicalities to social and business issues.

Systems originally replaced clerical activities on the basis of stand-alone applications. The data processing department's original role was to manage the delivery and operation of these predominantly back-room systems. When data became better integrated, and more management-orientated information was provided, the management services departments started concentrating on better management of their own house and on making links with other departments and functions of the business which needed systems. This trend, combined with the increased variety and availability of sophisticated and easier to use technology, has led to the users taking a more active role in developing their own systems.

Lately, since it is realized that information is an important resource which can be used in a novel way to enhance the competitive position of business, information technology and information systems are becoming strategically important for business. Information systems are moving out of the backroom, low-level support position, to emerge as the nerve centres of organizations and competitive weapons at the front end of businesses. The focus of attention moved from being tactical to becoming strategic, and changed the nature of systems and the system portfolio.

It is evident that activity in the information systems field will continue in many directions at once, driven by fashion and market forces, by organizational need and technical opportunity. However, it appears that the application of information technology is at the threshold of a new era, opening up new opportunities by using the technology strategically for the benefit of organizations and businesses. It is still to be seen how the technology and the developers will deliver against these new expectations.

References

Baker, F. T. (1972) Chief programmer team management of production programming. *IBM System Journal*, Spring.

Brooks, F. R., Jr. (1972) *The Mythical Man-Month*, Addison-Wesley, Reading, MA.

Codd, E. F. (1970) A relational model of data for large shared data banks. *Communications of the ACM*, **13**, 6.

Galliers, R. D. and Marshall, P. H. (1985) *Towards True End-User Computing: From EDP to MIS to DSS to ESE*, Working Paper, Western Australian Institute of Technology, Bentley, Western Australia.

Grosch, H. R. J. (1953) High-speed arithmetic: the digital computer as a research tool. *J. Opt. Soc. Am.*, April.

Keen, P. G. W. and Scott Morton, M. S. (1978) *Decision Support Systems: An Organizational Perspective*, Addison-Wesley, Reading, MA.

Land, F. F. (1983) Information Technology: The Alvey Report and Government Strategy. An Inaugural Lecture. The London School of Economics.

Sprague, R. H. and Carlson, E. D. (1982) *Building Effective Decision Support Systems*, Prentice Hall, New York.

Tofler, A. (1980) *The Third Wave*, Bantam Books.

Williams, G. and Welch, M. (1985) A microcomputing timetable. *BYTE*, **10**(9), September.

Reproduced from Somogyi, E. K. and Galliers, R. D. (1987) Applied information technology: from data processing to strategic information systems. *Journal of Information Technology*, **2**(1), March, 30–41. Reprinted by permission of the publishers, Routledge.

Postscript (R. D. Galliers and B. S. H. Baker)

Since this chapter first appeared in March 1987 there have, of course, been many developments in information technology, some of which are covered elsewhere in this book, and the new era presaged in the final paragraph has most certainly dawned. Some of the most important developments occurring in the interim are discussed below. The intention here is not to be comprehensive, but to give a flavour of the kind of developments that have taken place and, more importantly, their impact on present-day organizations.

1   The *object-oriented concept* involves the groupings of data and the program(s) that use that data, into self-contained functional capsules called objects. These objects can be regarded as 'building blocks' which can be put together with other objects to create new applications or enhancements to existing ones. Unlike previous system development tools and techniques the object-oriented concept allows for *growth* and *change*. The reusing of objects for different applications will not only increase development productivity but also will reduce maintenance and improve the overall quality of the software being produced. In particular, the object-oriented concept has significant practical implementation on distributed processing. Rymer (1993) identifies four strategic benefits arising from such applications: development of distributed applications is greatly simplified; objects can be reused in multiple environments; distributed objects facilitate interoperability and information sharing; and the environment supports multimedia and complex interactive applications. It has to be said, however, that a fundamental change in mindset is required to support a move to object-oriented applications. Planning and commitment of top management are needed in the long term as returns from this approach are unlikely to be gained in the shorter term. Systems development staff must be retrained to cope with the new concept and to fully understand the benefits it can convey.

2 *Client–server architecture* is a distributed approach to the organization of the IT infrastructure in which two or more machines 'collaborate' in fulfilling a user's request. The typical scenario is for workstations to be connected to local file servers and for these servers in turn to be connected to a central mainframe. The applications are divided between the client computer (i.e. the terminal and its end user) and the server (i.e. a dedicated machine running an application). However, at this time there is no standard or specific approach that identifies how the applications should be divided between the client and the server. This type of architecture enables resources to be more evenly spread across the network, improving response time for local requests by using the user's workstation to run part of the application. Besides the increase in user productivy gained through the improved response time, client–server architecture also provides ease of use with the performance, data integrity, security and reliability of a mainframe. This enables the information to be managed more effectively and provides greater flexibility (by allowing incremental growth) and control. One of the major problems, as with all new technologies or concepts, is the problem of implementation. There is a shortage of programmers who are skilled in network computing (Martin, 1992) and there is still a question as to the cost savings obtained despite some evidence that shows a benefit larger than initially expected (Cafasso, 1993). A distributed computing architecture often requires a complete reorganization of the IS function (LaPlante, 1992) because migration to a client–server architecture normally means downsizing or rightsizing. Therefore the transition must be carefully planned. The implementation of a client–server architecture will require not only retraining end-users, systems professionals and micro-oriented staff but also the overhauling of the data networks to provide the speed, integrity and reliability required by a distributed system.

3 *Data communications* form the backbone of modern computing networks. Local area networks (LANs) allow individuals to share information, printers and programs, improving the quality and accessibility of crucial information. Wide-area networks (WANs) allow communication of information between dispersed facilities (e.g. data centres or regional offices). There are two main problems associated with data communication between LANs and WANs: security and the management of local area network traffic across WANs. Encryption capabilities, public–private key algorithms and digital signatures are used to improve security helping to ensure that the information has not been tampered with during transmission. Integrated systems digital network (ISDN) promises to provide unprecedented flexibility in the interconnection of networks. ISDN is a way of transmitting data over the public telephone network without having to convert it to sound. This allows vast amounts of data to be sent down

a telephone line very quickly and with a high level of accuracy. However, to make enterprise networking a reality requires the inter-operability between disparate computer systems and networks. Electronic data interchange (EDI) seeks to address the former while value-added networks (VANs) seek to address the latter. Communication between organizations is possible through EDI. This is the standard technique which enables computers in different organizations to send business or information transactions successfully from one to the other, reducing paperwork and costs, improving lead times and accuracy of transactions. VANs provide two main services: first, they provide connectivity between the different types of networks in different organizations, and second, they can provide different types of external information services to the organization, information that previously was too expensive and/or difficult for organizations to collect themselves which help management to make more informative decisions. The access to such external information has opened up new opportunities and threats that previously did not exist due to the cost barriers imposed by data collection. Management now not only have to think more proactively about the type of data that needs to be gathered from within the organization to make their decisions, but also what external information is available and how it should be exploited.

4   *Image processing* technology allows documents to be stored in the form of pictures or images. These images can be indexed for efficient retrieval and transferred from one computer to another. It can change the way firms support marketing, design products, conduct training and distribute information. Since image processing helps to improve work methods it can also play a key role in reengineering an organization, thereby improving customer service and increasing productivity. It has been reported that, in the UK, 95 per cent of all business information is still held on paper (Ash, 1991). Storing this information in digitized form (normally on optical disk) can not only save floor space but can reduce labour costs and the time needed to search for and retrieve documents, improve data security, allow for multiple indexing of documents and eliminate the problem of misfiled or misplaced documents. It is also easy to integrate these electronic documents with related information and, whereas paper documents must be processed sequentially, electronic documents can be processed in parallel. Ash (1991) reports improvements in transaction volume per employee by 25–50 per cent and reductions in transaction times of between 50 and 90 per cent. Other reported savings are in staff reduction of up to 30 per cent and a reduction in the storage space requirements of up to 50 per cent. Image processing, however, suffers as do all of the areas mentioned in this section, from a lack of industry standards. In addition,

there are legal issues that need to be resolved with respect to document authentication.

5 *Multimedia applications* combine full-motion video images with sound, graphics and text, and are based on the integration of three existing technologies, namely the telephone, television and computer. Besides offering users a more human interface with their data, multimedia applications enable organizations to improve their productivity and customer service through the incorporation of different types of data (e.g. video) into their organizational systems. Conferencing applications (e.g. video conferencing) will probably be the first to benefit from this technology, bringing people who are physically miles apart electronically together in the same room. The most sophisticated example of a multimedia application is called *virtual reality*. This application takes the use of multimedia to its extreme. Computer-generated, interactive three-dimensional images (complete with sound and images) are used to enable users to become embedded in the reality that is being created on the screen in front of them. Although most applications are still at the research and development stage (due to such limitations as adequate computer power and developments in networking) some are beginning to find their way to the marketplace. The opportunities open to business through this application will be vast. Virtual reality will be able to offer benefits to business in the areas of training, design, assembly and manufacturing. Products or concepts will be able to be demonstrated in a way that would normally be impossible due to cost, safety or perception restrictions. Electronic databases will be able to be manipulated by hand or body movements, network managers will be able to repair technical network error without even having to leave their chair. Employees will be able to experience real-life situations within the training environment. These are just some of the applications of this technology. However, once again, one of the main problems with development in this area is the lack of standards.

6 A major development in recent years has been related to the whole question of *electronic commerce, the Internet* and the *World Wide Web (WWW)*. While electronic commerce applications began to appear on the scene in the early 1970s – with the electronic transfer of funds – we have witnessed many innovations in the period since the first edition of *Strategic Information Management* appeared in 1994, particularly with the advent of the Internet: 'Electronic commerce is an emerging concept that describes the buying and selling of products, services, and information via computer networks, including the Internet' (Turban *et al.*, 1998). Many different technologies enable electronic commerce, including electronic data interchange (EDI), smarts cards and e-mail, in addition to the Internet. There are very few medium to large organizations in the Western

world that do not have a corporate website these days, and most are very extensive. For example, 'in 1997, General Motors Corporation (www.gm.com) offered 16,000 pages of information that included 98,000 links to its products, services, and related topics' (*ibid.*).

References to postscript

Ash, N. (1991) Document image processing: who needs it? *Accountancy*, **108**(1176), August, 80–82.

Cafasso, R. (1993) Client-server strategies pervasive. *Computerworld*, **27**(4), 2 January, 47.

LaPlante, A. (1992) Enterprise computing: chipping away at the corporate mainframe. *Infoworld*, **14**(3), 20 January, 40–42.

Martin, M. (1992) Client-server: reaping the rewards. *Network World*, **9**(46), 16 November, 63–67.

Rymer, J. (1993) Distributed computing meets object-oriented technology. *Network World*, **10**(9). 1 March, 28–30.

Turban, E., McLean, E. and Wetherbe, J. C. (1998) *Information Technology for Management*, 2nd edn, Wiley, New York.

Questions for discussion

1 What significance does the increasing rate and pace of advances in information and communications technologies have for organizations?
2 What are your predictions about the state of information and communication technologies, based on the past changes, for the coming decade?
3 Why is it important that we understand the developments that have been and are taking place with respect to IT?

Part One

Information Systems Strategy

We begin our discussion of key aspects of strategic information management by focusing on information systems (IS) strategy, the inner circle of our conceptualization of the term, reproduced below as Figure I.1, and comprising:

- an information strategy
- an information technology (IT) strategy
- an information management strategy, and
- a change management strategy.

Information systems planning, the process by which IS strategies are formulated and/or emerge, is the subject of Part Two.

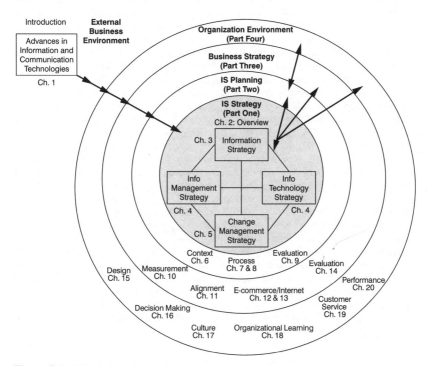

Figure I.1 *The focus of Part One: information systems strategy in context*

In our search for articles that focus on these components of IS strategy, it became clear that some aspects of the topic receive more attention than others; that there are various definitions and conceptualizations of strategy relating to information systems; that there is some confusion between the terms information systems strategy and information systems planning; and that there is little to be found on the context of IS strategy. Also, there are very few current articles focusing on IS strategy.* It would seem that IS strategy is now more important than ever, with flexible information infrastructures being a requirement for any organization hoping to grow efficiently and effectively (Ciborra *et al.*, 2000). In this part of the book, we set out to provide greater clarity as to the IS strategy domain, as well as to highlight key features and the results of recent research into the topic. Our overall orientation is to focus on the topic at a fairly general level rather than to look at the specifics, such as management of IS and the IS development process or the changing role and requisite capabilities/skills of IS managers and IS personnel generally. Useful sources of information covering these topics include Avison and Fitzgerald (1995) and Willcocks *et al.* (1997). Other important topics not covered in any depth here include infrastructural issues; sourcing IS services, and lessons from implementation failures. Useful references here include Gunton (1989), Ciborra *et al.* (2000), Ward and Griffiths (1996), Kwon and Zmud (1987), Willcocks and Lacity (1997), Lacity and Willcocks (2000), and Sauer (1993).

We commence, in Chapter 2, with a general overview of the topic by reflecting on the so-called 'stages of growth' concept as applied to IS/IT, first articulated by Nolan (Gibson and Nolan, 1974; Nolan, 1979), following Greiner's (1972) broader consideration of evolutionary and revolutionary phases of organizational development. The 'stages' model has come in for considerable criticism as a means of predicting future developments, its overly narrow technological focus, the original concept's grounding in the database technology of the mid- to late-1970s, and its lack of empirical support (e.g. Benbasat *et al.*, 1984; King and Kraemer, 1984), but its intuitive appeal to both IS and business executives is remarkably robust.

Galliers and Sutherland's original intention was to extend the earlier Nolan frameworks to counter criticisms of their narrow, and dated, technological orientation, by focusing on a broader set of strategic, organizational and managerial issues, as well as those related to IS *per se*. Their work was informed by the so-called 'Seven-S' concept popularized by McKinsey & Co., with a view to providing a closer 'fit' between IS and the business, and by a range of 'stages' models that had been developed during the latter half of the 1980s (including, e.g. Earl, 1986 and Hirschheim *et al.*, 1988). Experiences of applying the framework in many organizations since its original development give credence to the earlier claim regarding its robustness, in terms of its general applicability and time independence. Note, however, that the authors would not wish to claim that the framework represents *reality*; rather, it can be used to considerable effect in raising questions and awareness regarding key IS strategy and IS management issues across a range of stakeholders. The sociologist, Karl Weick, tells a story of a detachment of the Italian army lost in a blizzard in the Alps. After a period of uncertainty and no small amount of fear for their safety, and with no apparent means of knowing which route to take to get back to base camp, an old rumpled map is found at the bottom of someone's rucksack. A route is determined, and the group regain base camp with much relief. It is only under the brighter camplight that they realize the map is of the Pyrenees – not the Alps! Galliers and Sutherland's framework should be interpreted with this story in mind: it does not pretend to represent *reality*, but provides a means (a map) of obtaining some shared understanding as to what the key issues might be, and what might need to be done to move ahead. Further reading on applications of the framework may be found in Galliers (1991) and Galliers *et al.* (1994), for example.

---

* But see Earl (1999).

Chapter 3, by Smits, van der Poel and Ribbers, is the closest we found to an article representing our view of information strategy, as depicted in Figure I.1. Our intention was to include a chapter which focused attention on the strategic information required to enable the implementation of business strategy, *and* which would provide strategists with information that would enable the questioning of assumptions on which that strategy was based. This would include information from the business and technological environment, and feedback information concerned with the impact (both intended and unintended) of the strategy once implemented.

Smits and colleagues describe the information strategies of three major insurance companies in the Netherlands. The chapter includes reflections on the various stakeholders involved in the IS process, and on aligning IT to business goals and processes. A major finding, contrary to the above comment regarding necessary feedback information (and in our experience common to most organizations), was that none of the companies studied assess the effects of their information strategies at an organization-wide or business process level, and certainly not over time.

Chapter 4, by Karimi and Konsynski, focus attention on alternative structures associated with different global strategies and consider the need to align the information technology departmental structure with these alternatives in mind. Useful illustrations are given from various, very different, parts of the world including, for example, Finland and Singapore, as well as North America. Key issues associated with, for example, different regulatory environments and transborder data flows are highlighted. A key point that this chapter makes relates to the kind of relationship that should exist between considerations of organizational form and IT infrastructure, highlighted in the innermost circle of our conceptualization of strategic information management in Figure I.1. For further reading on transnational organizations and associated strategic management issues see, for example, Ohmae (1989).

In Chapter 5, we turn to the topic of managing change – a key feature in any IS strategy, as in any other strategy process (see, for example, Whittington, 1993). While strategy formulation (or formation) is one thing, implementation is quite another matter, suggest Markus and Benjamin! The authors focus on the role of IS professionals in the change process, their motivation being to 'stimulate IS specialists' efforts to become more effective – and more credible – agents of organizational change'. They describe – and critique – what they believe to be a commonly-held view of this role on the part of IS professionals, namely one which is embedded in technological determinism: a belief in 'the ability of *technology* (versus people) to cause change'.* Referring to the organizational design† literature, they propose two alternative models that might be more appropriate, and more successful, in the light of the rapidly changing nature and impact of modern IT: the 'facilitator' model and the 'advocate' model. As a result they propose new skills and career paths for IS personnel and IT managers, a revised research agenda for IS academics, and reform of IS educational curricula‡ to take account of the 'softer' skills necessary for the changed conditions pertaining in the late 1990s and into the twenty-first-century.

Chapter 5 brings Part One of the book, dealing with IS strategy, to a close. We trust that our treatment of this aspect of strategic information management has demonstrated just what a diverse and important topic this is – i.e. that it is much more broadly based than commonly

---

* A point taken up by Davenport (1996) in his critique of applications of the BPR concept (see also Chapter 14).

† See, for example, Cummings and Huse (1989), Schwarz (1994), Kanter *et al.* (1992) and Rogers (1995).

‡ Earlier calls for a more broadly based approach to IS education can be found in Buckingham *et al.* (1987).

assumed, often with the focus being little more than on information *technology* issues. Part Two then focuses on information systems planning, the means by which this more broadly based strategy may be developed.

References

Avison, D. and Fitzgerald, G. (1995) *Information Systems Development: Methodologies, Techniques and Tools*, 2nd edn, McGraw-Hill, London.

Benbasat, I., Dexter, A., Drury, D. and Goldstein, R. (1984) A critique of the stage hypothesis: theory and empirical evidence. *Communications of the ACM*, **27**(5), May, 476–485.

Buckingham, R. A., Hirschheim, R. A., Land, F. F. and Tully, C. J. (eds) *Information Systems Education: Recommendations and Implementation*, Cambridge University Press on behalf of the British Computer Society, Cambridge.

Ciborra, C.U. and Associates (2000) *From Control to Drift: The Dynamics of Corporate Information Infrastructures*, Oxford University Press, Oxford.

Cummings, T. G. and Huse E. F. (1989) *Organization Development and Change*, 4th edn, West Publishing, St Paul, MN.

Currie, W. I. and Galliers, R. D. (eds) (1999) *Rethinking Management Information Systems*, Oxford University Press, Oxford.

Davenport, T. (1996) Why reengineering failed. The fact that forgot people. *Fast Company*, Premier Issue, 70–74.

Earl, M. J. (1986) Information systems strategy formulation. In (1987), *Critical Issues in Information Systems Research* (eds R. J. Boland and R. A. Hirschheim, Wiley, Chichester. 157–178.

Earl, M. J. (1999) Strategy-making in the Information Age. In W. I. Currie and R. D. Galliers (eds), *op. cit.*, 161–174.

Galliers, R. D. (1991) Strategic information systems planning: myths, realities and guidelines for successful implementation, *European Journal of Information Systems*, **1**(1), 55–64.

Galliers, R. D., Pattison, E. M. and Reponen, T. (1994) Strategic information systems planning workshops: lessons from three cases. *International Journal of Information Management*, **14**, 51–66.

Gibson, R. and Nolan, D. (1974) Managing the four stages of EDP growth. *Harvard Business Review*, **52**(1), January–February.

Greiner, L. E. (1972) Evolution and revolution as organizations grow. *Harvard Business Review*, **50**(4), July–August.

Gunton, T. (1989) *Infrastructure: Building a Framework for Corporate Information Handling*, Prentice Hall, New York.

Hirschheim, R. A., Earl, M. J., Feeny, D. and Lockett, M. (1988) An exploration into the management of the information systems function: key issues and an evolutionary model. *Proceedings: Information Technology Management for Productivity and Strategic Advantage*, IFIP TC8 Open Conference, Singapore, March.

Kanter, R. M., Stein, B. A. and Jick, T. D. (1992) *The Challenge of Organizational Change: How Companies Experience It and Leaders Guide It*, Free Press, New York.

King, J. and Kraemer, K. (1984) Evolution and organizational information systems: an assessment of Nolan's stage model. *Communications of the ACM*, **27**(5), May.

Kwon, T. H. and Zmud, R. W. (1987) Unifying the fragmented models of information systems implementation. In R. J. Boland and R. A. Hirschheim (eds), (1987), *op cit.*, 227–251.

Lacity, M. C. and Willcocks, L. P. (2000) *Global IT Outsourcing*, Wiley, Chichester.

Nolan, R. (1979) Managing the crises in data processing. *Harvard Business Review*, **57**(2), March–April.

Ohmae, K. (1989) The global logic of strategic alliances, *Harvard Business Review*, **70**(2), March–April, 143–154.

Rogers, E. M. (1995) Diffusion of Innovations, 4th edn, Free Press, New York.

Sauer, C. (1993) *Why Information Systems Fail: A Case Study Approach*, Alfred Waller, Henley-on-Thames.

Schwarz, R. M. (1994) *The Skilled Facilitator: Practical Wisdom for Developing Effective Groups*, Jossey-Bass, San Francisco, CA.

Ward, J., Griffiths, P. (1997) *Strategic Planning for Information Systems*, 2nd edn, Wiley, Chichester.

Whittington, R. (1993) *What is Strategy? – And Does It Matter?* Routledge, London.

Willcocks, L. P., Feeny, D. and Islei, G. (1997) *Managing IT as a Strategic Resource*, McGraw-Hill, London.

Willcocks, L. P. and Lacity, M. C. (1997) *Strategic Sourcing of Information Systems: Perspectives and Practices*, Wiley, Chichester.

2 The Evolving Information Systems Strategy

Information systems management and strategy formulation: applying and extending the 'stages of growth' concept

R. D. Galliers and A. R. Sutherland

Introduction

For some time, reason has held that the organizational growth with respect to the use of Information Technology (IT) and the approach organizations take to the management and planning of information systems could be conceived of in terms of various, quite clearly defined, stages of maturity. Whilst there has been some criticism of the models that have been postulated, many view the various 'stages of growth' models as being useful in designating the maturity (in IT terms) of organizations. Four such 'stages of growth' models are described briefly below, i.e. those postulated by: (a) Nolan (1979); (b) Earl (1983; 1986, as amended by Galliers, 1987a, 1989*); (c) Bhabuta (1988), and (d) Hirschheim *et al.* (1988).

   The Nolan model is perhaps the most widely known and utilized of the four – by both practitioner and researcher alike. Despite its critics, by 1984 it had been used as a basis for over 200 consultancy studies within the USA by Nolan, Norton and Company, and had been incorporated into IBM's information systems planning consultancies (Nolan, 1984); Hamilton and Ives (1982) report that the original article describing the model (Gibson and Nolan, 1974) was one of the 15 most cited by information systems researchers.

---

* Galliers, R. D. (1989) The developing information systems organization: an evaluation of the 'stages of growth' hypothesis, paper presented at the London Business School, January 1989.

The Nolan model

Nolan's original four-stage model (Gibson and Nolan, 1974) was later developed into a six-stage model (Nolan, 1979), and it is this latter model which is most commonly applied. Like the models that followed it, it is based on the premise that the organizations pass through a number of identifiable growth phases in utilizing and managing IT. These 'stages of growth' are then used to identify the organization's level of maturity in this context, with a view to identifying key issues associated with further IT development.

Nolan posited that the growth phase could be identified primarily by analysing the amount spent on data processing (DP) as a proportion of sales revenue, postulating that DP expenditure would follow an S-curve over time. More importantly, however, it was claimed that this curve appeared to represent the learning path with respect to the general use of IT within the organization. As indicated above, the original four-stage model (Figure 2.1) was expanded into a six-stage model in 1979 with the addition of two new stages between 'control' and 'maturity', namely 'integration' and 'data administration'.

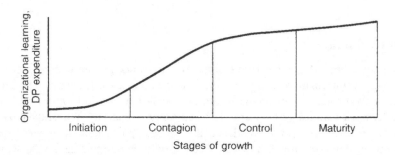

Figure 2.1 *Four stages of DP growth (amended from Gibson and Nolan, 1974; Earl, 1989, p.28)*

The six-stage model is illustrated in Figure 2.2. As can be seen, Nolan indicates that, in addition to DP expenditure, there are four major growth processes that can be analysed to identify the organization's stage of maturity with respect to IT use.

1 The scope of the *application portfolio* throughout the organization (moving from mainly financial and accounting systems to wider-ranging operational systems, to management information systems).
2 The focus of the *DP organization* (moving from a centralized, 'closed shop' in the early stages to data resource management in maturity).

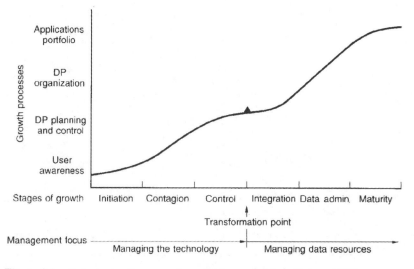

Figure 2.2 *Nolan's six-stage growth model (amended from Nolan, 1979)*

3 The focus of the *DP planning and control* activity (moving from a primarily internal focus in the first three stages to an external focus in the latter stages), and

4 The level of *user awareness* [moving from a primarily reactive stance (reactive, that is, to centralized DP initiatives) in the first two stages, to being a driving force for change in the middle stages, through to a partnership in maturity].

Nolan argues that the information systems management focus is very much concerned with technology *per se* during the earlier stages of growth, with a transformation point occurring at the completion of stage three, after which the focus is on managing the organization's data resources, utilizing database technology and methods.

As indicated earlier, the model has been criticized because it has not proved possible to substantiate its claims to represent reality, either as a means to describe the phases through which organizations pass when utilizing IT, or as a predictor of change (Benbasat *et al.*, 1984; King and Kraemer, 1984). In addition, its focus on database technology clearly dates the model. Earl (1989), for example, argues that organizations will pass through a number of different learning curves with respect to *different* ITs, as illustrated in Figure 2.3. In addition, it is now clear that different parts of a single organization may well be at different stages of growth with respect to a particular IT.

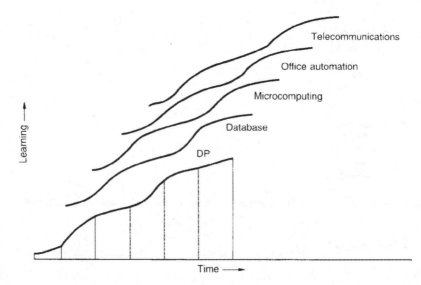

Figure 2.3   *Multiple learning curves (amended from Earl, 1989, p.31)*

The Earl model

Unlike Nolan's model, Earl's concentrates attention on the stages through which organizations pass in *planning* their information systems. First described in 1983 (Earl, 1983), the model has been revised on a number of occasions (Earl, 1986, 1988, 1989). The version presented here is based on the two earlier versions, as amended by Galliers (1987a, 1989), bearing in mind Earl's own subsequent changes. As can be seen from Table 2.1, Earl illustrates the changing agenda for information systems planning by concentrating attention on what is seen as the primary *task* of the process: its major *objective*, the *driving forces* of the planning process (in terms of those involved), the *methodological emphasis*, and the *context* within which the planning takes place. Following research on current information systems planning practice, Galliers adds to this a supplementary early stage of planning (which is essentially *ad hoc* in nature) and an additional factor, concerning the *focus* of the planning effort. In the latter context, he argues that the focus has tended to change over the years from a predominantly *isolated*, Information Systems function orientation, through an *organizational* focus, to a competitive, *environmental* focus.

Earl's argument is essentially that organizations begin their planning efforts by the first attempting to assess the current 'state of play' with respect to information systems coverage and IT utilization. Increasingly, the focus shifts

Table 2.1 *Earl's planning in stages model (amended from Earl, 1986, 1988, 1989) and Galliers (1987a, 1989)*

Factor	Stages					
	I	II	III	IV	V	VI
Task	Meeting demands	IS/IT audit	Business support	Detailed planning	Strategic advantage	Business-IT strategy linkage
Objective	Provide service	Limit demand	Agree priorities	Balance IS portfolio	Pursue opportunities	Integrate strategies
Driving force	IS reaction	IS led	Senior management led	User/IS partnership	IS/executive led; user involvement	Strategic coalitions
Methological emphasis	*Ad hoc*	Bottom-up survey	Top-down analysis	Two-way prototyping	Environmental scanning	Multiple methods
Context	User/IS inexperience	Inadequate IS resources	Inadequate business/IS plans	Complexity apparent	IS for competitive advantage	Maturity, collaboration
Focus	IS department		Organization-wide		Environment	

to management concern for a stronger linkage with business objectives. Finally, the orientation shifts to a strategic focus, with a balance being maintained in relation to the make-up of planning teams (between information systems staff, management and users), environmental and organizational information (with the likelihood of inter-organizational systems being developed, cf. Cash and Konsynski, 1985), and the range of approaches adopted (with multiple methods being accepted).

The Bhabuta model

Based on earlier work by Gluck *et al.* (1980), which proposes a four-stage process of evolution towards strategic planning, and a somewhat similar model of IT assimilation and diffusion postulated by McFarlan *et al.* (1982, 1983), Bhabuta (1988) developed a model which attempts to map the progress towards formal strategic planning of information systems. This is illustrated in Table 2.2.

Underpinning Bhabuta's argument is the contention that strategies based on productivity improvement (and the information systems needed to support them) 'will become the dominant paradigm in the turbulent and fiercely competitive markets of the next decade' (Bhabuta, 1988, p.1.72). His model is more widely focused than either the Nolan or Earl models, in that it attempts to bring together elements of, for example, strategy formulation, information systems, and the mechanisms by which the information systems function is managed. The value systems associated with each phase of the model are also identified (cf. Ackoff, 1981).

In interpreting the Bhabuta model, it should be noted that the categories used are not distinct nor absolute. With the maturing of IT utilization, and managerial sophistication with respect to IT, it can be expected that some of the attributes associated with, for example, Phase 3 and 4 organizations will emerge within Phase 1 and 2 organizations. This point takes account of some of the criticism of the Nolan model (Benbasat *et al.*, 1984), which is itself based on earlier work by Greiner (1972), regarding the discontinuities that organizations experience in growth.

The Hirschheim *et al.* model

The Hirschheim *et al.* (1988) model also builds on the earlier work of Nolan (1979) and arises from research, undertaken during the first half of 1986, into the evolution and management of the IT function in a number of British organizations. As a result of this research. Hirschheim and his colleagues contend that in companies where top management had begun to realize that information systems are vital to their business, organizations move through three evolutionary phases in their management of the IS/IT function. The three

Table 2.2 *Bhabuta's model linking the evaluation of strategic planning with information systems and the organization of the information systems function (amended from Bhabuta, 1988, p.l.76; Sutherland and Galliers, 1989, p.10)*

	Phase 1	Phase 2	Phase 3	Phase 4
Evolutionary phases of strategic planning	Basic financial planning	Forecast-based planning	Externally oriented planning	Strategic management
Value System	Meet the budget	Predict the future	Think strategically	Create the future
Competitive strategy mechanisms	Operational level productivity and diffuse innovation	Focused (niche) innovation and operational/tactical level productivity	Focused innovation and strategic productivity (quality focus)	Systemic innovation and productivity
Led by	Top management	Top and senior management	Entrepreneurial managers (top/senior/middle)	Corporate-wide employees
Application of IT/IS	Resource management Efficient operations Transaction processing Exception monitoring Planning and analysis	Effectiveness of divisional operations IT infrastructure Support key division makers	IT-based products and services Communications network Direct competitive tool	Inter-organizational IS (link buyers, suppliers, manufacturers, consumers). Facilitate organizational learning
Formalized IS and decision making	Processing of internal data	*Ad hoc* processing of external data	Systematic external data analysis	Link tactical/operational activities to external data analysis
Management of IT, location in hierarchy and scope	Technology management Individual projects Middle management responsibility	Formal planning of IS Data sharing and administration Focus on IT infusion Senior management responsibility	Couple IT and business planning IT planning at SBU/ corporate level Senior/Top management responsibility	Systemic support of organizational processes IT planning at SBU/ portfolio level Top management responsibility

phases are labelled 'delivery', 'reorientation' and 'reorganization' (see also Earl, 1989, p.197).

The 'delivery' phase is characterized by top management concern about the ability of the IS/IT function to 'deliver the goods'. Senior executives have begun to take the subject very seriously, but there is often dissatisfaction with the quality of the available information systems and the efficiency of the IS/IT function, together with mounting concern regarding IT expenditure and the consistency of hardware and infrastructure policies. It would appear that often this phase is initiated by replacing the DP manager with an external recruit with a good track record and substantial computing experience.

The emphasis in this phase is on the 'delivery' of information systems and, accordingly, the newly appointed IS executive spends most of the time on matters internal to the IS department. The primary role is to restore credibility to the function and/or to create confidence in user/top management that the function really is supporting current needs and is run efficiently. During this phase, IS education is sparse, but where it is provided, it is targeted on DP personnel with a view to improving skills, techniques and project management.

In the 'reorientation' phase, top management (or the Director ultimately responsible for IS) changes the focus of attention from the delivery of basic IS services to the exploitation of IT for competitive advantage. An attempt is made to align IS/IT investment with business strategy. In short, it is in this 'reorientation' phase that 'the business is put into computing'. With this change of direction/emphasis, it is common to appoint an IS executive over the DP Manager. The new post is filled, typically, by an insider: a senior executive who has run a business unit or been active in a corporate role, such as marketing or strategy formulation. They are likely to have only limited experience of DP, but are respected by top management for an ability to bring about change. The focus during this second phase is on the marketplace; on the external environment of the enterprise; on using IT for competitive advantage, and in extending the value chain through inter-organizational systems (cf. Cash and Konsynski, 1985).

In the 'reorganization' phase, the senior IS executive (by now the IT Director) is concerned with managing the interfaces or relationships between the IS function and the rest of the organization. Some areas will be strategically dependent on IS, others will be looking to IS more in a support role. Some will have significant IT capability, particularly with the advance of end-user computing, and some business executives will be driving IT and IS development. Increasingly IS will be managed along 'federal' lines (Edwards *et al.*, 1989) with IS capability in the centre *and* in business units/functions. These changed and changing relationships require careful management and often 'reorganization', and once again attention is focused on internal (organizational), as opposed to external (marketplace), concerns.

Table 2.3 *The Hirschheim et al. model of changing considerations towards information systems management (amended from Hirschheim et al., 1988, p.4.33; Sutherland and Galliers, 1989, p.11)*

Phase/factor	Delivery	Reorientation	Reorganization
IS executive	External IS recruit	Inside business	Same person
Management focus	Within IS/DP	Into the business	The interfaces
Education needs	Credibility	Strategy	Relationship
CEO posture	Concerned	Visionary/champion	Involved
Leadership	The board	The function	Coalition

The concerns and considerations associated with each of the phases of the Hirschheim *et al.* model are summarized in Table 2.3.

Towards a revised 'stages of growth' model

The major inadequacies of the early Nolan models relate to their lack of organizational and management focus, and the overly simplistic and subjective assumptions on which they were based. More importantly, they provided little help for the beleaguered DP manager attempting to create a successful IS function within the organization. This, as has been demonstrated, has been remedied in part by the subsequent work of Earl, Bhabuta and Hirschheim *et al.* In all but the latter case, however, the models described how an organization could place itself within a particular stage of IT planning maturity, rather than describing what is needed to be done in order to progress through to the more mature stages of growth.

The models that have been discussed thus far describe elements (technical, managerial and organizational) in the growth of 'computing' within an organization. Were these to be arranged and combined with a structure describing the important elements of an organization generally, then a model depicting the kinds of activities and organizational structures needed for an enterprise to move through IT growth stages (a more comprehensive and useful model) would result.

Such a model, dealing as it would with the growing maturity in the management and use of IT in an organization, would indicate how an organization might develop its use of the technology and its organization of the IS function. However, a means has to be found of bringing together a range of key elements associated with the operation and management of an organization generally in order that the revised model could be developed.

Table 2.4   *The Seven 'S's (Pascale and Athos, 1981, p.81)*

Strategy	Plan or course of action leading to the allocation of a firm's scarce resources, over time, to reach identified goals
Structure	Characterization of the organization chart (i.e. functional, decentralized, etc.)
Systems	Procedural reports and routine processes such as meeting formats
Staff	'Demographic' description of important personnel categories within the firm (i.e. engineers, entrepreneurs, MBAs, etc.). 'Staff' is *not* meant in line-staff terms
Style	Characterization of how key managers behave in achieving the organization's goals; also the cultural style of the organization
Skills	Distinctive capabilities of key personnel or the firm as a whole
Superordinate goals	The significant meanings or guiding concepts that an organization imbues in its members. Superordinate goals can be also described as the shared values or culture of the organization

After some considerable literature searching, the so-called Seven 'S's used by McKinsey & Company in their management consultancy (Pascale and Athos, 1981) were used to assist in the development of the model. The Seven 'S's used in analysis of organizational processes and management are summarized in Table 2.4.

Research method

As a first step, the elements of each of the Seven 'Ss' were considered in the context of each stage in the growth of IT utilization and management, according to the models described. In other words, a description of each of the 'S' elements was attempted in terms of the IT function and the provision of IT services generally, rather than the organization overall. Following a description of each of the 'S' elements in each stage of the model, an indication of what might be done to move into the next stage of the model can be provided. These indicators are based on what constitutes the Seven 'S's in the next stage.

Having produced a tentative model, it was then applied to four Perth-based organizations, and amendments made. The approach was to interview four or five senior executives from different areas in each of the organizations studied. These executives were, typically:

(a)   the Chief Executive Officer, or the Deputy
(b)   the Head of a Strategic Business Unit (SBU)
(c)   the IT Director, or Head of the IS function
(d)   the Head of Corporate Planning, or equivalent.

In some instances, for example, where the particular circumstances warranted broader coverage, more than one SBU head was interviewed. The interviews focused on the experiences of each organization in planning, managing and utilizing IT, and on their preparedness to utilize IT strategically. As a result of these interviews, the tentative model was continually refined and each organization eventually assessed in the context of the revised model. As a result of this assessment, conclusions were drawn as to what steps each organization might take (in relation to each of the Seven 'S's) in order to move on to later growth stages.

Since then, the model has been 'tested' by numerous participants at conferences and short courses, and by clients both in the UK and Australia. As a result it has been further refined.

Revised stages of growth model

The growth in IT maturity in an organization can be represented as six stages, each with its particular set of conditions associated with the Seven 'S's. These stages are described in Table 2.5.

Table 2.5   *Stages of IT growth in organizations (Sutherland and Galliers, 1989, p.14)*

Stage	Description
One	'Ad Hocracy'
Two	Starting the foundations
Three	Centralized dictatorship
Four	Democratic dialectic and cooperation
Five	Entrepreneurial opportunity
Six	Integrated harmonious relationships

The following sections describe each of the stages in the model in detail, using each of the Seven 'S's as a basis for the description. Each of the elements constitute an important aspect of how the IT function within the organization might operate at different stages of growth. The stages described are not intended to include any overt (nor covert) negative overtones associated with the early stages of the model. Some of the descriptions may appear to paint an uninviting and somewhat derogatory picture of IT utilization and management within organizations during earlier stages, especially in relation to the DP personnel involved. This is primarily due to the fact that the earlier stages tend to represent a historical perspective of how organizations first began to 'come to grips' with IT. Conversely, the latter stages are essentially a distillation of what are currently considered to be the best features of IS management as organizations begin to utilize IT more strategically.

In the past, few in the DP/IT profession paid much attention to the subtle organizational and psychological aspects of implementing and managing IT within organizations. The same could be said of management. Computing was seen as essentially a technical, support function for the most part. The situation is not quite so parlous at the present time, but some DP professionals still exhibit this type of behaviour, despite the increasing concern for IS professionals to exhibit 'hybrid' (i.e. a combination of managerial, organizational and business skills in addition to technical expertise) qualities (BCS, 1990).

Even with very aware DP staff, organizations will still display symptoms of the early stages. Indeed many aspects of the early stages, if implemented correctly, are actually quite important foundations. Correct implementation of IT during the early stages of development may well mean the difference between success or failure during the later stages of an organization's IT development. Indeed, organizations that attempt to move to later stages of the model too soon, without laying the appropriate groundwork of the earlier stages, are more likely to be doomed to IT failure.

Stage 1 'Ad hocracy'

Stage 1 of the model describes the uncontrolled, *ad hoc* approach to the use of IT usually exhibited by organizations initially. All organizations begin in Stage 1. This is not to say that all organizations remain in Stage 1 for any length of time. Some move very quickly to later stages. This may occur through pressure being exerted by a computer vendor, for example, actively attempting to push the client organization into a later stage of maturity.

Strategy

The major (only) strategy in this stage is to acquire hardware and software. Acquisition of IT staff and development of IT skills throughout the organization are for the most part disregarded by management in this initial start-up phase. There is a desire for simple applications to be installed, typically those relating to controlling financial aspects of the business (i.e. accounting systems). The 'strategy' normally employed at this stage is concerned with the acquisition of standard packages and, in many instances, external suppliers may be contracted to develop specific applications, rather than in-house applications being attempted (which would have been the norm prior to the 1980s).

Structure

There is no real organizational structure associated with IT in this stage. IT is simply purchased and installed wherever someone (usually with sufficient purchasing power) requires it to be used. As expenditure on IT represents a relatively large capital outlay for the typically small organizations currently at this stage of development, the CEO/owner is usually actively involved in purchasing. Little thought is given to the organizational impact of the IT, nor to the infrastructure necessary to manage its acquisition and use.

Systems

Any systems development that takes place during this stage tends to be *ad hoc*. Systems are most often unconnected (i.e. developed and operated in isolation). Development and operation of systems is uncoordinated, whether this is across the organization as a whole or within the area requiring the application. Systems tend to be operational in nature, concentrating on the financial aspects of the organization, rather than its core business. The *ad hoc* approach to development and use of information systems results in many being located within, and supporting, just one functional business area. Most of these systems will overlap and are inconsistent in operation and output. Manual systems are typically retained to 'backup' the computerized systems. Systems tend to cover only a limited aspect of the range of work required of the individuals within the area concerned.

Staff

IT staff typically consist of a small number of programmers. A number of programming staff may be employed, but often external contractors are used. Purchase of packaged software means that very few internal IT staff are deemed to be required.

Style

The predominant style associated with the utilization of IT in this stage is that of being unaware and, more significantly, unconcerned with being unaware. IT operates in a virtual vacuum, with almost total disregard as to how it will affect the organization, its processes and human resources. From the IT personnel perspective, the only issues that appear to be of any relevance are technical ones: nothing else is of significance so far as they are concerned. Much of this style can be attributed to the use of external contractors as IT staff. These external contractors will typically show little interest in the organization they are contracted to (they will not be there that long, and their future advancement does not depend on the organization or its management).

Skills

The skills associated with IT use tend to be of a technical nature and rather low level at that. The accent is well and truly on *technology*, as opposed to organizational, business or informational issues. Skills are individually based: while certain staff have or develop particular skills, these are jealously guarded from others. The only IT skills gained by user personnel relate very specifically to particular applications, whether this is a package or a bespoke development. Computers and computer applications tend to be so arcane that non-IT personnel find it extremely difficult to gain the requisite skills to be able to use the few systems that do exist. IT training provided by organizations in Stage 1 is virtually non-existent.

Superordinate goals

Given that very few people working in Stage 1 organizations have a clear conception of what is happening in the IT area (including the IT people themselves), it is difficult to ascribe a set of superordinate goals to this stage of the model. At best, one might describe these as being concerned with obfuscation. IT personnel typically keep whatever they may know and do hidden from those they are supposed to serve, either by design or through ignorance or misguided elitism (mostly the latter). A more unkind evaluation (although possibly a more accurate one!) would suggest that the practitioners in this stage are not capable of formulating well-constructed superordinate goals.

Stage 2   Starting the foundations

Stage 2 of the model marks the beginning of the ascendancy of an IT 'priesthood' in the organization.

Strategy

In this stage, the IT staff (for there is now a permanent cadre of such staff) attempt to find out about user needs and then meet them. This is the era of the IT Audit (cf. Earl, 1989), i.e. simply checking what has and is done, with the future seen simply as being a linear extension of the past. As indicated above, some systems have been installed in Stage 1 (typically packages), and these relate mostly to basic financial processes. Organizations in Stage 2 now concentrate on developing applications associated with other areas of the business. Although the emphasis is still on financial systems, they are now not so narrowly constrained. They are, however, still very much operational systems. No effective planning is performed, even though the IT staff may claim that they do at least plan their own work. What planning is undertaken is usually part of an annual budgetary process. The 'bottom-up' nature of ascertaining computing needs and the lack of adequate planning lead to the perception of a large backlog of systems still to be built, and demands for major increases in DP spending.

Structure

This is the first stage when a separate IT section within the organization is recognized. This section is given various names, but it is typically located under the Finance or Accounting function, as it reflects the main emphasis of IT applications within the organization. The IT section is still quite small, and provides limited services to the broad range of functions in the organization. The growth of internal IT staff usually heralds an era of reducing reliance on outside assistance. The internal IT staff now attempt to gain control of IT matters within the organization and do not usually welcome 'outside' interference.

Systems

Many more applications are developed (or purchased) and installed in the organization during this stage. Whereas Stage 1 may usually be quite short lived, Stage 2 may continue for quite some time. Early on, managers and staff in the organization begin to see computerized applications being installed after what may have been quite a lengthy period of waiting. This early delivery of applications provides an initial boost to the credibility of the IT function, thus lulling them and the rest of the organization into a false sense of security. The self-image of an important and powerful 'priesthood' is reinforced. Even though applications are being installed at a greater rate than previously, there are still substantial gaps in computerization in Stage 2 organizations. At the same time, many of the applications tend to overlap in purpose, function and data storage. Development and operation of applications is invariably centralized, spawning the development of the 'computer centre', and its attendants. Applications remain operational in nature, once again with the concentration being in the financial area, but with some other core business-orientated applications being attempted (although rarely completely imple-mented to the satisfaction of the end-user). The *ad hoc* and unprepared nature of going about building the first systems (in Stage 1 and early in Stage 2) also leads to a large maintenance load being placed on the IT section. This large maintenance load invariably leads to a growth in the number of IT staff. Usually this occurs in an uncontrolled manner, and leads, as this stage progresses, to a slowing of the pace in which new systems are developed.

Staff

This stage heralds the appearance of a DP Manager, who usually reports to the Financial Controller or equivalent. Apart from the programmers inherited from Stage 1, the DP Manager will be joined by Systems Analysts and Designers: people charged with the responsibility of ensuring that they have adequately understood the requirements of the 'user' and of designing appropriate systems.

Style

The predominant style of the IT staff in this stage is one of 'don't bother me (I'm too busy getting this system up and running at the moment)'. The pressure really is on these staff, and they show it. Their orientation is still technical. They assume that whatever they are doing is what they should be doing to assist the organization. Their job is to go about building the system as quickly as possible, and as technically competently as possible. Involvement with other staff in the organization, especially when these others attempt to be involved in building systems, is not welcomed, since users 'keep changing their minds about what they want'. In other words, the IT staff do not appreciate the changing nature of information needs at this stage (cf. Land, 1982; Oliver and Langford, 1984; Galliers, 1987b).

Skills

Rather than purely technical skills associated with the programming and installation of computing equipment, the IT staff now concentrate on skills associated with building and installing complete systems for the organization. Thus, expertise in systems development methodologies, structured techniques and the like become important at this stage.

Superordinate goals

There is now a cohesive set of superordinate goals shared within the IT function, concerned with the primacy and (in their terms) the inherent appropriateness of technological developments. The predominant situation elsewhere in the organization would be one of confusion, however. Many people are doing many things, but nobody quite knows exactly what is going on, and the whole picture of IT use in the organization is only dimly perceived.

Stage 3   Centralized dictatorship

Strategy

Stage 3 attempts to right the imbalances caused by the *ad hoc* nature of developments in Stage 1 and the 'blind' rush into systems of Stage 2. The need for comprehensive planning is recognized and embraced wholeheartedly by some (usually powerful) members of the management team (including some IT staff). IT is under central control up to this stage, but it is actually *out* of the control of those who are supposedly 'controlling' it. The answer is perceived to be in planning, and typically top-down planning. There is an awareness that many of the systems developed thus far do not actually meet real business needs. There is general recognition that IT should support the organization (rather than the converse) and as such, all IT development must be somehow linked to the corporate/business plans in a fundamentally linear manner. Thus, the overriding strategy is to ensure that a top-down, well-documented IT plan is put into place, from which future IT developments will emanate, and against which further development initiatives will be gauged.

Structure

A comprehensive DP department is incorporated into the organization at this stage. It is centralized, with all 'official' IT power invested in the department and its head (still the DP Manager). The latter may still report to the Financial Controller (Vice President Finance), but their standing in the management team will have grown slightly, although they are still treated as a technical person, and are not usually asked to participate in making 'business' decisions. Senior management have tended to renege on their responsibility to manage and control IT. This may be due to a number of factors, not the least being their almost total lack of understanding of IT, and in many instances, their unwillingness to begin to attempt to understand it. This attitude has then excluded DP staff from the organization's 'business' decision-making process, even though they may have wanted to participate, or may have been capable of making a positive contribution. The attitudes of Stage 2 are further developed in Stage 3, leaving a legacy which causes the DP Manager some discomfort. 'End users' have had some experience with IT for some time now and feel restless under the autocratic centralist regimes of the DP department. Typically, the DP Manager (and others in the department) will tend to ignore 'end users': in some instances letting them run free to do whatever they think fit (cf. Stage 1), but more likely attempting to exercise light control over any end-user developed system, with consequent ill feeling. The DP Manager and the DP department become out of touch with the 'ordinary' user in the organization, and problems in implementation and acceptance of systems developed centrally continue to manifest themselves.

Systems

Most systems are centrally developed, installed, operated and controlled by the DP department. By this stage, DP staff have implemented systems to cover most major operational activities in some form or another (they may not meet all the needs of the users, but they none the less operate in major business areas). At the same time, there are a number of systems which have been put together by end users in an uncontrolled, uncoordinated manner. These systems exhibit all the problems associated with Stage 1 developments, with the further difficulty that they have not been developed using technical expertise, and do not include all the elements that ensure a well-maintained ongoing success for the system in the future. For example, system security is a major problem here. When these systems fail (which they do regularly), the end users typically lay the blame at the feet of the DP Department and demand that they (the DP Department) fix and maintain the system.

Staff

Not only does the DP Department retain (and increase) the previous complement of staff (programmers, analysts, designers), but it grows further, with the addition of Information System Planners, and Database and Data Administration staff. Towards the end of this stage, the DP Manager may have a change in title to that of Information Systems/Technology Manager or the like. Similarly, the DP Department may be renamed the Information Systems (or Technology) Department.

Style

The predominant style at this stage is one of abrogation (or at least, delegation) of responsibility, from the DP department to other people in the organization, usually the end user. The view taken is that the latter can do whatever they like as regards IT acquisition and IS development – so long as they pay for it. The DP personnel see it as the users' problem if one of *their* systems malfunctions or fails. Similarly, the DP Manager will look to senior management for direction, requiring management commitment and guidance for new developments. Also, senior management of the organization have abrogated their ultimate responsibility for IT within the organization to the DP manager and personnel, despite the fact that they are becoming concerned about control and performance problems with IT.

Skills

Apart from the skills gained through the previous two stages, the major skill demonstrated in Stage 3 is that of project management. Those projects that are centrally instigated are normally well controlled, following strict project management guidelines. The major emphasis is to ensure that the systems that are to be built are built on time and within budget.

Superordinate goals

At this stage, the principal overriding values are those of senior management *concern* with the IT function. Senior management have seen substantial money invested in IT over the period of the first two stages and are now justifiably concerned about whether they will see an adequate return on its investment. As a result, they begin to attempt to ensure that this is achieved. The DP Department becomes defensive about adverse comments regarding how well it is performing, and often expresses how difficult it is to perform well, given the complexities and competing demands.

Stage 4   Democratic dialectic and cooperation

Strategy

The conflicting forces concerned with gaining centralized control and with the move towards end-user computing of the previous stage, has left IT in a state of disarray, with little coordination between the DP department and those using the technology. Thus, the emphasis of Stage 4 is towards integration and coordination. DP thus moves out of its defensive 'ivory tower' posture, into the real world turmoil of the business organization.

Structure

The emphasis in Stage 4 moves towards bringing all users back into the fold. In practice this means that the previously centralized DP department becomes a little more decentralized, with the addition of Information Centres, integration of Records Management, Office Automation (Word Processing) and Library Services to a group now known as the Information Systems or Information Services Department. The Information Systems (or Services) Manager (previously the DP Manager) often moves up a rung in the organizational structure (at the Vice President level or just below), and this often involves a change in title. The new title may be Information Resources Manager or, more commonly in America, the Chief Information Officer (Sobkowich, 1985). In many instances, a new manager is appointed as Information Systems Manager. The incumbent DP manager is overlooked, and is sometimes replaced (cf. Hirschheim *et al.*, 1988). The new IS Manager typically has more widespread business management experience, and may well not hail from the IT area. This new manager may come from another part of the organization, or may be recruited from external sources.

Systems

The organization now adopts a 'federal' approach to information systems management and development (cf. Edwards *et al.*, 1989). Line departments may (and usually do) gain control over the deployment of IT within their department. This results in miniature DP Departments spread throughout the organization. These exhibit characteristics of Stage 2 maturity. In Stage 4, Systems Analysts are now called Business Analysts. They know more about the business of the line department, but they perform much of the same role as the Systems Analyst of old. The Information Services Department now coordinates the use of IT throughout the organization and suggests methods which the separate DP departments should follow. Office Systems are now installed in an integrated and coordinated manner throughout the organization. Previously, they were implemented on a stand-alone basis, with no regard to integration considerations. Some Decision Support Systems (DSS) are attempted, but more often than not in an *ad hoc* manner. The organization is just coming to grips with working together with IT (rather than disparate groups pulling against each other), but a coordinated approach to DSS development through the organization is not as yet a reality.

Staff

As mentioned above, the traditional DP staff of analysts, designers and programmers are joined by Business Analysts. These staff are actually employed by the line departments they serve, but must closely interact with the rest of the DP department personnel. A higher level manager for the Information Services area is installed in the organization, usually at the Vice President level (or just below), as indicated above.

Style

The mood of the previous stage (defensiveness) has now changed to one of cooperation and collaboration. The Head of IT is deliberately chosen as being a person who can ensure that IT works in conjunction with, and to the benefit of, the rest of the organization. One of the major tasks allocated to this manager is to instil this sense of cooperation throughout the IT organization. This task is characterized by skills associated with a democracy. A dialectic is initiated and established throughout the organization for all IT-related issues. The dialectic ensures that proper understanding and cooperation are developed and maintained between IT staff and the rest of the organization. The dialectic can result in some constructive confrontation. Many IT personnel employed during the previous stages may be ill-equipped to handle this type of situation, and thus may be replaced or retrained.

Skills

The skills required of IT personnel in moving from Stage 3 to Stage 4 change dramatically. Although technical capabilities are still required, they are de-emphasized in relation to business skills, and to the overriding need for them to fit in with the rest of the organization (Galliers, 1990). Organizational integration is a major theme, with improved understanding between IT and other organization staff being the result. The IT function gradually gains an understanding of how the business works, and users finally gain a proper insight into IT-related issues. The IT function also gains some business-oriented management for its area, as opposed to the technoprofessional (isolated, defensive) attitude taken in the previous stages.

Supordinate goals

Cooperation is the prevailing attitude throughout Stage 4. All areas in the organization now attempt to gain an understanding of other areas and to work together for the common good and towards a common goal or set of related goals. This is possible only because of the intensive top-down planning work performed in Stage 3 (and carried through into Stage 4). Without the extensive and rigorous planning having been performed earlier, the gains made through the initiation of a dialectic could well be ephemeral.

Stage 5   Entrepreneurial opportunity

At last, the IT function is at the stage of coming out from under the burden of simply providing supporting services to other parts of the organization and can begin to provide a strategic benefit in its own right. The major operational systems are now in place, running relatively smoothly, and providing the opportunity to build strategic systems based on the foundations provided by these operational systems.

Strategy

The predominant strategy at this stage is actively to seek opportunities for the strategic use of IT, to provide a competitive advantage for the organization. This strategy involves substantial environmental scanning. The forces driving IT are predominantly outward looking, with internal operations successfully delegated to other managers.

Structure

Rather than comprising a relatively fixed structure, be it centralized or decentralized, coalitions are now formed between IT and business units in the organization. The 'federal' organization has come of age. Many coalitions are formed, each of them separate, but fitting within the overall plans of the organization, and driven by strategic, corporate (and subsidiary IT) plans. These strategic coalitions flow relatively freely into and out of existence, allowing the organization to respond to changing environmental pressures more readily. The necessary infrastructure (combining elements of both centralization and decentralization) has been put into place in the previous stages to ensure that these fluid coalitions do in fact operate as required, and produce results, both in the short term and the long term (i.e. from a maintenance and an enhancement point of view).

Systems

Systems are now more market-orientated than before. IT is used in an attempt to add value to organizational products and services. This factor, combined with the coalition aspect of the organizational structure in this phase, means most new systems are basically decentralized but with proper central coordination and control. Systems intended to provide a strategic advantage to the organization or to a business unit are developed in this stage. Most of these systems rely heavily on gathering and processing external data in addition to internal data. But in most instances, there is still a distinct lack of real integration between external and internal data. Decision Support Systems (DSS) for senior staff are developed and implemented at this stage. These DSS are possible only because necessary operational systems are in place and integrated appropriately. Most staff have had enough experience associated with IT to be able to specify effectively and use DSS and other Executive Information Systems (EIS).

Staff

The new role at this stage is that of a combined Business and Information Systems Planner. These people are responsible for recognizing and planning for strategic information systems, for the organization as a whole and for individual business units. They have had some years' experience, both in the business (or very similar businesses), and in the IT area (cf. the 'hybrid' concept). They may have come from either area, but are definitely cross-disciplinary.

Style

The predominant style is that of the Product Champion, the rugged individual who conceives of a good idea and pushes it through the necessary approval procedures in order to get it off the ground and working. In this case the idea is for information systems that will lead to a strategic advantage for the organization. Such systems are typically very hard to justify on a standard cost–benefit analysis basis. They require the whole-hearted support of powerful members of the organization to ensure that they are implemented (and even then, they run the risk of being stalled in mid-development).

Skills

This is the stage where IT moves out of the era of being a second string service and support unit, into being an integral part of the successful operation of the organization. The skills required to manage this transition are those of a senior executive. Entrepreneurial and marketing skills within selected IT personnel are also the basic requirements for ensuring success in this stage. Very knowledgeable IT users become quite commonplace. Successful organizations use these people to their full potential, as there is no longer any defensiveness about users acquiring in-depth knowledge about IT use.

Superordinate goals

Opportunity is pre-eminent during this stage. An entrepreneurial (as well as intrapreneurial) attitude is positively encouraged. Everyone is willing to identify and act on opportunities for strategic advantage.

Stage 6   Integrated harmonious relationships

Stage 6 is now reached, the dawning of a new age of sophistication and use of IT. At this stage, one notices harmonious working relationships between IT personnel and other staff in the organization. IT is deeply embedded throughout every aspect of the organization.

Strategy

During this stage, management is concerned with maintaining the comparative strategic advantage that has been hard won in the previous stage(s). This involves a constant reassessment of all uses of IT, both within the organization and in its marketplace(s). Cooperative strategies (strategic alliances) are also in place. Interactive planning, involving monitoring both likely futures as well as present circumstances (cf. Ackoff, 1981), is the focus of strategy formulation.

Structure

The strategic coalitions between IT and business units were somewhat separate and relatively uncontrolled in the previous stage. In this stage, however, they are now centrally coordinated (although not necessarily 'controlled' in any strict sense). An overall corporate view is integrated with the individual business unit views (both the operational and the IT viewpoint).

Systems

Building on the outward-looking strategic systems of the previous stage, IT now embarks on implementing *inter*-organizational systems (with suppliers, customers, government, etc.). New products and services may now be developed which are IT-based (rather than the technology being first a supporting element).

Staff

During this stage, the IT Head becomes a member of the Board of Directors. This is not a token measure for providing the occasional piece of advice when asked, but rather, as a full member of the Board, the IT Head will play an active part in setting strategic directions. Strategic decisions will then have the required IT element when appropriate from the very beginning, rather than as an afterthought.

Style

The style is now one of interdependence, with IT being but one part of the business team, working together towards making and keeping the organization successful.

Skills

All the skills required of a member of a Board, together with being a senior manager who understands IT and its potentialities, as well as the business, are necessary at this stage. And in keeping with the team approach, IT personnel are very much in tune with the needs and aspirations of the strategic business units with which they work.

Superordinate goals

Interactive planning, harmonious relationships and interdependent team work are the predominant values associated with this stage. The internal focus is on collaborative IT initiatives between groups, brought together to develop strategic information systems products. The external focus is on strategic alliances utilizing shared information systems, and the value chain is extended to include suppliers and customers.

This revised 'stages of growth' model is summarized in Table 2.6.

Application of the revised model

Application of the revised model in the context of the four Perth-based organizations is described in more detail elsewhere (Galliers and Sutherland, 1991). In this context, however, and in subsequent applications, the model has proved useful not only in clarifying the location of each organization in IT maturity terms, but also in providing insights into aspects of IS management and planning which appear to require particular attention. Specific insights into the model's application include the following:

1   Any organization is likely to display characteristics associated with a number of stages for each of the Seven 'S' elements. It is unlikely that any particular organization will find itself entirely within one stage. In addition, it is most likely that different parts of a single organization will be at different stages of growth at any one time. Use of the model in this context provides management with insights into areas/elements requiring particular attention.

2   Elements in early stages of the model must be adequately addressed before related elements in later stages are likely to be successfully undertaken. For instance, Decision Support Systems (DSS) or Executive Information Systems (EIS) are extremely unlikely to be effective without the right kind of basic operational systems/databases in place. Furthermore, an organization simply trying to overcome the large backlog and heavy maintenance load of systems (associated with Stage 2) is unlikely to be able to develop substantial strategic information systems, without further development in, for example, skill levels and planning approaches.

3   Organizations do not need to work slavishly through all the elements of each stage, making the same mistakes as many organizations have done in the past. For example, 'young' organizations can make effective use of top-down information systems planning to circumvent some of the pitfalls associated with this aspect of the first two stages. Typically, however 'skipping' portions of the model can only be successfully accomplished when the senior management of the organization has already experienced the conditions that affect performance in the earlier stages, and thus understand the benefit/advantages of following 'correct' procedures.

Table 2.6 A revised 'stages of growth' model (Sutherland and Galliers, 1989, p.23, reproduced in Galliers, 1991, pp. 61–62)

Element	Stage					
	1 Ad hocracy	2 Foundations	3 Centralized	4 Cooperation	5 Entrepreneurial	6 Harmonious
Strategy	Acquisition of hardware, software, etc.	IT audit Find out and meet user needs (reactive)	Top-down IS planning	Integration, coordination and control	Environmental scanning and opportunity seeking	Maintain comparative advantage Monitor futures Interactive planning
Structure	None	IS often subordinate to accounting or finance	Data processing department Centralized DP shop End-users running free at Stage 1	Information centres, library records, etc. in same unit Information services	SBU coalition(s) (many but separate)	Centrally coordinated coalitions (corporate and SBU views concurrently)
Systems	Ad hoc unconnected Operational Manual and computerized IS Uncoordinated Concentration in financial systems Little maintenance	Many applications Many gaps Overlapping systems Centralized Operational Mainly financial systems Many areas unsatisfied Large backlog Heavy maintenance load	Still mostly centralized Uncontrolled end-user computing Most major business activities covered Database systems	Decentralized approach with some controls, but mostly lack of coordination Some DSS-ad hoc Integrated office technology systems	Decentralized systems but central control and coordination Added value systems (more marketing oriented) More DSS-internal, less ad hoc Some strategic systems (using external data) Lack of external and internal data integration of communications technologies with computing	Inter-organizational systems (supplier, customer, government links) New IS-based products External-internal data integration

Table 2.6 *Continued*

Element		Stage				
	1 Ad hocracy	*2 Foundations*	*3 Centralized*	*4 Cooperation*	*5 Entrepreneurial*	*6 Harmonious*
Staff	Programmers/ contractors	Systems analysts DP Manager	IS planners IS Manager Data Base Administrator Data Administrator Data analysts	Business analysts Information Resources Manager (Chief Information Officer)	Corporate/business/IS planners (one role)	IS Director/member of board of directors
Style	Unaware	Don't bother me (I'm too busy)	Abrogation/ delegation	Democratic dialectic	Individualistic (product champion)	Business team
Skills	Technical (very low level), individual expertise	Systems development methodology	IS believes it knows what the business needs Project management	Organizational integration IS knows how the business works Users know how IS works (for their area) Business management (for IS staff)	IS Manager – member of senior executive team Knowledgeable users in some IS areas Entrepreneurial marketing skills	All senior management understand IS and its potentialities
Superordinate goals	Obfuscation	Confusion	Senior management concerned DP defensive	Cooperation	Opportunistic Entrepreneurial Intrapreneurial	Interactive planning

4   The positive aspects of earlier stages of the model are not discarded
    when moving through to the later stages. More 'mature' organizations
    will incorporate those elements from all proceeding stages to the degree
    that they are consistent with the later stages. Thus, organization at Stage
    5 will still perform Information Systems Planning, they will still have a
    DP function (of sorts) and will be likely to require Information Centres.
    The more mature organization will be flexible enough to determine
    the most appropriate nature of IT use and organization, rather than
    blindly following the structures and procedures adopted by other
    organizations.
5   To be effective, organizations should consolidate in most elements up to a
    particular stage, and then select certain key elements (in accordance with
    their own planning critiera/priorities), which they should then address in
    moving to the next stage. Indeed, all elements should be addressed in
    order to pass more smoothly on to the following stage.
6   It is not necessarily the case that organizations will develop *automatically*
    towards the more mature stages. Indeed, it has been found that
    organizations move 'backwards' at times, as a result of a change in
    personnel or managerial attitudes, see Galliers (1991) for example.
    Furthermore, it has proved useful at times to chart the development of the
    organization over a period of time by identifying when (i.e. in what year)
    each particular stage was reached.

The model has been found to be particularly useful in that it takes a holistic
view of information systems management issues, dealing as it does with the
development of information systems applications and information systems
planning/strategy formulation, the changing nature of required skills,
management style/involvement, and organizational structures. While the
model cannot pretend to give all the *answers*, it does provide a framework
which enables appropriate *questions* to be raised when setting out an
appropriate strategy for information systems, giving pointers as to what is
feasible as well as desirable in this regard.

Further testing and refinement of the model is taking place, but after two
years of application, the authors are confident that the model is sufficiently
refined to provide both IT and general management with a usable and useful
framework to assist in the task of marshalling their IT resources in line with
business imperatives.

While one might argue with the precise detail of the contents of each
element at each stage of the model, this does appear not to affect the utility.
Its key contribution is in focusing management attention onto a broad range
of issues associated with the planning and management of information
systems, in surfacing assumptions and attitudes held by key executives about
the role IT does and might play in achieving/supporting business objectives

and thereby enabling a shared understanding/vision to be achieved, and (most importantly) providing an easily understood means of putting IS/IT management on the senior and middle management agenda.

References

Ackoff, R. L. (1981) *Creating the Corporate Future*, Wiley, New York.

British Computer Society (1990) *From Potential to Reality: 'Hybrids' – A Critical Force in the Application of Information Technology in the 1990s*. A Report by the British Computer Society Task Group on Hybrids, 2 January.

Benbasat, I., Dexter, A., Drury, D. and Goldstein, R. (1984) A critique of the stage hypothesis: theory and empirical evidence. *Communications of the ACM*, **27**(5), 476–485.

Bhabuta, L. (1988) Sustaining productivity and competitiveness by marshalling IT. In *Proceedings: Information Technology Management for Productivity and Strategic Advantage*, IFIP TC-8 Open Conference, Singapore, March.

Cash, J. I. (Jr.) and Konsynski, B. R. (1985) IS Redraws competitive boundaries. *Harvard Business Review*, **63**(2), March–April, 134–142.

Earl, M. J. (1983) Emerging trends in managing new information technologies, Oxford Centre for Management Studies Research Paper 83/4. In *The Management Implications of New Information Technology*. (ed. N. Peircy), 1986, Croom Helm, London.

Earl, M. J. (1986) Information systems strategy formulation. In *Critical Issues in Information Systems Research* (eds R. J. Boland and R. A. Hirschheim) (1987), Wiley, Chichester.

Earl, M. J. (ed.) (1988) *Information Management: The Strategic Dimension*, The Clarendon Press, Oxford.

Earl, M. J. (1989) *Management Strategies for Information Technology*, Prentice Hall, Hemel Hempstead.

Edwards, B., Earl, M. and Feeny, D. (1989) Any way out of the labyrinth of managing IS? RDP89/3, Oxford Institute of Information Management Research and Discussion Paper, Templeton College, Oxford University.

Galliers, R. D. (1987a) Information systems planning in the United Kingdom and Australia: a comparison of current practice. In *Oxford Surveys in Information Technology* (ed. P. I. Zorkorczy), Vol. 4, Oxford University Press, Oxford, pp. 223–255.

Galliers, R. D. (ed.) (1987b) *Information Analysis: Selected Readings*, Addison-Wesley, Wokingham.

Galliers, R. D. (1990) Problems and answers of the IT skills shortage. *The Computer Bulletin*, **2**(4), 25 May.

Galliers, R. D. (1991) Strategic information systems planning: myths, reality and guidelines for successful implementation. *European Journal of Information Systems*, 1, 55–64.

Galliers, R. D. and Sutherland, A. R. (1991) Organizational learning and IT: steps towards managing and planning strategic information systems. *Warwick Business School Working Paper*, University of Warwick, January.

Gibson, D. and Nolan, R. L. (1974) Managing the four stages of EDP growth. *Harvard Business Review*, **52**(1), January–February.

Gluck, F. W., Kaufman, S. P. and Walleck, A. S. (1980) Strategic management for competitive advantage. *Harvard Business Review*, **58**(4), July–August.

Greiner, L. E. (1972) Evolution and revolution as organisations grow. *Harvard Business Review*, **50**(4), July–August.

Hamilton, S. and Ives, B. (1982) Knowledge utilisation among MIS researchers. *MIS Quarterly*, **6**(12), December.

Hirschheim, R., Earl, M., Feeny, D. and Lockett, M. (1988) An exploration into the management of the information systems function: key issues and an evolutionary model. *Proceedings: Information Technology Management for Productivity and Strategic Advantage*, IFIP TC-8 Open Conference, Singapore, March.

King, J. and Kraemer, K. (1984) Evolution and organizational information systems: an assessment of Nolan's stage model. *Communications of the ACM*, **27**(5), May.

Land, F. F. (1982) Adapting to changing user requirements. *Information and Management*, **5**, Reproduced in Galliers, R. D. (ed.) (1987) *Information Analysis: selected readings*, Addison-Wesley, Wokingham, pp. 203–229.

McFarlan, F. W. and McKenney, J. L. (1982) The Information archipelago: gaps and bridges. *Harvard Business Review*, **60**(5), September–October.

McFarlan, F. W., McKenney, J. L. and Pyburn, P. (1983) The information archipelago: plotting a course. *Harvard Business Review*, **61**(1), January–February.

Nolan, R. (1979) Managing the crises in data processing. *Harvard Business Review*, **57**(2), March–April.

Nolan, R. (1984) Managing the advanced stages of computer technology: key research issues. In *The Information Systems Research Challenge* (ed. F. W. McFarlan), Harvard Business School Press, Boston, pp. 195–214.

Oliver, I. and Langford, H. (1984) Myths of demons and users. *Proceedings: Australian Computer Conference*, Australian Computer Society Inc., Sydney, November. Reproduced in Galliers, R. D. (ed.) (1987) *Information Analysis: selected readings*, Addison-Wesley, Wokingham, pp. 113–123.

Pascale, R. T. and Athos, A. G. (1981) *The Art of Japanese Management*, Penguin, Harmondsworth.

Sobkowich, R. (1985) When the company picks a CIO, will you be IT? *Computerworld*, 24 June.

Somogyi, E. K. and Galliers, R. D. (1987a) Applied information technology: from data processing to strategic information systems. *Journal of Information Technology*, **2**(1), 30–41, March.

Somogyi, E. K. and Galliers, R. D. (1987b) *Towards Strategic Information Systems*, Abacus Press, Cambridge MA.

Sullivan, C. H. (1985) Systems planning in the information age. *Sloan Management Review*, Winter.

Sutherland, A. R. and Galliers, R. D. (1989) An evolutionary model to assist in the planning of strategic information systems and the management of the information systems function. *School of Information Systems Working Paper*. Curtin University of Technology, Perth, Western Australia, February.

Ward, J., Griffiths, P. and Whitmore, P. (1990) *Strategic Planning for Information Systems*, Wiley, Chichester.

Reproduced from Galliers, R. D. and Sutherland, A. R. (1991) Information systems management and strategy formulation: the 'stages of growth' model revisited. *Journal of Information Systems*, **1**(2), 89–114. Reprinted by permission of the Publishers, Blackwell Scientific Ltd.

Questions for discussion

1   The authors, in describing the Nolan model, state that 'different parts of a single organization may well be at different stages of growth with respect to a single IT'. What implications does this have for the management of IT and for IT strategy?

2   The authors describe several prior models to IT evolution in organizations. What are the relative strengths of the models in (a) their applicability to describe actual situations, and (b) in their usefulness for managers of IT?

3   Do you agree with the underlying assumption that moving through the stages represents a desired advancement in the use of IT in an organization?

4   Can you think of some contextual factors that might predict in which phase an organization would be placed regarding their management of IT and whether they move slowly or quickly through the phases?

5   What implications does the increasing pace of technology advances and the increasingly networked world have for the revised stages of growth model?

3 Information Strategy

Assessment of information strategies in insurance companies

M. T. Smits, K. G. van der Poel and P. M. A. Ribbers

This chapter describes the information strategies of three major insurance companies in the Netherlands. A research model was developed as an aid to describe how managers nowadays deal with information strategy. We report on the linkages between information strategies and business strategies, the roles of the stakeholders involved, and how the results are perceived. We found that in all three companies the executive board, IT management and line management are heavily involved in the information strategy process. The main focus in the three companies is on adjusting IT to business goals and processes, with only some attention directed towards creating a competitive advantage with IT. With respect to the effects of information strategy, we found that none of the three companies systematically evaluate the effects of information strategies on an organizational or a business process level. More case study research is required to look into the evolutionary changes of information strategies within organizations, and the effects of information strategies on the business processes and the use of IT over time.

1 Introduction

The concept of 'strategy' carries several connotations. Its roots in military tradition indicate innovative leadership and bold visions. Anthony (1965) has defined strategic planning as the definition of goals and objectives. Ansoff (1984) sees strategy as a mechanism for coping with a complex and changing environment. Mintzberg (1980) views strategy in five different ways: as a plan (rules leading to a goal); a ploy (a trick to beat competitors); a pattern (a way of behaving); a position (a safe place); and a perspective (a vision, a set of assumptions). Andrews (1980) defines strategy as: 'the pattern of decisions

... that determines ... goals, produces principal policies and plans and defines the range of business'.

In general, the concept of strategy relates to corporate strategy, which is the strategy that guides the corporation or enterprise as a whole. Business units within large organizations have business strategies related to their specific product-market situation (Porter, 1987). From corporate or business strategy derives the notion of functional strategies such as marketing strategy, manufacturing strategy, personnel strategy, financial strategy and information strategy. Of interest are the linkages between the functional strategies and the business strategies. Specifically, business strategy and information strategy can be linked in several ways (Parker *et al.*, 1989; Henderson and Venkatraman, 1993).

In this chapter we investigate whether these (theoretical) linkages exist in organizations with a substantial level of sophistication and interest in information management. We describe how managers in these organizations formulate information strategies in practice, which stakeholders are involved, how it links to business strategy, and how the results are perceived. This is done within the context of previous information strategy activities, looking for possible changes in the approach to information strategy. Our purpose is to learn how information intensive organizations make plans with respect to the demand and supply of information, and how this relates to the planning of IT. The research question in this chapter is three-fold: (i) how can the practice of information strategy in an organization be analysed; (ii) what is the actual practice in the insurance industry; and (iii) how does information strategy relate to business strategy?

After scanning the literature we decided to carry out case studies within a small number of organizations, based on interviews with both IS managers as well as general managers, in order to provide a richness in understanding strategy that cannot be obtained via a survey approach (Chan and Huff, 1992). We describe the planning process for information strategies as well as the contents of the plans, as suggested by King (1988) and Walsham and Waema (1994). A framework to analyse an organization's information strategy was derived from the literature and used to gather information from both informants and secondary sources, e.g. company documents. The following section summarizes the information strategy literature, while Section 3 provides an overview of the model used in this research. The final two sections use this model to analyse the information strategy within three major insurance organizations and compare the findings with related research, respectively.

2 Literature on information strategy

Information strategy began to attract interest at the beginning of the 1970s, and many terms have been used since then to address the alignment of information systems and business strategy. Similar terms are, for example, information systems strategy (ISS), information systems strategic planning (ISSP) and strategic information systems planning (SISP). For an extensive review of the literature we refer to Earl (1989), Ward *et al.* (1990), Galliers (1993) and Fitzgerald (1993).

A frequently used term, related to information strategy, is strategic information systems planning (SISP), defined as 'the process of deciding the objectives for organizational computing and identifying potential computer applications which the organization should implement' (Lederer and Sethi, 1988). However, Galliers (1991) views information strategy as only a part of SISP, together with information technology (IT) strategy, information management (IM) strategy, management of change strategy, and human resources strategy. Earl (1989) sees SISP as a combination of information systems strategy (aligning IS with business goals, and exploiting IT for competitive advantage), IM strategy and IT strategy.

In this study we used the term information strategy, and define it as: 'a complex of implicit or explicit visions, goals, guidelines and plans with respect to the supply and the demand of formal information in an organization, sanctioned by management, intended to support the objectives of the organization in the long run, while being able to adjust to the environment'. The definitions might look similar, but strict comparison shows that the SISP definition tends to focus on explicit objectives and on applications and technology. Our definition concentrates on the use and importance of information in an organization, starting with the planning of information (in the end influencing IT, as well as influenced by IT). Therefore we preferred this definition as a starting point to investigate how contemporary organizations deal with their needs for information and the planning of IT. The other three definitions mentioned were subsequently used to complete the research model and to develop the questionnaires, as described in Section 3.

Of particular importance is the linkage between the information strategy and the business strategy in an organization (Parker *et al.*, 1989). Henderson

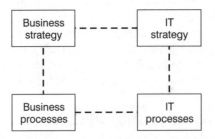

Figure 3.1   *Strategic alignment model (Parker et al., 1989; Henderson and Venkatraman, 1993)*

and Venkatraman (1993) propose the strategic alignment model (Figure 3.1) covering the linkages between four domains in an organization: (i) the business strategy domain (BS); (ii) the business processes domain (BP); (iii) the IT strategy domain (ITS); and (iv) the IT processes domain (ITP). They distinguish two main perspectives on how the alignment between the domains can take place. In the first perspective business strategy is the driving force for BP or ITS, ultimately affecting ITP. In the second perspective IT strategy is the driving force for ITP or BS, ultimately affecting BP.

We have analysed the linkages between information strategy and business strategy in several ways: by looking at the attitudes of senior managers (as a part of the information strategy environment), by analysing the information strategy process (with roles, methods and coordination), by analysing the content of the strategy, and by looking at how the effects are evaluated. As a support for these analyses we used the research model, explained in the next section.

3 Research model

The purpose of the model is to provide a framework for case study research into the actual practice of information strategy in contemporary organizations. We wanted to use the model as guideline for structured interviews with managers from various departments and levels, and as a framework to categorize the findings. The model used in this study focuses on four issues: environment, process, form and content, and effects of information strategy. The four components of the model are related to each other in several ways. The main relationship is that the environment influences the process which produces the content (being the output of the strategy process), which yields the effects, which change the environment (the impact or outcome of the strategy) and so close the loop.

There is a fair amount of similarity between this model and the input – process – output (IPO) model of King (1988): the planning process (P) converts several inputs (I) from the environment into a set (O) of mission,

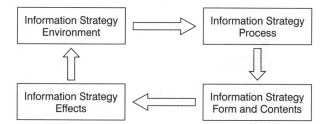

Figure 3.2 *Research model describing four components of information strategy*

Table 3.1　*Summary of the information strategies in three insurance companies*

		Information strategy		
Components/aspects		In company A	In company B	In company C
Environment	Position in the industry	Second tier	Dominant/ niche	Top
	Main distribution channel	Bank	Direct writer	Intermediaries
	Special factor	Recently merged	About to merge	Partner in ADN
	Company revenue	$2000M	$2000M	$3000M
	Employees	2000	2000	4000
	Business strategy	Explicit, known	Explicit, known	Explicit, known
	Internal organization	Product oriented	Market oriented	Product oriented
	Management attitude to IT	Positive	Very positive	Very positive
	IT expenditures/ revenue	<2%	>2%	<2%
	Existing architecture	Central/ decentral	Two tiered	Centralized
Process	Process type	Mech/problem	Political/mech	Mech/political
	Overall methodology	No	No	No
	IT scanning	Yes	Informal	Informal
	SWOT	Informal	Occasionally	Informal
	CSF	No	Occasionally	No
	Role top management	Dominant	Active	Active
	Line management	Active	Active	Present
	IT management	Active	Dominant	Dominant
	Planning specialist	One	–	–
	External consultant	–	–	–
	Alignment	Yes	Yes	Yes
	Impact	Not clear	Yes	Yes
	Organizational learning	No	Some	Some

Table 3.1 *Continued*

		Information strategy		
Components/aspects		*In company A*	*In company B*	*In company C*
Form and content	Time horizon	Five years	Three years	Three years
	Scope	IS/IT	IS/IT/telecom	IS/IT
	Objectives	Very specific	Explicit	Implicit
	Systems architecture	Evolving	Extensive, clear	Implicit
	Technical architecture	Evolving	Clear	Clear
	Organizational architecture	Clear	Clear	Clear
	Rules, alliances	Implicit, few	Implicit, few	Implicit, strict
	Plans	Projects	Projects, budgets	Projects, budgets
Effects	User satisfaction	Not measured	Not measured	Not measured
	Project results	Evaluated	Evaluated	Evaluated
	Bottom line results	Not measured	Tentative	Not measured

objectives, strategies, goals, resource allocations, information architectures and strategic programmes. The main difference is that the IPO model is more prescriptive (specifying components and relationships that should exist in SISP) whereas our model is descriptive and intended to provide structure to the collection of data from interviews and company documents.

The model in Figure 3.2 is based on the ideas of contextualism (Pettigrew, 1987) to consider a strategy in terms of three interrelated components: context, process and content. In contextualism, the main focus of research is to trace the dynamic interlinking between aspects of the components over time. This can be done via longitudinal studies, or, as in the present study, by indepth retrospect analysis of case material and interviews (Orlikowsky and Baroudi, 1991; Walsham and Waema, 1994). One important link is how previous strategies affect the actual environment, and how this again influences the strategy process and content. In our model, the context is split into the information strategy environment and the information strategy effects. In this way we could discriminate in our interviews between: (i) 'circumstances influencing the strategy process'; (ii) 'effects and impact of current and previous strategies'; and (iii) 'how (ii) influences the current process'.

In the case of information strategy, contextualism encompasses also the relationships between aspects of information strategy, the IT processes, the business strategy and the business processes (Figure 3.1). A comparison of our model with the model in Figure 3.1 shows that we focus on four components of information strategy, and that business strategy, business processes and IT processes form parts of the two (left side) components. Together these two form the context of information strategy. In Sections 3.1, 3.2, 3.3 and 3.4 the aspects of the four components of the model and the linkages are described in more detail. An overview of the aspects of the four components is given in Table 3.1.

3.1   The information strategy environment

The environment is defined here as all those facts and conditions which are not part of the information strategy itself, nor of the information strategy process, but that can or should influence either of those. There are two distinct views in the literature on factors that are important in the environment. One view categorizes organizations, and describing factors common to all organizations in a category. The second view does not try to group organizations, but just lists environmental factors.

The first view is, for instance, contained in the strategic grid (McFarlan, 1984), namely that conditions in the industry in which a firm operates largely set the scene for its information strategy. The external conditions in the line of industry determine the amount of strategic importance of current and future IT applications for organizations in the industry. Explicit emphasis on the environment is also described by Earl (1989), who distinguishes four types of companies with particular traits and preferences for IT, labelled as delayed, drive, dependent and delivery.

The second view in the literature encompasses those authors that search for 'success factors' (or the inverse: 'causes for failure'), to the extent that they attempt to relate the success or failure of information strategies to external factors. Many authors pay attention to specific factors, and several authors give lists and descriptions of factors, such as 'clarity of corporate strategy', 'IT planning resources', 'IT budget', 'future impact of IT', 'present impact of IT' (Premkumar, 1992); 'internal and external political power', 'importance of information', 'experience in planning', 'attitudes to change' (Hopstaken and Kranendonk, 1985); 'uncertainty of IS benefits', 'availability of IT' (Wilson, 1989).

In the context of this study it is not possible to investigate all potential influences, but we provide some structure by dividing the environment of information strategy in four aspects, as shown in Table 3.2:

- *IT opportunities*. These do not indicate only hardware, but also the capabilities of contractors and available services. As IT expands and

Table 3.2 *Four aspects of the environment of information strategy*

	Technological environment	Organizational environment
External environment	IT opportunities	Position in industry
Internal environment	IT resources	Nature of the organization

breaks into sub-specializations, organizations might want to use some form of technology scanning to evaluate the capabilities.

• *The position in the industry*, also including competitive and cooperative forces at work in the industry, such as market segmentation and barriers to entry or existing EDI networks.

• *The nature of the organization* includes simple to measure factors such as the size and the financial results of the company, but also factors more difficult to express, such as the organizational structure, the nature and clarity of the corporate strategy and the awareness and attitude of senior management towards IT.

• *The IT resources* reflect past investments in systems, hardware, procedures and people. They are the results of previous information strategies and now determine the competence of the organization to realize the chosen strategy. A specific category is formed by the resources available for the information strategy process, in terms of time, manpower and organizational attention.

3.2 The information strategy process

The information strategy process describes the way in which the information strategy is created or changed. The process dimension of information strategy is borrowed from the step by step methodologies summarized by Theeuwes (1987), King (1988), and others. Added to this are ideas about the importance of the linkage between corporate strategy and information strategy, in the form of 'impact' and 'alignment' (Parker *et al.*, 1989; Henderson and Venkatraman, 1993). This component of the model also distinguishes four main aspects.

An overriding aspect is what is called *process type* (Earl, 1993). Here we employ the typology of Schwenk (1988), who distinguishes three types of strategy process. First, the mechanical type describes a typical mechanistic approach: strategy is the result of a systematic stepwise process, consisting of the right people in the right positions, one group being the engine and another group manipulating the steering wheel. Second, the problem-oriented type describes strategy as the result of the more informal and continuous (learning) process of seeing opportunities and solving problems. Third, the political type describes strategy as the result of personal, political power relations in the organization. A typical statement of a manager in the political model, indicating the personal power and culture, is 'IT strategy? That's me!'.

The core of the information strategy process is defined on the one hand by *methodologies and tools* and on the other hand by *participants and their roles*. These two aspects are closely related, as methodologies often imply certain tools and roles. Methodologies, such as, for example, BSP (Zachman, 1982), typically divide the process into a number of steps and also define the tools or instruments that should be used, such as SWOT analysis (Johnson and Scholes, 1989) or CSF analysis (Rockart, 1979). An important determinant of the information strategy process is the distribution of the responsibility and the roles between the main participants in the process. A distinction is generally made between top management, IS management and line management, but participation by outsiders such as consultants or planning specialists may also be a factor. Two other issues stand out and require attention in this context: the use and functioning of steering committees and the mechanisms used for, and the effectiveness of the linkage between business strategy and information strategy. Both issues have recently been the subject of research (Feeney and Edwards, 1992; Saaksjarvi, 1994).

The final aspect is how and to what extent *organizational learning* is explicitly recognized as part of the strategy process. Presumably, organizations will always learn something from strategic experiences. The question we asked here is whether any mechanisms such as controlled experiments, executive seminars or analysis of the results of previous strategies are part of the information strategy process? The use of such learning activities has been described by Ruohonen (1991) and Lane (1992).

3.3　The information strategy form and content

Ideas about the form and content of an information strategy were derived from several models from the literature, describing relations between IS, IT and organization. The form of the information strategy defines some formal characteristics, such as the degree of formality, regularity of the documentation, the number of documents and pages used for expressing and communicating the strategy, and the time horizon (Mintzberg, 1991).

The content describes the subject areas or 'issues' for which the strategy is meant to provide solutions or directions. This is likely to be reflected in the contents page of the strategy documentation. The main aspects of the content of the information strategy are scope, objectives, architectures, rules and plans (e.g. Earl, 1989). Scope denotes the range of specific types of IT covered in the information strategy (for example, only transaction processing and management information systems, or also telecommunications, office automation or manual information processing) (Blumenthal, 1969; Theeuwes, 1987).

Objectives are conceived as specific and quantified. They are the targets set for the information function, and the linkages between these targets and the business objectives (Parker *et al.*, 1989; Scott Morton, 1991). The *architectures* can be divided into three parts: systems (or applications), technical and organizational. The applications architecture is sometimes equated to the information strategy and may indeed be the core of it. The technical architecture defines the hardware elements that support the information strategy, notably in the form of an infrastructure. The organizational architecture indicates the distribution of tasks and responsibilities for IT and IS (Theeuwes, 1987). *Rules* include guidelines and standards (or policies) which set a framework for decisions, such as a hurdle rate for investments. It also includes alliances, an increasingly important category of rules concerning make-or-buy decisions (Parker *et al.*, 1989). *Plans* in an information strategy are normally limited to priorities and budgets and do not include detailed designs and project plans (Theeuwes, 1987).

3.4 The information strategy effects

It is important to have effective information strategy planning and effective information strategies, in order to obtain effective IT in organizations (Henderson and Sifonis, 1988; Fitzgerald, 1993; Premkumar and King, 1991). However, measuring the effects of information strategies is very difficult, for several reasons, typically related to the evaluation of strategies in general (King, 1988).

First, there is the time aspect: effects cannot be determined reliably at one moment in time, nor over a fixed period, because the effects can vary significantly over the year(s). Second, there is an allocation aspect: it is very difficult to allocate the costs, benefits, people, products, etc. to the specific effects of the information strategy. Third, there is an evolutionary aspect: the information strategy in organizations changes over time, and can only be examined by using 'historical documents' or by 'looking back interviews'. Both are highly subjective sources. Fourth, there is the scope aspect: the effects of an information strategy can be measured from several scopes of vision, such as:

- the (narrow) scope of one systems development project as result of the information strategy
- the (narrow) scope of changes in the business strategy as results of the information strategy
- the (intermediate) scope of the performance (quality) of the systems development function
- the (intermediate) scope of the performance (quality) of a specific information system, and

- the (broad) scope of (all) information services in the organization (Laudon and Laudon, 1996).

The aspects for which each scope can be measured range from user satisfaction to costs and profits, or market performance of the business unit or the entire organization. We have asked the respondents 'if and how the effects of information strategy are measured'.

3.5   Research method

The model is an aid during the interviews, and structures the description of the information strategy in an organization. It is not a normative model, giving a prescription for the most effective strategy. The model was used to develop two questionnaires to be used in interviews with managers involved with information strategy. The first questionnaire is highly structured (along the aspects of the four components of the model as described in Sections 3.1, 3.2, 3.3 and 3.4), and contains open-ended as well as 'yes–no' questions. It is intended to obtain both factual and attitudinal information from people functionally involved with information strategy (typically IS managers and functional managers). The second questionnaire consists mainly of open-ended questions. It leads from questions about factual decisions taken in the previous years to the discussion of the value and appreciation of information strategy. The second questionnaire is intended to steer interviews with top executives. These relatively open interviews were held after analysis of company documents and the interview results of the first questionnaire. The second questionnaire deals with:

- the key (IS related) decisions taken in the previous years (reasons, effects)
- the information strategy process and the roles of different parties in the organization, and
- the value of the information strategy activities.

The following procedure was followed to investigate the practice of information strategy in each insurance company.

Step 1:   Structured interviews (based on the first questionnaire) with the senior IS manager and a senior manager(s) from the business domain.

Step 2:   Analysis of written materials (information plans and business plans). The plans were also screened for approximately five specific key decisions.

Step 3:   An interview with a member of the executive board (based on the second questionnaire).

Step 4:   All collected materials were used to write a detailed case description.

Each interview was taken by two interviewers. The results of each step were returned to the respondents for comments and adjustments. The final result is a validated case description, describing and assessing the information strategy from different perspectives. This procedure resembles the Delphi procedure (Turoff, 1970), whereby several persons are interviewed individually and afterwards confronted anonymously with the variety of responses. Based on the comments, the case descriptions are adjusted several times, until they are acceptable to the parties involved. In the three cases we investigated all respondents gave feedback at least once, participated sincerely, and added notably to the case descriptions. By following these procedures a validated view is obtained from complex subjects such as strategy (Turoff, 1970).

3.6 Three cases in a competitive environment

To select suitable cases for our purpose, we looked for: (i) substantial organizations, with a vested interest in information systems, so that it may be expected that both concepts and practice of information strategy are reasonably familiar; (ii) a branch of industry or commerce where information plays a substantial role; and (iii) an independent organization or business unit with complete or near complete control over its own information strategy. These criteria resulted in the selection of three organizations in the insurance industry, identified as A, B and C. To provide some background about the insurance industry, a sketch of the competitive environment is given below.

Insurance is a sizeable industry in the Netherlands. The total insurance market (excluding pension funds and health insurance) in the Netherlands is nearly $2000 per inhabitant, in total about $30 billion per year. The insurance market in the Netherlands is dominated by about 10 large firms. Insurance companies differentiate themselves through their distribution channels. An insurance company can sell its policies by means of 'direct marketing' (directly to the public and to professional clients), or via 'agents' or independent intermediaries, such as brokers, shops or banks. In particular the bank channel has become very important due to the recent changes in Dutch legislation which has permitted closer cooperation between banks, insurance companies and other financial institutions. As a consequence of the new legislation, several insurance companies have entered into mergers or alliances with banks.

The opening of the Common Market has broadened competition amongst insurance companies in Europe. This has been a factor in the trend towards greater concentration in the industry, as evidenced by takeovers and mergers between insurance companies on a national as well as on a European scale, combining specific (niche) markets and distribution channels.

The primary process of an insurance company relies heavily on information processing. Next to data processing in the back office, recently communication technology has also been used to link the various parties in the value chain. Of importance is the development of the 'assurance data network' (ADN). ADN is a value-added wide area network between insurance companies and their intermediaries. Insurance companies are also known to experiment with and use other advanced information technologies, such as the linking of voice and data processing facilities, and the use of expert systems to support decision making.

4   Findings

In Section 4.1 we give a relatively detailed description of our findings on the information strategy in company A. In Section 4.2 we summarize the findings in the three companies.

4.1   Company A

4.1.1   The information strategy environment

Company A is a large-to-medium sized insurance company, located and active in the Netherlands and dominant in certain niche markets. In 1991 its revenue was over $2000 million and it employed over 2000 people. It has traditionally strong links with one of the large banks in the Netherlands and the offices of that bank form an important distribution channel. In 1991 the company made profits of around $70 million, and it has had a steady development of revenue and profits during the period under investigation.

The corporate position of company A has changed significantly over the last few years. The volume of business has more than doubled, partly by growth, and partly by takeover of specialist and regional competitors. In the wake of the changes in the legal framework for financial and insurance organizations in the Netherlands, the company has entered into a complex merger with a large bank, thus formalizing and intensifying the already existing cooperation. The merger has been reflected in the appointment of some new directors.

The interviewees indicated that they considered the corporate mission and objectives of the company to be clear and well known. Corporate objectives are established annually by the board of directors after an extensive and formal process of consultation. This process was instituted in 1989 and involves a cycle of documentation, conferences and review. Top-management appears to be well aware of the importance of information technology and intend to promote its use, as witnessed by the following statement in the annual report over 1991: 'Information technology is of increasing importance in the financial services industry. An important competitive advantage can be created by making the company distinguish itself from other service providers by means of information technology'.

The main organizational structure of company A consists of a division life insurance and a division short-term (damages) insurance. These divisions have profit responsibility and have their own directors. There is a department of organization and information (O&A) which has a central responsibility for information systems and automation resources. Overall responsibility rests with the Board of Directors. One of the directors holds the portfolio 'automation'. The incumbent has held this position since 1992.

The O&A department consists of around 150 people, including one staff position for strategic planning. A few years ago, when it was last reported, automation expenditure was 2.3 per cent of revenue. Until 1985, the IT infrastructure consisted of large (IBM) mainframes. Since then, separate facilities for office automation have been added and a network of PCs and workstations has been installed. Recently, the data communication facilities with the offices of the partner-bank are being strengthened.

4.1.2   The information strategy process

The first impression of the information strategy process was of a mechanistic process type. The production of the annual 'information plan' is part of the strictly formalized and scheduled corporate planning process. Plans are conceived and written by O&A management and are (after extensive comment by other departments) sanctioned by the board. This was the way in which O&A management saw information strategy. However, subsequent discussions brought to light that during the year many new initiatives with a highly strategic content were taken. This usually happened in response to problems or suggestions from one of the operating divisions and was debated at board level. The portfolio holder in the board of directors played an active role in this. In this sense, the information strategy process was at least partly of the problem-driven type.

Company A did not use a 'commercial' methodology for information strategy, but from time to time used methods such as environmental scanning and SWOT analysis in a more or less formal manner. The O&A department participated in the information strategy process through involvement of the senior manager and of the special staff assistant. Their role was largely to analyse and to make proposals. Line managers from other departments influenced the process directly and indirectly, by making their needs and wishes known, sometimes to the point of insisting on a particular solution. The board had a very significant input and involved itself frequently and emphatically. There were no consultants involved, but there was a beginning of harmonization with the partner-bank. There was some attention to organizational learning, e.g. in the form of an evaluation of the effects of plans, but there was little evidence of conscious development or exploitation of experiences.

4.1.3   The information strategy form and content

There is much emphasis on formal documentation. Four planning documents were studied, covering the period 1986–1997, in total 218 pages. The plans cover information systems and office automation, but not telecommunications. The planning documents cover overlapping periods of 3–5 years. The plans are explicitly anchored in the corporate strategy and make reference to the corporate goals. Increasingly explicit goals and objectives are specified for the IS function, particularly in the most recent planning document. The plans give much prominence to application system development, without demonstrating a clear application architecture. Most attention goes to the production-oriented systems. There is no explicit attention to systems for competitive advantage, but implicitly this is present in attention to cost saving and close cooperation with the partner-bank. The hardware architecture or the organizational structures form implicit parts of the plans, but are not explicitly developed. There is some apparent tension in the jurisdiction over decentralized hardware and systems staff. Over the years the responsibilities slowly shift to the operating divisions, but the manager O&A retains overall responsibility.

Rules and controls are most of the time not a point of discussion in the plans. There is no mention of a steering committee or any other rules or mechanisms to guide IS efforts. However, the last plan specifies quantitative goals that are intended to be evaluated at the end of the planning period. There is a two-vendor hardware policy, but other forms of alliances are not discussed. The increasingly close relationship with the partner-bank is accepted as fact.

To characterize the strategic issues with which the management of company A was most concerned, four key decisions that dominated the information strategy agenda in the past few years were identified. They were:

1   Continuous support for the company-specific client/server model for interaction between corporate offices and intermediaries. Though the real costs had exceeded the original budget by many millions of dollars, the company had stuck to the concept and expected to reap the benefits in terms of competitive position in the next few years.

2   Partial decentralization of control over system development resources, which gave the operating divisions control over priorities for system development, leaving the IS department in a secondary role.

3   Deviation from the in-house development tradition by purchasing a comprehensive application package for the life insurance division.

4 Initiation of discussions with the partner-bank about information strategy issues. This might eventually lead to a decrease in the level of independence of the information strategy.

Finally, the manager O&A indicated his concern about the tension over the distribution of responsibilities for IT by adopting the battle cry 'Divide et impera' ('distribute and control').

4.1.4 The information strategy effects

Company A has developed a substantial IT infrastructure in the course of time. The core of the hardware architecture is formed by the central mainframes with the attached terminal network. More recently some decentralized processing capability has been added. The application architecture is extensive and has been painstakingly developed over the years. However, the application architecture no longer satisfies the requirements, and there is substantial pressure to make rapid enhancements. To this end experiments with software packages have been initiated, started and managed by the operating divisions. These pressures on the application architecture are largely due to new ways of doing business, particularly through the relationship with the partner-bank. Due to these pressures, the O&A organization is also under pressure. The new demands often do not match the available capabilities and the general atmosphere is certainly not relaxed.

Company A carefully screens and justifies all IT projects. However, cost overruns do occur, causing substantial concern at board level. No formal overall evaluation is made and opinions of users are not formally sampled. The board and the management of O&A are both aware of certain misgivings about the IT services in the company, but are convinced that IT is an essential and in the long run a beneficial investment. They are somewhat more dubious about the benefits of the effort spent on the preparation of formal information planning documents.

Management does not consider it possible to relate the investments in IT directly to corporate performance. The ratio of administrative expenses to premium income has decreased a little over the last few years, but it is not considered possible to assign this to automation efforts alone. The net profit margin is currently 3 per cent, but this tends to fluctuate under the influence of developments in damage claims.

4.1.5 Reflection

This case shows the importance of the clarification of terminology. In several interviews time needed to be taken, both at the beginning and during the discussions, to establish a common vocabulary. Without this, the wrong conclusions could easily be drawn. Also, different views on the real issues of the information strategy needed to be reconciled (in our case study research as well as in the company itself). This was inevitable, as various managers contributed to the information strategy from their own interest and expertise. Information strategy also proved to be a sensitive subject and it took some time and mutual trust before true facts and opinions came on the table.

The dominant attitude at company A appeared to be one of concern. The underlying culture was cooperative and collegial, but recent (merger) events had introduced a sense of coming change of which the direction was not yet clear.

Linkage between information strategy and business strategy appears to be assured, because of the diverse group of managers involved in the process, the high amount of time (20 per cent) spent to information strategy by the board of directors, and partial decentralization of system development resources. The impact and importance of IT is acknowledged in the business strategy documents, but no clear examples were found of the translation of IT possibilities into business processes.

4.2   Summary of the findings

It takes considerable time and effort to break through the language and terminology barrier of an information strategy. For example, in one instance it took half the first interview to establish that information strategy can mean more than the annual information plan. The various aspects of the model helped to bring the subject gradually into focus. Without a common terminology, it is easy to obtain misleading responses. It took a period of approximately 10 weeks, and about 50 man hours work, to finish a case study (steps 1–4) for one organization. Answers and explanations given in the interviews in step 1 are clarified and adjusted in the next steps. For example, functional managers indicated that the executive board spent only about 1 day each year on information strategy. The executive board member corrected this to 'more than 20 per cent of my time'. Input from multiple respondents and various levels thus contributes to an accommodated, calibrated view of information strategy.

In the previous section company A was described in detail. An overview of the findings in all three companies is given in Table 3.1. The companies all give IT substantial and high-level attention, more than, perhaps, the percentage of total revenue devoted to IT would suggest. The results can be summarized as follows:

• *Environment.* Information strategy awareness is high for all parties in the organizations. Attitudes of general managers and functional managers towards IT were generally positive and deviated little from each other.

- *Process.* Linkage between corporate strategies and information strategies is well established, certainly in the sense of alignment to business goals, but also (though less evident) in the sense of impact of technology on corporate strategies. The use of information technology in the organizations is not an activity that is planned or ruled from one specific department or person. Information strategy is influenced by many parties, partly historically and personally based. Formal methods play a supporting role in the information strategy process. Comprehensive methodologies are not used. SWOT analysis and other techniques tend to be used periodically as building blocks. Technology scanning is seldom done formally. Information strategy typically evolves through a problem-driven process, with both top-down and bottom-up inputs from IT managers as well as from general managers.
- *Form and contents.* The regularly produced 'information plan' serves as a means of communication within the information systems department and the rest of the organization. The annual planning cycle is a 'staging post' in a continuous information strategy process. Whereas the emphasis is generally on the (application) architectures and plans, reformulation of objectives occasionally received intense attention. Policies and guidelines on aspects such as investment criteria, risk management, security standards and alliances are an essential part of the information strategy, but remain often implicit and are assumed to be known. The strategies of all three organizations are more oriented to information systems and services than to the use of technology or infrastructures.
- *Results.* The companies put increasing emphasis on sophisticated methods to determine and control costs and benefits at the project and implementation level of information strategy. Organizations do not (or only tentatively, in the case of company B) systematically assess the effects and consequences of an information strategy at the business level, nor at the level of a single business process.

5 Comparison with related research

Mantz *et al.* (1991) report on a postal survey among about 350 Dutch organizations (both profit and non-profit). We note the following significant differences between the reported results of this survey and conclusions from our own research:

1 It is stated that in 47 per cent of the cases the IS manager is responsible for the identification of strategic applications. We find in all cases a sharing of this responsibility between top executives, IS managers and line managers, The difference may be due to the fact that we only investigated the insurance industry, or to an underestimation of the involvement of top

executives by the single respondents in the Mantz survey, as we encountered.

2   Sixty-one per cent of organizations are reported to use consultants in the information strategy process. We do not encounter this in any significant way. The confusion may have arisen as the process in the Mantz surveys also includes system development and implementation.

3   Sixty-eight per cent claim to require a formal 'control concept', defining the lines and mechanisms as a prerequisite for an information strategy. We found that managers in the insurance industry involved with information strategy are intimately aware of the functioning of their company and do not require such constructs.

Premkumar and King (1991) investigated 245 US business organizations, also by mailing questionnaires. We note the following differences and similarities between our findings and those of Premkumar and King:

1   Low use of standard planning methodologies is reported (22 per cent). We agree. Methodologies such as BSP were previously used, but were abandoned. Companies opt for a continuous and largely informal process, with great personal input from various levels.

2   Low effort spent on information strategy. We find that top executives, as well as senior IS managers in the insurance industry spend a substantial amount of time on information strategy. The survey may come to its conclusion by (implicity) only taking the effort of specialist staff into account, which is indeed a relatively low percentage.

3   A direct link is suggested between observable input to the information strategy and corporate results, such as return on investment. We find that such links are very tenuous and tend to be obscured by other factors. Senior executives do not believe in the possibility of measuring such links and are not inclined to spend serious effort in quantifying them.

Conrath *et al.* (1992) performed a (postal) survey among 67 Canadian top companies. The following differences and similarities are noted between the results of this survey and our findings:

1   Thirty per cent of respondents say that they do not link their information strategy with business strategy. This is contrary to our experience in the insurance industry, where a clear link between the two is established, in the sense of impact as well as of alignment. The explanation may be a preoccupation with formal, written business strategies by the respondents of the survey.

2   Only few companies were found to make a comparison between plan and performance. We agree that explicit evaluation appears to be the exception rather than the rule.

3 Only few companies were found to make a formal analysis of competitors' actions. This is also found in the insurance industry in the Netherlands. However, informally, competing companies tend to know each other very well. Several of the executives we interviewed were personally acquainted with each other. The explanation may be that the need for a formal analysis usually does not arise.

Saaksjarvi (1988) describes the relations between the process of information planning and the success of the planning, judged by IS managers of 100 large industrial and financial organizations in Finland. The planning process and success were measured by using a questionnaire. It was concluded that 44 per cent of the organizations had already integrated IS planning and corporate planning. According to the judgement of the IS managers, successful planning depends on the effective cooperation between general and IS management. In the present study we describe how general and IS management deal with information strategy, the processes and the goals they use in the insurance industry.

Summarizing, this comparison demonstrates that our model-based investigation of information strategy runs parallel to and is flanked by closely related research. However, there are significant differences between the findings in 'postal surveys' and our findings in the cases. Some differences (e.g. on the use of consultants) can be explained because we focus on the insurance industry. Other differences (e.g. 'linkages between information strategy and business goals', and 'effort spent on information strategy') can be explained by the limited power of postal surveys to enlighten complex issues such as information strategy.

6 Conclusions

The research questions were: (i) how can the practice of information strategy in an organization be analysed; (ii) what is the actual practice in the insurance industry; and (iii) how does information strategy relate to business strategy? We also looked for possible changes in the approach to information strategy over a period of about four years.

With respect to the research methods employed, we conclude, in line with Earl (1993), Walsham and Waema (1994) and others, that the analysis of information strategy should not be based on the results of only one interview with one (senior) manager, nor should it be based on postal surveys alone. It requires significant effort to obtain an accurate view on information strategy in an organization, due to the complex and often implicit meaning of the concept of information strategy. Our study in a substantial and representative part of the insurance industry in the Netherlands shows significant differences with findings based on surveys reported in the literature: we found more participants involved with, and more effort spent on information strategy, and more efforts to link information strategy to business strategy and processes.

We found that information strategy is a well-known and important concept, with often an implicit meaning to the managers involved. Senior management is heavily involved in information strategy: the members of the executive board in two companies in this study spent up to 20 per cent of their time. This is also reported by Walsham and Waema (1994): the CEO of a building company (500 employees) was involved in information strategy 25 per cent of his time.

We find it peculiar that the organizations spend significant efforts in information strategies but do not evaluate their effects, nor try to learn from previous information strategy planning experiences and effects. The reasons for this might be that managers are not used to evaluating strategies, and, obviously related to this, do not expect to gain useful insights.

Henderson and Venkatraman (1993) described the linkages between business strategy and information strategy in the strategic alignment model (Figure 3.1). In the model they distinguish four (linked) domains in an organization: (i) the business strategy domain; (ii) the business processes domain; (iii) the IT strategy domain; and (iv) the IT processes domain. We have found in the three cases that serious attention to information strategy is paid by various managers from all four domains. The main role can be played by the chief executive from the business strategy domain, or by the senior IT manager, but in each case all domains play an active and important role.

Of importance is how the information strategy and the business strategy are aligned, or linked (Parker *et al.*, 1989; Henderson and Venkatraman, 1993). There are two main perspectives on how alignment can take place. In the first perspective the business strategy is the driving force for the business processes or for the IT strategy, ultimately affecting the IT processes. In the second perspective it is the other way around: the IT strategy is the driving force for the IT processing or the business strategy, ultimately affecting the business processes. In the three cases we encountered mainly the first perspective. More specifically, the business processes and (in a lesser extent) the business strategy are the driving force for the IT processes, which subsequently influence the information strategy. We have not found clear examples indicating a more immediate influence of business strategy on information strategy, or vice versa.

An added dimension to information strategy is offered by the insight in the evolution through the years of the information strategy of the three companies. We found some indications that the roles, responsibilities and influence of the various managers in the three cases change over time, but more case studies are needed to be able to look into the developments of information strategies (Smits and van der Poel, 1996). Additional research, also in other lines of business, is needed to compare and further clarify the relations between the environment, the process, the content, and the effects of information strategy.

References

Andrews, K. R. (1980) *The Concept of Corporate Strategy*, RD Irwin, Boston, MA.

Ansoff, H. I. (1984) *Implanting Strategic Management*, Prentice Hall, London.

Anthony, R. N. (1965) *Planning and Control Systems, a Framework for Analysis*, Harvard University Press, Boston, MA.

Blumenthal, S. C. (1969) *MIS: a Framework for Planning and Development*, McGraw-Hill, New York.

Chan, Y. E. and Huff, S. L. (1992) Strategy, an information systems research perspective. *Journal of Strategic Information Systems*, **1**(4), 191–204.

Conrath, D. W., Ang, J. S. K. and Mattay, S. (1992) Strategic planning for information systems: a survey of Canadian organisations. *Infor*, **30**(4), 364–378.

Earl, M. J. (1989) *Management Strategies for Information Technology*, Prentice Hall, London.

Earl, M. J. (1993) Experiences in strategic information systems planning. *MIS Quarterly*, **17**(1), 1–24.

Feeney, D. F. and Edwards, B. (1992) Understanding the CEO/CIO relationship. Proceedings of the 13th ICIS Conference, pp. 119–126.

Fitzgerald, E. P. (1993) Success measures for information systems strategic planning. *Journal of Strategic Information Systems*, **2**(4), 335–350.

Galliers, R. D. (1991) Strategic information systems planning, myths and reality. *European Journal of Information Systems*, **1**(1), 55–64.

Galliers, R. D. (1993) Towards a flexible information architecture: integrating business strategies, information systems strategies and business process redesign. *Journal of Information Systems*, **3**(3), 199–213.

Henderson, J. C. and Sifonis, J. G. (1988) The value of strategic IS planning: understanding consistency, validity, and IS markets. *MIS Quarterly*, **12**(2), 186–200.

Henderson, J. C. and Venkatraman, N. (1993) Strategic alignment: leveraging information technology for transforming organizations. *IBM Systems Journal*, **32**(1), 4–16.

Hopstaken, B. A. A. and Kranendonk, A. (1985) Informatieplanning: een eenvoudige aanpak voor een complex probleem. *Informatie*, **27**(11), 988–998.

Johnson, G. and Scholes, K. (1989) *Exploring Corporate Strategy*, Prentice Hall, New York.

King, W. R. (1988) How effective is your information systems planning? *Long Range Planning*, **21**(5), 103–112.

Lane, D. C. (1992) Modelling as learning: a consultancy approach. *European Journal of Operations Research*, **59**, 64–84 (special issue).

Laudon, K. C. and Laudon, J. P. (1996) *Management Information Systems*, 4th edn, Prentice Hall, New York.

Lederer, A. L. and Sethi, V. (1988) The implementation of strategic ISP methodologies. *MIS Quarterly*, **12**(3), 445–461.

Mantz, E. A., Kleijne, D. and van der Zijden, F. A. P. (1991) Planning en realisatie informatievoorzieningen nog ver uit elkaar. *Informatie*, **33**(12), 847–855.

McFarlan, F. W. (1984) Information technology changes the way you compete. *Harvard Business Review*, **62**(1), 98–103.

Mintzberg, H. (1980) Opening up the definition of strategy. In *The Concept of Corporate Strategy* (ed. R. Andrews), RD Irwin, Boston, MA.

Mintzberg, H. (1991) *Strategy Formulation, Schools of Thought*, Prentice Hall, London.

Orlikowsky, W. and Baroudi, J. (1991) Studying information technology in organizations: research approaches and assumptions. *Information Systems Research*, **2**(1), 1–28.

Parker, M. M., Trainor, H. E. and Benson, R. J. (1989) *Information Strategy and Economics*, Prentice Hall, London.

Pettigrew, A. M. (1987) Context and action in the transformation of the firm. *Journal of Management Studies*, **24**(6), 649–670.

Porter, M. E. (1987) From competitive advantage to corporate strategy. *Harvard Business Review*, **65**(5), 43–59.

Premkumar, G. (1992) An empirical study of IS planning characteristics among industries. *Omega*, **20**(5), 611–629.

Premkumar, G. and King, W. R. (1991) Assessing strategic information systems planning. *Long Range Planning*, **24**, 41–58.

Rockart, J. F. (1979) Chief executives define their own data needs. *Harvard Business Review*, **57**(3), 81–93.

Ruohonen, M. (1991) Information management education in human resource strategy. *International Journal of Information Management*, **11**(2), 126–143.

Saaksjarvi, M. (1988) Information systems planning: what makes it succesful. *Proceedings of the ACC*, pp. 524–542.

Saaksjarvi, M. (1994) The roles and success of IS steering committees. *Proceedings of ECIS*, pp. 119–130.

Schwenk, C. R. (1988). *The Essence of Strategic Decision Making*, D. C. Heath, Lexington, MA.

Scott Morton, M. S. (1991) *The Corporation of the 1990s: IT and Organizational Performance*, Oxford University Press, New York.

Smits, M. T. and van der Poel, K. G. (1996) The practice of information strategy in six information intensive organizations in the Netherlands. *Journal of Strategic Information Systems*, **5**, 93–110.

Theeuwes, J. A. M. (1987) *Informatieplanning*, Kluwer, Deventer.

Turoff, M. (1970) The design of a policy Delphi. *Technological Forecasting and Social Change*, **2**(2), 149–171.

Walsham, G. and Waema, T. (1994) Information systems strategy and implementation: a case study of a building society. *ACM Transactions on Information Systems*, **12**(2), 150–173.

Ward, J., Griffiths, P. and Whitmore, P. (1990) *Strategic Planning for Information Systems*, Wiley, Chichester.

Wilson, T. D. (1989) The implementation of IS strategies in UK companies. *International Journal of Information Management*, **9**(4), 245–258.

Zachman, J. A. (1982) Business system planning and business information control study: a comparison. *IBM Systems Journal*, **21**, 35–45.

Reproduced from Smits, M. T., van der Poel, K. G. and Ribbers, P. M. A. (1997) Assessment of information strategies in insurance companies in the Netherlands. *Journal of Strategic Information Systems*, **6**(2), June, 129–148.

Reprinted by permission of the publishers, Elsevier Science NL.

Questions for discussion

1   Consider the authors' definition of information strategy: 'a complex of implicit or explicit visions, goals, guidelines, and plans with respect to the supply and the demand of formal information in an organization sanctioned by management, intended to support the objectives of the organization in the long run, while being able to adjust to the environment'. How does this differ from the notion of information strategy depicted in Figure 0.1 in the Preface? The authors treat information strategy, IS strategy, IS strategic planning, strategic IS planning as the same thing. How might these be differentiated?

2   The authors examine the link between IS strategy and business strategy by considering the attitudes of senior managers, analysing the information strategy process, analysing the content and forms of the strategies, and looking at how effects are evaluated. What are the limitations of each individually as indicators of the link and what other methods might we use to determine how well IS is linked to business strategy?

3   The authors state that 'attitudes of general managers and functional managers toward IT were generally positive and deviated little from each other'. How generalizable do you think this finding is?

4   The authors state that 'technology scanning is seldom done formally. Information strategy typically evolves through a problem-driven process, with both top-down and bottom-up inputs from IT managers as well as from general managers'. Consider why formal scanning might not be done. What would be the merits of conducting formal scanning?

5   The authors state that organizations do not systematically evaluate the effects and consequences of information strategy, in part because senior managers do not believe in the possibility to measure such links. Suggest an alternative explanation.

6   Consider two perspectives on how alignment can take place: (i) business strategy driving business processes which in turn drive IT strategy which affect IT processes; (ii) IT strategy driving IT processes which ultimately affect business process and business strategy. Discuss the merits of these two approaches.

4 The Information Technology and Management Infrastructure Strategy

Globalization and information management strategies

J. Karimi and B. R. Konsynski

1 Introduction

Recently, the globalization of competition has become the rule rather than the exception for a number of industries.[39] To compete effectively, at home or globally, firms often must coordinate their activities on a worldwide basis. Although many global firms have an explicit global business strategy, few have a corresponding strategy for managing information technology internationally. Many firms have information interchange protocols across their multinational organizational structures, but few have global information technology architectures. A global information management strategy is needed as a result of (1) *industry globalization*: the growing globalization trend in many industries and the associated reliance on information technologies for coordination and operation, and (2) *national competitive posture:* the aggregation of separate domestic strategies in individual countries that may contend with coordination. While Procter and Gamble contends with the need to address more effectively its global market in the branded packaged goods industry, Singapore requires improved coordination and control of trade documentation in order to compete more effectively in the cross-industry trade environment that is vital to the economic health of that nation. Each approach recognizes the growing information intensity in their expanding markets. Each in turn must meet the challenges brought about by the need for cross-cultural and cross-industry cooperation.

Globalization trends demand an evaluation of the skills portfolio that organizations require in order to participate effectively in their changing markets. Porter[41] suggests that coordination among increasingly complex networks of activities dispersed worldwide is becoming a prime source of competitive advantage: global strategies frequently involve coordination with coalition partners as well as among a firm's own subsidiaries. The benefits associated with globalization of industries are not tied to countries' policies and practice. Rather, they are associated with how the activities in the industry value chain are performed by the firm's worldwide systems. These systems involve partnerships[31] with independent entities that involve information and management process interchange across legal organization boundaries, as well as across national boundaries.

For a global firm, the coordination concerns involve an analysis of how similar or linked activities are performed in different countries. Coordination[31] involves the management of the exchange of information, goods, expertise, technology, and finances. Many business functions play a role in such coordination – logistics, order fulfilment, financial, etc. Coordination involves sharing and use, by different facilities, of information about the activities within the firm's value chain.[30] In global industries, these skills permit a firm to (1) be flexible in responding to competitors in different countries and markets, (2) respond in one country (or region) to a change in another, (3) scan markets around the world, (4) transfer knowledge between units in different countries, (5) reduce costs, (6) enhance effectiveness, and (7) preserve diversity in final products and in production location. The innovations in information technology (IT) in the past two decades have greatly reduced coordination costs by reducing both the time and cost of communicating information. Market and product innovation often involves coordination and partnership across a diverse set of organizational and geographically dispersed entities. Several studies[26,27,38,42] suggest ways in which companies/nations achieve competitive advantage through innovation.

Organizations must begin to manage the evolution of a global IT architecture that forms an infrastructure for the coordination needs of a global management team. The country-centered, multinational firm will give way to truly global organizations that will carry little national identity.[49,50] It is a major challenge to general management to build and manage the technical infrastructure that supports a unique global enterprise culture. This chapter deals with issues that arise in the evolution of a global business strategy and its alignment with the evolving global IT strategy.

Below we present issues related to the radical changes taking place in both the global business environment and the IT environment, with changes in one area driving changes in the other. Section 2 describes changes taking place in the global business environment as a result of globalization. It highlights elements from previous research findings on the effects of globalization on the organizational strategies/structures and coordination/control strategies. Section 3 deals with the information technology dimension and addresses the issue of development of a global information systems (GIS) management strategy. The section emphasizes the need for 'alignment' of business and technological evolution as a result of the radical changes in the global business environment and technology. Section 4 summarizes and presents other challenges to senior managers that are emerging in the global business environment.

2 Globalization and changes in the business environment

Since the Second World War, a number of factors have changed the manner of competition in the global business community. The particular catalyst for globalization and for evolving patterns of international competition varies among industries. Among the causative factors are increased similarity in available infrastructure, distribution channels, and marketing approaches among countries, as well as a fluid global capital market that allows large flows of funds between countries. Additional causes include falling political and tariff barriers, a growing number of regional economic pacts that facilitate trade relations, and the increasing impact of the technological revolution in restructuring and integrating industries. Manufacturing issues associated with flexibility, labor cost differentials, and other factors also play a role in these market trends.

Widespread globalization is also evident in a number of industries that were once largely separate domestic industries, such as software, telecommunications, and services.[9,32,40] In the decade of the 1990s, the political changes in the Soviet Union and the Eastern European countries, plus the evolution of the European Common Market toward a single European market without national borders or barriers,[13] also have led to growing international competition. Other factors are changing the economic dynamics in the Pacific Rim area, with changes in Hong Kong, Japan, China and Taiwan, Korea, Singapore, and the reentry of certain nations to the global economic community (e.g. Vietnam).

Previous research indicates that significant changes have taken place in organizational strategies/structure during the 1980s because of ever-increasing global competition and growth in the communications and information-processing industry. Researchers in international business have pointed out that the structure of a global firm's value chain is the key to its strategy: its fit with the environmental requirements that determine economic performance.[3,15,37,40] Another study found that, in successful global firms, organization structure and strategy are matched by selecting the most efficient or lowest cost structure that satisfies the information-processing requirements inherent in the strategy.[12] That is, the firm's strategy and its information-processing requirements must be in alignment with the firm's organizational structure and information-processing capabilities. To understand changes in organizational designs for global forms, these changes are highlighted in relation to the changes in strategies.

2.1   Evolution of the global firm's strategy/structure

Global strategy is defined by Porter[40] as strategy from which 'a firm seeks to gain competitive advantage from its international presence through either a concentrated configuration of activities, or coordinating among dispersed activities, or both'. Configuration involves the location(s) in the world where each activity in the value chain is performed, it characterizes the organizational structure of a global firm. A global firm faces a number of options in both configuration and coordination for each activity in the value chain. As implied by these definitions, there is no one pattern of international competition, neither is there one type of global strategy.

Bartlett[3,4] suggests that for a global firm value-chain activities are pulled together by two environmental forces: (1) national differentiation, i.e. diversity in individual country-markets; and (2) global integration, i.e. coordination among activities in various countries. For global firms, forces for integration and national differentiation can vary depending on their global strategies. Table 4.1 shows the evolution of the global firms' strategy/structure and their coordination/control strategies as a result of globalization of competition. The vocabulary of Bartlett[4] and Porter[40] will be further used in our framework.

Under a *multinational* strategy, a firm might differentiate its products to meet local needs to respond to diverse interests. In such an approach, the firm might delegate considerable operating independence and strategic freedom to its foreign subsidiaries. Under this *decentralized* organizational structure, highly autonomous national companies are often managed as a portfolio of offshore investments rather than as a single international business. A subsidiary is focused on its local market. Coordination and control are achieved primarily through personal relationships between top corporate management and subsidiary managers than by written rules, procedures, or a formal organizational structure. Strategic decisions are decentralized and top management is involved mainly in monitoring the results of foreign operations. Figure 4.1 presents this organizational strategy/structure.

This model was the classic strategy/structure adopted by most European-based companies expanding before the Second World War. Examples include Unilever in branded packaged products, Phillips in consumer electronics, and ITT in telecommunications switching. However, much changed for European companies in the 1970s with the reduction of certain tariff barriers by the EEC* and with the entrance of both American and Japanese firms into local markets.

*The EEC was the forerunner to the European Union (EU)

Table 4.1 *Global business environment – strategy/structure and coordination control*

Business strategy/ structure	Strategic management processes	Tactical business processes	Coordination and control processes
Multinational/ decentralized – federation	Informal HQ-subsidiary relationships; strategic decisions are decentralized	Mainly financial flows; capital out and dividends back	Socialization; careful recruitment, development, and acculturation of key decision makers
Global/centralized federation	Tight central control of decisions, resources and information	One-way flows of goods, resources and information	Centralization; substantive decision making by senior management
International/ coordinated – federation	Formal management planning and control systems allow tighter HQ – subsidiary linkages	Assets, resources, responsibilities decentralized but controlled from HQ	Formalization; formal systems, policies and standards to guide choice
Transnational/ integrated – network	Complex process of coordination and cooperation in an environment of shared decision making	Large flows of technology, finances, people, and information among interdependent units	Co-opting; the entire portfolio of coordinating and control mechanisms
Interorganizational/ coordinated federation of business groups	Share activities and gain competitive advantage by lowering costs and raising differentiation	Vertical disaggregation of functions	Formalization; multiple and flexible coordination and control functions

In the machine lubricant industry, automotive motor oil tends toward a multinational competitive environment. Countries have different driving standards and regulations and regional weather conditions. Domestic firms tend to emerge as leaders (for example, Quaker State and Pennzoil in the United States). At the same time, multinationals, with country subsidies (such as Castrol, UK) become leaders in regional markets. In the lodging industry,

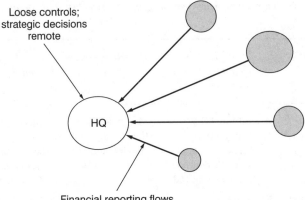

Loose controls;
strategic decisions
remote

HQ

Financial reporting flows

Figure 4.1   *Multinational strategy with decentralized organizational structure*

many segments are multinational as a result of the fact that a majority of activities in the value chain are strongly tied to buyer location. Further, differences associated with national and regional preferences and lifestyle lead to few benefits from global coordination.

Under a pure *global* strategy, a firm may seek competitive advantage by capitalizing on the economies associated with standardized product design, global-scale manufacturing, and a centralized control of world-wide operation. The key parts of a firm's value-chain activities (typically product design or manufacturing) are geographically concentrated. They are either retained at the center, or they are centrally controlled. Under this *centralized* organizational structure, there are primarily one-way flows of goods, information, and resources from headquarters to subsidiaries; key strategic decisions for worldwide operations are made centrally by senior management. Figure 4.2 depicts this organizational strategy/structure.

This export-based strategy was/is typical in Japanese-based companies in the postwar years. They typically require highly coordinated activities among subsidiaries. Examples include KAO in branded packaged products, Matsushita in consumer electronics, NEC in telecommunications switching, and Toyota in the automobile industry. Toyota started by capitalizing on a tightly controlled operation that emphasized worldwide export of fairly standardized automobile models from global-scale plants in Toyota City, Japan. Lately, because of growing protectionist sentiments and lower factory costs in less-developed countries, Toyota (among others) has found it necessary to establish production sites in less-developed countries in order to sustain its competitive edge. The marine engine lubricant industry is a global industry that requires a global strategy. Ships move freely around the world and require

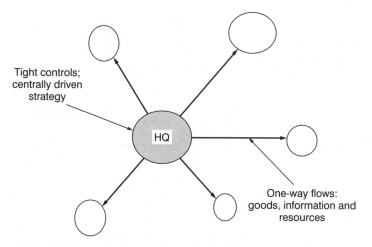

Figure 4.2   *Global strategy with centralized organizational structure*

that brand oil be available wherever they put into port. Brand reputations thus become global issues. Successful marine engine lubricant competitors (such as Shell, Exxon, and British Petroleum) are good examples of global enterprises.

In the area of business-oriented luxury hotels, competitors differ from the majority of hotel accommodations and the competition is more global. Global competitors such as Hilton, Marriott, and Sheraton have a wide range of dispersed properties that employ common brand names, common format, common service standards, and worldwide reservation systems to gain marketing advantage in serving the highly mobile business travelers. Expectations of global standards for service and quality are high.

Under an *international strategy*, a firm transfers knowledge and expertise to overseas environments that are less advanced in technology and market development. Local subsidiaries are often free to adapt new strategies, products, processes, and/or ideas. Under this *coordinated federation* organizational structure, the subsidiaries' dependence on the parent company for new processes and ideas requires a great deal more coordination and control by headquarters than under a classic multinational strategy. Figure 4.3 depicts this organizational strategy/structure.

This strategy/structure defines the managerial culture of many US-based companies. Examples include Procter and Gamble in branded packaged products, General Electric in consumer electronics, and Ericsson in tele-communications switching. These companies have a reputation for professional management that implies a willingness to delegate responsibility while retaining overall control through sophisticated systems and specialist

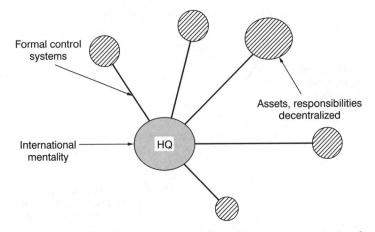

Figure 4.3   *International strategy with coordinated federation organizational structure*

corporate staffs. But, under this structure, international subsidiaries are more dependent on the transfer of knowledge and information than are subsidiaries under a multinational strategy; the parent company makes a greater use of formal systems and controls in its relations with subsidiaries.

Under a *transnational* strategy, a firm coordinates a number of national operations while retaining the ability to respond to national interests and preferences. National subsidiaries are no longer viewed as the implementors of centrally-developed strategies. Each, however, is viewed as a source of ideas, capabilities, and knowledge that can be beneficial to the company as a whole. It is not unusual for companies to coordinate product development, marketing approaches, and overall competitive strategy across interdependent national units. Under this *integrated network* organizational structure, top managers are responsible for: (1) coordinating the development of strategic objectives and operating policies, (2) coordinating logistics among operating divisions, and (3) coordinating the flow of information among divisions.[3] Figure 4.4 presents this organizational strategy/structure.

During the 1980s, forces of global competition required global firms to be more responsive nationally. As a result, the transnational strategies are being adopted by increasing numbers of global firms.[3] This adoption is becoming necessary because of the need for worldwide coordination and integration of activities upstream in the value chain (e.g. inbound logistics, operations) and because of the need for a greater degree of national differentiation and responsiveness at the downstream end (e.g. marketing, sales, and services). For example, adoption of a transnational mode allowed companies such as Procter and Gamble, NEC, and Unilever to respond effectively to the new and complex demands of their international business environments. They were able to replace exports with local manufacture and to develop more locally differentiated products.[3,9] In contrast, the inability to develop a similar organizational capability is seen by some to be a factor contributing to the strategic and competitive difficulties faced by companies such as ITT, GE, and KAO.

Special situations relate to another form of the *coordinated federation* organizational structure, *interorganizational* design, which is a particular form of the organizational framework represented in Figure 4.4. An inter-organizational design consists of two or more organizations that have chosen to cooperate by combining their strengths to overcome individual weaknesses.[51] There are two modes of interorganizational design: equity and non-equity collaboration. *Equity collaborations* are seen in joint ventures, minority equity investments, and franchises. *Non-equity collaborations* are seen in forms of licensing arrangements, marketing and distribution agreements, and interorganizational systems.[2,21,30,31] For example, in the airline industry, achieving the economies of scale in developing and managing a large-scale reservation system are now beyond the capacities of the medium-sized airlines. In Europe, two major coalitions have been created, the Amadeus Coalition and the Galileo Coalition. Software for Amadeus is built around System One, the computer reservation system for Continental and Eastern. Galileo makes use of United's software. Even the largest carriers have

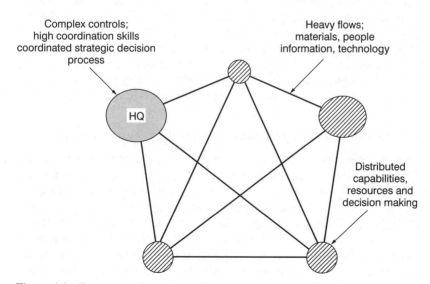

Figure 4.4   *Transnational strategy with integrated-network organizational structure*

acknowledged their inability to manage a large-scale reservation system by themselves; they have joined coalitions.[31]

Another highly visible example that demonstrates the notion of regional or national coordination in order to compete in a global market is the paper industry of Finland. The nineteen Finnish paper companies comprise a $3 billion industry that is heavily dependent on exports. Recently they determined that, to compete effectively in that service-oriented business, they must provide online electronic data interchange (EDI) interfaces with key customers and their sales offices. The Finnpap organization combined the efforts of the mill owners to develop an information system that reaches around the globe. The initial budget estimate of $40 million for five years has grown to an annual commitment of $10 million for the foreseeable future. None of the individual companies in the Finnish paper industry had the size, skills, and/or financial strength to create and deliver the world-class services necessary to compete against the large American, Canadian, and other global competitors. A regional cooperation was needed among the competitors in order to compete in the global market.

There has been a virtual explosion in the use of interorganizational designs for both global and domestic firms as a result of increased global competition during the 1980s. In 1983 alone, the number of domestic joint ventures announced in communications and information systems products and services industries exceeded the sum of all previously announced joint ventures in those sectors.[17] Research suggests that interorganizational designs can lead to (1) 'vertical disaggregation' of functions (e.g. marketing, distribution) typically conducted within the boundaries of a single organization performed independently by the organizations within the network, (2) the use of 'brokers,' or structure-independent organizations, to link together the different organizational units into 'business groups' for performance of specific tasks, and (3) the substitution of 'full disclosure information systems' in traditional organizations for lengthy trust-building processes based on experience.[36]

2.2 Evolution of the global firm's coordination control strategies

Strategic control is considered to be the key element for the 'integration' of a firm's value-chain activities; it is defined as 'the extent of influence that a head office has over a subsidiary concerning decisions that affect subsidiary strategy'.[10] Previous research found that, as resources such as capital, technology, and management become vested in the subsidiaries, head offices cannot continue to rely on control over these resources as means of influencing subsidiary strategy.[1,10,44] The nature of strategic control by the head office over its subsidiaries shifts with time; there is a need for new forms of administrative control mechanisms such as those offered through improved information management strategies.

In a study of nine large worldwide companies and by interviewing 236 managers both in corporate headquarters and in a number of different national subsidiaries, Bartlett and Ghoshal[4] found that many companies had reached a coordination crisis by 1980. New competitive pressures were requiring the global firms to develop multiple strategic capabilities, even as other environment forces led them to reconfigure their historical organization structures. Many familiar means of coordination (e.g. socialization, centralization, and formalization – shown in Table 4.1) characteristically proved inadequate to this new challenge.

The study further reports that European companies began to see the power and simplicity of more centralized coordination of subsidiaries. The Japanese increasingly adopted more formal systems, routines, and policies to supplement their traditional time-consuming, case-by-case negotiations. American managers took new interest in shaping and managing the previously ignored informal processes and value systems in their firms. The study also found that the challenge for many global firms was not to find the organizational structure that provided the best fit with their global strategies, but to build and manage the appropriate decision-making processes that can respond to multiple changing environmental demands. Furthermore, because of evolving global strategies from multinational to transnational, decision making is no longer concentrated at corporate headquarters. Today's global firm must be able to carry a great deal of complex information to diverse locations in its integrated network of operations.

As we have seen, research on international business suggests that globalization has caused a change in the coordination/control needs of global firms. As a result, new organizational designs are created to meet new organizational coordination needs and to deal with increased organizational complexity and size. The traditional organizational designs[18,29] such as functional, multidivisional, and matrix forms, are largely inappropriate for today's global firms.

Research further suggests that different organizational strategies/structures are necessary across products or businesses with diverse (global) environment demands. In response, there have been two relatively new trends in organizational strategies: (1) a shift from a multinational strategy with decentralized organizational structures to a transnational strategy and globally integrated networks of operations, and (2) a rapid proliferation of interorganizational designs and structurally independent organizational units and business groups.

In short, the success in global competition depends largely on (1) a proper fit between an organization's business strategy and its structure, (2) an organization's ability to adapt its structure in order to balance the environmental forces of national differentiation and global integration for its value-chain activities, and (3) the manner of coordination/control of the organization's value-chain activities. As presented above, the globalization of competition and the evolving business environment suggest that the success of today's global firms' business and its coordination/control strategies may be linked to a global information management strategy. In the following section, the roles and characteristics of global information systems (GIS) and their differences with traditional distributed data-processing systems are discussed. A global information system management strategy is proposed. The need for 'alignment' of the organization's business strategy/structure with its information system management strategy is emphasized as part of this strategy.

3   Global information systems

Due to the dramatic changes in IT, and the increased skills in organizations to deploy and exploit those advances, there are an increasing number of applications of IT by global firms in both service and manufacturing industries. The earliest were in international banking, airline, and credit authorization. However, during the 1980s, due to rapid improvements in communication and IT, more and more activities of global firms were coordinated using information systems. At the same time, patterns in the economies of IT development are changing.[19,22,38] The existence or near completion of public national data networks and of public or quasi-public regional and international networks in virtually all developed (and a few developing) countries has resulted in rapid growth in data-service industries, e.g. data processing, software, information storage and retrieval, and telecommunications services.[26,46]

Today global firms not only rely on data-service industries and IT to speed up message transmission (e.g. for ordering, marketing, distribution, and invoicing), but also to improve the management of corporate systems by: (1) improving corporate functions such as financial control, strategic planning, and inventory control, and (2) changing the manner in which global firms actually engage in production (e.g. in manufacturing, R&D, design and engineering, CAD/CAM/CAE).[46] Therefore, more and more of global firms' mechanisms for planning, control and coordination, and reporting depend on information technology. According to the head of information systems at the $35 billion chemical giant, information systems will either be a facilitator or an inhibitor of globalization during the 1990s.[35]

A *global information system* (GIS) is a distributed data-processing system that crosses national boundaries.[7] There are a number of differences between domestic distributed systems[25] and GISs. Because GISs cross national boundaries, unlike domestic distributed systems, they are exposed to wide variations in business environments, availability of resources, and technological and regulatory environments. These are explained briefly below.

Business Environment. From the perspective of the home-base country, there are differences in language, culture, nationality, and professional management disciplines among subsidiary organizations. Due to differences in local management philosophy, business/technology planning responsibilities are often fragmented rather than focused in one budgetary area. Business/ technology planning, monitoring, and control and coordination functions are often difficult and require unique management skills.[24]

Infrastructure. The predictability and stability of available infrastructure in a given country are major issues when making the country a hub for a global firm: 'It is a fact of life that some countries are tougher to do business in than others.'[8] Regional economic dependence on particular industry and cross-industry infrastructure may be informative. Singapore[26] has provided, through TradeNet, a platform for fast, efficient trade document processing. Hong Kong,[27] on the other hand, is still dealing with its unique position as the gateway to the People's Republic of China, and its historic 'free port' policies in developing its TradeLink platform. Lufthansa, Japan Airlines, Cathay Pacific, and other airlines are trying to pool their global IT infrastructure in order to deliver a global logistics system. At the same time, global banks are exploring the influence their IT architectures have on the portfolio of instruments they can offer on a global basis.[37]

Resource availability can vary due to import restrictions or to lack of local vendor support. Since few vendors provide worldwide service, many firms are limited in choice of vendors in a single project, because of operational risk. Finally, availability of telecommunications equipment/technology (e.g. LAN, private microwave, fiber optic, satellite earth stations, switching devices, and other technologies) varies among countries and geographic regions.

Regulatory Environments. Changes in government, economy, and social policy can lead to critical changes in the telecommunications regulations that pose serious constraints on the operation of GISs. The price and availability of service, and cross-border data-flow restrictions vary widely from one country to another.

The PTT (post, telephone, and telegraph) in most countries sets prices based on volume of traffic rather than based on fixed-cost leased facilities. By doing so, the PTT increases its own revenues and, at the same time, prevents global firms from exploiting economies of scale. The nature of the internal infrastructure systems may also influence the interest and ability to leverage regulation.[38,49,50]

There are regulations restricting usage of leased lines or import of hardware/software for GISs. These affect the GIS options possible in different countries: restrictions on connections between leased lines and public telephone networks, the use of dial-up data transmission, and the use of electronic mail systems for communications. It is not unusual for some companies to build their own 'phone company' in order to reduce dependence on government-run organizations.[8] Hardware/software import policies also make local information processing uneconomical in some countries. For example, both Canada and Brazil have high duties on imported hardware, and there are software import valuation policies in France, Saudi Arabia, and Israel.[6]

Transborder Data Flow (TBDF) regulations, in part, govern the content of international data flows.[5] Examples are requirements to process certain kinds of data and to maintain certain business records locally, and the fact that some countries don't mind data being 'transmitted in' but oppose interactive applications in which data are 'transmitted out'. Although the major reasons for regulating the content of TBDF are privacy protection and economic and national security concerns, these regulations can adversely affect the economies of GISs by forcing global firms to decentralize their operations, increase operating costs, and/or prohibit certain applications.

Standards. International, national, and industry standards play a key role in permitting global firms to 'leverage' their systems development investment as much as possible. Telecommunication standards vary widely from one country to another concerning the technical details of connecting equipment and agreements on formats and procedures. However, the conversion of the world's telecommunications facilities into an integrated digital network (IDN) is well underway, and most observers agree that a worldwide integrated digital network and the integrated services digital network (ISDN) will soon become a reality.[34,48] The challenge is not a problem of technology – the necessary technology already exists. Integration depends on creating the necessary standards and getting all countries to agree.

Telecommunications standards are set by various domestic governments or international agencies, and by major equipment vendors (e.g. IBM's System Network Architecture (SNA), Wang's Wangnet, Digital Equipment's DecNet, etc). There are also standards set by groups of firms within the same industry, such as SWIFT (Society for Worldwide International Funds Transfer) for international funds transfers and cash management, EDI (Electronic Data Interchange) for formatted business transactions such as purchase orders between companies (ANSI, EDIFACT, etc.),[16] and SQL (Structured Query Language) as a common form of interface for coordinating data across many databases.

3.1   Global information management strategy

Table 4.2 shows the alternative information systems management strategy/ structure as a result of the evolution in global business environment and technology. New information technologies are allowing closer integration of adjacent steps on the value-added chain through the development of electronic markets and electronic hierarchies.[33] As that study reports, the overall effect

Table 4.2 *Alignment of global and information management strategies*

Business strategy/ structure	Coordination control strategy	Coordination control mechanisms	IS strategy structure
Multinational decentralized – federation	Socialization	*Hierarchies*; managerial decisions determine the flow of materials and services	Decentralization/ standalone databases and processes
Global/centralized – federation	Centralization		Centralization/ centralized databases and processes
International and interorganizational/ coordinated federation	Formalization	*Markets*; market forces determine the flow of materials and services	IOS/linked databases and processes
Transnational integrated network	Co-opting		Integrated architecture/shared databases and processes

of technology is the change of coordination mechanisms. This will result in an increase in the proportion of economic activities coordinated by markets rather than by hierarchies. This also supports and explains change in global firms' strategies from multinational, global strategies to international (interorganizational), transnational strategies.

The task of managing across corporate boundaries has much in common with that of managing across national borders. Managing strategic partnerships, coalitions, and alliances has forced managers to shift their thinking from the traditional task of controlling a hierarchy to managing a network.[11,31,43] As discussed earlier, managers in transnational organizations must gather, exchange, and process large volumes of information; formal strategies/structures, cannot support such huge information-processing needs. Because of the widespread distribution of organizational units and the relative infrequency of direct contacts among those in disparate units in a transnational firm, top management has a better opportunity to shape relationships among managers simply by being able to influence the nature and frequency of contacts by using a proper information system management strategy.

The strategy should contain the senior management policy on corporate information systems architecture (ISA). Corporate ISA (1) provides a guide for systems development, (2) facilitates the integration and data sharing among applications, and (3) supports development of integrated, corporate systems that are based on a data resource with corporate-wide accessibility.[19] Corporate ISA for a global firm is a high-level map of the information and technology requirements of a firm as a whole; it is composed of network, data, and application and technology architectures. In the international environment, the network and data architectures are generally considered to be the key enabling technologies because they are the highway systems for a wide range of traffic.[24]

A new GIS management strategy needs to address organizational structural issues related to coordination and configuration of value-chain activities, by proper ISA design. The key components of a GIS management strategy are (1) a centralized and/or coordinated business/technology strategy on establishing data communications architecture and standards, (2) a centralized and/or coordinated data management strategy for creation of corporate databases, and (3) alignment of global business and GIS management strategy. These are explained below.

3.1.1   Network management strategy and architecture

Network architecture describes where applications are executed, where databases are located, and what communications links are needed among locations. It also sets standards ensuring that all other ISA components are interrelated and working together. The architecture is important in providing standards for interconnecting very different systems instead of requiring commonality of systems. At present, the potential for network architecture is determined more often by vendors than by general industry or organizational standards.[24]

Architecture. Research on international business points out that the structure of a global firm's value chain is the key to its strategy; its fit with environmental requirements derives economic performance. However, the environments of GISs are external to their global firms and thus cannot be controlled. Services provided by GISs must be globally coordinated, integrated, standardized, and tailored to accommodate national differences and individual national markets.

Deciding on appropriate network architecture is a leading management and technology issue. Research in the global banking industry found that an international bank providing a wide range of global electronic wholesale banking services has some automated systems that need to be globally standardized (e.g. global balance reporting system), while others (e.g. global letter of credit system) need to be tailored to individual countries' markets.[37]

The research also suggests that appropriate structure for GISs may vary for different product and service portfolios: uniform centralization/decentralization of strategy/structure may not be appropriate for all GIS applications. Further, the research found that international banks cannot expect to optimize the structure of environmentally diverse information systems with a symmetrical approach to GIS architecture, since any such approach may set limits on the product and service portfolios called for by the bank's global business strategy. An asymmetrical approach, structuring each system to suit the environmental needs of the service delivered, although more complex, can significantly improve international banks' operational performance. Such an approach may, however, significantly increase coordination costs.

Standards. Use of standards is an important strategic move for most companies, since many of today's companies limit the number of inter-company formats they support. With the success in the development and adoption of global standards, in particular in narrow areas (e.g. EDIFACT), it is much harder to make standards mistakes than was possible several years ago. By using standards, companies can broaden their choice of trading partners in the future. Absence of uniform data and communications standards in international, national, and industry environments means that no single product can address more than a fraction of the hardware and communications protocols scattered throughout a firm.

Standards are often set by government rules and regulations, major computers and communications vendors, and/or cooperative arrangements within an industry. Regardless of how the standards are set, they are critical to the operations of GISs. Because standards are the key to connectivity of a set of heterogeneous systems, explicit senior management policy on standards is important to promote adoption and compliance. There should be one central policy regarding key technologies/standards (e.g. EDI, SQL). This policy should include a management agenda for understanding both standards and the standard-setting process within industry, national, and international environments.[23] Such a central policy accomplishes several objectives, reducing cost, avoiding vendor viability, achieving economies of scale, reducing potential interface problems, and facilitating transborder data flow. Therefore, decisions about the components of network architectures and standards require a move toward centralized, corporate management coordination and control. However, decisions regarding adding traffic need decentralized planning; they require conformity by IS managers to data communications standards.

3.1.2 Data management strategy and architecture

Data architecture concerns the arrangement of databases within an organization. Although every organization that keeps data has a data architecture, in most organizations it is the result of evolution of application databases in its various departments and not the result of a well-planned data management strategy.[14,45] Data management problems are amplified for large global firms with diverse product families. For a global firm with congested data highways, the problems of getting the right data in the right amount to the right people at the right time multiply as global markets emerge.[8]

Lack of a centralized information management strategy often causes corporate entities (e.g. customers and products) to have multiple attributes, coding schemes, and values across databases.[14] This makes linkages or data sharing among value activities difficult at best; establishing linkages requires excessive time and human resources; costs and performance of other data-related activities within the value chain are affected. These factors make important performance and correlation data unavailable to top management for decision making, thereby creating important obstacles to the firm's competitive position and its future competitive advantage.

Strategy/Architecture. To increase coordination among a global firm's value-chain activities, its data architecture should be designed based on an integrated data management strategy. This strategy should mandate creation of a set of *corporate databases* derived from the firm's value-chain activities. A recent study has pointed out the significance of a firm's value-chain activities in deploying IT strategically;[20] however, no specific information management strategy is proposed.

Corporate data is used by more than one functional area within the value-chain activities. In contrast, department data is often used mainly by departments within the functional area that comprises a value-chain activity. Corporate data is used by departments across functions.

Corporate databases should be based on business entities involved in value-chain activities rather than around individual applications. A firm must define (1) appropriate measures of performance for each value activity (e.g. sales volume by market by period), (2) corporate entities by which the performance is measured (e.g. product, package type), (3) relationships among the entities defined, (4) entities' value sets, coding schemes, and attributes, (5) corporate databases derived from the entities, and (6) relationships among the corporate databases. For example, for a direct value-adding activity such as marketing and sales within a firm's value chain, the corporate databases may include: advertisement, brand, market, promotion, sales.

Given this data management strategy, corporate databases are defined independent of applications; they are accessible by all potential users. This data management strategy allows a firm's senior management to (1) integrate and coordinate information with the value-adding and support activities within the value chain, (2) identify significant trends in performance data, and (3) compare local activities to activities in other comparable locations.

This data management strategy creates an important advantage for a global firm, because activities used for the firm's strategic business planning are used to define the corporate databases. The critical establishment of linkage between strategic business planning and strategic information systems planning is possible when this strategy is used, because the activities that create value for the firm customers also create data the firm needs to operate. However, the strategy does not imply that all application databases should be replaced by corporate databases. Application databases should remain (directly or indirectly) as long as the applications exist; but there should be a disciplined flow of data among corporate, functional, and application databases.

3.1.3 *Alignment of global business and GIS management strategy: a plan for action*

One challenge facing management today is the necessity for the organization to align its business strategy/structure to its information systems management/ development strategy. A proper design of critical linkages among a firm's value-chain activities results in an effective business design involving information technology and an improved coordination with coalition partners, as well as among a firm's own subsidiaries. Previous research has emphasized the benefits of establishing proper linkages between business-strategic planning and technology-strategic planning for an organization.[22,28] Among these are proper strategic positioning of an organization, improvements in organizational effectiveness, efficiency and performance, and full exploitation of information technology investment.

Establishing the necessary alignment requires the involvement of and co-operation with both the senior business planner and the senior IS technology manager. This results in a new set of responsibilities and skills for both. For the senior business planner, new sets of responsibilities include (1) formal integration of the strategic business plan with the strategic IS plan, (2) examination of the business needs associated with a centralized and/or coordinated network, technology, and data management strategy, (3) review of the network architecture as a key enabling technology for the firm's competitive strategy and assessment of the impact of network alternatives on business strategy, (4) awareness of key technologies/standards and standard-setting processes at the industry, national, and international levels, (5) championing the rapidly expanding use of industry, national, and international standards.

For the senior information technology manager, new and critical responsibilities include (1) awareness of the firm's business challenges in the changing global environment and involvement in shaping the firm's leverage of information technology in its global business strategy, (2) preparing a systems development environment that recognizes the long-term company-wide perspective in a multi-regional and multi-cultural environment, (3) planning the development of the application portfolio on the basis of the firm's current business and its global strategic posture in the future, (4) making the 'business purpose' of the strategic systems development projects clear in a global business context, (5) selecting and recommending key technologies/standards for linking systems across geographic and cultural boundaries, (6) setting automation of linkages among the internal/external activities within the firm's value chain as goals and selling them to others, (7) designing corporate databases derived from the firm's value-chain activities, accounting for business cultural differences, and (8) facilitating corporate restructuring through the provision of flexibility in business services.

4 Summary and conclusions

Changes in technologies and market structures have shifted competition from national to a global scope. This has resulted in the need for new organizational strategies/structures. Traditional organizational designs are not appropriate for the new strategies, because they evolved in response to different competitive pressures. New organizational structures need to achieve both flexibility and coordination among the firm's diverse activities in the new international markets.

Globalization trends have resulted in a variety of organizational designs that have created both business and information management challenges. A global information systems (GIS) management strategy is required.

The key components of a GIS management strategy should include: (1) a centralized and/or coordinated business/technology strategy on establishing data communications infrastructure, architecture, and standards, (2) a centralized and/or coordinated data management strategy for design of corporate databases, and (3) alignment of global business and GIS management strategy. Such a GIS management strategy is appropriate today because it facilitates coordination among a firm's value-chain activities and among business units, and because it provides the firm with the flexibility and coordination necessary to deal effectively with changes in technologies and market structures. It also aligns information systems management strategy with corporate business strategy as it provides a foundation for designing information systems architecture (ISA).

In addition to the global enterprise's competitive posture, globalization also refers to the competitive posture of nations and city-states.[26,27] The issues related to coordination and control in the global enterprise also invest the nation/state to review the alignment of its cross-industry competitive posture.[31,42] It is incumbent on governments to seek appropriate levels of intervention in the business practices of the state that influence the state's competitive position in the global business community.

The challenges to general managers in the emerging global economic environment extend beyond the IT infrastructure. At the same time, with the information intensity in the markets (products, services, and channel systems) and the information intensity associated with coordination across geographic, cultural, and organizational barriers, global general managers will rely increasingly on information technologies to support their management processes. The proper alignment of the evolving global information management strategy and the global organizational strategy will be important to the positioning of the global firm in the global economic community.

References

1   Baliga, B. R. and Jaeger, A. M. Multinational corporations, control systems and delegation issues. *Journal of International Business Studies*, 15, 2 (Fall 1984), 25–40.

2   Barrett, S. and Konsynski, B. Interorganizational information sharing systems. *MIS Quarterly*, special issue (1982), 93–105.

3   Bartlett, C. A. and Ghoshal, S. Organizing for worldwide effectiveness: the transnational solution. *California Management Review*, 31, 1 (1988), 1–21.

4   Bartlett, C. A. and Ghoshal, S. *Managing across Borders: The Transnational Solution*. Boston: Harvard Business School Press, 1989.

5   Basche, J. Regulating international data transmission: the impact on managing international business. Research report no. 852 from the Conference Board. New York, 1983.

6   *Business Week*. Special report on telecommunications: the global battle (October 1983).

7   Buss, M. Managing international information systems. *Harvard Business Review*, special series (1980).

8   Carlyle, R. E. Managing IS at multinationals. *Datamation* (March 1, 1988), 54–66.

9   Chandler, A. D. The evolution of modern global competition. In [39], 405–488.

10 Doz, Y. L. and Prahalad, C. K. Headquarters influence and strategic control in MNCs. *Sloan Management Review* (Fall 1981), 15–29.

11 Eccles, R. G. and Crane, D. B. Managing through networks in investment banking. *California Management Review*, 30 (Fall 1987), 176–195.

12 Engelhoff, W. Strategy and structure in multinational corporations: an information processing approach. *Administrative Science Quarterly*, 27, 3 (1982), 435–458.

13   Frenke, K. A. The European community and information technology. *Communications of the ACM* (special section the EC '92), 33, 4 (1990), 404–412.

14   Goodhue, D. L., Quillard, J. A. and Rockart, J. F. Managing the data resource: a contingency perspective. *MIS Quarterly*, 12, 3 (September 1988), 372–391.

15   Ghoshal, S. and Noria, N. International differentiation within multi-national corporations. *Strategic Management Journal*, 10, 4 (July/August 1989), 323–337.

16   Hansen, J. V. and Hill, N. C. Control and audit of electronic data inter-change. *MIS Quarterly*, 13, 4 (December 1989), 403–413.

17   Harrigan, K. R. *Strategies for Joint Ventures*. Lexington, MA: 1985.

18   Huber, G. P. The nature and design of post industrial organization. *Management Science*, 30 (1984), 928–951.

19   Iramon, W. H. *Information Systems Architecture*. Englewood Cliffs, NJ: Prentice-Hall, 1986.

20   Johnston, H. R. and Carrico, S. R. Developing capabilities to use information strategically. *MIS Quarterly*, 12, 1 (March 1988), 36–48.

21   Johnston, H. R. and Vitale, M. Creating competitive advantage with interorganizational information systems. *MIS Quarterly*, 12, 2 (June 1988), 152–165.

22   Karimi, J. Strategic planning for information systems: requirements and information engineering methods. *Journal of Management Information Systems*, 4, 4 (Spring 1988), 5–24.

23   Keen, P. G. An international perspective on managing information technologies. ICIT Briefing Paper no. 4101, 1987.

24   Keen, P. G. *Competing in Time: Using Telecommunications for Competitive Advantage*. Cambridge, MA: Ballinger Publishing Co., 1988.

25   King, J. Centralized vs. decentralized options. *Computing Surveys* (December 1983).

26   King, J. and Konsynski, B. Singapore TradeNet: a tale of one city. NI-191–009, Harvard Business School, 1990.

27   King, J. and Konsynski, B. Hong Kong TradeLink: news from the second city. N1-191–026. Harvard Business School, 1990.

28   King, W. R. Strategic planning for IS: the state of practice and research. *MIS Quarterly*, 9, 2 (June 1985), Editor's comment, vi–vii.

29   Knight, K. Matrix organization: a review. *Journal of Management Studies*, 13 (1976), 111–130.

30   Konsynski, B. and Warbelow, A. Cooperating to compete: modeling interorganizational interchange, Harvard Business School working paper 90–002, 1989.

31   Konsynski, B. and McFarlan, W. Information partnerships – shared data, shared scale. *Harvard Business Review* (September/October 1990), 114–120.
32   Lu, M. and Farrell, C. Software development: an international perspective. *The Journal of Systems and Software*, 9 (1989), 305–309.
33   Malone, T. W., Yates, J. and Benjamin, R. I. Electronic markets and electronic hierarchies. *Communications of the AGM*, 30, 6 (June 1987), 484–497.
34   Martin, J. and Leben, J. *Principles of Data Communications.* Englewood Cliffs, NJ: Prentice-Hall, 1988.
35   Mead, T. The IS innovator at DuPont. *Datamation* (April 15, 1990), 61–68.
36   Miles, R. E. and Snow, C. C. Organizations: new concepts for new forms. *California Management Review*, 28 (1986), 62–73.
37   Mookerjee, A. S. Global Electronic Wholesale Banking Delivery System Structure. PhD thesis, Harvard University, 1988.
38   O'Callaghan, R. and Konsynski, B. Banco Santander: el banco en casa, 9–189–185, Harvard Business School, 1989.
39   Porter, M. E. *Competition in Global Industries.* Boston, MA: Harvard Business School Press, 1986.
40   Porter, M. E. Competition in global industries: a conceptual framework. In [39], 15–59.
41   Porter, M. E. From competitive advantage to corporate strategy. *Harvard Business Review* (May/June 1987), 43–59.
42   Porter, M. E. The competitive advantage of nations. *Harvard Business Review* (March/April 1990), 73–92.
43   Powell, W. Hybrid organizational arrangements. *California Management Review*, 30 (Fall 1987), 67–87.
44   Prahalad, C. K., and Doz, Y. L. An approach to strategic control in MNCs. *Sloan Management Review* (Summer 1981), 5–13.
45   Romero, V. Data Architecture: The Newsletter for Corporate Data Planners and Designers, 1, 1 (September/October 1988).
46   Sauvant, K. International transactions in services: the politics of transborder data flows. *The Atwater Series on World Information Economy*, I. Boulder: Westview Press, 1986.
47   Selig, G. J. A framework for multinational information systems planning. *Information and Management*, 5 (June 1982), 95–115.
48   Stallings, W. *ISDN: An Introduction.* New York: Macmillan, 1989.
49   Warbelow, A., Kokuryo, J. and Konsynski, B. Aucnet: TV auction network system. 9–190–001, Harvard Business School, 1989, p. 19.
50   Warbelow, A., Fjeldstad, O. and Konsynski, B. Bankenes Betalings-Sentral A/S: the Norwegian bank giro. N9–191–037, Harvard Business School, 1990, p.17.

51   Zammuto, R. *Organization Design: Structure, Strategy, and Environment*. The Dryden Press, forthcoming.

Questions for discussion

1   Evaluate the organizational strategies the authors present. What are the implications for IT architecture?
2   Do you agree with the major premise that 'the globalization of competition and the evolving business environment suggest that the success of [a] global firms' business and its coordination/control strategies may be linked to a global information management strategy'?
3   Will changes taking place in Europe (e.g. pan-European legislation, the introduction of the Euro) reduce the impact of some of the factors complicating international IS, such as the business environment, infrastructure, regulations, transborder dataflow, and standards?
4   The authors present a one-on-one alignment of IT strategy and organizational strategy. Is this realistic? Are there other effective alignments? How might effective alignment be achieved?
5   Assuming different stages of growth in different countries, what might be the appropriate role of the central IT group in a large multinational organization?

5 Change Management Strategy

Change agentry – the next information systems frontier

M. L. Markus and R. I. Benjamin

We wrote this chapter to stimulate Information Systems (IS) specialists' efforts to become more effective – and more credible – agents of organizational change. It describes what we believe to be a view of the IS specialists' change-agent role that is very commonly held by IS specialists. We believe that this role, while well-intentioned and supported by structural conditions in IS work, often has negative consequences for organizations and for the credibility of IS specialists. Further, it does not fit the emerging structural conditions of IS. We describe two alternative models of what it means to be a change agent, their potential consequences, and the structural conditions that support or inhibit behavior in that role. We conclude that increased behavioral flexibility of IS specialists – the ability to switch roles in different circumstances – would improve organizational effectiveness and IS specialist credibility. Finally, we discuss the implications of our analysis for research, teaching, and practice.

Introduction

We believe that IS specialists generally need to become better agents of organizational change than most are today (Benjamin and Levinson, 1993). In our research and consulting, we have seen many exceptional change agents among the IS ranks. But we have also seen many whose approach to introducing new technology into organizations is ineffective or counterproductive.

Why do IS specialists need to become better agents of organizational change? There are three primary reasons. First, new Information Technology (IT) is an organizational intervention (i.e. an attempt to create change). A vast body of research literature shows that how IT is 'implemented' (e.g. how it is specified, designed, or selected; how it is described or 'sold'; how people, facilities, structures, and processes are prepared to accommodate the change) is a major factor in the results organizations achieve from new ITs. Yet, despite our vast knowledge of this dynamic, many organizations continue to fail in IT implementations (Majchrzak, 1992; Markus and Keil, 1994), often at great cost in money, organizational competitiveness, and individual careers.

This same literature also shows that IS specialists *alone* cannot achieve IT implementation success. Executives and managers must do their part, and individual 'users' must do theirs. Why, then, should *IS specialists* improve their change management skills? Shouldn't we just continue to exhort senior business executives to give IT projects better 'top management support'? The answer is that we *do* continue to urge business leaders do their part in IT change management. However, when they do *not*, or when they are not as effective as they should be, IS specialists *who are effective change managers* can often tip the odds of IT projects toward success, whereas those who are technically skilled, but ineffective as change agents, cannot.

Second, IS specialists need to become better organizational change agents because change agentry will most likely become the largest and most important part of intraorganizational IS work in the future. Twenty years ago, almost all IS work was done 'in-house', meaning that IS specialists were employees of the organizations that consumed their products and services. This was the case, in large part, because the software and professional services sectors of the computer world were immature. Today, however, these sectors are strong and growing. Organizations are increasingly outsourcing application development, computer operations, even IS management. Although precise statistics are unavailable, most observers believe that a significant portion of all IS work is now performed by external consultants and vendors.

Transaction cost considerations suggest that IS work that does not require organizational loyalty and/or specialized organizational knowledge and skill will migrate to the marketplace. In essence, this theory predicts that all purely technical IS work will cease to be performed in-house. Conversely, any IS work where organizational loyalty and insider knowledge of the organization – personalities, business process, culture, and politics – are essential or advantageous, will be less vulnerable to outsourcing. IT implementation (introduction, not 'coding') and change management are likely to remain in-house, because this work involves organization-specific knowledge and concern for the best interests of the organization and its members. Further, IT implementation and change management issues are unlikely to diminish in importance or difficulty with time, even if all IS technical work is outsourced and all IT challenges are tamed. And, if change management does indeed become *the* job of IS specialists, then IS specialists need to be able to do this job extremely well – better than most of them are doing it today.

Third, becoming better change agents is bound to improve IS specialists' organizational credibility. Many people think IS specialists have low credibility. CIO, the acronym for chief information officer, is often said to stand for 'career is over'. Outsourcing researchers acknowledge that low credibility of in-house IS specialists is often a factor in the decision to turn the job over to an external specialist. Paul Strassman, former CIO for the Department of Defense and noted IS consultant, says:

> It just happens that the IT community has consistently ranked in surveys as one of the least admired corporate functions. IT therefore becomes an attractive target when there is a quota on how many bodies must leave. (Strassman, 1995a)

We believe there is a strong mutual relationship between credibility and change management skill. First, effective change management *requires* credibility. If managers do not trust IS specialists, they will not let themselves be influenced by their technical competence. On the other hand, effective change management behavior *builds* credibility. When managers see IS specialists behaving in effective ways, they are more likely to trust them and adopt their proposals.

In our experience, ineffective IS specialists often blame their ineffectiveness on their low credibility: 'If only the CEO would tell everyone to listen to us, we could make a difference'. By contrast, effective IS specialists accept the negative stereotypes and quietly work to prove them wrong. By refusing to act within the 'box' created by formal structures and policies and informal expectations about how IS is supposed to do its job, these effective change agents transform not only their interpersonal relationships with their clients, but also the behavior of managers and users in IT projects and decision making. Organizational success and improved IS credibility result.

These are our reasons for believing that IS specialists need to become better change agents. So, what does this really mean? To answer this question, we reread the IS and change management literatures, we interviewed practising IS specialists, we conducted new case studies, and reanalyzed old ones. We learned that there are two basic issues at work.

First, there is substantial disagreement in both theory and practice about what it means to be 'an agent of organizational change'. In fact, we found three completely different definitions of what change agents do and why. The first definition reflects the views of many practising IS specialists, according to our own and others' research. The second model can be identified in various Organizational Development (OD) texts, such as Schwarz (1994) and Cummings and Huse (1989). The third model comes from the innovation, management, and change politics literatures (e.g. Kanter *et al.*, 1992; Rogers, 1995).

Table 5.1 *Comparison of three models of change agentry*

Agentry model	Traditional IS model	Facilitator model	Advocate model
Role orientation (the change agent's attitudes, beliefs, behaviors)	• Technology causes change • IS specialist has no change responsibilities beyond building technology • Specialist is an agent of change by building technology that causes change; specialist is a technical expert • Specialist is an agent of change by serving the objectives of others; specialist is the manager's pair-of-hands • Specialist does not hold self responsible for achieving change or improvements in organizational performance	• Clients make change using technology; technology alone does not • Facilitator promotes change by helping increase clients' capacity for change • Facilitator avoids exerting expert or other power over clients • Facilitator serves interests of all clients, not just funders and direct participants • Facilitator values clients' informed choice about conditions of facilitator's work; works to reduce client dependence on facilitator • Facilitator does not hold self responsible for change or improvements in organizational performance; clients are	• People, including the change advocate, make change • Advocate influences change targets in direction viewed as desirable by advocate • Advocate increases targets' awareness of the need for change • Advocate champions a particular change direction • Advocate tactics include communication, persuasion, shock, manipulation, power • Advocate and change targets are responsible for change and performance improvements • Advocate shares credit or avoids taking full credit for outcomes
Consequences of model applied to IS work (for professional credibility, project success, etc.)	• Widespread system failures for social reasons • Key systems success factors defined as outside IS role and influence • Technical organizational change blocked by IS • Low IS credibility • IS resistance to role change	• Greater attention to building user capacity might increase project success and IS credibility • Emphasis on client self-sufficiency would reduce client resentment and increase IS credibility • Many new ITs offer more scope to IS specialists who act as facilitators than to those who act as experts/builders	• Role fits a need in situations where IS specialists have or could have better ideas than clients about effective business uses of technology • Role might increase IS credibility; role emphasizes communication, which is a key factor in credibility

Table 5.1 *Continued*

Agentry model	Traditional IS model	Facilitator model	Advocate model
Structural conditions compatible with role orientation	• IS is sole-source provider of services • Clients have limited technical and sourcing options • Low IS budget pressure exists • IS is centralized, responsible for many clients • IS is 'staff' function – responsible and rewarded for expert/functional performance, not business performance • IS holds 'control' role – with delegated authority over certain processes, decisions, behaviors • IS builds systems	• Facilitator is not a client group member • Facilitator's function lies outside the hierarchical chain-of-command • Facilitator's function is not formally responsible for business results, though some functional responsibility is inevitable	• One type of change advocate has no formal managerial authority and no delegated control, but may have valued resources to dispense • Another type of change advocate has line authority over the change targets and responsibility for achieving business outcomes • A third type of advocate occupies staff positions in the organizations for which change targets work; those who lack delegated control authority have much greater credibility than those who have it
IS Structural conditions, incompatible with role orientation	• Decentralized IS • Outsourced IS • Purchased systems • Diversity of client technology and sourcing options • Strong IS budget pressure • New technologies that demand different 'implementation' activities	• Valuable expertise in technical or business subject matters • Formal responsibility for business or technical results • Staff control over clients' processes, decisions, behaviors • Concerns about locus of employment	• Absence of managerial authority over target • Staff control over target's processes, decisions, behavior

This very lack of consensus about what it means to be a change agent is an impediment to progress because it creates misunderstandings when talked about. Further, given their definitions of what it means to be a change agent, some IS specialists may legitimately see no need for change in their behavior.

Second, we learned that the different change agent roles grow out of, and are maintained by, various structural conditions (cf. Orlikowski, 1992). *Structural conditions* are social and economic arrangements, e.g. reporting relationships and policies, that influence the processes of IS work (e.g. which activities are done by in-house specialists and which by vendors and/or clients) and the outcomes of IS work (e.g. how successful IT projects are and how clients view specialists' credibility and effectiveness). An example is the organizational policy, common 20 years ago but virtually extinct today, requiring all information systems to be built in-house rather than by outside vendors (Friedman, 1989).

Structural conditions help us understand why the IS role is what it is today, and they help us understand why the IS role is difficult (though not impossible) to change. They also tell us where and how we need to intervene to make a difference – for instance, by changing official organizational policies that define the IS function's role and by education and training programs.

This chapter presents three different models of change agentry. The models should be understood as 'ideal types', rather than as empirical categories. Thus, any particular individual or group might exhibit some mix of the models, either at the same time or in different situations. Nevertheless, we believe these models broadly characterize dominant beliefs in each of the three different practice domains explored. In all three models, IS change agentry is understood as a basic orientation toward the goals and means of IS work that shapes what the practitioner does and how she or he does it. Change agentry is not something a specialist might do *instead* of doing IS work. Rather, it is part and parcel of IS work, as it is performed by specialists who are employees of the organizations for which the work is done. Thus, we see change agentry skill as essential to the successful performance of in-house IS work.

For each ideal type, the general role orientation, the probable consequences in terms of client satisfaction and project success, and structural conditions that enable or hinder IS specialists adopting it are described (see Table 5.1 for a summary). The chapter concludes with a discussion of the implications of our analysis for IS research, education, and practice.

The traditional IS change-agent model

In our interviews, IS specialists frequently referred to themselves as change agents. 'I've always thought of myself as an agent of change' is a fairly typical statement. But, when we probed, we found that many IS specialists view information technology as the real cause of change. Despite widespread academic debates on technological determinism – the ability of *technology* (versus people) to cause change – the belief that technology alone can make a big difference is widely held, both in academic and practical circles. For instance, Silver (1990) defines as 'change agents' computer systems with particular characteristics.

IS specialists, it seems, consider themselves change agents because they identify psychologically with the technology they create. Because technology can be relied on to make change, IS specialists don't have to 'do' anything to make change other than build systems or install technology (McWhinney, 1992).

An additional premise of the traditional IS point of view is that the specific goals of technical change should be set by others, usually organizational managers. This allows the specialist to assign responsibility for any unintended or negative consequences of IT to the people who set the goals. (Managers, however, often blame IS specialists for creating or failing to avert unwanted IT impacts.)

We summarize the role orientation of the IS specialist as follows:

> IT changes people and organizations by enabling them to do things they couldn't previously do and by constraining them to work in different ways than they worked in the past. I am an agent of *change* because I design and build the systems that enable and constrain people and organizations. My role is that of designing and building systems that, when they are used by people and organizations, will produce desirable organizational change. I am also an *agent* of change, because I do not set the goals for organizational change. I do not determine what is a desirable organizational outcome. I act as an agent for the managers of the organization by building systems that, when used, will achieve *their* objectives. I am not responsible for setting the objectives or for achieving them, but only for providing the technological means by which managers and systems users can achieve their objectives. I am an expert in technological matters, not in business matters or in the behavioral issues involving the use of systems.

Consequences

It must be emphasized that an occupational role is not the sole creation of the occupation's members. It is a joint product of what specialists do and what is *done to them* by their clients and others. But obviously, these two things are related. If people feel themselves to have been treated poorly, they often respond in kind.

It is undeniable that many organizations have achieved great results from IT and that much of the success of these undertakings has been due to the efforts of IS specialists. At the same time, we in the IS field owe it to ourselves to analyze dispassionately whether the traditional IS role (as a joint product of IS and clients) has enabled organizations to achieve the maximum possible benefits from their investments in IT. If we have in any way contributed to a shortfall in total benefits, we need to ask if and how we should change. In this context, to identify negative consequences that result from the traditional IS role is not to condemn the role occupants, *but to build a case for changing* the IS role.

Computer historian Andrew Friedman (1989) argues persuasively that in managing their relationships with users over time in various ways (with the obvious collaboration of users and managers), IS specialists have not effectively coped with the human and organizational issues in IT implementation. Building on his work, we see three negative consequences that can be traced, at least in part, to the traditional IS role.

Many IT failures

First, IT failures attributable primarily to 'implementation' problems rather than technical problems abound. Decades of implementation research have confirmed a variety of social success factors for systems (cf. Walton, 1989), but most of them have been defined as outside the traditional IS role (Markus and Keil, 1994). For instance, despite the large and growing literature on end user training and learning (Compeau *et al.*, 1995), it is our observation that most IS units consider training to be a relatively minor part of their mission (in terms of resources allocated to it). Many IS departments outsource responsibility for systems training to human resources specialists and external vendors. Whatever the economic and practical rationales for these decisions, we believe they reflect deeply-held beliefs (probably shared by managers and human resource specialists, among others) about what is really IS work. By-and-large, those who subscribe to the traditional IS view believe that building systems is IS work, while training users is not.

An excellent example of crucial systems success factors defined as outside the IS job can be seen in a study of groupware implementation. Organizational culture and reward mechanisms inhibited consultants from sharing information in Lotus Notes databases, but IS implementors maintained a deliberate hands-off policy except for technical matters:

> We're [the IS group is] a common carrier – we make no guarantees about data quality. As for the problem of obsolescence, if they [the users] don't know it by now it is not my job to tell them. (Orlikowski and Gash, 1994)

IS inhibiting change

Another consequence of the traditional IS change agentry role is that it can ironically *inhibit* desirable organizational change rather than promote it (Beath, 1991; Markus and Robey, 1995; Nance, 1995). As technical experts,

IS specialists are often stereotyped as being in love with technical change. And many of the IS specialists we spoke to described their understandable pleasure in learning new technologies. But this interest does not always mean that new technologies are made available to clients and users, even when the latter *want* them.

IS specialists know that clients always complain about something. A common complaint is that the technical environment is changing too fast for them to keep up. But an equally common complaint is exactly the opposite: that IS isn't moving as fast as clients want in adopting new technologies – for instance, PCs in the 1980s, client–server in the 1990s. And IS specialists often have very good organizational reasons for moving slowly with innovations, such as the benefits that derive from waiting until standards emerge and the desire not to disrupt users' problem-free operating environments.

But IS specialists also have personal/group interests in addition to organizational ones. As is true of all other organizational members, these group and organizational interests occasionally conflict, and IS specialists occasionally place their own goals ahead of organizational ones. Some things they do knowingly. For instance, one specialist told us that he often lied to his clients about the compatibility of technologies they wanted to purchase to limit the range of systems he had to support. But other times, we suspect that IS specialists are unaware of real differences of interests among themselves, clients, and users. They believe that what is in *their* interests is in the organizations' interests, when it is not. For instance, one CIO told us that in his experience most IS managers believe that anything that reduces the IS operating budget is in the interests of the organization. He explained that this is not true. There are numerous ways to reduce the IS budget that shift costs onto user departments and many things that would improve an organization's total performance picture that would require the IS function to change the way it does business. But these changes do not happen because the organization measures only IS functional cost, not total business process cost.

We believe that it is normal and rational behavior for IS specialists to act in line with their own interests and incentives. We also think that doing so is occasionally not in the best interests of the organization in which they work. The most effective practitioners in any occupational group, in our view, are aware of ethical dilemmas posed by conflicts of interest, can discuss them openly as questions of values and ethics (not just as questions of technology and economics), and sometimes, even often, find a win-win solution or subordinate their own needs. By contrast, we found that many IS specialists do not confront these issues directly, relying on organizational standards, persuasion, and manipulation of technical information to get their own way.

The **symptoms** are clients complaining about IS specialists blocking needed technical change, while IS specialists are desiring higher budgets to study new technologies. The **root cause**, in our view, is differences in interests about technical change. Even though technical change is ostensibly what IS specialists are all about, technical change creates problems and vulnerabilities as well as career development for them. Our **interpretation** is that many IS specialists fear that new technologies *in the hands* of users are a threat to their professional credibility and self-esteem. New technology makes them feel vulnerable: Unless they know everything about it, they will look technically incompetent when users inevitably experience problems. Further, even when a new technology's problems are known and tractable, the shakedown period increases their workload and working hours. The **solution**, in our view, is enlargement of IS specialists' roles to encompass change management skill in addition to technical expertise.

Reduced IS credibility

Perhaps *the* major consequence of the traditional IS change management role is credibility erosion. We have already cited Strassmann's (1995a) remark about the IT community as one of the least admired corporate functions. He said this in context of a discussion of IT outsourcing. He found that most of the companies that outsourced IT were poor financial performers – not the result he expected in light of the benefits claimed by IT outsourcing advocates.

In addition to poor organizational financial performance, the poor technical performance of IS departments explains some outsourcing decisions (Earl and Feeny, 1994; Lacity and Hirschheim, 1993). But we have seen numerous instances where IS credibility is low even when technical performance is excellent. Low credibility, despite technical excellence, can be traced to the poor interpersonal relationships that arise between IS specialists and their clients when specialists define their role in the traditional, technology-centered way. We found support for this argument in academic research and the writings of professional consultants.

Several loosely connected streams of research on innovation, impression management, and personal perception suggest that credibility is imperfectly related to technical competence and job skill. Change agents may have low credibility because clients perceive them to be 'heterophilous' (different in background, beliefs systems, interests) (Rogers, 1995) or to lack 'value congruence' (Sitkin and Roth, 1993). Conversely, trust can often be built and maintained through strategies that focus on interpersonal relationships between IS specialists and their clients after some threshold of technical performance has been achieved (Bashein, 1994; Bashein and Markus, 1995).

Similarly, a noted consultant argues that technical specialists can play three different roles in the course of their work for clients: the 'expert' role, the 'pair-of-hands' role, and the 'collaborator' role (Block, 1981). In Block's typology, the essential difference is which party takes the active role and which party takes the inactive role in defining the problem and specifying its solution. In the expert role, the specialist calls the shots, and the client acquiesces. In the pair-of-hands role, the client is in charge, and the specialist does whatever the client tells him or her to do. The collaborator role requires client and specialist to diagnose the problem jointly and to agree on a course for its solution. Although there are times when specialists are required to play the expert and pair-of-hands roles, Block explains that the collaborator role often yields the best results by producing a valid understanding of the problem and greater client willingness to implement the solution.

The other two roles have some advantages from the perspective of the specialist. But these advantages often exact a high price in terms of project success and specialist credibility. Consider the 'expert' role. Experts often have high status, and they feel good when their expertise is used. However, people may distrust and withhold data from those who set themselves up as experts, leading to incorrect diagnoses and solutions. Further, people may lack commitment to implementing solutions proposed by experts. And they may become dependent on experts, which in turn generates resentment and resistance. Dependent clients may fail to acquire routine and simple skills for themselves, thus preventing experts from pursuing opportunities for skill enhancement or promotions. In short, the expert role can reduce specialists' credibility and produce reactions that thwart project success, even when the specialist has great technical skills and professional qualifications. Similarly, Block shows that the pair-of-hands role does not exempt the specialist from client blame when the solution the client wants fails to work.

IS specialists can often be observed to adopt the expert and the pair-of-hands roles in IS development and reengineering projects (Markus and Robey, 1995). The conclusion is that the role behavior of IS specialists is a probable contributor to the high failure rates of projects involving IT. Lawrence (1969) makes a similar point in his classic work: resistance is often people's reaction to the change *agents*, not necessarily to the change itself.

This chapter focuses on the IS specialist's role in IT-enabled organizational change. Thus, our analysis differs somewhat from Block's, which focuses particularly on who (specialist, client, or both collaboratively) should specify what the change should be. Nevertheless, we agree with Block that the roles played by IT specialists while they do their technical work can profoundly affect the quality of the solution, client satisfaction with the solution and willingness to do what it takes to make it a success, and client satisfaction with, and belief in, the competence of the specialist (i.e. the specialists' credibility).

Structural conditions

The traditional IS worldview is highly consistent with the ways in which IS work has historically been structured and managed and is still in many organizations. In the past, the work of internal IS specialists was shaped by three factors (Friedman, 1989):

- policies that established internal IS specialists as sole providers of computer services
- technologies and structures that limited the number of options available to clients and users
- lack of external competition, which protected IS departments from budget cuts

Further, IS specialists typically worked in large centralized IS departments. While many IS managers tend to think of themselves as 'line' managers, because they have huge budgets and run large production facilities, the fact remains that most IS units do not have responsibility for key *organizational* results (e.g. profitability). Instead, they are measured and rewarded for functional unit goals, such as 'delivering usable systems on time, on budget', in the words of the head of a major academic IS department. 'Real' line managers stereotype them as 'staff' – a term with the highly pejorative connotations of 'out of touch with our needs' and 'telling us to do things that don't make business sense'.

These negative perceptions (that is, poor IS credibility) do have a basis in structural conditions. Since IS units were required to support many different organizational groups, they could not be expected to know all their clients' needs well and to serve all their individuals interests equally well. And the functional incentives of IS departments are known to promote goal displacement, such as the cultivation of technical expertise for its own sake and the substitution of functional unit goals for the enterprise goal of performance improvement.

In short, structural conditions make a good explanation for how the IS role evolved to its present form over time. They also make a good prediction of what the IS role is likely to be in the future, under two (unlikely) conditions: (1) that structural conditions stay the same, and (2) that IS specialists do not actively try to change their role. Further, structural conditions tell us a lot about why IS specialists might not want to try to change their role: structural conditions represent the obstacles they face in trying to do so. A former CIO of Dupont recounted how he spent the first five years of his tenure achieving a reliable operation, and the next five unsuccessfully trying to unleash an entrepreneurial, 'help the business', culture. The seeds of his failure lay in his own past success.

On the other hand, we believe there is a very good case for voluntary IS role change. As presented above, the case is that (leaving aside all past blame and all past success) the traditional IS has some consequences that *IS specialists perceive* as negative. An example is 'Career is over'.

Further, the structural conditions that shaped the IS role in the past are changing in ways that demand a proactive change in the IS role. We have already mentioned the trend toward outsourcing. In addition, many organizations that retain IS work in-house have radically decentralized the IS function, giving responsibility for applications development and other IT-related decisions to business unit managers. Finally, many new information technologies – from groupware to the World Wide Web – are acquired as packages, not developed in-house. While they may require customization and content, they don't require the same sorts of development activities that IS specialists have traditionally performed for transaction processing and decision support systems (Farwell *et al.*, 1992).

Where the structural conditions of IS work have changed – for example, where IS is decentralized or outsourced and where systems are bought, not built – the old IS worldview seems distinctly dated. So, when we studied a company that had recently decentralized its IS personnel to the business units, both the CEO and the IS manager told us in no uncertain terms and in almost exactly the same words: 'There are no *systems* projects here, only *business* projects.' We conclude that the IS role *must* change, despite the structural conditions that make it difficult to do so.

In summary, the traditional IS view of change agentry assumes that technology does all the work of organizational change and that 'change agents' only need to change the technology (slowly). This model rationalizes a narrow focus on *building* technology, rather than a broader focus on achieving business results. The next section describes an alternative view of the change agent, coming from the literature and practice of organizational development.

The facilitator model

The Organizational Development (OD) literature (e.g. Cummings and Huse, 1989; Schwarz, 1994) depicts the change agent's role something like this:

> Organizational change is brought about by people (not technology). In order to make real and lasting change, people in organizations need to be able to make informed choices on the basis of valid information (about others' views, not just about the business issues), and they need to accept responsibility for their own behavior, including the success of the actions they take to create change. I am an agent of change because I help people create the conditions of informed choice, valid information, and personal responsibility. I have an obligation to increase people's capacity to create these conditions so that they do not become or remain

dependent on my helping them to do so. I have expertise in various subject matters (such as group dynamics and the effects of rewards on human motivation), but my primary role is one of facilitating the group and organizational processes by which people work on *content* (the particular business issues facing a group, such as the need for an information system). When I act as a process facilitator, I must avoid acting as a content expert and should not express my views about the specific technical or business issues at hand. In performing my role, it is often, maybe always, the case that different parties have different goals, objectives, and interests in change. Therefore, I must always serve the interests of the 'total client system' (e.g. the organization and its external stakeholders), even when this is in conflict with the interests of the particular managers who 'hired' me as a consultant or with my own personal and professional interests.

This facilitator model of change agentry has several important points of difference from the traditional IS model. The first is belief about what causes change. OD practitioners believe that it is people (clients) who create change, not themselves as change agents or their change 'technology' (e.g. OD interventions). Therefore, OD practitioners intervene in (facilitate) group and organizational processes in ways intended to increase the capacity and skills of the clients to create change. (This is analogous to an IS department defining its role as one of teaching clients and users how to select and build systems for themselves, rather than doing systems building and selection for them.) Further, OD practitioners believe that this increased capacity should extend to the domain of OD work, so that the professional services of OD practitioners are not permanently required by a specific client. OD practitioners do, however, agree with traditional IS specialists in not accepting personal responsibility for whether change actually happens or performance improvement occurs. 'So long as they act effectively, facilitators are not responsible for the group's ineffective behavior or its consequences' (Schwarz, 1994). The client group or organization itself is believed responsible for results (Argyris, 1990).

Second, the facilitator model of change agentry differs from the traditional IS model in how it handles technical or business expertise. OD practitioners view themselves as experts in 'process' (in the sense of behavioral or group process, not in the sense of 'business' process), not as experts in the 'content' of the technical or business issue the client is dealing with. OD practitioners are repeatedly cautioned not to provide factual information, opinions, or recommendations that are unrelated to how the group tackles the problem (Schwarz, 1994). Making the analogy to the IS situation, the *facilitator* (in our change agentry sense) of a JAD session would feel free to describe the next stages of the JAD process or the evidence of an interpersonal conflict in the team, but not to discuss the relative merits of client-server versus mainframe computing or to recommend which software to buy.

A third key difference between the facilitator model and the traditional IS model of change agentry concerns OD practitioners' explicit awareness of their power and the dangers to the client of their using it. (See Markus and Bjørn-Andersen, 1987, for discussion of similar issues in IS.) OD practitioners know that their personal and professional interests do not always coincide with those of a particular client or the 'whole client system' (Schwarz, 1994). And they consider it unethical to use their power in ways that undermine clients' abilities to be informed and responsible. This is why they believe that acting as a content expert (e.g. giving technical advice) is incompatible with the facilitator role: it may exert undue influence on the client's choice.

There is increasing IS interest in, and research on, the facilitation of technology-mediated group meetings and decisions. This is important work, but the parallels between it and our facilitation model of change agentry are imperfect for two reasons: First, our concern is with the facilitation of organizational change, not the facilitation of group meetings *per se* (although much organizational change is, of course, planned in meetings). Second, there is a technical component of Group Support Systems (GSS) facilitation, e.g. running the software, that is irrelevant to our concerns here.

Consequences

Why might IS specialists benefit from moving in the direction of the facilitator model of the change agent role? First, the OD approach to change agentry reduces some of the known points of friction in IS-client relations. For example, clients frequently complain about the imposition and enforcement of IT standards and about slow deployment of new ITs. In the traditional role, IS specialists tend to focus on why such policies are technically correct. This enrages their clients, who see it as self-serving behavior. By adopting more of a facilitator role, IS specialists would do things differently (leaving aside potential future changes in the structures of standards and policy setting). First, the IS specialists would focus on providing full and valid information about the alternatives. This means both pros and cons for each alternative, indicating who benefits and who pays. Second, the IS specialists would disclose their own group interests while encouraging open discussion of differences.

This requires a bit more explanation. One common OD intervention in negotiation situations involves helping people to distinguish between 'positions' (or proposed solutions) and 'interests' (or criteria by which a party judges a solution). When people become emotionally attached to their own positions, they often fail to see that another solution satisfies their interests as well or better, while at the same time meeting others' needs. It is very much easier to satisfy a client who says, 'I want to minimize users' and my relearning costs' than it is for the one who says, 'I want brand X'. Similarly, it's much easier for clients to accommodate IS specialists who say, 'We're afraid that you'll blame us for not meeting budget, schedule, and reliability targets if we go with a client/server architecture where we don't have much experience' than for those who say, 'The mainframe solution is better for this type problem'.

A second advantage of IS adopting more of a facilitator role is that it legitimizes IS responsibility for IT education and training for clients and users. As noted earlier, education, training, and other implementation activities are generally viewed as outside the IS role, in part because formal authority for training usually is assigned elsewhere (e.g. Human Resources). Yet, research and theory suggest that these factors have a profound, if not driving, influence on IS project success (Markus and Keil, 1994; Soh and Markus, 1995). Therefore, the IS function must *take responsibility* to ensure that IT training gets done right, regardless of who is officially in charge of training. Here we are making a distinction between what one CIO called 'an area of responsibility versus an area of active management'. IS specialists may not actively manage (design, deliver, contract for) IT training. Yet, IS units that take responsibility for this critical success factor (by facilitating its effective accomplishment) are much more successful as organizational change agents than those that do not. To do this job effectively, they need to know almost as much about technical learning, training, and communication as they do about IT.

The facilitator model of change agentry also places a value on making clients self-sufficient or independent of practitioner interventions. Dependence breeds resentment, and resentment destroys working relationships and professional credibility. We believe that clients' perceived dependence on IS specialists (whether it reflects a real lack of client skill or is an artifact of organizational IT sourcing policies) is a major factor in the poor credibility of many IS departments and CIOs today. Improved client self-sufficiency might turn this situation around.

A final advantage in movement toward the facilitator model is that many new information technologies provide greater opportunities to IS specialists who act as facilitators than to IS specialists who act as systems builders and technical experts. Interviews with IS specialists suggest that many new information technologies are not viewed as 'part of IS'. Examples include: digital telephony and voice mail, videoconferencing, the World Wide Web, etc. Probing reveals that these technologies are often considered as not part of IS because they are 'boxes'. That is, they provide minimal opportunities for building and development. Yet, many of these pre-programmed new technologies, such as group support systems, require considerable change facilitation skills for their effective deployment and use (in addition to software use facilitation). IS specialists who facilitate their clients' ability to make free, informed, and responsible decisions about IT adoption and use provide a valuable service, even if this work does not display IS technical expertise.

Structural conditions

OD practitioners recognize that certain structural conditions are necessary or at least useful for maintaining their role. They believe that, to be effective, they cannot be members (neither managers nor ordinary members) of the groups they facilitate. Of course, managers and members can successfully practice many facilitation techniques, but membership in the client system prevents them from acting formally as a neutral third-party. In the OD field, much attention is paid to the difficulties of being an internal practitioner. Internal practitioners strive to deal with these difficulties by removing themselves as far as possible from the formal chain-of-command. Ideally, they are organizationally separate from the human resource function and report directly to the chairman or CEO.

These structural conditions can be observed in the methodologies developed for systems development and reengineering projects by people from the OD tradition (cf. Bancroft, 1992; Mumford and Weir, 1979; Walton, 1989). OD-oriented methodologies differ considerably from traditional IS Systems Development Life Cycle (SDLC) manuals or reengineering bibles. One striking difference is that IS specialists are never recommended to facilitate the OD-designed processes (although they may in fact do so (cf. Davidson, 1993)). As experts, IS specialists are viewed as ineligible for the facilitator role and consigned to ordinary group membership. By contrast, in the 'user-led design' processes designed by IS specialists, IS specialists often lead the user teams. When they do, they often depart from the prescribed facilitation role in numerous ways (Davidson, 1993). We think this divergence may result in part from the conflict between the IS specialists' role as technical experts and the demands of neutral, third-party facilitation.

In general, the structural conditions that support the facilitator model of change agentry – avoidance of expertise displays, non-member status, lack of line or staff authority over people or performance, etc. – are quite different from the structural conditions under which most internal IS specialists operate. In particular, the following structural conditions present in much IS work create potentially serious obstacles to IS adoption of the facilitator role:

- *Technical expertise.* IS specialists have valuable technical expertise. The facilitator role does not give them a way to use it.
- *Authority for organizational control.* Many IS departments have some organizationally delegated or mandated ability to control the behavior of

their clients or to influence clients' decisions on technology issues, such as standards. As setters and enforcers of these rules and policies, IS specialists would be sending mixed messages if they tried, as OD practitioners try, to increase their clients' ability to make their own informed decisions.

- *Authority for technical outcomes.* IS specialists are generally measured, rewarded, and punished for the results they achieve on IS departmental or project budgets, project schedules, and the maintenance of reliable operations. According to the OD worldview, these responsibilities may prevent the practitioner from acting in the best interests of the client system, and thus may inhibit desired change. For instance, IS specialists may occasionally make decisions with the effect of reducing IS departmental budget expenses, while increasing the costs borne by users.
- *Concerns about employment opportunities.* The facilitator model of change agentry places a high value on increasing client self-sufficiency, reducing client dependence, and practitioners working themselves out of a job. If diligently practised, this value would work to promote downsizing and/or outsourcing of IS departments. These potential outcomes conflict with the personal interests many internal IS specialists have in their continuity of employment with a particular company.

In summary, the facilitator model of change agentry has the potential to reduce friction between IS specialists, clients, and users, thereby enabling better systems and IT management and enhanced IS credibility. These advantages make it worthwhile to consider how to move toward the facilitator model, despite obvious structural barriers. A third model of change agentry, drawn from the innovation and business change literature, also has some interesting potential advantages in the context of IS work.

The advocate model

A third model of the change agent role can be seen in the writings of innovation theorists, some line managers and consultants, academics from the organizational change management school, and change champion researchers (cf. Beath, 1991; Kanter *et al.*, 1992; Rogers, 1995; Semler, 1993). The distinguishing feature of this model is that change advocates work to influence people's behavior in particular directions that the change agents view as desirable, whether or not the change 'targets' themselves hold similar views. Thus, the advocate model differs sharply both from the traditional IS model, in which the change agent attempts to satisfy users' goals, and from the facilitator model, in which the change agent attempts to help clients realize their goals. By contrast, the advocate attempts to induce change targets – both individuals and groups – to adopt and internalize the change agent's views about what is needed to serve the organization's best interests.

Several recent articles in the trade press provide vivid descriptions of the advocate model. A consultant who has studied organizational change claims that roughly one-third of most companies' middle ranks should be composed of 'change leaders'. Change leaders are not necessarily the people who would be tapped for top management positions; they're 'the funny little fat guys with thick glasses who always get the job done' by operating with more than one leadership style and by doing whatever works (Katzenbach, cited in Sherman, 1995). A recent article by a manager in a software development company provides a window into the advocate model that is interesting because of its IS technical content (Allen, 1995). Similar descriptions of the advocate model of change agentry can be found in the business autobiography of Ricardo Semler (1993), among others.

The advocate model can be summarized as follows:

> I cannot make change alone. Change is made through the actions of many people. But people often don't question the way things are done today. I am an agent of change because I see what needs to be done differently and I try to find a way to change people's minds about the need for change in the way we do things today. I often try to change their minds by creating an exciting vision of the future, talking to people about it, and by modeling desired behaviors. But I may also try to shock them with outrageous actions that bring their heads up. Once they see the need for change and adopt my vision of what to change to, they will make the changes themselves. But I'll probably need to remain steadfast in support of my vision of change over long periods of time before they all catch on. And if my position and resources permit, I may need to stabilize and reinforce the change by replacing certain individuals who retard change and by promoting or otherwise rewarding those whose behavior embodies the desired values.

Like the facilitator model of change agentry, the advocate holds that people, not technology, are the causal factors in change. However, the advocate differs from the facilitator in beliefs about the need for participation in identifying the nature and direction of change. Indeed, the advocate thinks of people more as targets of the advocate's interventions than as clients with purposes of their own. In addition, the advocate is much more flexible than the facilitator about the acceptable means of change. The advocate's approach can be summarized as 'whatever works'. The advocate does not insist that the targets make an informed choice based on valid information and does not hesitate to use overt persuasion, covert manipulation, symbolic communication, and even the naked exercise of formal power to achieve a desired change (Buchanan and Boddy, 1992). The most effective advocates pursue changes that serve the organizations' best interests, even when their personal or professional interests conflict.

Consequences

Why might IS specialists benefit from moving in the direction of the advocate model of change agentry? The primary advantage of this model is captured in the old 'programmer's lament': 'Users don't know what they want, and what they want is not what they need.' One of the real sticking points in the line taking leadership over IS (Rockart, 1992) is that many managers remain unaware of how IT can most effectively be deployed in their organizations (although this appears to be changing). So, for example, a CIO of a large, diversified electronics company with 20 years tenure told us that his most successful change strategy was to build small demonstration systems (e.g. client/server prototypes) as vehicles for discussing organizational improvement opportunities with his internal clients. Another sticking point is that many line managers share the traditional IS specialists' belief in the magical power of technology to create organizational change. Thus, IS specialists can add business value by advocating process change and user skill training as key components of IT-enabled organizational performance improvement. While the advocacy of socio-technical change is not the exclusive province of IS specialists (since line executives have an important role here too), there is certainly more room for IS specialists to expand their role in this direction.

Another advantage of the proactive advocate role is its emphasis on communication. In our research and consulting, we have often been struck by the relatively infrequent communications between CIOs and CEOs, between CIOs and the heads of other organizational units, between IS analysts and users, and so forth. We have also heard frequent complaints about the IS function's lack of credibility. We think these two issues are related. One cannot be a successful advocate of major change without many, many interactions and discussions with the change targets. To put it in sports language, change agentry is a contact sport. According to the research literature (Bashein, 1994), credibility is often a side-effect of frequent, pleasurable communication. Therefore, it seems quite likely that IS professional credibility would improve substantially if IS specialists treated good communication with clients as central to their role.

Third, the advocate role may fit the issues of IT infrastructure better than either of the other two models. The major challenge of many in-house IS specialists today is to ensure threshold levels of commonality and interoperability to support internal and external communication and future flexibility. In economists' terms, this is a public goods problem (Markus and Connolly, 1990): because everyone benefits from IT infrastructure, no one wants to pay for it. Therefore, neither rational persuasion based on technical expertise nor a participatory, consensus decision-making approach may result in the optimal organizational result. Most organizations need considerable assistance to negotiate the political shoals of IT infrastructure development (Keen, 1991; Davenport *et al.*, 1992; Strassman, 1995b).

Structural conditions

Various assumptions are made about the structural conditions defining the change advocate's role. Early diffusion of innovation research was largely government funded and focused on change agents who worked for public agencies organizationally independent of the targets (cf. Rogers, 1995). Lacking formal managerial authority over targets, such advocates are structurally unable to mandate or enforce the desired change. (They may, however, have potentially valuable resources to dispense, such as funds, equipment, advice, and positive regard.) For the most part, these advocates are limited to tactics that include: communicating frequently with change targets; empathizing with targets; gaining targets' confidence by stressing their similarity with the targets in social station and attitudes; and working through the targets' 'opinion leaders'.

A second assumption, more common in the management and change literatures, is that the advocate is a line manager with direct authority over the change targets. In this case, the assumption is that the manager theoretically could mandate and enforce the desired change in behavior. However, effective managerial change advocates know this strategy is not likely to be effective, either because the desired change requires people's internalized commitment or because the targets may have good reasons to resist the desired change. (For example, the targets may honestly believe that the change is not in their own best interests or the interests of their firm.) Therefore, these advocates try to create change by behavior modeling and changing organizational symbols, and use displays of power primarily to reinforce and stabilize the change rather than to initiate it.

Later research in the technology and innovation management tradition (cf. Dean, 1987) has focused on internal change champions who occupy staff positions (sometimes in line departments, cf. Beath, 1991) in the organizations where the targets of change are employed. These change agents have some of the same resources that external agents do: access to funds for development, for example, or valuable expertise. And they similarly lack line management authority. Often, however, they have delegated authority from line managers to control certain aspects of their clients' behavior (Block, 1993).

While staff specialists groups often greatly prize their delegated authority, it can seriously undermine their ability to act as effective change agents (Block, 1993). From the targets' point of view, change agents with delegated (versus line) authority to reward and punish targets' behavior lack credibility and legitimacy to a much greater extent than staff advocates without the power to control them (or than line managers with legitimate authority). Staff specialists with control power are universally viewed as people with a particular axe to grind, with interests unaligned with those of the organizations in which they work.

Many internal IS specialists occupy this unenviable position. They lack direct line authority over users and the managers who fund systems projects. But they often have delegated authority to serve as 'guardians of the data resource', 'enforcers of technology standards', and 'approvers of requests for systems, software, and services'. As a result, they may not be able to fill the change advocate role as effectively as external change agents or as staff members (like OD practitioners) who lack or decline to exercise organizational control.

This structural position translates into enormous difficulties when line managers abdicate their essential roles as change advocates and champions in IT infrastructure projects and business process redesign projects. Almost all projects of this sort are believed to require senior executives to initiate and support the change effort (Hammer and Stanton, 1995). Nevertheless, they often cop out of this role. When they do so, CIOs and IS managers may try to fill the gap. While there is undoubtedly much scope for IS specialists as change advocates, many IS advocates in these big projects are undone by their low credibility (due to their delegated control authority) coupled with their peers' perceptions that senior executives will not back them up. When such projects fail, as they almost invariably do, IS specialists make the perfect fall guys. On the other side of the dilemma, IS specialists may also be blamed for failing to step into the breach left by abdicating executives.

Implications

In sorting out the implications of our analysis, we note that our models apply at two levels: the in-house IS function as a whole and the individual IS specialist (e.g. the CIO or a business analyst). We conclude that, for the inhouse function as a whole, the traditional IS model is rapidly becoming unviable. (Davenport *et al.*, 1992, have similarly concluded that 'technocracy' is the least effective model of information management.) Our reasons are several: First, the structural conditions that originally shaped the traditional IS role are changing in directions that undercut its effectiveness. Second, the traditional role undermines the credibility of IS specialists. Third, high credibility is needed for in-house IS specialists to contribute to positive organizational change.

On the other hand, neither alternative role clearly dominates. The facilitator role appears to be most useful with respect to black box technologies that don't need user-organization programming (e.g. personal digital assistants and integrated enterprise packages) and for some process reengineering projects; the advocate role appears to be most needed for IT infrastructure and possibly reengineering. The required new IS role may actually be some mix of all three models:

> Our role as the in-house IS function is to help our organization improve, that is, to change in a positive direction relative to the whole organization's best interests. To do this, we must recognize that our view of the organization's best interests does not always coincide with those of others. Therefore, we must sometimes use political advocacy, sometimes employ third-party facilitation skills, and sometimes invoke our technical expertise.

We see several major obstacles to adopting this new role – overreliance on technical expertise, authority to control or influence users' IT decisions, and responsibility for technical outcomes. Technical expertise involves knowing and telling 'the right answer'. But technically right answers can sometimes (often?) be wrong for social or political reasons. Insisting on technically right answers can actually prevent progress by inhibiting a workable organizational consensus around a technically adequate, if somewhat inferior, solution. In order to facilitate consensus, change agents must at least temporarily shelve their expertise and professional interests, because these factors can blind them to technically inferior solutions that are better because they can work (in the social or organizational sense). Similarly, control in the absence of line authority is a weapon that often backfires on those who use it. Control activity makes a staff unit into a political player with a vested interest in the outcome and therefore a prime a target of others' political might, when the unit tries to negotiate an enterprise-wide solution. Finally, responsibility for systems development budgets and schedules can divert IS specialists' attention and interests from bottom line organizational performance (Markus and Keil, 1994).

The first of these obstacles can probably be removed just by a change of mind. If experts can acknowledge that technical excellence is only one of several competing criteria for an effective solution, they will better be able to know when the technical best is not good enough. The second and third obstacles, may, however, require formal change in IT governance policies and structures. To be really effective as an agent of organizational change, the IS unit may have to eschew control authority, e.g. by pushing responsibility for IT standards back to business units or to some consensus organizational decision-making process. At the very least, IS units should probably separate as far as possible those individuals and subunits who perform the control role (e.g. budget approvals) from those whose activities involve IT-related organizational improvement work (e.g. system selection or specification, process reengineering, etc.). Similarly, Markus and Keil (1994) have recommended changes in the way IS units are measured and rewarded to reduce the dysfunctional effects of goal displacement.

Even very small IS departments have some internal job specialization. This suggests that not every IS specialist may have the same degree of client contact or the same involvement in bringing about organizational change. Thus, there is probably some argument for having different individuals specialize in our three change agent roles. And undoubtedly some of this would occur naturally, because of differences in individual skills and temperaments. But our tentative conclusion is that all IS specialists who do or could work with in-house clients need to be intellectually familiar with, and behaviorally skilled in, all three roles in order to be most credible and most able to contribute to organizational success with information technology. In our view, the most effective IS specialists are those who can shift rapidly from one model to another depending on the circumstances. Our following recommendations for research, teaching, and practice reflect this, as yet unconfirmed, hypothesis.

A research agenda

Our analysis suggests the need for new branches of computer personnel and IT management research that builds on work by various researchers such as Farwell *et al.* (1992), Trauth *et al.* (1993) and Todd *et al.* (1995) on IS skills and career paths; Iacono *et al.* (1995) on internal IS relationship managers (also known as internal consultants, client executives, or account managers); Buchanan and Boddy (1992) on project managers; Beath (1991) on IT champions; and Davenport *et al.* (1992) on IT governance.

There are descriptive, explanatory, and prescriptive questions to be answered. Descriptively, we need to know how in-house IS departments and in-house IS specialists in various job types view their roles as agents of change. It would also, of course, be interesting to explore differences between IS specialists who work in-house and those who do similar work as consultants or vendors.

Explanatory research is needed to determine the relationships between the roles IS departments and specialists adopt and (1) organizational or individual differences, (2) structural conditions, and (3) particular types of IT-enabled change situations (e.g. traditional systems development, emerging IT, reengineering projects, infrastructure development). Similarly, we need to determine the relationships between change agent roles and the important outcomes of IS specialist and departmental credibility and organizational success with IT projects. The research in this category would build upon and extend past research in the areas of IS management, particularly the centralization/decentralization/distribution debate. The majority of prior research in that area has emphasized cost and firm financial performance as the key outcome variables of interest (cf. Rockart and Benjamin, 1991; von Simson, 1990) rather than IS credibility and organizational success with IT projects.

Normatively, we also need research on how best to bring about change in IS roles and/or the structural conditions that underpin them. This research lends itself to field quasiexperiments and action research. Academics who partner with IS managers attempting to change practice might make important contributions to theoretical knowledge as well.

Educational reform

One dimension of change agentry is often called interpersonal or 'soft' skills. (Knowledge of organizational behavior and intervention skills is also involved in change agentry.) There is a perennial debate about the place of soft skills training in IS and other technical curricula. We have attended numerous business meetings over the last few years where IS and business executives have complained about the lack of interpersonal skills in their new IS hires. On the other hand, we have heard numerous objections from our academic colleagues, not least of which is that, whatever IS executives say about the need for soft skills, they always hire the most technical students. Furthermore, colleagues who have helped develop or teach in IS curricula with a large soft skills component have told us that these programs often collapse over time because of the technical orientations of new faculty members.

Clearly, there are many unanswered questions about the need for, and the efficacy of, interpersonal effectiveness training in IS curricula. We don't know, for example, whether such training would benefit all students or whether it would benefit only those with particular career plans. We also don't know whether IS faculty have the knowledge and skills to teach such courses, even if good educational materials are available.

Despite the unanswered questions, we believe that the IS academic community should engage the soft skills education issue proactively. Some of the answers will undoubtedly emerge from experience. Nevertheless, we have some initial thoughts about the relevant content and program structure.

First, in Table 5.2, we propose an outline of content areas for a 'course' on change agentry. This course has as its objective the development of cognitive, affective, and behavioral knowledge and skill. This means that, in addition to 'content inputs', e.g. lectures and readings on the topics, there should be opportunities for students to practise different role behaviors in circumstances where they can get constructive feedback about the effects of their behavior on others. We find that role plays (with video playback and small group critique) using case scenarios of realistic IS job situations are the best ways to foster affective and behavioral learning. We have seen relatively few published materials that are suitable for this purpose. Boddy and Buchanan's (1992) book on interpersonal skills for project managers is a useful model, but the examples are not tailored specifically to IS situations. We think that IS-tailored materials are essential for students to perceive the course as directly

Table 5.2 *Proposed educational program on change agentry*

Topic	Objectives • *to promote cognitive, affective, and behavioral learning about*:
Change agentry	• IT as an organizational intervention • What it means to be a change agent regarding IT in organizations • Different types of change agents • Structural conditions that support/hinder IS change agents • Change process and the role of the change agent • Professional credibility and its role in change agent effectiveness • Routine difficulties that derail change processes • How change agents can/should cope with routine change difficulties • Professional, emotional, and ethical dilemmas of change agents • Explicit/implicit change contracts between agents and clients/targets
The Technical Expert	• The history and sociology of professionalism; the role of professional societies legislation, etc. • Why the IS specialist lacks full status as a professional • The pros and cons of professionalism • Recent trends in medicine, law, accounting, and implications for IS • 'Personality' characteristics of technical experts/IS specialists • Technical experts in organizations: the roles and relationships of 'staff'/IS departments • When and how IS technical expertise is appropriately/inappropriately used • How expertise generates defensiveness in both experts and clients • How to cope with defensiveness to avoid derailing change
The Facilitator	• The history of facilitation in psychotherapy and organizational development • IS facilitation examples: JAD, GSS, strategic planning, reengineering • The goals and values of facilitation • The benefits and limitations of IS facilitation • Structural conditions and organizational issues of IS facilitation • The facilitation process and how to facilitate • When IS facilitation is appropriate/inappropriate • The ethical dilemmas of facilitators and how to deal with them
The Change Advocate	• The history of change advocacy in grass roots ('radical') politics • The goals, values, and ethics of change advocates • The general manager as change advocate • The IS specialist as change advocate • The tactics of change advocates and how they can be used in IS situations • Credibility/ethical issues in IS change advocacy and how to deal with them

relevant to their career success. We have had some luck developing such scenarios by using excerpts from newspaper and magazine articles, qualitative research reports, and interview transcripts. We call the scenarios 'credibility crunches' because they illustrate how IS specialists can enhance or reduce their own professional credibility by their responses to various situations that occur routinely in IS work. Much simplified examples include:

- The client insists that you acquire/build a system with specific features. You know that the intended hands-on users will find the system too hard to learn or else they will resist using it because of the way it changes familiar tasks or redistributes some important political resources. What do you do?
- You support several different client groups. Your clients have told you their priorities, but your boss in IS has given you a different set of marching orders. What do you do?
- Your client has just discovered that her project is late and seriously over budget. She comes in screaming at you (literally) and threatens to get you fired. What do you say to her?

In short, such a course already assumes a level of business experience and personal development that many young IS students may not have. Therefore, we do not recommend that a course in change agentry be offered to beginning IS students. However, a change agentry course would likely have little impact on students if it were offered at the very end of a program with no prior related work. This, we believe, is also the fate of other 'broadening' subjects, like 'computers and society', when they are left to the end of curricula. Therefore we recommend that a change agentry course be the final course in a small track geared to 'professional development'. The first in the track, we believe, should be the 'computers and society' course. We would offer this in the first year of an IS specialist curriculum for two reasons. First, many early IS students are stronger cognitively than behaviorally or affectively, and this course can effectively engage them at the intellectual level, setting the stage for later behavioral and affective growth. Second, this course promotes the development of insight and perspective before the student takes more technical subjects such as systems analysis, and so should precede, rather than follow, those subjects.

The second course in the professional development track would introduce experiential methods to complement cognitive skills development. The focus of this course would be interpersonal skills in the IS context. As with the change agent course, it would make heavy use of IS-specific exercises and role plays. At the content level, it would cover:

- individual differences (cognitive, affective, behavioral) and the student's own personal styles

- active listening skills, interpersonal conflict, interviewing techniques
- recognition of, and intervention in, group and intergroup dynamics.

This course would be a mandatory prerequisite for the course in change agentry, the last in the soft skills track.

Changes in practice

There are two areas of practice in which we see the need for initiatives, in addition to changing the structural conditions governing in-house IS work: (1) in-house training and development for IS specialists, and (2) IS professional ethics.

Recently, one of us had the opportunity to conduct a workshop on professional credibility for a group of high-level staff executives from a variety of disciplines (accounting, HR, IS) in different firms. The participants had many common concerns about their need for credibility to perform change management well and about the structural aspects of their jobs that jeopardized their credibility. The experience led us to believe that these issues should be incorporated into internal development and training programs for IS specialists. Here are our suggestions:

- Partner with internal training staff, organizational development specialists, and/or academics to design and conduct the training. Select trainers who are perceived as neutral (not able to evaluate the participants' job performance) and skilled at giving feedback and dealing with emotional topics.
- Make participation in this type of training voluntary and avoid including bosses and their subordinates in the same training session. (Also avoid large differences in participants' status.) Start experimentally with the most interested participants before trying to craft a large-scale program.
- Don't worry excessively about training materials at first. Experienced professionals can easily generate their own. Before the first workshop, the trainers should interview participants about difficult situations they have faced in the past. These 'critical incidents' can be sanitized and written up to serve as the basis for discussions and role plays of effective and ineffective behaviors. Over time, a much richer set of instructional materials and methods will evolve naturally.
- Document and disseminate some of the key lessons learned from the training sessions. The resulting document can be circulated to people who did not participate directly, sensitizing them to the issues and building their interest in attending the training.

A second area of practice that needs to be revisited in the light of our analysis is IS professional ethics. In-house IS change agentry immediately raises profound ethical dilemmas to a much greater extent than other computer-related work, e.g. hardware development. For instance, when interests differ, as they almost always do, whose interests are to be served: those of the IS specialist or function, those of the user, those of the person or unit paying the bill, those of the organization as a whole? When we examined the ethical guidelines prepared by OD practitioners (cf. Cummings and Huse, 1989), we found that these issues are squarely addressed. But when we examined ethical codes prepared for the computer science community (Anderson *et al.*, 1993; Oz, 1994), we found that they are not. In-house IS specialists clearly must concern themselves with the ethical issues that computer science codes cover well, such as intellectual property rights, privacy, risks, occupational health and safety, etc. But in-house IS specialists face additional ethical dilemmas arising from their change agent role that are not now addressed in relevant ethical codes.

To us, the conclusion is clear. The IS community needs a separate code that specifically addresses the ethical dilemmas faced by in-house IS professionals. It can incorporate the ACM and similar codes, but it should also go beyond them to tackle in-house change agentry. We would like to see AIS, SIM, and other leading IS institutions champion this initiative.

Conclusion

We undertook this research to stimulate IS specialists' efforts to become more effective agents of organizational change. We discovered a variety of obstacles. First, we found widely differing views about what it means to be a change agent. Unless these differences are acknowledged directly, miscommunication is likely to arise, inhibiting progress. We found, further, that many IS specialists do not see any need to change, because they already view themselves as effective change agents. However, their definition of the IS change-agent role does not fit the emerging structural conditions of inhouse IS work, and this role erodes the credibility of the in-house IS function. In addition, we found several structural barriers to change in the IS change-agentry role, especially overreliance on technical expertise, control authority, and an inappropriate reward system.

Despite these obstacles, we remain optimistic about the prospects for change in the role of the in-house IS specialist. IS managers and executives have the structural ability to act as effective change advocates inside IS departments. Further, IS managers and executives are likely to be effective change advocates with their peers and superiors when the topic is structural change in the IS function. Voluntary efforts on the part of IS departments to relinquish or share the control that their clients so resent could substantially increase IS credibility and influence in major enterprise change efforts.

Acknowledgements

We gratefully acknowledge the assistance of the members of IS366 at the Claremont Graduate School (Spring 1995) in our investigations. This work has benefited greatly from the helpful comments of Bob Zmud and two anonymous reviewers, Chris Sauer, Christina Soh, Ang Soon, Sung Juhn, Carole Agres, Larisa Preiser-Houy, Dan Manson, Jeanne Ross, and Michael Vitale.

References

Allen, C. D. (1995) Succeeding as a clandestine change agent. *Communications of the ACM*, **38**(5), 81–86.

Anderson, R. E., Johnson, D. G., Gotterbarn, D. and Perrolle, J. (1993) Using the new ACM code of ethics in decision making. *Communications of the ACM*, **36**(2), February, 98–107.

Argyris, C. (1990) *Overcoming Organizational Defenses: Facilitating Organizational Learning*, Prentice-Hall, Inc., Englewood Cliffs, NJ.

Bancroft, N. H. (1992) *New Partnerships for Managing Technological Change*, John Wiley & Sons, New York.

Bashein, B. J. (1994) Reengineering the credibility of information systems specialists. Unpublished doctoral dissertation, The Claremont Graduate School, Claremont, CA.

Bashein, B. J. and Markus, M. L. (1995) Reengineering the credibility of information systems specialists. Working paper (available from the first author), California State University, San Marcos, CA.

Beath, C. M. (1991) Supporting the information technology champion. *MIS Quarterly*, **15**(3), September, 355–377.

Benjamin, R. I. and Levinson, E. (1993) A framework for managing IT-enabled change. *Sloan Management Review*, Summer, 23–33.

Block, P. (1981) *Flawless Consulting: A Guide to Getting Your Expertise Used*, Pfeiffer, San Diego, CA.

Block, P. (1993) *Stewardship – Choosing Service Over Self-Interest*, Berrett-Koehler Publishers, San Francisco, CA.

Boddy, D. and Buchanan, D. (1992) *Take the Lead: Interpersonal Skills for Project Managers*, Prentice Hall, New York.

Buchanan, D. and Boddy, D. (1992) *The Expertise of the Change Agent: Public Performance and Backstage Activity*, Prentice Hall, New York.

Compeau, D., Olfman, L., Sein, M. and Webster, J. (1995) End-user training and learning. *Communications of the ACM* **8**(7), July, 24–26.

Cummings, T. G. and Huse, E. F. (1989) *Organization Development and Change*, 4th edn, St. Paul, MN.

Davenport, T. H., Eccles, R. C. and Prusak, L. (1992) Information politics. *Sloan Management Review*, **34**(1), 53–65.

Davidson, E. J. (1993) An exploratory study of joint application design (JAD) in information systems delivery. *Proceedings of the Fourteenth International Conference on Information Systems*, Orlando, FL, pp. 271–283.

Dean, J. W., Jr. (1987) Building for the future: the justification process for new technology. In *New Technology as Organizational Innovation* (eds J. M. Pennings and A. Buitendam), Ballinger, Cambridge, MA, pp. 35–58.

Earl, M. J. and Feeny, D. F. (1994) Is your CIO adding value? *Sloan Management Review*, Spring, 11–20.

Farwell, D., Kuramoto, L., Lee, D., Trauth, E. and Winslow, C. (1992) A new paradigm for MIS: implications for IS professionals. *Information Systems Management*, **9**(2), 7–14.

Friedman, A. L. (1989) *Computer Systems Development: History, Organization and Implementation*, John Wiley & Sons, Chichester, UK.

Hammer, M. and Stanton, M. A. (1995) *The Reengineering Revolution: A Handbook*, Harper Business, New York.

Iacono, C. S., Subramani, M. and Henderson, J. C. (1995) Entrepreneur or intermediary: the nature of the relationship manager's job. *Proceedings of the Sixteenth International Conference on Information Systems*, Amsterdam, The Netherlands, pp. 289–299.

Kanter, R. M., Stein, B. A. and Jick, T. D. (1992) *The Challenge of Organizational Change: How Companies Experience It and Leaders Guide it*, The Free Press, New York.

Keen, P. G. W. (1991) *Shaping the Future: Business Design Through Information Technology*, Harvard Business School Press, Boston, MA.

Lacity, M. C. and Hirschheim, R. (1993) *Information Systems Outsourcing: Myths, Metaphors, and Realities*, John Wiley & Sons, Chichester, UK.

Lawrence, P. R. (1969) How to deal with resistance to change. *Harvard Business Review*, January–February (originally published in 1954), 4–12, 176.

Majchrzak, A. (1992) Management of technological and organizational change. In *Handbook of Industrial Engineering* (ed. G. Salvendy), John Wiley & Sons, New York, pp. 767–797.

Markus, M. L. and Bjørn-Anderson, N. (1987) Power over users: its exercise by system professionals. *Communications of the ACM*, **30**(6), June, 498–504.

Markus, M. L. and Connolly, T. (1990) Why CSCW applications fail: problems in the adoption of interdependent work tools. *Proceedings of the Conference on Computer-Supported Cooperative Work*, Los Angeles, CA, pp. 371–380.

Markus, M. L. and Keil, M. (1994) If we build it they will come: designing information systems that users want to use. *Sloan Management Review*, Summer, 11–25.

Markus, M. L. and Robey, D. (1995) Business process reengineering and the role of the information systems professional. In *Business Process Reengineering: A Strategic Approach* (eds V. Grover and W. Kettinger), Idea Group Publishing, Middletown, PA, pp. 569–589.

McWhinney, W. (1992) *Paths of Change: Strategic Choices for Organizations and Society*, Sage Publications, Newbury Park, CA.

Mumford, E. and Weir, M. (1979) *Computer Systems in Work Design – The ETHICS Method*, John Wiley & Sons, New York.

Nance, W. D. (1995) The roles of information technology and the information systems group in organizational change. Working paper available from author at San Jose State University, San Jose, CA.

Orlikowski, W. J. (1992) The duality of technology: rethinking the concept of technology in organizations. *Organizational Science*, **3**(3), April, 398–427.

Orlikowski, W. J. and Gash, D. C. (1994) Technological frames: making sense of information technology in organizations. *ACM Transactions on Information Systems*, **12**(2), April, 174–207.

Oz, E. (1994) *Ethics for the Information Age*, Wm. C. Brown Communications, Dubuque, IA.

Rockart, J. F. (1992) The line takes the leadership – IS management in a wired society. *Sloan Management Review*, **33**(4), December, 47–54.

Rockart, J. F. and Benjamin, R. I. (1991) The information technology function of the 1990's: a unique hybrid. CISR WP No. 225, Sloan School of Management, Massachusetts Institute of Technology, Cambridge, MA.

Rogers, E. M. (1995) *Diffusion of Innovations*, 4th edn, Free Press, New York.

Schwarz, R. M. (1994) *The Skilled Facilitator: Practical Wisdom for Developing Effective Groups*, Jossey-Bass, San Francisco, CA.

Semler, R. (1993) *Maverick: The Success Story Behind the World's Most Unusual Workplace*, Warner Books, New York.

Sherman, S. (1995) Wanted: company change agents. *Fortune*, 11 December, 197–198.

Silver, M. S. (1990) Decision support systems: directed and nondirected change. *Information Systems Research*, **1**(1), 47–70.

Sitkin, S. B. and Roth, N. L. (1993) Explaining the limited effectiveness of legalistic 'remedies' for trust/distrust. *Organization Science*, **4**(3), August, 367–392.

Soh, C. and Markus, M. L. (1995) How IT creates business value: a process theory synthesis. *Proceedings of the Sixteenth International Conference on Information Systems*, Amsterdam, The Netherlands, pp. 29–41.

Strassman, P. A. (1995a) Outsourcing: a game for losers. *Computerworld*, 75, 21 August.

Strassman, P. A. (1995b) *The Politics of Information Management: Policy Guidelines*, The Information Economics Press, New Caanan, CT.

Todd, P. A., McKeen, J. D. and Gallupe, B. R. (1995) The evolution of IS job skills: a content analysis of IS job advertisements from 1970 to 1990. *MIS Quarterly*, **19**(1), March, pp. 1–27.

Trauth, E. M., Farwell, D. W. and Lee, D. (1993) The IS expectation gap: industry expectations versus academic preparation. *MIS Quarterly*, **17**(3), September, 293–307.

von Simson, E. M. (1990) The 'centrally decentralized' IS organization. *Harvard Business Review*, July-August, 158–162.

Walton, R. E. (1989) *Up and Running: Integrating Information Technology and the Organization*, Harvard Business School Press, Boston, MA, 1989.

Questions for discussion

1 Do you agree or disagree with the proposal that change agentry is a role for the IS specialist? Why?

2 Assess the authors' opinion that 'change agentry will most likely become the largest and most important part of intra-organizational IS work in the future.'

3 Given the authors' claim that low credibility is a problem facing IT in-house, how can IT managers be effective change agents? Keeping in mind the authors' assertion that they have seen 'numerous instances where IS credibility is low even when technology performance is high', what causes low credibility?

4 Give some examples that support the view of technology determinism (the ability of technology, as opposed to people, to cause change). What are some contravening examples?

5 Discuss the three models of the role of IT in change and what each role implies for the IT manager. What do the roles suggest for IS strategy? What might determine which model is most appropriate in a given organization?

6 Can the IT group, as the authors assume, move from one model to another at will? What model might be appropriate at the different stages of growth (see Table 2.6). Discuss the advantages of 'movement toward the facilitator role'. Should IT departments try to move to the facilitator or agent model? Why or why not?

Part Two

Information Systems Planning

Having considered information systems (IS) strategy and its various component parts, we turn, in Part Two to that aspect of strategic information management concerned with information systems planning (cf., the shaded portion of Figure II.1 below) which, as already noted, we view as the means by which an IS strategy may be developed. We first place IS planning in context and then consider various approaches to and the process of IS planning. We conclude Part Two with the vexed question of evaluating the outcomes of the IS planning process. For further reading on IS planning see, for example, Earl (1989) and Ward and Griffiths (1996).

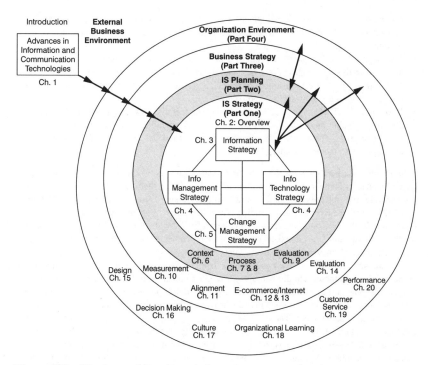

Figure II.1 *The focus of Part Two: information systems planning*

We begin with Chapter 6, by Palvia and Palvia. This chapter addresses key issues facing the management of Information Technology (IT) in various countries and analyses patterns in IT challenges by the level of economic development in the country in which an organization operates. This is particularly important as businesses become increasingly international in their operations. Often, though, we hear quite trite messages about the global reach and impact of IT. While, of course, the technological reach is there for all to see, as the authors argue, 'it cannot be applied uniformly across the world'. The reasons for this do include some technological barriers, such as the lack of an advanced telecommunications infrastructure in certain countries. More important, however, are some of the different values and concerns that need to be understood when dealing with a variety of cultures. To this end, and in the context of IS management issues, Palvia and Palvia reflect on a range of studies that have been conducted in a variety of countries, on different continents, regarding the key issues identified by those responsible for IT in their organizations. While there are some similarities, as one might expect, among the English-speaking nations of the Western world, there are also some marked differences, certainly as compared to countries in Asia, for example. As a result of their analysis, Palvia and Palvia present a model of what they term the global IT environment, which has echoes of the phases of IT development presented in Chapter 1, and the stages of growth framework introduced in Chapter 2. This time, though, the model relates to the level of IT adoption and the extent to which key issues are infrastructural, operational, managerial or strategic *vis-à-vis* the level of economic growth of a country or region. For further reading on aspects of IT in a global context, see Walsham (2001).

We turn next to the different approaches being adopted by organizations in undertaking IS planning. Chapter 7, by Earl, identifies five generic approaches being undertaken by leading firms on both sides of the Atlantic:

*   *Technology driven*: The development of IT architectures as a foundation for expected application needs (equivalent to our interpretation of IT strategy, and sometimes called a 'bottom-up' approach).
*   *Method driven*: The use of techniques – often a consultant's methodology – to identify IS needs by analysing business processes and objectives (see also Business-led, below).
*   *Administrative* The establishment of an IT capital and expense budget to satisfy approved projects (essentially a 'wish list' approach).
*   *Business-led*: The analysis of business plans to identify how and where IS/IT can most effectively enable these plans to be implemented (often called a 'top-down' approach).
*   *Organizational* The identification of key themes for IS/IT projects (cf. Rockart's, 1979 critical success factor concept).

In addition, Earl presents results from field research involving interviews with IS managers, general managers and line managers with a view to identifying their respective opinions *vis-à-vis*, for example, the objectives of undertaking, benefits arising from, and factors contributing to successful – and unsuccessful – IS planning. The results are remarkably similar to earlier research conducted in the UK and Australia by Galliers (1987), with, for example, top management involvement and support, the existence of a business strategy, and emphasis on business rather than technological imperatives, all being cited.

The chapter that follows, by Lederer and Sethi, remains one of the most comprehensive accounts of the methods actually being used by US companies in their IS planning efforts, and also details some of the problems they are facing. The authors provide, in addition, some guidance regarding ways in which these problems may be overcome. Four popular IS planning methods are also described in some detail. These are: BSP (Business Systems Planning, developed by IBM); PROplanner (Holland Systems Corp.); Information Engineering (IE, by KnowledgeWare), and Method/1 (Andersen Consulting). There are many other methods in use, of course, far too numerous to mention here, but it should be noted that these four are all, almost by definition, of the method-driven variety identified by Earl in the previous chapter. An example of Earl's favoured – thematic – approach (organization-led to use his terminology), might be IBM (UK)'s Executive Information Planning (EIP), whereas IBM's Process Quality Management (PQM) approach combines elements of the method-driven, business-led and thematic approaches. For more detail on EIP and PQM, see Lincoln (1990) and Hardaker and Ward (1987).

One of the issues identified in Chapter 8 as being of considerable concern to information systems planners related to the implementation and assessment of the outcomes of information systems planning efforts – a concern shared by many a senior business executive, as the following quote amply demonstrates: 'I still worry enormously, both about the amount we spend on IT and the increasing difficulty of justifying that expense in terms of the bottom line' (Sir Denys Henderson, Chairman of ICI, quoted in Grindley, 1991). Thus, the topic with which we close Part Two, and the subject of Chapter 9, is concerned with the vexed question of IT evaluation. The author, Leslie Willcocks, has written extensively on this topic (see, for example, Willcocks and Lester, 1998; Willcocks *et al.*, 1998). In this chapter he focuses attention on the problems associated with IT evaluation, and details and evaluates a number of alternative approaches and techniques. Further reading on this important topic, including the concept of considering investments of a synergistic nature as a 'bundle' rather than individual isolated investments within a 'bundle' (Hendricks *et al.*, 1992; Miller and O'Leary, 1994), can be found in Farbey *et al.* (1995); see also Segars and Grover (1998).

Following Part Two we move on, in Part Three, to a consideration of the information systems strategy – business strategy relationship – the topic of aligning IT with the business in other words, which is undoubtedly another topic central to strategic information management.

References

Earl, M. J. (1998) *Management Strategies for Information Technology*, Prentice Hall, New York.

Farbey, B., Targett, D. and Land, F. (1995) *Hard Money – Soft Outcomes: Evaluating and Managing IT Investments*, Alfred Waller Ltd, Henley-on-Thames.

Galliers, R. D. (1987) Information systems planning in the United Kingdom and Australia: a comparison of current practice. In *Oxford Surveys in Information Technology* (ed. P. I. Zorkoczy), Oxford University Press, Oxford, 223–255.

Grindley, K. (ed.) (1991) *Information Technology Review 1991/92*. Price Waterhouse, London.

Hardaker, M. and Ward, B. K. (1987) How to make a team work. *Harvard Business Review*, **65**(6), November/December.

Hendricks, J. A., Bastian, R. C. and Sexton, T. L. (1992) Bundle monitoring of strategic projects. *Management Accounting*, 31–35.

Lincoln, T. (ed.) (1990) *Managing Information Systems for Profit*, Wiley, Chichester.

Miller, P. and O'Leary, T. (1994) Accounting, 'economic citizenship' and the spatial reordering of manufacture. *Accounting, Organisations and Society*, **19**(1), 15–43.

Rockart, J. F. (1979) Chief executives define their own data needs. *Harvard Business Review*, **27**(4), September-October, 267–289.

Segars, A. H. and Grover, V. (1998) Strategic information systems planning: an investigation of the construct and its measurement. *MIS Quarterly*, **22**(2), June, 139–163.

Walsham, G. (2001) *Making a World of Difference: IT in a Global Context*, Wiley, Chichester.

Ward, J. and Griffiths, P. (1996) *Strategic Planning for Information Systems* (2nd edn), Wiley, Chichester.

Willcocks, L. P., Graeser, V. and Lester, S. (1998) Cybernomics and IT productivity: not business as usual, *European Management Journal* **16**(2), June.

Willcocks, L. P. and Lester, S. (eds) (1998) *Beyond the IT Productivity Paradox: Assessment Issues*, Wiley, Chichester.

6 Information Systems Plans in Context: A Global Perspective

Understanding the global information technology environment: representative world issues

P. C. Palvia and S. C. Palvia

As an increasing number of businesses expand their operations into international markets, in order to succeed they need to understand the considerable cultural, economic, and political diversity that exists in different parts of the world. For these reasons, while information technology is a critical enabler and many times a driver of global business expansion, it cannot be applied uniformly across the world. This chapter is aimed at analyzing the key information systems/technology (IS/IT) issues identified during the last decade in different regions of the world. Spurred by periodic key IS issues studies in the USA, several researchers have attempted to do the same for many other countries. We summarize many of their findings, and provide insights into the various differences and similarities among countries. A precursory model is developed to help understand the underlying causes into the nature of the issues. Elements of a more detailed model, worthy of further exploration, are also presented.

Introduction

During the past few years, the world has witnessed an unprecedented expansion of business into global markets. The idea of a 'global village', envisioned by McLuhan (1964), has finally come true. At the same time there is realization that information technology (IT) has played a crucial role in the race towards globalization. IT has been a critical enabler of globalization in most cases and a driver in some cases. Today, multinational corporations and governments increasingly rely on information technology (IT) for conducting international business. Therefore, in order to exploit fully the vast potential of IT, it is extremely important for corporate executives and chief information officers to understand the nature of the global information technology environment. In this chapter, we aim to provide not only this understanding, but also provide insights into the nature of world IT issues.

Reports of key management information systems (MIS or IS) and IT* management issues have continually appeared in the United States. For example, a stream of articles on MIS issues in the USA has appeared in the *MIS Quarterly* (Ball and Harris, 1982; Brancheau *et al.*, 1987; Dickson *et al.*, 1984; Niederman *et al.*, 1991). A study by Deans *et al.* (1991) identified and prioritized international IS issues in US-based multinational corporations. As technology is assimilated into other countries, researchers have begun to identify IS/IT issues in these countries. Several such studies have appeared recently: representative examples include: North American and European issues (CSC Index, 1995), Canada issues (Carey, 1992), Australia issues (Watson, 1989), Hong Kong issues (Burn *et al.*, 1993), India issues (Palvia and Palvia, 1992), and Singapore issues (Rao *et al.*, 1987). Such studies are perceived to be of value as they not only identify issues critical to determining strategies for organizations, but also provide direction for future MIS education, practice, and research.

A comparison of the cited studies reveals that the key IS issues in different countries vary to a considerable degree. In order to exploit fully IT for global business, it is imperative that the key IS issues of different countries are identified and dealt with appropriately in the conduct of international business. While an examination of IS issues of the entire world is impractical and infeasible, and even the data are not readily available, we summarize issues from a few countries selected on the basis of their level of economic development. Four categories of economic development are defined: advanced, newly industrialized, developing (operational), and under-developed. This classification is somewhat parallel to that used by many international agencies (e.g. the United Nations). Countries discussed in this chapter loosely fit this classification.

While some level of generalization is possible based on the countries discussed herein and is intended, we need to clearly point out the limitations. The chapter does not cover the entire world. Only a few countries are surveyed and while they may represent many other countries, they do not

---

* The terms: management information systems (MIS), information systems (IS), and to some degree information technology (IT) are used interchangeably.

represent all. Second, the classification of a country into one of the above four classes may be disputable, and furthermore, there is certainly a range within each class. Lastly, some countries may simply defy our classification scheme (e.g. Russia and the former socialist nations).

Key MIS issues in advanced nations

Advanced and industrialized nations include the United States, Western European countries, Japan, and Australia among others. Key IS issues have been systematically and periodically researched in the United States over the past fifteen years (Ball and Harris, 1982; Brancheau *et al.*, 1987; Dickson *et al.*, 1984; Hartog and Herbert, 1986; Niederman *et al.*, 1991). As of this writing, an effort is underway at the MIS Research Center at the University of Minnesota to compile a contemporary list of key IS issues in the USA based on a Delphi study to obtain opinions from IS executives (Janz *et al.*, 1994). Preliminary rankings from an intermediate step of this study are shown in Table 6.1. While a few new issues have appeared in the new list (e.g. business process re-engineering), there is not a substantial departure from the 1991 list of issues reported by Niederman *et al.* (1991). Also, as reported by CSC Index (1995), the IS issues in Western Europe are very similar to the North American issues (Tables 6.2 and 6.3). This similarity is also seen in Australian issues (Table 6.4) and West Europe issues that were reported by Watson and

Table 6.1 *Key issues in information systems management – USA (1994)*

Rank	Description of the issue
#1	Building a responsive IT infrastructure
#2	Facilitating and managing business process redesign
#3	Developing and managing distributed systems
#4	Developing and implementing an information architecture
#5	Planning and managing communication networks
#6	Improving the effectiveness of software development
#7	Making effective use of the data resource
#8	Aligning the IS organization within the enterprise
#9	Recruiting and developing IS human resources
#10	Improving IS strategic planning
#11	Managing the existing portfolio of legacy applications
#12	Measuring IS effectiveness and productivity

Source: Janz, B. D., Brancheau, J. C. and Wetherbe, J. C. Key information systems management issues. MISRC Working Paper, University of Minnesota, 1994.

Table 6.2 *Key issues in information systems management –*
North America (1995)

Rank	Description of the issue
#1	Aligning IS and corporate goals
#2	Instituting cross-functional information systems
#3	Organizing and utilizing data
#4	Re-engineering business processes through IT
#5	Improving the IS human resource
#6	Enabling change and nimbleness
#7	Connecting to customers/suppliers
#8	Creating an information architecture
#9	Updating obsolete systems
#10	Improving the systems-development process
#11	Educating management on IT
#12	Changing technology platforms
#13	Using IS for competitive advantage
#14	Developing an IS strategic plan
#15	Capitalizing on advances in IT
#16	Integrating systems
#17	Cutting IS costs
#18	Providing help-desk services
#19	Moving to open systems
#20	Improving leadership skills of IS management

Source: The Eighth Annual Survey of IS Management Issues, 1995.
CSC Index Group.

Brancheau (1991). As the 1991 issues study by Niederman *et al.* is well-known, meets methodological rigor, and is widely distributed, it will be discussed below as representative of IS issues of advanced nations.

Key issue ranks

A ranked list of IS management issues as reported by Niederman *et al.* (1991) is shown in Table 6.5. These issues were captured by a three-round Delphi survey of senior IS executives in the US. It should be noted these ranks represent the opinions of the members of the Society for Information Management (SIM). Typically, the SIM membership comprises large private organizations. The top ten issues are reviewed below. The review draws heavily from the Niederman *et al.* article.

Table 6.3 *Key issues in information systems management – Europe (1995)*

Rank	Description of the issue
#1	Instituting cross-functional information systems
#2	Improving the IS human resource
#3	Re-engineering business processes through IT
Tie	Cutting IS costs
#5	Creating an information architecture
#6	Aligning IS and corporate goals
#7	Improving the systems-development process
#8	Educating management on IT
#9	Organizing and utilizing data
Tie	Changing technology platforms
#11	Integrating systems
#12	Using IS for competitive advantage
Tie	Enabling change and nimbleness
#14	Developing an IS strategic plan
#15	Connecting to customers/suppliers
Tie	Providing help-desk services
#17	Moving to open systems
#18	Updating obsolete systems
#19	Determining the value of information systems
#20	Capitalizing on advances in IT

Source: The Eighth Annual Survey of IS Management Issues, 1995. CSC Index Group.

Table 6.4 *Key issues in information systems management – Australia (1993)*

Rank	Description of the issue
#1	Improving IS strategic planning
#2	Building a responsive IT infrastructure
#3	Aligning the IS organization with that of the enterprise
#4	Promoting effectiveness of the data resource
#5	Using IS for competitive advantage
#6	Developing an information architecture
#7	Improving data integrity and quality assurance
#8	Improving the quality of software development
#9	Increasing the understanding of the role and contribution of IS
#10	Planning for disaster recovery

Source: Pervan, G. P. Results from a study of Key Issues in Australian IS Management. 4th Australian Conference on Information Systems. September 28, 1993. University of Queensland, St. Lucia. Brisbane, Queensland.

Table 6.5   *Key issues in information systems management (1991)*

Rank	Description of the issue
#1	Developing an information architecture
#2	Making effective use of the data resource
#3	Improving IS strategic planning
#4	Specifying, recruiting, and developing IS human resources
#5	Facilitating organizational learning and use of IS technologies
#6	Building a responsive IT infrastructure
#7	Aligning the IS organization with that of the enterprise
#8	Using information systems for competitive advantage
#9	Improving the quality of software development
#10	Planning and implementing a telecommunications system
#11	Increasing understanding of role and contribution of IS
#12	Enabling multi-vendor data interchange and integration
#13	Developing and managing distributed systems
#14	Planning and using CASE technology
#15	Planning and managing the applications portfolio
#16	Measuring IS effectiveness and productivity
#17	Facilitating and managing decision and executive support systems
#18	Facilitating and managing end-user computing
#19	Improving information security and control
#20	Establishing effective disaster recovery capabilities

Source: Niederman, F., Brancheau, J. C. and Wetherbe, J. C. Information systems management issues for the 1990's. *MIS Quarterly*, December 1991.

- *Rank 1. Information architecture.* An information architecture is a high level map of the information requirements of an organization. Also called the enterprise model, it provides the overall framework to guide application development and database development. It includes the major classes of information (i.e. entities), and their relationships to the various functions and processes in the organization. The steps included in enterprise modeling include functional decomposition, entity-relationship diagrams, and planning matrices (McFadden and Hoffer, 1994).
- *Rank 2. Data resource.* Data should be regarded as a vital resource for an organization, especially for the information systems function and application development. Data and information are corporate resources, and not in the domain of an individual or a subgroup, but for the benefit of the entire organization. Firms collect massive amounts of not only internal data but also vast amounts of data from external sources, such as customers, suppliers, government and other firms. These data should be properly

harnessed and leveraged for optimizing the benefit to the organization. The establishment of large corporate databases, as well as the emergence of firms specializing in specific types of databases (e.g. Dow Jones, Compuserve, Compustat, Data Resources, etc.) underscores the value of the data resource.

- *Rank 3. Strategic planning.* Strategic IT planning refers to IT planning that supports business goals, missions, and strategy. With the role of IT elevated to a strategic tool for obtaining competitive advantage and achieving superior performance, the need for strategic IT planning is of paramount importance. Yet, strategic planning remains a thorny issue for both senior IS and non-IS executives. The rate of technological change requires the ability to develop quick courses of action at economical costs, before they become obsolete. Further exacerbating the situation is rapid organizational change as well as environmental change outside the organization. Perhaps because of the difficulties, this issue has remained one of the top issues in all previous key issue studies.

- *Rank 4. IS human resources.* Human resources for IS include technical as well as managerial personnel. This issue reappeared in the top ten list, after an absence in the previous study of 1986. This factor includes such concerns as planning for human resources, hiring, retaining, and developing human resources. While there is no acute shortage of IS talent, the rapid technological change creates shortage of specialized skills. For example, object oriented programmers are in short supply and in great demand at the present time. Another phenomenon of the last decade which has serious implications for human resources is IS downsizing and outsourcing. Organizations need to decide which IS functions can be outsourced to external vendors and which need to be retained in-house. These decisions have strategic implications for the company.

- *Rank 5. Organizational learning.* This issue calls for continued organizational learning about the applications of information technology, and productive use of information systems. Historically, information systems have been initiated by IS managers, and they have been the purveyors of information technology. However, the organizations that prosper will have to make proper use of information technologies and will have to use IT in the whole organization. As recent examples will indicate, line managers are taking initiatives for the development of IT applications, and end user computing is becoming pervasive. These trends bode well for organizational IT learning; however, such applications need to expand to a broader range of companies.

- *Rank 6. Technology infrastructure.* Infrastructure includes such components as organization's diverse computers, telecommunication networks (both LANs and WANs), databases, operating systems, system software, and business applications. A new issue that emerged in the 1991 study, it refers to the development of a sound technology infrastructure that will support business strategy and organizational goals. The appearance of this issue may have again been driven by strategic concerns. A lack of a coordinated strategy for technology infrastructure may have prevented companies from taking timely advantage of business opportunities as they emerged.

- *Rank 7. IS organization alignment.* The organizational positioning of the IS department within the company has a direct impact on its effectiveness. In early days of computing, IS was relegated to Accounting or Personnel departments, and had the image of a service/overhead function. While that image has been mostly erased, there are still issues relating to its proper alignment. For those who view IS as a strategic function, the IS department has moved up in the organizational hierarchy. Large companies today have positions such as Chief Information Officer (CIO) and vice-president of information technology. Another issue relating to alignment is the question of centralized, decentralized, or distributed IS organization. Technology can effectively support any option; the key issue is that the IS organization should be consistent with the company organization and philosophy.

- *Rank 8. Competitive advantage.* Information technology and information systems in a firm can be used in ways that provide a decided advantage over its competitors. Early examples of firms using IT in such manner include American Airlines, United Airlines, American Hospital Supply Co., and Merrill Lynch. The 1980s provided a major thrust for using information technology as a source of competitive advantage. This issue still ranks among senior IS executives as one of the top issues. Information systems dubbed as 'strategic information systems' are targeted towards customers, suppliers, or competitors, and are an essential part of a company's competitive strategy. While targeting information systems at external entities is one source of competitive advantage, other sources include using IT for organizational redesign, improving organizational effectiveness, streamlining of business processes, and integration of business activities.

- *Rank 9. Software development.* The development of software represents a major expenditure for the IS organization, yet it remains fraught with problems of poor quality, unmet needs, constant delays, and exceeded budgets. At the same time, the organization is presented with more options: in-house development, software packages, and outsourcing. Newer developments, e.g. software engineering methodologies, prototyping and CASE tools, promise to provide some much-needed help. However, organizations are further challenged as they have to constantly evaluate new technologies and development paradigms, such as distributed processing, visual languages and object oriented programming. For example, much of the new development is being done using the C++ or similar programming languages.

- *Rank 10. Telecommunication systems.* Telecommunication systems provide the backbone for an organization to do business anywhere anytime, without being constrained by time or distance. While the earlier focus in telecommunication systems was on connecting users to a centralized mainframe computer, the renewed emphasis is on providing connectivity between different computing centers and users, who are widely dispersed geographically, and many times globally. Telecommunication networks also need to substantially multiply their bandwidth in order to carry all types of signals: data, graphics, voice, and video. Challenges that face the implementation of telecommunication systems include huge financial investments and lack of common industry standards. Yet, for those who have implemented backbone networks, the rewards have been tremendous.

Other issues

Issues ranked just below the top ten include understanding the role of IS, multi-vendor data interchange and integration, managing distributed systems, and planning and using CASE technology. It is apparent that these issues have a strategic orientation, and relate to planning and successful use of emerging technologies in the organization.

Key MIS issues in newly industrialized nations

Several countries have made rapid economic growth in just over a decade. These countries have emerged as the 'newly industrialized countries' (NICs) and are now beginning to prosper. While the precise categorization of any country into any class is somewhat contentious, and is also subject to movement over time, countries like Taiwan, Hong Kong, Ireland, South Korea, and Singapore fall into this group. The latest key issue results that are available from some of these countries are included in the chapter. Singapore issues were reported by Rao *et al.* (1987), Hong Kong issues by Burn *et al.* (1993), and Taiwan issues by Wang (1994) and Palvia and Wang (1995). The Singapore results are shown in Table 6.6, and Hong Kong results in Table 6.7. Once again, there is a certain degree of similarity between these country issues. We discuss only the Taiwan issues as representative of issues of newly industrialized countries, as it is the most recent study of all, and one of the authors was directly involved with it.

Key issue ranks

The key IS issues in Taiwan were obtained by conducting a survey of senior managers in Taiwan, who were well-versed in technology (Wang, 1994; Palvia and Wang, 1995). Responses were obtained from 297 managers on a

Table 6.6   *Key issues in information systems management – Singapore (1987)*

Rank	Description of the issue
#1	Measuring and improving IS effectiveness
#2	Facilitating and managing end-user computing
#3	Keeping current with new technology and systems
#4	Integrating OA, DP, and telecommunications
#5	Training and educating DP personnel
#6	Security and control
#7	Disaster recovery program
#8	Translating IT into competitive advantage
#9	Having top management understand the needs and perspectives of MIS department (IS role and contribution)
#10	Impact of new technology on people and their role in the company

Source: Rao, K. V., Huff, F. P. and Davis, G. B. Critical issues in the management of information systems: a comparison of Singapore and the USA. *Information Technology*, 1:3, 1987, pp. 11–19.

Table 6.7   *Key issues in information systems management – Hong Kong (1989)*

Rank	Description of the issue
#1	Retaining, recruiting and training MIS/IT/DP personnel
#2	Information systems/technology planning
#3	Aligning MIS/DP organization
#4	Systems reliability and availability
#5	Utilization of data resources
#6	Managing end-user/personal computing
#7	Application software development
#8	Information systems for competitive advantage
#9	Telecommunications technology
#10	Integrating of data processing, office automation, and telecommunications
Tie	Software quality assurance standards

Source: Burn, J., Saxena, K. B. C., Ma, Louis and Cheung, Hin Keung. Critical issues of IS management in Hong Kong: a cultural comparison. *Journal of Global Information Management*, Vol. I, No.4, Fall 1993, pp. 28–37.

7-point Likert scale on 30 issues. The majority of the respondents were IS executives. A wide range of organizations, both in terms of size and type of business, were represented in the study. The ranked list is provided in Table 6.8. Once again, we focus on the top ten issues.

- *Rank 1. Communication between IS department and end users.* Communication between these two groups of people is necessary as one group is the user and the other the builder. End users in Taiwan seem to be unable to specify their information needs accurately to the IS group. They also have an unrealistic expectation of the computer's capabilities and expect the IS staff to quickly automate all of their operations. At the same time, IS employees may lack a good understanding of the organization's business processes, and use terminology that end users do not understand. The communication problem between the users and the

Table 6.8   *Key issues in information systems management – Taiwan (1994)*

Rank	Description of the issue
#1	Communication between the IS department and end users
#2	Top management support
#3	IS strategic planning
#4	Competitive advantage
#5	Goal alignment
#6	Computerization of routine work
#7	IT infrastructure
#8	System integration
#9	Software development productivity
#10	System friendliness
#11	Security and control
#12	Software development quality
Tie	IS standards (tie)
#14	Data resource
#15	IS funding level
#16	IS role and contribution
#17	User participation
#18	Recruit, train, and promote IS staff
#19	Information architecture
#20	Placement of IS department

Source: Palvia, P. and Wang, Pien. An expanded global information technology issue model: an addition of newly industrialized countries. *Journal of Information Technology Management*, Vol. VI, No.2, 1995, pp. 29–39.

IS community is further aggravated due to the low level of communication skills among IS graduates.

- *Rank 2. Top management support.* Top management support is required as IS projects require major financial and human resources. They also may take long periods of time to complete. As such, the call for top management support is pervasive in the MIS literature. Taiwan is no exception. Top management support was found to be especially important in encouraging the use of microcomputers in Taiwan (Igbaria, 1992). Senior management is expected to demonstrate its support by both allocating a suitable budget for the IS department, and by showing leadership and involvement. At the same time, top management support will strengthen the IS department by helping acquire the support of other functional departments. Without strong top management endorsement and support, the IS department would have little chance to achieve its mission.
- *Rank 3. IS strategic planning.* IS strategic planning in Taiwan is difficult due to rapid changes in technology, lack of familiarity with IS planning methodologies, inadequate understanding of business processes, short term orientation of firms, absence of successful domestic planning models, top management's unwillingness to provide adequate funding to implement strategy, and lack of top management support for the planning process. Lack of appropriate strategic planning in other countries has had the effect of producing system failures and creating uncoordinated 'islands of automation'.
- *Rank 4. Competitive advantage.* In the private sector, several retail, wholesale, transportation, and media firms have begun to build information systems that can be utilized to make new inroads, create business opportunities, and enable an organization to differentiate itself in the marketplace. Even public organizations have made progress. Stories of how public organizations (e.g. a government-run hospital and the administrative office of a village) use IT to improve their administrative effectiveness and reduce the waiting time of clients, have been reported. The aggressive promotion of IT by the government has helped to raise further the IS practitioner's consciousness of the competitive impacts of information technology.
- *Rank 5. Goal alignment.* The needs and goals of the IS department can often be at odds with the organizational goals. A major incongruence results in potential conflicts and sub-optimization of IS resources. IS staff are often interested in developing large scale and technically advanced systems which may not meet the needs of the business and the end users. In order to assure goal alignment, senior management needs to clearly communicate the organization's goals, policies, and strategies to the IS staff. In fact, a carefully crafted IS strategic planning process (issue #3) would facilitate goal alignment.

- *Rank 6. Computerization of routine work.* In the USA, computerization of routine work (such as accounting functions and transaction processing) was the first priority and was done in the 1960s and 1970s. Even though Taiwan is classified as a newly industrialized country, the extent of computer usage in business is far behind that in USA. As a paradox, the production of IT products has had a striking growth in Taiwan, while the businesses themselves have been slow in adopting the technology. In a sense, the IS evolution in many organizations is still in Nolan's initial stages (Nolan, 1979). For these organizations, automation of routine work (i.e. transaction processing systems) is evolving, yet critical.
- *Rank 7. IT infrastructure.* In vibrant economies, a responsive IT infrastructure is vital to the flexibility and changing needs of a business organization. The technology infrastructure issue is exacerbated by a combination of evolving technology platforms, integration of custom-engineered and packaged application software, and the rigidity of existing applications. Many Taiwanese organizations are gradually realizing that building an infrastructure, which will support existing business applications while remaining responsive to changes, is a key to long-term enterprise productivity.
- *Rank 8. System integration.* Integration of various system components into a unified whole provides benefits of synergy, effectiveness, and added value to the user. Many IS managers in Taiwan are recognizing the need to integrate the 'islands of automation' (e.g. data processing, office automation, factory automation) into an integrated single entity. In the past, the execution of systems integration had encountered great difficulty due to lack of IS standards, insufficient technical ability, and inadequate coordination among functional departments. However, open systems, networks, client/server architecture, and standardization of IT products (promoted by the government) are expected to make systems integration easier in the future.
- *Rank 9. Software development productivity.* Productivity is measured simply by the ratio of outputs to inputs. On both outputs, e.g. the quality and magnitude of software produced, and inputs, e.g. total time to complete a project and total person-hours, IS has had a dismal record. In interviews conducted during the research process, both IS professionals and end users complained that it takes excessively long to build and modify applications. The speed of development is not able to keep pace with changing business needs. Possible explanations and reasons that were stated include: insufficient technical skills, high IS staff turnover, lack of use of software productivity tools, and inadequate user participation. However, new software technology seems to offer hope, e.g. CASE tools, object oriented languages and visual programming languages.

- *Rank 10. System friendliness.* Ease of use and user-oriented features are essential to the success and continued use of a software product, as the popularity of graphical user interface (GUI) will testify. Unfriendly and difficult-to-use systems encounter strong resistance from end users at all managerial levels in Taiwan. The development of a friendlier interface is critical not only for the success of the software and hardware vendors, but also for the ultimate acceptance by the end user. Two reasons can be given for the significance of this issue in a non-advanced country. First, the users may be comparatively unfamiliar and untrained in the use of information technology. Second, a lot of software is imported from the advanced nations of the West and may not necessarily meet the human factor requirements of the host nation.

Other issues

Issues rated just below the top ten included: information security and control, and software development quality. As organizations in Taiwan increase the use of IT for business operations, there is a greater risk of disclosure, destruction, and contamination of data. The high turnover of IS professionals causes great concern for managers that proprietary information may be disclosed to competitors. Probable reasons associated with software quality problems include: lack of business process understanding and technical skills of the IS staff, high turnover among IS staff, and inadequate user participation. Issues rated at the bottom include: open systems, distributed systems, tele-communications, CASE, and expert systems. While these technologies have been introduced in Taiwan, their implementation is in a primitive stage. Also, end-user computing was rated low as it is not prevalent in the country. However, as employees and the general population acquire greater computer literacy, due partly to government efforts, this issue is expected to become more prominent.

Key MIS issues in developing nations

Countries which can be loosely described as developing countries include: Argentina, Brazil, India, and Mexico. These countries have been using information technology for a number of years, yet their level of IT sophistication and types of applications may be wanting in several respects. For example, La Rovere *et al.* (1996) report that Brazil faces several difficulties in network diffusion. Much of this is caused by lack of integrated policy towards informatics and telecommunication industries, and paucity of quality training programs. Similar obstacles are faced by many of the other Latin American countries. In Pakistan, Hassan (1994) describes environmental and cultural constraints in utilizing information technologies. With the emergence of many eastern block countries out of closed and guarded environments, and the general trend towards globalization, information is now available about the IT readiness of these countries. Much of this information is derived from individual experiences, general observations, and case studies (e.g. Chepaitis, 1994; Goodman, 1991). Yet, many of them seem to face similar problems.

Russia and other former Soviet Union countries defy a natural classification into any of our four classes. In fact, the World Bank places the former socialist countries in a distinctly separate category. In their commentary, Goodman and McHenry (1991) described two sectors of Soviet computing: the state sector which included development and deployment of a full range of highly sophisticated computers, and the mixed sector of private, state, foreign and black-market activities which were struggling in the sustained use of information technology. Roche (1992) and Roche et al. (1992) made similar observations. While giant centrally planned enterprises were created that emulated technological developments of the West, little computer equipment was either designed for or used by management and consumers. Thus, while Russia and former Soviet Union countries have made great strides in selected technological areas (e.g. the space program and aerospace industry) the general consumer sector and management have lagged behind significantly in IT utilization. As many reports would indicate, Russian IT issues are therefore characteristic of issues in developing countries. According to Chepaitis (1994), lack of adequate supply of quality information and poor information culture are IS issues reflective of Russia.

A prioritized list of ranked issues based on a systematic study is available for India. We present these results as an example of issues from a developed country.

Key issue ranks

The key IS issues in India were obtained by Palvia and Palvia (1992) and were based on data collection from top-level and middle-level Indian managers. These managers either worked directly with computers and information systems, or had been exposed to them by other means. The issues were first generated using the nominal grouping technique and brainstorming, and were then ranked by participant managers in two seminars in India. A fully ranked list is provided in Table 6.9; the top issues are discussed below. The discussion draws primarily from Palvia and Palvia (1992) and Palvia *et al.* (1992).

- *Rank 1. Understanding and awareness of MIS contribution.* An appreciation of the benefits and potential applications of MIS is absolutely necessary for successful IT deployment. There is a general lack of

Table 6.9   *Key issues in information systems management – India (1992)*

Rank	Description of the issue
#1	Understanding/awareness of MIS contribution
#2	Human resources/personnel for MIS
#3	Quality of input data
#4	Educating senior managers about MIS
#5	User friendliness of systems
#6	Continuing training and education of MIS staff
#7	Maintenance of software
Tie	Standards in hardware and software
#9	Data security
#10	Packaged applications software availability
Tie	Cultural and style barriers
#12	Maintenance of hardware
#13	Aligning MIS with organization
#14	Need for external/environmental data
#15	MIS productivity/effectiveness
#16	Applications portfolio
#17	Computer hardware
#18	MIS strategic planning
#19	Effect of political climate of country
#20	Telecommunications

Source: Palvia, P. and Palvia, S. MIS issues in India and a comparison with the United States: Technical Note. *International Information Systems*, Vol. I, No. 2, April 1992, pp. 100–110.

knowledge among Indian managers as to what management information systems can do for their business. The need for computer-based systems is neither a high priority nor widely recognized. Unless the potential contribution of MIS is clearly understood, advances in technological resources are not likely to be of much help. The lack of understanding is partly due to the traditional reliance on manual systems. The ready availability of a large number of semi-skilled and skilled personnel makes the operation of manual systems satisfactory, and prevents management from looking at superior alternatives.

- *Rank 2. Human resources and personnel for MIS.* Higher national priorities and lower priorities assigned to IS development have caused the neglect of IS human resource development. India is somewhat of an enigma in this regard. In the last several years, India has become a primary location for international outsourcing contracts; yet there is a great demand and shortage within the country for those trained in developing business information systems. While many universities and educational institutes are attempting to meet the burgeoning demand, some of these efforts may be misdirected from an IS point of view. The current emphasis on education seems to be on technological aspects rather than on the application of IS concepts to business needs.

- *Rank 3. Quality of input data.* Information systems rely on accurate and reliable data. The age-old adage of GIGO (Garbage In Garbage Out) is well known in MIS, and directly impacts the quality of IS. This issue has also been seen in Russia (Chepaitis, 1994) and other developing countries. While not reported as a key issue in US studies, it appears that developing countries have inferior input data due to several reasons: lack of information literacy and information culture among workers as well as a less-than-adequate infrastructure for collecting data. Some managers reported experiences of excessive errors in data transcription as well as deliberate corruption of data. The underlying causes may be mistrust of and intimidation caused by computer processing, resulting in carelessness, apathy and sabotage.

- *Rank 4. Educating senior managers about MIS.* This issue suggests a possible response to the top-ranked issue dealing with the lack of understanding and awareness of the role of MIS in organizations. It appears that senior managers do not truly understand the full potential of information technology. They need to be educated not so much about the technology *per se*, but more so about its many applications in business. For example, besides transaction processing, IT can be used for building executive information systems and strategic systems. Exposure to such possibilities by way of education and training can provide new and innovative ideas to managers to utilize IT fruitfully. In the authors' opinion, any education must be supplemented with business cases and some hands-on training.

- *Rank 5. User friendliness of systems.* The appearance of this issue in a developing nation may be attributed to several factors. First, the users in a developing nation are generally novices and untrained in the use of information technology; thus they may not be at ease with computer interfaces. Second, much of the software and systems are imported from Western and advanced nations. This software is geared to the needs of their people and may not be user-friendly in regard to the needs and cultural backgrounds of users in the importing nation. A hypothesis can be made that the ergonomic characteristics of an information system are at least partially dependent on the cultural and educational background of the people using them.

- *Rank 6. Continuing training and education of the MIS staff.* The education issue comes up once again, this time in the context of MIS personnel. Rapid advances in technology and a lower level of IT preparedness in developing countries put further pressure on MIS personnel to keep pace with the technology. Another challenge here is to not only provide training on the technology but to be able to do that from a business perspective. Specifically, two of the problems reported were: many current training plans attempt to train a large number of people simultaneously at the expense of quality, and there is a lack of proper training available for MIS professionals in business functions.

- *Rank 7 (tie). Maintenance of software, and standards in hardware and software*. These two related issues were tied in rank. Maintenance refers to fixing and updating production software when there are bugs or new requirements. Maintenance is a problem because of inadequate resources and competition for resources from new applications. Compared to developed nations, developing nations suffer from an inadequate supply of trained programmers. The problem is compounded if the majority of the software is purchased as packaged software. The maintenance effort is likely to be high if the quality and applicability of the purchased system is low. The quality of a system depends, in part, on the existence and enforcement of hardware and software standards, which brings us to the next issue.

  The issue of standards in hardware and software is an important one in developing countries as much software and hardware (especially hardware) is imported from other countries. The problems of hardware/ software standards are compounded significantly when buying hardware and software produced by different vendors in different nations, each with its own proprietary systems. While some international standards exist (e.g. in programming languages and telecommunications); the ultimate challenge will be to develop an exhaustive set of standards, and then to be able to enforce them.

- *Rank 9. Data security*. An organization's data is a valuable corporate resource, and needs to be protected else it may be abused to the organization's detriment. Data contained in manual systems was not very vulnerable to breach of security due to either unavailability of ready access or inordinately long access times. As a result, many information workers have developed poor practices and habits in data handling. With computerized systems, this attitude can cause severe data security and integrity problems. Newer controls and security provisions, which were unheard of in manual systems, may need to be built which may themselves cause resistance in adoption.

- *Rank 10 (tie). Packaged Applications Software Availability, and Cultural Barriers*. These two issues were tied in rank. Off-the-shelf packaged application software provides an inexpensive alternative to in-house development. All around the world, a lot of software is purchased off-the-shelf. An inadequate supply of MIS personnel (an issue discussed earlier) further necessitates an increased reliance on packaged software. While much packaged software is now being made available, there is need to develop more that meets the specific business requirements unique to developing nations.

Culture plays a role in the application of information technology (Ein-Dor *et al.*, 1993), albeit sometimes in subtle ways. For example, in one governmental office, secretaries and clerical people were mandated to use word-processing equipment. But as soon as the mandate was removed, they went back to typewriters and manual procedures. Apparently, they trusted the familiar equipment more, and it gave them a greater sense of control. Chepaitis (1994) provides the example of Russia, where people have never gathered, shared, and managed bountiful information. As a result, information is often hoarded for personal gain rather than freely shared or invested.

Other issues

Issues ranked just after the ones discussed above included maintenance of hardware and alignment of MIS with the organization. Many organizations are buying personal computers, and their maintenance sometimes becomes a problem due to limited vendor presence and delays in procuring parts. Aligning of MIS with the organization is an issue of moderate importance. According to an Indian manager, beyond alignment, the organizational culture and philosophy itself has to change to accept the role of MIS. Applications portfolio is not a major issue as most businesses are in the initial stages of information systems growth and are in the process of computerizing basic operations. For the same reasons, MIS strategic planning was not rated high, and telecommunications was considered not of immediate interest but more a concern of the future.

Key MIS issues in underdeveloped nations

Underdeveloped or basic countries are characterized by low or stagnant economic growth, low GNP, high levels of poverty, low literacy rates, high unemployment, agriculture as the dominant sector, and poor national infrastructure. While precise categorization is difficult, subjective and arguable, countries like Bangladesh, Cuba, Haiti, Jordan, Kenya, Nigeria, Iran, Iraq, and Zimbabwe may be included in this group. Note that countries may move in and out of a particular class over time. In this chapter, we use two African countries: Kenya and Zimbabwe as examples of underdeveloped nations.

Key issue ranks

The key MIS issues of Kenya and Zimbabwe were reported by Palvia *et al.* (1992), and were based on a study completed by Zigli in 1990. The methodology used in Zigli's study was based on the India study by Palvia and Palvia (1992). The same questionnaire, with minor modifications, was used to collect the data. A number of in-depth personal interviews with senior information systems executives were conducted utilizing the questionnaire for data collection and as the basis for discussions. Information was also gathered from local trade publications and other secondary sources.

The computing industry in both countries at the time appeared to be competing in an environment that was strongly influenced by government and a lack of 'hard' foreign currency. The hard currency situation was exacerbated by the virtual absence of indigenous hardware and software production, resulting in an inventory of outdated hardware and software. In addition, IT was accorded a very low priority by the government. As a result, purchases of equipment were being made from wherever possible, leading to mixed vendor shops and associated problems. Given the basic nature of IT adoption in these countries, only seven issues emerged with any degree of consensus. These are shown in Table 6.10 and are discussed in line with the 1990 study reported in Palvia *et al.* (1992).

- *Rank 1. Obsolescence of computing equipment.* Of greatest concern was the state of obsolescence of most computer equipment. The need for state

Table 6.10   *Key issues in information systems management – underdeveloped nations of Africa (1992)*

Rank	Description of the issue
#1	Obsolescence of computing equipment (hardware)
Tie	Obsolescence of operating and applications computer programs (software) (tie)
#3	Proliferation of mixed vendor shops (hardware and software)
#4	Availability of skilled MIS personnel and opportunities for professional development for MIS managers and non-managers
#5	Possible government intervention/influence in computer market
#6	Establishment of professional standards
#7	Improvement of IS productivity

Source: Palvia, P., Palvia, S. and Zigli, R. M. Global information technology environment: key MIS issues in advanced and less developed nations. In *The Global Issues of Information Technology Management*, edited by S. Palvia, P. Palvia and R. M. Zigli, Idea Group Publishing, 1992.

of the art equipment is urgent and was a critical concern for the IS executives. The current inventory is aging fast and simply does not meet the requirements of most businesses. A major contributing factor is the balance of trade and more specifically, the shortage of 'hard' foreign currency. These computers were state of the art twenty years ago but no longer. Not much progress has been made in twenty years. In fact, some regression may have occurred. These computers have now gone through two or three iterations of emulations, and both efficiency and effectiveness have suffered. The short-fall of computer equipment not only affects the private sector but the public sector as well. Overall, national infrastructures of both countries appear ill-prepared to advance information technology to bring them on a par with the rest of the world.

- *Rank 2. Obsolescence of software.* The inventory of software (including operating systems and application programs) is also quite dated. Most of the packages are of the word processor and spreadsheet variety, or their emulations. Only recently have relational databases been introduced into both countries. The acute shortage of 'hard' foreign currency precludes firms from purchasing software from overseas vendors, and further leads to exceptionally high rates of software piracy (especially for microcomputers). Major systems development is a rare occurrence. There seems to be simply no concept of integrated business systems, e.g. in manufacturing or accounting. However, some contemporary software is being introduced on a limited scale. For example, the relational database package Oracle is now being distributed in both countries by local software firms.

- *Rank 3. Proliferation of mixed vendor shops.* There are many vendors to choose from within one country, let alone the number of vendors in the entire world. While competition among vendors should raise the quality and reduce the cost of technology acquisition, it may also cause severe problems if vendor selection is not done carefully. Due to lack of coherent policies on the part of government and firms, many purchases of hardware and software are made on an opportunistic and *ad hoc* basis from whatever source and vendor that happens to be available at the time. This has led to the proliferation of mixed vendor shops. Of course, mixed vendor shops have added to the problems of IS management, operation, and maintenance. Mixed vendor shops were seen as a major detriment to efficiency and productivity by a number of firms in the interview sample.

- *Rank 4. Availability of skilled MIS personnel and professional development.* There is a shortage of people with computing and systems skills. Finding trained personnel and keeping existing information systems people current with the latest advances in IT are vital concerns of information systems managers in these less developed nations. There are too few qualified people and they are being spread too thin. This issue has implications for the educational system of underdeveloped nations: they must incorporate education and training in high technology areas, do it fast, and keep their programs constantly updated lest they become obsolete again.

- *Rank 5. Possible government intervention in the computer industry.* In economies dominated by government control, there is always the risk of government intervention in the computer industry, thereby threatening to reduce competition and increasing the probability of a monopoly. While a selected few may benefit from government actions, the larger business community tends to suffer. Such intervention may occur in the form of issuance of import licenses to new, local businesses in an effort to encourage their growth. Unfortunately, these new firms sell their licenses to existing, larger vendors. Both the sellers and the buyers realize substantial profits. Another example of government action is the mandated markups on imported parts and equipment. As a result of these markups (equaling or exceeding 100%), virtual cartels have emerged, and the cost of computers, computer peripherals and computer software has become one of the highest in the world.

- *Rank 6. Establishment of professional standards.* The lack of professional standards threatens the entry of non-professionals and untrained people into the MIS field, thereby further aggravating the IS quality issue. Therefore, the professional data processing societies in these two countries are very anxious to gain 'official' approval authorizing them to establish or participate in the establishment of standards of behavior and expertise for MIS professionals. The establishment of such standards will go a long way towards the development of better quality IS products. It should also improve productivity, the subject of the next issue.

- *Rank 7. Improvement of IS productivity.* Productivity is a concern in these two nations as a result of lack of professionalism, lack of access to state of the art productivity tools, and deteriorating hardware and software. In general, the productivity concern seems to extend to all aspects and areas of information systems. Over the last decade, there has been considerable emphasis on productivity in the advanced nations, and serious efforts have been made to enhance productivity (e.g. in the use of fourth generation languages, and CASE tools). However, in the less-developed countries, while being recognized as a problem, productivity appears to take a back seat to often more pressing problems.

Other issues

The existence of archaic hardware and software and the inability to acquire modern resources have caused an ever-widening technological gap and thereby a loss of competitiveness of the domestic businesses that depend upon such equipment. Erosion of the competitive position of firms was an issue expressed by several local executives. Another issue cited by some executives is the question of the local manufacture of hardware and software. This appears to be a polarizing issue. The foreign based vendors, as one would expect, oppose local manufacture, while users and the government favor it. However, software development may be a prime determinant in the evolution of information technology in less-developed nations, as in the case of India and the Philippines.

What was perhaps surprising were the issues not mentioned by the participants. For example, understanding of MIS by senior executives did not emerge as an issue of significant concern. Using IS for competitive advantage is another issue that did not surface in the interview process. In general, the strategic dimensions of information technology do not seem to be as important as the operational issues.

A model of global information technology environment

In summary, we have presented key IS management issues for representative countries in each of the four classes, and made comments about several other countries. Space considerations prevent us from discussing results from other countries that might be available. For example, key issues not discussed in this chapter, but investigated and available in the literature, include the following countries: United Kingdom (Galliers *et al.*, 1994), Gulf countries (Badri, 1992), Estonia (Dexter *et al.*, 1993), and Slovenia (Dekeleva and Zupancic, 1993).

In any case, our discussion shows that there can be major differences between issues of different countries, and few commonalties. There are more common issues between USA and Taiwan, and fewer between other countries. As an overall impression, it seems that advanced countries are driven by strategic needs, developing countries by operational needs, and under-developed countries by infrastructural needs. Based on this observation, Palvia *et al.* (1992) posited an initial model of country specific MIS issues based on economic development of the country. This model classified countries into three categories based on the level of economic growth. These categories are: advanced countries (e.g. United States, Canada, Japan), developing/operational countries (e.g. India, Russia, Argentina, Brazil), and underdeveloped/basic countries (e.g. Kenya, Chile, Iran, Nigeria). They acknowledged that the placement of a country into a particular category is subject to some debate, and that countries may change categories over time. Nevertheless, they were able to make some broad generalizations on the nature of IS issues based on economic growth of a nation. According to the model, the level of information technology adoption increases from one stage to the next, i.e. from underdeveloped to developing to advanced nations. Quite striking are the types of MIS issues at each stage of economic development. In the underdeveloped countries, the infrastructural issues dominate (e.g. the very availability of computer hardware, operating and applications software, and human resources for MIS). In the developing countries, operational issues are paramount (e.g. management's awareness of MIS capabilities, human resource development for MIS, quality of data, standards). Advanced country issues are characterized by strategic needs (e.g. information architecture, data resource management, strategic planning for MIS, organizational learning).

While the Palvia *et al.* (1992) model appears to be generally sound, the Taiwan study included in this chapter and experience from other countries has led us to refine the model (Figure 6.1). Another class of countries has been added to the original three-way classification. Several countries have emerged as the newly industrialized countries (NICs) in the last decade and are now prospering. Examples of such countries include Taiwan, South Korea, Hong Kong and Singapore. If we extrapolate the Taiwan issues to NICs in general, then the majority of NIC issues are somewhat unique and different from other classes. To reiterate, representative NIC issues include: communication between IS department and end users, top management support, software development productivity, goal alignment, and security and control. Clearly, most of these issues are above the routine operational and infrastructural issues faced by organizations in underdeveloped and developing nations. Yet, they are lower in their strategic orientation as compared to the advanced

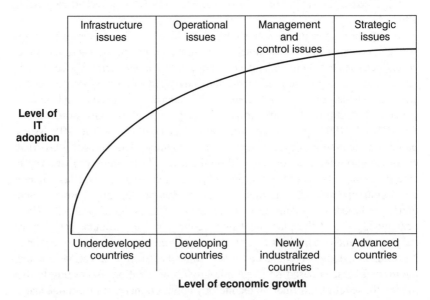

Figure 6.1   *A model of the global information technology environment*

nations. These issues then can most appropriately labeled as 'management and control' issues reflective of growing technology adoption. In a sense, the refined 'global information technology environment' model is similar to the Nolan stage model (1979), which posited the need for a control stage to contain and manage the proliferation of IS activities in an organization. The main difference is that our model explains the nature of IT conditions and practices based on economic conditions in different countries.

The addition of NICs into the model is also supported by the 'management and control' oriented policies being exercised in these countries. For example, Taiwan, Singapore, and South Korea have one or two government agencies which have coordinated and implemented explicit national IT plans since the 1980s. These three country governments explicitly promote and manage the production and use of IT products. Computerization is a national goal and essential to maintaining the competitiveness of the national economy in the global environment.

The model depicted in Figure 6.1 provides a first attempt in understanding the complex global IT environment. We recognize that there are limitations and other elements may be necessary for a deeper understanding of the global IT environment, or the environment of any particular country. For example, the inclusion of Russia and socialist countries under the 'developing operational' country class may be an object of concern for some. Singapore might also be a special case, as it is not really a country, but a city-state, and has a benevolent ruler form of government. Nevertheless, the above model may be a starting point for an organization considering expansion into other world markets, and attempting to evaluate the role and use of information technology in its pursuit.

Basic elements of a more complete model for global IT environment are offered in Figure 6.2. Some summary comments are made about this model here; more elaboration and expansion are subjects of further investigation. Besides level of economic growth, other factors critical to information technology adoption by firms in a country include its culture and political system. National culture comprises the values, beliefs, and behavior patterns dominant in a country, and has a strong influence on institutional and organizational patterns of behavior. Ein-Dor *et al.* (1993) presented a framework for the role of culture in IS, and presented some culturally sensitive findings. Shore and Venkatachalam (1995) explored the impact of culture on systems analysis and design issues. Based on the emerging literature on international and cross-cultural IS, it is a reasonable argument to make that national culture would have an impact on IS priorities.

The political system and government policies also have an impact on the IT readiness of a nation, as can be seen in the startling differences found among western countries, Russia, Eastern European countries, and Pacific Rim countries. Government, inspired by its political beliefs, may take a hands-off

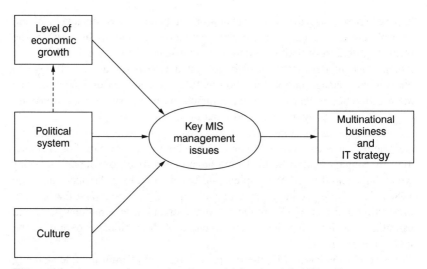

Figure 6.2　*A proposed comprehensive model for the global IT environment*

(yet supportive) approach towards IT developments (as in the USA and other free economies). At the other extreme, in spite of all good intentions, the government may impose a wide array of overly restrictive policies (as in some communist countries). As another alternative, government may pursue an aggressive policy of rapid technology growth, and provide necessary incentives and infrastructure to firms (as in Taiwan, Singapore, and South Korea). The dotted line shown in Figure 6.2 indicates that the political system of a nation also has an influence on its economic growth. Finally, as shown in the model, a good understanding of the global IT environment will be a key factor in the development of a suitable business and IT strategy of the multinational firm.

Conclusions

Reports of information systems management issues in different parts of the world are useful to organizations as they begin to plan and implement IT applications across the world. In this chapter, we have presented IS issues for many countries, and have examined the issues in USA, Taiwan, India, and Kenya and Zimbabwe in greater depth. The world is a large place, and attempting to understand the critical issues in every single country, or even selected countries, would be an arduous, perhaps an imprudent task. Instead, we have divided countries into four classes, and have provided an example in each class. An elementary model for the global IT environment has been postulated based on this categorization. While generalizations are fraught with risks, the provision of such a model will help practitioners and researchers alike in a preliminary assessment of the criticality of the various IT issues in different regions of the world. In closing, we would like to exhort others to pursue the following lines of investigation:

1 Develop and validate sound models that seek to explain the country issues. A simple model was presented in Figure 6.1. Elements of a more comprehensive model may include economic growth, national culture, and political system as causal factors, among others (as in Figure 6.2).
2 Evaluate the predictive capability of such models as well as report on the use of the models for prediction. While descriptive studies are helpful in identifying the key issues of individual countries at a point in time, this can be an enormous and time-consuming proposition given the number of countries in the world and the temporal nature of the issues. However, if the determinants of the key issues are known, then a preliminary estimation of the issues will be easier to make.
3 Use the model for focused research. For example, if culture is identified as one of the factors influencing IT needs, then it can be explored in more detail both in terms of culture components and IT components that are influenced by it.
4 Develop a comprehensive universal instrument and methodology that can be applied globally to identify the key IS issues. This instrument should then be administered simultaneously (or approximately in the same time frame) by a group of researchers in different countries. One of the limitations of previous 'key issue' studies is that they have used different questionnaires, different time frames, and different methods to assess the issues. While difficult, this undertaking will be very helpful in obtaining reliable results.
5 Develop specific practical implications and uses of the 'key issues' results. How can they be incorporated into the formulation of national policy, corporate policy or IS policies within an organization?

References

Badri, M. A. (1992) Critical issues in information systems management: an international perspective. *International Journal of Information Management*, **12**, 179–191.

Ball, L. and Harris, R. (1982) SMIS members: a membership analysis. *MIS Quarterly*, **6**(1), March, 19–38.

Brancheau, J. C. and Wetherbe, J. C. (1987) Key issues in information systems management. *MIS Quarterly*, March, 23–46.

Burn, J., Saxena, K. B. C., Ma, L. and Cheung, H. K. (1993) Critical issues of IS management in Hong Kong: a cultural comparison. *Journal of Global Information Management*, **1**(4), Fall, 28–37.

Carey, D. (1992) Rating the top MIS issues in Canada. *Canadian Datasystems*, June, 23–26.

Chepaitis, E. V. (1994) After the command economy: Russia's information culture and its impact on information resource management. *Journal of Global Information Management*, 2(1), Winter, 5–11.

CSC Index (1995) *Critical Issues Information Systems Management for 1995*, Cambridge, Massachusetts.

Deans, P. C., Karawan, K. R., Goslar, M. D., Ricks, D. A. and Toyne, B. (1991) Identification of key international information systems issues: U.S.-based multinational corporations. *Journal of Management Information Systems*, 27(4), Spring, 27–50.

Dekeleva, S. and Zupancic, J. (1993) Key issues in information systems management: a Delphi study in Slovenia. In DeGross J. I., Bostrom, R. P. and Robey, D., Eds. *Proceedings of the Fourteenth International Conference on Information Systems*, Orlando, Fl.

Dexter, A. S., Janson, M. A., Kiudorf, E. and Laast-Laas, J. (1993) Key information technology issues in Estonia. *Journal of Strategic Information Systems*, June, 2(2), 139–152.

Dickson, G. W., Leitheiser, R. L., Nechis, M. and Wetherbe, J. C. (1984) Key information systems issues for the 1980's. *MIS Quarterly*, 8(3), September, 135–148.

Ein-Dor, P., Segev, E. and Orgad, M. (1993) The effect of national culture on IS: implication for international information systems. *Journal of Global Information Management*, Winter, 33–44.

Galliers, R. D., Merali, Y. and Spearing, L. (1994) Coping with information technology? How British executives perceive the key information systems management issues in the mid-1990s. *Journal of Information Technology*, 9(3), 223–238.

Goodman, S. E. (1991) Computing and the resuscitation of Romania. *Communications of the ACM*, 34(9), September, 19–22.

Goodman, S. E. and McHenry, W. K. (1991) The Soviet computer industry: A tale of two sectors. *Communications of the ACM*, 34(6), June, pp. 25–29.

Hartog, C. and Herbert, M. (1986) 1985 opinion survey of MIS managers: key issues. *MIS Quarterly*, December, 351–361.

Hassan, S. Z. (1994) Environmental constraints in utilizing information technologies in Pakistan. *Journal of Global Information Management*, 2(4), Fall, 30–39.

Igbaria, M. (1992) An examination of microcomputer usage in Taiwan. *Information & Management*, 22, 19–28.

Janz, B., Brancheau, J. and Wetherbe, J. (1994) Key issues in IS management. Working Paper, *MIS Research Center*, University of Minnesota.

La Rovere, R. L., Tigre, P. B. and Fagundes, J. (1996) Information networks diffusion in Brazil: global and local factors. In *Global Information*

Technology and Systems Management: Key Issues and Trends (eds, P. Palvia, S. Palvia and E. Roches), Ivy League Publishing, New Hampshire.

McFadden, F. R. and Hoffer, J. A. (1994) *Modern Database Management*, 4th edn, Benjamin Cummings Pub. Co., California.

McLuhan, M. (1964) *Understanding Media: The Extensions of Man*, McGraw-Hill, New York.

Niederman, F., Brancheau, J. C. and Wetherbe, J. C. (1991) Information systems management issues for the 1990s. *MIS Quarterly*, December, 475–495.

Nolan, R. L. (1979) Managing the crises in data processing. *Harvard Business Review*, **57**(2), March-April, 115–126.

Palvia, P. and Palvia, S. (1992) MIS issues in India, and a comparison with the United States. *International Information Systems*, April, 100–110.

Palvia, P., Palvia, S. and Zigli, R. M. (1992) Global information technology environment: key MIS issues in advanced and less developed nations. In *The Global Issues of Information Technology Management* (eds S. Palvia, P. Palvia and R. M. Zigli), Idea Group Publishing, Harrisburg, PA.

Palvia, P. and Wang, P. (1995) An expanded global information technology issues model: an addition of newly industrialized countries. *Journal of Information Technology Management*, **VI**(2), 29–39.

Rao, K. V., Huff, F. P. and Davis, G. B. (1987) Critical issues in the management of information systems: a comparison of Singapore and the USA. *Information Technology*, **1**(3), 11–19.

Roche, E. M. (1992) *Managing Information Technology in Multinational Corporations*, Macmillan Pub. Co., New York.

Roche, E. M., Goodman, S. E. and Chen, H. (1992) The landscape of international computing. *Advances in Computers*, **35**, Spring.

Shore, B. and Venkatachalam, A. R. (1995) The role of national culture in systems analysis and design. *Journal of Global Information Management*, **3**(3), Summer, 5–14.

Wang, P. (1994) Information management systems issues in the Republic of China for the 1990s. *Information and Management*, **26**, 341–352.

Watson, R. T. (1989) Key issues in information systems management: an Australian perspective – 1988. *Australian Computer Journal*, **21**(3), 118–129.

Watson, R. T. and Brancheau, J. C. (1991) Key issues in information systems management: an international perspective. *Information and Management*, **20**, 213–223.

Questions for discussion

1   For each of the four groups (industrialized, newly industrialized, developing, underdeveloped),
    –   were you surprised by any of the issues included or by any issues not included?
    –   what changes would you expect to see now (given that the chapter first appeared in 1996)?
    –   over which issues does an IT manager have control, or not have control?
2   What are the implications of the different key issues for IT management in a multinational firm?
3   What are the implications for the so-called networked world?
4   Why would you expect different key issues in different major economic segments?
5   What are the implications of these key issues for small-medium sized local firms?
6   Consider similarities of Figure 6.1 with the 'stages of growth' model, discussed in Chapter 2. Is it basically the same conceptualization but just at a different level of analysis?

Further background reading

Watson, R. T., Kelly, G. G., Galliers, R. D., and Brancheau, J. C. (1997). Key issues in Information Systems Management: An international comparison, *Journal of Management Information Systems*, **13**(4), Spring, 91–115.

7 Approaches to Information Systems Planning

Experiences in strategic information systems planning*

M. J. Earl

Strategic information systems planning (SISP) remains a top concern of many organizations. Accordingly, researchers have investigated SISP practice and proposed both formal methods and principles of good practice. SISP cannot be understood by considering formal methods alone. The processes of planning and the implementation of plans are equally important. However, there have been very few field investigations of these phenomena. This study examines SISP experience in 27 companies and, unusually, relies on interviews not only with IS managers but also with general managers and line managers. By adopting this broader perspective, the investigation reveals companies were using five different SISP approaches: Business-Led, Method-Driven, Administrative, Technological, and Organizational. Each approach has different characteristics and, therefore, a different likelihood of success. The results show that the Organizational Approach appears to be most effective. The taxonomy of the five approaches potentially provides a diagnostic tool for analyzing and evaluating an organization's experience with SISP.

Introduction

For many IS executives, strategic information systems planning (SISP) continues to be a critical issue.[1] It is also reportedly the top IS concern of chief executives (Moynihan, 1990). At the same time, it is almost axiomatic that information systems management be based on SISP (Synott and Gruber, 1982). Furthermore, as investment in information technology has been

* An earlier version of this chapter was published in *Proceedings of the International Conference on Information Systems*, Copenhagen, Denmark, December 1990.

promoted to both support business strategy or create strategic options (Earl, 1988; Henderson and Venkatraman, 1989), an 'industry' of SISP has grown as IT manufacturers and management consultants have developed methodologies and techniques. Thus, SISP appears to be a rich and important activity for researchers. So far, researchers have provided surveys of practice and problems, models and frameworks for theory-building, and propositions and methods to put into action.[2]

The literature recommends that SISP target the following areas:

- aligning investment in IS with business goals
- exploiting IT for competitive advantage
- directing efficient and effective management of IS resources
- developing technology policies and architectures

It has been suggested (Earl, 1989) that the first two areas are concerned with information systems strategy, the third with information management strategy, and the fourth with information technology strategy. In survey-based research to date, it is usually the first two areas that dominate. Indeed, SISP has been defined in this light (Lederer and Sethi, 1988) as 'the process of deciding the objectives for organizational computing and identifying potential computer applications which the organization should implement' (p. 445). This definition was used in our investigation of SISP activity in 27 United Kingdom-based companies.

Calls have been made recently for better understanding of strategic planning in general, including SISP, and especially for studies of actual planning behavior in organizations (Boynton and Zmud, 1987; Henderson and Sifonis, 1988). As doubts continue to be raised about the pay-off of IT, it does seem important to examine the reality of generally accepted IS management practices such as SISP. Thus, in this investigation we used field studies to capture the *experiences* of large companies that had attempted some degree of formal IS planning.[3]

We were also interested as to whether any particular SISP techniques were more effective than others. This question proved difficult to answer, as discussed below, and is perhaps even irrelevant. Techniques were found to be only one element of SISP, with process and implementation being equally important. Therefore, a more descriptive construct embodying these three elements – the SISP *approach* – was examined. Five different approaches were identified; the experience of the organizations studied suggests that one approach may be more effective than the others.

Methodology

In 1988–89, a two-stage survey was conducted to discover the intents, outcomes, and experiences of SISP efforts. First, case studies captured the history of six companies previously studied by the author. These retrospective case histories were based on accounts of the IS director and/or IS strategic planner and on internal documentation of these companies. The cases suggested or confirmed questions to ask in the second stage. Undoubtedly, these cases influenced the perspective of the researcher.

In the second stage, 21 different UK companies were investigated through field studies. All were large companies that were among the leaders in the banking, insurance, transport, retailing, electronics, IT, automobile, aerospace, oil, chemical, services, and food and drink industries. Annual revenues averaged £4.5 billion. They were all headquartered in the UK or had significant national or regional IS functions within multi-national companies headquartered elsewhere. Their experience with formal SISP activities ranged from one to 20 years.[4] The scope of SISP could be either at the business unit level, the corporate level, or both. The results from this second stage are reported in this chapter.

Within each firm, the author carried out in-depth interviews, typically lasting two to four hours, with three 'stakeholders'. A total of 63 executives were interviewed. The IS director or IS strategic planner was interviewed first, followed by the CEO or a general manager, and finally a senior line or user manager. Management prescriptions often state that SISP requires a combination or coalition of line managers contributing application ideas or making system requests, general managers setting direction and priorities, and IS professionals suggesting what can be achieved technically. Additionally, interviewing these three stakeholders provides some triangulation, both as a check on the views of the IS function and as a useful, but not perfect, cross-section of corporate memory.

Because the IS director selected the interviewees, there could have been some sample bias. However, parameters were laid down on how to select interviewees, and the responses did not indicate any prior collusion in aligning opinions. Respondents were supposed to be the IS executives most involved with SISP (which may or may not be the CIO), the CEO or general manager most involved in strategic decisions on IS, and a 'typical' user line manager who had contributed to SISP activities.

Interviews were conducted using questionnaires to ensure completeness and replicability, but a mix of unstructured, semi-structured, and structured interrogation was employed.[5] Typically, a simple question was posed in an open manner (often requiring enlargement to overcome differences in organizational language), and raw responses were recorded. The same question was then asked in a closed manner, requesting quantitative responses using scores, ranking, and Likert-type scales. Particular attention was paid to anecdotes, tangents, and 'asides'. In this way, it was hoped to collect data sets for both qualitative and quantitative analysis. Interviews focused on intents, outcomes, and experiences of SISP.

It was also attempted to record experiences with particular SISP methodologies and relate their use to success, benefits and problems. However, this aim proved to be inappropriate (because firms often had employed a variety of techniques and procedures over time), and later was jettisoned in favor of recording the variety and richness of planning behavior the respondents recalled. This study is therefore exploratory, with a focus on theory development.[6]

Interests, methods, and outcomes

Data were collected on the stimuli, aims, benefits, success factors, problems, procedures, and methods of SISP. These data have been statistically examined, but only a minimum of results is presented here as a necessary context to the principal findings of the study.[7]

Respondents were asked to state their firms' current *objectives* for SISP. The dominant objective was alignment of IS with business needs, with 69.8 percent of respondents ranking it as most important and 93.7 percent ranking it in their top five objectives (Table 7.1). Interview comments reinforced the importance of this objective. The search for competitive advantage applications was ranked second, reflecting the increased strategic awareness of IT in the late 1980s. Gaining top management commitment was third. The only difference among the stakeholders was that IS directors placed top management commitment above the competitive advantage goal, perhaps reflecting a desire for functional sponsorship and a clear mandate.

Table 7.1   *Objectives of SISP*

Rank order	Objective	Respondents selecting (n = 63)	Primary frequency	Sum of ranks	Mean rank
1	Aligning IS with business needs	59	44	276	4.38
2	Seek competitive advantage from IT	45	8	161	2.55
3	Gain top management commitment	36	6	115	1.83
4	Forecast IS resource requirements	35	1	80	1.27
5	Establish technology path and policies	30	2	77	1.22

Table 7.1 suggests that companies have more than one objective for SISP; narrative responses usually identified two or three objectives spontaneously. Not surprisingly, the respondents' views on benefits were similar and also indicated a multidimensional picture (Table 7.2). All respondents were able to select confidently from a structured list. Alignment of IS again stood out, with 49 percent ranking it first and 78 percent ranking it in the top five benefits. Top management support, better priority setting, competitive advantage applications, top management involvement, and user-management involvement were the other prime benefits reported.

Respondents also evaluated their firm's *success* with SISP. Success measures have been discussed elsewhere (Raghunathan and King, 1988). Most have relied upon satisfaction scores (Galliers, 1987), absence of problems (Lederer and Sethi, 1988), or audit checklists (King, 1988). Respondents were given no criterion of success but were given scale anchors to help them record a score from 1 (low) to 5 (high), as shown in Appendix B.

Ten percent of all respondents claimed their SISP had been 'highly successful', 59 percent reported it had been 'successful but there was room for improvement', and 69 percent rated SISP as worthwhile or better. Thirty-one percent were dissatisfied with their firm's SISP. There were differences between stakeholders; whereas 76 percent of IS directors gave a score above 3, only 67 percent of general managers and 57 percent of user mangers were as content. Because the mean score by company was 3.73, and the modal company score was 4, the typical experience can be described as worthwhile but in need of some improvement.

Table 7.2   *SISP benefits*

Rank order	Benefit	Respondents selecting (n = 63)	Primary frequency	Sum of ranks	Mean rank
1	Aligning IS with business needs	49	31	208	3.30
2	Top management support	27	7	94	1.49
3	Better priority setting	35	3	75	1.19
4	Competitive advantage applications	21	4	67	1.06
5	Top management involvement	19	3	60	0.95
6	User/line management involvement	21	2	58	0.92

A complementary question revealed a somewhat different picture. Interviewees were asked in what ways SISP had been *unsuccessful*. Sixty-five different types of disappointment were recorded. In such a long list none was dominant. Nevertheless, Table 7.3 summarizes the five most commonly mentioned features contributing to dissatisfaction. We will henceforth refer to these as 'concerns'.

It is apparent that concerns extend beyond technique or methodology, the focus of several researchers, and the horizon of most suppliers. Accordingly we examined the 65 different concerns looking for a pattern. This inductive and subjective clustering produced an interesting classification. The cited concerns could be grouped almost equally into three distinct categories (assuming equal weighting to each concern): method, process, and implementation, as shown in Table 7.4. The full list of concerns is reproduced in Appendix C.

Method concerns centered on the SISP technique, procedure, or methodology employed. Firms commonly had used proprietary methods, such as Method 1, BSP, or Information Engineering, or applied generally available techniques, such as critical success factors or value chain analysis. Others had

Table 7.3 *Unsuccessful features of SISP*

Rank order	Unsuccessful features
1	Resource constraints
2	Not fully implemented
3	Lack of top management acceptance
4	Length of time involved
5	Poor user-IS relationships

Table 7.4 *SISP concerns by stakeholder*

	Total citations	%	IS directors (n = 21)		General managers (n = 21)		User managers (n = 21)	
			Citations	%	Citations	%	Citations	%
Method	45	36	14	36	18	44	13	28
Process	39	31	9	23	11	27	19	41
Implementation	42	33	16	41	12	29	14	31
	126	100	39	100	41	100	46	100

invented their own methods, often customizing well-known techniques. Among the stated concerns were lack of strategic thinking, excessive internal focus, too much or too little attention to architecture, excessive time and resource requirements, and ineffective resource allocation mechanisms. General managers especially emphasized these concerns, perhaps because they have high expectations but find IS strategy making difficult.

Implementation was a common concern. Even where SISP was judged to have been successful, the resultant strategies or plans were not always followed up or fully implemented. Even though clear directions might be set and commitments made to develop new applications, projects often were not initiated and systems development did not proceed. This discovery supports the findings of earlier work (Lederer and Sethi, 1988). Evidence from the interviews suggests that typically resources were not made available, management was hesitant, technological constraints arose, or organizational resistance emerged. Where plans were implemented, other concerns arose, including technical quality, the time and cost involved, or the lack of benefits realized. Implementation concerns were raised most by IS directors, perhaps because they are charged with delivery or because they hoped SISP would provide hitherto elusive strategic direction of their function. Of course, it can be claimed that a strategy that is not implemented or poorly implemented is no strategy at all – a tendency not unknown in business strategy making (Mintzberg, 1987). Indeed, implementation has been proposed as a measure of success in SISP (Lederer and Sethi, 1988).

Process concerns included lack of line management participation, poor IS-user relationships, inadequate user awareness and education, and low management ownership of the philosophy and practice of SISP. Line managers were particularly vocal about the management and enactment of SISP methods and procedures and whether they fit the organizational context.

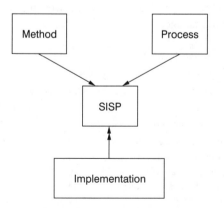

Figure 7.1 *Necessary conditions for successful SISP*

Analysis of the reported concerns therefore suggests that method, process, and implementation are all necessary conditions for successful SISP (Figure 7.1). Indeed, when respondents volunteered success factors for SISP based on their organization's experience, they conveyed this multiple perspective (see Table 7.5). The highest ranked factors of 'top management involvement', and 'top management support' can be seen as process factors, while 'business strategy available' and 'study the business before technology' have more to do with method. 'Good IS management' partly relates to implementation. Past research has identified similar concerns (Lederer and Mendelow, 1987), and the more prescriptive literature has suggested some of these success factors (Synott and Gruber, 1982). However, the experience of organizations in this study indicates that no single factor is likely to lead to universal success in SISP. Instead, successful SISP is more probable when organizations realize that method, process, and implementation are all necessary issue sets to be managed.

In particular, consultants, managers, and researchers would seem well advised to look beyond method alone in practising SISP. Furthermore, researchers cannot assume that SISP requires selection and use of just one method or one special planning exercise. Typically, it seems that firms use several methods over time. An average of 2.3 methods (both proprietary and in-house) had been employed by the 21 companies studied. Nine of them had tried three or more. Retrospectively isolating and identifying the effect of a method therefore becomes difficult for researchers. It may also be misleading because, as discovered in these interviews, firms engage in a variety of strategic planning activities and behavior. This became apparent when respondents were asked the open-ended question, 'Please summarize the approach you have adopted in developing your IS strategy (or identifying which IT applications to develop in the long run)'. In reply they usually recounted a rich history of initiatives, events, crises, techniques, organizational changes, successes, and failures all interwoven in a context of how IS resources had been managed.

Table 7.5　*Success factors in SISP*

Rank order	Success factor	Respondents selecting	Primary frequency	Sum of ranks	Mean rank
1	Top management involvement	42	15	160	2.55
2	Top management support	34	17	140	2.22
3	Business strategy available	26	9	99	1.57
4	Study business before technology	23	9	87	1.38
5	Good IS management	17	1	41	0.65

Prompted both by the list of concerns and narrative histories of planning-related events, the focus of this study therefore shifted. The object of analysis became the SISP *approach*. This we viewed as the interaction of method, process, and implementation, as well as the variety of activities and behaviors upon which the respondents had reflected. The accounts of interviewees, the 'untutored' responses to the semi-structured questions, the documents supplied, and the 'asides' followed up by the interviewer all produced descriptive data on each company's approach. Once the salient features of SISP were compared across the 21 companies, five distinct approaches were identified. These were then used retrospectively to classify the experiences of the six case study firms.

SISP approaches

An approach is not a technique *per se*. Nor is it necessarily an explicit study or formal, codified routine so often implied in past accounts and studies of SISP. As in most forms of business planning, it cannot often be captured by one event, a single procedure, or a particular technique. An approach may comprise a mix of procedures, techniques, user-IS interactions, special analyses, and random discoveries. There are likely to be some formal activities and some informal behavior. Sometimes IS planning is a special endeavor and sometimes it is part of business planning at large. However, when members of the organization describe how decisions on IS strategy are initiated and made, a coherent picture is gradually painted where the underpinning philosophy, emphasis, and influences stand out. These are the principal distinguishing features of an approach. The *elements* of an approach can be seen as the nature and place of method, the attention to and style of process, and the focus on and probability of implementation.

The five approaches are labelled as Business-Led, Method-Driven, Administrative, Technological, and Organizational. They are delineated as ideal types in Table 7.6. Several distinctors are apparent in each approach. Each represents a particular philosophy (either explicit or implicit), displays its own dynamics, and has different strengths and weaknesses. Whereas some factors for success are suggested by each approach, not all approaches seem to be equally effective.

Business-led approach

The *Business-led Approach* was adopted by four companies and two of the case study firms. The underpinning 'assumption' of this approach is that current business direction or plans are the only basis upon which IS plans can be built and that, therefore, business planning should drive SISP. The emphasis is on the business leading IS and not the other way around. Business plans or strategies are analyzed to identify where information systems are most required. Often

Table 7.6 *SISP approaches*

	Business-Led	Method-Driven	Administrative	Technological	Organizational
Emphasis	Business	Technique	Resources	Model	Learning
Basis	Business plans	Best method	Procedure	Rigor	Partnership
Ends	Plan	Strategy	Portfolio	Architecture	Themes
Methods	Ours	Best	None	Engineering	Any way
Nature	Business	Top-down	Bottom-up	Blueprints	Interactive
Influencer	IS planner	Consultants	Committees	Method	Teams
Relation to business strategy	Fix points	Derive	Criteria	Objectives	Look at business
Priority setting	The board	Method recommends	Central committee	Compromise	Emerge
IS role	Driver	Initiator	Bureaucrat	Architect	Team member
Metaphor	It's common sense	It's good for you	Survival of the fittest	We nearly aborted it	Thinking IS all the time

this linkage is an annual endeavor and is the responsibility of the IS director or IS strategic planner (or team). The IS strategic plan is later presented to the board for questioning, approval, and priority-setting.

General managers see this approach as simple, 'business-like', and a matter of common sense. IS executives often see this form of SISP as their most critical task and welcome the long overdue mandate from senior management. However, they soon discover that business strategies are neither clear nor detailed enough to specify IS needs. Thus, interpretation and further analysis become necessary. Documents have to be studied, managers interviewed, meetings convened, working papers written, and tentative proposals on the IS implications of business plans put forward. 'Home-spun' procedures are developed on a trial and error basis to discover and propose the IT implications of business plans. It may be especially difficult to promote the notion that IT itself may offer some new strategic options. The IS planners often feel that they have to 'take the lead' to make any progress or indeed to engage the business in the exercise. They also discover that some top executives may be more forceful in their views and expectations than others.

Users and line managers are likely to be involved very little. The emphasis on top-level input and business plans reduces the potential contribution of users and the visibility of local requirements. Users, perceiving SISP as remote, complain of inadequate involvement. Because the IS strategy becomes the product of the IS function, user support is not guaranteed. Top management, having substantially delegated SISP to the specialists, may be unsure of the recommendations and be hesitant to commit resources, thus impairing implementation.

Nevertheless, some advantages can accrue. Information systems are seen as a strategic resource, and the IS function receives greater legitimacy. Important strategic thrusts that require IT support can be identified, and if the business strategy is clearly and fully presented, the IS strategy can be well-aligned. Indeed, in one of the prior case study companies that adopted this approach, a clear business plan for survival led to IT applications that were admired by many industry watchers. However, despite this achievement, the IS function is still perceived by all three sets of stakeholders as poorly integrated into the business as a whole.

Method-driven approach

The *Method-Driven Approach* was present in two companies and two of the case study firms. Adherents of this approach appear to assume that SISP is enhanced by, or depends on, use of a formal technique or method. The IS director may believe that management will not think about IS needs and opportunities without the use of a formal method or the intervention of consultants. Indeed, recognition or anticipation of some of the frustrations typical of the Business-Led Approach may prompt the desire for method. However, any method will not do. There is typically a search for the 'best method', or at least one better than the last method adopted.

Once again, business strategies may be found to be deficient for the purpose of SISP. The introduction of a formal method rarely provides a remedy, however, because it is unlikely to be a strong enough business strategy technique. Also, the method's practitioners are unlikely to be skilled or credible at such work. Furthermore, as formal methods are usually sponsored by the IS department, they may fail to win the support or involvement of the business at large. Thus, a second or third method may be attempted while the IS department tries to elicit or verify the business strategy and to encourage a wider set of stakeholders to participate. Often, a vendor or consultant plays a significant role. As the challenges unfold, stakeholders determine the 'best' method, often as a result of the qualities of the consultants as much as the techniques themselves. The consultants often become the drivers of the SISP exercise and therefore have substantial influence on the recommendations.

Users may judge Method-Driven exercises as 'unreal' and 'high level' and as having excluded the managers who matter, namely themselves. General managers can see the studies as 'business strategy making in disguise' and thus become somewhat resistant and not easily persuaded of the priorities or options suggested by the application of the method. IS strategic plans may then lose their credibility and never be fully initiated. The exercises and recommendations may be forgotten. Often they are labelled the 'xyz' strategy, where 'xyz' is the name of the consulting firm employed; in other words, these strategies are rarely 'owned' by the business.

Formal methods do not always fail completely. Although a succession of methods achieved little in the companies studied, managers judged that each method had been good in some unanticipated way for the business or the IS department.[8] For example, in one firm it showed the need for business strategies, and in another it informed IS management about business imperatives. In the former firm, IS directors were heard to say the experience had been 'good for the company, showing up the gaps in strategic thinking!' Nevertheless, formal strategy studies could leave behind embryonic strategic thrusts, ideas waiting for the right time, or new thinking that could be exploited or built upon later in unforeseen ways.

Administrative approach

The *Administrative Approach* was found in five companies. The emphasis here is on resource planning. The wider management planning and control procedures were expected to achieve the aims of SISP through formal procedures for allocating IS resources. Typically, IS development proposals were submitted by business units or departments to committees who examined project viability, common system possibilities, and resource consequences. In some cases, resource planners did the staff work as proposals ascended the annual hierarchical approval procedure. The Administrative Approach was the parallel of, or could be attached to, the firm's normal financial planning or capital budgeting routine. The outcome of the approach was a one-year or multi-year development portfolio of approved projects. Typically no application is developed until it is on the plan. A planning investment or steering committee makes all decisions and agrees on any changes.

Respondents identified significant down sides to the Administrative Approach. It was seen as not strategic, as being 'bottom-up' rather than 'top-down'. Ideas for radical change were not identified, strategic thinking was absent, inertia and 'business as usual' dominated, and enterprise-level applications remained in the background. More emotional were the claims about conflicts, dramas, and game playing – all perhaps inevitable in an essentially resource allocation procedure. The emphasis on resource planning sometimes led to a resource-constrained outcome. For example, spending limits were often applied, and boards and CEOs were accused of applying cuts to the IS budget, assuming that in doing so no damage was being done to the business as a whole.

Some benefits of this approach were identified. Everybody knew about the procedure; it was visible, and all users and units had the opportunity to submit proposals. Indeed, an SISP procedure and timetable for SISP were commonly published as part of the company policy and procedures manual. Users, who were encouraged to make application development requests, did produce some ideas for building competitive advantage. Also, it seemed that radical, transformational IT applications could arise in these companies despite the apparently bottom-up, cautious procedure. The most radical applications emerged when the CEO or finance director broke the administrative rules and informally proposed and sanctioned an IS investment.

By emphasizing viability, project approval, and resource planning, the administrative approach produced application development portfolios that were eventually implemented. Not only financial criteria guided these choices. New strategic guidelines, such as customer service or quality improvement, were also influential. Finally, the Administrative Approach often fitted the planning and control style of the company. IS was managed in congruence with other activities, which permitted complemetary resources to be allocated in parallel. Indeed, unless the IS function complied with procedures, no resources were forthcoming.

Technological approach

The *Technological Approach* was adopted by four companies and two of the case study firms. This approach is based on the assumption that an information systems-oriented model of the business is a necessary outcome of SISP and, therefore, that analytical modelling methods are appropriate. This approach is different from the Method-Driven Approach in two principal characteristics. First, the end product is a business model (or series of models). Second, a formal method is applied based on mapping the activities, processes, and data flows of the business. The emphasis is on deriving architectures or blueprints for IT and IS, and often Information Engineering terminology is used. Architectures for data, computing, communications, and applications might be produced, and computer-aided software engineering (CASE) might be among the tools employed. A proprietary technology-oriented method might be used or adapted in-house. Both IS directors and general mangers tend to emphasize the objectives of rigorous analysis and of building a robust infrastructure.

This approach is demanding in terms of both effort and resource requirements. These also tend to be high-profile activities. Stakeholders commented on the length of time involved in the analysis and/or the implementation. User managers reacted negatively to the complexity of the analysis and the outputs and reported a tendency for technical dependencies to displace business priorities. In one case, management was unsure of the validity and meaning of the blueprints generated and could not determine what proposals mattered most. A second study of the same type, but using a different technological method, was commissioned. This produced a different but equally unconvincing set of blueprints.

These characteristics could lead to declining top management support or even user rebellion. In one firm, the users called for an enterprise modelling exercise to be aborted. In one of the case study firms, development of the blueprint applications was axed by top management three and a half years after initiation. In another, two generations of IS management departed after organizational conflict concerning the validity of the technological model proposed.

Some success was claimed for the Technological Approach. Benefits were salvaged by factoring down the approach into smaller exercises. In one case this produced a database definition, and in another it led to an IT architecture for the finance function. Some IS directors claimed these outcomes were valuable in building better IT infrastructures.

Organizational approach

The *Organizational Approach* was used in six companies and one of the case study firms. The underpinning assumption here is quite different. It is that SISP is not a special or neat and tidy endeavor but is based on IS decisions being made through continuous integration between the IS function and the organization. The way IT applications are identified and selected is described in much more multi-dimensional and subtle language. The approach is not without method, but methods are employed as required and to fit a particular purpose. For example, value analysis may be used, workshops arranged, business investigation projects set up, and vendor visits organized. The emphasis, however, is on process, especially management understanding and involvement. For some of these companies, a major SISP method had been applied in the past, but in retrospect it was seen to have been as much a process enabler as an analytical investigation. Executive teamwork and an understanding of how IT might contribute to the business were often left behind by the method rather than specific recommendations for IS investment. Organizational learning was important and evident in at least three ways.

First, IS development concentrated on only one or two themes growing in scope over several years as the organization began to appreciate the potential benefits. Examples of such themes included a food company concentrating on providing high service levels to customers, an insurance company conentrating on low-cost administration, and a chemical company concentrating on product development performance. Second, special studies were important. Often multidisciplinary senior executive project teams or full-time task forces were assigned to tackle a business problem from which a major IS initiative would later emerge. The presence of an IS executive in the multidisciplinary team was felt to be important to the emergence of a strategic theme because this person could suggest why, where, and how IT could help. Teamwork was the principal influence in IS strategy making. Third, there was a focus on implementation. Themes were broken down into identifiable and frequent deliverables. Conversely, occasional project cost and time overruns were acceptable if they allowed evolving ideas to be incorporated. In some ways, IS strategies were discovered through implementation. These three learning characteristics can be seen collectively as a preference for incremental strategy making.

The approach is therefore *organizational* because:

1 Collective learning across the organization is evident.
2 Organizational devices or instruments (teams, task forces, workshops, etc.) are used to tackle business problems or pursue initiatives.
3 The IS function works in close partnership with the rest of the organization, especially through having IS managers on management teams or placing IS executives on task forces.
4 Devolution of some IS capability is common, not only to divisions, but also to functions, factories, and departments.
5 In some companies SISP is neither special nor abnormal. It is part of the normal business planning of the organization.

6   IS strategies often emerge from ongoing organizational activities, such as trial and error changes to business practices, continuous and incremental enhancement of existing applications, and occasional system initiatives and experiments within the business.

In one of the companies, planning was 'counter-cultural'. Nevertheless, in the character described above, planning still happened. In another company there were no IS plans, just business plans. In another, IS was enjoying a year or more of low profile until the company discovered the next theme. In most of these firms, IS decisions were being made all the time and at any time.

Respondents reported some disadvantages of this approach. Some IS directors worried about how the next theme would be generated. Also, because the approach is somewhat fuzzy or soft, they were not always confident that it could be transplanted to another part of the business. Indeed, a new CEO, management team, or management style could erode the process without the effect being apparent for some time. One IS director believed the incrementalism of the Organizational Approach led to creation of inferior infrastructures.

The five approaches appear to be different in scope, character, and outcome. Table 7.7 differentiates them using the three characteristics that seem to help other organizations position themselves. Also, slogans are offered to capture the essence of each approach. Strengths and weaknesses of each approach are contained in Table 7.8.

It is also possible to indicate the apparent differences of each approach in terms of the three factors suggested in Figure 7.1 as necessary for success: method, process, and implementation. Table 7.9 attempts a summary.

In the Business-Led Approach, method scores low because no formal technique is used; process is rated low because the exercise is commonly IS dominated; but implementation is medium because the boards tend to at least approve some projects. In the Method-Driven Approach, method is high by definition, but process is largely ignored and implementation barely or rarely initiated. In the Administrative Approach, only a procedure exists as method. However, its dependence on user inputs suggests a medium rating on process. Because of its resource allocation emphasis, approved projects are generally implemented. The Technological Approach is generally method-intensive and insensitive to process. It can, however, lead to some specific implementation of an infrastructure. The Organizational Approach uses any method or devices that fit the need; it explicitly invests in process and emphasizes implementation.

Preliminary evaluations

The five approaches were identified by comparing the events, experiences, and lessons described by the interviewees. As the investigation proved to be

Table 7.7 *Five approaches summarized*

	Business-Led	*Method-Driven*	*Administrative*	*Technological*	*Organizational*
Underpinning assumption	Business plans and needs should drive IS plans	IS strategies will be enhanced by use of a formal SISP method	SISP should follow and conform with the firm's management planning and control procedures	SISP is an exercise in business and information modelling	SISP is a continuous decision-making activity shared by the business and IS
Emphasis of approach	Business leads IS and not vice versa	Selection of the best method	Identification and allocation of IS resources to meet agreed needs	Production of models and blueprints	Organizational learning about business problems and opportunities and the IT contribution
Major influence of outcomes	IS planners	Practitioners of the method	Resource planning and steering committees	Modelling method employed	Permanent and *ad hoc* teams of key managers, including IS
Slogan	Business drives IS	Strategy needs method	Follow the rules	IS needs blueprints	Themes with teams

Table 7.8 *Strengths and weaknesses of SISP approaches*

	Business-Led	Method-Driven	Administrative	Technological	Organizational
Strengths	Simple	Provides a methodology	System viability	Rigor	Becomes normal
	Business first	Plugs strategy gaps	System synergies	Focus on infrastructure	Emphasis on implementation
	Raises IS status	Raises strategy profile	Encourages user input	Favors integrated tools	Promotes IS-user partnership
Weaknesses	*Ad hoc* method	User involvement	Non-strategic	Lacks management support	Generation of new themes
	Lacks management commitment	Too influenced by method	Bureaucratic	Only partial implementation	Soft methodology
	Depends on quality of business strategy	Implementation unlikely	Resource-constrained	Complexity	Architecture becomes difficult

Table 7.9 *SISP approaches vs. three conditions for success*

	Business-Led	Method-Driven	Administrative	Technological	Organizational
Method	Low	High	Low	High	Medium
Process	Low	Low	Medium	Low	High
Implementation	Medium	Low	High	Medium	High

exploratory, the classification of approaches is descriptive and was derived by inductive interpretation of organizational experiences. Table 7.6, therefore, should be seen as an ideal model that caricatures the approaches in order to aid theory development. One way of 'validating' the model is to compare it with prior research in both IS and general management to assess whether the approaches 'ring true'.

Related theories

Difficulties encountered in the Business-Led Approach have been noted by others. The availability of formal business strategies for SISP cannot be assumed (Bowman *et al.*, 1983; Lederer and Mendelow, 1986). Nor can we assume that business strategies are communicated to the organization at large, are clear and stable, or are valuable in identifying IS needs (Earl, 1989; Lederer and Mendelow, 1989). Indeed, the quality of the process of business planning itself may often be suspect (Lederer and Sethi, 1988). In other words, while the Business-Led Approach may be especially appealing to general managers, the challenges are likely to be significant.

There is considerable literature on the top-down, more business-strategy-oriented SISP methods implied by the Method-Driven Approach, but most of it is conjectural or normative. Vendors can be very persuasive about the need for a methodology that explicitly connects IS to business thinking (Bowman *et al.*, 1983). Other researchers have argued that sometimes the business strategy must be explicated first (King, 1978; Lederer and Mendelow, 1987). This was a belief of the IS directors in the Method-Driven companies, but one general manager complained that this was 'business strategy making in disguise'. The Administrative Approach reflects the prescriptions and practices of bureaucratic models of planning and control. We must turn to the general management literature for insights into this approach. Quinn (1977) has pointed out the strategy-making limitations of bottom-up planning procedures. He argues that big change rarely originates in this way and that, furthermore, annual planning processes rarely foster innovation. Both the political behavior stimulated by hierarchical resource allocation mechanisms and the business-as-usual inertia of budgetary planning have been well-documented elsewhere (Bowers, 1970; Danziger, 1978).

The Technological Approach may be the extreme case of how the IT industry and its professionals tend to apply computer science thinking to planning. The deficiencies of these methods have been noted in accounts of the more extensive IS planning methods and, in particular, of Information Engineering techniques. For instance, managers are often unhappy with the time and cost involved (Goodhue *et al.*, 1988; Moynihan, 1990). Others note that IS priorities are by definition dependent on the sequence required for architecture building (Hackathorn and Karimi, 1988; Inmon, 1986). The voluminous data generated by this class of method has also been reported (Bowman *et al.*, 1983; Inmon, 1986).

The Organizational Approach does not fit easily with the technical and prescriptive IS literature, but similar patterns have been observed by the more behavioral studies of business strategy making. It is now known that organizations rarely use the rational-analytical approaches touted in the planning literature when they make significant changes in strategy (Quinn, 1978). Rather, strategies often evolve from fragmented, incremental, and largely intuitive processes. Quinn believed this was the quite natural, proper way to cope with the unknowable – proceeding flexibly and experimentally from broad concepts to specific commitments.

Mintzberg's (1983) view of strategy making is similar. It emphasizes small project-based multiskilled teams, cross-functional liaison devices, and selective decentralization. Indeed, Mintzberg's view succinctly summarizes the Organizational Approach. He argues that often strategy is formed, rather than formulated, as actions converge into patterns and as analysis and implementation merge into a fluid process of learning. Furthermore, Mintzberg sees strategy making in reality as a mixture of the formal and informal and the analytical and emergent. Top managers, he argues, should create a context in which strategic thinking and discovery mingle, and then they should intervene where necessary to shape and support new ways forward.

In IS research, Henderson (1989) may have implicitly argued for the Organizational Approach when he called for an iterative, ongoing IS planning process to build and sustain partnership. He suggested partnership mechanisms such as task forces, cross-functional teams, multi-tiered and cross-functional networks, and collaborative planning without planners. Henderson and Sifonis (1988) identify the importance of learning in SISP, and de Geus (1988) sees all planning as learning and teamwork as central to organizational learning. Goodhue *et al.* (1988) and Moynihan (1990) argue that SISP needs to deliver good enough applications rather than optimal models. These propositions could be seen as recognition of the need to learn by doing and to deliver benefits. There is therefore a literature to support the Organizational Approach.

Data assessment

The field data itself can be used to assess the suggested taxonomy of approaches. Questions that arise are: do the approaches actually exist, and is it possible to clearly differentiate between them? Analysis of variance tests on reported success scores indicated that differences between approaches are significant, but differences between stakeholder sets are not.[9] This is one indication that *approach* is a distinct and meaningful way of analyzing SISP in action.

A second obvious question is whether any approaches are more effective than others. It is perhaps premature to ask this question of a taxonomy suggested by the data. Caution would advise further validation of the framework first, followed by carefully designed measurement tests. However, this study provides an opportunity for an early, if tentative, evaluation of this sort.

For example, as shown in Table 7.10, success scores can be correlated with SISP approach. Overall mean scores are shown, as well as scores for each stakeholder set. No approach differed widely from the mean score (3.73) across all companies. However, the most intensive approach in terms of technique (Technological) earned the highest score, perhaps because it represents what respondents thought an IS planning methodology should look

Table 7.10 *Mean success scores by approach*

	Business- Led	Method- Driven	Administrative	Technological	Organizational
Total means	3.25	3.83	3.60	4.00	3.94
IS directors	3.50	4.50	3.60	4.25	4.00
General managers	3.00	4.00	3.40	4.00	4.17
Line managers	3.25	3.00	3.80	3.75	3.66
Number of firms	4	2	5	4	6

Note: 5 = high; 1 = low.

like. Conversely, the Business-Led Approach, which lacks formal method-ologies, earned the lowest scores. There are, of course, legitimate doubts about the meaning or reliability of these success scores because respondents were so keen to discuss the unsuccessful features.

Accordingly, another available measure is to analyze the frequency of concerns reported by firm, assuming each carries equal weight. Table 7.11 breaks out these data by method, process, and implementation concerns. The Organizational Approach has the least concerns attributed to it in total. The Business-Led Approach was characterized by high dissatisfaction with method and implementation. The Method-Driven Approach was perceived to be unsuccessful on process and, ironically, on method, while opinion was less harsh on implementation, perhaps because implementation experience itself is low. The Administrative Approach, as might be predicted, is not well-regarded on method. These data are not widely divergent from the qualitative analysis in Table 7.9.

Table 7.11 *SISP concerns per firm*

	Business-Led	Method-Driven	Administrative	Technological	Organizational
Method	2.75	2.50	2.80	1.75	1.33
Process	0.75	3.00	1.60	2.50	2.16
Implementation	2.75	1.00	1.60	3.00	1.83
Total	6.25	6.50	6.00	7.25	5.32
Number of Firms	4	2	5	4	6

Another measure is the potential of each approach for generating competitive advantage applications. Respondents were asked to identify and describe such applications and trace their histories. No attempt was made by the researcher to check the competitive advantage claimed or to assess whether the applications deserved the label. Although only 14 percent of all such applications were reported to have been generated by a formal SISP study, it is interesting to compare achievement rates of the firms in each approach (Table 7.12). Method-Driven and Technological Approaches do not appear promising. Little is ever initiated in the Method-Driven Approach, while competitiveness is rarely the focus of the Technological Approach. The Administrative Approach appears to be more conducive, perhaps because user ideas receive a hearing. Forty-two percent of competitive advantage applications discovered in all the firms originated from user requests. In the

Table 7.12 *Competitive advantage propensity*

Approach	Competitive advantage application frequency
Business-Led	4.0 applications per firm
Method-Driven	1.5 applications per firm
Administrative	3.6 applications per firm
Technological	2.5 applications per firm
Organizational	4.8 applications per firm

Business-Led Approach, some obviously necessary applications are actioned. In the Organizational Approach, most of the themes pursued were perceived to have produced a competitive advantage.

These three qualitative measures can be combined to produce a multi-dimensional score. Other scholars have suggested that a number of performance measures are required to measure the effectiveness of SISP (Raghunathan and King, 1988). Table 7.13 ranks each approach according to the three measures discussed above (where 1 = top and 5 = bottom). In

Table 7.13 *Multidimensional ranking of SISP approaches*

	Business-Led	Method-Driven	Administrative	Technological	Organizational
Success score ranking	5	3	4	1	2
Least concerns ranking	2	3	4	5	1
Competitive advantage potential ranking	2	5	3	4	1
Sum of ranks	9	11	11	10	4
Overall ranking	2	4	4	3	1

summing the ranks, the Organizational Approach appears to be substantially superior. Furthermore, all the other approaches score relatively low on this basis.

Thus, both qualitative and quantitative evidence suggest that the Organizational Approach is likely to be the best SISP approach to use and, thus, a candidate for further study. The Organizational Approach is perhaps the least formal and structured. It also differs significantly from conventional prescriptions in the literature and practice.

Implications for research

Many prior studies of SISP have been based on the views of IS managers alone. A novel aspect of this study was that the attitudes and experiences of general managers and users were also examined. In reporting back the results to the respondents in the survey companies, an interesting reaction occurred. The stakeholders were asked to select which approach best described their experience with SISP. If only IS professionals were present, their conclusions often differed from the final interpretative results. However, when all three stakeholders were present, a lively discussion ensued and, eventually, unprompted, the group's views moved toward an interpretation consistent with both the data presented and the approach attributed to the firm. This is another soft form of validation. More important, it indicates that approach is not only a multi-dimensional construct but also captures a multi-stakeholder perspective. This suggests that studies of IS management practice can be enriched if they look beyond the boundaries of the IS department.

Another characteristic of prior work on SISP is the assumption that formal methods are used and in principle are appropriate (Lederer and Sethi, 1988; 1991). A systematic linkage to the organization's business planning procedures is also commonly assumed (Boynton and Zmud, 1987; Karimi, 1988). The findings of this study suggest that these may be false assumptions and that, besides studying formal methods, researchers should continue to investigate matters of process while also paying attention to implementation. Indeed, in the field of business strategy, it was studies of the process of strategy making that led to the 'alternative' theories of the strategic management of the firm developed by Quinn (1978) and Mintzberg (1987).

The Organizational Approach to SISP suggested by this study might also be seen as an 'alternative' school of thought. This particular approach, therefore, should be investigated further to understand it in more detail, to assess its effectiveness more rigorously, and to discover how to make it work.

Finally, additional studies are required to further validate and then perhaps develop these findings. Some of the parameters suggested here to distinguish the approaches could be taken as variables and investigated on larger samples to verify the classification. Researchers could also explore whether different approaches fit, or work better in, different contexts. Candidate situational factors include information intensity of the sector, environmental uncertainty, the organization's management planning and control style, and the maturity of the organization's IS management experience.

Implications for practice

For practitioners, this study provides two general lessons. First, SISP requires a holistic or interdependent view. Methods may be necessary, but they could fail if the process factors receive no attention. It is also important to explicitly and positively incorporate implementation plans and decisions in the strategic planning cycle.

Second, successful SISP seems to require users and line managers working in partnership with the IS function. This may not only generate relevant application ideas, but it will tend to create ownership of both process and outcomes. The taxonomy of SISP approaches emerging from this study might be interpreted for practice in at least four different ways. First, it can be used as a diagnostic tool to position a firm's current SISP efforts. The strengths and weaknesses identified in the research then could suggest how the current approach could be improved. We have found that frameworks used in this way are likely to be more helpful if users and general managers as well as IS professionals join together in the diagnosis.

Second, the taxonomy can be used to design a situation-specific (customized) approach on a 'mix-and-match' basis. It may be possible to design a potentially more effective hybrid. The author is aware of one company experimenting at building a combination of the Organizational and Technological Approaches. One of the study companies that had adopted the Organizational Approach to derive its IS strategy also sought some of the espoused benefits of the Technological Approach by continuously formulating a shadow blueprint for IT architecture. This may be one way of reconciling the apparent contradictions of the Organizational and Technological Approaches.

Third, based on our current understanding it appears that the Organizational Approach is more effective than others. Therefore, firms might seriously consider adopting it. This could involve setting up mechanisms and responsibility structures to encourage IS-user partnerships, devolving IS planning and development capability, ensuring IS managers are members of all permanent and *ad hoc* teams, recognizing IS strategic thinking as a continuous and periodic activity, identifying and pursuing business themes, and accepting 'good enough' solutions and building on them. Above all, firms might encourage any mechanisms that promote organizational learning about the scope of IT.

Another interpretation is that the Organizational Approach describes how most IS strategies actually are developed, despite the more formal and rational endeavors of IS managers or management at large. The reality may be a continuous interaction of formal methods and informal behavior and of intended and unintended strategies. If so, SISP in practice should be eclectic, selecting and trying methods and process initiatives to fit the needs of the time. One consequence of this view might be recognition and acceptance that planning need not always generate plans and that plans may arise without a formal planning process.

Finally, it can be revealing for an organization to recall the period when IS appeared to be contributing most effectively to the business and to describe the SISP approach in use (whether by design or not) at the time. This may then indicate which approach is most likely to succeed for that organization. Often when a particularly successful IS project is recalled, its history is seen to resemble the Organizational Approach.

Conclusions

This study evolved into a broad, behavioral exploration of experiences in large organizations. The breadth of perspective led to the proposition that SISP is more than method or technique alone. In addition, process issues and the question of implementation appear to be important. These interdependent elements combine to form an approach. Five different SISP approaches were identified, and one, the Organizational Approach, appears superior.

For practitioners, the taxonomy of SISP approaches provides a diagnostic tool to use in evaluating the effectiveness of their SISP efforts and in learning from their own experiences. Whether rethinking SISP or introducing it for the first time, firms may want to consider adopting the Organizational Approach. Two reasons led to this recommendation. First, among the companies explored, it seemed the most effective approach. Second, this study casts doubt on several of the by now 'traditional' SISP practices that have been advocated and developed in recent years.

The 'approach' construct presented in this chapter, the taxonomy of SISP approaches derived, and the indication that the least formal and least analytical approach seems to be most effective all offer new directions for SISP research and theory development.

Notes

1 See, for example, surveys by Dickson *et al.* (1984), Hartog and Herbert (1986), Brancheau and Wetherbe (1987), and Niederman *et al.* (1991).

2 Propositions and methods include Zani's (1970) early top-down proposal, King's (1978) more sophisticated linkage of the organization's IS strategy set to the business strategy set, and focused techniques such as critical success factors (Bullen and Rockart, 1981) and value chain analysis

(Porter and Millar, 1985). These are supplemented by product literature such as Andersen's (1983) Method 1 or IBM's (1975) Business System Planning. The models and frameworks for developing a theory of SISP include Boynton and Zmud (1987), Henderson and Sifonis (1988), and Henderson and Venkatraman (1989). Empirical works include a survey of practice by Galliers (1987), analysis of methods by Sullivan (1985), investigation of problems by Lederer and Sethi (1988), assessment of success by Lederer and Mendelow (1987) and Raghunathan and King (1988), and evaluation of particular techniques such as strategic data planning (Goodhue *et al.*, 1992).

3   Prior work has tended to use mail questionnaires targeted at IS executives. However, researchers have called for broader studies and for surveys of the experiences and perspectives of top managers, corporate planners, and users (Lederer and Mendelow, 1989; Lederer and Sethi, 1988; Raghunathan and King, 1988).

4   Characteristics of the sample companies are summarized in Appendix A.

5   Extracts from the interview questionnaires are shown in Appendix B.

6   This exploration through field studies was in the spirit of 'grounded theory' (Glaser and Strauss, 1967).

7   Fuller descriptive statistics can be seen in an early research report (Earl, 1990).

8   Methods employed included proprietary, generic, and customized techniques.

9   Differences between approaches are significant at the 10 percent level (f = 0.056). Differences between stakeholder sets are not significant (f = 0.126). No interaction was discovered between the two classifications.

References

Arthur Andersen & Co. (1983) *Method/1: Information Systems Methodology: An Introduction*, The Company, Chicago, IL.

Bowers, J. L. (1970) *Managing the Resource Allocation Process: A Study of Corporate Planning and Investment*, Division of Research, Graduate School of Business Administration, Harvard University, Boston, MA.

Bowman B., Davis, G. and Wetherbe, J. (1983) Three stage model of MIS planning. *Information and Management*, **6**(1), August, 11–25.

Boynton, A. C. and Zmud, R. W. (1987) Information technology planning in the 1990's: directions for practice and research. *MIS Quarterly* **11**(1), March, 59–71.

Brancheau, J. C. and Wetherbe, J. C. (1987) Key issues in information systems management. *MIS Quarterly*, **11**(1), March, 23–45.

Bullen, C. V. and Rockart, J. F. (1981) A primer on critical success factors. CISR Working Paper No. 69, Center for Information Systems Research, Massachusetts Institute of Technology, Cambridge, MA, June.

Danziger, J. N. (1978) *Making Budgets: Public Resource Allocation*, Sage Publications, Beverly Hills, CA.

de Geus, A. P. (1988) Planning as learning. *Harvard Business Review*, **66**(2), March-April, 70–74.

Dickson, G. W., Leitheiser, R. L., Wetherbe, J. C. and Nechis, M. (1984) Key information systems issues for the 1980's. *MIS Quarterly*, **10**(3), September, 135–159.

Earl, M. J. (ed.) (1988) *Information Management: The Strategic Dimension*, Oxford University Press, Oxford.

Earl, M. J. (1989) *Management Strategies for Information Technology*, Prentice Hall, London.

Earl, M. J. (1990) Strategic information systems planning in UK Companies early results of a field study. Oxford Institute of Information Management Research and Discussion Paper 90/1, Templeton College, Oxford.

Galliers, R. D. (1987) *Information Systems Planning in Britain and Australia in the Mid-1980's: Key Success Factors*, unpublished doctoral dissertation, London School of Economics, University of London.

Glaser, B. G. and Strauss, A. L. (1967) *The Discovery of Grounded Theory: Strategies for Qualitative Research*, Aldine Publishing Company, Chicago, IL.

Goodhue, D. L., Quillard. J. A. and Rockart, J. F. (1988) Managing the data resource: a contingency perspective. *MIS Quarterly*, **12**(3), September, 373–391.

Goodhue, D. L., Kirsch, L. J., Quillard, J. A. and Wybo, M. D. (1992) Strategic data planning: lessons from the field. *MIS Quarterly*, **16**(1), March, 11–34.

Hackathorn, R. D. and Karimi, J. (1988) A framework for comparing information engineering methods. *MIS Quarterly*, **12**(2), June, 203–220.

Hartog, C. and Herbert, M. (1986) 1985 opinion survey of MIS managers: key issues. *MIS Quarterly*, **10**(4), December, 351–361.

Henderson, J. C. (1989) Building and sustaining partnership between line and I/S managers. CISR Working Paper No. 195. Center for Information Systems Research, Massachusetts Institute of Technology, Cambridge, MA, September.

Henderson, J. C. and Sifonis, J. G. (1988) The value of strategic IS planning: understanding consistency, validity, and IS markets. *MIS Quarterly*, **12**(2), June, 187–200.

Henderson, J. C. and Venkatraman, N. (1989) Strategic alignment: a framework for strategic information technology management. CISR

Working Paper No. 190, Center for Information Systems Research, Massachusetts Institute of Technology, Cambridge, MA, August.

IBM Corporation (1975) *Business Systems Planning – Information Systems Planning Guide*, Publication #GE20–0527–4, White Plains, NY.

Inmon, W. H. (1986) *Information Systems Architecture*, Prentice Hall, Englewood Cliffs, NJ.

Karimi, J. (1988) Strategic planning for information systems: requirements and information engineering methods. *Journal of Management Information Systems*, **4**(4), Spring, 5–24.

King, W. R. (1978) Strategic planning for management information systems. *MIS Quarterly*, **2**(1), March, 22–37.

King, W. R. (1988) How effective is your information systems planning? *Long Range Planning*, **1**(1), October, 7–12.

Lederer, A. L. and Mendelow, A. L. (1986) Issues in information systems planning. *Information and Management*, **10**(5), May, 245–254.

Lederer, A. L. and Mendelow, A. L. (1987) Information resource planning: overcoming difficulties in identifying top management's objectives. *MIS Quarterly*, **11**(3), September, 389–399.

Lederer, A. L. and Mendelow, A. L. (1989) Co-ordination of information systems plans with business plans. *Journal of Management Information Systems*, **6**(2), Fall, 5–19.

Lederer, A. L. and Sethi, V. (1988) The implementation of strategic information systems planning methodologies. *MIS Quarterly*, **12**(3), September, 445–461.

Lederer, A. L. and Sethi, V. (1991) Critical dimensions of strategic information systems planning. *Decision Sciences*, **22**(1), Winter, 104–119.

Mintzberg, H. (1983) *Structure in Fives: Designing Effective Organizations*, Prentice Hall, Englewood Cliffs, NJ.

Mintzberg, H. (1987) Crafting strategy. *Harvard Business Review*, **66**(4), July-August, 66–75.

Moynihan, T. (1990) What chief executives and senior managers want from their IT departments. *MIS Quarterly*, **14**(1), March, 15–26.

Niederman, F., Brancheau, J. C. and Wetherbe, J. C. (1991) Information systems management issues for the 1990s. *MIS Quarterly*, **15**(4), December, 475–500.

Porter, M. E. and Millar, V. E. (1985) How information gives you competitive advantage. *Harvard Business Review*, **66**(4), July-August, 149–160.

Quinn, J. B. (1977) Strategic goals: plans and politics. *Sloan Management Review*, **19**(1), Fall, 21–37.

Quinn, J. B. (1978) Strategic change: logical incrementalism. *Sloan Management Review*, **20**(1), Fall, 7–21.

Raghunathan, T. S. and King. W. R. (1988) The impact of information systems planning on the organization. *OMEGA*, **16**(2), 85–93.

Sullivan, C. H., Jr. (1985) Systems planning in the information age. *Sloan Management Review*, **26**(2), Winter, 3–11.

Synott, W. R. and Gruber, W. H. (1982) *Information Resource Management: Opportunities and Strategies for the 1980's*, J. Wiley and Sons, New York.

Zani, W. M. (1970) Blueprint for MIS. *Harvard Business Review*, **48**(6), November–December, 95–100.

Appendix A: Field study companies

Descriptive statistics for field study companies

Company		Annual revenue (£B)	Annual IS expenditure (£M)	Years of SISP experience
1	Banking	1.7*	450	4
2	Banking	1.9*	275	2
3	Retailing	4.2	80	4
4	Retailing	0.56	8	4
5	Insurance	2.8†	30	11
6	Insurance	0.9†	15	15
7	Travel	0.75	8	4
8	Electronics	1.35	25	3
9	Aerospace	4.1	120	17
10	Aerospace	2.1	54	20
11	IT	3.9	77	21
12	IT	0.6	18	11
13	Telecommunications	0.9	50	6
14	Automobile	0.5	14	9
15	Food	4.5	40	1
16	Oil	55.0	1000	6
17	Chemicals	2.18	5	10
18	Food	1.4	20	8
19	Accountancy/Consultancy	0.55	1	5
20	Brewing	1.7	23	9
21	Food/Consumer	2.5	27	1

* Operating costs.
† premium income.

Appendix B: Interview questionnaire

Structured (closed) questions

1	What prompted you to develop an IS/IT strategy?	(RO)
3	What were the objectives in developing an IS/IT strategy?	(RO)
4a	What are the outputs of your IS/IT strategy development?	(MC)
4b	What are the content headings of your IS strategic plan or strategy?	(MC)
5	What methods have you used in developing your IS strategy; when; why?	(MC)
7	What have been the benefits of strategic information systems planning?	(RO)
8	How successful has SISP been?	(LS)
9	What have you found to be key success factors in SISP?	(RO)
10	How is your SISP connected to other business planning processes?	(MC)
11	How do you review your IS strategies?	(MC)
12	What are the major problems you have encountered in SISP?	(RO)

All these questions were asked using multiple-choice lists (MC), Likert-type scale (LS), or rank-order lists (RO).

Example rank-order questions

3 What were the objectives in developing an IS/IT strategy?

Tick		*Rank*
......	Align IS development with business needs	......
......	Revamp the IS/IT function	......
......	Seek competitive advantage from IT	......
......	Establish technology path and policies	......
......	Forecast IS requirements	......
......	Gain top management commitment	......
......	Other (specify)	......

Example multiple-choice questions

5   What methods have you used in developing your IS strategy; when, why?

When	*Method*	*Why*
......	Critical success factors	......
......	Stages of growth	......
......	Business systems planning	......
......	Enterprise modelling	......
......	Information engineering	......
......	Method 1	......
......	Other proprietary (specify)	......
......	In-house IS strategy	......
......	In-house business strategy	......
......	In-house application search techniques	......
......	Informal	......
......	Other (specify)	......

Example Likert-type scale question

8a   How successful has SISP been on the following scale?

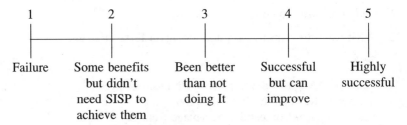

Semi-structured (open) questions

2a   Please summarize the approach you have adopted in developing your IS strategy (or in identifying and deciding which IT applications to develop in the long run).

2b   What are the key elements of your IS strategy?

6a   Have you developed any applications that have given competitive advantage in recent years? If so, what?

6b   How was each of these applications identified and developed?

8b   In what ways has SISP been unsuccessful?

13   Can you describe any key turning points in your SISP experience, such as changes in aims, approach, method, benefits, success factors or problems?

Appendix C: Concerns or unsuccessful features of SISP

Method concerns

1   It did not lead to management identifying applications supportable at a cost
2   No regeneration or review
3   Failed to discover our competitors' moves or understand their improvements
4   Not enough planning; too much emphasis on development and projects
5   It was not connected to business planning
6   It was too internally focused
7   Sensibly allocating resources to needs was a problem
8   Business needs were ignored or not identified
9   Not flexible or reactive enough
10 Not coordinated
11 Not enough consideration of architecture
12 Priority-setting and resource allocation were questionable
13 The plans were soon out of date
14 Business direction and plans were inadequate
15 Not enough strategic thinking
16 The thinking was too functional and applications-oriented and not process-based
17 It was too technical and not business-based
18 It was overtheoretical and too complicated
19 It could have been done quicker; it took too long
20 It developed a bureaucracy of its own
21 We have not solved identification of corporate-wide needs
22 The architecture was questionable; people were not convinced by it
23 We still don't know how to incorporate and meet short-term needs
24 We did not complete the company-entity model
25 We found it difficult justifying the benefits
26 It was too much about automating today's operations
27 It was too ad hoc; insufficient method
28 Many of the recommendations did not meet user aspirations

Process concerns

1   Some businesses were less good at, and less committed to, planning than others
2   The exercise was abrogated to the IS department
3   Inadequate understanding across all management
4   Line management involvement was unsatisfactory

5   Lack of senior management involvement
6   No top management buy-in
7   The strategy was not sold or communicated enough
8   We still have poor user-IS relationships
9   Too many IS people have not worked outside of IS
10 Poor IT understanding of customer and business needs
11 Line management buy-in was low
12 Little cross-divisional learning
13 IS management quality was below par
14 Senior executives were not made aware of the scale of change required
15 Users lacked understanding of IT and its methods
16 It was too user-driven in one period
17 We are still learning how to do planning studies
18 Planning almost never works; there are too many 'dramas'
19 The culture has not changed enough
20 We oversold the plan
21 Too much conflict between organizational units

Implementation concerns

1   We have not broken the resource constraints
2   We have not implemented as much as we should
3   It was not carried through into resource planning
4   The necessary technology planning was not done
5   We have not achieved the system benefits
6   We made technical mistakes
7   Some of the needs are still unsatisfied
8   Appropriate hardware or software was not available
9   Cost and time budget returns
10 We were not good at specifying the detailed requirements
11 Defining staffing needs was a problem
12 We have not gotten anything off the ground yet
13 We had insufficient skilled development resources
14 Regulatory impediments
15 We were overambitious and tried to change too much
16 We still have to catch up technically

Questions for discussion

1 Consider the success factors listed in Table 7.5 – is it worth undertaking SISP without top management involvement?
2 Compare the author's concept of SISP to that of information strategy from Smits *et al.* (in Chapter 3).
3 Debate the strengths and weaknesses of the approaches to SISP. Assuming time constraints prevent an 'everything goes' approach, which approach:
   - might help improve IS credibility?
   - might do the most to align IT with business strategy?
   - might do the most to enable the competitive uses of IT?
   - might do the most to achieve organization-wide vision?
   - might be more appropriate at the different stages of growth?
   - might best deal with management of change issues?
4 The author states that 'successful SISP seems to require users and line managers working in partnership with the IS function'. Who should be involved in SISP and how should those involved be determined?
5 Given the alternative approaches identified in this chapter, think of a possible hybrid approach (keeping in mind time, resource and people constraints).

8 The Information Systems Planning Process

Meeting the challenges of information systems planning

A. L. Lederer and V. Sethi

Introduction

Strategic information systems planning (SISP) is a critical issue facing today's businesses. Because SISP can identify the most appropriate targets for computerization, it can make a huge contribution to businesses and to other organizations. Effective SISP can help organizations use information systems to implement business strategies and reach business goals. It can also enable organizations to use information systems to create new business strategies. Recent research has shown that the quality of the planning process significantly influences the contribution which information systems can make to an organization's performance.[1] Moreover, the failure to carry out SISP carefully can result in lost opportunities and wasted resources.[2]

To perform effective SISP, organizations conventionally apply one of several methodologies. However, carrying out such a process is a key problem facing management.[3]

SISP also presents many complex technical questions. These deal with computer hardware, software, databases, and telecommunications technologies. In many organizations, as a result of this complexity, there is a tendency to let the computer experts handle SISP.

However, SISP is too important to delegate to technicians. Business planners are increasingly recognizing the potential impact of information technology, learning more about it, and participating in SISP studies despite their lack of technical experience.

This chapter defines and explains SISP. It illustrates four popular SISP methodologies. Then, based on a survey of 80 organizations, we discuss the problems of carrying out SISP. We also suggest some potential actions which business planners can take to deal with the problems.

What is SISP?

Information systems planning has evolved over the last 15 years. In the late 1970s, its primary objectives were to improve communication between computer users and MIS departments, increase top management support for computing, better forecast and allocate information system resource requirements, determine opportunities for improving the MIS department and identify new and higher payback computer applications.[4]

More recently, two new objectives have emerged. They are the identification of strategic information systems applications[5] – those that can give the organization a competitive edge – and the development of an organization-wide information architecture.[6]

While the importance of identifying strategic information systems applications is obvious, the importance of the organization-wide information architecture of information systems that share common data and communicate easily with each other is highly desirable. Just as new business ventures must mesh with the organization's existing endeavours, new systems applications must fit with the existing information architecture.

Unfortunately, an organization's commitment to construct an organization-wide information architecture vastly complicates SISP. Thus organizations have often failed to build such an architecture. Instead, their piecemeal approach has resulted in disjointed systems that temporarily solved minor problems in isolated areas of the organization. This has caused redundant efforts and exorbitant costs.

Thus, this chapter embraces two distinct yet usually simultaneously performed approaches to SISP. On one hand, SISP entails the search for high-impact applications with the ability to create an advantage over competitors.[7] Thus, SISP helps organizations use information systems in innovative ways to build barriers against new entrants, change the basis of competition, generate new products, build in switching costs, or change the balance of power in supplier relationships.[8] As such, SISP promotes innovation and creativity. It might employ idea generating techniques such as brainstorming,[9] value chain analysis,[10] or the customer resource life cycle.

On the other hand SISP is the process of identifying a portfolio of computer-based applications to assist an organization in executing its current business plans and thus realizing its existing business goals. SISP may mean the selection of rather prosaic applications, almost as if from a predefined list that would best fit the current and projected needs of the organization. These applications would guide the creation of the organization-wide information architecture of large databases and systems of computer programs. The distinction between the two approaches results in the former being referred to as attempting to *impact* organizational strategies and the latter as attempting to *align* MIS objectives with organizational goals.

Carrying out SISP

To carry out SISP, an organization usually selects an existing methodology and then embarks on a major, intensive study. The organization forms teams of business planners and computer users with MIS specialists as members or as advisors. It is likely to use the SISP vendor's educational support to train the teams and consulting support to guide and audit the study. It carries out a multi-step procedure over several weeks or months. The duration depends on the scope of the study. In addition to identifying the portfolio of applications, it prioritizes them. It defines databases, data elements, and a network of computers and communications equipment to support the applications. It also prepares a schedule for developing and installing them.

Organizations usually apply one of several methodologies to carry out this process. Four popular ones are Business Systems Planning[11] PROplanner,[12] Information Engineering,[13] and Method/1.[14] These will be described briefly as contemporary, illustrative methodologies although the four undergo continuous change and improvement. They were selected because, together, they accounted for over half the responses to the survey described later.

Business Systems Planning (BSP), developed by IBM, involves *top-down* planning with *bottom-up* implementation. From the top-down, the study team first recognizes its firm's business mission, objectives and functions, and how these determine the business processes. It analyses the processes for their data needs. From the bottom-up, it then identifies the data currently required to perform the processes. The final BSP plan describes an overall information systems architecture comprised of databases and applications as well as the installation schedule of individual systems. Table 8.1 details the steps in a BSP study.

BSP places heavy emphasis on top management commitment and involvement. Top executive sponsorship is seen as critical. MIS analyses might serve primarily in an advisory capacity.

PROplanner, by Holland Systems Corp. in Ann Arbor, Michigan, helps planners analyse major functional areas within the organization. They then define a Business Function Model. They derive a Data Architecture from the Business Function Model by combining the organization's information requirements into generic data entities and broad databases. They then identify an Information Systems Architecture of specific new applications and an implementation schedule.

Table 8.1 *Description of BSP study steps*

Enterprise Analysis The team documents the strategic business planning process and how the organization carries it out. It presents this information in a matrix for the executive sponsor to validate.

Enterprise Modelling The team identifies the organization's business processes, using a technique known as value chain analysis, and then presents them in a matrix showing each's relationship to each business strategy (from the Enterprise Analysis). The team identifies the organization's entities (such as product, customer, vendor, order, part) and presents them in a matrix showing how each is tied to each process.

Executive Interviews The team asks key executives about potential information opportunities needed to support their enterprise strategy (from the Enterprise Analysis), the processes (from the Enterprise Modelling) they are responsible for, and the entities (from the Enterprise Modelling) they manage. Each executive identifies a value and priority ranking for each information opportunity.

Information Opportunity Analysis The team groups the opportunities by processes and entitles to separate 'quick fix' opportunities. It then analyses the remaining information opportunities, develops support recommendations, and prioritizes them.

I/S Strategies and Recommendations The team assesses the organization's information management in terms of its information systems/enterprise alignment, ongoing information planning, tactical information planning, data management, and application development. It then defines new strategies and recommends them to executive management.

Data Architecture Design The team prepares a high level design of proposed databases by diagramming how the organization uses its entities in support of its processes (entities and processes were defined during Enterprise Modelling) and identifying critical pieces of information describing the entities.

Process Architecture Design The team prepares a plan for developing high priority applications and for integrating all proposed applications. It does this by tying business processes to their proposed applications.

Existing Systems Review The team reviews existing applications to evaluate their technical and functional quality by interviewing users and information systems specialists.

Implementation Planning The team considers the quality of existing systems (from the Existing Systems Review) and the proposed applications (from the Process Architecture Design) and develops a plan identifying those to discard, keep, enhance, or re-develop.

Information Management Recommendations The team develops and presents a series of recommendations to help it carry out the plans that it prepared in Implementation Planning.

PROplanner offers automated storage, manipulation, and presentation of the data collected during SISP. PROplanner software produces reports in various formats and levels of detail. *Affinity* reports show the frequencies of accesses to data. *Clustering* reports guide database design. Menus direct the planner through on-line data collection during the process. A data dictionary (a computerized list of all data on the database) permits planners to share PRO planner data with an existing data dictionary or other automated design tools.

Information Engineering (IE), by Knowledge Ware in Atlanta, provides techniques for building Enterprise Models, Data Models, and Process Models. These make up a comprehensive knowledge base that developers later use to create and maintain information systems.

In conjunction with IE, every general manager may participate in a critical success factors (CSF) inquiry, the popular technique for identifying issues that business executives view as the most vital for their organization's success. The resulting factors will then guide the strategic information planning endeavour by helping identify future management control systems.

IE provides several software packages for facilitating the strategic information planning effort. However, IE differs from some other methodologies by providing automated tools to link its output to subsequent systems development efforts. For example, integrated with IE is an application generator to produce computer programs written in the COBOL programming language without handcoding.

Method/1, the methodology of Andersen Consulting (a division of Arthur Andersen & Co.), consists of ten phases of work segments that an organization completes to create its strategic plan. The first five formulate information strategy. The final five further formulate the information strategy but also develop action plans. A break between the first and final five provides a top management checkpoint and an opportunity to adjust and revise. By design, however, a typical organization using Method/1 need not complete all the work segments at the same level of detail. Instead, planners evaluate each work segment in terms of the organization's objectives.

Method/1 focuses heavily on the assessment of the current business organization, its objectives, and its competitive environment. It also stresses the tactics required for changing the organization when it implements the plan.

Method/1 follows a layered approach. The top layer is the methodology itself. A middle layer of techniques supports the methodology and a bottom layer of tools supports the techniques. Examples of the many techniques are focus groups, Delphi studies, matrix analysis, dataflow diagramming and functional decomposition. FOUNDATION, Andersen Consulting's computer-aided software engineering tool set, includes computer programs that support Method/1.

Besides BSP, PRO planner, IE and Method/1, firms might choose Information Quality Analysis,[15] Business Information Analysis and Integration Technique,[16] Business Information Characterization Study,[17] CSF, Ends/ Means Analysis,[18] Nolan Norton Methodology,[19] Portfolio Management,[20] Strategy Set Transformation,[21] Value Chain Analysis, or the Customer Resource Life Cycle. Also, firms often select features of these methodologies and then, possibly with outside assistance, tailor their own in-house approach.[22]

Problems with the methodologies

Planners have long recognized that SISP is an intricate and complex activity fraught with problems.[23] Several authors have described these problems based on field surveys, cases, and conceptual studies. An exhaustive review of their most significant articles served as the basis of a comprehensive list of the problems for our research.

To organize the problems, we classified them as tied to resources, process, or output. Resource-related problems address issues of time, money, personnel, and top management support for the initiation of the study. Process-related problems involve the limitations of the analysis. Output-related problems deal with the comprehensive and appropriateness of the final plan. We derived these categories from a similar scheme used to define the components of IS planning. (Research Appendix 1 lists the problems studied in the surveys, cases and conceptual studies. The problems have been paraphrased, simplified, and classified.)

A survey of strategic information systems planners

To understand better the problems of SISP, we developed a questionnaire with two main parts. In the first part, respondents identified the methodology they had used during an SISP study. They also rated the extent to which they had encountered each of the aforementioned problems as 'not a problem', 'an insignificant problem', 'a minor problem', 'a major problem', or 'an extreme problem'. Similar studies have used this scale.

The second part asked about the implementation of plans. Planners indicated the extent to which different outputs of the plan had been affected. This conforms to the recommendation that a criterion for evaluating a planning system is the extent to which the final plan actually guides the strategic direction of an organization. In this part, the subjects also answered questions about their satisfaction with various aspects of the SISP experience.

We mailed the questionnaire to 251 organizations in two groups. The first included systems planners who were members of the Strategic Data Planning

Institute, a Rockville, Maryland group under the auspices of Barnett Data Systems. The second was another group of systems planners.[24]

While 163 firms returned completed surveys, 80 (or 32 per cent) had carried out an SISP study and they provided usable data. Considering the length and complexity of the questionnaire, this is a high response rate.

Evidence of SISP problems: carrying out plans

In general, the respondents were fairly satisfied with their SISP experience. Their average rating for overall satisfaction with the SISP methodology was 3.55 where a neutral score would have been 3.00 (on the scale of zero to six in which zero was 'extremely dissatisfied' and six was 'extremely satisfied'). Satisfaction scores for the different dimensions of SISP were also only slightly favourable. Satisfaction was 3.68 with the SISP process, 3.38 with the SISP output, and 3.02 with the SISP resource requirements.

However, satisfaction with the carrying out of final SISP plans was lower (2.53). In fact, only 32 per cent of respondents were satisfied with the extent of carrying them out while 53 per cent were dissatisfied. Table 8.2 summarizes the respondents' satisfaction with these aspects of the SISP.

Table 8.2   *Overall satisfaction with SISP*

	Average	Satisfied	Neutral	Dissatisfied
The methodology	3.55	54%	23%	23%
The resources	3.02	38%	24%	38%
The process	3.68	48%	17%	25%
The output	3.38	55%	17%	28%
Carrying out the plan	2.53	32%	15%	53%

Further evidence focusing on the plan implementation problem stems from the contrast between the elapsed planning horizon and the degree of completion of SISP recommended projects. The average planning horizon of the SISP studies was 3.73 years while an average of 2.1 years had passed since the studies' completion. Thus, 56 per cent of the planning horizons had elapsed. However, out of an average of 23.4 projects recommended in the SISP studies, only 5.7 (24 per cent) had been started. Hence, it appears that firms were failing to start projects as rapidly as necessary in order to complete them during the planning horizon. There may have been insufficient project start-ups in order to realize the plan.

In addition to *not* starting projects in the plan, organizations instead had begun projects that were *not* part of their SISP plan. These latter projects were about 38 per cent of all projects started during the 2.1 years after the study.

Actions for planners

Below are the 18 most severe problems – which at least 25 per cent of the respondents described as an 'extreme' or 'major' problem. Because each can be seen as closely tied to Leadership, Implementation, or Resource issues, they are categorized into those three groups. They are then ordered within the groups by their severity. (Research Appendix 2 ranks all of the reported problems. The 'Extreme or Major Problem' column in the table shows the percentage of subjects rating the problem as such. The 'Minor Problem' displays the similar percentage. Subjects could also rate each as 'Insignificant' or 'Not a Problem'.)

We offer an interpretation of each problem and suggestions to both top management and other business planners considering an SISP study. Many of the suggestions are based on the successful SISP experiences of Raychem Corp., a world-wide materials sciences company based in Menlo Park, California with over 10 000 employees in 41 countries. Raychem conducted SISP studies in 1978 and 1990.[25] The company thus had the chance to carry out and implement an SISP study, and to learn from the experience.

The interpretations and suggestions provide a checklist for debate and discussion, and eventually, for improved SISP.

Leadership issues

It is Difficult to Secure Top Management Commitment for Implementing the Plan (No. 1 – the Most Serious – of the 18)

Over half the respondents called this an extreme or major problem. It means that once their study was completed and in writing, they struggled to convince top management to authorize the development of the recommended applications. This is consistent with the percentages in the previous section.

Such a finding suggests that top management might not understand the plan or might lack confidence in the MIS department's ability to carry it out. It thus suggests that top management carefully consider its commitment to implementing a plan even before authorizing the time and money needed to prepare the plan.

Likewise, planners proposing an SISP study should assess in advance the likelihood that their top management will refuse to fund the newly recommended projects. They may also want to determine tactics to improve the likelihood of funding. In Raychem's 1978 study, the CEO served as sponsor and hence the likelihood of implementing its findings was substantially improved.

The Success of the Methodology is Greatly Dependent on the Team Leader (No. 3)

If the team leader cannot convince top management to support the study or cannot obtain a top management mandate to convince functional area management and MIS management to participate, the study is probably doomed. The team leader motivates team members and pulls the project along. The team leader must be a respected veteran in the organization's business and a dynamic leader comfortable with current technology.

Organizations should reduce their dependency on their team leader. One way to do so is by using a well-structured and well-defined methodology to simplify the team leader's job. Likewise, by obtaining as much visible, top management support as possible, the organization will depend less on the team leader's personal ties to top management. In Raychem's case, dependency on the team leader was reduced because the team consisted of members with broad, corporate rather than parochial, departmental views. Such members can enable the team leader to serve as a project manager rather than force the individual to be a project champion.

It is Difficult to Find a Team Leader who Meets the Criteria Specified by the Methodology (No. 4)

As with the previous item, management will have to look hard to find a business-wise and technology-savvy leader. Such people are scarce. Management must choose that person carefully.

It is Difficult to Convince Top Management to Approve the Methodology (No. 8)

It is not only difficult to convince top management to implement the final plan (as in the first item above) but also difficult to convince top management to even fund the initial SISP study. SISP is slow and costly. Meanwhile, many top managers want working systems immediately, not plans for an uncertain future. Thus, advocates of SISP should prepare convincing arguments to authorize the funding of the study.

In Raychem's case, four executives – including two vice presidents – from different areas of the firm met several times with the CEO in 1978. Because he felt that information technology was expensive but was not sufficiently providing him with the information required to run the company, the executives were able to convince him to approve the SISP study and be its sponsor.

Implementation issues

Implementing the Projects and the Data Architecture Identified in the Plan Requires Substantial Further Analysis (No. 2)

Nearly half the respondents found this an extreme or major problem. SISP often fell short of providing the analysis needed to start the design and programming of the individual computer applications. The methodology did not provide the specifications necessary to begin the design of the recommended projects. This meant duplicating the investigation initially needed to make the recommendations.

This result suggests that prospective strategic information systems planners should seek a methodology that provides features to guide them into implementation. Some vendors offer such methodologies. Otherwise, planners should be prepared for the frustrations of delays and duplicated effort before seeing their plans reach fruition.

In Raychem's case, the planners drew up a matrix showing business processes and classes of data. The matrix reduced the need for further analysis somewhat by helping the firm decide the applications to standardize on a corporate basis and those to implement in regional offices. As another means of reducing the need for more analysis, Raychem set up model databases for all corporate applications to access.

The Methodology Fails to Take into Account Issues Related to Plan Implementation (No. 7)

The exercise may produce an excellent plan. It may produce a list of significant, high-impact applications.

However, as in earlier items, the planning study may fail to include the actions that will bring the plan to fruition. For example, the study might ignore the development of a strategy to ensure the final decisions to proceed with specific applications. It might fail to address the resistance of those managers who oppose the plan.

Again, planners need to pay careful attention to ensure that the plan is actually followed and not prematurely discarded.

The Documentation does not Adequately Describe the Steps that Should be Followed for Implementing the Methodology (No. 12)

The documentation describing some proprietary SISP methodologies is inadequate. It gives insufficient guidance to planners. Some of it may be erroneous, ambiguous, or contradictory.

Planners who purchase a proprietary methodology should read its documentation carefully before signing the contract. Planners who develop their own methodology should be prepared to devote significant energy to its documentation.

In Raychem's case, it chose BSP in 1978 simply because there were no other methodologies at the time. For its 1990 study, Raychem planners interviewed a number of consulting companies with proprietory methodologies before choosing the Index Group from Boston. Raychem then used extensive training to compensate for any potential deficiencies in the documentation.

The Strategic Information Systems Plan Fails to Provide Priorities for Developing Specific Databases (No. 13)

Both top management and functional area management must agree with the plan's priorities. For example, they must concur on whether the organization builds a marketing database, a financial database, or a production database. They must agree on what to do first and what to delay.

Without top management agreement on the priorities of the targeted databases, the plan will never be executed. Without functional area management concurrence, battles to change the priorities will rage. Such changes can result in temporarily halting ongoing projects while starting others. One risk is pre-eminent: Everything is started but nothing is finished.

Planners should be certain that the plan stipulates priorities and that top management and functional area management sincerely accept them.

Raychem approached this problem by culling 10 agreed upon, broad initiatives from 35 proposals in the 1990 study. Instead of choosing to establish database priorities during the study, it later established priorities for the numerous projects spawned by the initiatives.

The Strategic Information Systems Plan Fails to Determine an Overall Data Architecture for the Organization (No. 14)

Although the major objective of many SISP methodologies is to determine an overall data architecture, many respondents were disappointed with their success in doing so. They were disappointed with the identification of the architecture's specific databases and with the linkages between them. To many respondents, despite the huge effort, the portfolio of applications may appear piecemeal and disjointed.

Although these may appear to be technical issues, planners should still understand major data architecture issues and should check to be sure that their SISP will provide such an overall, integrated architecture, and not just a list of applications.

The Strategic Information Systems Plan Fails to Sufficiently Address the Need for Data Administration in the Organization (No. 18)

Because long-range plans usually call for the expansion of databases, the need for more data administration personnel – people whose sole role is ensuring that databases are up and working – is often necessary. In many organizations, the data administration function has grown dramatically in recent years. It may continue to expand and the implications of this necessary growth can be easy to ignore. Planners should thus be sure that their long-range plan includes the role of data administration in the organization's future. In Raychem's case, a data administration function was established as a result of its 1978 study.

Resource issues

The Methodology Lacks Sufficient Computer Support (No. 5)

SISP can produce reams of reports, charts, matrices and diagrams. Planners cannot manage that volume of data efficiently and effectively without automated support.

When planners buy an existing methodology, they should carefully scrutinize the vendor's computer support. They should examine the screens and reports. On the other hand, if they customize their own methodology, they must be certain not to underestimate the need for such support. In some organizations, the expense of developing computer support in-house might compel the organization to then buy an existing methodology rather than tailor its own.

The Planning Exercise Takes Very Long (No. 6)

The study takes weeks or even months. This may be well beyond the span of attention of many organizations. Too many business managers expect results almost immediately and lose interest if the study drags on. Moreover, many organizations undergo major changes even during the planning period.

Most importantly, an overrun during the planning exercise may reduce top management's confidence in the organization's ability to carry out the final plan. Hence planners should strive to keep the duration of the planning study as short as possible.

Raychem's 1978 study required three months but its 1990 study required nine. In 1990, planners chose to risk the consequences of a longer study because it enabled them to involve more senior level executives albeit on a part-time basis. Planners could have completed a briefer study with lower level executives on a full-time basis. However, the planners felt the study under such circumstances would have been less credible. They clearly felt that the potential problem of insufficient top management commitment described above was more serious than the problem of a lengthy study!

The Strategic Information Plan Fails to Include an Overall Personnel and Training Plan for the MIS Department (No. 8)

Many MIS departments lack the necessary skills to carry out the innovative and complex projects recommended by an SISP study. A strategic information systems plan thus needs to consider new personnel to add to the MIS Department. The SISP study will probably recommend additions to existing positions, permanent information systems planners, and a variety of such new positions as expert systems specialists, local area and wide area network specialists, desktop-publishers, and many others. An SISP study also often recommends training current MIS staff in today's personal computer, network, and database technologies.

Planners will need to be certain that their study accurately assesses current MIS department skills and staffing. They will also need to allocate the time and resources to ensure the presence of critical new personnel and the training of existing personnel. Raychem included a statement supporting such training in its 1990 study.

It is Difficult to Find Team Members who Meet the Criteria Specified by the Methodology (No. 10)

Qualified team members, in addition to team leaders (as in an earlier item above), are scarce. Team members from functional area departments must feel comfortable with information technology while computer specialists need to understand the business. Both need excellent communication skills and must have the time to participate. Hence, management should check the credentials of their team members carefully and be certain that their schedules allow them to participate fully in the planning process.

To find qualified team members, Raychem's planners in its 1990 study first drew up lists of business unit functions and geographical locations. They used it to identify a mix of team members from a variety of units in various locations. World-wide, senior managers helped identify team members who would be seen as leaders with objective views and diverse backgrounds. Such team members made the final study more credible.

The Strategic Information Systems Plan Fails to Include an Overall Financial Plan for the MIS Department (No. 11)

Responsible top management frequently demands financial justification for new projects. Because computer projects appear different from other capital projects, planners might treat them differently. Because top management will scrutinize and probably challenge costs and benefits in the long-range plan, planners must be sure that any costs and benefits are defensible.

In 1990, Raychem did not provide specific cost and benefit figures because of its concern that technological change would render them inaccurate later on. However, the firm did use various financial tests to reduce its initially suggested initiatives from 35 to 10. Moreover, planners did cost justify individual projects as they were spawned from the initiatives.

The Planning Exercise is Very Expensive (No. 15)

The planning exercise demands an exorbitant number of hours from top management, functional area management, and the MIS department. These are often the organization's busiest, most productive, and highest paid managers, precisely the people who lack the time to devote to the study.

Hence, management must be convinced that the planning study is both essential and well worth the time demanded of its top people.

The Strategic Information Systems Plan Fails Sufficiently to Address the Role of a Permanent MIS Planning Group (No. 16)

Like general business planning, strategic systems planning is not a one-time endeavour. It is an ongoing process where planners periodically review the plan and the issues behind it. Many information systems planners feel that a permanent planning group devoted solely to the information systems is essential, but that their planning endeavours failed to establish one.

As with many other planning efforts, planners should view the SISP exercise as an initial effort in an ongoing process. They should also consider the need for a permanent planning function devoted to SISP. In Raychem's 1978 study, the company formed a planning committee of executives from around the company. In their 1990 study, the management refined their procedures to ensure that planning committee members would serve as sponsors of each of the 10 initiatives and that they also report progress on them to the CEO.

Many Support Personnel are Required for Data Gathering and Analysis During the Study (No. 17)

To understand the current business processes and information systems support, many staff members must collect and collate data about the organization. Planners are concerned about their time and expense.

Planners should be sceptical if the vendor of a methodology suggests that staff support will be negligible. Moreover, planners may want to budget for some surplus staff support. Raychem controlled the cost of data gathering and analysis by having team members gather and analyse the data in the business units with which they were familiar.

Implications

There are two broad approaches to SISP. The *impact* approach entails the identification of a small number of information systems applications that can give the organization a competitive edge. It involves innovation and creativity in using information systems to create new business strategies by building barriers against new entrants, changing the basis of competition, generating new products, building in switching costs, or changing the balance of power in supplier relationships.

The *align* approach entails the development of an organization-wide information architecture of applications to guide the creation of large databases and computer systems to support current business strategies. It typically involves identifying a larger number of carefully integrated conventional applications that support these strategies.

Some organizations may attempt to follow both approaches equally while others may follow one more so than the other. Thus the two approaches suggest that perhaps the different groups of problems may carry different weights during the SISP process. The matrix in Figure 8.1 shows the approaches, categories with summarized problem statements, and weights in each cell.

For example, when seeking new and unconventional applications under the impact approach, leadership may play a more critical role. Without experienced, articulate and technology savvy leadership in the SISP study, it may be difficult to convince top management to gamble on radical innovation. This does not suggest that leadership is unimportant when attempting to plan applications for alignment but rather that it may be more critical under the impact approach.

Because the align approach typically affects larger numbers of lower-level employees, the potential for resource problems is perhaps greater. The possible widespread effects increase the complexity of the align approach. Thus resource issues are probably of more critical concern in this approach.

Finally, regardless of whether the approach is 'impact' or 'alignment', implementation is still often perceived as the key to successful SISP. Thus whether an organization is attempting to identify a few high-impact applications or many integrated and conventional ones, implementation issues remain equally important.

Approaches

Issues	'Impact'	'Align'
LEADERSHIP Difficult to Secure Top Management Commitment for Implementation Success Dependent on Team Leader Difficult to Find Team Leader Meeting Criteria Difficult to Obtain Top Management Approval	Critical	Important
IMPLEMENTATION Requires Further Analysis Ignores Plan Implementation Issues Documentation is Inadequate for Implementation No Priorities for Developing Databases No Overall Data Architecture is Determined No Data Administration Need Addressed	Very important	Very important
RESOURCES Methodology Lacks Sufficient Computer Support Planning Exercise Takes Long Time No Training Plan for IS Department Difficult to Find Team Members Meeting Criteria No Financial Plan for IS Department Very Expensive No Permanent IS Planning Group Many Support Personnel Required	Important	Critical

Figure 8.1 *Where information systems planning fails*

Conclusion

Effective SISP is a major challenge facing business executives today. It is an essential activity for unlocking the significant potential that information technology offers to organizations. This chapter has examined the challenges of SISP.

In summary, strategic information systems planners are not particularly satisfied with SISP. After all, it requires extensive resources. Top management commitment is often difficult to obtain. When the SISP study is complete, further analysis may be required before the plan can be executed. The execution of the plan might not be very extensive. Thus, while SISP offers a great deal – the potential to use information technology to realize current business strategies and to create new ones – too often it is not satisfactorily done.

In fact, despite its complex information technology ingredient, SISP is very similar to many other business planning endeavours. For this reason alone, the involvement of top management and business planners has become increasingly indispensable.

References

1   G. Premkumar and W. R. King. Assessing strategic information systems planning. *Long Range Planning.* October (1991).
2   W. R. King. How effective is your information systems planning? *Long Range Planning.* **21**(5), 103–112 (1988).
3   A. L. Lederer and A. L. Mendelow. Issues in information systems planning. *Information and Management.* pp. 245–254. May (1986); A. L. Lederer and V. Sethi. The implementation of strategic information systems planning methodologies. *MIS Quarterly.* **12**(3), 445–461. September (1988); and S. W. Sinclair. The three domains of information systems planning. *Journal of Information Systems Management.* **3**(2), 8–16. Spring (1986).
4   E. R. McLean and J. V. Soden. *Strategic Planning for MIS.* John Wiley and Sons. Inc. (1977).
5   PRISM. Information systems planning in the contemporary environment final report. December (1986). Index Systems. Inc. Cambridge, MA and M. R. Vitale, B. Ives and C. M. Beath. Linking information technology and corporate strategy an organizational view. *Proceedings of the Seventh International Conference on Information Systems.* pp. 265–276. San Diego. CA. 15–17 December (1986).
6   R. Moskowitz. Strategic systems planning shifts to data-oriented approach. *Computerworld.* pp. 109–119, 12 May (1986).
7   E. K. Clemons. Information systems for sustainable competitive advantage. *Information and Management.* **1**(3), 131–136. October (1986). B. Ives and G. Learmonth. The information system as a competitive weapon. *Communications of the ACM.* **27**(12), 1193–1201. December (1985). F. W. McFarlan. Information technology changes the way you compete. *Harvard Business Review.* **62**(3), 98–103. May–June (1984). G. L. Parsons. Information technology: a new competitive weapon. *Sloan Management Review.* **25**(1), 3–14. Fall (1983): and C. Wiseman. *Strategy and Computer Information Systems as Competitive Weapons.* Dow Jones-Irwin, Homewood. IL (1985).

8   M. E. Porter. *Competitive Advantage Creating and Sustaining Superior Performance.* New York, Free Press (1985).

9   N. Rackoff, C. Wiseman and W. A. Ulrich. Information systems for competitive advantage and implementation of planning process. *MIS Quarterly.* **9**(4), 285–294. December (1985).

10 M. E. Porter. *Competitive Advantage Creating and Sustaining Superior Performance.* Free Press, New York (1985).

11 IBM Corporation. *Business Systems Planning – Information Systems Planning Guide*, Publication No GE20 0527–4 (1975).

12 Holland Systems Coporation. *4FRONT strategy Method Guide.* Ann Arbor. MI (1989).

13 J. Martin. *Strategic Information Planning Methodologies.* Prentice-Hall Inc. Englewood Cliffs. NJ (1989).

14 Andersen Consulting. *Foundation Method/1 Information Planning.* Version 8.0. Chicago. IL (1987).

15 J. R. Vacca. IBM's information quality analysis. *Computerworld.* 10 December (1984).

16 W. M. Carlson. Business information analysis and integration technique (BIAIT) a new horizon. *Data Base.* 3–9. Spring (1979).

17 D. V. Kerner. Business information characterization study. *Data Base.* 10–17, Spring (1979).

18 J. C. Wetherbe and G. B. Davis. Strategic Planning through Ends/Means Analysis. MISRC Working Paper. 1982. University of Minnesota.

19 R. Moskowitz. Strategic systems planning shifts to data-oriented approach. *Computerworld.* pp. 109–119, 12 May (1986).

20 F. W. McFarlan. Portfolio approach to information systems. *Harvard Business Review.* **59**(5), 142–150, September–October (1981).

21 W. R. King. Strategic planning for management information systems. *MIS Quarterly.* pp. 27–37, March (1978).

22 C. H. Sullivan Jr. An evolutionary new logic redefines strategic systems planning. *Information Strategy. The Executive's Journal.* **3**(2), 13–19. Winter (1986).

23 F. W. McFarlan. Problems in planning the information system. *Harvard Business Review.* **49**(2), 75–89, March–April (1971).

24 J. R. Vacca. BSP How is it working? *Computerworld.* March (1983).

25 Interviews with Paul Osborn, an executive at Raychem, who provided details about the firm's SISP experiences.

Related reading

M. Hosoda, CIM at Nippon Seiko Co. *Long Range Planning.* **23**(5), 10–21 (1990).

G. K. Janssens and L. Cuyvers. EDI – A strategic weapon in international trade. *Long Range Planning.* **24**(2), 46–53 (1991).

Research Appendix 1: SISP survey items: resources, processes and output

Resources

1   The size of the planning team is very large.
2   It is difficult to find a team leader who meets the criteria specified by the methodology.
3   It is difficult to find team members who meet the criteria specified by the methodology.
4   The success of the methodology is greatly dependent on the team leader.
5   Many support personnel are required for data gathering and analysis during the study.
6   The planning exercise takes very long.
7   The planning exercise is very expensive.
8   The documentation does not adequately describe the steps that should be followed for implementing the methodology.
9   The methodology lacks sufficient computer support.
10 Adequate external consultant support is not available for implementing the methodology.
11 The methodology is not based on any theoretical framework.
12 The planning horizon considered by the methodology is inappropriate.
13 It is difficult to convince top management to approve the methodology.
14 The methodology makes inappropriate assumptions about organization structure.
15 The methodology makes inappropriate assumptions about organization size.

Process

The Methodology

1   fails to take into account organizational goals and strategies;
2   fails to assess the current information systems applications portfolio;
3   fails to analyse the current strengths and weaknesses of the IS department;
4   fails to take into account legal and environmental issues;
5   fails to assess the external technological environment;
6   fails to assess the organization's competitive environment;
7   fails to take into account issues related to plan implementation;
8   fails to take into account changes in the organization during SISP;
9   does not sufficiently involve users;

10   managers find it difficult to answer questions specified by the methodology;
11   requires too much top management involvement;
12   requires too much user involvement;
13   the planning procedure is rigid; and
14   does not sufficiently involve top management.

SISP Output:

1   fails to provide a statement of organizational objectives for the IS department;
2   fails to designate specific new steering committees;
3   fails to identify specific new products;
4   fails to determine a uniform basis for priorities projects;
5   fails to determine an overall data architecture for the organization;
6   fails to provide priorities for developing specific databases;
7   fails to sufficiently address the need for Data Administration in the organization;
8   fails to include an overall organizational hardware plan;
9   fails to include an overall organizational data communications plan;
10   fails to outline changes in the reporting relationships in the IS department;
11   fails to include an overall personnel and training plan for the IS department;
12   fails to include an overall financial plan for the IS department;
13   fails to sufficiently address the role of a permanent IS planning group;
14   plans are not flexible enough to take into account unanticipated changes in the organization and its environment;
15   is not in accordance with the expectations of top management;
16   implementing the projects and the data architecture identified in the SISP output requires substantial further analysis;
17   it is difficult to secure top management commitment for implementing the plan;
18   the experiences from implementing the methodology are not sufficiently transferable across divisions;
19   the final output document is not very useful; and
20   the SISP output does not capture all the information that was developed during the study.

Research Appendix 2: Extent of SISP problems

Abbreviated problem statement

Item No		Extreme or major problem	Minor problem
017	Difficult to secure top management commitment	52%	16%
016	Requires further analysis	46%	31%
R4	Success dependent on team leader	41%	30%
R2	Difficult to find team leader meeting criteria	37%	17%
R9	Methodology lacks sufficient computer support	36%	27%
R6	Planning exercise takes long time	33%	30%
P7	Ignores plan implementation issues	33%	18%
R13	Difficult to obtain top management approval	32%	36%
O11	No training plan for IS department	30%	29%
R3	Difficult to find team members meeting criteria	30%	24%
O12	No financial plan for IS department	29%	28%
R8	Documentation is inadequate	28%	33%
O6	No priorities for developing databases	27%	26%
O5	No overall data architecture is determined	27%	22%
R7	Very expensive	26%	29%
O13	No permanent IS planning group	26%	24%
R5	Many support personnel required	26%	23%
O7	No data administration need addressed	26%	16%
O18	Experiences not sufficiently transferable	24%	19%
09	No organizational data communications plan	22%	38%
O10	No changes in IS reporting relationships	22%	31%
O4	No prioritization scheme provided	22%	19%
O15	Output belies top management expectations	22%	15%
P3	No analysis of IS department strengths/weaknesses	21%	32%
O8	No hardware plan	20%	36%
P11	Heavy top management involvement	20%	21%

Item No		Extreme or major problem	Minor problem
O14	Resulting plans are inflexible	20%	18%
P5	No analysis of technological environment	19%	20%
P12	Too much user involvement	18%	28%
O19	Final output document not very useful	18%	20%
P10	Questions difficult for managers to answer	17%	39%
O20	Information during study not captured	17%	25%
P4	Methodology ignores legal/environmental issues	14%	16%
R14	Bad assumptions about organization structure	14%	14%
P8	Ignores organization changes during P8 SISP	13%	25%
O1	No objectives for IS department are provided	13%	21%
P9	Insufficient user involvement	13%	5%
R1	Very large planning team required	12%	21%
P6	Methodology ignores competitive environment	12%	19%
O3	No new projects identified in final plans	12%	13%
O2	Output fails to designate new steering committees	11%	18%
P13	Rigidity of planning procedure	9%	17%
P2	No assessment of current applications portfolio	9%	16%
P14	Lack of top management involvement	9%	13%
P1	Ignores organizational goals and strategies	8%	10%
R12	Inappropriate planning horizon	6%	7%
R10	Inadequate consultant support	5%	11%
R15	Inappropriate size assumptions	4%	8%
R11	No theoretical framework	3%	5%

Questions for discussion

1 How might the appropriate planning process vary according to the context of IT and to the stage of growth (c.f. Chapter 2)?

2 Do you agree that the 'quality of the planning process significantly influences the contribution which IS can make to an organization's performance'?

3 The authors state that 'an organization's commitment to construct an organization-wide information architecture vastly complicates SISP. Thus, organizations have often failed to build such an architecture'. What are other factors, aside from commitment, that affect whether an organization has constructed an organization-wide information architecture?

4 Of the two major goals of SISP – impact (the search for high-impact applications and the creation of competitive advantage) and alignment (the identification of a portfolio of computer-based applications to assist an organization in executing business plans) – which do you recommend? Should the SISP also vary according to the stage of growth? Is it possible consciously to plan for strategic IS (i.e. the 'impact' goal)?

5 The authors state that 'advocates of SISP should prepare convincing arguments to authorize the funding of the study'. What are some convincing arguments for why SISP should be carried out?

6 What would be the role of a permanent planning group? How might such a group overcome some of the major problems of SISP raised by the authors?

9 Evaluating the Outcomes of Information Systems Plans

Managing information technology evaluation – techniques and processes*

L. P. Willcocks

As far as I am concerned we could write off our IT expenditure over the last five years to the training budget. (Senior executive, quoted by Earl, 1990)

. . . the area of measurement is the biggest single failure of information systems while it is the single biggest issue in front of our board of directors. I am frustrated by our inability to measure cost and benefit. (Head of IT: AT & T quoted in Coleman and Jamieson, 1991)

Introduction

Information Technology (IT) now represents substantial financial investment. By 1993, UK company expenditure on IT was exceeding £12 billion per year, equivalent to an average of over 1.5% of annual turnover. Public sector IT spend, excluding Ministry of Defence operational equipment, was over £2 billion per year, or 1% of total public expenditure. The size and continuing growth in IT investments, coupled with a recessionary climate and concerns over cost containment from early 1990, have served to place IT issues above the parapet in most organizations, perhaps irretrievably. Understandably, senior managers need to question the returns from such investments and whether the IT route has been and can be, a wise decision.

This is reinforced in those organizations where IT investment has been a high risk, hidden cost process, often producing disappointed expectations.

* An earlier version of this chapter appeared in the *European Management Journal*, Vol. 10, No. 2. June, pp. 220–229.

This is a difficult area about which to generalize, but research studies suggest that at least 20% of expenditure is wasted and between 30% and 40% of IT projects realize no net benefits, however measured (for reviews of research see Willcocks, 1993). The reasons for failure to deliver on IT potential can be complex. However major barriers, identified by a range of studies, occur in how the IT investment is evaluated and controlled (see for example Grindley, 1991; Kearney, 1990; Wilson, 1991). These barriers are not insurmountable. The purpose of this chapter is to report on recent research and indicate ways forward.

Evaluation: emerging problems

Taking a management perspective, evaluation is about establishing by quantitative and/or qualitative means the worth of IT to the organization. Evaluation brings into play notions of costs, benefits, risk and value. It also implies an organizational process by which these factors are assessed, whether formally or informally.

There are major problems in evaluation. Many organizations find themselves in a Catch 22. For competitive reasons they cannot afford not to invest in IT, but economically they cannot find sufficient justification, and evaluation practice cannot provide enough underpinning, for making the investment. One thing all informed commentators agree on: there are no reliable measures for assessing the impact of IT. At the same time, there are a number of common problem areas that can be addressed. Our own research shows the following to be the most common:

• inappropriate measures
• budgeting practice conceals full costs
• understating human and organizational costs
• understating knock-on costs
• overstating costs
• neglecting 'intangible' benefits
• not fully investigating risk
• failure to devote evaluation time and effort to a major capital asset
• failure to take into account time-scale of likely benefits.

This list is by no means exhaustive of the problems faced (a full discussion of these problems and others appears in Willcocks, 1992a). Most occur through neglect, and once identified are relatively easy to rectify. A more fundamental and all too common failure is in not relating IT needs to the information needs of the organization. This relates to the broader issue of strategic alignment.

Strategy and information systems

The *organizational investment climate* has a key bearing on how investment is organized and conducted, and what priorities are assigned to different IT investment proposals. This is affected by:

- the financial health and market position of the organization
- industry sector pressures
- the organizational business strategy and direction
- the management and decision-making culture.

As an example of the second, 1989–90 research by Datasolve showed IT investment priorities in the retail sector focusing mainly on achieving more timely information, in financial services around better quality service to customers, and in manufacturing on more complete information for decision-making. As to decision-making culture, senior management attitude to risk can range from conservative to innovative, their decision-making styles from directive to consensus-driven (Butler Cox, 1990). As one example, conservative consensus-driven management would tend to take a relatively slow, incremental approach, with large-scale IT investment being unlikely. The third factor will be focused on here, that is creating a strategic climate in which IT investments can be related to organizational direction. Shaping the context in which IT evaluation is conducted is a necessary, frequently neglected prelude to then applying appropriate evaluation techniques and approaches. This section focuses on a few valuable pointers and approaches that work in practice to facilitate IT investment decisions that add value to the organization.

Alignment

A fundamental starting point is the need for alignment of business/ organizational needs, what is done with IT, and plans for human resources, organizational structures and processes. The highly publicized 1990 Landmark Study tends to conflate these into alignment of business, organizational and IT strategies (Scott Morton, 1991; Walton, 1989). A simpler approach is to suggest that the word 'strategy' should be used only when these different plans are aligned. There is much evidence to suggest that such alignment rarely exists. In a study of 86 UK companies, Ernst and Young (1990) found only two aligned. Detailed research also shows lack of alignment to be a common problem in public sector informatization (Willcocks, 1992b). The case of an advertising agency (cited by Willcocks and Mason, 1994) provides a useful illustrative example:

Case: An advertising agency

In the mid-1980s, this agency installed accounting and market forecasting systems at a cost of nearly £100,000. There was no real evaluation of the worth of the IT to the business. It was installed largely because one director had seen similar systems running at a competitor. Its existing systems had been perfectly adequate and the market forecasting system ended up being used just to impress clients. At the same time as the system was being installed, the agency sacked over 36 staff and asked its managers not to spend more than £200 a week on expenses. The company was taken over in 1986. Clearly there had been no integrated plan on the business, human resource, organizational and IT fronts. This passed on into its IT evaluation practice. In the end, the IT amplifier effect may well have operated. IT was not used to address the core, or indeed any, of the needs of the business. A bad management was made correspondingly worse by the application of IT.

One result of such lack of alignment is that IT evaluation practice tends to become separated from business needs and plans on the one hand, and from organizational realities that can influence IT implementation and subsequent effectiveness on the other. Both need to be included in IT evaluation, and indeed are in the more comprehensive evaluation methods, notably the information economics approach (see below).

Another critical alignment is that between what is done with IT and how it fits with the information needs of the organization. Most management attention has tended to fall on the 'technology' rather than the 'information' element in what is called IT. Hochstrasser and Griffiths (1991) found in their sample no single company with a fully developed and comprehensive strategy on information. Yet it would seem to be difficult to perform a meaningful evaluation of IT investment without some corporate control framework establishing information requirements in relationship to business/organizational goals and purpose, prioritization of information needs and, for example, how cross-corporate information flows need to be managed. An information strategy directs IT investment, and establishes policies and priorities against which investment can be assessed. It may also help to establish that some information needs can be met without the IT vehicle.

IT Strategic grid

The McFarlan and McKenney (1983) grid is a much-travelled, but useful framework for focusing management attention on the IT evaluation question: where does and will IT give us added value? A variant is shown below in Figure 9.1.

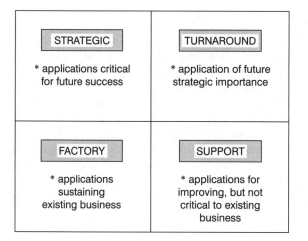

Figure 9.1   *Strategic grid analysis*

Cases: Two manufacturing companies

Used by the author with a group of senior managers in a pharmaceutical company, it was found that too much investment had been allowed on turnaround projects. In a period of downturn in business, it was recognized that the investment in the previous three years should have been in strategic systems. It was resolved to tighten and refocus IT evaluation practice. In a highly decentralized multinational mainly in the printing/publishing industry, it was found that most of the twenty businesses were investing in factory and support systems. In a recessionary climate, competitors were not forcing the issue on other types of system, the company was not strong on IT know-how, and it was decided that the risk-averse policy on IT evaluation, with strong emphasis on cost justification should continue.

The strategic grid is useful for classifying systems then demonstrating, through discussion, where IT investment has been made and where it should be applied. It can help to demonstrate that IT investments are not being made into core systems, or into business growth or competitiveness. It can also help to indicate that there is room for IT investment in more speculative ventures, given the spread of investment risk across different systems. It may also provoke management into spending more, or less, on IT. One frequent outcome is a demand to reassess which evaluation techniques are more appropriate to different types of system.

Value chain

Porter and Millar (1991) have also been useful in establishing the need for value chain analysis. This looks at where value is generated inside the organization, but also in its external relationships, for example with suppliers and customers. Thus the primary activities of a typical manufacturing company may be: inbound logistics, operations, outbound logistics, marketing and sales, and service. Support activities will be: firm infrastructure, human resource management, technology development and procurement. The question here is what can be done to add value within and across these activities? As every value activity has both a physical and an information-processing component, it is clear that the opportunities for value-added IT investment may well be considerable. Value chain analysis helps to focus attention on where these will be.

IT investment mapping

Another method of relating IT investment to organizational/business needs has been developed by Peters (1993). The basic dimensions of the map were arrived at after reviewing the main investment concerns arising in over 50 IT projects. The benefits to the organization appeared as one of the most frequent attributes of the IT investment (see Figure 9.2).

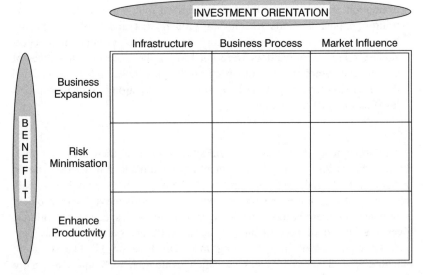

Figure 9.2   *Investment mapping*

Thus one dimension of the map is benefits ranging from the more tangible arising from productivity enhancing applications to the less tangible from business expansion applications. Peters also found that the orientation of the investment toward the business was also frequently used in evaluation. He classifies these as *infrastructure*, e.g., telecommunications, software/hardware environment; *business operations*, e.g., finance and accounts, purchasing, processing orders; and *market influencing*, e.g., increasing repeat sales, improving distribution channels. Figure 9.3 shows the map being used in a hypothetical example to compare current and planned business strategy in terms of investment orientation and benefits required, against current and planned IT investment strategy.

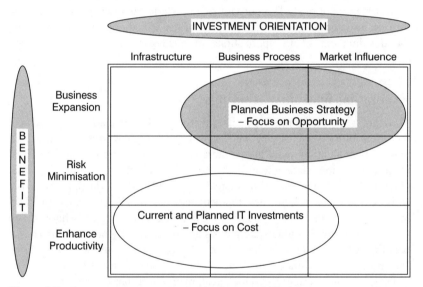

Figure 9.3 *Investment map comparing business and IT plans*

Mapping can reveal gaps and overlaps in these two areas and help senior management to get them more closely aligned. As a further example:

> a company with a clearly defined, product-differentiated strategy of innovation would do well to reconsider IT investments which appeared to show undue bias towards a price-differentiated strategy of cost reduction and enhancing productivity.

Multiple methodology

Finally, Earl (1989) wisely opts for a multiple methodology approach to IS strategy formulation. This again helps us in the aim of relating IT investment more closely with the strategic aims and direction of the organization and its key needs. One element here is a *top-down approach*. Thus a critical success factors analysis might be used to establish key business objectives, decompose these into critical success factors, then establish the IS needs that will drive these CSFs. *A bottom-up evaluation* would start with an evaluation of current systems. This may reveal gaps in the coverage by systems, for example in the marketing function or in terms of degree of integration of systems across functions. Evaluation may also find gaps in the technical quality of systems and in their business value. This permits decisions on renewing, removing, maintaining or enhancing current sysems. The final leg of Earl's multiple methodology is *'inside-out innovation'*. The purpose here is to 'identify opportunities afforded by IT which may yield competitive advantage or create new strategic options'. The purpose of the whole threefold methodology is, through an internal and external analysis of needs and opportunities, to relate the development of IS applications to business/organizational need and strategy.

Evaluating feasibility: findings

The right 'strategic climate' is a vital prerequisite for evaluating IT projects at their feasibility stage. Here, we find out how organizations go about IT feasibility evaluation and what pointers for improved practice can be gained from the accumulated evidence. The picture is not an encouraging one. Organizations have found it increasingly difficult to justify the costs surrounding the purchase, development and use of IT. The value of IT/IS investments are more often justified by faith alone, or perhaps what adds up to the same thing, by understating costs and using mainly notional figures for benefit realization (see Farbey *et al.*, 1992; PA Consulting, 1990; Price Waterhouse, 1989; Strassman, 1990; Willcocks and Lester, 1993).

Willcocks and Lester (1993) looked at 50 organizations drawn from a cross-section of private and public sector manufacturing and services. Subsequently this research was extended into a follow-up interview programme. Some of the consolidated results are recorded in what follows. We found all organizations completing evaluation at the feasibility stage, though there was a fall off in the extent to which evaluation was carried out at later stages. This means that considerable weight falls on getting the feasibility evaluation right. High levels of satisfaction with evaluation methods were recorded. However, these perceptions need to be qualified by the fact that only 8% of organizations measured the impact of the evaluation, that is, could tell us whether the IT investment subsequently achieved a higher or lower return than other non-IT investments. Additionally there emerged a range of inadequacies in evaluation practice at the feasibility stage of projects. The most common are shown in Figure 9.4.

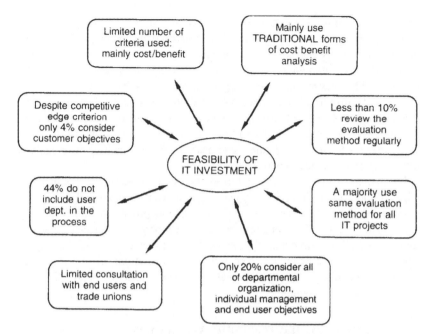

Figure 9.4 *IT evaluation: feasibility findings*

Senior managers increasingly talk of, and are urged toward, the strategic use of IT. This means doing new things, gaining a competitive edge, and becoming more effective, rather than using IT merely to automate routine operations, do existing things better, and perhaps reduce the headcount. However only 16% of organizations used over four criteria on which to base their evaluation. Cost/benefit was used by 62% as their predominant criterion in the evaluation process. *The survey evidence here suggests that organizations may be missing IS opportunities, but also taking on large risks, through utilizing narrow evaluation approaches that do not clarify and assess less tangible inputs and benefits.* There was also little evidence of a concern for assessing risk in any formal manner. However the need to see and evaluate risks and 'soft' hidden costs would seem to be essential, given the history of IT investment as a 'high risk, hidden cost' process.

A sizable minority of organizations (44%) did not include the user department in the evaluation process at the feasibility stage. This cuts off a vital source of information and critique on the degree to which an IT proposal is organizationally feasible and will deliver on user requirements. Only a small minority of organizations accepted IT proposals from a wide variety of groups and individuals. In this respect most ignored the third element in Earl's multiple methodology (see above). Despite the large amount of literature emphasizing consultation with the workforce as a source of ideas, know-how and as part of the process of reducing resistance to change, only 36% of organizations consulted users about evaluation at the feasibility stage, while only 18% consulted unions. While the majority of organizations (80%) evaluated IT investments against organizational objectives, only 22% acted strategically in considering objectives from the bottom to the top, that is, evaluated the value of IT projects against all of organization, departmental, individual management, and end-user objectives. This again could have consequences for the effectiveness and usability of the resulting systems, and the levels of resistance experienced.

Finally, most organizations endorsed the need to assess the competitive edge implied by an IT project. However, somewhat inconsistently, only 4% considered customer objectives in the evaluation process at the feasibility stage. This finding is interesting in relationship to our analysis that the majority of IT investment in the respondent organizations were directed at achieving internal efficiencies. It may well be that not only the nature of the evaluation techniques, but also the evaluation process adopted, had influential roles to play in this outcome.

Linking strategy and feasibility techniques

Much work has been done to break free from the limitations of the more traditional, finance-based forms of capital investment appraisal. The major concerns seem to be to relate evaluation techniques to the type of IT project, and to develop techniques that relate the IT investment to business/ organization value. A further development is in more sophisticated ways of including risk assessment in the evaluation procedures for IT investment. *A method of evaluation needs to be reliable, consistent in its measurement over time, able to discriminate between good and indifferent investments, able to measure what it purports to measure, and be administratively/organization-ally feasible in its application.*

Return on management

Strassman (1990) has done much iconoclastic work in the attempt to modernize IT investment evaluation. He concludes that:

> Many methods for giving advice about computers have one thing in common. They serve as a vehicle to facilitate proposals for additional funding ... the current techniques ultimately reflect their origins in a technology push from the experts, vendors, consultants, instead of a 'strategy' pull from the profit centre managers.

He has produced the very interesting concept of Return on Management (ROM). ROM is a measure of performance based on the added value to an organization provided by management. Strassman's assumption here is that, in the modern organization, information costs are the costs of managing the enterprise. If ROM is calculated before then after IT is applied to an organization then the IT contribution to the business, so difficult to isolate using more traditional measures, can be assessed. ROM is calculated in several stages. First, using the organization's financial results, the total value-added is established. This is the difference between net revenues and payments to external suppliers. The contribution of capital is then separated from that of labour. Operating costs are then deducted from labour value-added to leave management value-added. ROM is management value-added divided by the costs of management. There are some problems with how this figure is arrived at, and whether it really represents what IT has contributed to business performance. For example, there are difficulties in distinguishing between operational and management information. Perhaps ROM is merely a measure in some cases, and a fairly indirect one, of how effectively management information is used. A more serious criticism lies with the usability of the approach and its attractiveness to practising managers. This may be reflected in its lack of use, at least in the UK, as identified in different surveys (see Butler Cox, 1990; Coleman and Jamieson, 1991; Willcocks and Lester, 1993).

Matching objectives, projects and techniques

A major way forward on IT evaluation is to match techniques to objectives and types of projects. A starting point is to allow business strategy and purpose to define the category of IT investment. Butler Cox (1990) suggests five main purposes:

1 surviving and functioning as a business;
2 improving business performance by cost reduction/increasing sales;
3 achieving a competitive leap;
4 enabling the benefits of other IT investments to be realized;
5 being prepared to compete effectively in the future.

The matching IT investments can then be categorized, respectively, as:

1 *Mandatory investments*, for example accounting systems to permit reporting within the organization, regulatory requirements demanding VAT recording systems; competitive pressure making a system obligatory, e.g., EPOS amongst large retail outlets.
2 *Investments to improve performance*, for example, Allied Dunbar and several UK insurance companies have introduced laptop computers for sales people, partly with the aim of increasing sales.
3 *Competitive edge investments*, for example SABRE at American Airlines, and Merrill Lynch's cash management account system in the mid-1980s.

4   *Infrastructure investments.* These are important to make because they give organizations several more degrees of freedom to manoeuvre in the future.

5   *Research investments.* In our sample we found a bank and three companies in the computer industry waiving normal capital investment criteria on some IT projects, citing their research and learning value. The amounts were small and referred to case tools in one case, and expert systems in the others.

There seems to be no shortage of such classifications now available. One of the more simple but useful is the sixfold classification shown in Figure 9.5.

Once assessed against, and accepted as aligned with required business purpose, a specific IT investment can be classified, then fitted on to the cost benefit map (Figure 9.5 is meant to be suggestive only). This will assist in identifying where the evaluation emphasis should fall. For example, an 'efficiency' project could be adequately assessed utilizing traditional financial investment appraisal approaches; a different emphasis will be required in the method chosen to assess a 'competitive edge' project. Figure 9.6 is one view of the possible spread of appropriateness of some of the evaluation methods now available.

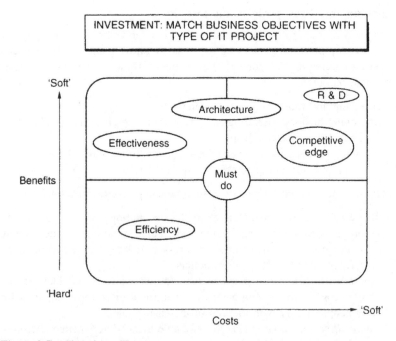

Figure 9.5   *Classifying IT investments*

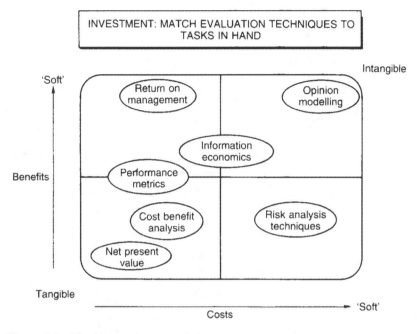

Figure 9.6 *Matching projects to techniques*

From cost-benefit to value

A particularly ambitious attempt to deal with many of the problems in IT evaluation – both at the level of methodology and of process – is represented in the information economics approach (Parker *et al.* 1988). This builds on the critique of traditional approaches, without jettisoning where the latter may be useful.

Information economics looks beyond benefit to value. Benefit is a 'discrete economic effect'. Value is seen as a broader concept based on the effect IT investment has on the business performance of the enterprise. How value is arrived at is shown in Figure 9.7. The first stage is building on traditional cost benefit analysis with four highly relevant techniques to establish an enhanced return on investment calculation. These are:

(a) *Value linking.* This assesses IT costs which create additional benefits to other departments through ripple, knock-on effects.
(b) *Value acceleration.* This assesses additional benefits in the form of reduced time-scales for operations.
(c) *Value restructuring.* Techniques are used to measure the benefit of restructuring a department, jobs or personnel usage as a result of

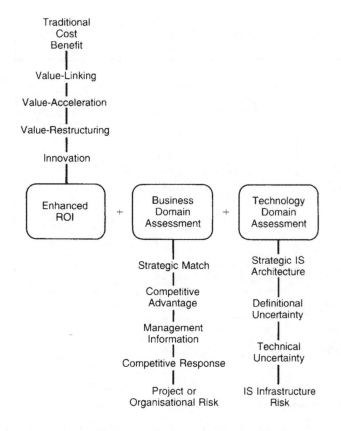

Figure 9.7   *The information economics approach*

introducing IT. This technique is particularly helpful where the relationship to performance is obscure or not established. R&D, legal and personnel are examples of departments where this may be usefully applied.

(d)   *Innovation valuation.* This considers the value of gaining and sustaining a competitive advantage, while calculating the risks or cost of being a pioneer and of the project failing.

Information economics then enhances the cost-benefit analysis still further through business domain and technology domain assessments. These are shown in Figure 9.7. Here *strategic match* refers to assessing the degree to which the proposed project corresponds to established goals; *competitive advantage* to assessing the degree to which the proposed project provides an advantage in the marketplace; *management information* to assessing the contribution toward the management need for information on core activities; *competitive response* to assessing the degree of corporate risk associated with not undertaking the project; and *strategic architecture* to measuring the degree to which the proposed project fits into the overall information systems direction.

Case: Truck leasing company

As an example of what happens when such factors and business domain assessment are neglected in the evaluation, Parker *et al.* (1988) point to the case of a large US truck leasing company. Here they found that on a 'hard' ROI analysis, IT projects on preventative maintenance, route scheduling and despatching went top of the list. When a business domain assessment was carried out by line managers, customer/sales profile system was evaluated as having the largest potential effect on business performance. An important infrastructure project – a Database 2 conversion/installation – also scored highly where previously it was scored bottom of eight project options. Clearly the evaluation technique and process can have a significant business impact where economic resources are finite and prioritization and drop decisions become inevitable.

The other categories in Figure 9.7 can be briefly described:

- *Organizational risk* – looking at how equipped the organization is to implement the project in terms of personnel, skills and experience.
- *IS infrastructure risk* – assessing how far the entire IS organization needs, and is prepared to support, the project.
- *Definitional uncertainty* – assessing the degree to which the requirements and/or the specifications of the project are known. Incidentally, research into more than 130 organizations shows this to be a primary barrier to the effective delivery of IT (Willcocks, 1993). Also assessed are the complexity of the area and the probability of non-routine changes.
- *Technical uncertainty* – evaluating a project's dependence on new or untried technologies.

Information economics provides an impressive array of concepts and techniques for assessing the business value of proposed IT investments. The concern for fitting IT evaluation into a corporate planning process and for bringing both business managers and IS professionals into the assessment process is also very welcome.

Some of the critics of information economics suggest that it may be over-mechanistic if applied to all projects. It can be time-consuming and may lack credibility with senior management, particularly given the subjective basis of much of the scoring. The latter problem is also inherent in the process of arriving at the weighting of the importance to assign to the different factors before scoring begins. Additionally there are statistical problems with the suggested scoring methods. For example, a scoring range of 1/5 may do little to differentiate between the ROI of two different projects. Moreover, even if a project scores nil on one risk, e.g. organizational risk, and in practice this risk may sink the project, the overall assessment by information economics may cancel out the impact of this score and show the IT investment to be a reasonable one. Clearly much depends on careful interpretion of the results, and much of the value for decision-makers and stakeholders may well come from the raised awareness of issues from undergoing the process of evaluation rather that from its statistical outcome. Another problem may lie in the truncated assessment of organizational risk. Here, for example, there is no explicit assessment of the likelihood of a project to engender resistance to change because of, say, its job reduction or work restructuring implications. This may be compounded by the focus on bringing user managers, but one suspects not lower level users, into the assessment process.

Much of the criticism, however, ignores how adaptable the basic information economics framework can be to particular organizational circumstances and needs. Certainly this has been a finding in trials in organizations as varied as British Airports Authority, a Central Government Department and a major food retailer.

Case: Retail food company

In the final case, Ong (1991) investigated a three-phase branch stock management system. Some of the findings are instructive. Managers suggested including the measurement of risk associated with interfacing systems and the difficulties in gaining user acceptance of the project. In practice few of the managers could calculate the enhanced ROI because of the large amount of data required and, in a large organization, its spread across different locations. Some felt the evaluation was time-independent; different results could be expected at different times. The assessment of risk needed to be expanded to include not only technical and project risk but also the risk impact of failure to an organization of its size. In its highly competitive industry, any unfavourable venture can have serious knock-on impacts and most firms tend to be risk-conscious, even risk-averse.

Such findings tend to reinforce the view that information economics provides one of the more comprehensive approaches to assessing the potential value to the organization of its IT investments, but that it needs to be tailored, developed, and in some cases extended, to meet evaluation needs in different organizations. Even so, information economics remains a major contribution to advancing modern evaluation practice.

CODA: From development to routine operations

This chapter has focused primarily on the front-end of evaluation practice and how it can be improved. In research on evaluation beyond the feasibility stage of projects, we have found evaluation variously carried on through four main additional stages. Respondent organizations supported the notion of an evaluation learning cycle, with evaluation at each stage feeding into the next to establish a learning spiral across time – useful for controlling a specific project, but also for building organizational know-how on IT and its management (see Figure 9.8). The full research findings are detailed elsewhere (see Willcocks and Lester, 1993). However, some of the limitations in evaluation techniques and processes discovered are worth commenting on here.

We found only weak linkage between evaluations carried out at different stages. As one example, 80% of organizations had experienced abandoning projects at the development stage due to negative evaluation. The major reasons given were changing organizational or user needs and/or 'gone over

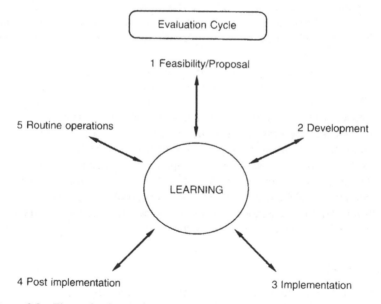

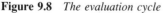

Figure 9.8 *The evaluation cycle*

budget'. When we reassembled the data, abandonment clearly related to underplaying these objectives at the feasibility stage. Furthermore, all organizations abandoning projects because 'over budget' depended heavily on cost-benefit in their earlier feasibility evaluation, thus probably understating development and second-order costs. We found only weak evidence of organizations applying their development stage evaluation, and indeed their experiences at subsequent stages, to improving feasibility evaluation techniques and processes.

Key stakeholders were often excluded from the evaluation process. For example, only 9% of organizations included the user departments/users in development evaluation. At the implementation stage, 31% do not include user departments, 52% exclude the IT department, and only 6% consult trade unions. There seemed to be a marked fall-off in attention given to, and the results of, evaluation across later stages. Thus 20% do not carry out evaluation at the post-implementation stage, some claiming there was little point in doing so. Of the 56% who learn from their mistakes at this stage, 25% do so from 'informal evaluation'. At the routine operations stage, only 20% use in their evaluation criteria systems capability, systems availability, organizational needs and departmental needs.

These, together with our detailed findings, suggest a number of guidelines on how evaluation practice can be improved beyond the feasibility stage. At a minimum these include:

1   Linking evaluation across stages and time – this enables 'islands of evaluation' to become integrated and mutually informative, while building into the overall evaluation process possibilities for continuous improvement.
2   Many organizations can usefully reconsider the degree to which key stakeholders are participants in evaluation at all stages.
3   The relative neglect given to assessing the actual against the posited impact of IT, and the fall-off in interest in evaluation at later stages, mean that the effectiveness of feasibility evaluation becomes difficult to assess and difficult to improve. The concept of learning would seem central to evaluation practice, but tends to be applied in a fragmented way.
4   The increasing clamour for adequate evaluation techniques is necessary, but may reveal a quick-fix orientation to the problem. It can shift attention from what may be a more difficult, but in the long term more value-added area, which is getting the process right.

Conclusions

The high expenditure on IT, growing usage that goes to the core of organizational functioning, together with disappointed expectations about its impact, have all served to raise the profile of how IT investment can be evaluated. It is not only an underdeveloped, but also an undermanaged area which organizations can increasingly ill-afford to neglect. There are well-established traps that can now be avoided. *Organizations need to shape the context in which effective evaluation practice can be conducted. Traditional techniques cannot be relied upon in themselves to assess the types of technologies and how they are increasingly being applied in organizational settings. A range of modern techniques can be tailored and applied. However, techniques can only complement, not substitute for developing evaluation as a process, and the deeper organizational learning about IT that entails.* Past evaluation practice has been geared to asking questions about the price of IT. Increasingly, it produces less than useful answers. The future challenge is to move to the problem of value of IT to the organization, and build techniques and processes that can go some way to answering the resulting questions.

References

Butler Cox (1990) Getting value from information technology. Research Report 75, June, Butler Cox Foundation, London.

Coleman T. and Jamieson, M. (1991) Information systems: evaluating intangible benefits at the feasibility stage of project appraisal. Unpublished MBA thesis, City University Business School, London.

Earl, M. (1989) *Management Strategies for Information Technology*, Prentice Hall, London.

Earl, M. (1990) Education: The foundation for effective IT strategies. IT and the new manager conference. *Computer Weekly/Business Intelligence*, June, London.

Ernst and Young, (1990) Strategic Alignment Report: UK Survey, Ernst and Young, London.

Farbey, B., Land, F. and Targett, D. (1992) Evaluating investments in IT. *Journal of Information Technology*, **7**(2), 100–112.

Grindley, K. (1991) *Managing IT at Board Level*, Pitman, London.

Hochstrasser, B. and Griffiths, C. (1991) *Controlling IT Investments: Strategy and Management*, Chapman and Hall, London.

Kearney, A. T. (1990) *Breaking the Barriers: IT Effectiveness in Great Britain and Ireland*, A. T. Kearney/CIMA, London.

McFarlan, F. and McKenney, J. (1983) *Corporate Information Systems Management: The Issues Facing Senior Executives*, Dow Jones Irwin, New York.

Ong, D. (1991) Evaluating IS investments: a case study in applying the information economics approach. Unpublished thesis, City University, London.

PA Consulting Group (1990) *The Impact of the Current Climate on IT – The Survey Report*, PA Consulting Group, London.

Parker, M., Benson, R. and Trainor, H. (1988) *Information Economics*, Prentice Hall, London.

Peters, G. (1993) Evaluating your computer investment strategy. In *Information Management: Evaluation of Information Systems Investments* (ed. L. Willcocks), Chapman and Hall, London, pp. 99 –112.

Porter, M. and Millar, V. (1991) How information gives you competitive advantage. In *Revolution in Real Time: Managing Information Technology in the 1990s* (ed. W. McGowan), Harvard Business School Press, Boston, pp. 59–82.

Price Waterhouse (1989) *Information Technology Review 1989/90*, Price Waterhouse, London.

Scott Morton, M. (ed.) (1991) *The Corporation of the 1990s*, Oxford University Press, Oxford.

Strassman, P. A. (1990) *The Business Value of Computers*, The Information Economics Press, New Canaan, CT.

Walton, R. (1989) *Up and Running*, Harvard Business School Press, Boston.

Willcocks, L. (1992a) Evaluating information technology investments: research findings and reappraisal. *Journal of Information Systems*, **2**(3), 242–268.

Willcocks, L. (1992b) The manager as technologist? In *Rediscovering Public Services Management* (eds L. Willcocks and J. Harrow), McGraw-Hill, London.

Willcocks, L. (ed.) (1993) *Information Management: Evaluation of Informations Systems Investments*, Chapman and Hall, London.

Willcocks, L. and Lester, S. (1993) Evaluation and control of IS investments. OXIIM Research and Discussion Paper 93/5, Templeton College, Oxford.

Willcocks, L. and Mason, D. (1994) *Computerising Work: People, Systems Design and Workplace Relations*, 2nd edn, Alfred Waller Publications, Henley-on-Thames.

Wilson, T. (1991) Overcoming the barriers to implementation of information systems strategies. *Journal of Information Technology*, **6**(1), 39–44.

Adapted from Willcocks, L. (1992) IT evaluation: managing the catch 22. *The European Management Journal*, **10**(2), 220–229. Reprinted by permission of the author and Elsevier Science.

Questions for discussion

1 The value of IT/IS investments is more often justified by faith alone, or perhaps what adds up to the same thing, by understanding costs and using

mainly notional figures for benefit realization. Discuss the reasons for which IT evaluation is rendered so difficult.

2   Evaluate the three major evaluation techniques the author discusses – ROM, matching objectives, projects and techniques, and information economics.

3   Again refer back to the revised stages of growth model introduced in Chapter 2: might different evaluation techniques be appropriate at different phases?

4   Who should be involved in the IT evaluation process?

5   Given the two approaches to SISP (impact and alignment) proposed by Lederer and Sethi in Chapter 8, what evaluation approach might be appropriate for the two SISP approaches?

Part Three

The Information Systems Strategy–Business Strategy Relationship

We now turn, in Parts Three and Four, to the contexts within which both information systems planning and information systems strategy take place. First, in Part Three, we consider the information systems strategy–business strategy relationship, while in Part Four we consider information systems strategy in the wider organizational environment. As can be seen from Figure III.1 (cf. the shaded portion of the diagram), our focus in Part Three is on aspects of the

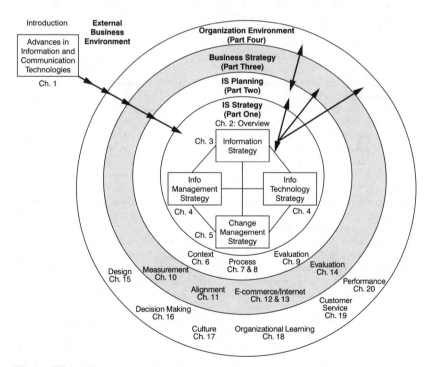

Figure III.1 *The focus of Part Three: the information systems strategy–business strategy relationship*

relationship itself (Chapters 10 and 11), on key strategic issues that have exercised minds in recent years, namely electronic commerce and the impact of the Internet (Chapters 12 and 13), and on the ever important issue of how to evaluate IS investment proposals.

In the first edition of *Strategic Information Management* we included an article by Clemons and Row (1991), which reflected the then state-of-the-art thinking on the attainment of competitive advantage from the astute utilization of information technology. This article was representative of many on this topic that appeared in the period from the mid-1980s through to the 1990s. The earlier articles focused on the issue of *obtaining* competitive advantage from IT (see, for example Ives and Learmonth, 1984; McFarlan, 1984; Cash and Konsynski, 1985; Porter and Millar 1985; Copeland and McKenney, 1988), while concerns in the latter part of the period were directed more towards *sustaining* that advantage (see, for example, Feeny and Ives, 1990, 1997; Mata *et al.*, 1995). In the second edition of *Strategic Information Management*, we changed the focus somewhat by reflecting more of the thinking of the 1990s on this important topic. Now, with the third edition, we focus on recent thinking in relation to the important issues of alignment, eBusiness and IT evaluation. All but one of the articles appearing in Part Three are new to this edition.

We begin in Chapter 10 with an article by Reich and Benbasat that examines factors that influence alignment between business and IT objectives. Reich and Benbasat consider social alignment as a state in which business and IT executives have a shared understanding and commitment to the business and IT mission, objectives and plans. Using data gathered from ten business units in the Canadian life insurance industry, they looked at four factors: shared domain knowledge between business and IT executives; IT implementation success; communication between business and IT executives, and connections between business and IT planning processes. All these four factors influence short-term alignment whereas only shared domain knowledge appears to influence long-term alignment. Reich and Benbasat further our understanding of what alignment entails and what factors are important in obtaining alignment.

Whereas Reich and Benbasat focus on the question of what influences alignment, Sabherwal, Hirschheim and Goles in Chapter 11 focus on the question of how alignment is actually achieved. In contrast to the approach in Chapter 10, Chapter 11 employs a qualitative analysis of three case studies to highlight the value of a punctuated equilibrium model of alignment. They use the case studies to explain the way in which alignment evolves through modifications to an existing alignment pattern, punctuated by periodic transitions to a different alignment pattern. The transitions can be of an evolutionary or revolutionary character. Unlike prior research in the area of alignment, Sabherwal *et al.* find that evolutionary periods of organizational change may or may not entail a high level of alignment and that revolutionary change does not always increase alignment. The chapter helps to challenge one to consider the question of whether managers can exercise strong control over alignment, or whether in fact alignment can ever be achieved in an ever-changing organizational climate.

It is interesting to note that many organizations created separate eBusiness units, rather than housing eBusiness initiatives under the IT organization. This was done partly out of a concern that an eBusiness unit reporting through IT would be unable to achieve rapid response to the demands of the market. One wonders whether chief executives did not feel IT could truly meet their strategic agendas in the area of eBusiness. In other companies, IT played and continues to play a significant role in envisioning eBusiness strategies. Chapter 12 is an early article discussing electronic markets. By Lee and Clarke, this article offers many lessons on the conditions under which electronic markets will succeed. We believe this article provides lessons that are equally valuable today as when it first was published. This chapter provides us with an intriguing view of four cases where electronic market systems have been adopted: two successful, and two failed. Noting the potential of IT in reducing transaction costs and increasing market efficiency, the authors demonstrate how economic benefits from such adoptions can be achieved. Conversely, adoption barriers are also identified 'by analyzing transaction risks and resistance resulting from reengineering'. As a result of this analysis, the authors claim that successful deployment of electronic markets and redesign of market processes using electronic commerce solutions is less about information technology *per se*, much more about understanding and managing the barriers and the projected economic benefits. For further classic readings on aspects of electronic commerce, see, for example, Rayport and Sviokla (1995); Benjamin and Wigand (1995), and Holland (1998). See also Elliott (2002).

Following Lee and Clarke's presentation of two eBusiness success stories and two failures, we include the article recently published in the *Harvard Business Review* wherein Porter presents his well-known five forces model of industry structure and his model of the value chain in the context of the Internet. He identifies areas where eBusiness might rightfully have major impacts on industry structures and on the organizational value chain. While the article might have been considered controversial had it been written several years earlier, few are likely to challenge the basic premises today: distorted market signals and the illusion of new rules of business led to gross exaggerations of the potential of the Internet to transform businesses, and to unwise investments. However, Porter does not argue that the eBusiness should be abandoned, but that companies should systematically consider eBusiness strategy in much the same way they develop organizational strategy, by carefully reflecting upon the current and future nature of their respective industries and by carefully examining the strengths and weaknesses in their own value chains, in order to identify those areas in which eBusiness has the potential to offer the organization important competitive returns.

While the eBusiness era gave the impression that many were investing in IT with little consideration for the ultimate outcome, as the pace of change seemed to demand rapid IT development and implementation, Chapter 14 offers a compelling example of how an organization can assess an IT proposal, even if the benefits are largely non-quantifiable. Irani and Love offer the story of a leading UK manufacturing organization during its adoption of a vendor-supplied Manufacturing Resource Planning (MRP) information system. Initially, led by a young, enthusiastic, but inexperienced management team, the company made an 'act of faith' decision to invest because they deemed the calculation of financial returns unachievable. The management team used a simplistic cost/benefit analysis where the perceived project costs and benefits were listed, but no attempt to assign financial values to these costs and benefits were made. Unfortunately for the team, the project ultimately ended in failure. Irani and Love caution against the argument that financial values cannot be assigned and counsel us not to make IT investments based solely on intuition.

References

Benjamin, R. I. and Wigand, A. (1995) Electronic markets and the virtual value chains on the Information Superhighway. *Sloan Management Review*, Winter.

Cash, Jr., J. I. and Konsynski, B. R. (1985) IS redraws competitive boundaries. *Harvard Business Review*, 63(2), March/April, 134–142.

Clemons, E. K. and Row, M. C. (1991) Sustaining Information Technology advantage: the role of structural differences. *MIS Quarterly*, **15**(3), September, 275–292. Reproduced in Galliers, R. D. and Baker, B. S. H (1994), *op cit.*, 167–192.

Copeland, D. G. and McKenney, J. L. (1988) Airline reservation systems: lessons from history. *MIS Quarterly*, **12**(3), September, 353–370.

Elliott, S. (ed.) (2002) *Electronic Commerce: B2C Strategies and Models*, Wiley, Chichester.

Feeny, D. F. and Ives, B. (1990) In search of sustainability: reaping long-term advantage from investments in Information Technology. *Journal of Management Information Systems*, **7**(1), Summer.

Feeny, D. F. and Ives, B. (1997) IT as a basis for sustainable competitive advantage. In Willcocks, L. *et al.* (1997), *op cit.*, 43–63.

Feeny, D. F. Edwards, B. and Simpson, K. (1992) Understanding the CEO/CIO relationship. *MIS Quarterly*, **16**(4), 435–448.

Holland, C. (ed.) (1998) Special Issue of the *Journal of Strategic Information Systems* on Electronic Commerce, **7**(3), September.

Ives, B. and Learmonth, G. P. (1984) Information Systems as a competitive weapon. *Communications of the ACM*, **27**(12), December, 1193–1201.

McFarlan, F. W. (1984) Information technology changes the way you compete. *Harvard Business Review*, **62**(3), May/June, 98–102.

Mata, F. J., Fuerst, W. L. and Barney, J. B. (1995) Information Technology and sustained competitive advantage: a resource-based analysis. *MIS Quarterly*, **19**(4), December, 487–505.

Porter, M. and Millar, V. E. (1985) How information gives you competitive advantage. *Harvard Business Review*, **63**(4), July/August, 149–160.

Rayport, J. F. and Sviokla, J. J. (1995) Exploiting the virtual value chain. *Harvard Business Review*, **73**(6), November/December, 75–85.

Willcocks, L., Feeny, D. and Islei, G. (1997) *Managing IT as a Strategic Resource*, McGraw Hill, London.

10 Measuring the Information Systems–Business Strategy Relationship

Factors that influence the social dimension of alignment between business and information technology objectives

B. H. Reich and I. Benbasat

The establishment of strong alignment between information technology (IT) and organizational objectives has consistently been reported as one of the key concerns of information systems managers. This chapter presents findings from a study which investigated the influence of several factors on the social dimension of alignment within ten business units in the Canadian life insurance industry. The social dimension of alignment refers to the state in which business and IT executives understand and are committed to the business and IT mission, objectives and plans.

The research model included four factors that would potentially influence alignment: (1) shared domain knowledge between business and IT executives, (2) IT implementation success, (3) communication between business and IT executives, and (4) connections between business and IT planning processes. The outcome, alignment, was operationalized in two ways: the degree of mutual understanding of current objectives (short-term alignment) and the congruence of IT vision (long-term alignment) between business and IT executives.

A total of 57 semi-structured interviews were held with 45 informants. Written business and IT strategic plans, minutes from IT steering committee meetings, and other strategy documents were collected and analyzed from each of the ten business units.

All four factors in the model (shared domain knowledge, IT implementation success, communication between business and IT executives, and connections between business and IT planning) were found to influence short-term alignment. Only shared domain knowledge was found to influence long-term alignment. A new factor, strategic business plans, was found to influence both short- and long-term alignment.

The findings suggest that both practitioners and researchers should direct significant effort toward understanding shared domain knowledge, the factor which had the strongest influence on the alignment between IT and business executives, There is also a call for further research into the creation of an IT vision.

Introduction

In the last decade, the *alignment of information technology plans with organizational objectives* has consistently been among the top concerns reported in surveys of information systems managers and business executives (Brancheau *et al.*, 1996; *Business Week*, 1994; *Computerworld*, 1994; Galliers *et al.*, 1994; Neiderman *et al.*, 1991; Rodgers, 1997). Academics have also devoted attention to the issue of alignment for a long time (Davis and Olson 1985; Henderson and Venkatraman, 1992; King, 1978). Several researchers have investigated the means of attaining alignment and its impact on organizational outcomes (e.g. Baets, 1996; Chan *et al.*, 1997; Das *et al.*, 1991; Kearns and Lederer, 1997; Nelson and Cooprider, 1996; Subramani *et al.*, 1999). Although there has been much attention paid to alignment, no comprehensive model of this construct is commonly used. In this study, we add to the body of knowledge by focusing on the antecedents that influence alignment.

In the broadest sense, information technology (IT) management can be conceptualized as a problem of *aligning* the relationship between the business and IT infrastructure domain in order to take advantage of IT opportunities and capabilities (Sambamurthy and Zmud, 1992). In the research literature, there seem to be two approaches to the subject of alignment. The first concentrates on examining the strategies, structure, and planning method- ologies in organizations (e.g. Chan *et al.*, 1997; Henderson and Sifonis, 1988; Tallon and Kraemer, 1998; Zviran, 1990). The second investigates the actors in organizations, examining their values, communications with each other, and ultimately their understanding of each other's domains (Dougherty, 1992; Nelson and Cooprider, 1996; Subramani *et al.*, 1999).

Support for this duality of approach is found in Horovitz (1984), who suggested that there were two dimensions to strategy creation: the intellectual dimension and the social dimension. Research into the intellectual dimension is more likely to concentrate on the content of plans and on planning methodologies. Research into the social dimension is more likely to focus on the people involved in the creation of alignment.

An earlier paper defined alignment as the degree to which the information technology mission, objectives, and plans support and are supported by the business mission, objectives and plans (Reich and Benbasat, 1996). In this definition alignment is conceptualized as a state or an *outcome** (Broadbent and Weill, 1991; Chan *et al.*, 1997). Determinants of alignment are likely to be *processes*, for example, communication and planning.

Combining the Horovitz duality with the notion that alignment is an outcome, the *intellectual dimension* of alignment is defined as 'the state in which a high-quality set of interrelated IT and business plans exists.' The *social dimension* of alignment is defined as 'the state in which business and IT executives within an organizational unit understand and are committed to the business and IT mission, objectives and plans' (Reich and Benbasat, 1996).

Although it is believed that both dimensions are important to study and are necessary for an organization to achieve high levels of alignment, the focus of the research reported here is solely on understanding the *social dimension* of alignment and the factors that influence it. This dimension of alignment has not been accorded the same degree of attention by IT researchers, even though the creation and maintenance of organizational understanding and commitment may be more problematic than developing IT and business plans in the first place.

There is support in the literature for studying the social dimension. For example, as Taylor-Cummings (1998) notes, the 'culture gap' between IT and business people has been identified as a major cause of system development failures. Mintzberg (1993) notes that formal planning is not the only way to create strategy. He suggests that relying on the strategic vision and strategic learning approaches, the latter based on integrating the views and visions of a number of actors, is a better means to cope with uncertain environments. Boynton and Zmud (1987) state that the current planning literature is based mainly on a rational model of organizational decision making. They note, however, that other models such as the political behavioral model or the resource dependency model also provide robust descriptions of the IT planning processes. In particular, the resource dependency model views these decision-making processes as 'an organized anarchy where actors, their solutions, problems, and resources are intertwined to create an organizational structure where unpredictable outcomes regularly emerge' (p. 69).

---

* Yetton *et al.* (1995, p. 5) state that 'most of the organizational theory literature on fit examines cross-sectional data and analyses states of fit.' Work by Miles and Snow (1984) and Yetton *et al.* in strategic IT change are exceptions that examine fit as a process.

Another theoretical perspective supporting the concept of the social dimension of alignment is the social construction of reality (Berger and Luckmann, 1967). This view would suggest that, in addition to studying artifacts (such as plans and structures) to predict the presence or absence of alignment, one should investigate the contents of the players' minds: their beliefs, attitudes, and understanding of these artifacts. This research attempts to measure the executives' understanding of IT and business plans.

Other studies have also investigated the social dimension of alignment (e.g., Nelson and Cooprider, 1996; Subramani *et al.*, 1999). The approach in those studies was to use statistical methods on a large sample in order to measure relationships between independent variables and alignment. A more interpretive approach (Klein and Myers, 1999) is taken here to discover how certain critical factors interact to create conditions that enable or inhibit alignment. While initially identifying a set of factors that have the potential to influence alignment, we are aware that there is no well accepted theory of the social aspects of alignment. Therefore, the research was exploratory. The approach to data collection and interpretation was open to revealing new factors and processes that might emerge as influential in affecting alignment. The units in the sample were examined in a holistic fashion, focusing on more than just the variables initially identified from previous literature, in order to understand the full context within which the various outcomes emerged.

The overall research goal was to (1) define the alignment construct, (2) develop measures for alignment, and (3) investigate the organizational factors and events that influence alignment. This chapter is primarily concerned with the third topic (the first two are described in Reich and Benbasat, 1994, 1996). The research reported herein is an in-depth investigation of the factors influencing alignment within ten business units of three Canadian life insurance companies.

The next section of this chapter presents the theoretical framework of the study and the propositions derived. The third section outlines the research methodology and measurement issues, and the fourth presents the findings. The final section discusses the major outcomes and provides some suggestions for research and practice.

The research model and propositions

A review of prior research (reported in Reich and Benbasat 1994) did not find a commonly accepted model to investigate the social dimension of alignment. Several categories of factors were identified that, according to the theoretical and empirical literatures, have the potential to influence alignment: external influences, IT characteristics, connections between IT and business planning systems, communication between IT and business executives, and implementation of previous IT plans. For the purposes of this research, to the extent possible, 'external influences' were controlled by collecting data from organizations in the same industry (life and health insurance). 'IT characteristics' were controlled by sampling from companies in which IT was accorded high strategic value, as measured by the IT budget and the proximity of the CIO to the CEO.

In addition, the concept of one of the subfactors, called 'IT-knowledgeable line managers,' was expanded and made a factor. The result was a factor called 'shared domain knowledge,' which refers both to IT-knowledgeable business managers and business-knowledgeable IT managers.

Using relationships reported in prior literature, factors were organized into the research model shown in Figure 10.1, which contains five constructs at three levels. *Shared domain knowledge* and *IT implementation success* are expected to affect both the *communication between IT and business executives* and the *connections between business and IT planning*, which in turn will influence (the social dimension of) *alignment*. In theory, the model in Figure 10.1 should be valid for any organizational unit in which the IT and business executives have the autonomy to develop their own strategic plans. A limitation of the model is that there is likely to be recursive causality between factors in complex organizations (Jang, 1989). While acknowledging this limitation, the model was used to guide the research. Also expected was that other relationships and constructs might emerge during the investigation.

Interestingly, the model is supported by one developed independently by Rockart *et al.* (1996) who, based on their observations and their adaptation of a framework by Earl and Feeny (1994), propose a set of relationships that parallel the ones in Figure 10.1. In their model, 'increased business knowledge' and 'IT performance track record' influence 'IT/business executive relationships,' which in turn influence a 'focus on business imperatives.' These variables parallel 'shared knowledge,' 'IT implementation success,' 'communication between business and IT executives,' and 'alignment' respectively in the current model. However, while the model by Rockart *et al.* has its focus on the IT side of the business (being a model of the key attributes of effective CIOs), the current model considers both the IT and business side, given that the definition of alignment used here refers to IT supporting, and being supported by, business.

It is important to compare the current model to prior research efforts in order to identify its unique contributions to the literature. Two other studies examined the social dimensions of alignment. Nelson and Cooprider (1996) found that mutual trust and mutual interest between IT and business people influence their shared knowledge, which in turn affects IT performance. Subramani *et al.* (1999) defined a 'user gap' as the difference between the user group's perspective on issues and the IT group's assessment of the user

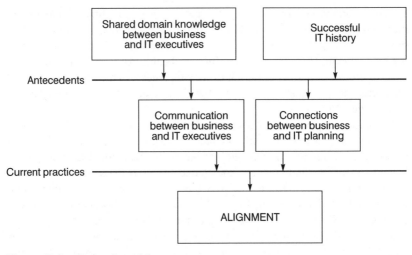

Figure 10.1   *Research model*

group's perspective. 'IT gaps' were defined in a similar way. They found that both the IT and user gaps were inversely related to the operational as well as service performance of IT; however, the IT related gaps had a stronger effect on IT performance than the user gaps.

These studies differ from the current one in that their focus is mainly on the relationship between alignment and IT performance (Chan *et al.*, 1997; Subramani *et al.*, 1999), or between shared knowledge and IT performance (Nelson and Cooprider, 1996). In contrast, the main interest of the current study is on identifying the factors that create or inhibit alignment. Another difference is that Nelson and Cooprider investigate the factors (mutual trust and interest) that lead to shared knowledge, whereas the current model does not investigate the antecedents of shared knowledge.

The following subsections discuss each of the potentially influential constructs in Figure 10.1. Each construct is introduced and propositions are generated to show the expected relationships between the constructs. Measurement approaches for each construct are discussed in the section on research methodology.

Communication between business and IT executives

There is ample evidence in the literature that communication leads to mutual understanding or alignment. Boynton *et al.* (1994) suggest that the effective application of IT depends on the interactions and exchanges that bind IT and line managers. Rogers (1986, p. 199) states that participants create and share information with each other to reach a mutual understanding. Such information sharing over time leads the individuals to converge or diverge from each other in their mutual understanding of a certain topic.

Clark and Fujimoto (1987) note that successful linking depends on 'direct personal contacts across functions, liaison roles at each unit, cross-functional task forces, [and] cross-functional protect teams. Littlejohn (1996) notes that as communication increases it is more likely that group members will share common ideas. Rockart *et al.* (1996) suggest that communication ensures that business and IT capabilities are integrated into the business effectively. Empirical support for the connection between communication frequency and convergence in understanding was reported in Lind and Zmud (1991). Luftman (1997) reported that the degree of personal relationship between IT and non-IT executives is a major factor influencing alignment.

Proposition 1: The level of communication between business and IT executives will positively influence the level of alignment.

Connections between business and IT planning

Much of the literature on alignment implicitly or explicitly assumes that the IT planning process is the crucial time during which alignment is forged. Partial support for this hypothesis was reported in a study showing that IT executives who participate more in business planning believe they have a better understanding of top management's objectives than those who participate less (Lederer and Burky, 1989). Support for the importance of connections in planning is also found in Zmud (1988), who argues that structural mechanisms (e.g., steering committees, technology transfer groups) associated with communications and management systems (e.g., planning and control mechanisms) are needed to build IT-line partnerships for the successful introduction of new technologies.

Proposition 2: The level of connection between business and IT planning processes will positively influence the level of alignment.

Shared domain knowledge between business and IT executives

Shared domain knowledge is defined here as *the ability of IT and business executives, at a deep level, to understand and be able to participate in the others' key processes and to respect each other's unique contribution and challenges*. Nelson and Cooprider's (1996, p. 411) shared knowledge construct, developed concurrently, (i.e., *an understanding and appreciation among IT and line managers for the technologies and processes that affect their mutual performance*) is very similar, although their operationalization differed.

There is evidence in the organizational behavior literature about the importance of shared knowledge. Cohen and Levinthal (1990) note that common knowledge improves communication. Dougherty (1992) posited a relationship between 'shared understanding' and innovation. The shared domain knowledge construct has also been of interest to IT academics for more than a decade. Vitale *et al.* (1986) suggested ways to develop IT-knowledgeable line managers. There is empirical evidence on the importance of shared knowledge for IT-line partnerships (Henderson 1990), for IT performance (Nelson and Cooprider, 1996) and for IT use (Boynton *et al.*, 1994). Rockart *et al.* (1996) indicate that increased business knowledge influences (and is influenced by) IT/business executive relationships.

> **Proposition 3:** The level of shared domain knowledge within a business unit will positively influence communication between business and IT executives and connections between business and IT planning processes.

IT implementation success

There is evidence to indicate that past failures reduce the credibility of IT departments and the confidence line managers have in the competence of IT departments (Lucas, 1975). Failures also pose a threat to the working relationships between IT and business executives by lowering trust, cooperation, and support from users and management (Brown, 1991; Senn, 1978). On the other hand, a successful history of IT contribution is expected to increase the interest of business executives to communicate with IT executives and to have IT considered more fully and carefully in business planning because of the high value expected from IT utilization. Rockart *et al.* (1996) note that a successful IT track record improves business relationships at all levels.

> **Proposition 4:** The level of IT implementation success will positively influence the level of communication between business and IT executives and the connections between business and IT planning processes.

Research methodology

Sample, informants, and data gathered

The sample for this project consisted of business units within three large Canadian-based insurance companies. These organizations offered similar products, primarily individual and group life, term, and health insurance. Their US divisions were not investigated. Their asset bases respectively were Canadian $1, $10, and $20 billion and all had a large national network of agents and brokers. Although budgets are not easily comparable, all three companies spent more than 15% of their operating expenses on IT. In the two companies that had IT steering committees, they were chaired by the CEO. This selection of organizations was made to reflect Yin's (1989) strategy of 'literal replication' in which all cases are theoretically the same.

Within these three companies, ten business units were studied, with four taken from each of the two larger companies and two from the smaller company. Each business unit had responsibility for setting its own strategic goals and plans, and each had an IT department contained within it which designed and built its information systems. All of these IT units were supported by a corporate IT unit with responsibility for developing standards, technology infrastructure, and the communications network. Although not all of the IT units had been stable in size during the last few years, all senior IT executives had at least ten years of experience and all had worked for most of their career in the insurance industry. Table 10.1 contains the demographic characteristics of the business units studied, the number of executives interviewed, and the written documents gathered.

Informants having the following roles within the business unit were interviewed: senior vice presidents of the business unit; vice presidents of marketing, administration, and new business; IT vice presidents and assistant vice presidents, and directors of systems development or IT planning. Also interviewed were members from all of the IT steering committees, and heads of the IT research function. Although each person interviewed was asked a core set of questions concerning the factors and alignment, each role was expected to produce unique data on the site and 'role questions' were included in the interview. For example, IT executives were asked to talk about the formation of the IT plan. The senior IT executives were interviewed several times, since they were the people most knowledgeable about the IT implementation success within the organization.

In total, 45 long (two to three hours) interviews with 37 informants were conducted. In addition, a wealth of written material was collected from each site, including annual reports, the most recent one and five year business and IT plans, minutes of IT and management committee meetings, and IT strategy papers (see Table 10.1).

Measurement of constructs

An earlier measurement paper (Reich and Benbasat, 1996) identified two aspects of the social dimension of alignment, namely *short-term* and *long-term* alignment. While short-term alignment refers to shared understanding of short-term goals, long-term alignment refers to shared understanding of IT vision. These two dimensions were found to be distinct because some organizations had achieved high levels of one while rating low on the other.

Table 10.1 Business unit (BU) characteristics and data gathered

BU	# of IT	Line of business	Executives interviewed	Written data gathered–reports and minutes from meetings
1	100	Individual insurance	3 BU Executives 2 IT Executives	Five year business strategy, five year operating plan, annual plan, minutes from BU planning meetings; draft IT strategy.
2	100	Group insurance	3 BU Executives 2 IT Executives	Five year business strategy, annual plan; annual IT plan, four IT strategy reports.
3	45	Retirement Assets	3 BU Executives 2 IT Executives	Draft five year business strategy, annual plan; two years of annual IT plans.
4	29	Investment	1 BU Executive 1 IT Executive	Draft annual business plan, previous year's business plan; two annual IT plans, previous IT strategy.
5	17	Individual insurance	2 BU Executives 1 IT Executive	Annual business plan; IT project plan.
6	26	Group insurance	2 BU Executives 1 IT Executive	Annual business plan; annual IT plan.
7	40	Individual insurance	2 BU Executives 1 IT Executive	Five year business strategy, annual plan; five year IT plan, annual IT strategy and project plan, six months of IT steering committee minutes.
8	24	Group insurance	2 BU Executives 1 IT Executive	Five year business strategy, annual plan; annual IT plan, five months of IT steering committee minutes.
9	15	Retirement Assets	3 BU Executives 1 IT Executive	Two five year strategic business plans, annual plan; annual IT plan, three months of IT steering committee minutes, IT directions document.
10	9	Reinsurance	2 BU Executives 2 IT Executives	Five year business strategy, annual plan; two months of IT steering committee minutes, IT strategy.

Short-term alignment is defined as the state in which business and IT executives understand and are committed to* each other's short-term (one to two year) plans and objectives. This aspect was operationalized by interviewing senior business and IT executives, asking them to identify both current business and IT objectives/plans, and measuring the level of understanding that IT executives have of current business plans and business executives have of current IT plans.†

Long-term alignment is defined as the state in which business and IT executives share a common vision of the way(s) in which IT will contribute to the success of the business unit. This aspect of alignment was operationalized by asking business and IT executives to articulate their visions for IT and the authors measured the degree of congruence between these visions.

Examples of alignment ratings have been placed in Appendix A, since they repeat material in the previous chapter.

Measuring communication between business and IT executives

Galbraith's (1977) typology of seven techniques, thought to increase communication between two separate units, can be used to capture many of the ways in which IT and business executives interact. The six most pertinent techniques are listed below, in order of the degree (according to Galbraith) to which they contribute to connecting the objectives of two organizations:

1 Direct communication (e.g., communication between business and IT executives, such as regular or *ad hoc* meetings, electronic mail or written memos).
2 Liaison roles (e.g., a named person as liaison between IT and a line function).
3 Temporary task forces (e.g., IT project team, new product development team).
4 Permanent teams/committees (e.g., IT steering committee)
5 Integrating roles (e.g., IT person leads the business quality team).
6 Managerial linking roles (e.g., product management role).

The typology was used in this study to formulate interview questions identifying the type and number of these techniques employed in any one

---

* 'Commitment was added to the definition after the study had begun and, therefore, 'understanding' but not commitment was measured. This limitation is discussed as a future research project.
† The previous study examined several measures of alignment and showed that elicitation of objectives from executives provided the most reliable and practical measure, although it is based on the researcher's subjective judgment.

business unit. Data were collected from individuals in interviews and corroborated with written documents (e.g., minutes from meetings). These strategies allowed identification of much of the recurring business communication between business and IT executives. These data were used to identify business units with 'low,' 'moderate' or 'high' levels of communication between business and IT executives.

Measuring the connections between business and IT planning

Several descriptive and prescriptive typologies (Galliers, 1987; Henderson and Venkatraman, 1992; Jang, 1989; Kottemann and Konsynski, 1984) have converged on five generic types of IT planning. From these, a five-level scale of planning styles (shown in Table 10.2) was developed based on the degree of connection between business and IT planning processes. Each level is progressively higher in its 'level of connection' between business and IT objectives and its potential to create alignment.

Each informant in the business unit was asked to describe the steps in the most recent IT and business planning processes. Using their descriptions, we classified the connection between business and IT planning processes, based on the typology shown in Table 10.2. Level 1 was characterized as being

Table 10.2   *Scale of connection between business and IT business planning processes*

Conn. rating	Level	Name	Dominant characteristics
Low	1	Isolated	IT and business plans are developed separately, or not at all,
Mod.	2	Architected	IT plans are developed from data and application architectures.
Mod.	3	Derived	IT plans are developed during a top-down analysis beginning with business objectives.
High	4	Integrated	IT plans are developed and ratified at the same time as other business objectives are. Business and IT executives are both present in the planning.
High	5	Proactive	IT objectives precede the formulation of business objectives and are used as input to their development. IT is considered to be significant in changing the basis of competition.

'low,' levels 2 and 3 as being 'moderate,' and levels 4 and 5 as being 'high' levels of connection.

Measuring shared domain knowledge

Shared domain knowledge was operationalized as work experience and measured by assessing the actual amount of IT experience among the business executives and the actual amount of business experience among the IT executives.

Business knowledge was conceptualized as the aggregate of two dimensions: (1) experience in the insurance industry and (2) experience as a line supervisor or manager. It was felt that both dimensions were important to one's ability to participate in strategic decisions within a line insurance unit. IT knowledge was also conceptualized as having two core dimensions: (1) familiarity with new technology and (2) experience in implementing IT projects. If a line manager possessed both of these dimensions, the feeling was that he/she could identify opportunities for the utilization of new IT and could implement agreed-upon projects within the business unit.

Each interviewee's entire education and work history was elicited and shared knowledge was rated using the scales shown in Table 10.3. The years

Table 10.3 *Measuring the shared domain knowledge (SDK) factor*

Type of SDK	Variables	High level	Moderate level	Low level
Business knowledge	Insurance Experience	>10 years in line roles	Between 5 and 10 years	Under 5 years
	Line Management Experience	>5 years	Between 3 and 5 years	Under 3 years
IT knowledge	IT Management Experience	>2 years in IT management	Management of a large IT project	User level involvement only
	Awareness of new information technologies	Frequent reader of IT periodicals and experimenter with IT	Occasional reader or experimenter with IT	Seldom reads IT periodicals or experiments with IT

used to separate the rating categories had been reviewed and validated by a focus group of IT executives.

The first two variables were aggregated to indicate the level of 'business knowledge' of each IT executive, and the last two, taken together, indicated the level of 'IT knowledge' of the business executive. Because the objective was to represent the entire business unit executive group with this rating, interviewees were asked their opinions of other executives who were not interviewed. Then, an aggregate rating of 'high,' 'moderate,' or 'low' was assigned to the *business unit* which represented the level of shared domain knowledge among the executives. If both business and IT executives rated highly, the business unit would rate 'high.' If neither rated highly, the business unit was rated 'low.' If there were mixed levels of knowledge, the unit was rated 'moderate.'

Measuring IT implementation success

To assess the previous IT implementation success, each interviewee was asked several questions about IT activities during the last two years, including.

1   Name the major projects started in the past two years.
2   How successful were each of the major projects?
3   Overall, how well were the IT plans implemented?

In addition, open ended questions about the general IT history within the business unit were asked. Major IT decisions were discussed to determine whether they were characterized as successes or failures. These questions resulted in a rich understanding of the details of past projects and the various opinions about IT implementation success up to a decade before the interviews. The remarks of the interviewees in each business unit were analyzed and aggregated, and the overall level of success in IT implementation was assigned a 'high,' 'moderate' or 'low' rating.

Data collection and analysis

Data collection and analysis took approximately 12 months, full-time, for the first author. Within-unit analysis accounted for seven months of this time and across-unit analysis for four months.

Within-unit analysis

The data collection and analysis process for each business unit consisted of two major phases: (1) preparation of the site report and (2) verification of the site report. The preparation of the site report phase consisted of the following steps:

- perusal of written documents and customization of interview guides with local 'jargon,'
- conducting interviews and creating field notes,
- analysis of transcribed interview tapes, field notes, and written documents to prepare a site report.

The site reports, single spaced, were between 15 and 35 pages long. The first author prepared the site reports, each of which contained the following sections: business background, IT background, alignment measures, factor measures, and interpretive causal analysis. The intent was too look for explanations, based on data originating either from the informants or inferred by the researchers, that would link constructs together in plausible ways.

Steps were taken to ensure that the interview data collected, especially those dealing with the more factual aspects of the organization's history, could be verified to the extent possible. Based on an analysis of written documents; important events, including major decisions and projects, were identified. These were used in the interviews to investigate in more detail the actions of the interviewees, and others in the organization, with respect to these events. Specific details of behavior (e.g., the number of meetings attended or names of committees one served on) were requested to ascertain whether the data collected were accurate and reliable.

Data for the causal analysis were gathered during interviews, as informants proffered explanations for or were asked about situations that seemed unusual. For example, in BU 7, business executives were asked to explain why the IT executive participated in so many non-IT task forces. In BU 9 the head of the unit was asked to explain why he could not recall any of the IT objectives. These questions and the informants' natural tendency to explain and interpret their actions resulted in many causal statements (e.g., 'moving closer to the business people has made a lot of difference to our communication . . . We see them at coffee and in the hallway'). These data were included in the site report when they were in line with prior expectations, when they were novel but plausible, or when they were mentioned by more than one informant. The first author also 'created' causal chains based on the data and her interpretations of it (e.g., *the IT director has no insurance experience AND attends no meetings with the business executives, **therefore** cannot explain the business objectives*).

The second phase, verification of site reports, consisted of an analysis of the site report by the second author, who questioned the credibility of the conclusions and probed for missing data. Each report contained quotes from interviews, quotes from written documents, and interpretive comments in order to expose the second author to as much raw data as possible (Sviokla, 1986; Yin, 1989) so that he could follow the line of reasoning and thus check the credibility of the conclusions reached. Transcripts of the audio interviews were also made available to the second author. In a few cases, the second author requested a re-analysis and this was done.

After this step, the site report was amended by removing direct quotes and other data which would breach the anonymity of individual informants, and then sent to the senior IT executive, who was asked to check the reports for factual errors and to comment on the causal analysis. Realizing that wider organizational review would have been optimal, this was left to the IT executive to arrange if he/she so desired. Eight informants annotated and returned their write-ups and two of the ten sites were debriefed verbally. One site requested changes based on missing information. A follow-up phone interview and meeting were held to correct the site report.

Across-unit analysis

The next phase was the *analysis across business units*. There were three steps: (1) a re-examination of the ratings for each factor, (2) a within-company analysis, and (3) an evaluation of the influence of each factor on alignment.

First, each factor, including alignment, was examined across all sites to ensure that the scales had been applied consistently. Approximately three months were spent in re-examining the raw data and re-rating the sites. This effort resulted in a few adjustments in the ratings, some recalibration of scales (reported in the following section) and increased reliability of the interpretive analysis.

Second, a within-company analysis was performed to identify any company-level factors which might have influenced either the short or long-term alignment ratings. Within each of the three companies (BUs 1 through 4, 5 and 6, and 7 through 10 belonged to the three companies respectively), there was little consistency in the short-term alignment ratings. Each of the large companies had at least one business unit which rated high, moderate, and low on short-term alignment. The smaller company (BUs 5 and 6) had only moderate ratings. It was thus concluded that company characteristics did not influence short-term alignment.

Two of the companies exhibited wide variance in the long-term alignment ratings for their business units. However, in the third, there was some consistency in the long-term alignment ratings. The four business units in this company (BUs 7 through 10) reported low, low, moderate and no IT vision, respectively. There may be some connection between the consistency of results and the overall performance of this company. Although it had enjoyed many decades of superior performance, the last two years had been difficult. Poor investments and a bad experience with US health care products had weakened the company to the point where its parent company had begun looking for a buyer. While no one in any of the interviews alluded to this fact,

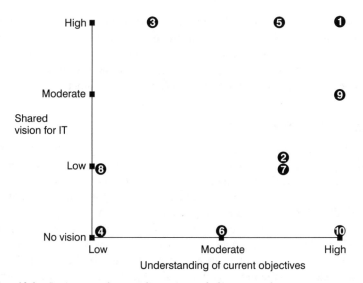

Figure 10.2 *Ratings on the two dimensions of alignment (short-term), understanding of current objectives and (long-term), shared vision for IT*

it may have undermined their confidence for the future and may have influenced our low long-term alignment findings.

Third, the ratings on alignment were used to create four groups of business units. These were the high or low performers on short and long-term alignment, respectively. Data on the factors and on the history of each business unit were interpreted to create 'lines of reasoning' (Yin, 1989). Resulting explanatory models of short and long-term alignment were constructed. No statistical analysis was done due to the exploratory, interpretive, and qualitative nature of these investigations (Miles and Huberman, 1994).

Results

In Figure 10.2, each circle represents a business unit in the study and its rating on long- and short-term alignment*

To understand more about factors that may have influenced these alignment ratings, business units were separated into four groups for analysis. The groups represented the extreme cases, that is, the business units which achieved either a high or a low rating on short or long-term alignment. Causal

---

* The data for all business units was re-evaluated and re-rated in preparation for this chapter. One significant change resulted: the long-term alignment of BU 2 was downgraded from high to low in recognition of the two competing IT visions within this unit.

analysis was used to determine if the constructs in the model could be used to explain alignment. Results are presented next with detailed data from two of the business units BU 1 and BU4, used throughout the presentation to illustrate the analysis. Findings associated with short-term alignment are discussed first, followed by findings on long-term alignment.

Short-term alignment

Three business units (1, 9, and 10), were rated as having a high level of short-term alignment; three business units (3, 4, and 8) were rated low or low/moderate. Data on the constructs in the research model are shown in Table 10.4. High values are shown without shading, moderate values are bold and italicized, and low values are bold, italicized, and have heavy borders.

Data across the business units shown in Table 10.4 seemed to show general support for the research model. Each business unit was examined to see if there was evidence to allow causal inferences to be drawn. In the next sections, data from the most extreme cases, BU 1 and BU 4, will be used to illustrate how these factors can interrelate and influence short-term alignment. BUs 9, 10, and 3, which showed only partial support for the model, will then be discussed and conclusions drawn. BU 8 is not discussed since it adds little to our understanding of the phenomena.

Causal analysis of Business Unit 1

Business Unit 1 sells life and health insurance to individuals in North America through independent life insurance agents. The 700 agents in Canada are managed out of twenty agency offices. There are five vice presidents below the senior vice president in BU 1, one in charge of new business, three in charge of the agency offices, and one in charge of both client services (administration) and systems. Therefore, the senior person in charge of systems is also in charge of administering the inforcement of insurance policies, and providing service to the policyholders. This organizational structure gives the VP of IT more positional power than any other head of IT in the study sample. There are over 100 professionals within the systems department, grouped into agency systems and administrative systems areas.

Within BU 1, the level of shared domain knowledge and IT Implementation success were extremely high. Interview data revealed a decade of effort to produce these results and strong indications that they had influenced communication and short-term alignment.

An abbreviated history of BU 1 is shown in Table 10.5.

A spiral whereby one success leads to another can be seen in BU 1. First, early implementation success and business knowledge in the head of systems led to high levels of communication. Second, deliberate creation of shared

Table 10.4 Factors for BUs with high or low ratings on short-term alignment (high values are shown in normal font, moderate values in bold italics, and low values in bold italics inside heavy borders).

Alignment, BU	Communication	Connections in planning	Shared domain knowledge	IT implementation success
HIGH BU 1	Two days of executive meetings per month, two other cross-functional teams. IT visits to each of 20 sales branches several times per year.	All projects, including IT, are discussed and voted on at the same meeting.	IT VP has 10 years line experience. Five administrative managers are ex-IT people.	Leader in use of IT in Sales, stable administrative backbone in place.
HIGH BU 9	IT executives sit on several permanent cross-functional teams.	BU objectives drive all planning; IT and line projects are integrated.	Line executives have some IT experience. IT executives have years of line experience.	*BU is trying to catch up after several flawed implementations. Partial progress.*
HIGH BU 10	Two cross functional teams. High level of direct contact between IT manager and executives.	*IT plan is created after business plan is drafted.*	*Low level of cross-functional experience.*	Successful IT implementations, innovative PC systems.
LOW-MOD BU 3	Six frequently-meeting permanent teams include both IT and line managers.	IT director is in charge of business planning. Tight connections between all areas.	Most line executives have managed IT projects. One IT executive has line experience.	*This young BU has mixed success to date.*
LOW BU 8	*One permanent management team, meets weekly. Otherwise infrequent contact between IT and line managers.*	IT plans are derived from SVP's overview plan. No integrated planning.	Line executives have no IT experience. IT executive has line experience but in another unit.	Mixed success with IT implementation.
LOW BU 4	*No regular meetings of executives and IT director.*	*Each executive makes his/her own plan, submits only budgets for discussion.*	*IT manager is a career IT person; no line person has direct IT experience.*	*EIS was discontinued, large strategic IT project is 2 years late and 500% over budget.*

Table 10.5 *Processes and events influencing short-term alignment within BU 1*

Time	Processes and events within BU 1	Interpretation
1954–1982	Career path of head of systems for BU 1: 10 years in policyholder services; eight years of liaison between his unit and IT; 10 years in corporate IT.	**Result:** IT head acquires both business and IT knowledge before joining BU 1.
1979–1982	BU 1 successfully implements a large database system to support policy administration. As soon as it is installed, BU 1 is one of the first companies in Canada to give agents PCs and access to policy data.	**Result:** IT group has high credibility in BU 1.
1983	IT group is decentralized into Individual business units from corporate IT. The new head of systems has several duties. *'When I moved over to Individual* [from corporate IT]*, the SVP thought the best way to insure that there was good integration between systems and the line was to give me responsibility for the business planning function, I also wanted some involvement with a line function. So when I moved over, I was responsible for line of business planning, sales compensation, and systems.'*	**Reason:** Cross-functional responsibilities resulted from his high level of business knowledge and the successful IT implementations. **Result:** Communication between IT and line is improved and planning processes between IT and line units are integrated.
1982–1992	Head of systems promotes shared domain knowledge by encouraging IT people to do the FLMI program (10 insurance courses). To date, 90% of senior IT people have it. He also hires line people into IT positions. *'We don't let somebody work on a project if they don't understand the business purpose of the project.'*	**Result:** Level of shared domain knowledge was systematically increased within BU 1.
1987	Head of systems is promoted to being VP, client services and systems.	**Reason:** Promotion is due in part to his shared domain knowledge. **Result:** Large increase in cross-functional communication since the IT manager is now in charge of all policy administration.

Table 10.5 *Continued*

Time	Processes and events within BU 1	Interpretation
1987–1992	VP of systems institutes a practice whereby IT people visit each of 20 sales branches at least once a year and the director of sales systems goes to sales conferences four times a year. The SVP told us how unusual this practice was: *'I asked the question* [to 20 heads of IT from the top individual life carriers in North America], *how many people have been in an agency office in the last year? And [my head of Systems] was the only one that held up his hand.'*	**Reason:** IT people are welcomed into branches because they have some business knowledge. **Result:** These visits improve shared domain knowledge and communication.
By 1992	Business and IT planning processes are indivisible. One meeting is held at which all projects (including IT, marketing, new products, etc.) are considered and voted on.	**Result** All units hear about and discuss the Sales system which represents their long-term vision.
By 1992	IT implementation success is high; *Certainly on the administrative side, we've grown very substantially while we were holding staff pretty well level. Where I would also say we've done an excellent job, well ahead of the industry in Canada, is on support for the sales process … agents are pretty enthusiastic about what we've done … we have one of the best retention rates.*	**Reason:** IT people are widely respected for their business knowledge. This increases the likelihood of mutual support and therefore success during the IT implementation process.
By 1992	Very high level of mutual understanding of objectives (short-term alignment) between IT and line executives.	**Reasons:** Short-term alignment is due to multiple channels of communication and integrated planning processes.

knowledge within IT led to more success in implementation. Consequently, IT people were welcomed onto cross-functional teams and into remote sales branches. This also increased the level of communication, which then led to higher levels of understanding between IT and business executives.

Causal analysis of Business Unit 4

Insurance companies rely on investment profits to cover the gap between the cost of selling insurance policies and the revenue that this business generates. BU 4 is responsible for investing the monies that are generated by the life and health insurance product lines. In the year of the interviews, this business unit generated $2 billion in net investment income, an increase of 9% over the previous year's results. They were a successful unit.

The business unit is structured so that the various types of investments are headed up by four vice presidents and the service functions of accounting and systems report to the senior vice president. The director of systems manages an IT staff of 25 employees.

Within BU 4, we rated the level of short-term alignment as low. The director of systems rated alignment as:

Lower than low. Right off the scale. I've been the guy with complete control over the budget, its priorities and what exactly we work on, other than the most recent fire. And it scares the hell out of me, because it's absolutely wrong. It smacks of having no tie to the business direction.

A line vice president concurred, rating alignment as:

Low, because the systems people are working in a vacuum, they have no sponsorship, no business input, they are spending a lot of money, and there is no acceptance of line management responsibility.

The history of IT within BU 4 was traced back five years and some evidence was found that the lack of shared domain knowledge and a lack of IT implementation success had played an influential role. An abbreviated history of BU 4 is shown in Table 10.6

In BU 4, a situation exists in which an experienced IT manager joins the business unit as head of systems. He has no real access to business unit management, because he does not sit on the senior committees. He does not understand core investment work, which is focused on decision support, access to data, and desktop tools. He has no line experience and no insurance courses and his counterparts, the line executives, have very little experience with IT projects. The first new IT project, an executive information system, fails. The second project is a disaster in terms of budget and time. Line management takes no responsibility. According to the business executive:

There's a built-in bias here when the group closes ranks. Because there's no one [i.e. no IT person] at the meetings to scream, 'There's no business input in this

Table 10.6 *Processes and events influencing short-term alignment within BU 4*

Time	Processes and events within BU 4	Interpretation
1969–1987	Career path of head of systems for BU 4: 18 years in corporate IT. For 7 years before he joined the BU, he developed mainframe systems for BU 4.	**Result:** IT head has a good knowledge of mainframe investment systems, but has no line experience.
1982–1987	BU 4 executives are not involved in the IT projects, spend some time in developing PC-based systems for analysis of investment options.	**Result:** BU 4 executives are more conversant with PC technology, have little large systems experience.
1987	IT group is decentralized into investment business unit from corporate IT. First IT event is a demonstration of new mainframe transactions and algorithms. Not much interest is shown in this.	**Result:** Executives see no reason to talk to IT people, no channels are created. Head of systems does not sit on the management team.
1988–1990	Two IT Initiatives are commenced: a giant asset-matching mainframe system and an Executive IS. The EIS had mixed support and was cancelled when the champion was transferred. The mainframe system was starved of resources and made little progress.	**Reason:** Executives have no experience in championing large projects. IT director has no access to executives, no real understanding of the workings of the BU.
1990–1992	During the project, IT cannot communicate with line managers. As a line VP remembers: *'we hear a lot about it [the big systems project], we don't see very much. We know it's been delayed, we know it's overrun on costs, we don't know what the problems are, we've had people try to explain them to us, and never understood it at all. Most times, when systems people come in to explain something, the tendency is to lapse into the jargon and it just ... whew! ... right over our heads. And you tend to fall asleep in the process. So you say, well, it must be working, somebody says it's going to come together, and I guess ... we'll find out.*	**Reason:** No shared language has been established; no trust exists between the line and IT. **Result:** The project lurches along. Budget was originally $1 million, expenses are at $7 million, projected to double. IT is isolated within the BU. *'There's an overall reputation an IT project takes twice as long and costs twice as much, and never does what it's supposed to do ... which is a real bad reputation.*
By 1992	Very low level of mutual understanding of objectives (short-term alignment). *'Right now, the responsibility is all on him [the head of systems] to do a mind read of everybody, do it in a way that somehow sees something that the other guy doesn't even know exists, and comes up with the right answer. Impossible. But we sit back as management and say, 'You systems people, boy.' It's kind of a no-win situation.'*	**Reason:** Low levels of shared knowledge has led to low levels of IT implementation success and low levels of alignment.

... project,' everyone says, 'Those systems people screwed up again. And you can just shift the whole blame off to the other guy. He's not even in the meeting, so you can really beat him about the head. And everybody feels so much better after they've done that.

When interviewed, the executives exhibited very low levels of mutual understanding of objectives.

BU 4 also exhibits very low connections between IT and business planning. This could be interpreted as a result of the low level of shared domain knowledge or the lack of IT success. However, a wider appraisal of BU 4 planning practices reveals that very few strategy meetings of any type are held in BU 4. Budgets are discussed, strategies are not. Therefore, what initially looks like strong confirmation of the model is an artifact of the absence of a planning culture within BU 4.

The strongest influences in this business unit seem to be from the lack of shared knowledge between the IT and the business managers. They cannot speak each other's language and, as a result, leadership is abdicated and IT projects fall. IT managers are kept out of the decision-making loop with the result that no shared understanding is created.

Business Units 9 and 10: contingent findings

BUs 9 and 10 exhibited mixed support for the model and were investigated further to try to determine the causalities within them.

In BU 9, the interest was in what impact a low level of IT implementation success had on an otherwise successful organization, since the model suggested that such a lack might inhibit alignment. The analysis revealed that the very high level of shared domain knowledge among executives had resulted in opening up many channels of communication between them. The vice president was committed to information technology (*IT is the competitive advantage in our business ... I am a complete believer that technology can radically change the cost structure and the way we do work*). Even though the recent implementations had been only partially successful, their mutual respect and belief in IT had led them to a redoubling of efforts rather than a pulling away from IT or a deterioration in communication. When interviewed, BU 9 executives exhibited a high level of mutual understanding of objectives. The conclusion was that the high level of shared domain knowledge had mitigated the expected influence of poor IT implementation success. This finding is shown on Figure 10.3 with a dotted line.

BU 10 was an opposite case (low shared domain knowledge, high IT success, high level of mutual understanding of objectives), and an investigation was undertaken to determine the effect of his low shared domain knowledge. The peculiarity of this case was in the nature of its IT history. Within this small business unit, both business managers and IT people had

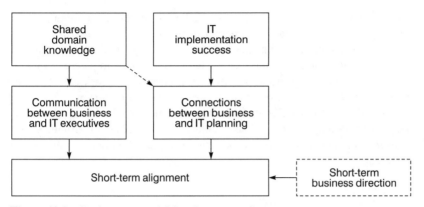

Figure 10.3   *Explanatory model for short-term alignment*

worked for the last five years to implement PC-based technology in direct contravention of corporate IT policy. They had the first local area network in this large organization and used it very successfully for production systems and low-cost local e-mail. This and other accomplishments seemed to have bound the IT and line people together into a highly cohesive team. Unfortunately, the method of rating shared domain knowledge as cross-functional experience used in this study seemed to be too restrictive for this business unit because their very close cooperation on projects over a long period of time had imbued both the head of the business unit and the IT manager with a deep understanding of each others' domain. A more holistic scale for shared domain knowledge might have resulted in a different score. Therefore, the finding from this business unit was that the scale for shared domain knowledge should reflect long-term working relationships as well as job transfers.

Business Unit 3: a lack of business direction

The previous discussion developed the argument that a high level of shared domain knowledge or a high level of IT implementation success would lead business units to high levels of communication and, through this mechanism, to high levels of short-term alignment. BU 3 is an anomaly to this argument, in that it displays high or moderate levels of the preconditions, but low levels of short-term alignment.

BU 3 was a newly created business unit and was just in the process of formulating a set of one to two year objectives. When questioned, executives could not articulate these, thereby achieving a low rating on short-term alignment. Consideration was given to eliminating BU 3 from the data set because it was younger than the other business units and therefore might contaminate the findings. However, the belief is that there are more reasons than age that could create the situation of unarticulated short-term business plans (for example, a recent industry 'shock' or a recent negative shift in organizational fortunes). In these cases, the business units might be of mature age but not exhibit any short-term alignment because of a lack of short-term objectives. *The existence of a short-term business direction was therefore added to the model* (see Figure 10.3). This direction would consist of a set of one to two year objectives, either found in written plans or articulated by management. This is believed to be a necessary precondition for short-term alignment.

Conclusions: short-term alignment

When the data were analyzed within each business unit shown in Table 10.4, the strongest resulting explanatory model contained five influential elements: shared domain knowledge, IT implementation success, communication, connections in planning and short-term business direction. The relationships suggested by the data are shown in Figure 10.3.

Apart from the prerequisite factor of a short-term business direction, the biggest distinction found between business units with high and low levels of short-term alignment was the frequency of structured and unstructured communication between IT and line executives. The conclusion was that, over time, executives in a business unit create the kind of communications environment that is comfortable for them. Those who are respected are able to get involved in activities that are well outside their sphere of influence. Those who are not respected tend to get left out, either by not being invited onto senior committees or by not being involved in discussions about important business issues.

How do IT people gain admission to cross-functional committees and informal discussions? From BUs 1 and 4, it can be seen that two factors, shared domain knowledge and IT implementation success, can interact to produce high or low levels of communication. From BU 9 and 10, the conclusion is that having both a high level of IT implementation success and a high level of shared domain knowledge may not be necessary for high levels of communication. It seems that high levels of either can result in high levels of communication, and through this mechanism, lead to high levels of short-term alignment. Further, it seems that very high levels of shared domain knowledge can compensate for the expected influence of a low level of IT implementation success.

The connections in the planning construct had a moderate influence on short-term alignment, but no strong evidence could be found that planning practices were influenced by shared domain knowledge or IT implementation success. Contrary to communication patterns, which resulted from a mix of organizational and individual preferences, connections in planning seemed to reflect only organizational practices. In other words, if a shared planning process existed between IT and the line, one would also expect to find shared planning between most other units in the organization. If no planning process was found in IT, most likely there would be little planning done in the business units. The problems encountered in measuring and gauging the influence of this construct will be further discussed in the long-term alignment section.

Long-term alignment

Three business units (1, 3, and 5), were rated as having a high and three (4, 6, and 10) as having a very low level of long-term alignment (i.e. no vision). Data on the constructs in the research model are shown in Table 10.7. High values are unshaded, moderate values are bold and italicized, and low values are bold, italicized, and have heavy borders.

As can be seen from an examination of the data, there is some general support for the model, but only the shared domain knowledge construct unambiguously distinguishes the high achievers from low achievers in creating a shared vision for IT. The data from each business unit were examined to look for evidence of causality.

Since the history of BU 1 and BU 4 was discussed earlier in the context of short-term alignment, only aspects that relate directly to long-term alignment will be examined here. BUs 5 and 6, which showed only partial support for the model, will then be discussed and conclusions drawn. BUs 3 and 10 are not discussed since their stories support the model.

Before beginning the discussion about long-term alignment, it should be noted that the respondents in business units with a high level of long-term alignment were not aware of or could not communicate exactly when their IT vision had been formed, it seemed to be just an accepted fact that they would spend most of their IT development resources in one part of their business. No insight was found about a particular time, either during a planning session or a senior management meeting, when the strategy was created.

Causal analysis of Business Unit 1

BU 1's long-term vision for IT was to concentrate on empowering the salespeople with information analysis tools, and the ability to complete transactions at the customer's site. Implementation of this sales system would make the company a world leader in individual life sales processes. An interesting aspect of this goal is that it focused on only the major parts of the organization (sales; new business) of which the VP of IT was *not* in charge (he was also the VP of administration).

Table 10.7 Factors for BUs with 'High' or 'No Vision' Ratings on Long-term Alignment (high values are shown in normal font, moderate values in bold italics, and low values in bold italics inside heavy borders.)

Alignment, BU	Communication	Connections in planning	Shared domain knowledge	IT implementation success
HIGH BU 1	Two days of executive meetings per month, two other cross-functional teams. IT people visit each sales branch several times/year.	All projects, including IT, are discussed and voted on at the same meeting.	IT VP has 10 years line experience. Five administrative managers are ex-IT people.	Leader in use of IT in sales, stable administrative backbone in place.
HIGH BU 3	Six frequently-held-meetings permanent teams include both IT and line managers.	IT director is in charge of business planning. Tight connections between all areas.	Most line executives have managed IT projects. One IT executive has line experience.	*This young BU has mixed success to date.*
HIGH BU 5	*One permanent team with IT and line executives. Lots of direct contact between SVP and IT executives.*	*IT plans are derived from business plans. No integrated planning or review.*	SVP has Master's in Computer Science; IT manager has line experience.	*Implementation success has been very mixed, mainly negative.*
NO Vision BU 6	Frequent contact between IT manager and SVP. IT executive is also in charge of administration (similar to BU 1).	Agents have input into the type and the priority of IT projects. Offsite planning includes IT manager.	*One executive has a high level of IT experience. IT manager is also in charge of administration.*	*Although BU6 was successful in the mid-1980s, their recent IT projects have not been successful.*
NO Vision BU 10	Two cross-functional teams. High level of direct contact between IT manager and executives.	*IT plan is created after business plan is drafted.*	*Low level of cross-functional experience.*	Successful IT implementations, Innovative PC systems.
NO Vision BU 4	No regular meetings of executives and IT director.	*Each executive makes his/her own plan, submits only budgets for discussion.*	*IT manager is a career IT person; no line person has direct IT experience.*	*The EIS was discontinued; a large strategic IT project is two years late and 500% over budget.*

No evidence was found to suggest that the planning meetings within BU 1 were the critical times at which the IT vision was formulated. In fact, there were no separate IT planning meetings. At the business planning meetings, although the sales system project was thoroughly discussed and endorsed, vision did not appear to originate there.

The construct that helped in understanding how they could have forged this vision was communications. Because the IT people were regularly visiting the sales offices (unlike IT people in most other insurance organizations in North America) there seemed to have been a deep understanding formed within IT that this area offered the most leverage to the business. A dialogue had ensued with business executives about the exact nature of the support that was required. Over time, the ideas become more focused and clear and resulted in a sales support vision that was taken to the planning meetings. It has already been explained how the shared domain knowledge within IT and a high level of IT implementation success influenced the communications process, so they too must be seen to influence long-term alignment, albeit indirectly.

Therefore, for BU 1, all constructs in the model played a part, but the ongoing communications between IT people and agency people generated and sustained the shared IT vision, our measure for long-term alignment.

Causal analysis of Business Unit 4

Within BU 4 there were silos, in which each line executive was working in isolation and the IT director had no strong connection with any of them. The IT director's previous experience was centered on the mainframe, whereas the line executives primarily used PC systems to analyze trading and investment data. The IT and business executives were worlds apart. The most recent IT strategic plan, formulated three years before the interviews, was never circulated to management and only one of the four projects suggested in it was actually pursued. They had not identified a long-term business direction, so a consultant had been hired to create one.

It was no surprise to find a lack of vision about how IT might leverage the business. The findings suggested that executives within BU 4 were quite uninformed about how IT could be used to improve their results. Their current strategic business planning initiative did not include IT. The conclusion reached was that this attitude, at least in part, was the result of a very low level of shared domain knowledge and low levels of communication between IT and line management. They had no way to get internal advice about IT and no respect for an IT director who did not understand their business.

Business Unit 5: an unusual leader

Two other units, BU 5 and BU 6, are interesting in that they seem to refute most of the assumptions inherent in the model. In BU 5, most of the factors are rated only moderate; however, the business unit was rated as having a high level of long-term alignment. In BU 6, most of the factors were rated as being high or moderate, however, the business unit was rated as having no vision. The analysis centered on two questions: (1) were any constructs in the original model instrumental in explaining the results and (2) were there other constructs that might help in understanding the apparent anomalies?

In BU 5, there was a high level of agreement among executives about the role that IT could play in their future. They needed better access to internal data to support marketing decisions such as pricing and product features. However, the rating of the model elements (moderate levels of IT success, communication, and connections in planning) make this high level of IT vision interesting. In analyzing the causal links within BU 5, it was found that the influence of the head of the business unit was stronger than the more 'institutional' factors represented in the model.

This senior vice president had a Master's degree in Computer Science and was, by far, the most IT-experienced senior executive within the sample of ten business units. Because of his strong computing background, he (unlike virtually all of his peers in the business units) was willing to set a direction for the IT part of the business and was very clear about how IT should be used. Because of the power of his position in the organization and the level of his expertise, his views prevailed and required few formal communication channels or planning processes to entrench them as the dominant vision. Therefore, an unusual level of shared domain knowledge (primarily in the senior line manager, although it was also present in the IT manager) seemed to be the most important construct in explaining long-term alignment in BU 5.

Business Unit 6: no long-term business direction

In BU 6, there was no agreement whatsoever about the future direction for IT. This was especially interesting because IT had made this business unit a market leader in the early 1980s. They had created an IT system to support their insurance product and this system had helped them capture over 60% of the Canadian market. Unfortunately, the makeup of the industry had changed since then and several very strong competitors had copied the software, given better price breaks to the customers, and taken away half of the market. Their attempt to regain competitive advantage through improved software had floundered because of a combination of poor project management and a low level of customer adoption.

When the BU 6 executives were interviewed, they were suffering a crisis of confidence. Not only had their market share been slashed by competitors but their strategic weapon, information technology, had also failed to provide the promise of recovery.

So, although BU 6 had created strong communication links between IT and senior line managers, and their IT and business planning was highly integrated, these management processes had not yet shown them a way out of their strategic dilemma. The analysis concluded that low levels of success in their IT implementation, coupled with a lack of long-term business direction, were the constructs which most strongly influenced their lack of IT vision.

Conclusion: long-term alignment

When the data were analyzed for each business unit within Table 10.7, the strongest resulting explanatory model contained one influential element from the model: shared domain knowledge. In addition, long-term business direction was added to the model as a necessary antecedent for long-term alignment. Although communication was seen to be influential in BU 1, 3 and 4, there was less support for it in other business units and it was not included in the model.

In Figure 10.4, a heavy dotted line has been drawn between shared domain knowledge and long-term alignment. The thickness of the line represents the strength of the relationship, the dotted format represents the indirect nature of the relationship. Although the belief is that there are intervening factors between these two constructs, they were not discovered in this research. There is no strong evidence that a vision for IT is created through the communication events tracked. In addition, no evidence could be found that planning processes actually contributed to the creation of an IT vision. The planning processes seemed to be useful only for validation and funding once the vision had been created.

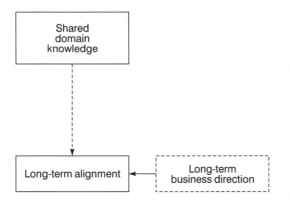

Figure 10.4 *Explanatory model for long-term alignment*

Conclusions

Overall, substantial parts of the research model were corroborated for short-term alignment, one element proved to be influential in creating long-term alignment, and one new construct, existence of a business direction, emerged from the data. In the next section, the findings are related back to previous research and new propositions are suggested. A discussion of the limitations of the study and implications for future research follows. The chapter concludes with recommendations for practitioners.

Summary of results regarding short- and long-term alignment

In general, it was relatively easy to discover the influence of constructs on the creation of short-term alignment. Organizational stories, minutes from meetings, respondents' explanations, and the researchers' interpretations often converged to create plausible causal explanations. The origin of the short-term business or IT objectives could be traced and the meetings at which they were discussed by IT and business executive identified. How the level of shared domain knowledge had influenced communication and the understanding that IT and business executives displayed toward each other's objectives, could also be explained.

Such linkages were not apparent when it came to explaining the presence or absence of long-term alignment. The one construct that seemed to predict long-term alignment was shared domain knowledge, but a causal explanation for its influence was not found. One significant issue was that how or when IT visions were created could not be found. Actions by individuals seemed to strongly influence the creation and dissemination of vision, and vision itself was difficult for respondents to articulate, and difficult to measure. Apart from measurement problems, it is possible that creation of a shared, long-term vision for IT would be better explained with process analysis rather than factor models. The suspicion is that there are several paths to a shared IT vision and that a longitudinal, ethnographic study is required to illuminate the antecedents of this construct.

The relationships between findings and prior empirical work are shown in Table 10.8.

One observation was that IT implementation success cannot be used to predict the level of communication or connections in planning without taking into account the level of shared domain knowledge. A high level of shared domain knowledge may moderate the expected negative influence of a low level of IT implementation success on the other two factors.

In simpler language, managers within a business unit with high levels of shared domain knowledge understand and respect each others' contribution and trust that each is giving their best effort. Even in the presence of a seriously derailed major IT project, these units may exhibit high levels of communication and short-term alignment. In units without high levels of shared domain knowledge, failed or failing IT projects result in finger-pointing, reduced levels of communication, and low levels of short-term alignment.

Another conclusion was that planning practices are not predicted by intra-unit factors, such as shared domain knowledge or IT implementation success. They seem to be influenced by macro organizational level policies and, in some cases by senior individuals within business units. Business and IT planning processes seem to be events at which business direction is set, IT plans are discussed, and budgets are ratified. While these events influence short-term alignment by getting the short-term objectives understood by all, and funded, they do not seem to play a role in the creation of an IT vision. Although a high level of shared domain knowledge in organizations with long-term alignment was expected, there may be other, as yet unknown, factors that influence this outcome. When we as researchers understand more clearly how IT visions are created, these other factors could likely be identified.

Limitations and ideas for future research

There were several measurement problems associated with this study, the most notable being the measurement of connections in planning and IT vision. These issues are discussed below as well as the issue of generalizability and future research investigating shared domain knowledge. In addition, future researchers should investigate the notions of 'trust' and 'commitment' that this study was unable to pursue.

Connections between business and IT planning

A measurement problem inhibited the full investigation of the relationships between connections in planning and other constructs. Of the ten business units rated, six had a 'derived' level of connection between IT and business planning, meaning that their IT plans were derived from their business plans. This rating did not differentiate between proactive and reactive planners at the business level or the IT level and units with very different potential for long-term alignment were grouped together. For example, one unit, which was executing IT projects based on an eight-year-old business plan, was rated the same as another, which was executing a two-year-old business plan. Quite predictably, the former had a lower level of IT vision, but the planning scale could not predict this difference.

It may take different research approaches to determine the predictive power of the planning construct. For example, a large statistical study may determine that the highest levels of connections in planning (i.e., integrated or proactive)

Table 10.8 *Summary of findings for each proposition and support literature*

Proposition	Short-term alignment	Long-term alignment	Literature supporting the proposition
1. **The level of communication between business and IT executives will influence the level of alignment.**	**Supported** Anomaly: In one unit, there was no short-term business direction and therefore, no short-term alignment, regardless of a high level of communication.	**Not supported** Two units with high levels of communication exhibited a 'no vision' rating on long-term alignment.	Cohen and Levinthal (1990); Rogers (1986); Clark and Fujimoto (1987); Zmud (1988); Lind and Zmud (1991); Littlejohn (1996)
2. **The level of connection between business and IT planning processes will influence the level of alignment.**	**Supported** Anomaly: In one unit, there was no short-term business direction and therefore no short-term alignment regardless of a high level of connections in planning.	**Not supported** Formal planning processes do not seem to create IT vision.	Lederer and Burky (1989): Zmud (1988
3a. **The level of shared domain knowledge will influence the level of communication between business and IT executives.**	**Supported** Anomaly: In one unit, the measurement of shared domain knowledge did not capture the implicit meaning of the construct. With a recalibration of the measure, to include an individual with both IT and business skills, the proposition was supported.	**Weak support** The relationship between shared domain knowledge and long-term alignment was strong, but the influence of intermediate constructs is unknown.	Cohen and Levinthal (1990); Henderson (1990); Dougherty (1992); Boynton et al. (1994); Rockart et al. (1996); indirectly predicted by Nelson and Cooprider (1996)

Table 10.8 *Continued*

Proposition	Short-term alignment	Long-term alignment	Literature supporting the proposition
3b. The level of shared domain knowledge will influence the level of connections between business and IT planning processes.	**Not supported** Although there was strong correlation between these two constructs, the conclusion was that planning processes reflected organization-wide policies rather than factors within the business units studied.	**Not supported** Same reasoning as with short-term alignment.	Same as above.
4a. Success in IT implementation will influence communication between business and IT executives.	**Generally supported** Anomaly: In two units, the presence of a high level of shared domain knowledge seemed to moderate the influence of a negative IT history.	**Not supported**	Indirectly predicted by Lucas (1975); Senn (1978); Brown (1991); Rockart et al. (1996)
4b. Success in IT implementation will directly influence connection between business and IT planning processes.	**Not supported** Planning processes seemed to reflect organization-wide policy rather than factors within the business unit.	**Not supported** Same reasoning as with short-term alignment.	Same as above

will predict long-term alignment. Alternatively, a scale with finer gradations may provide the differentiation needed to identify causality. With a longitudinal study, researchers may be able to assess if IT was leading, in synch, or lagging behind the strategic business planning process (Applegate 1993). Cross-sectional studies or those that focus on a limited duration may not identify the influence of business and IT planning practices on the creation of IT vision.

IT vision

After this study, when or where IT visions are cannot be identified and only a vague idea exists of how visions are nurtured and refined over time. To the extent that the study could find any origins for IT visions, they seemed to be created in one of two ways: either through sustained communication between a group of IT and business executives or by fiat from a senior business person with IT credibility. A future study that looked only at the creation of IT vision could pay more attention to both processes and individuals. Different methodologies such as long-term participant observation or a large survey could be tried to see if the process of creating vision or the factors that accompany it can be identified. In addition, it will be important to carefully identify the characteristics of an IT vision in order to interview or survey respondents.

*Generalizability**

Because the ten business units in this study shared certain characteristics, no insights were developed about their influence. One such characteristic is the location of the IT function. All of the business units had an IT group that was located within the unit. This study, therefore, investigated the alignment between a business unit IT group and the business unit executives. No insights were created about alignment between corporate IT and business unit executives.

All of the units were located in companies within the insurance industry. These companies wanted very much to use IT to its fullest potential and, therefore, the findings cannot easily be related to an organization that treats IT as a minor element in their strategy.

The insurance industry itself may cause generalizability issues in that it was in a state of flux with profits coming under pressure and units trying to update business practices and respond to competitive pressures. A study done in a

* Some researchers (e.g., Numagami 1998) believe that the issue of generalizability or external validity is not a relevant criterion for case study or interpretive research.

stable environment may produce slightly different results, especially with respect to the effect of planning processes.

As mentioned in the findings, it was not possible to determine the weight of influence of each construct, nor was it possible to identify more than a few interactions between constructs. The suspicion is that there are recursive relationships left undiscovered. Another suspicion is that there are more than one collection of factors which will predict alignment. It will take larger surveys to explore more complex relationships.

However, to the extent that business units share the common characteristics of units in this study, these findings should hold across other industries and in larger or smaller units. To the extent that communication is a characteristic of culture, the importance of communication may or may not hold in studies of other cultures.

Since shared domain knowledge proved to be a very influential antecedent to communication and alignment, more research is needed to investigate the ways in which shared domain knowledge is created. For example, can we identify at the time of initial hire the people who will become the innovators in an organization? Can we create knowledge through steering committees, job rotation, and elaborate planning processes?

Recommendations for practitioners

The most important direct predictor of alignment in this study was a high level of communication between IT and business executives. However, one cannot mandate meaningful communication between individuals. IT people have to earn the right to play a meaningful role in management forums. Based on findings from this study, one important way for an IT person to be heard is for him/her to devote the time necessary to develop shared domain knowledge, the most influential construct in the research model. An IT person needs to understand the leverage points of the industry, the history and current issues of the business units, and to learn to apply 'common sense' in the application of technology to business problems. This change in view would help focus their attention on those technologies and ideas that could produce the most benefit, rather than those that offer the most technical promise.

Creating an environment in which shared domain knowledge can grow may entail actions such as physically moving IT people into business units, making industry (i.e., non-IT) reading, course work, and conference attendance mandatory, and sending IT people on regular trips to visit sales offices and customers (Reich, *et al.*, 1997). Systems analysts can be encouraged to follow their applications into line areas, either temporarily or permanently. Other approaches would include bringing non-IT people into senior IT roles or hiring junior analysts with a broad education. All of these activities would be designed to change first the behaviors and second the attitudes of IT professionals toward the needs and the priorities of the business. Changes in hiring practices, assignments, and rewards must be put in place to reinforce the message that IT is an integral part of the business.

Line managers who have a deep knowledge both of the core business and applications of IT are the catalysts around which IT innovations seem to occur. In organizations where IT is critical to success, managers should be expected to exert the same influence over IT projects as they do over marketing and new product development. Organizations must recognize that IT knowledge is a 'core competence' (Prahalad and Hamel, 1990) for managers; therefore, management training programs should include a one or two year tour of duty working on a large IT project. This experience will develop in young managers one of the two dimensions of IT knowledge identified in this study: the ability to implement an important IT project. The other aspect – awareness of new information technology – can be fostered by attendance at IT presentations. Over time, the level of IT competence within the organization will grow, enabling most managers to participate fully in IT decision making.

Keil (1995) identified three resource-oriented reasons to avoid escalating commitment to a failed project. This study has shown that failure in IT implementation affects more than resources: it affects alignment, possibly by influencing confidence, trust, and risk-taking. Post-implementation reviews, which are seen by many as an exercise in retribution, should be viewed as an opportunity to create a shared learning about the positive and negative results of an IT project and help people to move past bad experiences by learning from them (Senge, 1990).

In the analysis of IT planning practices, one conclusion was drawn about the way in which connections in IT and business planning can be optimized. Planning processes that have a *connection event* (e.g., a meeting at which all projects, both business and IT, are prioritized), plus a regular re-evaluation of priorities are influential in ensuring high levels of short-term alignment of objectives. Top-down, or derived planning processes, are only adequate in business units with clear, unambiguous business objectives.

The importance of regular communication between IT and business executives cannot be overemphasized. Organizations must realize, however, that without some background of shared domain knowledge or shared beliefs, mechanisms such as IT steering committees may degrade into project review or budget approval committees. A strategic focus should be forged early in these committees, even though this process may reveal conflicting views about the role of IT within the company. Data from this study suggest a steering committee that isolates IT discussion from other organizational issues may be counterproductive and could act to lower the level of alignment.

In general, there are few 'quick fixes' emerging from this study. Like any other core competence IT proficiency within an organization takes time to develop. Management must act with deliberation and consistency over a significant period of time to develop the background for achieving alignment.

Acknowledgements

The authors are very grateful for financial support from the University of British Columbia HSS Research Grants program.

References

Applegate, L. *Frito-Lay, Inc.: A Strategic Transition (Consolidated)*. Harvard Business School 9–193–040, Boston, MA, 1993.

Baets, W. 'Some empirical evidence on IT strategy alignment in banking.' *Information and Management* (**30**:4), 1996, 155–177.

Berger, P. and Luckmann, T. *The Social Construction of Reality*, Anchor Books, New York, 1967.

Brancheau, J. C., Janz, B. D. and Wetherbe, J. C. Key issues in information systems management: 1994–95 SIM Delphi results. *MIS Quarterly* (**20**:2), June 1996, 225–242.

Boynton, A. C. and Zmud, R. W. Information technology planning in the 1990's: directions for practice and research. *MIS Quarterly* (**11**:1), March 1987, 59–71.

Boynton A. C., Zmud, R. W. and Jacobs, G. C. The influence of IT management practice on IT use in large organizations. *MIS Quarterly* (**18**:3), June 1994, 299–318.

Broadbent, M. and Weill, P. Developing business and information strategy alignment: a study in the banking industry. *Proceedings of the Twelfth International Conference on Information Systems*, J. I. DeGross, I. Benbasat, G. DeSanctis and C. M. Beath (eds), December 1991, 293–306.

Brown, R. Value-added associations: the IS/CEO relationship, *Systems/3X and AS World* (**19**:2), 1991, 28–35.

Business Week. Special issue on the Information Revolution, 12 July 1994.

Chan, Y. E., Huff, S. L., Barclay, D. W. and Copeland, D. G. Business strategy orientation, information systems orientation and strategic alignment. *Information Systems Research* (**8**:2), 1997, 125–150.

Clark, K. B. and Fujimoto, T. Overlapping problem solving in product development. Working Paper, Harvard Business School, 1987.

Cohen, W. M. and Levinthal, D. A. Absorptive capacity: a new perspective on learning and innovation. *Administrative Science Quarterly* (**35**), 1990, 128–152.

Computerworld. 19 May 1994, 84.

Das, S. R., Zahra, S. A. and Warkentin, M. E. Integrating the content and process of strategic MIS planning with competitive strategy. *Decision Sciences* (**22**:5), 1991, 953–984.

Davis, G. B. and Olson, M. H. *Management Information Systems: Conceptual Foundations, Structure, and Development* (2nd edn), McGraw-Hill, New York, 1985.

Dougherty, D. Interpretive barriers to successful product innovation in large firms. *Organization Science* (**3**:2), 1992, 179–202.

Earl, M. J. and Feeny, D. F. Is your CIO adding value? *Sloan Management Review*, Spring 1994, 11–20.

Galbraith, J. R. *Organization Design*. Addison-Wesley Publishing Company, Reading, MA, 1977.

Galliers, R. D. *Information System Planning in Britain and Australia in the Mid-1980s: Key Success Factors*. Unpublished PhD Dissertation, University of London, 1987.

Galliers, R. D., Merali, Y. and Spearing, L. Coping with information technology? How British executives perceive the key issues in the mid-1990's. *Journal of Information Technology* (**9**:4), 1994, 223–238.

Henderson, J. C. Plugging into strategic partnership. *Sloan Management Review* (**31**:3), Spring 1990, 7–18.

Henderson, J. C. and Sifonis, J. Understanding the value of IT planning: understanding consistency, validity and IT markets. *MIS Quarterly* (**12**:2), June 1988, 187–200.

Henderson, J. C. and Venkatraman, N. Strategic alignment: a model for organizational transformation through information technology. In *Transforming Organizations*, T. A. Kocham and M. Useem (eds), Oxford University Press, New York, 1992.

Horovitz, J. New perspectives on strategic management. *Journal of Business Strategy*, Winter 1984, 19–33.

Jang, S. Y. *The Influence of Organizational Factors on information Systems Strategic Planning*. Unpublished PhD Dissertation, University of Pittsburgh, 1989.

Keams, G. S. and Lederer, A. L. Alignment of information systems plans with business: the impact of competitive advantage. *Proceedings of the Second AIS Conference*, Indianapolis, IN, 1997, 840–842.

Keil, M. Pulling the plug: software project management and the problem of project escalation. *MIS Quarterly* (**19**:4), December 1995, 421–447.

King, W. Strategic planning for management information systems. *MIS Quarterly* (**2**:1), March 1978, 27–37.

Klein, H. K. and Myers, M. D. A set of principles for conducting and evaluating interpretive field studies in information systems. *MIS Quarterly* (**23**:1), March 1999, 67–94.

Kottemann, J. E. and Konsynski, B. R. Information systems planning and development: strategic postures and methodologies. *Journal of Information Systems* (**1**:2), Fall 1984, 45–63.

Lederer, A. and Burky, L. B. Understanding top management's objectives: a management information systems concern. *Journal of Information Systems*, Fall 1989, 49–66.

Lind, M. R. and Zmud, R. W. The influence of convergence in understanding between technology providers and users in information technology innovativeness. *Organization Science* (**2**:2), May 1991, 195–217.

Littlejohn, S. W. *Theories of Human Communication* (5th edn). Wadsworth, New York, 1996.

Lucas, H. C. *Why Information Systems Fail*, Columbia University Press, New York, 1975.

Luftman, J. N. Align in the sand. *Computerworld Leadership Series* (**3**:2), 17 February 1997, 1–11.

Miles, M. B. and Hubermann, A. M. *Qualitative Data Analysis* (2nd edn). Sage Publications, Newbury Park, CA, 1994.

Miles, R. and Snow, C. Fit, failure, and the hall of fame. *California Management Review* (**26**:3), 1984, 10–28.

Mintzberg, H. The pitfalls of strategic planning. *California Management Review*, Fall 1993, 32–47.

Nelson, K. M. and Cooprider, J. G. The contribution of shared knowledge to IT Group performance. *MIS Quarterly* (**20**:4), 1996, 409–432.

Niederman, F., Brancheau, J. and Wetherbe, J. Information systems management issues in the 1990's. *MIS Quarterly* (**15**:4). December 1991, 474–500.

Numagami, T. The infeasibility of invariant laws in management studies: a reflective dialogue in defense of case studies. *Organization Science* (**9**:1), 1998, 2–15.

Prahalad, C. K. and Hamel, G. The core competence of the corporation. *Harvard Business Review*, May-June 1990, 79–91.

Reich, B. H. and Benbasat, I. A model for the investigation of linkage between business and information technology objectives. *Research in Strategic Management and Information Technology* (**1**), 1994, 41–72.

Reich, B. H. and Benbasat, I. Measuring the linkage between business and information technology objectives. *MIS Quarterly* (**20**:1), March 1996, 55–81.

Reich, B. H., Chan, Y. E. and Bassellier, G. Investigating IT competence in business managers. SIM Workshop, Atlanta, December 1997.

Rockart, J. F., Earl, M. J. and Ross, J. Eight imperatives for the new IT organization. *Sloan Management Review*, Fall 1996, 43–55.

Rodgers, L. Alignment revisited. *CIO Magazine*, 15 May 1997, 44–45.

Rogers, E. M. *Communication Technology: The New Media in Society*. The Free Press, New York, 1986.

Sambamurthy, V. and Zmud, R. W. *Managing IT for Success: The Empowering Business Partnership.* Financial Executives Research Foundation, Morristown, NJ, 1992.

Senge, P. M. *The Fifth Discipline: The Art and Practice of the Learning Organization.* Doubleday/Currency, New York, 1990.

Senn, J. A. A management view of systems analysis: failures and shortcomings. *MIS Quarterly* (**2**:3), 1978, 25–32.

Subramani, M. R., Henderson, J. C. and Cooprider, J. Linking IS-user partnerships to IS performance: a socio-cognitive perspective. MISRC Working Paper WP99–01, University of Minnesota, 1999.

Sviokla, J. J. *Planpower, XCON, and Mudman: An In-Depth Analysis of Three Commercial Expert Systems in Use,* Unpublished Doctoral Dissertation, Harvard Business School, 1986.

Tallon, P. and Kraemer, K. A process-oriented assessment of the alignment of information systems and business strategy: implications for IT business value. In *Proceedings of the Association for Information Systems Americas Conference.* E. D. Hoadley and I. Benbasat (eds). Baltimore, MD, 14–16 August, 1998.

Taylor-Cummings, A. Bridging the user-IS Gap. A study of major information systems projects. *Journal of Information Technology* (**13**), 1998, 29–54.

Vitale, M. R., Ives, B. and Beath, C. Linking information technology and corporate strategy: an organizational view. In *Proceedings of the Seventh International Conference on Information Systems,* L. Maggi, R. Zmud and Wetherbe (eds), San Diego, CA, December 1986, 265–276.

Yetton, P. W., Craig, J. F. and Johnston, K. D. Fit, simplicity and risk: multiple paths to strategic IT change. In *Proceedings of the Sixteenth International Conference on Information Systems,* J. I. DeGross, G. Ariav, C. Beath, R. Hoyer and C. Kemerer (eds.), Amsterdam, December 1995, 1–11.

Yin, R. K. *Case Study Research: Design and Methods* (2nd edn). Sage Publications, Newbury Park, CA, 1989.

Zmud, R. W. Building relationships throughout the corporate entity. In *Transforming the IT Organization: The Mission, the Framework, the Transition,* J. Elam, M. Ginzberg, P. Keen and R. W. Zmud (eds), ICIT Press, Washington DC, 1988, 55–82.

Zviran, M. Relationship between organizational and information systems objectives: some empirical evidence. *Journal of Management Information Systems* (**7**:1), Summer 1990, 65–84.

Appendix A: Measuring alignment

The scale used for measuring short-term alignment has four levels: high, moderate, low and unknown, as shown in the following table.

Alignment rating	Scale used to measure understanding of current objectives (short-term alignment)
High: (IT and Business Executives)	The IT executives can identify the current objectives of the business unit. These objectives were the ones written in the business plan or articulated by senior business executives. The business executives can identify most or all of the current high priority projects of the IT group.
	Example of high congruence when executives are asked to list IT objectives:
	Head of business unit: *'Objectives are GOLD, BEN-NET. The head of IT may have his own objectives, like productivity.'*
	VP, finance: *'Bring GOLD in. BEN-NET. Development Productivity*
	VP, marketing: *'GOLD – realize benefits. More Productive Systems Development.'*
	Head of IT: *'GOLD, BEN-NET. I also have productivity initiatives underway.'*
	Another example of clear understanding of IT objectives exhibited by a business unit head:
	'Her strategies, you mean her goals? The main one is to get the Ceded Reinsurance admin system in by July 1 on budget. And then the other one is to get the Received Reinsurance system in . . . it probably won't be in by the end of this year, but to make enough progress so that it can be in by next year.'
Moderate (IT or Business)	The IT and business executives have only a general understanding of each other's current objectives but cannot identify specific, high-priority ones.

Alignment rating	*Scale used to measure understanding of current objectives (short-term alignment)*
Low (IT or Business)	Neither the IT nor the business executives can identify each other's major current objectives. Example: Head of business unit: *'The IT head probably has his own strategies. I probably haven't gotten around to reading them yet and I would think that they are in support of the ones we are looking at.'* Head of IT: *'I want to move to a broader technical platform, to get more effective use of PCs and to get into local area networks.'*
Unknown	No business or IT current objectives have been formulated.

To create a score for the business unit on short-term alignment, the following steps were taken: (1) a score for each individual was created, (2) scores for all IT interviewees were combined to create a representative score for IT, (3) scores for all business executives were combined to create a representative score for business, and (4) these two scores were averaged for the final short-term alignment rating (for more details see Reich and Benbasat, 1996).

The scale used to rate long-term alignment is shown in the following table. If the IT vision is anchored in an information system (as is the one shown in 'high' section of the table), it is an implementation that is expected to take a number of years and fundamentally change the way the business is conducted.

Alignment rating	*Scale used to measure congruence in shared vision for IT (long-term alignment)*
High	Business and IT executives agree on the overall role by which IT will contribute to the future of the business unit. Example of a congruent IT vision focused on the insurance agents: Head of business unit: *'The new system will change many aspects of the operation such as putting new business functions out to the agent'*

Alignment rating	Scale used to measure congruence in shared vision for IT (long-term alignment)
	VP, IT: *'The new system will change many things . . . many internal functions will disappear as they are replaced by the system or are moved to the agent.'*
Moderate	There is some agreement on how IT will contribute to the future of the business unit. Some executives might have conflicting or no visions for IT.
Low	The visions expressed for IT by the executives do not show any congruence. Several visions might be expressed, but they differ on the overall value of IT or on the business processes to which IT can be most effectively applied.
	Example 1 – no congruence in vision for IT:
	Head of the business unit: *'You sort of have to be as good as your competitor but you don't gain anything extra. You lose if you don't do it.'*
	Head of IT: *'I believe that technology is a thing to support decentralization . . . you can use technology to restructure the way we do business and achieve efficiencies.'*
	Example 2 – lots of conflicting visions, no congruence:
	Head of administration: *'Our vision is to have a paperless office'*
	Head of marketing: *'Two IT strategies are important: paying the agent early and issuing the policy on site.'*
	Head of IT: *'IT goals are flexibility, managed data redundancy, cooperative processing . . .'*
No vision	None of the executives have any clear vision for the role of IT within the business unit.

Reproduced from Reich, B. H. and Benbasat, I. (2000) Factors that influence the social dimension of alignment between business and information

Questions for discussion

1 Compare and contrast the findings reported in this chapter with those of Sabherwal *et al.* in Chapter 11. Are they complementary or conflicting, particularly in relation to short- and long-term alignment?

2 Reich and Benbasat define the social dimension of alignment as 'the state in which business and IT executives understand and are committed to the business and IT mission, objectives and plans'. How might you use the extended 'stages of growth' framework introduced in Chapter 2 in the light of this definition?

3 Provide a critique of the research model introduced in this chapter. What other factors might be considered when talking of alignment?

4 Consider the approaches to and challenges of information systems planning introduced in Chapters 7 and 8. How do the findings of this chapter compare?

5 The authors of this chapter conclude that 'high level communication between IT and business executives' is most important in establishing alignment. How would you go about improving communication between IT and business executives?

11 Information Systems–Business Strategy Alignment

The dynamics of alignment: insights from a punctuated equilibrium model

R. Sabherwal, R. Hirschheim and T. Goles

Several prior articles have emphasized the importance of alignment between business and information system (IS) strategies, and between business and IS structures. Seeking to advance our understanding of alignment, we examine the dynamics of changes in alignment through strategy/structure interactions in the business and IS domains. More specifically, we address the following question: *In what ways does alignment evolve over time?*

Changes in the strategic IS management profile (which includes business strategy, IS strategy, business structure, and IS structure) over time are examined using a punctuated equilibrium model, involving long periods of relative stability, or evolutionary change, interrupted by short periods of quick and extensive, or revolutionary, change. Case studies of changes in business and IS strategies and structure over long time periods in three organizations suggest that the punctuated equilibrium model provides a valuable perspective for viewing these dynamics.

The cases suggest that a pattern of alignment may continue over a long period, because either the level of alignment is high or the managers do not recognize the low alignment as a problem. Revolutions, involving changes in most or all dimensions of the strategic IS management profile, interrupt the evolutionary changes. However, organizations hesitate to make such revolutionary changes in strategic IS management profiles. Complete revolutions apparently require a combination of strong triggers. Finally, post-revolution adjustment to one dimension of the strategic IS management profile seems to follow revolutionary changes.

Introduction

The importance of alignment for effective organizational performance is now well recognized (e.g., Delery and Doty, 1996). Alignment among two or more organizational dimensions, which may be defined as the extent to which these dimensions meet theoretical norms of mutual coherence (Jarvenpaa and Ives, 1993; Nadler and Tushman, 1980), has been argued (e.g., Schoonhoven, 1981; Van de Ven and Drazin, 1985) and empirically found (e.g., Miller, 1992) to enhance performance. However, despite the recognition of the importance of alignment, there has been little research on the dynamics of alignment.

With a few exceptions (e.g., Brown and Magill, 1998), the literature on alignment treats it as a static end-state. However, Thompson (1967, p. 234) views alignment as 'a moving target' at which organizations shoot, while Jarvenpaa and Ives (1993, p. 570) suggest that it should be examined 'as an emergent process.' Clearly, the environment continues to change, slowly or rapidly, after alignment is achieved. If business strategy or structure is changed in response, would the other elements be altered in a synchronized fashion so as to maintain alignment, or would there be periods of low alignment until the other elements are realigned? This paper seeks to contribute to the literature on alignment by examining the following broad question: *in what ways does alignment evolve over time?* In addressing this question, our specific focus is on the strategic management of information systems (IS). However, our results should also provide insights into the dynamics of alignment in other contexts.

Much of the prior research on alignment in strategic IS management is limited in three ways. First, it has primarily taken a cross-sectional view (Henderson and Venkatraman, 1992). Second, with rare exceptions (Brown, 1997), it has focused on two dimensions, such as business and IS strategies (e.g., Chan *et al.*, 1997), or business and IS structures (e.g., Fiedler *et al.*, 1996). Finally, rather than using theory to identify, *a priori*, the expected alignment patterns, most prior studies empirically develop and test the 'ideal' alignment patterns (e.g., Sabherwal and Kirs, 1994). To address these limitations, this chapter: (a) dynamically incorporates the dimensions of alignment and the relationships among them; (b) examines alignment from a holistic perspective; and (c) develops a theoretical model of alignment patterns, and then compares it over time to a selection of organizations.

We conducted three detailed case studies of longitudinal changes in alignment. The cases seem to best fit the punctuated equilibrium model (e.g., Gersick, 1991; Tushman *et al.*, 1986), albeit with some modifications. Thus, this chapter integrates the literature from the areas of alignment and punctuated equilibrium, and offers some new insights into the dynamics of alignment. The rest of the chapter is organized as follows. We first develop the theoretical background for the paper, and then explain the research methodology. We then describe each case and draw some conclusions from them. Finally, the research findings, limitations, and implications are discussed.

Theoretical development

Alternative approaches for studying strategic IS management

The strategic IS literature contains several *universalistic theories*, which present one way of performing IS management and focus on the ways in which it can be improved. Universalistic theories provide valuable insights by focusing on an IS management approach, its contributions, and the ways in which it can be enhanced (e.g., Rackoff *et al.*, 1985). However, universalistic theories view the same approach as useful in all situations, rather than examining multiple approaches in alternative contexts. Consequently, they do not provide a sufficiently integrative view of the various aspects of organizations, and may be more appropriate for relatively narrow domains.

In contrast, articles taking a *contingency perspective* examine the effects of environmental, organizational, and IS contexts on IS management, or the alignment between certain aspects of IS management and the corresponding aspects of business management. This stream of literature argues (King, 1978; Sambamurthy and Zmud, 1992), and empirically shows (Chan *et al.* 1997; Sabherwal and Kirs, 1994), that greater alignment among dimensions from IS and/or business domains produces superior performance. Contingency models recognize the importance of alternative contexts, and thus provide a more integrative view of strategic IS management. However, they are usually static in nature, focusing on alignment at one point in time, and its short-term performance implications.

Several other theories take a more dynamic view of IS management. Nolan's (1979) stage hypothesis and other such theories (Galliers and Sutherland, 1991; Hirschheim *et al.*, 1988), may be characterized as *life-cycle theories* (Van de Ven and Poole, 1995, p. 515). These theories generally assume that (a) the changes in all organizations take place along the same path (i.e., the same stages); and (b) these changes are in a 'forward' direction toward a desired 'end goal,' such as the maturity stage in Nolan's model. These theories do not recognize the different contexts as important in determining the appropriateness of a particular model.

Strategic IS management may also be studied using the *punctuated equilibrium model*, which differs from the Darwinian model of change through gradual evolution by arguing that periods of gradual evolution are 'punctuated' by sudden revolutionary periods of rapid change (Elderidge and Gould, 1972; Van de Ven and Poole, 1995). Some prior models in IS research may be characterized as punctuated equilibrium models (Orlikowski, 1993;

Porra, 1996). For example, Newman and Robey (1992) model the IS development process in terms of episodes and encounters, which are similar to evolutionary and revolutionary periods, respectively. In contrast to universalistic theories, which focus on only one way of managing IS, the punctuated equilibrium model is open to alternative ways of managing IS over time. Moreover, unlike contingency theories, which implicitly assume stability, it recognizes that the long periods of stability are separated by short periods of considerable instability. Finally, the punctuated equilibrium model differs from lifecycle theories as it neither assumes that the same stages are universally followed nor implies a 'forward' direction of change toward a desired 'end goal.'

In the next subsection we draw upon prior research to develop the theoretical ideals for the strategic IS management profile. To assess alignment, an organization's actual strategic IS management profile may be compared to these theoretical ideals. The dynamics of alignment may be examined by viewing the changes in an organization's strategic IS management profile.

Strategic IS management profile

We view a company's IS management using its *strategic IS management profile*, including business and IS strategies, and business and IS structures, as shown in Figure 11.1. The strategic IS management profile resembles prior comprehensive models of IS alignment, especially Henderson and

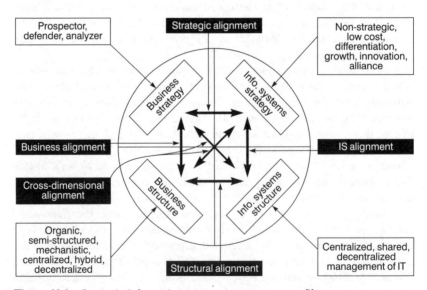

Figure 11.1   *Strategic information systems management profile*

Venkatraman (1992) and Broadbent and Weill (1990). We describe the alignment between business and IS strategies as 'strategic alignment' (Chan *et al.*, 1997), between business and IS structures as 'structural alignment' (Ein-Dor and Segev, 1982), between business strategy and structure as 'business alignment,' and between IS strategy and structure as 'IS alignment.' Finally, following Henderson and Venkatraman, we call the alignments between: (a) business structure and IS strategy; and (b) business strategy and IS structure, 'cross-dimension alignment.'

The dimensions of the strategic IS management profile

Business and IS strategies and structures can each be assessed using multiple constructs. The selection of one construct to describe a dimension is never definitive. We selected the constructs based on their prominence in the prior literature and our confidence in evaluating them based on the interview transcripts.

Business strategy may be examined using different typologies for the corporate-level strategy (i.e., which products and markets to compete in) and the business-level strategy (i.e., how to compete in a particular industry) (Beard and Dess, 1981). We assessed business strategy using the popular typology of Defenders, Analyzers, and Prospectors[1] (Miles and Snow, 1978; Miles *et al.*, 1978), which combines elements of both corporate and business level strategies,[2] and has also been used in prior IS research (Brown, 1997; Brown and Magill, 1998; Camillus and Lederer, 1985, Tavakolian, 1989).

Business structure was examined in terms of the decision making being organic or mechanistic (Burns and Stalker, 1961; Schoonhoven and Jelinek, 1990). Based on some later work (Jelinek and Schoonhoven, 1990; Brown and Eisenhardt, 1997), an intermediate structure, 'semistructure,' was also included. Exhibiting partial order, semistructures lie between the organic and mechanistic forms. Mechanistic and organic decision-making processes may be linked to centralized and decentralized processes, respectively (Brown and Magill, 1998). Therefore, we viewed business structures as being one of three: mechanistic and centralized; semistructured and hybrid (i.e., some business decisions at the corporate or central level and the others at the business unit or local level); or organic and decentralized.

IS structure was examined using a similar construct: centralized, shared, or decentralized management of IS (Brown and Magill, 1994). We assessed whether the locus of responsibility for IS management decisions belongs to a corporate or a central unit (centralization), a business unit or department (decentralization), or is shared by these groups (shared) (Camillus and Lederer, 1985; Tavakolian, 1989). Similar measures, albeit with greater complexity and attention to differences across decision types, have been used earlier (Brown, 1997; Brown and Magill, 1994, 1998).

Finally, *IS strategy* was assessed by examining the ways in which IS was being sought to impact the organization. This was done using the five strategic thrusts (low cost, differentiation, growth, alliance, and innovation) identified by Rackoff *et al.* (1985) and used in several prior studies (e.g., Bergeron *et al.*, 1991; Sabherwal and King, 1991). Recognizing that a firm may not consider IS to be strategic (e.g., Brown and Magill, 1998), we also included a sixth, 'nonstrategic' category.

Theoretical patterns of alignment

Three of the four dimensions are assessed using three types: Prospector, Analyzer, Defender (business strategy); organic/decentralized, semistructured/hybrid, mechanistic/centralized (business structure); and decentralized, shared, centralized (IS structure). The typology for the fourth dimension, IS strategy, includes six types. However, differentiation, growth, alliance, and innovation do not differ from each other in terms of alignment with the other dimensions. Previous research has also found it difficult to separate alliance and growth, and differentiation and innovation IS strategies (Sabherwal and King, 1991). Consequently, we combine the six types into four: (a) nonstrategic IS; (b) low-cost IS strategy; (c) differentiation, growth, innovation, or alliance IS strategy; and (d) a combination of low-cost *and* differentiation/growth/innovation/alliance IS strategy. A nonstrategic IS is considered to have *low* alignment with all the business strategies and structures, while the other three IS strategies can be aligned with the three types in each of the other dimensions (Brown and Magill, 1998).

Based on a careful review of the literature, as summarized in Table 11.1, the theoretical patterns were identified for the six types of alignment. Viewing these patterns in conjunction, we arrive at the three profiles, also shown in Table 11.1. When viewing alignment between any two dimensions, if they are both from the same row in Table 11.1 (i.e., within the same profile), alignment would be high. Alignment would be medium if the two dimensions are from consecutive rows (i.e., across Profiles 1 and 2, or across 2 and 3), and low if the two dimensions are two rows apart (i.e., across Profiles 1 and 3).[3]

Thus, some of the six types of alignment could be high, while the others are medium or low. In a similar situation, involving multiple contingencies affecting a dependent variable, Gresov (1989) examined several possibilities, three of which are important in the short term (Brown and Magill, 1998): the absence of any conflict (i.e., the contingencies reinforce each other), the presence of conflict (i.e., the contingencies work at cross-purposes), and the presence of a dominant imperative (i.e., one contingency dominates the rest). We propose that the overall alignment in a strategic IS profile is based on the six types of alignment. If the number of alignments that are high exceeds those that are low, the overall alignment would be high. This is closest to Gresov's

Table 11.1 *Theory-Based Ideal Alignment Patterns*

Type of alignment		Dimension 1	Dimension 2	Supporting references
Business alignment	#1	**Business strategy** Defender	**Business structure** Mechanistic, centralized	Miles *et al.* (1978), Miles and Snow (1978, 1996), Jelinek and Schöonhoven (1990), Das *et al.* (1991)
	#2	Analyzer	Mechanistic, centralized semistructured, Hybrid	
	#3	Prospector	Organic, decentralized	
Strategic alignment	#1	**Business strategy** Defender	**IS strategy**[a] Low cost	Camillus and Lederer (1985), Segev (1989)
	#2	Analyzer	Low cost AND differentiation/growth/alliance/innovation	
	#3	Prospector	Differentiation/growth/alliance/innovation	
Structural alignment	#1	**Business structure** Mechanistic, centralized	**IS structure** Centralized	Ein-Dor and Segev (1982), Jelinek and Schoonhoven (1990), Brown (1997)
	#2	Semistructured, hybrid	Shared	
	#3	Organic, decentralized	Decentralized	
IS alignment	#1	**IS structure** Centralized	**IS strategy** Low cost, nonstrategic[b]	Camillus and Lederer (1985), Jelinek and Schoonhoven (1990), Brown (1997)
	#2	Shared	Low cost AND differentiation/growth/alliance/innovation	
	#3	Decentralized	Differentiation/growth/alliance/Innovation	
Cross-dimensional alignment 1	#1	**Business structure** Mechanistic, centralized	**IS strategy**[c] Low cost	Camillus and Lederer (1985), Brown (1997), Brown and Magill (1998)
	#2	Semistructured, hybrid	Low cost AND differentiation/growth/alliance/innovation	
	#3	Organic, decentralized	Differentiation/growth/alliance/innovation	
Cross-dimensional alignment 2	#1	**Business strategy** Defender	**IS structure** Centralized	Camillus and Lederer (1985), Tavakolian (1989), Das *et al.* (1991)
	#2	Analyzer	Shared	
	#3	Prospector	Decentralized	

[a] 'Nonstrategic' IS would have LOW alignment with any of the three business strategies.

[b] The relationship of nonstrategic IS with centralized IS structure is based specifically on Brown and Magill (1998).

[c] 'Nonstrategic' IS would have LOW alignment with any of the three business structures.

'no conflict' situation. If the number of alignments that are high is less than those that are low, the overall alignment would be low. This is closest to Gresov's 'conflict' situation. Finally, if the number of alignments that are high equals the number of alignments that are low, the overall alignment would be medium. This lies between Gresov's 'no conflict' and 'conflict' situations. It may be noted that we considered all six types of alignment as equally important, and therefore did not pursue Gresov's 'dominant imperative.'[4]

The dynamics of alignment

Even after an organization has achieved alignment, its environment continues to change, slowly or rapidly. However, organizations may not be able to adjust their alignment patterns to accommodate environmental changes, due to two major reasons. First, an overemphasis on alignment could constrict the organization's outlook, inhibiting the recognition of alternative perspectives and reducing the ability to 'recognize and respond to the need for change' (Miller, 1996, p. 510). The second reason focuses on complacency and inertia. Alignment facilitates short-term success, which leads to intertia, and the inertia in turn leads to failure when the market conditions shift suddenly (Tushman and O'Reilly, 1996). Therefore, when organizations with a high level of alignment face sudden changes in industry conditions, they may find it necessary to make revolutionary changes (Greenwood and Hinings, 1996).

The *punctuated equilibrium model* is a potentially useful way of examining the dynamics of alignment. One key component of the punctuated equilibrium model is a deep structure, or 'the set of fundamental choices a system has made of (1) the basic parts into which the units will be organized and (2) the basic activity patterns that will maintain its existence' (Gersick, 1991, p. 14). Other key components of the punctuated equilibrium model are evolutionary periods during which the deep structures undergo little change, and revolutionary periods during which the deep structures are completely transformed. In the context of long-term changes in alignment, we propose that the strategic IS management profile represents the 'deep structure.' It reflects the organization's basic choices in terms of strategies and structural arrangements, in business and IS domains. Then, based on the punctuated equilibrium model, evolutionary changes would not have much effect on the strategic IS profile. Consistent with the earlier arguments, a high level of alignment may lead to inertia, necessitating revolutions, involving complete transformation of the strategic IS profile.

Evolutionary and revolutionary changes may also be understood using the two long-term possibilities identified by Gresov (1989). In the context of the strategic IS management profile, the conflict implied by low alignment may be resolved in the long run either by redesign or without redesign. Resolution by redesign, wherein the contingency factors are changed significantly to reduce the conflict among them, reflects revolutionary changes. In contrast, resolution without redesign, wherein actors reinterpret the contingency factors such that conflict disappears, characterizes evolutionary change.

Based on the above characteristics of evolutionary and revolutionary changes, we considered a *revolutionary change* in the strategic IS management profile to be one involving a categorical (i.e., from one type to another, such as from Prospector to Analyzer business strategy) change in three or more dimensions. We also distinguished between *complete revolutions*, wherein all four dimensions of the profile were changed in the same period, and *incomplete revolutions*, wherein only three dimensions were changed concurrently. *Evolutionary changes* were those involving only minor modifications (i.e., not representing a shift to another type, such as continuing to pursue a Prospector business strategy but doing so in a different fashion) along one or more dimensions. Finally, during the analysis of the case studies, we observed another kind of change, which we call *post-revolutionary changes*. These involve categorical changes in one of the four dimensions of the strategic IS management profile.

In summary, to pursue its goal of examining the dynamics of alignment, this chapter draws upon the punctuated equilibrium model. It uses an organization's strategic IS profile as the deep structure that undergoes changes over time. Consequently, changes occur in six types of alignment that together reflect overall alignment. The chapter examines whether these changes occur over time in an alternately evolutionary and revolutionary fashion as suggested by the punctuated equilibrium model.

Research methodology

To explore this supposition, we conducted multiple case studies. A qualitative approach was chosen due to the lack of prior research on dynamics of alignment, the desire to understand the strategic IS management profiles within the rich organizational contexts, and the sensitive nature of the data needed (Yin, 1984). Moreover, the focus of the study was on the events associated with changes in alignment over time. In order to understand the thought processes underlying major decisions made along the way, it was essential to incorporate the perspectives of senior business and IS executives. At the same time, in order to achieve some understanding of the different aspects of the changes in alignment, we wanted to examine them in multiple cases. Three detailed case studies were conducted.

The case sites were selected based on a combination of accessibility (to senior business and IS executives), interestingness (in the issues causing senior executives to reconsider the role and strategy of the IS organization), and cross-case diversity (in company size, industry, and issues). We use the pseudonyms[5] ENERGY, DIVFIN, and LEASE to represent the three companies. ENERGY and DIVFIN are large companies, whereas LEASE is small. ENERGY is international, with significant presence in the United States, LEASE is located in United States, and DIVFIN is Australian. One major subsidiary of ENERGY, which we call SUBSID, provides consulting and IS services to external organizations as well as other subsidiaries of ENERGY. ENERGY's IS group was a major portion of this subsidiary.

Data collection

Each case examined changes in both business and IS strategies and structures over extended time periods. The events were studied retrospectively through intensive, nondirective interviews with the executives involved in strategic IS management. We asked the informants to focus on specific critical events, but encouraged them to expand their comments into areas of personal interest concerning their company's strategic business and IS conditions. More vivid events were of special interest. Each interview was tape-recorded, with additional notes being taken when necessary and then transcribed.

In an effort to address the potential limitations of examining time-consuming phenomena through retrospective interviews, we interviewed multiple informants from different backgrounds and at varying hierarchical levels. This, along with the examination of internal company documents, provided multiple perspectives on the strategic IS profile and enabled cross-checking of the perceived relationships among its four dimensions. The interviews at LEASE were conducted during January–February 1996. DIVFIN was visited twice, while ENERGY was visited thrice. Most of the interviews were conducted during the first visit – in April 1996 at DIVFIN and in February–April 1996 at ENERGY. Later events were studied through follow-up visits – in July 1997 at DIVFIN and in June–July 1997 and April 1998 at ENERGY. A total 47 hours of interviews were conducted. We conducted five interviews at LEASE, with the chief financial officer (CFO), senior VP (Operations), VP (Accounting), VP (Marketing), and the former IS director. At DIVFIN, we conducted nine interviews with seven individuals: corporate CFO, corporate CIO, IT manager (later promoted to CIO), new IT manager (who joined after an outsourcing arrangement began), IT directors for financial services and property services, and IT project manager (who reports to IT director for property services). Finally, at ENERGY, we conducted 16 interviews with 13 executives, including the president and CEO of SUBSID, six of the nine individuals (including customer support managers) who directly report to SUBSID's CEO (one of these individuals is now the CEO), and six IT line of business managers.

Data analysis

At each company, we examined the way in which the strategic IS management profile changed over time, through rigorous analysis of extensive interview transcripts and company documentation. Being based on three cases, our results may seem particularistic. However, we tried to produce more general explanations (Eisenhardt, 1989) through 'analytic generalization' (Yin, 1984), where 'the generalization is of theoretical concepts and patterns' (Orlikowski, 1993, p. 310). The concepts and patterns were linked to the existing theory on punctuated equilibrium models and on alignment in strategic IS management. A four-step process was followed, as described below.

Step 1 – Initial analysis of transcripts

Each transcript was read carefully, and the informants' descriptions of, and explanations for, the various events were highlighted. The interviewee comments were also linked to business and IS strategies and structures, and to the relationship between two or more of these dimensions. Using this understanding of the processes through which the strategic IS management profiles evolved, we sought to identify a process theory (Van de Ven and Poole, 1995) best representing each case. In each case, the alternately slow and rapid pace of changes seemed to best conform to the punctuated equilibrium model. The periods of major change, and the intervening periods of relatively little change, were also identified in this step, and then subjected to a more rigorous analysis.

Step 2 – Formal interpretation of transcripts

The case transcripts were analyzed in a more structured fashion in this step. Each case was assigned to two authors, so that each of the three authors independently read the transcripts for two of the cases. This allowed the incorporation of two different perspectives for each case and minimized the likelihood that we missed something important.

In order to facilitate consistent interpretation, the three authors used a common set of brief definitions of the various business and IS strategies. We used a common electronic form to analyze transcripts, and moved interview comments to this form through 'copy' and 'paste' commands. The perceived nature of each comment was also indicated on this electronic form. The comment could concern one or more dimensions of the strategic IS profile (e.g., 'Move towards a centralized IS structure'), IS or business performance, a factor that may have triggered a major change, an important change in personnel, or some other potentially important aspect. The form also indicated the location of each comment on the transcript, the approximate date to which it was relevant, and any links to other comments. Thus, this step helped segment interview data into meaningful pieces of text (Tesch, 1990).

Step 3 – Analysis of the formal interpretations

Next, the electronic forms containing the assessments of the two raters for all the transcripts for each case were combined in an electronic spreadsheet. The spreadsheets were quite large, with the smallest one (for LEASE) having 310 rows. Each spreadsheet was sorted based on the nature of, and the time period relevant to, each comment.

Together, Steps 2 and 3 helped us to decontextualize the interviewee comments out of their original context, and then recontextualize them (i.e., assemble all the comments in a case about a particular aspect) (Tesch, 1990). The three sorted spreadsheets were used to identify the business and IS strategies and structures, the factors affecting them, and the changes in business and IS performance. Within each case, the strategic IS profiles at various times were viewed in the light of the ideal alignment patterns (see Table 11.1) to assess the six types of alignment. The changes in the four strategic dimensions were used to classify the overall change as evolutionary or revolutionary.

Step 4 – Cross-case analysis

While similar in the applicability of the punctuated equilibrium model to them, the three cases differed in several ways. Comparison of changes in strategic IS management profiles across the three cases, and the factors triggering the changes, revealed some patterns that generally conform to the punctuated equilibrium model. The results also include a few departures from the prior literature, which should be examined in future research.

Descriptions of cases

Case study 1: LEASE

Started in 1976 as an equipment sales company, LEASE became an independent equipment lessor in 1983. The case covers the period from 1986 until early 1996, during which time its net worth grew from $25 million[6] to $100 million, and the number of employees ranged from 90 to 275. As shown in Figure 11.2, we examined two revolutions that occurred in 1990 and 1993, and three evolutionary changes: before the first revolution, between the two revolutions, and following the second revolution.

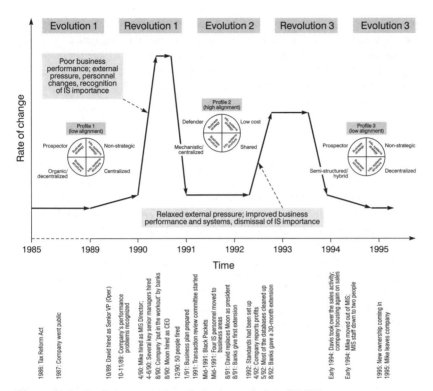

Figure 11.2   *Evolutionary and revolutionary periods at LEASE*

Evolutionary period 1

From the time of its creation, LEASE pursued a *Prospector* business strategy. Comprised of about two-thirds operating lease and about one-third direct finance lease, it grew quickly by aggressively pursuing a number of products. However, it operated with an *organic and decentralized* business structure, with few standards and minimal concern for proper records. The functional areas operated as 'little fiefdoms' (chief financial officer, or CFO) with no central control. LEASE had little information it could use for planning and control. Also, as it was not affiliated with a bank, it faced few external controls. In its desire to grow quickly, LEASE had paid little attention to systems. It had a small, centralized IS staff which was isolated from the business functions. Thus, a perception of IS as *nonstrategic* was accompanied by a *centralized* IS management structure.

When the 1986 Tax Reform Act was passed, certain tax benefits applicable to the leasing business were repealed. As a result, 'the buyers that formerly bought those deals from us no longer had an appetite' (CFO) for those previously more profitable arrangements. However, LEASE continued to conduct business as if the environment was the same as before. It also failed to recognize the sharp decline in mainframe computer prices due to the ascent of personal computers.[7] Unaware of the problems lying ahead, LEASE went public in 1987. In October 1989, David Garcey was hired as senior vice president (VP) (Operations) as the company started recognizing it was in trouble.

Revolutionary period 1

Following the entrepreneurs' recognition of LEASE's financial troubles, things moved quickly. Several senior executives, mainly from Garcey's previous company, were hired in April–June 1990. In 1990, LEASE had a debt of $100 million for equity of $60 million, and as it incurred further losses, the debt/equity ratio quickly rose to about three. In August 1990, LEASE was 'put in the workout' (VP, Accounting) by its lender banks. It now had to do monthly compliance reports. Recognizing the seriousness of the situation, the entrepreneurs hired Rick Moon, a banker, as CEO. The former IS director characterized this as 'fighting bankers with a banker.'

Soon after the new CEO arrived, the business strategy shifted to *Defender*. LEASE stopped growing and started cutting costs. In January 1991, a business plan was prepared. A few months later, a transaction review committee[8] was created to monitor all the sales deals. The CEO primarily concentrated on cutting costs, firing 50 people in December 1990 and another 20 a little later. Senior executives believed that Moon had a plan to cut costs, but lacked a plan to get the company back on track once costs were cut. In August 1991, the Board decided not to renew Moon's contract, and named David Garcey as president instead. An interviewee attributed this move partly to the banks' greater confidence in his abilities than in Rick Moon's. Garcey quickly centralized the business structure, instituted clear lines of reporting, and assumed a significant role in all major decisions.

The changes in top management, strategy, and structure on the business side were accompanied by major changes in IS. Moon and Garcey recognized the strategic role IS would play in *cutting costs*, especially in accounting. Moon hired Mike Adrian as IS director. When Adrian joined LEASE as IS director, it had 14 people in IS. He shifted the previously centralized IS management to a more *shared* form, moving four IS employees to the user areas. They participated in meetings with others in their area, played a major role in local IS decisions, and communicated weekly with Adrian.

Evolutionary period 2

In August 1991, the banks gave LEASE an extension. They had greater confidence in LEASE as several *mechanistic* controls, including a monthly flash report to management, were established. The transaction review committee met daily and approved all bids, credits, and major sales. LEASE also started a process called 'black packets'[9] to closely scrutinize each deal. For several months, employees worked hard examining the previous deals, setting standards, and cleaning databases. They frequently discovered new problems. The senior VP (Operations) remarked: 'It seemed like every time you asked a question, you turned a rock over and there was a bunch more ugliness underneath the rock.' Detailed standards had been set up by early 1992, and by May 1992 most of the databases had been cleaned up. In April 1992 LEASE reported profits, which led to banks granting it a 30-month extension, and allowing it to keep a certain formula amount of cash flows to invest in new business. This was a major landmark, as it allowed LEASE to generate new business, thereby garnering additional income and providing for future cash flows.

Revolutionary period 2

Following the turnaround, LEASE made major changes in business and IS strategies and structures. In addition to the traditional leasing of computer equipment, it began leasing other kinds of equipment (e.g., forklifts and trucks) as well. The common belief was that the back office had been taken care of, and now the front office needed to be focused on. David Garcey brought sales under his direct control in 1994, and emphasized the need to increase sales.

With the business strategy reverting back to *Prospector*, the lack of attention to mechanistic controls seemed to reemerge as well. Clear reporting structures and well-defined roles were being blurred, with people being rotated frequently across departments and tasks. The business structure had shifted toward a *semistructured and hybrid* form. The importance of IS was reduced again. Mike Adrian left the IS group, but continued on at LEASE, becoming 'quasi-advisory' to IS. The IS structure was in flux. Central IS staff, which had been trimmed toward the end of 1992, was now down to two people, with the individual departments assuming responsibility for various information technology (IT) functions. Vendors were hired for IS maintenance, and the IS budget was reduced to $300,000. Another individual took over as head of IS, but unlike Mike Adrian, was not given the title of IS director. Having made a strategic contribution to the corporate turnaround, IS was now nonstrategic again.

Evolutionary period 3

After these major changes, LEASE entered another period of minimal change. It sought to gradually build sales to enhance profitability. Adrian disagreed with some of the ongoing changes, and in late 1995, decided to leave LEASE. With only two individuals in the central IS group, and no one having the title of IS director, IS management became decentralized. Some senior executives were afraid that this reduced role of IS would come back to haunt them in the future.

Conclusions

The strategic IS management profile during Evolution 1 had high business and IS alignments. But the other types of alignment were low, and so the overall alignment was low as well. LEASE seemed to resolve the conflict in the alignment profile without redesign; convincing themselves that IS was not important due to the rapid growth, its managers focused on hiring salespersons and closing deals quickly without building essential systems. The business performance was good in the short term, but the long-term performance suffered, and LEASE ended up close to bankruptcy.

Revolution 1 was triggered by several factors, including the shift in the environment (changing tax laws, computer industry economics) and LEASE's inability to respond to it via evolution, deteriorating business performance, changes in top management (including two quick changes in CEO and the hiring of the first and last CIO), and the recognition of the importance of IS. LEASE underwent changes in all four dimensions of its strategic IS profile. Consequently, the overall alignment increased, with three of the six alignment measures being high and the other three being medium. The increased alignment apparently improved both business and IS performance. LEASE seemed to have finally succeeded in resolving the conflict in its alignment profile by redesigning the four dimensions.

Unfortunately, once the performance improved and the banks relaxed their controls, LEASE quickly underwent another revolution, reverting in three of the four dimensions to the strategic IS management profile before the first revolution. The importance of IS was dismissed again, the position of CIO was discontinued, the IS staff was drastically reduced, and the focus on sales without systems and controls resurfaced. Only one of the six alignments (IS structure-business strategy) was high, with another two (business, structural) being medium, and the rest being low. The conflict within the strategic IS management profile had thus reemerged, and the overall alignment was again low. Although the company was still performing well, concerns were expressed about its long-term future.

Case study 2: DIVFIN

DIVFIN is a diversified Australian company with annual revenue of about two billion dollars and after-tax profits of over $250 million. Its businesses include financial services, property services, capital services and investments, and group services. This case focused on a revolutionary change in which DIVFIN outsourced all its IS activities to a multinational IS vendor and obtained a 35 percent stake in the vendor's Australian unit. The case description is in terms of three periods: the revolutionary period (February 1994 to June 1995), and the evolutionary periods before and after this revolution.

Evolutionary period 1

As shown in Figure 11.3 DIVFIN grew considerably from 1980 to 1993. Pursuing a *Prospector* business strategy, it grew by getting into new areas, partly through external acquisitions. One major acquisition was of a large integrated financial services firm in 1985. Consistent with its growth by acquisition, DIVFIN included several companies managed in a decentralized and organic fashion. Characterized by a high level of entrepreneurship, DIVFIN was managed in an *ad hoc* fashion with few controls. IS management was highly decentralized, aiming to support the internal operations of the

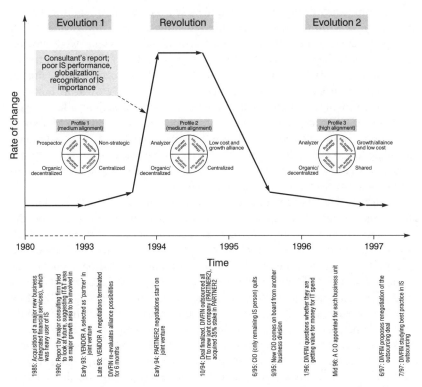

Figure 11.3 *Evolutionary and revolutionary periods at DIVFIN*

different companies within DIVFIN. Each business unit of DIVFIN had a separate IS unit. The business units differed vastly in the technologies used, probably due to historic differences, especially between financial and property divisions. However, IS was playing a nonstrategic role at DIVFIN. IS activities were driven by 'the techies,' according to a senior business executive, with little direction from the business side. Although the total money invested on IS was tightly maintained, there was a lack of control on specific activities. According to the IS executives we interviewed, the IS resources were used inappropriately, with too much expenditure on maintaining old systems.

In 1990, the CEO (Steve Avery) engaged a large consulting firm to catalog areas for future growth for DIVFIN. The consulting firm highlighted the importance of the IT industry, including the possibility of some form of joint venture. This focused attention on IS, which according to one senior IS executive 'had been historically much underfinanced.'

Revolutionary period

The revolutionary change began with the CEO and the other senior managers mandating a 35 to 40 percent expense reduction to allow for greater global competitiveness, especially as several international companies were moving into Australia. This caused a shift to an *Analyzer* strategy as DIVFIN searched for ways to simultaneously accomplish global competitiveness, drastic reduction in business expenses, and entry into the high-growth IS industry. The CEO sought to acquire a stake in the IS industry through an alliance with a major IS provider rather than purchasing an IS company. Moreover, outsourcing was expected to transform the management of IS. IS now became strategic to: (a) generating external revenues through stake in an IS company; and (b) significantly reducing business costs. Thus, IS strategy was to simultaneously seek *low cost and growth/alliance*.

In early 1993, DIVFIN initiated negotiations with a global IS vendor, but these discussions were severed in late 1993 due to disagreements on the structure of the joint venture. Six months later, another global IS vendor which was trying to enter the Australian market approached DIVFIN about the prospect of a joint venture. Having in part built its business on similar alliances in financial services and property development industries, DIVFIN found such an arrangement to be attractive. As part of the agreement, DIVFIN would outsource all of its IS to a new Australian company, in which it would have a 35 percent stake, with the global IS vendor having the other 65 percent stake. The contract was consistent with DIVFIN's past in some aspects, including the lack of controls, clear plans, or service-level agreements. It also reflected the company's past in that the focus was mainly on the external component of the alliance with the details of the internal management of the

IS function being ignored. However, the contract represented a shift in other ways. One change was that the decisions were made largely by the corporate CEO and CIO, and the historically independent business units had little say in the matter. This change in decision-making locus later caused problems in establishing realistic and meaningful service-level agreements. The joint venture company went online on 1 October 1994.

Evolutionary period 2

Inadequate definition of service levels was exacerbated by the apparent belief that by outsourcing IS, IS management had been outsourced as well. DIVFIN failed to place appropriate control mechanisms to monitor and administer the contract. Some individuals from the vendor acted as liaisons to translate and handle user needs, but they were not effective in coordinating and controlling the relationship. In transitioning DIVFIN's IS personnel to the vendor, only the former IS director of financial services was retained, and he left in June 1995. There was really no one from DIVFIN to handle IS from June 1995 to October 1995 when a corporate CIO, with the responsibility for managing the contract, was hired. This centralized IS management was a major departure from history.

Initially, there were several problems in the relationship with the vendor. They were attributed to inadequate management by DIVFIN, unrealistic expectations, and cultural differences. In sharp contrast to DIVFIN's laissez faire culture, the vendor was a machine bureaucracy. Some interviewees also viewed it as inadequately customer-oriented. Over time, DIVFIN has recognized the need to manage the contract better. IS management is now *shared* by DIVFIN and the business units,[10] with each unit now having its own CIO and its own people responsible for managing its part of the vendor contract.

The problem, however, is the contract, especially how to take the user requirements and fit them into the overall structure of the contract. DIVFIN had assumed that due to the nature of the alliance, the vendor would readily provide needed services whether or not they were identified in the original scope. As outsourcing vendors do not accept such interpretations, it is not surprising that the conflict continues. The vendor does want to deliver a high-quality service, but because the contract was poorly defined, and the business units' needs poorly understood, neither party is satisfied. This has led DIVFIN to seek to renegotiate the contract. The vendor is lukewarm to the overture. Seeing no point in rejecting such discussions outright, however, it has been arguing that the renegotiations would have to benefit both parties.

When we last visited DIVFIN (in July 1997), one of the newly appointed CIOs considered the IS outsourcing situation (in terms of the relationship between DIVFIN and the new company) to be getting better, but the overall service performance to be 'pretty ordinary.' While there has been a modest improvement in the vendor's service, 'there is still a long way to go.' One of DIVFIN's new IS managers also raised a concern about the increased external dependence. As there is no longer an internal IS group, DIVFIN's business units have no alternatives. Worse, he was worried about how the business unit managers will acquire the necessary understanding of IT to succeed in the future.

Conclusions

During Evolution 1, three types of alignment were high while the other three were low. Thus, the overall alignment was considered medium. All three mis-alignments concerned IS strategy, which is interesting considering that IS performance was criticized by most interviewees. In contrast, the three alignments among the other three dimensions (business strategy, business structure, and IS structure) were all high. The high levels of these types of alignment, especially business alignment, may be related to DIVFIN's good short-term and long-term business performance.

A consultant's report, combined with the increased recognition of the importance of IS and the need to cut costs due to increasing global competition, led to the revolutionary changes. The revolution was incomplete, as only three of the four dimensions of the strategic IS management profile (all except business structure) were changed. All six types of alignment changed somewhat, but the overall alignment remained medium. Structural alignment became low as IS management was centralized at the corporate level in sharp contrast to the highly decentralized business structure.

Following the revolution, DIVFIN underwent considerable changes in one dimension – IS structure. CIOs were hired for each strategic business unit, and some of the vendor's service-level agreements were moved from the corporate level to the business-unit level. These changes somewhat offset the change made in the revolution by moving the IS structure back to shared, which was between the earlier decentralized and the post-revolution centralized forms. These post-revolution changes increased structural alignment and increased the overall alignment to high. Thus, DIVFIN followed the incomplete revolution with post-revolution changes to further improve alignment. The IS performance problems were reduced as a result, and there seemed to be greater confidence about the future.

Case study 3: ENERGY

ENERGY is the United States subsidiary of an international organization performing the exploration, production, refining, and marketing of petroleum products. In 1995, its revenues exceeded $20 billion, with a net income of

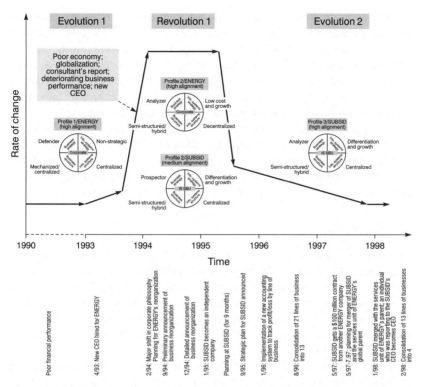

Figure 11.4 *Evolutionary and revolutionary periods at ENERGY*

over one billion dollars, and over 15,000 employees. As shown in Figure 11.4, we describe the case in terms of a revolutionary change (April 1993 to September 1995) in which ENERGY was restructured and several independent subsidiaries (including one with a considerable focus on IS) were formed, and the evolutionary periods preceding and following it.

Evolutionary period 1

Until 1993, ENERGY had been operating in a stable fashion, with little change in strategic orientation, organization structure, or corporate philosophy. It was historically very successful. It had been following a *Defender* strategy, maintaining its territory through low costs but not seeking opportunities for growth. However, the energy industry was becoming increasingly competitive, partly due to protracted low prices of crude oil and natural gas in the late 1980s and early 1990s. Projected future prices also showed no significant increase. ENERGY had a mechanistic and centralized structure based on what several interviewees called a 'command and control' model. As with other Defenders (Delery and Doty, 1996), there was an unwritten contract with the employees. They were expected to be loyal and work hard, while ENERGY promised a good salary, excellent benefits, and lifetime employment. However, the employees were constrained, or as one interviewee put it, 'mushroom capped' – that is, ENERGY exerted a paternalistic control over the employees, managing the employees' careers for them in terms of job assignments, training, and advancement.

During this period, IS management was highly centralized, with a central IS group serving the various business areas. The IS group played a nonstrategic role, supporting the business areas but doing so from a technological focus rather than a business-oriented one. They were perceived as telling business people how to do things rather than listening to their needs.

Revolutionary period

The primary risk with a Defender business strategy is the inability to respond to major market shifts (Miles *et al.*, 1978). ENERGY also suffered from this problem. It had a tendency to reinvent the wheel,[11] and also failed to respond to increasing competition. Continued success had seemingly led to a complacent, inward-looking, and inflexible corporate culture. ENERGY's financial performance in the early 1990s was therefore disappointing relative to other energy firms.

A new president and CEO, Paul Hill, was hired in April 1993. He discarded traditional solutions to ENERGY's problems, insisting instead on a corporate transformation. He commissioned a thorough evaluation of the company's mission, structure, and direction. The company's business strategy shifted toward *Analyzer* with greater attention to the market conditions and efforts to identify growth opportunities. In February 1994, Hill and four executive vice presidents mandated a major shift in corporate philosophy from a centralized 'command and control' structure, which was considered unsuitable for rapid market changes, to what they called 'federal governance' (a customer support manager).[12] Shifting the business structure toward a *semistructured and hybrid* form, decisions were moved to the lowest hierarchical level at which the necessary information was available. ENERGY departed from a *de facto* policy of life-long employment toward transient employment.[13]

On 1 January 1995, each subsidiary became an independent entity with individual profit and loss responsibility. Top management of ENERGY was performed by a leadership council, and a larger leadership group which included senior executives from the various subsidiaries. Similarly, each subsidiary's leadership group and council included one or more representatives from ENERGY.

One of the subsidiaries, SUBSID, employed about 1800 people, including approximately 800 in the IS group.[14] Its mission was to provide a variety of corporate services, including IS, not only to ENERGY subsidiaries, but also on the open market to other organizations not related to ENERGY (including other firms in the energy industry). SUBSID had an existing revenue base in excess of $300 million, mainly from other ENERGY subsidiaries. Its board included the CEO and three other senior executives from ENERGY, but not the heads of the other business units (to avoid conflict of interest). Moreover, SUBSID's CEO was one of the 14 members of ENERGY's leadership council. SUBSID's corporate siblings were free to look outside for IS services. IS accountability and decision making were pushed into the business units, and a CIO was appointed for each unit. The IS management structure for ENERGY was thus decentralized. The shift in IS structure was accompanied by increased recognition of the importance of IS, and a shift toward a combination of *low-cost and growth* IS strategy. ENERGY was seeking to reduce business and IS costs through efficiencies expected from market competition. In addition, it expected external revenue from SUBSID. SUBSID's corporate siblings continued to have some influence on SUBSID as its valued customers, as well as through ENERGY's top executives who were members of SUBSID's board.

Evolutionary period 2

Following the major upheaval, the subsidiaries settled down to fine-tune internal structures and strategies. SUBSID's senior executives spent nine months assessing strengths, weaknesses, market, and competition, completing the strategic plan in September 1995. SUBSID initially started with a *Prospector* strategy, seeking to get external business in a creative fashion. It sought business not only from IS development but also from selling surplus IS capacity and IS-related infrastructure. Its internal information systems, and superior IS skills, including advantages in subsurface information technology and infrastructure processing, were seen as potentially key in *differentiating* SUBSID from its competitors and enabling *growth* of its business. The September 1995 strategic plan led to a change in SUBSID's structure, from centralized cost-centers to a matrix structure including 21 lines of businesses. The semi-structured/hybrid business structure was aligned with SUBSID's new Prospector business strategy, emphasizing revenue growth and customer satisfaction.

SUBSID created the position of manager (Business Development) to pursue external contracts, made a customer support manager responsible for each of the ENERGY customers, and appointed a CIO for its internal systems. IS management within SUBSID was done in a centralized fashion by the CIO, who was responsible for deciding about the systems to be used by SUBSID's lines of businesses. The internal systems were also generally centralized.

SUBSID's strengths included industry knowledge and the ability to do oil and gas accounting at about half the industry cost. However, several factors offset these strengths. SUBSID was now competing for both existing and new business with large competitors, possessing strong deal-making and relationship-building skills, eager to get a foothold in the energy industry. Therefore, SUBSID started hiring commissioned salespersons for the first time in company history. However, established attitudes at SUBSID posed another problem; its personnel had to make a transition from viewing their ENERGY customers as a captive audience to treating them as free-market customers. Finally, SUBSID had no track record in the external market, and no list of references. The other major energy companies would also hesitate to do business with SUBSID due to the fear that this may help a competitor (i.e., ENERGY) through additional revenues and potential access to sensitive data.

Free to go elsewhere for IS services, ENERGY's other business units started investigating such possibilities. Based on the confidence that it could be very competitive with other service providers, at least in the energy industry, SUBSID viewed this as both an obstacle and an opportunity. The search for an external vendor led to a better appreciation of the value of SUBSID, and also enhanced SUBSID's credibility with other subsidiaries of ENERGY. Their assessments of SUBSID's performance improved as well, going up by five percentage points in 1997 in terms of overall satisfaction level.

The obstacles encountered in seeking external contracts, along with the difficulties other subsidiaries of ENERGY faced when they sought external vendors, led to a shift in SUBSID's strategy toward *Analyzer*. Instead of pursuing a Prospector strategy through increased external business, SUBSID now focused mainly on internal (within ENERGY or within its global parent company) customers. To pursue external opportunities, it decided to look for a strategic alliance with an IS vendor. Moreover, rather than trying to provide all kinds of IS-related solutions, SUBSID focused on systems development and delivery. In May 1997, SUBSID obtained a $100 million project from another ENERGY subsidiary. SUBSID was conducting this project along with an external vendor. In addition to the business from the ENERGY companies, SUBSID obtained several external projects, ranging from $100,000 to over five million dollars. Its revenues for 1996 were about $350 million, and $430 million in 1997.

When we last visited SUBSID in April 1998, it had continued its postrevolutionary changes along three basic lines. The biggest change had been the merger of SUBSID, based in United States, with other similar subsidiaries of ENERGY's global parent to form a single IS and business services subsidiary supporting all the business units of the global company. SUBSID was still pursuing an Analyzer business strategy, although its market focus had continued to shift somewhat from providing services to the general energy industry towards gaining a larger share of ENERGY's parent company's business. While SUBSID would continue to seek new opportunities outside its global parent, it planned to be less aggressive until it had explored all the internal opportunities for new business.

The second post-revolutionary change involved further consolidation of SUBSID's lines of business, first from 21 to 13 and then to four. The organizational structure continued to be semistructured/hybrid but had evolved into a three-dimensional matrix based on SUBSID lines of business, geographical regions, and the business units of ENERGY's global parent.

The third post-revolutionary initiative was a continuation of the search for acquiring new business skills related to marketing and relationship management, but with a slight twist. Although SUBSID was still hiring individuals with specific expertise in these areas, it was also exploring potential strategic partnerships to enhance its competencies and market attractiveness. For example, it was discussing a possible joint venture or partnership with a consulting firm for a wide range of services to the energy industry. It also had a continuing relationship with another consulting firm for building a knowledge base designed to capture the skills and competencies related to marketing its services to external customers. To oversee these partnerships, SUBSID had created a new executive position responsible for 'Strategic Relation Planning' on the same level as the CFO and CIO, reporting directly to the CEO.

Despite these changes, the underlying principle remained the same: Anything SUBSID did would be under the free-market umbrella. If it could not compete with the other service providers on a level playing field, or better opportunities surfaced elsewhere, the deal would not be completed.

Conclusions

The strategic IS management profile during the initial evolutionary period had a high level of overall alignment although IS was considered nonstrategic. While ENERGY enjoyed good short-term IS performance, its business performance was deteriorating, apparently due to ENERGY's failure to react to the changing environment (reduced prices, increased competition).

A new CEO and a consultant's report provided further impetus for the revolution in which all four dimensions were changed, but alignment was maintained at a high level. At that time, a subsidiary focusing primarily on IS, SUBSID, was created. The initial strategic IS management profile of SUBSID had medium overall alignment. SUBSID's Prospector business strategy was not well aligned with the other dimensions, and it therefore was no surprise that over the next several months, SUBSID encountered problems in pursuing this strategy. Recognizing its limitations in seeking external growth, SUBSID underwent postrevolutionary changes. Its business strategy changed to Analyzer, which was better suited to the other three dimensions. Consequently, the overall alignment became high. Short-term business performance seemed to have improved as a result of this revolution by redesign.

Discussion

This research has used a punctuated equilibrium model to examine the dynamics of alignment. Three case studies were used to better understand the way in which alignment evolves through modifications to an existing alignment pattern, punctuated by periodic transitions to an altogether different pattern of alignment. As discussed below, our results integrate prior literature and provide some new insights for organization science in general and for strategic IS management in particular.

Evolutionary periods and resolution without redesign

Each case had long periods of no change in the strategic IS management profile. Prior literature (e.g., Miles and Snow, 1996) suggests that these evolutionary periods are characterized by a high level of alignment. We did find the evolutionary period to have a high level of alignment at ENERGY, but low overall alignment at LEASE. The overall alignment was medium at DIVFIN, although all the misalignments concerned IS strategy. Thus, the research conforms to the punctuated equilibrium model, but differs in suggesting that the long evolutionary periods may sometimes have *low* alignment. The evolutionary periods at both DIVFIN and LEASE had misalignments which were apparently resolved without redesign, as both companies' top executives believed that IS was not strategic and so it did not need to be aligned with business.

Reluctance toward resolution by redesign

Our cases reveal a reluctance in organizations to make revolutionary changes through which all or most of the dimensions of the strategic IS management profile are modified. At ENERGY, the consultant and managers initially commissioned to suggest strategic changes proposed a structure that was simply an improved version of the previous structure. Following this tentative change, ENERGY did undergo a complete revolution, but only due to the strong stance taken by the new CEO. Similarly, at LEASE, the pressure from the lender banks caused a revolution. However, it followed some initial hiccups, and a change in the CEO. The second revolution at LEASE encountered less hesitation than the first, but it was essentially a step back toward the strategic profile that had existed prior to the first revolution. The reluctance to make revolutionary changes was also evident at DIVFIN. A consulting firm's report initiated thinking about alternative ways of improving performance, but DIVFIN took time to identify ways of doing so. Moreover, it first looked for a vendor that was similar to itself, and quite reluctantly entered into a partnership with a culturally different vendor.

Thus, the research suggests that occasional revolutionary changes in the deep structure (e.g., the strategic IS profile) may significantly help organizations in the long run, but such revolutions too may be inhibited by cultural or structural inertia (Tushman and O'Reilly 1996). Consequently, organizations sometimes change some dimensions of the deep structure, but not the remaining dimensions.

Revolutionary changes and resolution by redesign

All three cases suggest that evolutions are punctuated by revolutionary changes in the strategic IS profile. Each company made revolutionary changes to transform the alignment pattern that had continued for a long time. ENERGY and LEASE underwent complete revolutions, wherein all four dimensions were changed, whereas DIVFIN underwent an incomplete revolution as three dimensions were changed. This finding is consistent with the basic punctuated equilibrium model. Through evolutionary changes, managers incrementally alter strategies and structures to constrain the level of misalignment. However, 'sooner or later, discontinuities upset the congruence that has been a part of the organization's success' (Tushman and O'Reilly, 1996, p. 12).

Consistent with the reluctance to make revolutionary changes, we found all the revolutions to require some combination of five strong triggers – environmental shifts, sustained low performance, influential outsiders, new leadership, and perception transformation. At ENERGY, the strategic IS management profile during the initial evolutionary period had a high level of alignment. This profile had served ENERGY well for some time, but a new profile was needed when competition increased and prices declined. At LEASE, the initial strategic IS management profile was continued despite the low alignment, due to the belief that IS was not important. However, when the environment shifted with the new tax laws and changing economics of the IS industry, LEASE had to modify its strategic IS profile. All three cases indicated that alignment profiles may also be radically altered when the business or functional (IS in this case) performance deteriorates. For example, when faced with bankruptcy and the stringent controls enforced by the banks, LEASE quickly made large-scale changes in Revolution 1. As suggested by Gersick (1991, p. 27), the presence of influential outsiders also seemed to motivate revolutions. In all three cases, the revolutions were triggered by the actions of external agencies – the establishment and use of direct controls by the lending banks at LEASE, the consulting firm's report and the entry of international firms into the Australian market at DIVFIN, and the consulting firm's report at ENERGY. Moreover, the potency of these influential outsiders is amplified by changes in leadership (including a new CEO), which played a critical role in the revolutions at LEASE and ENERGY.

The above four factors – environmental shifts, sustained low performance, influential outsiders, and new leadership – have previously been discussed as possible triggers of revolutions (Haveman, 1992). However, we found another trigger, perceptual transformation, which does not seem to have been discussed earlier. We found revolutions to be triggered by significant changes in the perceptions concerning IS (at LEASE in both revolutions as well as at DIVFIN) or the organization's skills in a certain area (e.g., the lack of deal-making skills at SUBSID). It is possible that we discovered this trigger because we examined alignment across an overall business domain and a specific area (i.e., IS).

Possible ineffectiveness of resolution by redesign

It has been argued that if a low level of alignment, or conflict in the alignment profile, is responsible for the poor performance, organizations would seek to resolve this conflict by redesign (Gresov, 1989). As discussed above, we also found that resolution by redesign is used to resolve such conflict. However, we found that the resolution by redesign may or may not be effective. At DIVFIN, the revolution did not increase overall alignment; it increased some types of alignment but reduced others. At ENERGY, the alignment within the strategic IS profile was high both before and after the revolution, although the revolution did change all four dimensions of the profile. Finally, the first revolution at LEASE increased alignment considerably, but the second revolution undid the changes and led to low alignment. Thus, the resolution by redesign in revolutions may not lead to an increase in overall alignment, and sometimes may even reduce it.

Post-revolutionary changes

Because revolutions sometimes reduce alignment, they may be followed by further adjustments in alignment patterns. At DIVFIN, structural alignment decreased after the revolution, as the business structure had remained decentralized but IS management became centralized. This caused problems in implementing the outsourcing relationship. Consequently, the management of the relationship was re-decentralized (this increased structural alignment). At SUBSID, the overall alignment in postrevolution strategic IS management profile was medium. This was addressed by shifting business strategy to Analyzer and focusing on corporate siblings, while also seeking external revenues. No change to the strategic IS management profile was made at LEASE during the evolutionary period following the first revolution. However, shortly after the first revolution had produced the desired improvements, the second revolution caused the strategic IS profile to revert almost entirely (all three aspects except IS structure) to the profile before the first revolution.

Thus, this chapter suggests that revolutions may be followed by post-revolution adjustments to the strategic IS management profiles, either to reinforce them or to take a step back toward the pre-revolution situation. A revolution may take the organization too far in another direction, and the new alignment pattern may be inappropriate for its competencies, causing the organization to seek new competencies and further modify the alignment pattern. In some other cases, the revolution may not go far enough, and the changed strategic IS profile may be low in one or more kinds of alignment. This may cause the organization to further fine-tune the alignment pattern, possibly by reverting somewhat toward the prerevolution situation. Such post-revolution adjustments are consistent with Sastry's (1997) suggestion that trial periods, similar to our postrevolution adjustments, follow revolutions.

The above observations should be viewed in the light of the study's limitations, which restrict its generalizability. First, the chapter is limited due to the use of a small number of cases. The findings are based on only three companies, although they are of different sizes and from different industries. Second, the cases were studied retrospectively. The interviews were conducted during one to three visits at fairly close points in time, but our focus was on changes that occurred over long time periods. Third, although we collected the data using key informants at each organization, a wider set of informants may have provided additional insights. For example, only one non-IS executive was interviewed at DIVFIN. We also could not interview some important executives who were no longer at these companies.

The chapter has several implications for future research in the broad area of organization science. First, the approach of viewing alignment in conjunction with punctuated equilibrium models should be valuable in future research. Research on dynamics of alignment in other areas may similarly consider an alignment profile (involving strategy and structure of the overall business and a functional area) as the deep structure that undergoes evolutionary and revolutionary changes (Gersick, 1991).

Second, our use of Gresov's (1989) work on conflict among multiple contingencies should also be of interest to researchers in other aspects of organizations. This chapter has shown the value of Gresov's resolution by redesign and resolution without redesign approaches for viewing alignment in the long run. These approaches may also explain two deviations we found from prior research (e.g., Miles and Snow, 1996); unlike prior research we found that: (a) the evolutionary period may or may not be characterized by a high level of alignment; and (b) the revolutionary change does not always increase alignment. The use of resolution without redesign during evolutions could explain why some companies continue for a long time with what appears, at least to outsiders, as a low level of alignment. The use of resolution by redesign might explain why revolutionary changes do not increase alignment; it might reduce alignment among some dimensions and thereby offset increase in alignment among other dimensions. Further research on punctuated equilibrium models in other areas is needed to examine how resolution without redesign can help sustain low alignment in the absence of substantial performance degradation. Further research is also needed to examine the conditions that influence whether alignment will increase or decrease as a result of revolutions.

Third, we found strategic and structural changes during the revolution to be reinforced or offset by postrevolutionary changes. Such postrevolutionary changes have not been examined in prior field research. Further research is needed to validate or refine our classification of periods of changes in alignment profiles into evolutions, incomplete or complete revolutions, and postrevolutionary changes. Additional case studies examining changes in alignment profiles should help in doing so.

Finally, we found that revolutions may be triggered by a number of factors, one of which – perception transformation – has received little attention earlier. Studies of punctuated equilibrium models in other areas (e.g., research and development) may examine if substantial changes in perceptions about the importance of that area may similarly trigger revolutionary changes. Additional cases should also examine other causes that may trigger revolutionary changes.

This chapter also makes some potentially important contributions to the literature on strategic IS management by taking a dynamic, holistic, and theory-based view of alignment. Our examination of the changes over time in three cases is an initial step in making the transition from the earlier static view of alignment toward understanding the dynamics of alignment. By examining the cases individually and in comparison to each other in the light of a punctuated equilibrium model, the chapter provides insights into the ways in which alignment may possibly increase or decrease over time. Future research in this area should empirically test these findings, using additional cases as well as multistage surveys.

This chapter also contributes to the strategic IS literature by providing a more holistic view of strategic IS management. The strategic IS management profile included business and IS strategy and structure, unlike prior studies which have focused on only two of the four dimensions, such as business and IS strategy (e.g., Chan *et al.*, 1997) or business and IS structure (e.g., Fiedler *et al.*, 1996).

This study also differs from the prior work on IS alignment in its use of a deductive, theory-based view of alignment. Future studies of alignment in strategic IS management and other areas may benefit from a similar use of prior theory to identify the ideal alignment patterns. This approach, which has rarely been used in IS research (Jarvenpaa and Ives, 1993; Brown and Magill, 1998), is an attractive alternative to the more popular approach of empirically generating the ideal alignment patterns (e.g., Sabherwal and Kirs, 1994) because it allows replication and fosters cumulative research.

In conclusion, the study has attempted to advance our understanding of the dynamics of alignment. It suggests that claims about performance effects of alignment should be couched in explicitly longitudinal terms because the same alignment pattern may not be effective over extended periods. Based on the application of the punctuated equilibrium model to the three cases, the chapter suggests that the changes in alignment are, for the most part, small and evolutionary. These changes may prevent catastrophes by controlling misalignments, but they inhibit moving to an altogether different pattern of alignment. Therefore, managers should periodically scrutinize their organizations' IS alignment patterns, lest these patterns mask symptoms of future failure. Revolutionary changes in the strategic IS management profiles may be necessary to move the organization to a path that offers a greater performance potential, rather than continuing on the previous path by simply fine-tuning strategies and structures. Moreover, managers making revolutionary changes in their 'deep structures' should be prepared to fine-tune them even after (and especially, soon after) the revolution.

Acknowledgments

The authors are grateful to the editor-in-chief, the senior editor, and the two anonymous reviewers at *Organization Science* for their numerous suggestions on earlier drafts of this paper. We also greatly appreciate the valuable suggestions provided by the seminar participants at Florida State University.

Notes

1   Miles and Snow (1978) also described a fourth type of organization (Reactor), but considered it to be one that either lacks a viable strategy or is in transition from one of the three ideal strategies to another. Miles and Snow (1996) excluded Reactors in more recent descriptions of the typology. We therefore excluded Reactors, as was done in most empirical studies using this typology (e.g., Delery and Doty, 1996).

2   Miles *et al.* (1978) identify three broad types of problems (entrepreneurial, engineering, administrative) faced by organizations, and solving the

entrepreneurial problem in their model is equivalent to corporate-level decisions, while solving engineering and administrative problems corresponds to business-level decisions (Beard and Dess, 1981).

3   Nonstrategic IS was considered to have low alignment with all business strategies and structures.

4   This situation did not seem to surface in the cases either.

5   The names of all companies and individuals are disguised to maintain confidentiality.

6   All figures in all three cases are in United States dollars.

7   Similar to most leasing firms, LEASE made its profit by (a) charging an interest rate on its leases above its cost of money; (b) selling equipment returned to it at the end of a lease for more than the customer was credited. If the market price of used equipment tumbled, as was the case with mainframes, it lost money.

8   It included all senior managers who had anything to do with the sales deals.

9   'Black packets' were black vinyl folders containing everything about a lease, which were examined in great detail by a group of representatives from each department.

10   This happened somewhat differently across the business divisions, with the property services division bringing its own IS director on board before the financial services division.

11   For example, instead of using existing external knowledge bases and vendors, oil rigs and drilling platforms were designed and built inhouse, from scratch.

12   Zmud *et al.* (1986) discuss a similar 'federal governance' model of IS management.

13   It now placed greater emphasis on employee development, not only to improve performance but also to help the employees become more marketable.

14   The other people worked in non-IS lines of business. SUBSID worked primarily in IS, but also offered other services, such as financial services, accounting services, and distribution channel management.

References

Beard, D. W., G. G. Dess, 1981. Corporate-level strategy, business-level strategy, and firm performance. *Acad. Management J.* **24**(4) 663–688.

Bergeron, F., C. Buteau, L. Raymond, 1991. Identification of strategic information systems opportunities: Applying and comparing two methodologies. *MIS Quart.* **15**(1) 89–104.

Broadbent, M., P. Weill, 1990. Developing business and information strategy alignment: A study in the banking industry. J. I. DeGross, M. Alavi, H. J.

Oppelland, eds. *Proc. Eleventh International Conference on Inform. Systems*, Copenhagen, Denmark, 293–306.

Brown, C. V., 1997. Examining the emergence of hybrid IS governance solutions: Evidence from a single case site. *Inform. Systems Res.* **8**(1) 69–94.

——, S. L. Magill, 1994. Alignment of the IS functions with the enterprise. *MIS Quart.* **18**(4) 371–403.

——, ——, 1998. Reconceptualizing the context-design issue for the information systems function. *Organ. Sci.* **9**(2) 176–194.

Brown, S. L., K. M. Eisenhardt, 1997. The art of continuous change: Linking complexity theory and time-paced evolution in relentlessly shifting organizations. *Admin. Sci. Quart.* **42** 1–34.

Burns, T., G. M. Stalker, 1961. *The Management of Innovation.* Tavistock, London, U.K.

Camillus, J. C., A. L. Lederer, 1985. Corporate strategy and the design of computerized information systems. *Sloan Management Rev.* **26**(3) 35–42.

Chan, Y. E., S. L. Huff, D. W. Barclay, D. G. Copeland, 1997. Business strategic orientation, information systems strategic orientation, and strategic alignment. *Inform. Systems Res.* **8**(2) 125–150.

Das, S. R., S. A. Zahra, M. E. Warkentin, 1991. Integrating the content and process of strategic MIS planning with competitive strategy. *Decision Sci.* **22**(5) 953–984.

Delery, J., D. H. Doty, 1996. Modes of theorizing in strategic human resource management: Tests of universalistic, contingency, and configurational performance predictors. *Acad. Management J.* **39**(4) 802–835.

Ein-Dor, P., E. Segev, 1982. Organizational computing and MIS structure: Some empirical evidence. *MIS Quart.* **6**(3) 55–68.

Eisenhardt, K. M., 1989. Building theories from case study research. *Acad. Management Rev.* **14**(4) 532–550.

Elderidge, N., S. Gould, 1972. Punctuated equilibria: An alternative to phyletic gradualism. T. J. Schopf, ed. *Models in Paleobiology.* Freeman, Cooper, & Co., San Francisco, CA, 82–115.

Fiedler, K., V. Grover, J. T. C. Teng, 1996. An empirically derived taxonomy of information technology structure and its relationship to organization structure. *J. MIS.* **13**(1) 9–34.

Galliers, R. D., A. R. Sutherland, 1991. Information systems management and strategy formulation: The 'stages of growth' model revisited. *J. Inform. Systems* **1** 89–114.

Gersick, C. J. G., 1991. Revolutionary change theories: A multilevel exploration of the punctuated equilibrium paradigm. *Acad. Management Rev.* **16**(1) 10–36.

Greenwood, R., C. R. Hinings, 1996. Understanding radical organizational change: Bringing together the old and the new institutionalism. *Acad. Management Rev.* **21**(4) 1022–1054.

Gresov, C., 1989. Exploring fit and misfit with multiple contingencies. *Admin. Sci. Quart.* **34** 431–453.

Haveman, H. A., 1992. Between a rock and a hard place: Organizational change and performance under conditions of fundamental environmental transformation. *Admin. Sci. Quart.* **37**(1) 48–75.

Henderson, J. C., N. Venkatraman, 1992. Strategic alignment: A model for organizational transformation through information technology. T. A. Kochan, M. Useem, eds. *Transforming Organizations*. Oxford University Press, New York, 97–116.

Hirschheim, R., M. Earl, D. Feeny, M. Lockett, 1988. An exploration into the management of the information systems function: Key issues and an evolutionary model. C. K. Yuen, G. Davis, eds. *Proc.: Inform. Tech. Management for Productivity and Strategic Advantage*. IFIP TC-8 Open Conference, 4.15–4.38, Singapore.

Jarvenpaa, S. L., B. Ives, 1993. Organizing for global competition: The fit of information technology. *Decision Sci.* **24**(3) 547–580.

Jelinek, M., C. B. Schoonhoven, 1990. *The Innovation Marathon; Lessons from High Technology Firms*. B. Blackwell, Cambridge, MA.

King, W. R., 1978. Strategic planning for management information systems. *MIS Quart.* **2**(1) 27–37.

Lederer, A. L., A. L. Mendelow, 1989. Coordination of information systems plans with business plans. *J. MIS* **6**(2) 5–19.

Miles, R. E., C. C. Snow, 1978. *Organizational Strategy, Structure, and Process*. McGraw-Hill, New York.

———, ———, 1996. *Fit. Failure, and The Hall of Fame: How Companies Succeed or Fail*. The Free Press, New York.

———, ———, A. D. Meyer, H. J. Coleman, Jr., 1978. Organizational strategy, structure, and process. *Acad. Management Rev.* **3**(3) 546–562.

Miller, D., 1992. Environmental fit versus internal fit. *Organ. Sci.* **3**(2) 159–178.

———, 1996. Configurations revisited. *Strategic Management J.* **17**, 505–512.

Nadler, D., M. L. Tushman, 1980. A congruence model for diagnosing organizational behavior. *Resource Book in Macro Organizational Behavior*. Goodyear, Santa Clara, CA. 30–49.

Newman, M., D. Robey, 1992. A social process model of user-analyst relationships. *MIS Quart.* **16**(2) 249–266.

Nolan, R. L., 1979. Managing the crises in data processing. *Harvard Bus. Rev.* **57**(2) 115–126.

Orlikowski, W. J., 1993. CASE tools as organizational change: Investigating incremental and radical changes in systems development. *MIS Quart.* **17**(3) 309–340.

Porra, J., 1996. Colonial systems, information colonies, and punctuated prototyping. Unpublished PhD dissertation, Department of Computer Science, University of Jyvaskyla, Finland.

Rackoff, N., C. Wiseman, W. A. Ulrich, 1985. Information systems for competitive advantage: Implementation of a planning process. *MIS Quart.* **9**(4) 285–294.

Sabherwal, R., W. R. King, 1991. Towards a theory of strategic use of information resources: An inductive approach. *Inform. Management* **20** 191–212.

——, P. Kirs, 1994. The alignment between organizational critical success factors and information technology capability in academic institutions. *Decision Sci.* **25**(2) 301–330.

Sambamurthy, V., R. W. Zmud, 1992. *Managing IT for Success: The Empowering Business Partnership.* Financial Executives Research Foundation, Morristown, NJ.

Sastry, M. A., 1997. Problems and paradoxes in a model of punctuated organizational change. *Admin. Sci. Quart.* **42** 237–245.

Schoonhoven, C. B. 1981. Problems with contingency theory: Testing assumptions hidden within the language of contingency theory. *Admin. Sci. Quart.* **26** 349–377.

——, M. Jelinek, 1990. Dynamic tension in innovative, high technology firms: Managing rapid technological change through organization structure. M. A. Von Glinow, S. A. Mohrman, eds. *Managing Complexity in High Technology Organizations.* Oxford University Press, New York, 95–99.

Segev, E., 1989. A systematic comparative analysis and synthesis of two business-level strategic typologies. *Strategic Management J.* **10** 487–505.

Tavakolian, H., 1989. Linking the information technology structure with organizational competitive strategy: A survey. *MIS Quart.* **13**(3) 309–317.

Tesch, R., 1990. *Qualitative Research: Analysis Type and Software Tools.* The Falmer Press, New York.

Thompson, J. D., 1967. *Organizations in Action.* McGraw-Hill, Chicago, IL.

Tushman, M. L., W. H. Newman, E. Romanelli, 1986. Convergence and upheaval: Managing the unsteady pace of organizational evolution. *California Management Rev.* **29**(1) 29–44.

——, C. A. O'Reilly. 1996. Ambidextrous organizations: Managing evolutionary and revolutionary change. *California Management Rev.* **38**(4) 8–30.

Van de Ven, A. H., R. Drazin, 1985. The concept of fit in contingency theory. B. M. Staw, L. L. Cummings, eds. *Research in Organizational Behavior,* Vol. 7. JAI Press, Greenwood, CT, 333–365.

——, M. S. Poole, 1995. Explaining development and change in organizations. *Acad. Management Rev.* **20**(3) 510–540.

Yin, R. K., 1984. *Case Study Research: Design and Method*. Sage, Beverly Hills, CA.

Zmud, R. W., A. C. Boynton, G. C. Jacobs, 1986. The new information economy: A new perspective for effective information systems management. *Data Base* **18**(1) 17–23.

Questions for discussion

1   The authors of this chapter attempt to address the question of how alignment might evolve over time. How well do they address this issue? And how would you counter the argument that alignment is a lost cause anyway, given that business must continuously evolve and reinvent itself, while its IT architecture has, perforce, to remain relatively constant?

2   'The concept of alignment might be seen as being based on the (false) assumption that there is but one organization with which to align information systems and structures. But there are many, and many interpretations of the same organization(s).' Discuss this statement in the light of the findings presented by the authors of this chapter.

3   Consider organizations with which you are familiar. How has alignment fluctuated over time? Perhaps you might use the 'stages of growth' model(s) outlined in Chapter 2 as part of your analysis. Does alignment grow stronger or weaker at different stages? Does it fluctuate between stages?

4   Consider the different ways in which the authors assessed business strategy, business structure, IS structure and IS strategy. Given the manner in which these issues have been considered elsewhere in this book, what is your view of the robustness of the authors' treatment of each?

12   Strategies in Response to the Potential of Electronic Commerce

Market process reengineering through electronic market systems: opportunities and challenges

H. G. Lee and T. H. Clark

Over the past few years, various electronic market systems have been introduced by market-making firms to improve transaction effectiveness and efficiency within their markets. Although successful implementation of electronic marketplaces may be found in several industries, some systems have failed or their penetration pace is slower than was projected, indicating that significant barriers remain. This chapter analyzes the economic forces and barriers behind electronic market adoptions from the perspective of market process reengineering. Four cases of electronic market adoptions – two successful and two failed – are used for this analysis. Economic benefits are examined by investigating how the market process innovation enabled by information technology (IT) reduces transaction costs and increases market efficiency. Adoption barriers are identified by analyzing transaction risks and resistance resulting from the reengineering. Successful deployment of electronic market systems requires taking into account these barriers along with the economic benefits of adoption. The chapter presents suggestions based on these case studies, which are relevant to the analysis, design, and implementation of electronic market systems by market-making firms.

Introduction

Electronic markets have become increasingly popular alternatives to traditional forms of commerce as the costs of electronic communications decline and as the ability to convey complex information through networks increases.

The role of market-making firms, such as commodity exchanges or livestock auctions, is to reduce the cost of carrying out transactions. These organizations have emerged to facilitate their member traders' transactions and to establish trade rules governing the rights and duties of those carrying out transactions in their facilities.[11,21] Over the past decade, many market-making firms have adopted electronic market systems to increase transaction effectiveness and efficiency within their markets. One characteristic shared by these systems is the decoupling of the logistics (product flows) from the market transactions through on-line trading.

This chapter examines market-making firms' adoptions of electronic commerce by investigating the fundamental economic and social attributes that influence market efficiency and transaction risks. Although electronic marketplaces have been adopted successfully in several industries, the translation of technical possibilities into institutional realities is often slow or ends in failure. There are clearly barriers as well as opportunities. The key questions driving this research are: What are the major economic forces driving electronic market adoptions by market-making firms? What risks or barriers behind electronic market adoptions limit successful implementation? Why do electronic markets often fail, despite economic benefits that are well documented at the time of adoption? What strategies can market-making firms employ to reduce barriers and to avoid adoption failure?

Much has been written in recent years about changes in cooperative strategies and industry structures associated with electronic hierarchies and electronic markets. Malone, Yates and Benjamin suggested that the introduction of electronic commerce would lead to greater use of markets rather than hierarchies as IT reduced transaction costs.[27] Hess and Kemerer tested this electronic market hypothesis using a case study of computerized loan organization systems.[20] Gurbaxani and Whang integrated the transaction-cost argument with an internal agency cost to examine firm boundaries.[16] Many authors have pointed out that firms using electronic commerce often produced new forms of organization, such as networks[35] and value-adding partnerships,[22] instead of simply increasing firms' reliance on markets. Clemons, Reddi and Row argued that, when firms increased outsourcing, they did so with a limited number of long-term trading partners due to increased opportunistic and operational risks.[7,8] Bakos and Brynjolfsson included the concept of noncontractible investments in coordination costs to explain why buying firms limited the number of suppliers.[4,5]

The study of electronic commerce for market-making firms requires a different approach from these previous works. Neither the question of the economic coordination mechanism (hierarchies, networks, or markets) nor the question of firm boundaries (produce or outsource) is relevant. The analysis needs to begin with an understanding of traditional market processes and to investigate how conventional transaction methods are changed as a result of electronic market adoption. This chapter examines the evolution of electronic market systems from a reengineering perspective, which we call market process reengineering (MPR). That is, we view the introduction of the on-line trading system as a strategic move by market-making firms to innovate the transaction process within institutional markets.

The advantage of MPR is that it allows us to analyze both opportunities and barriers associated with electronic market adoptions. On the one hand, economic incentives can be examined by studying how the new transaction process, enabled by IT, improves market efficiency. On the other hand, analysis of resistance to the change can explain failed adoptions. This chapter investigates four cases of electronic market adoptions from various industries: CALM for livestock trading, AUCNET for used-car trading, Information Auctioning for potted plants trading, and CATS for meat trading. All of these systems have been introduced by existing or new market-making firms to bring innovation to traditional market processes. CALM and AUCNET have been successful since the beginning of their services. The other two systems ceased operations after only one or two years. By analyzing both successful and failed cases, we examine the barriers as well as the economic forces behind the adoption of electronic market systems, and develop suggestions and strategies for market-making firms to limit the risks of failure in adopting electronic commerce applications.

Market-making firms and electronic markets

Why organized markets emerge

We consider market-making firms as social institutions in which a large number of commodity exchanges of a specific type regularly take place, facilitated and structured by institutional rules governing the exchange. Market transactions involve contractual agreement and the exchange of property rights; market-making firms provide mechanisms to structure, organize, and legitimate these activities. An example of a market-making firm is an auction market, which involves the use of a specified method, custom, or routine for reaching agreement on a price (note 1). The auction organization offers trading rules that structure the bidding process and trade settlement, in addition to publicity, clerical work, bidding place, storage space, and so on. Thus, market-making firms provide not only places for exchanges but also institutional rules to standardize and legitimate exchanges made within their facilities.[21]

Transaction costs are the costs of obtaining relevant information, of bargaining and making decisions, and of policing and enforcing contracts.[10] They can be reduced if traders complete transactions in markets organized by market-making firms, rather than in fragmented, nonmarket exchange[21] (note 2). The costs of obtaining relevant information are reduced dramatically through the creation of an organized market since market-making firms help publicize prices as well as other relevant information. Regularized access to contacts within the market itself reduces costs by making it easier to find preferable trading counterparts. Bargaining costs can be reduced too as market-making firms help establish procedures and conventions for reaching a bargain, and traders more easily formulate their expectations about what kind of deal they may strike. Furthermore, deals are likely to be carried out more rapidly since the options for transacting with alternative buyers and sellers present in the market are clear to both parties. Policing and enforcement costs can be reduced because market-making firms bring norms of conduct and codes of practice for buyers or sellers. The individual is not alone in ensuring that the contract is carried out because market-making firms regulate all the transaction activities in great detail, such as the responsibilities of parties and the terms of settlements.

Electronic market systems for market-making firms

We differentiate electronic market adoptions by market-making firms from consumer electronic shopping systems over the Internet. The tremendous growth of the Internet, and particularly of the World Wide Web, has dramatically increased the number of new intermediaries such as Web Shop, Internet Mall, IndustryNet, and Internet Shopping Network, which interpose themselves between producers and customers in the industry value chain to take advantage of new types of economies of scale, scope and knowledge enabled by the Internet.[31] These intermediaries allow vendors to advertise their products to millions of prospective consumers, while allowing customers to place orders electronically.[19]

These new electronic intermediaries in cyberspace, however, do not include discovering the market price of goods,[25] although they have potential to influence retail prices by increasing competition among suppliers.[3] They usually employ posted-off pricing,[32] where producers list ask prices and consumers decide how many items to buy at the posted price. In these systems, suppliers are price makers and on-line trading systems help determine quantities traded at relatively fixed prices. This contrasts with market-making firms' electronic market systems, one of whose major functions is to determine the market price of goods. Sellers who join the market institutions (such as farmers in a livestock auction) have fixed quantities for supply without price tags: Sellers are price takers, not price makers, although they have a certain level of reserve prices. Electronic market systems play an important role in determining the market price of goods through either electronic auctions or electronic negotiations.[25]

In addition, buyers who purchase goods in market institutions are not end consumers but typically wholesalers who resell their purchased items to retailers. Since the quality of offered products varies widely (even products from the same producer differ in quality time to time, as in the case of agricultural products such as livestock or cut flowers), descriptions of the product quality are essential to buyers who regularly join the institutions to purchase goods at the wholesale level. In contrast, products sold in electronic shopping systems over the Internet are mostly standardized and mass-produced (products from one supplier are identical). These systems typically target retail consumers who purchase goods based on price tags and brand names.

Finally, traders completing transactions through market-making firms are subject to institutional rules established to reduce transaction uncertainties and to protect member traders against transaction conflicts. Agreement over the governing rules can be facilitated because the members meet frequently and deal in a restricted range of goods. It is possible to enforce the rules because the opportunity to trade on the exchange itself is of great value: withholding permission to trade is a sanction sufficiently severe to ensure compliance for most member traders. When the transaction facilities are scattered and owned by a vast number of people, as in the case of various on-line shopping systems over the Internet, the establishment and administration of a private legal system would be very difficult. Those who operate in these markets therefore have to depend on the legal system at the state level.

It is nevertheless possible for existing or new market-making firms to use the Internet to build electronic market systems. In the past, for example, the Federal Communications Commission (FCC) allocated radio spectra either by lottery or by comparative hearings (note 3). In an attempt to revamp the method of allocating public resources, the FCC implemented an Auction Bidding System (ABS) to sell broadband Personal Communications Service (PCS) licenses to public bidders.[40] Through a high-tech auction designed to maximize revenues quickly, the FCC sold 99 broadband PCS licenses for 51 market regions in 1995 and raised $7.7 billion for the US Treasury. Although the auction was held in Washington, DC, firms throughout the country used the on-line electronic messages to place their bids.[2] Unlike on-line shoppers for retail goods in the Internet, however, participants had to sign an agreement for trading rules that specify every detail of the bidding processes and responsibilities of bidders; anyone who violated the agreement was left out of the market.

Market process reengineering

Decoupling product flow from market transactions

Business process redesign (BPR), also known as reengineering, enables organizational transformation.[13,14,18] Firms embrace a BPR approach when a radical improvement can be achieved by realigning business process with information technology (IT) change. BPR requires a firm to step back from current business processes to consider its overall business objective; only then can it create radical change to realize improvements of any magnitude.[17] Information technology is usually a necessary but insufficient factor in achieving BPR. Successful reengineering is not an IT initiative but, rather, a business initiative, although IT has been described as both a strategic catalyst and an enabler of BPR.[15,34]

Market-making firms in various industries have used the BPR approach to redesign existing processes inside their firms. When goods arrive at the market for sale, a clerk enters information regarding the producer, product type and quantity into the control computer. Once transactions occur, either by face-to-face auction or negotiation, the computer consolidates all purchase information for settlement of accounts and generates transaction reports for buyers and sellers. Thus, IT is already being used to speed up existing transaction processes while reducing labor costs. However, the use of computers for BPR inside market-making firms does not necessarily require changing the market transaction process and associated institutional rules governing these market processes.

Market-making firms have come to understand that the market process can be redesigned using telecommunications as well as computers. In traditional transactions, suppliers had to bring their products to the marketplace and buyers wishing to purchase goods also had to be present at the market in order to inspect the goods and to participate in the bidding process. Goods sold by either auctions or negotiations were handed over to buyers who transported them back to the buyer's location. In the new approach, product flow is separated from the market transactions by connecting the central computer with terminals at member traders' locations using communication networks (Figure 12.1). In this new virtual marketplace, transactions are based on

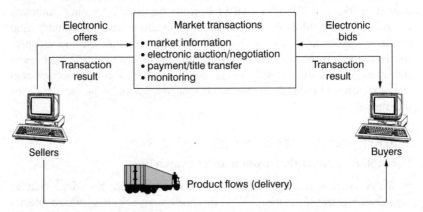

Figure 12.1 *Decoupling of product flows from market transactions*

information and products move from sellers directly to buyers only after on-line transactions are completed.

On-line trading is not automation of traditional market processes, but market process reengineering which brings innovation to the transaction process and to the role of market makers. Suppliers offer their products in electronic forms instead of transporting them to the markets. Buyers place electronic bids in their offices rather than coming to the market. Transactions are executed based upon information seen on computer terminals, with no need for products to be present physically. Goods remain at suppliers' locations and are not shipped until the transaction is completed.

Research framework and methodology

Our research model presumes that market makers adopting electronic market systems would encounter barriers to realizing the expected improvements in market efficiency (Figure 12.2). To implement electronic market systems successfully, adoption barriers must be identified and properly managed, along with implementing systems to improve transaction efficiency and effectiveness. The success of the adoption depends on creating and sustaining the identified economic gains while reducing potential barriers. This chapter identifies economic gains and barriers resulting from electronic market adoptions and examines how firms can manage risks and barriers in the course of market process reengineering.

Increased transaction effectiveness and efficiency

Every market transaction consists of *information gathering, contract formation* and *trade settlement*.[25] Information gathering reflects the process by which traders obtain information on potential trading counterparts that best fit their preferences. Once trading opportunities are discovered, traders move on to contract formation, such as reaching an agreement on transaction prices. If potential trading parties fail to agree on transaction terms, negotiations may have to be repeated with many firms before a contract is finally formulated.

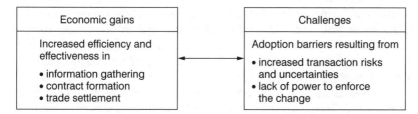

Economic gains	Challenges
Increased efficiency and effectiveness in • information gathering • contract formation • trade settlement	Adoption barriers resulting from • increased transaction risks and uncertainties • lack of power to enforce the change

Figure 12.2 *Opportunities and challenges of electronic market adoptions*

Many market-making firms adopt auction mechanisms to expedite this bargaining procedure and to find the market value of goods promptly. The trade settlement process clears transactions through physical exchange of goods and payment. The economic benefits from electronic market adoptions can be investigated to reveal how IT improves these three transaction processes.

For information gathering, electronic markets typically offer pre-trading and post-trading information that can be accessed by market participants at any time. Traders who could get information regarding available trading partners upon their arrival at the market are now better informed in advance about the prospective trading partners. Furthermore, most electronic market systems provide an electronic bulletin board that displays information on recent transactions, including quantities of products recently sold, product quality characteristics and prices paid by buyers. This post-trading information keeps traders well informed on the market price of goods with specific characteristics of interest to buyers or sellers, thereby facilitating selling and buying decisions. Since traders can obtain this information and execute transactions without coming to markets, they save both time and money.

For contract formation, sellers in open markets often establish reservation prices for exchanges because they do not have perfect information about the consequences of their actions in markets. The reservation price plays a role as sequentially rational rules under incomplete market information.[33] Suppliers who brought their products to traditional markets often had to accept prices lower than their reservation prices. This is common with perishable products or when the transportation costs of bringing the products back home are high. If product flows are separated from the market transactions, sellers can keep their reservation prices relatively firm unless they urgently need cash for their products. Thus, electronic markets can strengthen supplier power in some market environments, resulting in increased average prices for their goods.

Electronic markets can become a national marketplace by eliminating geographical constraints and can broaden the range of choices for buyers. Traditional markets (such as auctions for agricultural products) typically consist of several regional markets scattered around the country. Regional markets are limited in transaction volume since they need to hold inventory until the moment of sale. The transaction depends on the pool of products held or stored in the regional market. Electronic markets allow the pool of product offers to be enlarged without expanding physical infrastructure, such as storage capacity. The establishment of national, as opposed to regional, markets increases the buyers' chances of finding preferred trading parties in terms of prices and product quality.

Electronic markets can also benefit the trade settlement process. Since goods are delivered directly from suppliers to buyers after an on-line transaction, the transportation logistics from suppliers to the markets are eliminated. Often, direct shipping reduces product damage during packaging, loading, and unloading. Furthermore, the use of electronic markets facilitates electronic auditing, which helps firms monitor transactions.

Barriers of electronic market adoptions

For traders used to coming to a market for exchange of goods, the idea of separating logistics from the market transaction through on-line trading is revolutionary. Anything associated with the new transaction method – institutional rules, market structures, management systems, relationships with member traders and technical complexity – must be redesigned to accommodate the change. Many member traders' longstanding policies and traditions may be affected, and innovation leaders often encounter resistance from those who prefer the status quo. Market-making firms that initiate electronic market systems are thus likely to face two types of adoption barriers: (1) *transaction risks* created by the new alternative market form, and (2) *lack of the market power* necessary to enforce the change.

Two important assumptions of human behaviors in transaction-cost analysis are bounded rationality and opportunism, which result in the risks and uncertainties of transactions in open markets[37,38] (note 4). As discussed earlier, one of the primary functions of market-making firms is to reduce transaction risks through institutional rules. However, the adoption of electronic markets is likely to increase transaction risks or uncertainties. For instance, buyers have to make purchasing decisions based on information without physically inspecting products, thus facing the risk of incomplete and distorted information. Sellers may doubt that their goods would be appropriately valued in the unproved market system, particularly when there is a strong possibility that they would suffer from lower prices due to inactive trading at the newly created electronic markets. When market participants perceive these risks or uncertainties involved with the change exceed the benefits expected using the new approach, they will be reluctant to adopt the new transaction process (note 5).

BPR generally requires a top-down approach.[14,18] The inertia of old processes and structures often makes it extremely difficult to introduce radical changes. BPR therefore needs to be initiated by top management, who has the authority to lead the reengineering through the organization. Market process reengineering is also likely to encounter resistance from market participants. The resistance may be nothing more than inertia, but it also stems from a healthy suspicion of new and unproven market systems. Furthermore, parties affected adversely by the change are expected to fight reengineering efforts. Unlike BPR within a firm, however, market-making firms can hardly impose a top-down style of reengineering. Although they can initiate the reengineering process, market-making firms generally lack sufficient power to force adoption. Without the active participation of member traders, the reengineering effort is doomed. The only way for market-making firms to achieve their reengineering objective is to convince their member traders of benefits of the new process.

The next two sections discuss four cases of electronic market adoptions – their economic incentives and adoption barriers, respectively – within our research framework. The data are gathered from interviews as well as secondary sources. Two cases (CALM and AUCNET) were published as successful adoptions in the early 1990s.[6,36] Although our analysis refers to these publications, further data have been gathered by interviews, in particular from the market process reengineering perspective. The analysis for the two failed cases is based on interviews and internal documents from the companies involved in these efforts.

Economic forces of electronic market adoptions

This discussion of four cases focuses on market process reengineering (how electronic markets have brought innovation to traditional market transaction processes) and its resulting economic gains (increased market efficiency). The improvement of transaction effectiveness and efficiency, enabled by electronic market systems, is investigated along the three transaction process dimensions discussed above: information gathering, contract formation and trade settlement. Table 12.1 compares the four cases in terms of trading items, traditional transaction methods, initiating market-making firms, operation period, system throughout, new price discovery methods and their evaluations. The observed values of the electronic market adoptions are summarized in Table 12.2.

CALM for livestock trading in Australia

The pastoral industry remains important to Australia, which is the largest beef exporter in the world and has the largest sheep population of any country. Australia currently has a population of about 26 million cattle, 121 million sheep/lambs and 2.7 million pigs. In 1995, about 10 million cattle, 34 million sheep/lambs and 5 million pigs were traded at US$4.1 billion. The profitability of the pastoral industry depends on effective and efficient trading in livestock. The need to sell many animals several times during their lives increases the importance of effective livestock trading within the pastoral value chain (note 6).

Livestock is traded among local producers; there is also 'farmgate' trading where traveling buyers negotiate contracts with producers on-site. This offers the producer convenience but does not necessarily result in a competitive

Table 12.1 *Four cases*

	CALM	AUCNET	IA	CATS
Traded items	Livestock (cattle, sheep/ lambs, pigs)	Used cars	Potted plants	Fresh meat
Traditional trading method	Saleyard auction (on-site auction)	Auto auction (on-site auction)	Flower auction (on-site auction)	Negotiations/ formula pricing
Market-making firms	Australian Meat and Livestock Corporation	AUCNET Inc.	VBA (the largest flower auction in Holland)	American Meat Exchange
Operation period	July 1987-present	June 1985-present	January 1994-October 1995	June 1981-June 1982
Throughput	2.1 million livestock heads in 1995	232 000 cars listed in 1995	10 percent of transaction for potted plants within VBA	109 transactions during the service
Pricing in electronic markets	Electronic auction	Electronic auction	Dutch auction	Electronic negotiation
Evaluation	Success with growth rate of 20 percent in throughput	Success with growth rate of 26 success in throughput	Failed adoption (ceased operation)	Failed adoption (ceased operation)

price. Thus, for many years, the dominant mechanism for livestock sales has been saleyard trading where farmers can market their products through face-to-face auctions. There are over 100 saleyard auctions throughout Australia. Suppliers are typically local farmers who bring their products to auctions for sale. Buyers are usually meat exporters/processors, wholesalers, meat retailers (supermarket chains), and agencies that purchase the store stock for their client farmers.

In the early 1980s, the Australian Meat and Livestock Corporation (AMLC), an industry statutory authority responsible for marketing livestock in Australia and overseas, initiated a reengineering project for the livestock trading process.[6] The objective was to establish a network for electronic sale

Table 12.2   *Observed economic gains (increased market efficiency)*

	Information gathering	Contract formation	Trade settlement
CALM	Market intelligence service (post-trading information) facilitates traders' selling and buying decisions	Farmers are no longer forced to sell their products at prices lower than reserve prices Buyers have more choices than in regional saleyard auctions	Direct shipping from farmers to buyers reduces transportation costs and damages to products
AUCNET	Auction schedule distributed in advance saves dealers' time involved with bidding Dealers can download the images/data and talk with clients about offered products	Trading volume can be increased without parking spaces at auction sites Buyers enjoy more vehicle choices not available in traditional auto auctions	Unsold vehicles do not have to be brought back to sellers' locations
IA	Pre-trading information enables wholesalers to consult with retailers and to establish a bidding strategy in advance	Growers can keep reserve prices firm Buyers can specify packaging requirements before delivery	Growers' direct delivery to buyers relieves auction of storage and traffic problems
CATS	Traders can browse listed bids/offers to select trading counterparts Summarized information on transaction history helps traders negotiate prices	Nationwide database of bids and offers induces more competitive market prices than formula-based pricing Small firms can bypass brokers for transactions	

of cattle, sheep/lambs, and pigs in order to improve market efficiency and the match between product characteristics and market demands. After a trial system in 1983 in the New England region of Australia, AMLC formed a new division in 1985, Computer Aided Livestock Marketing (CALM), to lead the industry toward electronic market systems. CALM service was commercially launched in July 1987.

CALM is an electronic auction system for buying and selling cattle, sheep/lambs and pigs on the basis of product descriptions, while the stock remain on the farmers' property or feedlot. Buyers can bid electronically from anywhere in Australia. Traders link their workstations to the central computer using Telecom Australia's X.25 packet-switching network. To list a lot on a CALM auction, a vendor arranges for a CALM-accredited assessor to prepare an assessment of his or her lot. The information about products that will be auctioned off is normally released one clear working day ahead of the auction. The electronic auction takes the form of either sequential auction or simultaneous auction.[6] Once sold by CALM, the products are shipped directly to buyers.

CALM has significantly reduced the cost of obtaining market information on livestock trading. CALM market intelligence service, available since mid-1991, comprises a number of components, including statistical reports on CALM transactions, historical trends in CALM sale prices and market commentaries on domestic and overseas market details. During contract formation, CALM has decreased the pressure on the producer to sell at whatever price is being offered at the saleyard because failure to sell incurs effort or cost for returning the stock to their feedlot. CALM listed over 2.1 million livestock in 1995, far more than were offered in any single regional market, thus enabling buyers to purchase products that better fit their preferences. Finally, the livestock does not have to travel to a saleyard in CALM; thus, there is no transportation cost of bringing the stock to the saleyard. This lowers the stress on the animals and reduces handling and the resultant bruising, and so brings higher-quality product to the buyer.

Since CALM service was launched, the number of livestock traded through CALM has increased at a compound annual growth rate of 20 percent. In 1995, CALM sold 234 000 cattle, 1 840 000 sheep/lambs and 82 500 pigs through the electronic auction, with just 252 employees. This transaction accounts for US$109 million (60 percent for cattle, 32 percent for sheep/lambs and 8 percent for pigs). The CALM throughput is expected to grow at over 15 percent per year during the next decade, further penetrating the traditional saleyard auction trading.

AUCNET for used-car trading in Japan

Japanese consumers generally purchase second-hand cars from licensed dealers. A complex web of title registration and regulation makes direct trading of used cars between individuals difficult. Avoiding the risks of hidden defects and securing financial loans also lead Japanese consumers to prefer dealing with reliable and substantial used-car dealers. If a vehicle desired by a consumer is not in their inventory, a used-car dealers typically go to the auctions, rather than rely on their competitors' inventory. In 1995, over 3.6 million used cars worth ¥1482 billion (US$15 billion) were sold through 144 auto auctions in Japan.

In a traditional auto auction, vehicles, buyers and sellers are assembled at auction sites. Traders are typically used-car dealers who either seek vehicles for their clients or wish to sell trade-ins. Cars are brought onto the auction floor one at a time, and buyers bid by holding up their hand. Although cars are inspected prior to the auction by auto mechanics, an estimated 80 to 90 percent of the buyers personally inspect the cars prior to the auction. Thus, the product flow is coupled with the auction process.

AUCNET was introduced in 1986 by an entrepreneurial used-car dealer who realized that computers and advanced communication technology could eliminate an immense amount of time wasted in the search for cars. The AUCNET system is a centralized on-line wholesale market in which cars are sold using video images, character-based data and a standardized inspector rating.[36] Sellers must have their vehicles inspected by AUCNET mechanics, who assess damage and summarize the quality rank in a single number (from 1 to 10). A car sold through AUCNET remains at the seller's location until the transaction is completed. Then, a transport company typically delivers it directly to the buyer. During the electronic auction, sellers and buyers are linked to AUCNET's central host computer via satellite.

AUCNET's advantage over traditional auto auctions is its ability to help dealers gather information. Attending conventional auto auctions is time-consuming. Because there is no precise schedule for when certain cars will be sold, a dealer might spend an entire day at a traditional auction to bid on one or two cars. Since used-car dealers usually are salespeople themselves, they lose sales opportunities while attending traditional auctions. Since the AUCNET auction schedule is distributed in advance, used-car dealers can download the data and images of offered cars through the satellite network and can limit their time spent in the auction process to only the cars they are interested in buying. Dealers can also show the information to customers and include these cars in their bidding list based on clients' requests.

Most traditional auto auctions in Japan are held in metropolitan areas where parking spaces for used-car sales is becoming increasingly sparse and expensive. Traditional auctions therefore are limited in the number of used cars they can accommodate for sales. AUCNET created the largest auto auction without using a single parking space; in 1995, it listed over 230 000 used cars. AUCNET can easily accommodate increasing sales volume, with an expected annual growth rate of 15 percent projected over the next five years. As a result, buyers in AUCNET enjoy greater vehicle choices than are available in regional auto auctions and for this reason are willing to pay higher average prices. Furthermore, used-car sellers in the past had to carry significant transportation costs to move a car to the auction site and back again if it was not sold. About 45 percent of cars brought to the auto auction sites remained unsold. AUCNET eliminated such costs by decoupling the logistics from the market transactions.

With these advantages over traditional auto auctions, AUCNET's through-put has increased at an annual compound growth rate of 26 percent since its initial operation. In 1995, when AUCNET listed over 230 000 used cars, the company recorded an operating profit of ¥1.8 billion (US$18 million) on sales of ¥6.1 billion (US$61 million) with just 136 employees. The membership network among dealers has continued to expand at a rate of about 100 per quarter, reaching 4,150 at the end of 1995.

Information auctioning for potted plant trading in Holland

The florist industry, associated with the cultivation and trading of cut flowers and potted plants, is a major economic sector in the Netherlands. The Dutch flower industry, which has almost an 80 percent share of the world export market, produced over US$3.5 billion transactions in 1995. Auction organizations, which are typically cooperatives of growers and are obliged to sell all their member farmers' products through their auction processes, are key institutions for coordinating global supplies and demands. For example, Bloemenveiling Aalsmeer (VBA), the largest auction market with 43 percent of market share of eleven flower auctions, is a cooperative of about 5,000 growers. Buyers are typically large organizations, such as exporters, whole-salers, and retail chains.

Because cut flowers are perishable goods, fast market transaction and delivery are vital in the supply chain. In traditional flower auctions, cut flowers and potted plants are brought to the market the night before the auction. Upon arrival, products are inspected by the auction's own inspectors (the flower master) and kept in large cooling areas until the moment of auction. The flower master's inspection remarks are recorded in computers so that they can be displayed during the auction. The auction normally starts early in the morning and continues until all the products are sold by Dutch auction rules, where an auctioneer begins by asking a high price and gradually lowers the price until some bidder takes the offer. Cut flowers and potted plants are carried through the auction hall during the auction so that buyers can make purchasing decisions based on what they see. After sale, the lots are driven out and loaded into vans or trucks arranged by buyers. In this way, products auctioned in the morning can be sold the same evening or the next morning at florists and retailers in Europe, North America, and practically any other part of the world.

In January 1994, VBA launched Information Auctioning to reengineer the traditional auction process of potted plants.[23] The sheer scale of individual transactions required large storage spaces and generated substantial traffic to and from the VBA auction house. VBA realized that this traffic would be unmanageable within the decade, given a 10 percent annual growth rate, since the available space for expansion was already nearly exhausted. The objective of Information Auctioning was to separate the logistics of potted plants from the auction process. In Information Auctioning, growers send a sample, rather than the entire quantity available, along with information about the main supply to VBA. Buyers bid for the main supply based on the product sample in auction halls. The main supply remains at growers' locations to be packaged and shipped to the buyer after transactions are completed. Growers, buyers and auctioneers use electronic communications to coordinate all the information exchanged in this process.

Information Auctioning does not completely separate product flow from the market transactions. A sample lot of the offered product must still be sent to the market, and buyers still personally attend the bidding at the auction halls. VBA decided to adopt this approach in order to work as practically as possible within existing transaction conventions. Because it is difficult to describe florist products electronically, VBA feared that buyers might balk at a radical transition to completely on-line trading. VBA assumed that Information Auctioning would serve as a milestone for its long-term reengineering goal of completely separating logistics from market transactions.

Information Auctioning enables buyers to browse the entire database of offered products the day before the auction. This contrasts with traditional auctions, where buyers could get the information of available products only on the day of auction. This pre-trading information is a significant benefit to wholesalers (buyers). The prices of cut flowers and potted plants change significantly day by day depending on supply and demand, often varying up to 20 or 30 percent in sequential trading days. Wholesalers (buyers) can communicate with retailers, based upon this information, to come up with bidding strategies, such as what to buy, how many lots to buy, and how much to pay.

In traditional auction markets, growers have to sell out their perishable products regardless of the market price received. Since Information Auctioning decouples the product flows of the main supply from the market process, a grower can keep their reservation price relatively firm. If no buyer is willing to pay higher than the grower's reserve price, the grower may withdraw the products from the market and offer them again later on, since products are not harvested until sold. In return, buyers benefit because they can specify the packaging requirement for delivery (note 7). Information Auctioning also expected to resolve storage and traffic problems for VBA. Direct delivery of goods from growers to buyers would allow VBA to increase its transaction volume without expanding its physical storage capacity.

Despite all these expected benefits, however, the penetration rate of Information Auctioning was disappointing for the first several months of operation. VBA undertook various rule changes to induce traders to switch to the new transaction method. Even so, Information Auctioning executed only 10 percent of the product sales – much less than the planned goal of 45 percent. VBA officially stopped the Information Auctioning service in September 1995. VBA encountered unexpected resistance and failed to deal with the barriers it faced; these are discussed later.

CATS for meat trading in the United States

Wholesaling is a vital link in the marketing process of the US meat industry. Wholesale trading of fresh meat takes place for a variety of reasons. Because of the perishability of the meat products, the market transactions rely heavily on cooler and holding capacity, which is more easily available in wholesalers. Regulations, such as the late 1920s Consent Decree, prohibit some meat packers from retailing, thus necessitating wholesaling for market transactions. In 1995, over 135 million slaughtered cattle, hogs and sheep were distributed by wholesalers for domestic consumption and export to foreign markets. In 1981, when CATS was introduced, the US meat industry produced more than 39 billion pounds of meat.

In wholesale markets, fresh meat is generally traded either on a negotiated basis or on a formula basis. A negotiated trade is a transaction where delivery, quality, quantity and price are agreed on at one time by a seller and a buyer. A formula-priced transaction differs in that the transaction price is based on prices published by a market reporting service on the day prior to shipping.

Formula pricing, which accounts for 80 percent of all meat trading, has been questioned on the grounds of market price manipulation and adequacy of market information. Formula prices are based on prices that are reported voluntarily, and the reporting mechanism involves personal discretion on the part of the market information services. Thus, large firms could use market reporting services to affect prices in a self-serving manner that may be detrimental to other market participants, including consumers and farm producers. Another problem was the adequacy of market information. A large percentage of negotiated transactions is not reported to market reporting services. It is estimated that sales data on less than 2 percent of US federally inspected slaughter is reported to market reporting services.[30] A considerable portion of the market is insulated from use as a source of price information, further increasing the potential of market price manipulation by large firms.

The Computer Assisted Trading System (CATS), an electronic meat trading system at the wholesale level, was introduced in 1981 by American Meat Exchange (AME) to address concerns about the accuracy and adequacy of market information.[30] AME, one of the three market reporting service companies at that time, thought that the redesign of the meat market process using electronic networks would create desirable conditions for a competitive market and greater pricing efficiency. In CATS, a trader could place bids and offers using terminals connected to the central computer through local telephone or toll-free WATS lines. This order information was then made available to all other eligible traders. Unlike the other three cases discussed here, however, all of which employ auction mechanisms for discovering value of goods, the transaction price in CATS was determined by several rounds of electronic negotiations. The electronic communications between trading parties continued until either a transaction was consummated or a party withdrew from the negotiation.

CATS enabled traders to review selected bids and offers and helped them obtain pre-trading information. It also supplied traders with daily transaction information, a chronological (or otherwise sorted) listing of transactions for each region and a summary of price and quantity information for each item. Price and quantity information was summarized for product and transaction type to facilitate the traders' market analysis.

CATS was expected to resolve the *thin* market problem of formula-based trading by increasing competition among buyers and sellers. Since CATS was capable of connecting many buyers and sellers, and reporting market information to traders regardless of their geographical location or market power, it was expected to *thicken* the market and to provide competitive pricing. In addition, CATS was intended to allow traders to bypass brokers to locate potential trading partners. AME thought that this would encourage relatively small farmers and buyers who relied on brokerage agencies to join the system, and that it would result in more fair and competitive pricing than formula-pricing, which was dominated by a few large firms.

The AME's electronic market adoption, failed, however. AME launched the CATS service in June 1981 and suspended its operation in November of the same year. During this period, 981 bids and 1693 offers were placed and 109 transactions were executed through the CATS. The disappointed AME officially terminated the CATS operation in June 1982. Like Information Auctioning, AME failed to foresee and prepare for certain barriers and resistance to new electronic market adoptions.

Analysis of adoption barriers

Market-making firms initiated the electronic market systems with clear visions of their potential economic benefits. Why, then, did Information

Table 12.3 *Adoption barriers and tactics to overcome them*

	Observed barriers	Tactics to overcome them
CALM	Transaction disputes over misinformation of products Thin market may result in transaction penalties for both farmers and buyers	Establishment of AUS-MEAT for standard product descriptions and on-site product inspection Industry-wide commitment and promotions
AUCNET	Buyers may mistrust electronic description of used cars Retaliation from JUCDA	Standardization of car inspection and rigorous inspection process Antitrust complaints and publicity
IA	Quality uncertainty of offered products Inactive trading may hurt both growers and buyers	Use of sample lots to represent the main supply Various auction rule changes
CATS	Quality uncertainty of offered products Resistance from big wholesalers due to their loss of market price control	Use of NAMP's Meat Buyer Guide without on-site inspection Resolution of trade disputes through bilateral negotiations between buyer and seller

Auctioning and CATS fail, despite tangible benefits comparable to those of CALM and AUCNET? The difference between successful and failed adoptions lies in the management of barriers introduced by the change. We identify three types of adoption barriers that prevent market-making firms from implementing successful electronic market systems. Table 12.3 summarizes observed barriers or uncertainties that result from the establishment of electronic marketplaces in these four cases, together with tactics employed to reduce these barriers by the initiating market-making firms.

Electronic product description

Market process reengineering requires that buyers purchase products from descriptions (information) without physically inspecting them. This creates new uncertainties for buyers since it can magnify information asymmetry (note 8). If the market-making firms fail to ensure that product information properly reflects the original products or if they are not equipped to protect buyers from misinformation, buyers will resist the new system. Product evaluation (inspection) becomes a challenging task when product flows are separated from market transactions. Unlike traditional markets, where all products are brought to a central site and can be easily inspected, initiating market institutions need to decentralize their inspection structures for market process reengineering.

The major concern of CALM developers was that product misinformation in the system might discourage buyers from purchasing livestock based on the information provided. To address this issue, AMLC established the Authority for Uniform Specification of Meat and Livestock (AUS-MEAT) in 1985 to focus on quality standards and provide accurate and consistent descriptions of livestock. CALM requires that all supply lots be inspected by CALM-accredited assessors who describe the quality of livestock using four-level standard measures. CALM's institutional rules also include arbitration procedures that can be used to resolve disputes arising from product misinformation.

Standard car ratings and rigorous inspection processes have been fundamental to the success of AUCNET. Used-car sellers must have their vehicles inspected by AUCNET mechanics. The inspection results are summarized in a single number, between 1 and 10 (10 indicates a new car; 5 or 6 could be resold to the consumer without additional work). For most buyers, this number is the key decision variable when buying a car, even though they may have access to more detailed inspection results. In addition, AUCNET targets relatively high-quality cars in an attempt to further reduce buyers' risks. A car rated lower than 4 cannot be sold on AUCNET. The average price of a car sold on AUCNET is ¥1 280 000 (US$13 000), compared with ¥670 000 (US$7000) for traditional auctions; these numbers indicate that the vehicles sold in AUCNET are relatively late models.

When VBA launched Information Auctioning, it hoped that the use of samples could solve the problem of product description. Most buyers, however, did not trust the samples to represent the entire product supply adequately: samples were always assumed to be the best lots out of the main supply. Without well-standardized product rating and inspection for the main supply, the use of samples increased the risk of information asymmetry.

CATS adopted the National Association of Meat Purveyors (NAMP) Meat Buyer Guide to represent meat products whose qualities vary widely depending on cutting methods and specifications. However, CATS had no instruments to check the reliability of data entered by sellers. Buyers had to assume that the description, entered by suppliers, was a proper representation of the offered products. Furthermore, CATS failed to provide the clearinghouse function, leaving responsibility for resolving trade disputes to individual traders.

Thin market

Traders who take their orders to a new, less active and less liquid market face uncertain execution and liquidity penalty.[9] In the absence of significant order flow, when their orders will be executed is uncertain. In addition, attempts to buy and sell in a thin market may create an imbalance of demand and supply, which may hurt prospective buyers or sellers. If the new system fails to provide a critical mass large enough to induce traders to switch to a new market form, traders will not join the system because of economic penalties of inferior execution (note 9).

CALM was introduced by AMLC, a statutory authority with the power to lead the livestock industry into electronic trading. AMLC started the CALM operation using funds from the industry levy that applied to all animals slaughtered or exported live in Australia. CALM enjoyed industry-wide commitment to its service from the beginning, as well as strong support from the Minister and the Department of Primary Industry and Energy. Its active promotions, such as free insurance for products traded over the CALM, also helped CALM promptly achieve the initial critical mass necessary for the impacts of electronic markets to be felt.

Information Auctioning lagged behind its intended market penetration rate because of the lack of significant order flows. Despite its advantages over traditional auctions, the benefits of shifting trading into this new market form were not strongly felt by participants, partly because there were not enough market counterparts. The thin market resulted in lower prices than those of traditional auctions. As a result, growers had to bear costs to modify packaging to suit the buyers but received no extra compensation for their services. In response, VBA established a price floor (minimum price) to reduce price volatility and auctioned the main supply prior to the sample lots in an attempt to make the new market more active. The change of rules did not make the new market active enough to overcome the thin-market problem, however.

Resistance to change

The inertia resulting from large investments in existing infrastructures and the reluctance of traders to embark on a new round of organizational learning may serve as barriers to successful implementation of electronic marketplaces. The change of the transaction process using computer and communications technology can generate confusion and discomfort to traders if they have limited IT knowledge. Opponents often argue that traditional markets serve as an important socialization venue and thus cannot be replaced by electronic marketplaces. Moreover, firms affected adversely by an electronic market are expected to resist and oppose the system.

As a new market institution, AUCNET faced retaliation from traditional auction markets, which felt threatened by the new system. In the beginning of its service, AUCNET secured about 1000 reservations from used-car dealers. Then, the Japanese Used Car Dealer Association (JUCDA), which ran most traditional auto auctions, announced it was against AUCNET and threatened that members who joined AUCNET would be stripped of their membership in JUCDA. When more than half of the reservations were withdrawn, AUCNET used antitrust complaints and publicity in the press to get the government to prevent JUCDA from blocking AUCNET.

CATS was introduced by AME, a private company that lacked the market power to enforce the change in the meat industry. It began its services without industry-wide commitment. The objective of CATS was to make the market more competitive by reducing the large firms' influence on meat pricing (formula pricing). Large wholesalers, whose participation was critical to its success, were not enthusiastic about the new process. CATS both lacked regulatory power to overcome the large firms' resistance and failed to offer them strong enough incentives to join the system.

Implications for management

The central claim of this chapter is that successful deployment of electronic markets requires consideration of the barriers resulting from market process reengineering along with the projected economic benefits. To blame immature technologies in the early 1980s for the failure of CATS is unreasonable since the IT used by CATS had already been used successfully by the cotton industry in the TELCOT system, which began operation in 1978.[26] Likewise, IT was not a major impediment to Information Auctioning, which was launched more recently and used well-proven technologies. Most risks, uncertainties and barriers stem from social and economic factors, rather than IT-related obstacles. This finding is consistent with many BPR research results:[15,34] IT is a necessary but insufficient factor for reengineering. The success of electronic market adoptions is as dependent on the management of barriers as it is on the economic benefits enabled by the IT. Some cautious suggestions can be made on the basis of the four case studies to assist market-making firms in the analysis, design and implementation of electronic market systems.

Standard product quality rating and inspection

Recent advances in multimedia technology allow more product groups to be traded electronically. Although the use of multimedia representation may help buyers make purchasing decisions, by itself it will not eliminate the product uncertainty encountered by buyers in electronic markets. Before Information

Auctioning, another flower auction market in the Netherlands introduced Video Auctioning, where the physical presence of cut flowers was replaced by pictures displayed on a big screen during the auction process.[23] That system also failed. Similarly, Slide Auction was implemented before the advent of AUCNET by traditional Japanese used-car auctions.[36] The Slide Auction, designed to hold auctions by using 35mm color slides, also ended in failure. None of these failed systems provided adequate product quality specifications and assurances.

There are two features that are crucial for reducing the uncertainties involved in product descriptions in electronic markets: (1) certain standards for product ratings and (2) a trusted party to carry out product inspection. The failures of Information Auctioning, Video Auctioning and Slide Auction were due to the lack of standardized quality ratings. CATS used an industry-wide standard for meat product descriptions but did not employ an inspection procedure to verify the sellers' descriptions. The emphasis on building standard product ratings and rigorous inspection process accounts for much of the success of CALM and AUCNET (note 10).

Quick achievement of critical mass

Participation externality affects the dynamics of the introduction and adoption of electronic market systems.[24,25] The benefits realized by individual participants in an electronic market system increase as more organizations join the system. Without a critical mass of users, an electronic market system is unlikely to spread its usage and may be extinguished. The quick achievement of initial critical mass accounts for much of the success in CALM and AUCNET. Within two years of its operation, CALM listed over 110,000 cattle and 517,000 sheep/lambs, and secured more than 5,000 registered users. AUCNET focused on the participation externality and managed to list over 44,000 vehicles in two years.

CALM was able to accomplish critical mass partly thanks to industry-wide commitment and government support. In the case of AUCNET, the new market institution induced a large number of traders to switch to the electronic marketplace by providing strong incentives to join the system without any support from a third party. With or without government support, the planning of strategies to obtain a critical mass of early adopters is crucial so that participation externalities can make the impact of the new process felt.

Preparation for resistance and retaliation

In view of the inertia of old transaction processes and structures, the strain of implementing a market process reengineering plan can hardly be over-estimated. Since traders need to be aware of the advantages of the new transaction process, education and promotion of the concept, including IT-related technical supports, must be a prominent part of the plan. Opponents of electronic markets often proclaim the disadvantages of electronic market-places compared with traditional markets, since traders cannot capture all the market information on traditional transaction methods.[28] In financial trading, for instance, it is important to know who is bidding, who is offering and who is trading with whom. This information gives a trader some guidance regarding the nature of trading activity and price movements. Thus, initiating firms need to design the electronic market system carefully so that traders can use their terminals to garner as much information as is available (or more) on the traditional trading floor.

Firms that are affected adversely by an electronic market can be expected to fight the system. For instance, AUCNET had to rely on government authority to overcome JUCDA's retaliatory efforts (note 11). Retaliation is more likely when there are many firms whose power is relatively equal or when the affected parties are able to unite against the initiating firm. Without a strategy to deal with potential retaliations, the initiating firm may be caught without an appropriate response and therefore jeopardize its investments.

Conclusion

We expect the adoption of electronic commerce applications by existing or new market makers to grow rapidly as the cost of communicating information between firms decreases. We have investigated here the evolution of electronic market adoption by such market-making firms. The implementation of electronic markets is viewed as market process reengineering aimed at decoupling product flow from market transactions through on-line trading. We have taken a close look at how IT-enabled reengineering increases market efficiency as well as barriers.

Firms interested in redesigning market processes using electronic commerce solutions need to plan carefully to overcome adoption barriers that could cast a shadow over the benefits of the proposed new market processes. By examining the barriers and facilitators of success in the case studies presented, market makers can be better prepared to design electronic markets that increase market efficiency and overcome barriers to adoptions.

Notes

1   Market-making firms can also be established in formats other than the auction. In NASDAQ and the London Stock Exchange, for instance, investors trade with financial intermediaries (dealers) based on dealers' quoted prices. Both NASDAQ and the London Stock Exchange are

governed by detailed trading rules, including responsibility of inter-mediary roles such as affirmative obligations.[12]

2 In transaction cost economics, first suggested by Coase[10] and expanded by Williamson,[37,38,39] transaction costs are used to explain why firms (or hierarchies) emerge. The transaction cost economics suggests that the costs and difficulties associated with market transactions sometimes favor hierarchies (or in-house production) over markets as an economic governance structure. Hodgson[21] employs the transaction cost theory to address the question of why organized markets, or market institutions, are favored against fragmented, less-organized markets, without institutional rules.

3 With open lotteries, nearly 400,000 applications for cellular licenses were received, and the FCC had to bear significant processing costs. Moreover, it required lengthy delays to introduce services since many licenses were resold to other cellular providers. After this lottery fiasco, the FCC used comparative hearings to award cellular licenses in thirty markets, but this took almost two years and millions of dollars spent on lobbying by firms attempting to influence the outcome.

4 In addition to these two behavioral assumptions, Williamson presented three characteristics of transactions – uncertainty, frequency of transactions and asset specificity – to explain the economic governing mechanisms between markets and hierarchies.

5 Our use of the term 'transaction risks' has a narrower, system-oriented focus compared with its use in References 7 and 8, which study transaction risks extensively in the context of interorganizational information systems. In these previous works, transaction risks are those risks accruing from firms' reliance on coordination with independent partners. In contrast, we address the transaction risks that are newly created as a result of the electronic market adoption within market institutions.

6 Livestock is sold either for slaughter or for breeding stock. Products traded in breeding purposes include store stocks for medium-term resale and feedlotting stocks for short-term resale. These stocks may be resold later in the market by different traders.

7 There are three methods for potted plant packaging. In traditional auctions, purchased products may not be packaged in a way preferred by the buyer. Since products are not packaged yet at the moment of the transaction, buyers in Information Auctioning can specify their packaging preferences before delivery.

8 Akerlof[1] presents transactions in second-hand cars as an example of markets with asymmetric information. It would be very costly for a buyer of a second-hand car to determine accurately its true quality. There is certainly no guarantee that the owner of the car would disclose his or her

knowledge about its history and quality during the transaction, particularly if the vehicle is a 'lemon' that the seller is eager to unload.

9   In the financial market literature, this phenomenon is called the 'liquidity trap' or 'central market defense', and represents a crucial economic dynamic for new market designs, including electronic trading systems, because of the importance of the liquidity in financial exchanges.[9,12]

10   Another example is TELCOT, an electronic market system introduced by the Plain Cotton Cooperative Association (PCCA) for cotton trading.[26] In TELCOT, cotton farmers send six-ounce samples of each bale (500-pound cotton package) to the Department of Agriculture, which determines the grades of cotton based on well-standardized measures. The standard attributes assessed by the government enable buyers to purchase cotton before seeing it.

11   The experience of HAM (the Hog Auction Market), an electronic market system for pig trading in Singapore, offers another example of retaliation from affected parties. When HAM was introduced, pig importers who were afraid of being squeezed out of the pig market process by HAM, understandably protested the system by boycott and legal injunction.[29] The government, convinced that HAM would ultimately benefit local consumers, had to resort to regulatory powers to overcome the brokers' court injunction, which would have killed the HAM system.

References

1   Akerlof, G. A. The market for 'lemons': qualitative uncertainty and the market mechanism. *Quarterly Journal of Economics*, 84 (August 1970), 488–500.

2   Anthes, G. H. FCC auction built on client/server: software enables simultaneous bidding. *Computerworld* (3 April 1995), 58.

3   Bakos, J. A strategic analysis of electronic marketplaces. *MIS Quarterly*, 15, 3 (September 1991), 295–310.

4   Bakos, J. and Brynjolfsson, E. From vendors to partners: information technology and incomplete contracts in buyer-seller relationships. *Journal of Organizational Computing*, 3, 3 (1993), 301–328.

5   Bakos, J. and Brynjolfsson, E. Information technology, incentives, and the optimal number of suppliers. *Journal of Management Information Systems*, 10, 2 (Fall 1993), 37–53.

6   Clarke, R. and Jenkins, M. The strategic intent of on-line trading systems: a case study in national livestock marketing. *Journal of Strategic Information Systems*, 2, 1 (March 1993), 57–76.

7   Clemons, E., Reddi, S. P. and Row, M. The impact of information technology on the organization of economic activities: the 'move to the

middle' hypothesis. *Journal of Management Information Systems*, 10, 2 (Fall 1993), 9–35.

8   Clemons, E. and Row, M. Information technology and industrial cooperation: the changing economics of coordination and ownership. *Journal of Management Information Systems*, 9, 2 (Fall 1992), 9–28.

9   Clemons, E. and Weber, B. Evaluating the prospects for alternative electronic securities market. *Proceedings of the 12th International Conference on Information Systems*. New York: 1991, pp. 53–61.

10   Coase, R. H. The nature of the firm. *Economica N. S.*, 4 (1937), 386–405.

11   Coase, R. H. *The Firm, the Market and the Law*. Chicago: University of Chicago Press, 1988.

12   Cohen, K. J., Maier, S. F., Schwartz, R. A. and Whitcomb, D. K. *The Microstructure of Securities Markets*. Englewood Cliffs, NJ: Prentice-Hall, 1986.

13   Davenport, T. H. *Process Innovation*. Boston: Harvard Business School Press, 1993.

14   Davenport, T. H. and Short, J. E. The new industrial engineering: information technology and business process redesign. *Sloan Management Review*, 31, 4, (Summer 1990), 11–27.

15   Davenport, T. H. and Stoddard, D. B. Reengineering: business change of mythic proportions? *MIS Quarterly*, 18, 2 (June 1994), 121–127.

16   Gurbaxani, V. and Whang, S. The impacts of information systems on organizations and markets. *Communications of the ACM*, 34, 1 (January 1991), 59–73.

17   Hammer, M. Reengineering work: don't automate, obliterate. *Harvard Business Review*, 68, 4 (July–August 1990), 104–112.

18   Hammer, M. and Champy, J. *Reengineering the Corporation*. New York: Harper Business, 1993.

19   Hayes, C. Cashing in on the home shopping boom. *Black Enterprise*, 25, 7 (July 1995), 120–133.

20   Hess, C. M. and Kemerer, C. F. Computerized loan organization system: an industry case study of the electronic markets hypothesis. *MIS Quarterly*, 18, 3 (September 1994), 251–274.

21   Hodgson, G. M. *Economics and Institutions*. Philadelphia: University of Pennsylvania Press, 1988.

22   Johnston, R. and Lawrence, P. Beyond vertical integration: the rise of the value-adding partnership. *Harvard Business Review*, 66, 4 (July–August 1988), 94–101.

23   Kambil, A. and van Heck, E. Information technology, competition and market transformations: re-engineering the Dutch flower auctions. Working Paper (Stern no. IS-95-1), Center for Research on Information Systems, New York University, January 1995.

24   Katz, M. L. and Shapiro, C. Network externalities, competition and compatibility. *American Economic Review*, 75 (Spring 1985), 70–83.

25   Lee, H. G. and Clark, T. Impacts of electronic marketplace on transaction cost and market structure. *International Journal of Electronic Commerce*, 1, 1 (1996), 127–149.

26   Lindsey, D., Cheney, P., Kasper, G. and Ives, B. TELCOT: an application of information technology for competitive advantage in the cotton industry. *MIS Quarterly*, 14, 4 (December 1990), 347–357.

27   Malone, T., Yates, J. and Benjamin, R. Electronic markets and electronic hierarchies. *Communications of the ACM*, 30, 6 (June 1987), 484–497.

28   Massimb, M. N. and Phelps, B. D. Electronic trading, market structure and liquidity. *Financial Analysis Journal* (January–February 1994), 39–50.

29   Neo, B. S. The implementation of an electronic market for pig trading in Singapore. *Journal of Strategic Information Systems*, 1, 5 (December 1992), 278–288.

30   Sarhan, M. E. and Nelson, K. E. Evaluation of the pilot test of the computer assisted trading system, CATS, for wholesale meat in the US. Project report of Department of Agricultural Economics, University of Illinois at Urbana-Champaign, 1983.

31   Sarkar, M. B., Bulter, B. and Steinfield, C. Intermediaries and cybermediaries: a continuing role for mediating players in the electronic marketplace. *Journal of Computer-Mediated Communication*, 1, 3 (1996), http://www.usc.edu/dept/annenberg/journal.html.

32   Smith, V. L. and Williams, A. W. Experimental market economics. *Scientific American*, 267 (December 1992), 116–121.

33   Stigler, G. J. Public regulation of the securities markets. *Journal of Business*, 37 (April 1964), 117–134.

34   Stoddard, D. B. and Jarvenpaa, S. L. Business process redesign: tactics for managing radical change. *Journal of Management Information Systems*, 12, 1 (Summer 1995), 81–107.

35   Thorelli, H. B. Networks: between markets and hierarchies. *Strategic Management Journal*, 7 (1986), 37–51.

36   Warbelow, A. and Kokuryo, J. AUCNET: TV Auction Network System. Harvard Business School Case Study, 9–190–001, July 1989.

37   Williamson, O. Transaction-cost economics: the governance of contractual relations. *Journal of Law and Economics*, 22, 2 (October 1979), 233–261.

38   Williamson, O. The economics of organization: the transaction cost approach. *American Journal of Sociology*, 87, 3 (November 1981), 548–577.

39   Williamson, O. *The Economic Institutions of Capitalism*. New York: Free Press, 1985.

40   Young, D. The PCS auction: a post-game wrap-up. *Telecommunications* (July 1995), 21–24.

Questions for discussion

1   Identify other electronics markets that have been successful or unsuccessful and explain why.
2   Figure 12.2 lists two challenges to electronic markets: (a) increased transaction risks and uncertainties, and (b) lack of power to enforce the change. Think of some others. In the case of electronic shopping, what are the major challenges? What are the risks from both the buyer and seller perspective?
3   How can some of the barriers be overcome (such as lack of trust in information, thin markets, and resistance to change), both in the context of electronic markets and electronic shopping?
4   The authors state that 'most risks, uncertainties and barriers stem from social and economic rather than IT-related obstacles'. What are some of the IT-related obstacles?
5   For organizations considering electronic commerce, what are some of the implications from these cases?

13 The Strategic Potential of the Internet

Strategy and the Internet

M. E. Porter

Many have argued that the Internet renders strategy obsolete. In reality, the opposite is true. Because the Internet tends to weaken industry profitability without providing proprietary operational advantages, it is more important than ever for companies to distinguish themselves through strategy. The winners will be those that view the Internet as a complement to, not a cannibal of, traditional ways of competing.

The Internet is an extremely important new technology, and it is no surprise that it has received so much attention from entrepreneurs, executives, investors, and business observers. Caught up in the general fervor, many have assumed that the Internet changes everything, rendering all the old rules about companies and competition obsolete. That may be a natural reaction, but it is a dangerous one. It has led many companies, dot-coms and incumbents alike, to make bad decisions – decisions that have eroded the attractiveness of their industries and undermined their own competitive advantages. Some companies, for example, have used Internet technology to shift the basis of competition away from quality, features, and service and toward price, making it harder for anyone in their industries to turn a profit. Others have forfeited important proprietary advantages by rushing into misguided partnerships and outsourcing relationships. Until recently, the negative effects of these actions have been obscured by distorted signals from the marketplace. Now, however, the consequences are becoming evident.

The time has come to take a clearer view of the Internet. We need to move away from the rhetoric about 'Internet industries,' 'e-business strategies,' and a 'new economy' and see the Internet for what it is: an enabling technology – a powerful set of tools that can be used, wisely or unwisely, in almost any industry and as part of almost any strategy. We need to ask fundamental questions: Who will capture the economic benefits that the Internet creates?

Will all the value end up going to customers, or will companies be able to reap a share of it? What will be the Internet's impact on industry structure? Will it expand or shrink the pool of profits? And what will be its impact on strategy? Will the Internet bolster or erode the ability of companies to gain sustainable advantages over their competitors?

In addressing these questions, much of what we find is unsettling. I believe that the experiences companies have had with the Internet thus far must be largely discounted and that many of the lessons learned must be forgotten. When seen with fresh eyes, it becomes clear that the Internet is not necessarily a blessing. It tends to alter industry structures in ways that dampen overall profitability, and it has a leveling effect on business practices, reducing the ability of any company to establish an operational advantage that can be sustained.

The key question is not whether to deploy Internet technology – companies have no choice if they want to stay competitive – but how to deploy it. Here, there is reason for optimism. Internet technology provides better opportunities for companies to establish distinctive strategic positionings than did previous generations of information technology. Gaining such a competitive advantage does not require a radically new approach to business. It requires building on the proven principles of effective strategy. The Internet *per se* will rarely be a competitive advantage. Many of the companies that succeed will be ones that use the Internet as a complement to traditional ways of competing, not those that set their Internet initiatives apart from their established operations. That is particularly good news for established companies, which are often in the best position to meld Internet and traditional approaches in ways that buttress existing advantages. But dot-coms can also be winners – if they understand the trade-offs between Internet and traditional approaches and can fashion truly distinctive strategies. Far from making strategy less important, as some have argued, the Internet actually makes strategy more essential than ever.

Distorted market signals

Companies that have deployed Internet technology have been confused by distorted market signals, often of their own creation. It is understandable, when confronted with a new business phenomenon, to look to marketplace outcomes for guidance. But in the early stages of the rollout of any important new technology, market signals can be unreliable. New technologies trigger rampant experimentation, by both companies and customers, and the experimentation is often economically unsustainable. As a result, market behavior is distorted and must be interpreted with caution.

That is certainly the case with the Internet. Consider the revenue side of the profit equation in industries in which Internet technology is widely used. Sales figures have been unreliable for three reasons. First, many companies have subsidized the purchase of their products and services in hopes of staking out a position on the Internet and attracting a base of customers. (Governments have also subsidized on-line shopping by exempting it from sales taxes.) Buyers have been able to purchase goods at heavy discounts, or even obtain them for free, rather than pay prices that reflect true costs. When prices are artificially low, unit demand becomes artificially high. Second, many buyers have been drawn to the Internet out of curiosity; they have been willing to conduct transactions on-line even when the benefits have been uncertain or limited. If Amazon.com offers an equal or lower price than a conventional bookstore and free or subsidized shipping, why not try it as an experiment? Sooner or later, though, some customers can be expected to return to more traditional modes of commerce, especially if subsidies end, making any assessment of customer loyalty based on conditions so far suspect. Finally, some 'revenues' from on-line commerce have been received in the form of stock rather than cash. Much of the estimated $450 million in revenues that Amazon has recognized from its corporate partners, for example, has come as stock. The sustainability of such revenue is questionable, and its true value hinges on fluctuations in stock prices.

If revenue is an elusive concept on the Internet, cost is equally fuzzy. Many companies doing business on-line have enjoyed subsidized inputs. Their suppliers, eager to affiliate themselves with and learn from dot-com leaders, have provided products, services, and content at heavily discounted prices. Many content providers, for example, rushed to provide their information to Yahool for next to nothing in hopes of establishing a beachhead on one of the Internet's most visited sites. Some providers have even paid popular portals to distribute their content. Further masking true costs, many suppliers – not to mention employees – have agreed to accept equity, warrants, or stock options from Internet-related companies and ventures in payment for their services or products. Payment in equity does not appear on the income statement, but it is a real cost to shareholders. Such supplier practices have artificially depressed the costs of doing business on the Internet, making it appear more attractive than it really is. Finally, costs have been distorted by the systematic understatement of the need for capital. Company after company touted the low asset intensity of doing business on-line, only to find that inventory, warehouses, and other investments were necessary to provide value to customers.

Signals from the stock market have been even more unreliable. Responding to investor enthusiasm over the Internet's explosive growth, stock valuations became decoupled from business fundamentals. They no longer provided an accurate guide as to whether real economic value was being created. Any company that has made competitive decisions based on influencing near-term share price or responding to investor sentiments has put itself at risk.

Distorted revenues, costs, and share prices have been matched by the unreliability of the financial metrics that companies have adopted. The executives of companies conducting business over the Internet have, conveniently, downplayed traditional measures of profitability and economic value. Instead, they have emphasized expansive definitions of revenue, numbers of customers, or, even more suspect, measures that might someday correlate with revenue, such as numbers of unique users ('reach'), numbers of site visitors, or click-through rates. Creative accounting approaches have also multiplied. Indeed, the Internet has given rise to an array of new performance metrics that have only a loose relationship to economic value, such as pro forma measures of income that remove 'nonrecurring' costs like acquisitions. The dubious connection between reported metrics and actual profitability has served only to amplify the confusing signals about what has been working in the marketplace. The fact that those metrics have been taken seriously by the stock market has muddied the waters even further. For all these reasons, the true financial performance of many Internet-related businesses is even worse than has been stated.

One might argue that the simple proliferation of dot-coms is a sign of the economic value of the Internet. Such a conclusion is premature at best. Dot-coms multiplied so rapidly for one major reason: they were able to raise capital without having to demonstrate viability. Rather than signaling a healthy business environment, the sheer number of dot-coms in many industries often revealed nothing more than the existence of low barriers to entry, always a danger sign.

A return to fundamentals

It is hard to come to any firm understanding of the impact of the Internet on business by looking at the results to date. But two broad conclusions can be drawn. First, many businesses active on the Internet are artificial businesses competing by artificial means and propped up by capital that until recently had been readily available. Second, in periods of transition such as the one we have been going through, it often appears as if there are new rules of competition. But as market forces play out, as they are now, the old rules regain their currency. The creation of true economic value once again becomes the final arbiter of business success.

Economic value for a company is nothing more than the gap between price and cost, and it is reliably measured only by sustained profitability. To generate revenues, reduce expenses, or simply do something useful by deploying Internet technology is not sufficient evidence that value has been created. Nor is a company's current stock price necessarily an indicator of economic value. Shareholder value is a reliable measure of economic value only over the long run.

In thinking about economic value, it is useful to draw a distinction between the uses of the Internet (such as operating digital marketplaces, selling toys, or trading securities) and Internet technologies (such as site-customization tools or real-time communications services), which can be deployed across many uses. Many have pointed to the success of technology providers as evidence of the Internet's economic value. But this thinking is faulty. It is the uses of the Internet that ultimately create economic value. Technology providers can prosper for a time irrespective of whether the uses of the Internet are profitable. In periods of heavy experimentation, even sellers of flawed technologies can thrive. But unless the uses generate sustainable revenues or savings in excess of their cost of deployment, the opportunity for technology providers will shrivel as companies realize that further investment is economically unsound.

So how can the Internet be used to create economic value? To find the answer, we need to look beyond the immediate market signals to the two fundamental factors that determine profitability:

- *industry structure*, which determines the profitability of the average competitor; and
- *sustainable competitive advantage*, which allows a company to outperform the average competitor.

These two underlying drivers of profitability are universal; they transcend any technology or type of business. At the same time, they vary widely by industry and company. The broad, supra-industry classifications so common in Internet parlance, such as business-to-consumer (or 'B2C') and business-to-business (or 'B2B') prove meaningless with respect to profitability. Potential profitability can be understood only by looking at individual industries and individual companies.

The Internet and industry structure

The Internet has created some new industries, such as on-line auctions and digital marketplaces. However, its greatest impact has been to enable the reconfiguration of existing industries that had been constrained by high costs for communicating, gathering information, or accomplishing transactions. Distance learning, for example, has existed for decades, with about one million students enrolling in correspondence courses every year. The Internet has the potential to greatly expand distance learning, but it did not create the industry. Similarly, the Internet provides an efficient means to order products, but catalog retailers with toll-free numbers and automated fulfillment centers have been around for decades. The Internet only changes the front end of the process.

Whether an industry is new or old, its structural attractiveness is determined by five underlying forces of competition: the intensity of rivalry among existing competitors, the barriers to entry for new competitors, the threat of substitute products or services, the bargaining power of suppliers, and the bargaining power of buyers. In combination, these forces determine how the economic value created by any product, service, technology, or way of competing is divided between, on the one hand, companies in an industry and, on the other, customers, suppliers, distributors, substitutes, and potential new entrants. Although some have argued that today's rapid pace of technological change makes industry analysis less valuable, the opposite is true. Analyzing the forces illuminates an industry's fundamental attractiveness, exposes the underlying drivers of average industry profitability, and provides insight into how profitability will evolve in the future. The five competitive forces still determine profitability even if suppliers, channels, substitutes, or competitors change.

Because the strength of each of the five forces varies considerably from industry to industry, it would be a mistake to draw general conclusions about the impact of the Internet on long-term industry profitability; each industry is affected in different ways. Nevertheless, an examination of a wide range of industries in which the Internet is playing a role reveals some clear trends, as summarized in the exhibit 'How the Internet Influences Industry Structure.' Some of the trends are positive. For example, the Internet tends to dampen the bargaining power of channels by providing companies with new, more direct avenues to customers. The Internet can also boost an industry's efficiency in various ways, expanding the overall size of the market by improving its position relative to traditional substitutes.

But most of the trends are negative. Internet technology provides buyers with easier access to information about products and suppliers, thus bolstering buyer bargaining power. The Internet mitigates the need for such things as an established sales force or access to existing channels, reducing barriers to entry. By enabling new approaches to meeting needs and performing functions, it creates new substitutes. Because it is an open system, companies have more difficulty maintaining proprietary offerings, thus intensifying the rivalry among competitors. The use of the Internet also tends to expand the geographic market, bringing many more companies into competition with one another. And Internet technologies tend to reduce variable costs and tilt cost structures toward fixed cost, creating significantly greater pressure for companies to engage in destructive price competition.

While deploying the Internet can expand the market, then, doing so often comes at the expense of average profitability. The great paradox of the Internet is that its very benefits – making information widely available; reducing the difficulty of purchasing, marketing, and distribution allowing buyers and sellers to find and transact business with one another more easily – also make it more difficult for companies to capture those benefits as profits.

We can see this dynamic at work in automobile retailing. The Internet allows customers to gather extensive information about products easily, from detailed specifications and repair records to wholesale prices for new cars and average values for used cars. Customers can also choose among many more options from which to buy, not just local dealers but also various types of Internet retail networks (such as Autoweb and AutoVantage) and on-line direct dealers (such as Autobytel.com, AutoNation and CarsDirect.com). Because the Internet reduces the importance of location, at least for the initial sale, it widens the geographic market from local to regions to national. Virtually every dealer or dealer group becomes a potential competitor in the market. It is more difficult, moreover, for on-line dealers to differentiate themselves as they lack potential points of distinction such as showrooms, personal selling, and service departments with more competitors selling largely undiffer-entiated products, the basis for competition shifts ever more toward price. Clearly, the net effect on the industry's structure is negative.

That does not mean that every industry in which Internet technology is being applied will be unattractive. For a contrasting example, look at Internet auctions. Here, customers and suppliers are fragmented and thus have little power. Substitutes, such as classified ads and flea markets, have less reach and are less convenient to use. And though the barriers to entry are relatively modest, companies can build economies of scale, both in infrastructure and, even more important, in the aggregation of many buyers and sellers, that deter new competitors or place them at a disadvantage. Finally, rivalry in this industry has been defined, largely by eBay, the dominant competitor, in terms of providing an easy-to-use marketplace in which revenue comes from listing and sales fees, while customers pay the cost of shipping. When Amazon and other rivals entered the business, offering free auctions, eBay maintained its prices and pursued other ways to attract and retain customers. As a result, the destructive price competition characteristic of other on-line businesses has been avoided.

EBay's role in the auction business provides an important lesson: industry structure is not fixed but rather is shaped to a considerable degree by the choices made by competitors. EBay has acted in ways that strengthen the profitability of its industry. In stark contrast, Buy.com, a prominent Internet retailer, acted in ways that undermined its *industry*, not to mention its own potential for competitive advantage. Buy.com achieved $100 million in sales faster than any company in history, but it did so by defining competition solely on price. It sold products not only below full cost but at or below cost of goods sold, with the vain hope that it would make money in other ways. The company had no plan for being the low-cost provider; instead, it invested

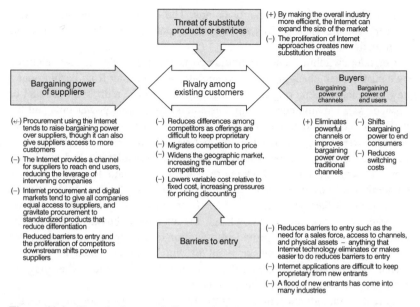

Figure 13.1 *How the Internet influences industry structure*

heavily in brand advertising and eschewed potential sources of differentiation by out-sourcing all fulfillment and offering the bare minimum of customer service. It also gave up the opportunity to set itself apart from competitors by choosing not to focus on selling particular goods; it moved quickly beyond electronics, its initial category, into numerous other product categories in which it had no unique offering. Although the company has been trying desperately to reposition itself, its early moves have proven extremely difficult to reverse.

The myth of the first mover

Given the negative implications of the Internet for profitability, why was there such optimism, even euphoria, surrounding its adoption? One reason is that everyone tended to focus on what the Internet could do and how quickly its use was expanding rather than on how it was affecting industry structure. But the optimism can also be traced to a widespread belief that the Internet would unleash forces that would enhance industry profitability. Most notable was the general assumption that the deployment of the Internet would increase switching costs and create strong network effects, which would provide first movers with competitive advantages and robust profitability. First movers would reinforce these advantages by quickly establishing strong new-economy brands. The result would be an attractive industry for the victors. This thinking does not, however, hold up to close examination.

Consider switching costs. Switching costs encompass all the costs incurred by a customer in changing to a new supplier – everything from hashing out a new contract to reentering data to learning how to use a different product or service. As switching costs go up, customers' bargaining power falls and the barriers to entry into an industry rise. While switching costs are nothing new, some observers argued that the Internet would raise them substantially. A buyer would grow familiar with one company's user interface and would not want to bear the cost of finding, registering with, and learning to use a competitor's site, or, in the case of industrial customers, integrating a competitor's systems with its own. Moreover, since Internet commerce allows a company to accumulate knowledge of customers' buying behavior, the company would be able to provide more tailored offerings, better service, and greater purchasing convenience – all of which buyers would be loath to forfeit. When people talk about the 'stickiness' of Web sites, what they are often talking about is high switching costs.

In reality, though, switching costs are likely to be lower, not higher, on the Internet than they are for traditional ways of doing business, including approaches using earlier generations of information systems such as EDI. On the Internet, buyers can often switch suppliers with just a few mouse clicks, and new Web technologies are systematically reducing switching costs even further. For example, companies like PayPal provide settlement services or Internet currency – so-called e-wallets – that enable customers to shop at different sites without having to enter personal information and credit card numbers. Content-consolidation tools such as OnePage allow users to avoid having to go back to sites over and over to retrieve information by enabling them to build customized Web pages that draw needed information dynamically from many sites. And the widespread adoption of XML standards will free companies from the need to reconfigure proprietary ordering systems and to create new procurement and logistical protocols when changing suppliers.

What about network effects, through which products or services become more valuable as more customers use them? A number of important Internet applications display network effects, including e-mail, instant messaging, auctions, and on-line message boards or chat rooms. Where such effects are significant, they can create demand-side economies of scale and raise barriers to entry. This, it has been widely argued, sets off a winner-take-all competition, leading to the eventual dominance of one or two companies.

But it is not enough for network effects to be present; to provide barriers to entry they also have to be proprietary to one company. The openness of the Internet, with its common standards and protocols and its ease of navigation, makes it difficult for a single company to capture the benefits of a network effect. (America Online, which has managed to maintain borders around its on-line community, is an exception, not the rule.) And even if a company is lucky enough to control a network effect, the effect often reaches a point of diminishing returns once there is a critical mass of customers. Moreover, network effects are subject to a self-limiting mechanism. A particular product or service first attracts the customers whose needs it best meets. As penetration grows, however, it will tend to become less effective in meeting the needs of the remaining customers in the market, providing an opening for competitors with different offerings. Finally, creating a network effect requires a large investment that may offset future benefits. The network effect is, in many respects, akin to the experience curve, which was also supposed to lead to market-share dominance – through cost advantages, in that case. The experience curve was an oversimplification, and the single-minded pursuit of experience curve advantages proved disastrous in many industries.

Internet brands have also proven difficult to build, perhaps because the lack of physical presence and direct human contact makes virtual businesses less tangible to customers than traditional businesses. Despite huge outlays on advertising, product discounts, and purchasing incentives, most dot-com brands have not approached the power of established brands, achieving only a modest impact on loyalty and barriers to entry.

Another myth that has generated unfounded enthusiasm for the Internet is that partnering is a win–win means to improve industry economics. While partnering is a well-established strategy, the use of Internet technology has made it much more widespread. Partnering takes two forms. The first involves complements: products that are used in tandem with another industry's product. Computer software, for example, is a complement to computer hardware. In Internet commerce, complements have proliferated as companies have sought to offer broader arrays of products, services, and information. Partnering to assemble complements, often with companies who are also competitors, has been seen as a way to speed industry growth and move away from narrow-minded, destructive competition.

But this approach reveals an incomplete understanding of the role of complements in competition. Complements are frequently important to an industry's growth – spreadsheet applications, for example, accelerated the expansion of the personal computer industry – but they have no direct relationship to industry profitability. While a close substitute reduces potential profitability, for example, a close complement can exert either a positive or a negative influence. Complements affect industry profitability indirectly through their influence on the five competitive forces. If a complement raises switching costs for the combined product offering, it can raise profitability. But if a complement works to standardize the industry's product offering, as Microsoft's operating system has done in personal computers, it will increase rivalry and depress profitability.

With the Internet, widespread partnering with producers of complements is just as likely to exacerbate an industry's structural problems as mitigate them. As partnerships proliferate, companies tend to become more alike, which heats up rivalry. Instead of focusing on their own strategic goals, moreover, companies are forced to balance the many potentially conflicting objectives of their partners while also educating them about the business. Rivalry often becomes more unstable, and since producers of complements can be potential competitors, the threat of entry increases.

Another common form of partnering is outsourcing. Internet technologies have made it easier for companies to coordinate with their suppliers, giving widespread currency to the notion of the 'virtual enterprise' – a business created largely out of purchased products, components, and services. While extensive outsourcing can reduce near-term costs and improve flexibility, it has a dark side when it comes to industry structure. As competitors turn to the same vendors, purchased inputs become more homogeneous, eroding company distinctiveness and increasing price competition. Outsourcing also usually lowers barriers to entry because a new entrant need only assemble purchased inputs rather than build its own capabilities. In addition, companies lose control over important elements of their business, and crucial experience in components, assembly, or services shifts to suppliers, enhancing their power in the long run.

The future of Internet competition

While each industry will evolve in unique ways, an examination of the forces influencing industry structure indicates that the deployment of Internet technology will likely continue to put pressure on the profitability of many industries. Consider the intensity of competition, for example. Many dot-coms are going out of business, which would seem to indicate that consolidation will take place and rivalry will be reduced. But while some consolidation among new players is inevitable, many established companies are now more familiar with Internet technology and are rapidly deploying on-line applications. With a combination of new and old companies and generally lower entry barriers, most industries will likely end up with a net increase in the number of competitors and fiercer rivalry than before the advent of the Internet.

The power of customers will also tend to rise. As buyers' initial curiosity with the Web wanes and subsidies end, companies offering products or services on-line will be forced to demonstrate that they provide real benefits. Already, customers appear to be losing interest in services like Priceline.com's reverse auctions because the savings they provide are often outweighed by the hassles involved. As customers become more familiar with the technology, their loyalty to their initial suppliers will also decline; they will realize that the cost of switching is low.

A similar shift will affect advertising-based strategies. Even now, advertisers are becoming more discriminating, and the rate of growth of Web advertising is slowing. Advertisers can be expected to continue to exercise their bargaining power to push down rates significantly, aided and abetted by new brokers of Internet advertising.

Not all the news is bad. Some technological advances will provide opportunities to enhance profitability. Improvements in streaming video and greater availability of low-cost bandwidth, for example, will make it easier for customer service representatives, or other company personnel, to speak directly to customers through their computers. Internet sellers will be able to better differentiate themselves and shift buyers' focus away from price. And services such as automatic bill paying by banks may modestly boost switching costs. In general, however, new Internet technologies will continue to erode profitability by shifting power to customers.

To understand the importance of thinking through the longer-term structural consequences of the Internet, consider the business of digital marketplaces. Such marketplaces automate corporate procurement by linking many buyers and suppliers electronically. The benefits to buyers include low transaction costs, easier access to price and product information, convenient purchase of associated services, and, sometimes, the ability to pool volume. The benefits to suppliers include lower selling costs, lower transaction costs, access to wider markets, and the avoidance of powerful channels.

From an industry structure standpoint, the attractiveness of digital marketplaces varies depending on the products involved. The most important determinant of a marketplace's profit potential is the intrinsic power of the buyers and sellers in the particular product area. If either side is concentrated or possesses differentiated products, it will gain bargaining power over the marketplace and capture most of the value generated. If buyers and sellers are fragmented, however, their bargaining power will be weak, and the marketplace will have a much better chance of being profitable. Another important determinant of industry structure is the threat of substitution. If it is relatively easy for buyers and sellers to transact business directly with one another, or to set up their own dedicated markets, independent marketplaces will be unlikely to sustain high levels of profit. Finally, the ability to create barriers to entry is critical. Today, with dozens of marketplaces competing in some industries and with buyers and sellers dividing their purchases or operating their own markets to prevent any one marketplace from gaining power, it is clear that modest entry barriers are a real challenge to profitability.

Competition among digital marketplaces is in transition, and industry structure is evolving. Much of the economic value created by marketplaces derives from the standards they establish, both in the underlying technology platform and in the protocols for connecting and exchanging information. But once these standards are put in place, the added value of the marketplace may be limited. Anything buyers or suppliers provide to a marketplace, such as information on order specifications or inventory availability, can be readily provided on their own proprietary sites. Suppliers and customers can begin to deal directly on-line without the need for an intermediary. And new technologies will undoubtedly make it easier for parties to search for and exchange goods and information with one another.

In some product areas, marketplaces should enjoy ongoing advantages and attractive profitability. In fragmented industries such as real estate and furniture, for example, they could prosper. And new kinds of value-added services may arise that only an independent marketplace could provide. But in many product areas, marketplaces may be superseded by direct dealing or by the unbundling of purchasing, information, financing, and logistical services; in other areas, they may be taken over by participants or industry associations as cost centers. In such cases, marketplaces will provide a valuable 'public good' to participants but will not themselves be likely to reap any enduring benefits. Over the long haul, moreover, we may well see many buyers back away from open marketplaces. They may once again focus on building close, proprietary relationships with fewer suppliers, using Internet technologies to gain efficiency improvements in various aspects of those relationships.

The Internet and competitive advantage

If average profitability is under pressure in many industries influenced by the Internet, it becomes all the more important for individual companies to set themselves apart from the pack – to be more profitable than the average performer. The only way to do so is by achieving a sustainable competitive advantage – by operating at a lower cost, by commanding a premium price, or by doing both. Cost and price advantages can be achieved in two ways. One is operational effectiveness – doing the same things your competitors do but doing them better. Operational effectiveness advantages can take myriad forms, including better technologies, superior inputs, better-trained people, or a more effective management structure. The other way to achieve advantage is strategic positioning – doing things differently from competitors, in a way that delivers a unique type of value to customers. This can mean offering a different set of features, a different array of services, or different logistical arrangements. The Internet affects operational effectiveness and strategic positioning in very different ways. It makes it harder for companies to sustain operational advantages, but it opens new opportunities for achieving or strengthening a distinctive strategic positioning.

Operational effectiveness

The Internet is arguably the most powerful tool available today for enhancing operational effectiveness. By easing and speeding the exchange of real-time information, it enables improvements throughout the entire value chain, across almost every company and industry. And because it is an open platform with common standards, companies can often tap into its benefits with much less investment than was required to capitalize on past generations of information technology.

But simply improving operational effectiveness does not provide a competitive advantage. Companies only gain advantages if they are able to achieve and sustain higher levels of operational effectiveness than competitors. That is an exceedingly difficult proposition even in the best of circumstances. Once a company establishes a new best practice, its rivals tend to copy it quickly. Best practice competition eventually leads to competitive convergence, with many companies doing the same things in the same ways. Customers end up making decisions based on price, undermining industry profitability.

The nature of Internet applications makes it more difficult to sustain operational advantages than ever. In previous generations of information technology, application development was often complex, arduous, time consuming, and hugely expensive. These traits made it harder to gain an IT advantage, but they also made it difficult for competitors to imitate information systems. The openness of the Internet, combined with advances in software architecture, development tools, and modularity, makes it much easier for companies to design and implement applications. The drugstore chain CVS, for example, was able to roll out a complex Internet-based procurement application in just 60 days. As the fixed costs of developing systems decline, the barriers to imitation fall as well.

Today, nearly every company is developing similar types of Internet applications, often drawing on generic packages offered by third-party developers. The resulting improvements in operational effectiveness will be broadly shared, as companies converge on the same applications with the same benefits. Very rarely will individual companies be able to gain durable advantages from the deployment of 'best-of-breed' applications.

Strategic positioning

As it becomes harder to sustain operational advantages, strategic positioning becomes all the more important. If a company cannot be more operationally effective than its rivals, the only way to generate higher levels of economic value is to gain a cost advantage or price premium by competing in a distinctive way. Ironically, companies today define competition involving the Internet almost entirely in terms of operational effectiveness. Believing that

The six principles of strategic positioning

To establish and maintain a distinctive strategic positioning, a company needs to follow six fundamental principles.

First, it must start with the *right goal*: superior long-term return on investment. Only by grounding strategy in sustained profitability will real economic value be generated. Economic value is created when customers are willing to pay a price for a product or service that exceeds the cost of producing it. When goals are defined in terms of volume or market share leadership, with profits assumed to follow, poor strategies often result. The same is true when strategies are set to respond to the perceived desires of investors.

Second, a company's strategy must enable it to deliver a *value proposition*, or set of benefits, different from those that competitors offer. Strategy, then, is neither a quest for the universally best way of competing nor an effort to be all things to every customer. It defines a way of competing that delivers unique value in a particular set of uses or for a particular set of customers.

Third, strategy needs to be reflected in a *distinctive value chain*. To establish a sustainable competitive advantage, a company must perform different activities than rivals or perform similar activities in different ways. A company must configure the way it conducts manufacturing, logistics, service delivery, marketing, human resource management, and so on differently from rivals and tailored to its unique value proposition. If a company focuses on adopting best practices, it will end up performing most activities similarly to competitors, making it hard to gain an advantage.

Fourth, robust strategies involve *trade-offs*. A company must abandon or forgo some product features, services, or activities in order to be unique at others. Such trade-offs, in the product and in the value chain, are what make a company truly distinctive. When improvements in the product or in the value chain do not require trade-offs, they often become new best practices that are imitated because competitors can do so with no sacrifice to their existing ways of competing. Trying to be all things to all customers almost guarantees that a company will lack any advantage.

Fifth, strategy defines how all the elements of what a company does *fit* together. A strategy involves making choices throughout the value chain that are interdependent; all a company's activities must be mutually reinforcing. A company's product design, for example, should reinforce its approach to the manufacturing process, and both should leverage the way it conducts after-sales service. Fit not only increases competitive advantage but also makes a strategy harder to imitate. Rivals can copy one activity or product feature fairly easily, but will have much more difficulty duplicating a whole system of competing. Without fit, discrete improvements in manufacturing, marketing, or distribution are quickly matched.

Finally, strategy involves *continuity* of direction. A company must define a distinctive value proposition that it will stand for, even if that means forgoing certain opportunities. Without continuity of direction, it is difficult for companies to develop unique skills and assets or build strong reputations with customers. Frequent corporate 'reinvention,' then, is usually a sign of poor strategic thinking and a route to mediocrity. Continuous improvement is a necessity, but it must always be guided by a strategic direction.

For a fuller description, see M. E. Porter, 'What is Strategy?' (*Harvard Business Review*, November–December 1996).

no sustainable advantages exist, they seek speed and agility, hoping to stay one step ahead of the competition. Of course, such an approach to competition becomes a self-fulfilling prophecy. Without a distinctive strategic direction, speed and flexibility lead nowhere. Either no unique competitive advantages are created, or improvements are generic and cannot be sustained.

Having a strategy is a matter of discipline. It requires a strong focus on profitability rather than just growth, an ability to define a unique value proposition, and a willingness to make tough trade-offs in choosing what not to do. A company must stay the course, even during times of upheaval, while constantly improving and extending its distinctive positioning. Strategy goes far beyond the pursuit of best practices. It involves the configuration of a tailored value chain – the series of activities required to produce and deliver a product or service – that enables a company to offer unique value. To be defensible, moreover, the value chain must be highly integrated. When a company's activities fit together as a self-reinforcing system, any competitor wishing to imitate a strategy must replicate the whole system rather than copy just one or two discrete product features or ways of performing particular activities. (See the sidebar 'The six principles of strategic positioning.')

The absence of strategy

Many of the pioneers of Internet business, both dot-coms and established companies, have competed in ways that violate nearly every precept of good strategy. Rather than focus on profits, they have sought to maximize revenue and market share at all costs, pursuing customers indiscriminately through discounting, giveaways, promotions, channel incentives, and heavy advertising. Rather than concentrate on delivering real value that earns an attractive price from customers, they have pursued indirect revenues from sources such as advertising and click-through fees from Internet commerce partners. Rather than make trade-offs, they have rushed to offer every conceivable product, service, or type of information. Rather than tailor the value chain in a unique way, they have aped the activities of rivals. Rather than build and maintain control over proprietary assets and marketing channels, they have entered into a rash of partnerships and outsourcing relationships, further eroding their own distinctiveness. While it is true that some companies have avoided these mistakes, they are exceptions to the rule.

By ignoring strategy, many companies have undermined the structure of their industries, hastened competitive convergence, and reduced the likelihood that they or anyone else will gain a competitive advantage. A destructive, zero-sum form of competition has been set in motion that confuses the acquisition of customers with the building of profitability. Worse yet, price has been defined as the primary if not the sole competitive variable. Instead of emphasizing the Internet's ability to support convenience, service, specialization, customization, and other forms of value that justify attractive prices, companies have turned competition into a race to the bottom. Once competition is defined this way, it is very difficult to turn back. (See the sidebar 'Words for the unwise: the Internet's destructive lexicon.')

Even well-established, well-run companies have been thrown off track by the Internet. Forgetting what they stand for or what makes them unique, they have rushed to implement hot Internet applications and copy the offerings of dot-coms. Industry leaders have compromised their existing competitive advantages by entering market segments to which they bring little that is distinctive. Merrill Lynch's move to imitate the low-cost on-line offerings of its trading rivals, for example, risks undermining its most precious advantage – its skilled brokers. And many established companies, reacting to misguided investor enthusiasm, have hastily cobbled together Internet units in a mostly futile effort to boost their value in the stock market.

It did not have to be this way – and it does not have to be in the future. When it comes to reinforcing a distinctive strategy, tailoring activities, and enhancing fit, the Internet actually provides a better technological platform than previous generations of IT. Indeed, IT worked against strategy in the past. Packaged software applications were hard to customize, and companies were often forced to change the way they conducted activities in order to conform to the 'best practices' embedded in the software. It was also extremely difficult to connect discrete applications to one another. Enterprise resource planning (ERP) systems linked activities, but again companies were forced to adapt their ways of doing things to the software. As a result, IT has been a force for standardizing activities and speeding competitive convergence.

Internet architecture, together with other improvements in software architecture and development tools, has turned IT into a far more powerful tool for strategy. It is much easier to customize packaged Internet applications to a company's unique strategic positioning. By providing a common IT delivery platform across the value chain, Internet architecture and standards also make it possible to build truly integrated and customized systems that reinforce the fit among activities. (See the sidebar 'The Internet and the value chain.')

To gain these advantages, however, companies need to stop their rush to adopt generic, 'out of the box' packaged applications and instead tailor their deployment of Internet technology to their particular strategies. Although it remains more difficult to customize packaged applications, the very difficulty of the task contributes to the sustainability of the resulting competitive advantage.

The Internet as complement

To capitalize on the Internet's strategic potential, executives and entrepreneurs alike will need to change their points of view. It has been widely assumed that

---

Words for the unwise: the Internet's destructive lexicon

The misguided approach to competition that characterizes business on the Internet has even been embedded in the language used to discuss it. Instead of talking in terms of strategy and competitive advantage, dot-coms and other Internet players talk about 'business models.' This seemingly innocuous shift in terminology speaks volumes. The definition of a business model is murky at best. Most often, it seems to refer to a loose conception of how a company does business and generates revenue. Yet simply having a business model is an exceedingly low bar to set for building a company. Generating revenue is a far cry from creating economic value, and no business model can be evaluated independently of industry structure. The business model approach to management becomes an invitation for faulty thinking and self-delusion.

Other words in the Internet lexicon also have unfortunate consequences. The terms 'e-business' and 'e-strategy' have been particularly problematic. By encouraging managers to view their Internet operations in isolation from the rest of the business, they can lead to simplistic approaches to competing using the Internet and increase the pressure for competitive imitation. Established companies fail to integrate the Internet into their proven strategies and thus never harness their most important advantages.

---

the Internet is cannibalistic, that it will replace all conventional ways of doing business and overturn all traditional advantages. That is a vast exaggeration. There is no doubt that real trade-offs can exist between Internet and traditional activities. In the record industry, for example, on-line music distribution may reduce the need for CD-manufacturing assets. Overall, however, the trade-offs are modest in most industries. While the Internet will replace certain elements of industry value chains, the complete cannibalization of the value chain will be exceedingly rare. Even in the music business, many traditional activities – such as finding and promoting talented new artists, producing and recording music, and securing airplay – will continue to be highly important.

The risk of channel conflict also appears to have been overstated. As on-line sales have become more common, traditional channels that were initially skeptical of the Internet have embraced it. Far from always cannibalizing those channels, Internet technology can expand opportunities for many of them. The threat of disintermediation of channels appears considerably lower than initially predicted.

Frequently, in fact, Internet applications address activities that, while necessary, are not decisive in competition, such as informing customers, processing transactions, and procuring inputs. Critical corporate assets – skilled personnel, proprietary product technology, efficient logistical systems – remain intact, and they are often strong enough to preserve existing competitive advantages.

In many cases, the Internet complements, rather than cannibalizes, companies' traditional activities and ways of competing. Consider Walgreens,

The Internet and the value chain

The basic tool for understanding the influence of information technology on companies is the value chain – the set of activities through which a product or service is created and delivered to customers. When a company competes in any industry, it performs a number of discrete but interconnected value-creating activities, such as operating a sales force, fabricating a component, or delivering products, and these activities have points of connection with the activities of suppliers, channels, and customers. The value chain is a framework for identifying all these activities and analyzing how they affect both a company's costs and the value delivered to buyers.

Because every activity involves the creation, processing, and communication of information, information technology has a pervasive influence on the value chain. The special advantage of the Internet is the ability to link one activity with others and make real-time data created in one activity widely available, both within the company and with outside suppliers, channels, and customers. By incorporating a common, open set of communication protocols, Internet technology provides a standardized infrastructure, an intuitive browser interface for information access and delivery, bidirectional communication, and ease of connectivity – all at much lower cost than private networks and electronic data interchange, or EDI.

Many of the most prominent applications of the Internet in the value chain are shown in Figure 13.2. Some involve moving physical activities on-line, while others involve making physical activities more cost effective.

But for all its power, the Internet does not represent a break from the past; rather, it is the latest stage in the ongoing evolution of information technology.[1] Indeed, the technological possibilities available today derive not just from the Internet architecture but also from complementary technological advances such as scanning, object-oriented programming, relational databases, and wireless communications.

To see how these technological improvements will ultimately affect the value chain, some historical perspective is illuminating.[2] The evolution of information technology in business can be thought of in terms of five overlapping stages, each of which evolved out of constraints presented by the previous generation. The earliest IT systems automated discrete transactions such as order entry and accounting. The next stage involved the fuller automation and functional enhancement of individual activities such as human resource management, sales force operations, and product design. The third stage, which is being accelerated by the Internet, involves cross-activity integration, such as linking sales activities with order processing. Multiple activities are being linked together through such tools as customer relationship management (CRM), supply chain management (SCM), and enterprise resource planning (ERP) systems. The fourth stage, which is just beginning, enables the integration of the value chain and entire value system, that is, the set of value chains in an entire industry, encompassing those of tiers of suppliers, channels, and customers. SCM and CRM are starting to merge, as end-to-end applications involving customers, channels, and suppliers link orders to, for example, manufacturing, procurement, and service delivery. Soon to be integrated is product development, which has been largely separate. Complex product models will be exchanged among parties, and Internet procurement will move from standard commodities to engineered items.

In the upcoming fifth stage, information technology will be used not only to connect the various activities and players in the value system but to optimize its workings in real time. Choices will be made based on information from multiple activities and corporate entities. Production decisions, for example, will automatically factor in the capacity available at multiple facilities and the inventory available at multiple suppliers. While early fifth-stage applications will involve relatively simple optimization of sourcing, production, logistical, and servicing transactions, the deeper levels of optimization will involve the product design itself. For example, product design will be optimized and customized based on input not only from factories and suppliers but also from customers.

The power of the Internet in the value chain, however, must be kept in perspective. While Internet applications have an important influence on the cost and quality of activities, they are neither the only nor the dominant influence. Conventional factors such as scale, the skills of personnel, product and process technology, and investments in physical assets also play prominent roles. The Internet is transformational in some respects, but many traditional sources of competitive advantage remain intact.

---

1   See M. E. Porter and V. E. Millar 'How Information Gives You Competitive Advantage,' (*Harvard Business Review*, July–August 1985) for a framework that helps put the Internet's current influence in context.

2   This discussion is drawn from the author's research with Peter Bligh.

Firm infrastructure
• Web-based, distributed financial and ERP systems
• On-line investor relations (e.g. information dissemination, broadcast conference calls)

Human Resource Management
• Self-service personnel and benefits administration
• Web-based training
• Internet-based sharing and dissemination of company information
• Electronic time and expense reporting

Technology development
• Collaborative product design across locations and among multiple value-system participants
• Knowledge directories accessible from all parts of the organization
• Real-time access by R&D to on-line sales and service information

Procurement
• Internet-enabled demand planning; real-time available-to-promise/capable-to-promise and fulfillment
• Other linkage or purchase, inventory, and forecasting systems with suppliers
• Automated 'requisition to pay'
• Direct and indirect procurement via marketplaces, exchanges, auctions, and buyer-seller matching

Procurement	Operations	Outbound logistics	Marketing and sales	After-sales service
• Real-time integrated scheduling, shipping, warehouse management, demand management and planning, and advanced planning and scheduling across the company and its suppliers • Dissemination throughout the company of real-time inbound and in-progress inventory data	• Integrated information exchange, scheduling, and decision making in in-house plants, contract assemblers, and components suppliers • Real-time available-to-promise and capable-to-promise information available to the sales force and channels	• Real-time transaction of orders whether initiated by and end consumer, a sales person, or a channel partner • Automated customer-specific agreements and contract terms • Customer and channel access to product development and delivery status • Collaborative integration with customer forecasting systems • Integrated channel management including information exchange, warranty claims, and contract management (versioning, process control)	• On-line sales channels including Web sites and marketplaces • Real-time inside and outside access to customer information, product catalogs, dynamic pricing, inventory availability, on-line submission of quotes, and order entry • On-line product configurators • Customer-tailored marketing via customer profiling • Push advertising • Tailored on-line access • Real-time customer feedback through Web surveys, opt-in/opt-out marketing, and promotion response tracking	• On-line support of customer service representatives through e-mail response management, billing integration, co-browse, chat, 'call me now', voice-over-IP and other uses of video streaming • Customer self-service via Web sites and intelligent service request processing including updates to billing and shipping profiles • Real-time field service access to customer account review, schematic review, parts availability and ordering, work-order update, and service parts management

Figure 13.2   *Prominent applications of the Internet in the value chain*

the most successful pharmacy chain in the United States. Walgreens introduced a Web site that provides customers with extensive information and allows them to order prescriptions on-line. Far from cannibalizing the company's stores, the Web site has underscored their value. Fully 90% of customers who place orders over the Web prefer to pick up their prescriptions at a nearby store rather than have them shipped to their homes. Walgreens has found that its extensive network of stores remains a potent advantage, even as some ordering shifts to the Internet.

Another good example is W. W. Grainger, a distributor of maintenance products and spare parts to companies. A middleman with stocking locations all over the United States, Grainger would seem to be a textbook case of an old-economy company set to be made obsolete by the Internet. But Grainger rejected the assumption that the Internet would undermine its strategy. Instead, it tightly coordinated its aggressive on-line efforts with its traditional business. The results so far are revealing. Customers who purchase on-line also continue to purchase through other means – Grainger estimates a 9% incremental growth in sales for customers who use the on-line channel above the normalized sales of customers who use only traditional means. Grainger, like Walgreens, has also found that Web ordering increases the value of its physical locations. Like the buyers of prescription drugs, the buyers of industrial supplies often need their orders immediately. It is faster and cheaper for them to pick up supplies at a local Grainger outlet than to wait for delivery. Tightly integrating the site and stocking locations not only increases the overall value to customers, it reduces Grainger's costs as well. It is inherently more efficient to take and process orders over the Web than to use traditional methods, but more efficient to make bulk deliveries to a local stocking location than to ship individual orders from a central warehouse.

Grainger has also found that its printed catalog bolsters its on-line operation. Many companies' first instinct is to eliminate printed catalogs once their content is replicated on-line. But Grainger continues to publish its catalog, and it has found that each time a new one is distributed, on-line orders surge. The catalog has proven to be a good tool for promoting the Web site while continuing to be a convenient way of packaging information for buyers.

In some industries, the use of the Internet represents only a modest shift from well-established practices. For catalog retailers like Lands' End, providers of electronic data interchange services like General Electric, direct marketers like Geico and Vanguard, and many other kinds of companies, Internet business looks much the same as traditional business. In these industries, established companies enjoy particularly important synergies between their on-line and traditional operations, which make it especially difficult for dot-coms to compete. Examining segments of industries with characteristics similar to those supporting on-line businesses – in which customers are willing to forgo personal service and immediate delivery in order to gain convenience or lower prices, for instance – can also provide an important reality check in estimating the size of the Internet opportunity. In the prescription drug business, for example, mail orders represented only about 13% of all purchases in the late 1990s. Even though on-line drugstores may draw more customers than the mail-order channel, it is unlikely that they will supplant their physical counterparts.

Virtual activities do not eliminate the need for physical activities, but often amplify their importance. The complementarity between Internet activities and traditional activities arises for a number of reasons. First, introducing Internet applications in one activity often places greater demands on physical activities elsewhere in the value chain. Direct ordering, for example, makes warehousing and shipping more important. Second, using the Internet in one activity can have systemic consequences, requiring new or enhanced physical activities that are often unanticipated. Internet-based job-posting services, for example, have greatly reduced the cost of reaching potential job applicants, but they have also flooded employers with electronic résumés. By making it easier for job seekers to distribute résumés, the Internet forces employers to sort through many more unsuitable candidates. The added back-end costs, often for physical activities, can end up outweighing the up-front savings. A similar dynamic often plays out in digital marketplaces. Suppliers are able to reduce the transactional cost of taking orders when they move on-line, but they often have to respond to many additional requests for information and quotes, which, again, places new strains on traditional activities. Such systemic effects underscore the fact that Internet applications are not stand-alone technologies; they must be integrated into the overall value chain.

Third, most Internet applications have some shortcomings in comparison with conventional methods. While Internet technology can do many useful things today and will surely improve in the future, it cannot do everything. Its limits include the following:

- Customers cannot physically examine, touch, and test products or get hands-on help in using or repairing them.
- Knowledge transfer is restricted to codified knowledge, sacrificing the spontaneity and judgment that can result from interaction with skilled personnel.
- The ability to learn about suppliers and customers (beyond their mere purchasing habits) is limited by the lack of face-to-face contact.
- The lack of human contact with the customer eliminates a powerful tool for encouraging purchases, trading off terms and conditions, providing advice and reassurance, and closing deals.
- Delays are involved in navigating sites and finding information and are introduced by the requirement for direct shipment.

- Extra logistical costs are required to assemble, pack, and move small shipments.
- Companies are unable to take advantage of low-cost, nontransactional functions performed by sales forces, distribution channels, and purchasing departments (such as performing limited service and maintenance functions at a customer site).
- The absence of physical facilities circumscribes some functions and reduces a means to reinforce image and establish performance.
- Attracting new customers is difficult given the sheer magnitude of the available information and buying options.

Strategic imperatives for dot-coms and established companies

At this critical juncture in the evolution of Internet technology, dot-coms and established companies face different strategic imperatives. Dot-coms must develop real strategies that create economic value. They must recognize that current ways of competing are destructive and futile and benefit neither themselves nor, in the end, customers. Established companies, in turn, must stop deploying the Internet on a stand-alone basis and instead use it to enhance the distinctiveness of their strategies.

The most successful dot-coms will focus on creating benefits that customers will pay for, rather than pursuing advertising and click-through revenues from third parties. To be competitive, they will often need to widen their value chains to encompass other activities besides those conducted over the Internet and to develop other assets, including physical ones. Many are already doing so. Some on-line retailers, for example, distributed paper catalogs for the 2000 holiday season as an added convenience to their shoppers. Others are introducing proprietary products under their own brand names, which not only boosts margins but provides real differentiation. It is such new activities in the value chain, not minor differences in Web sites, that hold the key to whether dot-coms gain competitive advantages. AOL, the Internet pioneer, recognized these principles. It charged for its services even in the face of free competitors. And not resting on initial advantages gained from its Web site and Internet technologies (such as instant messaging), it moved early to develop or acquire proprietary content.

Yet dot-coms must not fall into the trap of imitating established companies. Simply adding conventional activities is a me-too strategy that will not provide a competitive advantage. Instead, dot-coms need to create strategies that involve new, hybrid value chains, bringing together virtual and physical activities in unique configurations. For example, E*Trade is planning to install stand-alone kiosks, which will not require full-time staffs, on the sites of some corporate customers. Virtual Bank, an on-line bank, is cobranding with corporations to create in-house credit unions. Juniper, another on-line bank, allows customers to deposit checks at Mail Box Etc. locations. While none of these approaches is certain to be successful, the strategic thinking behind them is sound.

Another strategy for dot-coms is to seek out trade-offs, concentrating exclusively on segments where an internet-only model offers real advantages. Instead of attempting to force the Internet model on the entire market, dot-coms can pursue customers that do not have a strong need for functions delivered outside the Internet – even if such customers represent only a modest portion of the overall industry. In such segments, the challenge will be to find a value proposition for the company that will distinguish it from other Internet rivals and address low entry barriers.

Successful dot-coms will share the following characteristics:

- Strong capabilities in Internet technology
- A distinctive strategy vis-à-vis established companies and other dot-coms, resting on a clear focus and meaningful advantages
- Emphasis on creating customer value and charging for it directly, rather than relying on ancillary forms of revenue
- Distinctive ways of performing physical functions and assembling non-Internet assets that complement their strategic positions
- Deep industry knowledge to allow proprietary skills, information, and relationships to be established

Established companies, for the most part, need not be afraid of the Internet – the predictions of their demise at the hands of dot-coms were greatly exaggerated. Established companies possess traditional competitive advantages that will often continue to prevail; they also have inherent strengths in deploying Internet technology.

The greatest threat to an established company lies in either failing to deploy the Internet or failing to deploy it strategically. Every company needs an aggressive program to deploy the Internet throughout its value chain, using the technology to reinforce traditional competitive advantages and complement existing ways of competing. The key is not to imitate rivals but to tailor Internet applications to a company's overall strategy in ways that extend its competitive advantages and make them more sustainable. Schwab's expansion of its brick-and-mortar branches by one-third since it started on-line trading, for example, is extending its advantages over internet-only competitors. The Internet, when used properly, can support greater strategic focus and a more tightly integrated activity system.

Edward Jones, a leading brokerage firm, is a good example of tailoring the Internet to strategy. Its strategy is to provide conservative, personalized advice to investors who value asset preservation and seek trusted, individualized guidance in investing. Target customers include retirees and small-business owners. Edward Jones does not offer commodities, futures, options, or other risky forms of investment. Instead, the company stresses a buy-and-hold approach to investing involving mutual funds, bonds, and blue-chip equities. Edward Jones operates a network of about 7,000 small offices, which are located conveniently to customers and are designed to encourage personal relationships with brokers.

Edward Jones has embraced the Internet for internal management functions, recruiting (25% of all job inquiries come via the Internet), and for providing account statements and other information to customers. However, it has no plan to offer on-line trading, as its competitors do. Self-directed, on-line trading does not fit Jones's strategy nor the value it aims to deliver to its customers. Jones, then, has tailored the use of the Internet to its strategy rather than imitated rivals. The company is thriving, outperforming rivals whose me-too internet deployments have reduced their distinctiveness.

The established companies that will be most successful will be those that use Internet technology to make traditional activities better and those that find and implement new combinations of virtual and physical activities that were not previously possible.

Traditional activities, often modified in some way, can compensate for these limits, just as the shortcomings of traditional methods – such as lack of real-time information, high cost of face-to-face interaction, and high cost of producing physical versions of information – can be offset by Internet methods. Frequently, in fact, an Internet application and a traditional method benefit each other. For example, many companies have found that Web sites that supply product information and support direct ordering make traditional sales forces more, not less, productive and valuable. The sales force can compensate for the limits of the site by providing personalized advice and after-sales service, for instance. And the site can make the sales force more productive by automating the exchange of routine information and serving as an efficient new conduit for leads. The fit between company activities, a cornerstone of strategic positioning, is in this way strengthened by the deployment of Internet technology.

Once managers begin to see the potential of the Internet as a complement rather than a cannibal, they will take a very different approach to organizing their on-line efforts. Many established companies, believing that the new economy operated under new rules, set up their Internet operations in stand-alone units. Fear of cannibalization, it was argued, would deter the mainstream organization from deploying the Internet aggressively. A separate unit was also helpful for investor relations, and it facilitated IPOs, tracking stocks, and spin-offs, enabling companies to tap into the market's appetite for Internet ventures and provide special incentives to attract Internet talent.

But organizational separation, while understandable, has often undermined companies' ability to gain competitive advantages. By creating separate Internet strategies instead of integrating the Internet into an overall strategy, companies failed to capitalize on their traditional assets, reinforced me-too competition, and accelerated competitive convergence. Barnes & Noble's decision to establish Barnesandnoble.com as a separate organization is a vivid example. It deterred the on-line store from capitalizing on the many advantages provided by the network of physical stores, thus playing into the hands of Amazon.

Rather than being isolated, Internet technology should be the responsibility of mainstream units in all parts of a company. With support from IT staff and outside consultants, companies should use the technology strategically to enhance service, increase efficiency, and leverage existing strengths. While separate units may be appropriate in some circumstances, everyone in the organization must have an incentive to share in the success of Internet deployment.

The end of the new economy

The Internet, then, is often not disruptive to existing industries or established companies. It rarely nullifies the most important sources of competitive advantage in an industry; in many cases it actually makes those sources even more important. As all companies come to embrace Internet technology, moreover, the Internet itself will be neutralized as a source of advantage. Basic Internet applications will become table stakes – companies will not be able to survive without them, but they will not gain any advantage from them. The more robust competitive advantages will arise instead from traditional strengths such as unique products, proprietary content, distinctive physical activities, superior product knowledge, and strong personal service and relationships. Internet technology may be able to fortify those advantages, by tying a company's activities together in a more distinctive system, but it is unlikely to supplant them.

Ultimately, strategies that integrate the Internet and traditional competitive advantages and ways of competing should win in many industries. On the demand side, most buyers will value a combination of on-line services, personal services, and physical locations over stand-alone Web distribution. They will want a choice of channels, delivery options, and ways of dealing with companies. On the supply side, production and procurement will be more effective if they involve a combination of Internet and traditional methods, tailored to strategy. For example, customized, engineered inputs will be bought directly, facilitated by Internet tools. Commodity items may be purchased via digital markets, but purchasing experts, supplier sales forces, and stocking locations will often also provide useful, value-added services.

The value of integrating traditional and Internet methods creates potential advantages for established companies. It will be easier for them to adopt and integrate traditional ones. It is not enough, however, just to graft the Internet onto historical ways of competing in simplistic 'clicks-and-mortar' configurations. Established companies will be most successful when they deploy Internet technology to reconfigure traditional activities or when they find new combinations of Internet and traditional approaches.

Dot-coms, first and foremost, must pursue their own distinctive strategies, rather than emulate one another or the positioning of established companies. They will have to break away from competing solely on price and instead focus on product selection, product design, service, image, and other areas in which they can differentiate themselves. Dot-coms can also drive the combination of Internet and traditional methods. Some will succeed by creating their own distinctive ways of doing so. Others will succeed by concentrating on market segments that exhibit real trade-offs between Internet and traditional methods – either those in which a pure Internet approach best meets the needs of a particular set of customers or those in which a particular product or service can be best delivered without the need for physical assets. (See the sidebar 'Strategic Imperatives for Dot-Coms and Established Companies.')

These principles are already manifesting themselves in many industries, as traditional leaders reassert their strengths and dot-coms adopt more focused strategies. In the brokerage industry, Charles Schwab has gained a larger share (18% at the ed of 1999) of on-line trading than E-trade (15%). In commercial banking, established institutions like Wells Fargo, Citibank, and Fleet have many more on-line accounts than Internet banks do. Established companies are also gaining dominance over Internet activities in such areas as retailing, financial information, and digital marketplaces. The most promising dot-coms are leveraging their distinctive skills to provide real value to their customers. ECollege, for example, is a full-service provider that works with universities to put their courses on the Internet and operate the required delivery network for a fee. It is vastly more successul than competitors offering free sites to universities under their own brand names, hoping to collect advertising fees and other ancillary revenue.

When seen in this light, the 'new economy' appears less like a new economy than like an old economy that has access to a nhew technology. Even the phrases 'new economy' and 'old economy' are rapidly losing their relevance, if they ever had any. The old economy of established companies and the new economy of dot-coms are merging, and it will soon be difficult to distinguish them. Retiring these phrases can only be healthy because it will reduce the confusion and muddy thinking that have been so destructive of economic value during the Internet's adolescent years.

In our quest to see how the Internet is different, we have failed to see how the Internet is the same. While a new means of conducting business has become available, the fundamentals of competition remain unchanged. The next stage of the Internet's evolution will involve a shift in thinking from e-business to business, from e-strategy to strategy. Only by integrating the Internet into overall strategy will this powerful new technology become an equally powerful force for competitive advantage.

Acknowledgements

The author is grateful to Jeffrey Rayport and to the Advanced Research Group at Inforte for their contributions to this article.

Questions for discussion

1   'Many have argued that the Internet renders strategy obsolete. In reality, the opposite is true.' In what ways do you think that this statement from Michael Porter is appropriate? And how would you provide a counter argument?

2 There are strong echoes in this chapter of Porter's seminal '5 forces' analysis of two decades ago. What has changed and what remains the same 20 or so years on (both in relation to Information & Communication Technology and to the competitive environment)?

3 Porter concludes this chapter by stating 'The next stage of the Internet's evolution will involve a shift in thinking from e-business to business, from e-strategy to strategy'. Do you agree? Why? Relate your answers to aspects of alignment considered, for example, in Chapter 11.

4 'Competitive analysis frameworks, such as the "5 forces" and "value chain" concepts propagated by Porter are ultimately redundant since competitor firms will draw the same conclusions as each other from their use and, in any event, strategy is "emergent" and the result of "tinkering" from the bottom-up.' Discuss this view in the light of arguments Porter puts forward in this chapter.

14 Evaluating the Impact of IT on the Organization

The propagation of technology management taxonomies for evaluating investments in information systems

Z. Irani and P. E. D. Love

The management of Information Technology (IT) and Information Systems (IS) is considered a complex exercise by academics and practitioners alike. The reason for this is that there are ubiquitous portfolios of tangible and intangible benefits that are offered to an organization following the adoption of IT/IS that, in turn, all need managing to ensure realization. Organization also have to take into account the direct and often larger indirect costs that are typically associated with IT/IS deployments. To provide managers with a critical insight into the management of new technology, this chapter uses a case study research strategy to examine the technology management experiences of a leading UK manufacturing organization during its adoption of a vendor-supplied Manufacturing Resource Planning (MRPII) information system. Following the lack of attention given to human and organizational technology management factors while implementing MRPII, the vendor-based information system was later abandoned and deemed a failure. In addressing those technology management factors that were later identified as important, it was found that key employees were able to overcome a number of organizational barriers and develop and implement a bespoke MRPII system that significantly improved the organization's competitive position. Technology management taxonomies that contributed to the *failure* and later *successful* implementation of MRPII are identified and discussed. The organization's experiences in solving the problems associated with the implementation of their IS offers a learning opportunity for those companies that are seeking a competitive advantage through technology management.

Introduction

The adoption of information technology (IT) and Information Systems (IS) remains a lengthy, time-consuming and complex process, so issues associated with its management would appear to be of paramount importance. Yet many companies appear to approach the whole management of technology in an unstructured or ad hoc manner throughout the systems' lifecycle. However, with capital investments in IT/IS such as Material Requirements Planning (MRPII), or its enhanced extension Enterprise Resource Planning (ERP) predicted to increase from $21.02 billion in 1998 to $72.63 billion in 2001, issues associated with technology management are appearing on management's agenda [11].

The effective management of technology needs to be viewed as a structured iterative business process, which offers organizational learning during the lifecycle of the technology. This feedback is necessary so as to offer businesses the opportunity to learn from their experiences, or mistakes. Technology management should be seen as a business process that facilitates the development of a comprehensive and robust technocentric infrastructure, consequently enhancing the delivery of accurate, timely, and appropriate services within an organization, which in turn increases the economic vitality of the business. There remains, however, a so-called 'technology management gap' within many businesses, which may result in a competitive advantage being jeopardized. Remenyi *et al.* [18] propose that technology management (when viewed from an evaluation perspective) may not be deployed in an effective manner in many businesses, and thus initiators of the new technology often become distanced from the development process. In addition, developers may lose sight of the business focus and as a result not deliver what was originally proposed and justified. Similarly, Irani *et al.* [14] suggest that technology management policies and procedures based on the use of traditional appraisal techniques have worked well for decisions concerning manufacturing capital equipment replacement, but are myopic for the appraisal of complex IT/IS such as MRPII or ERP. The reason for this is that the human and organizational implications associated with adopting new technology (and its management) are often overlooked, or simply ignored. Yet such factors can significantly impact the success or failure of IT/IS investments [5, 6, 13, 17, 20, 22].

Clearly, efficient and effective technology management has the scope to impact companies in a positive or negative way during the technology's lifecycle (i.e., feasibility, justification, requirements definition/engineering, system design, details design, test and preoperation, implementation, operation, maintenance, and post-implementation audit/evaluation). Furthermore, the multiple paths associated with technology management can often yield considerably different outcomes.

This chapter uses a case study to describe the experiences of a leading UK manufacturing organization that managed its technology through what were internally considered traditional approaches, that is, basing its investment justification for implementing a MRPII system around traditional appraisal processes. Such prescriptive methods, however, were unable to capture and accommodate the human and organizational dimensions of the investment, and as a result the vendor system was later abandoned and deemed a failure. Recognizing the need for an integrated IS that captures the idiosyncrasies of the organization and softer implications of the investment, key employees were able to later overcome human and organizational barriers and approach the adoption and management of MRPII from a new perspective. Technology management (human and organizational) taxonomies that contributed to the successful evaluation and implementation of a MRPII system are identified and discussed by the authors. In doing so, this chapter makes a contribution to the normative literature by describing how different approaches to the technology management process can yield different organizational outcomes. Two fundamentally different approaches of technology management are presented and discussed. As a result, the findings presented in the chapter provide a learning opportunity for those companies that are seeking a competitive advantage through the effective management of new technology.

Research methodology

Previous research suggests that an organization's failure with IT/IS is primarily attributable to not meeting user expectations, which underlines the significance of the soft human and organizational issues involved with IT/IS evaluation [19]. With this in mind, there was a need for a research methodology that would involve and enfranchise an organization and their staff, so that the theory and knowledge surrounding decision-making and the investment justification process of MRPII could be derived to develop effective technology management taxonomies. Considering the originality of this research, a case study strategy was adopted [8, 9, 23]. The case used for the research was not systematically sampled, so it is not possible to generalize the findings to a wider population of small to medium enterprises (SMEs) with similar characteristics found within the manufacturing industry.

Data collection

The data collection procedure has followed the major prescriptions in doing field-work research [1, 4, 7, 23]. A variety of secondary data sources were used to collect data with regard to the development of technology management taxonomies for evaluating MRPII investments, such as internal reports, budget reports, and filed accounts. A variety of data have been used to derive the findings presented in this chapter, which include interviews, observations, illustrative materials (e.g., newsletters and other publications that form part of the case study organization's history) and past project management documentation. The authors have extensive industrial experience in the manufacturing industry and have used this experience, together with a predefined interview protocol, to determine the data needed for the research.

Interviews

Interviews were conducted with the Managing Director (MD), Production Director (PD), Production Manager (PM), and Shop Floor employees. The duration of each interview was approximately 40 minutes, where every interview was conducted on a 'one-to-one' basis so as to stimulate conversation and break down any barriers that may have existed between the interviewer and interviewee. Furthermore, all interviews took place away from the normal office environment and resulting disruptions. (Interviews were conducted in the company's boardroom.)

The authors acted as a neutral medium through which questions and answers were transmitted and therefore endeavored to eliminate bias. Essentially, bias in interviews occurs when the interviewer tries to adjust the wording of the question to fit the respondent or records only selected portions of the respondent's answers. Most often, however, interviewer bias results from the use of probes. These are follow-up questions and are typically used by interviewers to get respondents to elaborate on ambiguous or incomplete answers [21]. Bearing this in mind, in trying to clarify the respondent's answers the interviewers were careful not to introduce any ideas that might form part of the respondent's subsequent answer. Furthermore, the interviewers were also mindful of the feedback respondents gained from their verbal and non-verbal responses. Thus the interviewer avoided giving overt signals such as smiling and nodding approvingly when a respondent failed to answer a question. It was decided that such actions could lead to respondents withholding responses to later questions. The interviewees reviewed the reports from the interviews and their views were invited to ensure the accuracy of the reports.

Case study validity

The use of interviews, documentary sources, and observations indicates that internal validity needed to be addressed. Interviews, in particular, were used to identify technology management 'failure' and 'success' factors related to MRPII implementation, which had been discovered through examining the interviews. Each interview was tape-recorded and subsequently transcribed. These were given to each person that had been interviewed to check and to resolve any discrepancies that may have arisen and eliminate any interviewer bias. Bearing in mind the array of evidence that was accumulated, great care was undertaken by the authors to ensure that the data collected converged on similar facts [15].

Case study

The case study presented in this section describes the experiences of a SME UK manufacturing organization that adopted a vendor-based MRPII system, which subsequently 'failed' to satisfy user requirements. The reason for this failure is attributed to a lack of consideration of human and organizational benefits and costs implications during the evaluation process [19]. Acknowledging the problems with the system, functional managers later developed and implemented a bespoke MRPII system, which took into account financial, human, and organizational cost and benefits. As a result, the system has proven to be very successful, as the organization was cited in the UK's top 100 for its best practices.

Background

The case study organization (which shall be referred to as Company V) is a precision subcontract job shop with about 150 employees and a turnover of just under £5 million. It produces a wide variety of made-to-order parts, products, and assemblies, for a large number of customers, in diverse industries. Essentially, Company V sells time and expertise using many different conventional and computer-controlled machines. Company V has a make-to-order inventory policy, with most component parts having a very low level of standardization and thus few common components. To produce these differing and often complex parts, a highly flexible production capability is required. This implies versatile manufacturing equipment, flexible employees, and a genuine need to maximize the utilization of technology, to continuously improve and innovate, and to remain competitive in manufacture. Typical components and assemblies within a jobbing shop environment tend to be diverse and have uncomplicated Bills of Material (BOM) and product structures. Furthermore, they are nearly always made to specifications supplied by the Original Equipment Manufacturer (OEM).

Orders for individual products tend to be small and their timing depends on the fluctuating needs of customers, who often use the company to 'off-load' capacity. Therefore, close communications and the integrity of information between Company V and its customers are necessary for responsive change. The company boasts of its agility and information management, and as such manufacturing lead times are short, which ensures that throughout production flow is maximized. Therefore, if there are changes in the requirements of customers or the marketplace then Company V is able to respond in an effective manner by retooling or reequipping their production facility.

Company V's management team is lean, with few functional divisions. The following personnel report directly to the managing director: a sales and marketing director, a finance director, an administrative/general director (to whom the purchasing, human resource, and IT/IS functions report), and a manufacturing director. On the shop floor, supervisors manage several self-directed work teams who comprise of 7 to 15 staff members, such as machine operators, assemblers, material handlers, receivers, and shippers.

Case findings and analysis

The 'success' of Company V's previous investments helped give them the encouragement and motivation they needed to introduce a computerized Production Planning and Control (PPC) system. The measure of 'success' used by Company V was the removal of 'procedural pain' – that is, if it was not considered painful to carry out the new computerized procedure, the project was considered a success. When asked to further elaborate on the issue of procedural pain, the measures of laborious, repetitive, boring, and time-consuming were all identified. However, it should be noted that these are all nontraditional 'subjective' intangible and nonfinancial measures, but according to Hyde [12], traditional criteria for judging IT project success are no longer correct and should be replaced by measures that reflect new approaches to system development and management.

Unlike other 'smaller' investments, the driving force behind the PPC project was the managing director, who ultimately sanctioned all investment decisions. When asked to evaluate the perceived impact of the proposed PPC system, the managing director replied:

> The scope of benefits from investing in IT appeared enormous, and only restricted by my imagination. . . . I was the main visionary leader and could see the long-term strategic implications of my decision to invest. I was sure the benefits would far outweigh the costs.

There appeared, however, to be other factors 'driving' this investment, with the managing director stating:

> We were under significant pressure by our customers to offer year on year cost reductions. . . . So, there were risks associated with not utilizing new technology to provide a competitive advantage.

The reason why Company V lacked a formal justification process was because they had not previously invested in projects that were outside the scope of traditional appraisal techniques. In particular, major strategic benefits such as perceived market leadership, leadership in new technology, and promotion of an 'open business culture' were not readily convertible in financial terms. Previous investments in Computer Numerically Controlled (CNC) equipment had been financed through loan agreements where cash flow projections and sensitivity analysis had been used to assess the impact and risk of the investment. Clearly, in such cases the focus is on direct financial benefits and costs, whereas the PPC system was viewed as providing a portfolio of benefits and costs, which were not easily accommodated within those appraisal techniques traditionally used by Company V.

Company V soon discovered that the accountancy frameworks that it has considerable experience in using were not suitable for investments with intangible and nonfinancial benefits and indirect costs, as they provided inappropriate information for rigorous evaluation. A new and inexperienced management team (which was unaware of the latest appraisal techniques, which could take into account qualitative costs and benefits) used a simplistic Cost/Benefit Analysis (CBA). Management's use of CBA allowed the listing of perceived project benefits and costs, but no assignments of financial values were made to the PPC implications identified. This was due to the complexity, subjectivity, and time-consuming nature of identifying and assigning arbitrary values to the intangible and nonfinancial benefits and costs associated with the PPC investment. Table 14.1 presents a taxonomy of strategic benefits identified as part of Company V's CBA, with Tables 14.2 and 14.3 presenting tactical and operational benefits, respectively. The interdependent nature of these taxonomies is also depicted in Figure 14.1.

In considering the proposed taxonomies of benefits identified in the tables, Harris [10] describes how investment decisions typically fall into three categories, these being strategic, tactical, and operational. Regarding the costs considered as part of Company V's CBA, they only identified direct financial costs, such as:

- uninterruptable power supply
- file servers, terminals, and printing facilities
- backup tape streamer
- key vendor software modules
- relational database software
- additional networking software
- consultancy support (partially grant funded)
- network wiring, junctions, and connectors
- installation and maintenance
- 'in-house' customizing time
- reengineering of business processes to suit software

Table 14.1   *Taxonomy of strategic production planning and control benefits*

Classification of MRPII benefits	Financial	Non-financial	Partly/totally intangible
Strategic Benefits			
Improved Growth and Success	X	X	X
Leader in New Technology			X
Improved Market Share	X		
Market Leadership	X	X	X
Enhanced Competitive Advantage	X	X	X

Table 14.2   *Taxonomy of tactical production planning and control benefits*

Classification of MRPII benefits	Financial	Non-Financial	Partly/totally Intangible
Tactical Benefits			
Improved Flexibility	X	X	X
Improved Response to Changes		X	
Improved Product Quality	X	X	X
Improved Teamwork			X
Promotes Open Culture			X
Improved Integration with other business Functions			X
Increased Plant Efficiency	X		
Reduced Delivery Lead-times		X	
Reduced Lead-times		X	
Improved Capacity Planning	X	X	X
Improved Data Management		X	X
Improved Manufacturing Control		X	X
Improved Accuracy of Decisions	X	X	X

Table 14.3   *Taxonomy of operational production planning and control benefits*

Classification of MRPII benefits	Financial	Non-financial	Partly/totally intangible
Operational Benefits			
Reduced Raw Material Inventory	X		
Reduced Levels of WIP		X	
Reduced Labor Costs	X		
Reduced Manufacturing Costs	X		
Increased Throughput	X		

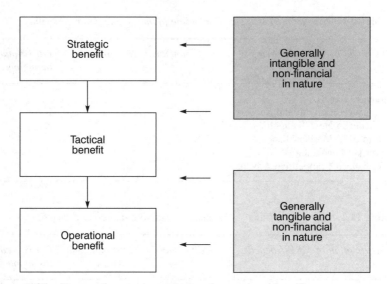

Figure 14.1   *Nature of strategic, tactical and operational benefits*

- running costs: electricity insurance premium rises
- consumables (e.g., toner cartridges disks, paper)
- database software course
- database user group fees
- hardware and software performance required to process types
- data volumes of transactions
- functions that are over and above a given user's immediate requirement (e.g., mandatory security facilities)
- balancing developmental costs against maintenance costs
- network architecture and associated hubs, routers, and gateways

As Company V was unable to calculate accurately the financial returns achievable, an 'act of faith' decision to invest was made. The basis for this investment strategy, although ad hoc, was that the company was unable to calculate accurately the scope and magnitude of the investments' benefits. In particular, the far-reaching implications of the intangible and nonfinancial benefits (together with the indirect costs that later appeared), added to the complexity and further justified the investment strategy. Interestingly enough, the British CIMA/IProdE [2] suggests that some benefits of IT/IS cannot be quantified, and stated that 'an act of faith that such systems are necessary may be required.' Therefore, it would appear that the British CIMA/IProdE advocates the adoption of an ad hoc justification strategy. Yet Kaplan [16] states that if companies invest in projects whose financial returns are unknown, or below their cost of capital, there is a chance they could become insolvent.

During the implementation of the core PPC module, it became evident that the vendor-supplied system required the data to fulfill its (the software's) needs, rather than fitting the way Company V operated. It is noteworthy that Cox and Clark [3] reported similar findings. Such circumstances had sought to be avoided by Company V, as the 'major' reengineering of business processes just to satisfy the software was considered expensive, non-value-adding, and time-consuming, as well as causing disruptions to production performance. Furthermore, these implications appeared as significant cost factors that had not been acknowledged within their CBA. The reengineering of processes, however, presented themselves as unavoidable, to achieve the necessary functionality for the effective use of the PPC system.

Employee resistance and a culture based on reactive isolation added to the implementation problems. People openly blamed the IS when things went wrong. The production director was regularly confronted with 'work-to lists' that usually had much data that seemed meaningless. He was ready to dismiss the system and go back to the old manual way of PPC. However, the production director was eventually convinced by the software selection and implementation team that computerized PPC was the only way forward if the company were to expand in the future. The team explained that the difficulties being experienced were attributable to the lack of a suitable reporting structure and data format and that the system needed time to 'settle down.'

It appeared that Company V's biggest problem was their core vendor-supplied PPC module, which worked extremely well if kept supplied with a continuous flow of 'clean data.' Nonetheless, if there was any 'hitch' in data recording or accuracy, the system became highly unstable and unreliable. Therefore, the need to alleviate this problem led the software selection and implementation team to investigate the purchase of a vendor shop floor data collection (SFDC) module. Furthermore, the purchase of the SFDC module seemed a natural progression toward achieving 'full' MRPII integration, which received the managing director's endorsement.

It was found that the operational workforce did not receive an orientation on the importance of PPC and on how the SFDC could make a contribution to the performance of the PPC function. In hindsight, however, the software selection and implementation team regretted not educating the workforce. This was particularly painful to the team because management considered this lack of education and training as a barrier to the program being accepted at an operational level. Skepticism and the implications of misuse resulted in 'unreliable' data, which brought 'noise' into the Master Production Schedule (MPS). Such issues later resulted in inaccurate customer delivery lead times being quoted, falls in productivity, and the loss of a customer base. These factors had a significant impact on the perceived success of the IS and were not acknowledged as implementation issues during the system's evaluation.

At this point the managing director (project champion) turned his attention to a new project, appearing to have either lost interest, due to the lack of success, or being driven by other organizational improvement initiatives. Responsibility for the implementation process was delegated to others, hoping that the by then well-established production director would take up the challenge. He had not been a key member of the software selection and implementation team, but had, rather, operated as an honoree, advising on technical issues when consulted. The production director therefore expected to take the lead in his role as head of the production department. He did not welcome the responsibility for ensuring project success of a half-implemented system, on which he had been given little opportunity for significant input. Still, he acknowledged the contribution that the PPC system was making (and could further make) toward the streamlining of the production function. In light of difficulties, the software selection and implementation team suddenly changed, from supporting to trying to apportion blame.

Many of the problems that the real-time shop floor data collection intended to alleviate appeared to be further complicated by the SFDC module, which, as the production director claimed, was because:

> We had not sat down in the first place and formalized our systems. . . . People were not informed of the impact the system would make on their job function(s) . . . nobody on the shop floor bought into ensuring the success of the system. They needed educating, not disciplining.

Furthermore, it appeared that at this point, the software selection and implementation team reached a stalemate. No clear direction could be decided, as there was no focused leadership within the team. Furthermore, the PPC software appeared to be dictating the need for a number of dedicated experts, to analyze, manipulate, and control the production function. This was not welcomed by the majority of the management team, who were trying to develop a corporate culture based on openness, through promoting the concepts of flexible, empowered teamwork. Thus the adoption of such a system clearly did not have the operational support necessary for its successful operation. Consequently, management, who were supported by the software selection and implementation team, advocated the development of a bespoke system, more suited to the idiosyncrasies of Company V's processes, and their by now perceived unique needs as a subcontract jobbing shop.

The development of a bespoke MRPII system

Driven by the need to develop an integrated is that would acknowledge the idiosyncrasies of Company V, key employees set about developing their own business solution. This investment was partially financed by two government-sponsored schemes. The development of bespoke software was perceived to give Company V a new opportunity to gain operational support for the successful implementation of MRPII. It would appear that human and organizational issues played a crucial part in the decision-making process to develop a bespoke software system. The decision by Company V to develop its own software was seen as a significant turnaround by many within the organization, and indeed it contradicted the managing director's initial justification for purchasing vendor software.

The majority of benefits originally envisaged as deliverables from implementing vendor software, such as those that were identified in Tables 14.1 through 14.3, appeared to have still remained relevant. However, the scope of costs associated with developing a bespoke MRPII system was considered greater than originally detailed. Therefore, as part of a revised CBA, Company V significantly increased its estimate of the costs it perceived would be incurred during the development, implementation, and operation of bespoke MRPII software. These new costs were in addition to the already realized direct costs that had been incurred during the earlier purchase of vendor software and complement those social subsystem costs reported by Ryan and Harrison [19]. Tables 14.4 and 14.5 identify the taxonomy of costs that have been classified as indirect organizational and human costs, respectively.

Acknowledging failure through loss of confidence and user participation, Company V decided to abandon the use of the vendor SFDC module due to the disappointing results obtained. This decision was made because of:

- poor data reliability
- swipe hardware terminal problems
- lack of employee support and discipline consistently to use the bar code system
- lack of interest in continuing the implementation process
- misalignment between the strategic direction of the vendor and the organization
- falls in productivity
- lack of clear project focus, leadership, and deliverables

Essentially, the company went back to basics and drew on their experiences. It was decided by the managing director to enlist the support of a consultancy company, as help was needed to facilitate the design, development, and implementation process. Before such processes commenced, Company V reassessed its strategic direction, organizational strengths, and weaknesses, and revised its business plan and developed a project strategy. Company V then began a series of intensive strategic education sessions and workshop training days. All functional managers were educated on the importance of MRPII, and on the impact that the investment

Table 14.4   *Taxonomy of indirect human costs*

Classification of indirect human costs	MRPII cost factors
Management/ Staff Resource	Integrating computerized production planning and control into work practices.
Management Time	Devising, approving and amending IT and manufacturing strategies.
Cost of ownership: System Support	Vendor support/trouble shooting costs.
Management Effort and Dedication	Exploring the potential of the system. Linking and integrating new systems together, e.g., CAM, DNC, CIM.
Employee Time	Detailing, approving and amending the computerization of product BOMs.
Employee Training	Being trained to manipulate vendor software and training others.
Employee Motivation	Interest in computerized production planning and control reduces as time passes.
Changes in Salaries	Pay increases based on improved employee flexibility.
Software Disposal	The removal of all software prior to disposal.
Staff Turnover	Increases in interview costs, induction costs, training costs based in the need for skilled human resource.

would make to their job function(s). A simplified course was also developed for shop floor stakeholders. This course not only addressed the educational issues associated with MRPII but also looked at the practical implications of such a system on their job function(s). In doing so, it clearly differentiated education from training. The subject and teaching media used varied, using as much imagination as possible. Teamwork was promoted, with all employees being mixed and grouped together. They were filmed and reviewed playing games, using Legos® and jigsaw puzzles, all with meaning for throughput production flow, communication, Just in Time (JIT) inventory management, and Total Quality Management (TQM). The workshop exercises appeared to be well received, and helped to win over skeptics. In parallel with the workshop training and education sessions, an information system design and development team was assembled.

Table 14.5 *Taxonomy of indirect organizational costs*

Classification of indirect organizational costs	MRPII cost factor
Productivity Losses	Developing and adapting to new systems, procedures, and guidelines.
Strains on Resource	Maximizing the potential of the new technology through integrating information flows and increasing information availability.
Business Process Reengineering	The redesign of organizational functions, processes, and reporting structures.
Hardware Disposal	The removal of all hardware prior to environmentally friendly disposal.
Organizational Restructuring	Covert resistance to change.

Where necessary, employees (subject to their acceptance) were sent on external training courses to develop new technical skills. In addition, students on industrial placements were temporarily employed to develop software. Students were placed at Company V for a period of six months or one year. During their placement each student was supervised by a member of staff from a university (implicitly resulting in technical academic support). This recruitment policy helped to keep system development costs down, thus reducing the need for expensive contract engineers. An additional benefit of having students on the project was to maintain a constant stream of innovation, inspiration, and motivation. However, closer supervision was needed to retain project focus than would have been needed if only general company employees performed the work. During the development of their bespoke IS, Company V schematically mapped out their entire business process using flowchart tools. In doing so, a top-level analysis of Company V's key business processes was performed, identifying processes and their order of occurrence.

This enabled processes to be reengineered and facilitated the removal of non-value-adding activities before any systems were computerized. This approach to reengineering was considerably different from earlier attempts in that previous processes appeared to be generic and were based around the functionality of the vendor-supplied software. The reengineering of business processes before bespoke system development allowed for the software being developed to be modeled on best practice jobbing shop activities. It was at this point that the expertise of the consultancy company and academic institutions proved invaluable.

Technology management factors: key learning issues

As a result of the case study findings, a number of technology management factors have been identified as having an impact on the failure/success of Company V's adoption of MRPII. These factors are presented in Table 14.6, where their contribution is identified toward the implementation of vendor software and the later development of a bespoke system.

The inability of traditional modes of financial analysis to justify IT/IS investments (which have strategic implications) has led a growing number of practitioners in calling for a moratorium on their use. The reason for this is that traditional approaches are considered to offer narrow levels of analysis, through their prescriptive focus on operational implications of the investment. This is further complicated, with many managers becoming preoccupied with financial appraisal insofar as practical strategic considerations have been overlooked and in some cases ignored. This inevitably results in many strategically important projects failing to 'pass' the financial justification stage of the evaluation process. Consequently, companies are often forced to adopt a myopic approach to IT/IS project justification. This is further complicated where the information system is modular and the system is purchased in stages, the implications being that the appraisal methods only consider the benefits and costs associated with the module being evaluated and are unable to account for benefits that the entire system brings.

Conclusions

The increased scope of new technology has not only provided organizations with enablers for change but also prompted companies to reassess the way they evaluate, manage, and exploit technology. The empirical results reported in this chapter have identified a case where traditional modes of investment appraisal were inappropriate when accounting for the implications of the investment, and as a result, did not support the efficient and effective deployment of new technology. Therefore, the strategy adopted by the case study when evaluating the MRPII investment was an 'act of faith,' and thus *ad hoc* in nature. This subsequently resulted in the system being considered a 'failure' as human and organizational factors were neglected during the evaluation and technology management process. The main reason for Company V's *ad hoc* approach to investment decision-making was that many of the benefits resulting from their investment were considered intangible and nonfinancial. Consequently, they could not be accommodated within traditional evaluation and management frameworks, which had been previously used for the justification of capital manufacturing equipment. The relatively new and inexperienced management team further complicated the justification process, as a result of their lack of knowledge on how to identify and manage

Table 14.6 *Comparative review of technology management processes*

Technology management factors	Vendor software	Bespoke software
Investment Strategy	Act of Faith	Educated Decision Without Financial Quantitative Analysis
Formal Project Management	No	Yes
Company Culture	Closed	Open
Concept Justification to Workforce	No	Yes
Workforce Educated/Trained	No	Yes
Management Educated/Trained	No	Yes
Appraisal Technique	Cost/Benefit Analysis	Cost/Benefit Analysis
Consultancy Support	No	Yes
Academic Involvement	No	Industrial Placement of Students
Continuous Project Evaluation	No	Monthly Management Review Meetings
Investment Integrated in Business Plan	No	Yes
Classification of Benefits	Strategic, Tactical, and Operational	Strategic, Tactical, and Operational
Nature of Benefits Identified	Financial, Nonfinancial, and Intangible	Financial, Nonfinancial, and Intangible
Classification of Costs Identified	Direct Costs	Direct and Indirect Costs
Nature of Costs Identified	Financial	Financial and Intangible
Risk Considered	Competitive Risk	Competitive Risk
Implementation Process	Implementation Team	Implementation Team with Contribution from Other Functions
Project Leader	Managing Director	Production Director
Development Scope	Short/Medium Term	Long Term
Human Factors	Not Considered	Addressed Where Possible
Organizational Implications	Not Considered and Not Considered Far-Reaching	Acknowledged as Being Far-Reaching
Implementation Documentation	*Ad hoc*	Formal Documentation Process
Stakeholder Analysis	No	Yes
Perceived Project Outcome	Failure	Success

IT/IS-related benefits and costs. There are also serious implications connected with the poor project management, which in part was exacerbated by indecisive and inconsistent leadership, thus questioning the appropriate positioning of project managers within the organizational structure. With management under increasing pressure to produce short-term financial savings through improved productivity, managers need to ensure that those projects with long-term strategic focuses were not excluded on the basis of their intangible and nonfinancial benefits. The case study points to the significance of human and organizational factors, and exemplifies the need to take account of such issues within any robust evaluation criteria, thus heightening the significance of the proposed technology management taxonomies.

Acknowledgements

The authors thank the case study company for its participation in this study. Without the cooperation and support of management and employees the research could not have been undertaken. The authors are also grateful to the five anonymous referees for their helpful and constructive comments, which helped improve this manuscript.

Note

The previously formed software selection and implementation team took the initiative to implement bespoke MRPII development. They perceived that the company would be more satisfied with the results of their 'own' system, rather than the implementation of 'rigid' vendor software.

References

1　Bonoma, T. V. Case research in marketing: opportunities, problems, and a process. *Journal of Marketing Research, 12* (1985), 199–208.
2　British CIMA/IProdE. *Justifying Investments in Advanced Manufacturing Projects.* London: Kogan Page, 1987.
3　Cox, J. F., and Clark, S. L. Problems in implementing and operating a manufacturing resource planning information system. *Journal of Management Information Systems, 1*, 1 (1984), 81–101.
4　Dane, F. C. *Research Methods.* Pacific Grove, CA: Brooks-Cole, 1990.
5　Ezingeard J.-N., Irani, Z. and Race, P. Assessing the value and cost implications of manufacturing information and data systems: an empirical study. *European Journal of Information Systems, 7*, 4 (1999), 252–260.

6   Farbey, B., Land, F. and Targett, D. *IT Investment: A Study of Methods and Practices*. Kent, UK: Management Today/Butterworth-Heinemann Ltd., 1993.

7   Fieldler, J. *Field Research: A Manual for Logistics and Management of Scientific Studies in Natural Settings*. San Francisco: Jossey-Bass, 1978.

8   Galliers, R. D. Choosing information systems research approaches. In R. D. Galliers (ed.), *Information Systems Research – Issues, Methods and Practice Guidelines*. Oxford, UK: Blackwell Scientific, 1992, pp. 144–162.

9   Hakim, C. *Research Design: Strategies and Choice in the Design of Social Research*. London: Allen and Unwin, 1987.

10 Harris, S. *Human Communication and Information Systems*. Oxford, UK: NCC Blackwell, 1996.

11 Heald, K., and Kelly, K. ARM research predicts EPR market will reach $72.63 billion by 2002, *ARM Research*, November 2d, 1998.

12 Hyde, A. Failure? – who says? *The Computer Bulletin*, 26–29 July, 2000.

13 Irani, Z., Ezingeard, J.-N. and Grieve, R. J. Integrating the costs of an IT/IS infrastructure into the investment decision making process. *The International Journal of Technological Innovation. Entrepreneurship and Technology Management (Technovation)*, *17*, 11–12 (1997), 695–706.

14 Irani, Z., Love, P. E .D. and Hides, M. T. *Investment Evaluation of New Technology: Integrating IT/IS Cost Management into a Model*, Association for Information System, 2000 Americas Conference on Information Systems (AMCIS 2000), CD Proceedings, 10–13 August 2000, Long Beach, CA.

15 Jick, T. D. Mixing qualitative and quantitative methods: triangulation in accumulation. *Administrative Science Quarterly*, *24*, 602–611, 1979.

16 Kaplan, R. S. Financial justification for the factory of the future. Working Paper, Harvard Business School, 1985.

17 Khalifa, G., Irani, Z. and Baldwin, L. P. IT Evaluation Methods: Drivers and Consequences, Association for Information System, 2000 Americas Conference on Information Systems (AMCIS2000), CD Proceedings, 10–13 August 2000, Long Beach, CA.

18 Remenyi, D., Money, A., Sherwood-Smith, M. and Irani, Z. *The Effective Measurement and Management of IT Costs and Benefits*, Professional Information Systems Text Books series, 2d ed., Kent, UK: Butterworth-Heinemann/Computer Weekly, 2000.

19 Ryan, S. D., and Harrison, D. A. Considering social subsystem costs and benefits in IT investment decisions: A view from the field of anticipated payoffs, *Journal of Management Information Systems*, *16*, 4 (2000), 11–40.

20   Serafeimidis, V. and Smithson, S. Information Systems Evaluation in
     Practice: a case study of organisational change. *Journal of Information
     Technology, 15*, 2 (2000), 93–105.
21   Shaughnessy, J. J. and Zechmeister, E. B. *Research Methods in
     Psychology*, 3d edn, Boston: McGraw-Hill, 1994.
22   Voss, C. A. Managing advanced manufacturing technology, *International
     Journal of Operations and Production Management, 6*, 5 (1986), 4–7.
23   Yin, R. K. *Case Study Research: Design and Methods*. Applied Social
     Research Methods Series, vol. 5. London: Sage Publications, 1994.

Questions for discussion

1   We often talk of tangible and intangible benefits when evaluating IS/IT
    investments. How useful is this distinction? Consider the case study
    discussed in this chapter and the benefits identified when answering this
    question. Can you think of other benefits – tangible or intangible – that
    might also have been identified by the authors?
2   In Chapter 20, Willcocks and Lester talk of the IT productivity paradox.
    Relate the conclusions to be drawn from this chapter and theirs.
3   Why do many organizations 'approach the whole management of
    [information] technology in an unstructured or *ad hoc* manner throughout
    the systems' lifecycle'? Why don't they view it 'as a structured iterative
    business process' as the authors of this chapter recommend?
4   How might a company use the findings from the case study research
    reported in this chapter in parallel with the kind of 'stages of growth'
    framework introduced in Chapter 2?
5   Compare and contrast the findings and recommendations reported in this
    chapter with those of Willcocks in Chapter 9.

Part Four

Information Systems Strategy and the Organizational Environment

The focus of this final part of the book is the outer shaded portion of our conceptualization of strategic information management, reproduced below as Figure IV.1. It is concerned with the wider context within which information systems strategy takes place: the organizational environment. As such, it reflects on such issues as information technology and the globalization

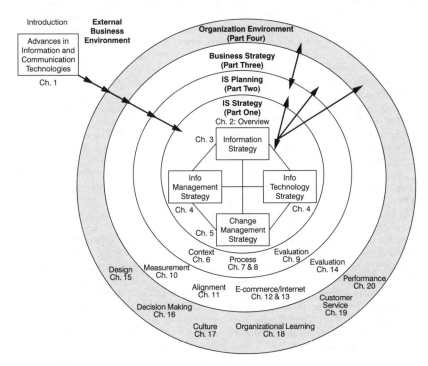

Figure IV.1 *The focus of Part Four: information systems strategy and the organizational environment*

of business;* alternative organizational arrangements; decision making in organizations, and organizational culture and knowledge management. New to this edition are chapters on the impact of IT on customer relationship management and the impact of IT on organizational learning.

Part Four commences, in Chapter 15, with an article by Lambert and Peppard that looks at IT and new organizational forms. By the latter they mean structure, systems, management style, cultures, roles, responsibilities, skills and the like. The authors remind us that 'Organizations must adopt a form that is appropriate to their strategy and the competitive position within which they find themselves', bearing in mind the opportunities afforded by IT. A range of alternative organizational forms are presented, as is a framework which should prove useful when dealing with the myriad complex issues associated with migrating towards an appropriate new form. Their framework pays considerable attention to change management issues (cf. once again, the innermost circle of our conceptualization of strategic information management, and Chapters 5 and 6). For further reading on the general topic of organizational transformation, see Kochan and Useem (1992), from which Chapter 5 is extracted. For more on IT and organizational transformation, see, for example, Scott Morton (1991) and Galliers and Baets (1997).

We turn our attention, in Chapter 16, to the effects of information technology on organizational decision making. Written by Huber, this chapter is not alone in this collection in being of particular relevance to MBA audiences, drawing, as it does, from a range of disciplines, in this instance from the worlds of organization science and communications, as well as information systems. As Gibbons (1995) has argued, it is through trans-disciplinary research of this kind that new knowledge is more likely to be obtained. Huber's intent is to reinvestigate components of organization theory, given that much of this had been formulated 'when the nature and mix of communication technologies were relatively constant, both across time and across organizations of the same general type'. Citing the advent of electronic mail, image transmission, computer conferencing, expert systems, external information retrieval systems, and the like, Huber sets out to explore how such new technologies as these might impact organizational forms, intelligence and decision making. A series of propositions are set forth, connected with constructs and concepts, from which a conceptual theory is developed. He concludes, *inter alia*, that researchers in organization science 'should study advanced information technology as . . . an intervention or jolt in the life of an organization that may have unanticipated consequences with respect to evolved organizational design'. The collective experiences of our readers are likely to conclude that he is right on this score! More positively, he also concludes that IT is likely to improve decision making and enable new organizational forms. Reasons for possible impediments to the former, however, are uncovered in Chapter 19 that then follows. For further reading on IT and organizational structure and decision making, see, for example, Fiedler *et al.* (1996), Leidner and Elam (1993, 1995), Molloy and Schwenk (1995), Orlikowski and Robey (1991) and Tavakolian (1989).

In Chapter 17, Leidner reflects on the issues associated with current attempts to implement knowledge management systems (KMS) in organizations and their, at times, limited impact, due to clashes with corporate culture. The author introduces the chapter with an insightful account of developments over the years in information systems designed to support managerial and operational activity in organizations, preceding the more recent developments in KMS. Providing a complementary account to that presented in Chapter 1, Leidner focuses attention on the implementation effects and requirements of various types of information system, from management information systems (MIS), to decision support systems (DSS), to executive information systems (EIS), to KMS. She notes a trend from a 'one system for all users', to a 'one system for one user', to an 'anyone, anywhere, anytime' information provision strategy in line with these developments. Reflecting on organizational culture issues, Leidner illustrates how the

---

* See also, for example, Walsham (2001) and Castells (2001).

necessity for user participation in the information systems development and design process has progressed, in the light of these developments, from involvement during earlier stages of analysis and design to active contribution of user knowledge with KMS. This is where her concept of information culture comes in, with a series of propositions that help illustrate, *inter alia*, the circumstances in which knowledge is more or less likely to be shared by actors in organizations, dependent on their view as to whether this information is an individual or corporate asset.

While knowledge management may be considered a relatively new topic, it is in essence an extension of the broader issue of organizational learning. Chapter 18 offers an interesting analysis of the introduction of IT in an organization and subsequent learning. Pentland views organizations as knowledge systems composed of a collection of knowledge processes, including constructing, organizing, storing, distributing, and applying. Pentland analyses the case of a small engineering consulting company that implemented a new information system to automate one of its core business activities. He shows how information systems influence not only the objects of knowledge but also the criteria for knowledge construction.

Chapter 19 introduces a topic new to this edition, that of improving customer support with information systems. El Sawy and Bowles provide insights for designing IT-enabled customer support processes that enable a company to meet the requirements of operating in a fast response, internetworked world. The system they describe provides an infrastructure for problem resolution that includes a customer support knowledge base whose structure is dynamically updated based on adaptive learning through customer interactions. Whereas the previous chapter focuses on individuals learning through information systems, this chapter poses the opportunity of systems learning through the information input by people. El Sawy and Bowles provide observations that can be useful starting points for any firm wanting to think of ways to utilize information technology to improve customer relationships.

We conclude, in Chapter 20, with a look at what has been termed the IT productivity paradox – the problem that many organizations face in obtaining business advantage from their IT, despite the dramatic developments in the technology that we have witnessed over recent years, and despite the considerable investment made in this technology by many companies. Written by Willcocks and Lester, it proposes a means of linking business and information systems strategy by prioritizing IT investments, setting interlinking performance measures and considering external IT services as well as internally developed solutions. In many ways, then, the holistic stance taken by the authors makes Chapter 20 an appropriate place to bring our consideration of strategic information management to a close, since it tries to integrate many – although by no means all – of the issues raised in the book. The overall intention of the chapter, as well as *Strategic Information Management* as a whole, has been to enable organizations to obtain greater business value from their investments in IT. This can only be achieved by executives understanding the issues, getting involved and taking responsibility in this key area. We hope we have gone some way in assisting in this process.

References

Castells, M. (2001). *The Internet Galaxy*, Oxford University Press, Oxford.

Fiedler, K. D. Grover, V. and Teng, J. T. C. (1996) An empirically derived taxonomy of Information Technology structure and its relationship to organizational structure. *Journal of Management Information Systems*, **13**(1), Summer, 9–34.

Galliers, R. D. and Baets, W. R. J. (1998) *Information Technology and Organizational Transformation: Innovation for the 21st Century Organization*, Wiley, Chichester.

Gibbons, M. (1995) *The New Production of Knowledge: The Dynamics of Science and Research in Contemporary Societies*, Sage, London.

Kochan, T. A. and Useem, M. (eds) (1992) *Transforming Organizations*, Oxford University Press, New York.

Leidner, D. E. and Elam, J. J. (1993) Executive information systems; their impact on executive decision making. *Journal of Management Information Systems*, **10**(3), 139–156.

Leidner, D. E. and Elam, J. J. (1995) The impact of executive information systems on organizational design, intelligence and decision making. *Organization Science*, **6**(6), 645–665.

Molloy, S. and Schwenk, C. R. (1995) The effects of Information Technology on strategic decision making. *Journal of Management Studies*, **32**(5), 283–311.

Orlikowski, W. and Robey, D. (1991) Information Technology and the structuring of organizations. *Information Systems Research*, **2**(2), 143–169.

Porter, M. E. (1990) *The Competitive Advantage of Nations*, Macmillan, Basingstoke.

Scott Morton, M. S. (ed.) (1991) *The Corporation of the 1990s: Information Technology and Organizational Transformation*, Oxford University Press, New York.

Tavakolian, H. (1989) Linking the Information Technology structure with organizational competitive strategy: a survey. *MIS Quarterly*, **13**(3), September, 309–319.

Walsham, G. (2001). *Making a World of Difference: IT in a Global Context*. Wiley, Chichester.

15 The Information Technology–Organizational Design Relationship

Information technology and new organizational forms

R. Lambert and J. Peppard

Throughout the 1980s there was a tremendous emphasis on business strategy. Many organizations developed sophisticated strategies with scant attention given to their ability and capability to deliver these strategies. Over the past few years a tremendous amount has been written about the organization of the 1990s, its characteristics and the key enabling role of information technology. While this presents us with a destination in general terms, little attention is given in how to get there. This chapter addresses this concern, beginning by reviewing six perspectives which best represent current thinking on new ways of organizing and outlines their characteristics. Having identified their key characteristics, three key issues which now dominate the management agenda are proposed. The vision: where do we want to be in terms of our organizational form? Gap analysis and planning: how do we get there? and Managing the migration: how do we manage this process of reaching our destination? Extending the traditional information systems/information technology strategic planning model, a framework is presented which addresses these concerns. This framework is structured around the triumvirate of vision, planning and delivery with considerable iteration between planning and delivery to ensure the required form is met.

Introduction

Academics, consultants and managers continually debate the most effective organizational form. (Organizational form includes structure, systems, management style, cultures, roles, responsibilities, skills, etc.) If there is agreement it is that there is no one best way to develop organizations to achieve the best mix of structure, systems, management style, culture, roles, responsibilities and skills. One lesson is clear and it is that organizations must adopt a form that is appropriate to their strategy and the competitive position within which they find themselves. Recently there has been a spate of papers challenging traditional ways of organizing and their underlying assumptions and proposing alternative approaches. Many of these approaches are dependent on opportunities provided by information technology (IT).

Clearly the situation within which organizations find themselves today is radically different than from earlier times. As we saw earlier, the 1990s have been characterized by globalization of markets, intensification of competition, acceleration of product life cycles, and growing complexity with suppliers, buyers, governments and other stakeholder organizations. Rapidly changing and more powerful technology provides new opportunities. To be competitive in these conditions requires different organizational forms than in more stable times. It is well recognized that responsiveness, flexibility and innovation will be key corporate attributes for successful organizations. Information plays a critical role in improving these within today's organization. However, traditional organizational forms have significant limitations in supporting the information-based organization.

Information technology must share responsibility for much of the rigidity and inflexibility in organizations. By automating tasks IT cemented hierarchy with reporting systems, and rigidified behaviour through standardization. Indeed, often technology has not resulted in fundamental changes in how work is performed: rather it has allowed it to be done more efficiently. The irony is that IT can also help us break out of traditional modes of organizing and facilitate new organizational forms which previously would have been impossible. The challenge therefore is not only to consider new organizational forms but also to identify the critical issues that must be managed to allow this transformation to begin.

It is our intention to map out some of the themes relating to new ways of organizing which have been emerging over the past decade. We also want to clear up the confusion which is often encountered when reading such literature where similar ideas are often shrouded with new names. In particular, we explore the role of IT in facilitating new ways of organizing.

In order to place this chapter in perspective, we begin by briefly tracing developments in organization theory. This review is not intended to be exhaustive, but to give a flavour of just some of the main themes which have emerged over the years. We then explore some of the perspectives that have been proposed in the recent management literature, identify the main themes of each, the critical management issues and combine these into a framework which we believe is useful in giving direction to managing the transformation process.

Historical viewpoint

Whenever people have come together to accomplish some task, organizations have existed. The family, the church, the military are examples of early organizations. Each had their own structure, hierarchy, tasks, role and authority. The modern business organization, however, is a relatively recent phenomenon whose evolution can be traced to two important historical inferences: the industrial revolution and changes in the law.

The industrial revolution, which occurred largely in England during the 1770s, saw the substitution of machine power for human work and marked the beginning of the factory system of work. It spawned a new way of producing goods and offered opportunities which saw business increase to a scale never previously possible. The early Company Acts provided limited liability for individuals who came together for business purposes. Both these events led to the emergence of the professional manager, i.e. someone who managed the business but who did not own it. The increase in scale of organizations required a management structure and organizational form.

Early attempts to formulate appropriate organization form focused on determining the anatomy of formal organization. This so-called classical approach was built around four key pillars: division of labour, functional processes, structure, and span of control (Scott, 1961). Included here is the scientific management approach pioneered by Frederick Taylor (1911) which proposed one best way of accomplishing tasks. The objective was to increase productivity by standardizing and structuring jobs performed by humans. It spawned mass production with its emphasis on economies of scale. Although initially the concept applied to factory-floor workers, its application spread progressively in most organizational activity. Harrington Emerson took Taylor's ideas and applied them to the organizational structure with an emphasis on the organization's objectives. He emphasized, in a set of organizational 'principles' he developed, the use of experts in organizations to improve organizational efficiency (Emerson, 1917).

This mechanistic view was subsequently challenged by an emerging view stressing the human and social factors in work. Drawing on industrial psychology and social theory, the behavioural school argued that the human element was just as important. Themes such as motivation and leadership dominated the writings of subscribers to this view (e.g. Maslow, 1943, 1954; Mayo, 1971; McClelland, 1976).

Over the past 40 years organizational theorists have been concerned with the formal structure of organization and the implications these structures have on decision-making and performance. Weber (1947), for example, argued that hierarchy, formal rules, formal procedures, and professional managerial authority would increase efficiency.

Ever since Adam Smith (1910) articulated the importance of division of labour in a developing economy this notion has become ingrained in the design of organizations. Functionalism due to specialization is a salient feature of most organizations. Too often, however, this had led to an ineffective organization with each functional unit pursuing its own objectives. To overcome inherent weaknesses in this view, both the systems approach and the strategy thesis seek to integrate diverse functional unit objectives.

The systems movement originated from attempts to develop a general theory of systems that would be common to all disciplines (Bertalanfy, 1956). Challenging the reductionist approach of physics and chemistry the focus was on the whole being greater than the sum of the parts. Organizations were conceptualized as systems composed of subsystems which were linked and related to each other. Indeed, the systems approach is the dominant philosophy in designing organizational information systems. Systems theory also made the distinction between closed systems, i.e. those that focus primarily on their internal operations, and open systems which are affected by their interaction with their external environment. Early organizational theories tended to adopt a closed systems view. However, by adopting a more open approach it was clear that environmental issues were equally important.

The strategy movement which originated from Harvard Business School in the 1950s highlighted the importance of having an overall corporate strategy to integrate these various functional areas and how the organization can best impact its environment. The argument was that without an overall corporate strategy, each functional unit would pursue its own goals very often to the detriment of the organization as a whole. The decade of the 1970s saw many formalized, analytical approaches to strategic planning being proposed such as the Boston Consulting Group's planning portfolio (Henderson, 1979) and Ansoff's product portfolio matrix (Ansoff, 1979). Competitor analysis and the search for competitive advantage was the dominant theme of the 1980s, greatly influenced by the work of Porter (1980, 1985).

Chandler (1962), in his seminal study of US industries, saw structure following strategy. His thesis was that different strategies required different organizational structures to support them. Organizations that seek innovation demand flexible structures. Organizations that attempt to be low cost operators must maximize efficiency and the mechanistic structure helps achieve this. However, theorists such as Mintzberg (1979) and Thompson (1961) have emphasized the systemic aspect of structure, showing how structure can influence strategy and decision-making while hindering adaptation to the external environment.

The contingency theorists argued that the form an organization took is a function of the environment (Lawrence and Lorsch, 1970). Mintzberg, Miller and others talk about organizational configurations that bring strategy, structure, and context into natural co-alignment (Miller, 1986, 1987; Miller and Mintzberg, 1984). They argue that key forces or imperatives explain and give rise to many common configurations. The form an organization would take would reflect its dominant imperative.

We are not arguing that these forms or perspectives were inappropriate. In their time they represented the best forms that supported contemporary management thinking. For instance, despite its neglect of human aspects, scientific management yielded vast increases in productivity. However, the dynamic element which precipitated many of these approaches has also rendered them ineffective. Where are many of the *excellent* companies which Peters and Waterman (1982) wrote about 10 years ago? Perhaps they stuck to the knitting and ran out of wool. Perhaps the competition started using knitting machines or, indeed, the market now no longer has the need for wool products.

Recently Mintzberg (1991) has refined his thinking on organizational form and considered another view of organizational effectiveness, in which organizations do not slot themselves into established images so much as continually to build their own unique solutions to problems.

Given today's competitive conditions it is clear that one of the challenges facing management in the 1990s is to develop more dynamic organizations harnessing the power and capability of IT. What form such organizations will take is yet unclear. However, a picture of what this form will look like and how to initiate its development is beginning to emerge.

New perspectives

Over the past few years there have been a number of papers calling for the reappraisal of the form taken by organizations and for the widely accepted assumptions governing organizations to be re-evaluated. *Fortune, International Management* and *Business Week* have recently run articles looking at the organization of the 21st century indicating clearly that this topic is on the general management agenda as well as a focus of academic studies. In our research we have identified six perspectives which we feel represent current thinking on new ways of organizing. These are: network organizations; task focused teams; networked group; horizontal organizations; learning organizations; and matrix management.

In the sections that follow, we examine these perspectives briefly, with reference to key articles and research findings, and we identify salient themes. We then synthesize these themes into a framework which presents the key issues to be considered in the transformation process to a new organizational form.

Network organization

In their early work Miles and Snow (1978) discuss how market forces could be injected into traditional organizational structures to make them more efficient and responsive. In so doing they exhibit characteristics of delayering, downsizing, and operating through a network of market-sensitive business units. The driving force towards such an organization form are competitive pressures demanding both efficiency and effectiveness and the increasing speed necessary to adopt to market pressures and competitors' innovations. In essence, the network organization is in response to market forces. Included in this perspective are outsourcing, value adding partnerships, strategic alliances and business network design.

With a network structure, one firm may research and design a product, another may engineer and manufacture it, distribution may be handled by another, and so on. A firm focuses on what it does well, outsourcing to other firms for resources that are required in addition (Figure 15.1). However, care must be exercised in outsourcing: Bettis *et al.* (1992) report that improper use of outsourcing can destroy the future of a business.

Three specific types of network organization are discussed by Snow *et al.* (1992):

- *Internal network*, typically arises to capture entrepreneurial and market benefits without having the company engage in much outsourcing. The basis logic is that internal units have to operate with prices set by the market instead of artificial transfer prices. They will constantly seek to innovate and increase performance.
- *Stable network*, typically employs partial outsourcing and is a way of injecting flexibility into the overall value chain.
- *Dynamic network*, provides both specialization and flexibility, with outsourcing expected.

Recent changes in the UK National Health Service (NHS) have seen the development of an internal market for health care as shown by General

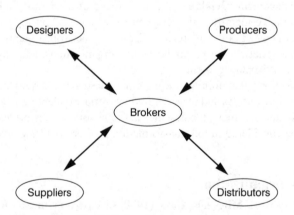

Figure 15.1   *Illustration of a network structure*

Practitioner Fund holders and the competitive role of NHS Trusts. The distinction between purchaser and provider organization represents the emergence of the networked organization. District Health Authorities now purchase health services based on the health needs assessment of the community from a variety of sources. Provider organizations need to be more cost and quality conscious.

In order for networks to exist, close relationships must be built with both suppliers and buyers along what Porter (1985) refers to as the value system. Johnson and Lawrence (1988) have coined the term value-adding partnerships (VAPs) to describe such relationships, which are more than just conventional electronic data interchange (EDI) links. They depend largely on the attitudes and practices of the participating managers. Asda Superstores and Procter and Gamble (P&G) now cooperate with each other beyond sending just orders and invoices via EDI. For instance Asda now provide forecasting information to P&G in an open way that was not previously management practice. In return, P&G are more responsive in meeting replenishment requirements. General Motors has renamed its purchasing department the 'supplier development' department.

For a network organization to exist it requires the capability of IT to facilitate communication and co-ordination among the various units. This is especially so when firms are operating in global markets. Further, IT facilitates VAPs; it does not create them.

Strategic alliances

Strategic alliances with both competitors and others in the industry value system are key strategies adopted by many organizations in the late 1980s (Hamel *et al.*, 1989; Nakomoto, 1992; Ohmae, 1989). McKinsey's estimate that the rate of joint venture formation between US companies and international partners has been growing by 27 per cent since 1985 (Ernst and Bleeke, 1993).

Collaboration may be considered a low cost route for new companies to gain technology and market access (Hamel *et al.*, 1989). Many European companies have developed pan-European alliances to help rationalize operations and share costs. Banks and other financial institutions use each others' communication networks for ATM transactions. Corning, the $3 billion-a-year glass and ceramics maker, is renowned for making partnerships. Among Corning's bedfellows are Dow Chemicals, Siemens (Germany's electronics conglomerate) and Vitro (Mexico's biggest glass maker). Alliances are so central to Corning's strategy that the corporation now defines itself as a 'network of organizations'. The multi-layered structure of today's computer industry and the large number of firms it now contains, means that any single firm, no matter how powerful, must work closely with many others. Often, this is in order to obtain access to technology or management expertise. A web of many joint ventures, cross-equity holdings and marketing pacts now entangles every firm in the industry.

Outsourcing

There is an argument that organizations should focus on core competencies and outsource all other activities. This has been a successful strategy followed by many companies. For example, Nike and Reebok have both prospered by concentrating on their strengths in designing and marketing high-tech fashionable sports footwear. Nike owns one small factory. Virtually all footwear production is contracted to suppliers in Taiwan, South Korea and other Asian countries. Dell Computers prospers by concentrating on two aspects of the computer business where the virtually integrated companies are vulnerable: marketing and service. Dell owns no plants and leases two small factories to assemble computers from outsourced parts. Figure 15.2 illustrates the relative success of electronics companies who outsource as against the vertically integrated companies.

Japanese financial-industrial groups are an advanced manifestation of a dynamic network. Called *keiretsu*, they are able to make long-term investments in technology and manufacturing, command the supply chain from components and capital equipment to end products and coordinate their strategic approaches to block foreign competition and penetrate world markets. There are also close relations between the banks and group companies, often cemented by banks holding company shares. It is interesting to note that many German companies have similar relations with their banks

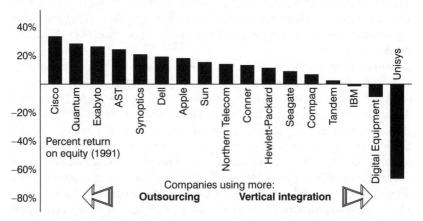

Figure 15.2 *Outsourcing versus integration in electronics companies (Source: Fortune, 8 February 1993)*

and very often bankers sit on the board of directors. *Business Week* (1992) recently reported that Ford has been making plans for what it would do with a bank if and when US legislation permits it to own one.

Business network redesign

The concept of business network redesign (BNR) has become increasingly popular where organizations seek to address major changes in the way they interface and do business with external entities. BNR represents using IT for 'designing the nature of exchange among multiple participants in a business network' (Venkatraman, 1991, p.140). The underlying assumption is that the sources of competitive advantage lie partly within a given organization and partly in the larger business network. Using IT, suppliers, buyers and competitors, are linked together via a strategy of electronic integration (Venkatraman, 1991).

BNR needs to be distinguished from EDI, which refers to the technical features, and inter-organizational systems (IOS), which refers to the characteristics of a specific system.

Redesigning an industry network is something akin to the dynamic structure of Snow *et al.* (1992) where an active relationship is cultivated between members of the network. Terms such as strategic alliance and value-adding partnerships are equally relevant here as they are with dynamic networks. Extending the industry network by introducing outsourcing is also feasible.

Task focused teams

Reich (1987) argues that a 'collective entrepreneurship' with few middle-level managers and only modest differences between senior management and junior staff is developing in some organizations. Drucker (1988) concurs and contends the organization of the future will be more information-based, flatter, more task oriented, driven more by professional specialists, and more dependent upon clearly focused issues. He proposes that such an organization will resemble a hospital or symphony orchestra rather than a typical manufacturing firm. For example, in a hospital much of the work is done in teams as required by an individual patient's diagnosis and condition. Drucker argues that these *ad hoc* decision-making structures will provide the basis for a permanent organizational form.

The emphasis on the team is a common theme which is emerging from the other perspectives on organizations. The team is seen as being the building block of the new organization and not the individual as has traditionally been the case. Katzenbach and Smith (1992) define a team as a 'small number of people with complementary skills who are committed to a common purpose, performance goals and approach for which they hold themselves mutually accountable'. They suggest that there is a common link between teams, individual behaviour change and high performance.

High performance teams play a crucial role within Asea Brown Boveri (ABB), the Swedish–Swiss conglomerate. Here, their T50 programme is seeking to reduce cycle time by 50 per cent. These teams were as a result of a major change of attitude in the organization. Management by directives was replaced by management by goals and trust; individual piece-rate payment changed to group bonuses; controlling staffs moved to support teams; and there was one union agreement for all employees.

Drucker's notion of teams echoes Burns and Stalker's (1961) organic organization as opposed to the more mechanistic type of organization. Table 15.1 contrasts these views and presents their distinguishing organizational characteristics.

Increasingly, firms are using teams to coordinate development across functional areas and thus reduce product development times (Krachenberg *et al.*, 1988; Lyons *et al.*, 1990). For example, if we look at pharmaceuticals and telecommunications, the traditional sequential flow of research, development, manufacturing and marketing is being replaced by synchrony: specialists from all these functions working together as a team. Terms such as 'concurrent engineering', 'design for manufacturability', 'simultaneous engineering', 'design-integrated manufacturing' and 'design-to-process' are being used increasingly in organizations to incorporate cross-functional teams and methodologies to integrate engineering and design with manufacturing process (Dean and Susman, 1989; Griffin *et al.*, 1991).

Since 1990 British Aerospace (BAe) has been actively promoting simultaneous engineering in its engineering division, having examined a number of initiatives. They saw the total quality management (TQM) message being difficult to get across and not very relevant to engineering. While process review was appealing it was limited in scope if only done inside engineering. For BAe, multifunctional teams are key to the success of their programmes. There is a clear focus on goals, the top level plan is robust to change, dependencies are less critical as they are dealt with by the team, members develop mutual role acknowledgement generating an achievement culture.

However, the notion of teams is nothing new. Value analysis and value engineering have been popular in many manufacturing firms since the 1950s. Although employees from various disciplines were brought together, the focus was on products; the new conceptualization is much broader. What is new about Drucker's vision is the role that IT will play. IT greatly facilitates task-based teams especially in enabling geographically dispersed groups to improve the coordination of their activities through enhanced electronic communication. Rockart and Short (1989) see self-governing units as being one of the impacts of IT.

Table 15.1   *Mechanistic versus organic organizations*

Element	Mechanistic organization	Organic organization
Channel of communication	Highly structured Controlled information flow	Open; free flow of information
Operating style	Must be uniform and restricted	Allowed to vary freely
Authority for decisions	Based on formal line-management position	Based on expertise of the individual
Adaptability	Reluctant, with the insistence holding fast to tried and tested principles in spite of changes in circumstances	Free, in response to changing circumstances
Work emphasis	On formal, laid down procedures	On getting things done unconstrained by formality
Control	Tight, through sophisticated control systems	Loose and informal, with emphasis on cooperation
Behaviour	Constrained, and required to conform to job description	Flexible and shaped the individual to meet the needs of the situation and personality
Participation	Superiors make decisions with minimum consultation and minimum involvement of subordinates	Participation and group consensus frequently used

Source: D. P. Slevin and J. G. Colvin (1990).

The networked group

According to Charan (1991) a network is a recognized group of managers assembled by the CEO and the senior executive team. The membership is drawn from across company functional areas, business units, from different levels in the hierachy and from different locations. Such a network brings together a mix of managers whose business skills, personal motivations, and functional expertise allow them to drive a large company like a small company. The foundation of a network is its social architecture, which differs in important ways from structure. As such, it differs from Miles and Snow's (1987) concept of network in that it is internally focused.

- networks differ from teams, cross-functional task forces or other assemblages designed to break hierarchy
- networks are not temporary; teams generally disband when the reason they were assembled is accomplished
- networks are dynamic; they do not merely solve problems that have been defined for them
- networks make demands on senior management.

In most organizations, information flows upwards and is thus prone to distortion and manipulation. In a network, especially a global network that extends across borders, information must be visible and simultaneous. Members of the network receive the same information at the same time. Not only must hard information be presented, but also more qualitative information, not just external information but members' experiences, successes, views and problems.

The single most important level for reinforcing behaviour in networks is evaluation. Every manager, regardless of position or seniority, responds to the criteria by which he or she is evaluated, who conducts the review, and how it is conducted. For a network to survive top management must focus on behaviour and horizontal leadership: Does a manager share information willingly and openly? Does he or she ask for and offer help? Is he or she emotionally committed to the business? Does the manager exercise informal leadership to energize the work of sub-networks?

Horizontal organizations

Questioning the validity of the vertical orientation of organizations a number of writers have proposed what they call the horizontal organization. Such organizations have clearly defined customer facing divisions and processes to improve performance.

Ostrof and Smith (1992) contend that performance improvements will be difficult to achieve for companies organized in a traditional vertical fashion. While the advantage of vertical organizations may be functional excellence it suffers from the problem of coordination. With many of today's competitive demands requiring coordination rather than functional specialization, traditional vertical organizations have a hard time responding to the challenges of the 1990s.

In the horizontal organization, work is primarily structured around a small number of business processes or work flows which link the activities of employees to the needs and capabilities of suppliers and customers in a way that improves the performance of all three.

Ostrof and Smith (1992) list ten principles at the heart of horizontal organizations which are listed in Table 15.2. Although not arguing for the

Table 15.2 *Blueprint for a horizontal organization*

- Organize around process not task
- Flatten hierarchy by minimizing the subdivision of work flows and non-value-added activities
- Assign ownership of processes and process performance
- Link performance objectives and evaluation to customer satisfaction
- Make teams, not individuals, the principal building blocks of organization performance and design
- Combine managerial and non-managerial activities as often as possible
- Treat multiple competencies as the rule, not the exception
- Inform and train people on a 'just-in-time to perform' basis not on a 'need to know' basis
- Maximize supplier and customer contact
- Reward individual skill development and team performance, not individual performance

Source: Ostrof and Smith (1992).

replacement of vertical organizations they recommend that each company must seek its own unique balance between the horizontal and vertical features needed to deliver performance.

BT was one of the early companies to recognize the ineffectiveness of the traditional vertical organization. Through project Sovereign and its process management initiatives, BT has reorganized itself into customer facing divisions and has embarked on significant performance improvement activity. Senior managers are now process owners with responsibility for service delivery as opposed to being functional heads. In a recent interview, BT's chairman revealed that AT&T, MCI and Deutsche Telecom have all restructured themselves following the BT model, setting up distinct business and personal communication divisions and separating network management from customer facing elements (Lorenz, 1993).

The horizontal design is seen as a key enabler to organizational flexibility and responsiveness. Time is critical in today's fast changing business environment (Stalk, 1988). Organizations need to be able to respond to customer demands with little delay and just-in-time (JIT) is just one manifestation of this. Kotler and Stonich (1991) have coined the term 'turbo marketing' to describe this requirement to make and deliver goods and services faster than competitors.

Multinational corporations face additional challenges making horizontal organizations work. As a result of their research Poynter and White (1990) have identified five activities needed to create and maintain a horizontal organization spanning a number of countries:

1 *Create shared values.* Collaborative decision making is not possible unless an organization has shared decision premises, a common culture or set of business values.

2 *Enabling the horizontal network.* To counteract the tendency for an organization to (re)assert vertical relationships, initiatives, such as giving headquarters' executives dual responsibilities, should be put in place.

3 *Redefine managers' roles.* The skills, abilities and approaches required for the horizontal organization are different than those from conventional vertical organizations. Fundamentally, senior managers must create, maintain and define an organization context that promotes lateral decision making oriented towards the achievement of competitive advantage world-wide.

4 *Assessing results.* Assignment of performance responsibility and availability for results within horizontal organizations is problematic. The people involved in horizontal collaborative efforts change over time and their individual contributions are difficult to measure.

5 *Evaluating people.* Evaluating executives in terms of their acceptance and application of a common set of beliefs is particularly appropriate for international management because of the shortcomings of orthodox vertical measures of evaluating people.

Business process redesign

This focus on process has become an important management focus over the past few years, with business process redesign (BPR) figuring highly on many corporate agendas (Dumaine, 1989; Butler Cox Foundation, 1991; Heygate and Breback, 1991; Kaplan and 'Murdock, 1991). BPR first entered the management nomenclature as a result of research conducted at MIT (Davenport and Short, 1990; Scott Morton, 1991). In their 'Management in the 1990s' research project they identified BPR as an evolutionary way of exploiting the capabilities of IT for more than just efficiency gains (Scott Morton, 1991).

Consider how IT is currently implemented in organizations: localized exploitation – typically to improve the efficiency of a particular task; and internal integration – integration of key internal applications to establish a common IT platform for the business.

With an internal focus, both of the above overlay on the existing tasks and activities thus retaining existing organization structures. This is what Hammer (1990) has referred to as 'paving the cow path'. Most IT systems design methodologies reinforce this view. BPR, however, questions the validity of existing ways of organizing work and is concerned with redesigning the organization around fundamental business processes.

BPR is the analysis and design of work flows and processes within organizations. It has also been called business re-engineering, process re-engineering, process innovation and core process redesign. The crucial element is the concentration on process rather than events or activities. A business process can be defined as a set of related activities that cuts across functional boundaries or specializations in order to realize a business objective. A set of processes is a business system.* Processes are seen to have two important characteristics: (i) they have customers, that is, processes have defined business outcomes and there are recipients of outcomes (customers can be either internal or external); (ii) they cross functional boundaries, i.e. they normally occur across or between organizational functional units. Examples include research and development, mortgage application appraisal, developing a budget, ordering from suppliers, creating a marketing plan, new product development, customer order fulfilment, flow of materials (purchasing, receiving, manufacturing).

Most companies still operate with thousands of specialists who are judged and rewarded by how well they perform their separate functions – with little knowledge or concern about how these fit into the complex process of turning raw material, capital and labour into a product or service. Activities and events are thus snap shots of a larger process. The Japanese realized that focusing on individual activities in the value chain was not sufficient. Superior performance was gained by focusing on the total process. So while Western managers focused on managing inventories, the Japanese saw that eliminating delays in the production process was the key to reducing instability, decreased cost, increased productivity and service.

However, BPR is not a new concept: its origins can be found in work study organization and methods (O&M) of the 1960s. It also has its roots in the quality revolution where the stress is on improving quality by identifying, studying, and improving the processes that make and deliver a product or service. The scope of quality management is often narrow, however, with responsibility lying in functional areas and thus not as rigorous as process redesign. The emphasis of BPR is on how different processes are carried out. The objective is to re-evaluate these processes and to redesign them so that they are aligned more closely to business objectives.

The philosophy of BPR is fundamentally different from the systems approach with which it might be confused. The systems approach is a theoretical framework which recognizes the interdependence of functional units and seeks to integrate them by integrating information flows. With BPR the emphasis is on processes which transcend functional units. It seeks to challenge existing assumptions relating to how the organization operates. It

---

* For a discussion on the 'process' notion see Chris Edwards and Joe Peppard, *Business Process Redesign: Hype, Hope or Hypocrisy?* Cranfield School of Management, Cranfield, Bedford, 1993.

emphasizes a top down customer focused approach often using IT as the mechanism for coordination and control.

The benefits of taking a process approach is to reduce costs, increase quality, while increasing responsiveness and flexibility. IT is often the essential ingredient by which the process concept can be turned into a practical proposition. Processes can also be redesigned to take account of the latest developments in technology.

Learning organizations

There has been renewed interest over the past few years in the learning organization (Garvin, 1993; Hayes *et al.*, 1988; Kochan and Useem, 1992; Stata, 1989; Senge, 1990a, 1990b, 1991; Quinn Mills and Friesen, 1992). The argument is that current patterns of behaviour in large organizations are typically 'hard wired' in structure, in information systems, incentive schemes, hiring and promotion practice, working practices, and so on. To break down such behaviour, organizations need the capability to harness the learning capabilities of their members. The learning organization is able to sustain consistent internal innovation or 'learning' with the immediate goals of improving quality, enhancing customer or supplier relationships, or more effectively executing business strategy (Quinn Mills and Friesen, 1992). This notion has similarities to the work of Argyris (1976, 1982).

Argyris identified two types of learning that can occur in organizations: adaptive learning and generative learning. Typically, organizations engage in adaptive or 'single-loop' learning and thus cope with situations within which they find themselves. For example, comparing budgeted against actual figures and taking appropriate action. Generative or double-loop learning, however, requires new ways of looking at the world, challenging assumptions, goals, and norms.

Implementing executive information systems (EIS) typically requires users to first adapt to using technology to obtain their required information, i.e. adaptive learning. However, to exploit the potential of EIS fully, systems users must proactively develop and test models of the use of EIS in the management process, i.e. double-loop learning. Zuboff's (1988) work refers to the criticality of line managers developing spatial models to exploit fully the potential of information systems available to them.

Mintzberg (1973) claims that the way executives use information that they collect is to develop mental images – models of how the organization and its environment function. Hedberg and Jonsson (1978) assert that to be able to operate at all, managers look at the world and intuitively create a myth or theory of what is happening in the world. With this in mind, they create a strategy to react to this myth so that they can form defence networks against information overflows from other myths and map information into definitions of their situations. They then test the strategy out on the world and evaluate its success.

Mason and Mitroff (1981) suggest that assumptions are the basic elements of a strategist's frame of reference or world view. Since assumptions form the basis of strategies, it is important that they be consistent with the information available to strategists (Schwenk, 1988). However, most decision-makers are unaware of the particular set of assumptions they hold and of methods that can help them in examining and assessing the strength of their assumptions (Mason and Mitroff, 1981; Mitroff and Linstone, 1993). The accuracy of these assumptions may be affected by their cognitive heuristics and biases. DeGeus (1988) suggests that planning is learning. However, planning is based on assumptions that should be constantly challenged.

Organization learning theory suggests that learning often cannot begin until unlearning has taken place (Burgelman, 1983). This requires a realization of the current position. Senge (1990a) talks about creative tension where a vision (picture of what might be) of the future pulls the organization from its current reality position. This is more than adaptation and is very much proactive.

Quinn Mills and Friesen (1992) list three key characteristics of a learning organization: (i) *It must make a commitment to knowledge.* This includes promoting mechanisms to encourage the collection and dissemination of knowledge and ideas throughout the organization. This may include research, discussion groups, seminars, hiring practices. (ii) *It must have a mechanism for renewal.* A learning organization must promote an environment where knowledge is incorporated into practices, processes and procedures. (iii) *It must possess an openness to the outside world.* The organization must be responsive to what is occurring outside of it.

Many organizations have implemented information systems in an attempt to improve organizational learning. For example, groupware products such as Lotus Notes or IBM's TeamFocus facilitate the sharing of ideas and expertise within an organization.

At Price Waterhouse they have 9000 employees linked together using Lotus Notes. Auditors in offices all over the world can keep up to date on relevant topics; anyone with an interest in a subject can read information and add their own contribution. By using groupware, Boeing has cut the time needed to complete a wide range of products by an average of 90 per cent or to one-tenth of what similar work took in the past.

Over the long run, superior performance depends on superior learning. The key message is that the learning organization requires new leadership skills and capabilities. The essence of the learning organization is that it is not just the top that does the thinking; rather it must occur at every level. Hayes *et al.* (1988) argue that in effect the organization of the 1990s will be a learning organization, one in which workers teach themselves how to analyse and solve problems.

Matrix management

Bartlett and Ghoshal (1990) argue that strategic thinking has far outdistanced organizational capabilities which are incapable of carrying out sophisticated strategies. In their search for a more effective form they argue that companies that have been most successful at developing multi-dimensional organizations first attend to the culture of the organization; then change the systems and relationships which facilitate the flow of information. Finally, they realign the organizational structure towards the new focus.

They call this matrix management although it is different from the 1970s concept of matrix management. They argue that while the notion of matrix management had appeal, it proved unmanageable – especially in an international context. Matrix management tended to pull people in several directions at once. Management needs to manage complexity rather than minimize it.

They contend that the most successful companies are those where top executives recognize the need to manage the new environmental and competitive demands by focusing less on the quest for an ideal structure and more on developing the abilities, behaviour and performance of individual managers. This has echoes of Peters and Waterman's (1982) bias for action.

People are the key to managing complex strategies and organizations. The 'organizational psychology' needs to be changed in order to reshape the understanding, identification, and commitment of its employees. Three principal characteristics common to those that managed the task most effectively are identified:

- *Build a shared vision.* Break down traditional mindsets by developing and communicating a clear sense of corporate purpose that extends into every corner of the company and gives context and meaning to each manager's particular roles and responsibilities.
- *Develop human resources.* Turn individual manager's perceptions, capabilities, and relationships into the building blocks of the organization.
- *Co-opting management efforts.* Get individuals and organizational groups into the broader vision by inviting them to contribute to the corporate agenda and then giving them direct responsibility for implementation.

While matrix management as a structural objective (the 1970s conceptualization) may not be possible, the essence can still be achieved. Management needs to develop a matrix of flexible perspectives and relationships in their mind.

A framework

Each of the perspectives presented above challenges traditional views of organizations. The arguments are based around a total re-evaluation of the assumptions which underlie organizational form, i.e. the best mix of structure, systems, management style, culture, roles, responsibilities and skills. From the different viewpoints presented we can get a glimpse of the characteristics of the 21st century organization. Key characteristics of these organizations are:

- constantly challenging traditional organizational assumptions
- evolution through learning at all levels
- multi-disciplinary self-managing teams with mutual role acknowledgement
- a reward structure based on team performance
- increased flexibility and responsiveness
- an achievement rather than blame culture
- an organizational wide and industry wide vision
- a vision of what kind of organizational form is required
- process driven with a customer focus
- fast response with time compression
- information based
- IT enabled.

This list of characteristics is perhaps not surprising. They have been advocated in both the academic and general management literature over recent years. Of course we cannot categorically say that organizations structured in a traditional way will not survive, although it is hard to see them thriving. We do suggest, however, that an organization critically reviews its form to determine whether it should incorporate some of these characteristics and the extent to which these should be adopted.

While we do have a destination in general terms there are three key issues which we feel need to be addressed in practice:

- *The vision.* The precise destination for a particular organization, i.e. where do we need to be? This is very much the visioning process where organizational requirements are determined. The precise final form will be unique to each organization depending on the organization itself and the context within which it exists. While form will depend on the strategy of the business many organizations fail to consider the organization's ability to deliver this strategy. This must go beyond defining structure and incorporate culture, reward systems, human resource requirements, etc. These in some sense could be seen as representing the organization form's critical success factors (CSFs).
- *Gap analysis.* A critical understanding of where the organization is now in relation to this organization vision should be established. The role which IT will play in the new organization should also be assessed. In short, we are attempting to describe the nature of the journey that needs to be undertaken. The concern here is with planning the business transformation.

- *Managing the migration.* How do we manage the migration from the existing organization form to a new form? The concern here is with the change management process which seeks to ensure the successful transition from the old form to the new form. A particularly difficult area to tackle here is an organization's ability to incorporate information systems/information technology (IS/IT) developments successfully where these involve significant business change.

A recurring problem faced by any organization engaging in redesign is determining an appropriate approach. Perhaps it is too ambitious to expect an existing method to be comprehensive enough to deal with all the issues involved. All organizations are different and changing an organization's form is more complex than simply identifying core processes and leveraging IT as many of the articles imply. The critical issue is to address broader themes such as culture, management development, IS/IT development, skills, reward systems, etc. These notions are complex, however, and do not subscribe to neat techniques but need to be managed carefully.

Traditionally, we have aligned IT with the business strategy, without much consideration to people issues or the organizational capability to deliver (Galliers, 1991). Macdonald (1991, 1993) provides a useful model high-lighting interrelationships between the business strategy, IS/IT and organizational processes. While checking for alignment of these variables and identifying issues, he outlines the topography but fails to provide any help in reaching the required destination.

It is much easier to embellish the characteristics of the organization of the 1990s than to define clear frameworks to achieve these characteristics. What we do not have is a road map to translate these aspirations into a workable design. Additionally, the road map needs to identify potential hazards and obstacles that are likely to be encountered en route and how these are to be dealt with.

Figure 15.3 illustrates some of the problems faced by an organization attempting to move from a current form to a new one. There are many forces which will drive it off course and it is essential that these are managed in order successfully to achieve the desired goal.

A key point is that, even when we identify the destination, the challenge is to negotiate the journey. Any route planning needs to explicitly address these issues. Questioning an organization's fundamental approach to the way that it does business can be risky and may confront too many entrenched interests among managers and employees to be worth doing unless an organization is in dire trouble. By then a complete overhaul is often too late to be of much use. It is often difficult to put across the idea that a successful organization should radically reconsider how it does business, however.

The issues can be fundamental and might include inappropriate IS/IT, management myopia, resistance, poor vision, etc. The stakes are high as is the

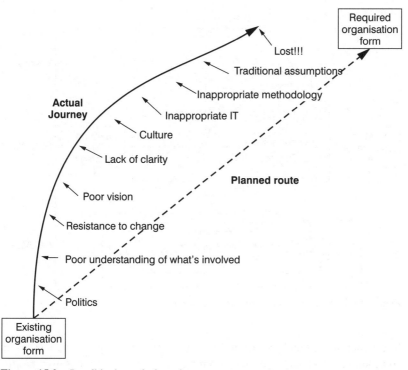

Figure 15.3 *Roadblocks and obstacles to a new organization*

need to manage them well particularly as many of them are central to people's value systems, such as power, politics and rewards. The characteristics of the new organization form, as described earlier, have a significantly different emphasis than those required by traditional forms, e.g. flexibility, process oriented, fast cycle response. In planning the migration we believe a fundamentally different paradigm should be used for managing this transition.

We have continually failed to provide an integrating framework to help in coordinating change and uncertainty. This uncertainty requires continual learning on the part of the organization both in terms of its destination and how to get there. A new multifaceted approach which integrates business strategy, IS/IT, organization design and human resources is needed.

In Figure 15.4 we present a framework for business transformation which we have found useful when approaching issues associated with the migration towards a new organizational form. This framework expands on the model of IS/IT strategy formulation popularized by Earl (1989), Galliers (1991) and Ward *et al.* (1990) and incorporates organizational and implementation issues.

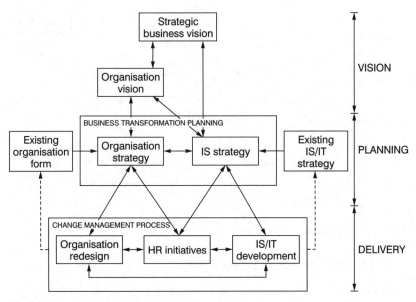

Figure 15.4   *Business transformation framework*

It is structured around the triumvirate of vision, planning and delivery with considerable iteration between planning and delivery to ensure that the required form is being met.

The underlying premise of this framework questions the traditional sequential IS/IT planning model where business strategy drives IS strategy which determines the organization's IT strategy. It incorporates an organization's ability to deliver fundamental business change, recognizing that increasingly this change is being enabled by IT.

Vision

The requirement for a clear business vision is well known and espoused by many scholars on strategy. However, equally important is a vision of the organization form that is necessary to deliver and support the achievement of that strategy. This organizational vision needs to be more than the traditional structural perspective of centralization, differentiation and formalization. Rather, it should define the organizational form CSFs in relation to culture, teamwork, empowerment, skills, reward systems and management style.

We define two types of visioning: business vision and organization vision. While business vision remains as currently practised by many organizations, the organization vision identifies the attributes and characteristics of the organization to achieve this business vision. Grand Metropolitan, for example, has an organization vision based on organizational competencies which are crucial to deliver its strategies. They believe that managerial and organizational competencies are more enduring and difficult to emulate than, what they call, 'the traditional structural strategies' of a conglomerate such as product portfolio, production sites and acquisition strategies. Having looked at the organizational CSFs for home banking, Midland Bank decided that their existing organization was not an appropriate vehicle for a home banking/telebanking organization, hence First Direct was set up. Acting 'independently' of the parent it articulated an organization vision of what was required organizationally to deliver this new service.

Business transformation planning

Business transformation planning demands two key activities: planning the organization strategy and developing an information systems strategy which facilitates this strategy but which is also closely aligned to business requirements. The conventional IS/IT planning framework does not explicitly consider the organization's ability and capability to deliver the business strategy.

A key concern of business transformation planning is a critical evaluation and understanding of the existing organization's characteristics and capabilities of how the current IS/IT strategy is being used to support them. The gap between existing and required can then be determined. It is important to emphasize that the relationship between both the organizing strategy and the IS strategy is bi-directional.

Organization strategy

An organization strategy involves more than simply considering the arrangement of people and tasks: what we typically call structure. It incorporates all the characteristics of organizational form which are encapsulated in the CSFs articulated in the organization vision. This will include what is needed in terms of skills, styles, procedures, values and reward systems. The organization strategy operationalizes these notions and will become the blueprint for the change management process.

A number of approaches to understand and evaluate aspects of organizational form have been proposed by many authors. For example, Johnson (1992) presents the cultural web as a means of assessing existing organization culture. The strategic alignment process of Macdonald is also useful in reviewing the alignment of strategy, organizational processes and IT.

It is important also at this stage to consider the opportunities which IT offers in relation to organizing work. Groupware, for example, greatly enhances team work and can lead to greater productivity. IT facilitates more customer-oriented service as the systems provide more comprehensive information. BT now has one point of contact with both business and personal customers. Queries can be dealt with more efficiently and work routed to the appropriate area where necessary. First Direct is only possible due to IT, which allows the telephone clerks to give almost immediate response to requests.

Distance effects are also minimized due to IT. People from diverse geographical locations can now work together in the same team creating the boundary-less corporation. Multinational corporations can adopt a more efficient horizontal structure. Technology is also blurring the distinction between organizations. With technology, business processes can now transcend traditional organizational boundaries. Strategic alliances and value added partnerships are becoming key strategies for many organizations and IT has a major role to play in facilitating the communication and coordination necessary to make these pay off.

Changing the way things are done will usually require investment in human resource initiatives in order to enhance team skills, customer service skills, information sharing and organization wide values. These can become critical barriers and deflect an organization in migrating to the new form.

IS strategy

Although the organization of the 1990s will be information-based, we believe that designing systems solely around information flows is flawed. The emphasis will not be on how tasks are performed (faster, cheaper, better) but rather in how firms organize the flow of goods and services through value-added chains and systems. Organizing around business processes permits greater focus on what the organization is trying to achieve and not on operationalizing objectives around existing activities.

IT has, for too long, been seen as a tool for improving efficiency and effectiveness. The new organizational shapes are dependent on the capability of information and communication technologies. EIS, for example, permit senior managers to delegate and decentralize while still maintaining overall control.

As mentioned above, aligning IS strategy with business strategy is only half the story. The IS strategy must also be compatible with how the business is organized to meet the business strategy. As a result of their research, Hayes and Jaikumar (1988) contend that acquiring any advanced manufacturing system is more like replacing an old car with a helicopter. By failing to understand and prepare for the revolutionary capabilities of these systems, they will become as much an inconvenience as a benefit – and a lot more expensive.

During the business transformation planning phase, the existing organiza- tion form and the existing IS/IT strategy will be reviewed and the transformation plans developed. The change strategy will be mapped out in terms of approaches to be used, the rate of change, how it is to be achieved, milestones and how the road-blocks and obstacles are to be negotiated. Of critical concern, is a clear statement of the final destination.

Change management process

Migration to the new form is a change process which implements the plans in the most appropriate way.

Organizational redesign

Organization redesign involves managing the migration to the new organizational infrastructure. In particular:

- the change from function to process orientation
- developing and implementing new ways of working
- redefining roles and responsibilities in line with the migration.

These must be closely aligned with human resource (HR) initiatives and IS/IT development.

Human resource initiatives

Central to the successful management change are the HR initiatives which are put in place. Many organizations try to accomplish strategic change by merely changing the system and structure of their organization. This is a recipe for failure. HR initiatives will be incorporated within the organization's overall HR strategy and will include education, management development programmes, training and reward structures. Probably one of the greatest barriers to the management of change is the assumption that it simply happens or that people must simply change because it is necessary to do so (Peppard and Steward, 1993).

HR development has a crucial challenging role to play in successfully 'orchestrating' strategic culture change (Burack, 1991). US Labor Secretary Robert Reich recently urged American companies to treat their workers as assets to be developed rather than as costs to be cut.

Many barriers to change are not tangible, and although are propagated by organizations, they exist in the mind of the manager. Indeed, such an initiative would also contribute towards the learning capability of organizations, although there is a distinction between learning as an individual phenomenon and an organization's capability to learn by the systematization of knowledge.

Management needs to be taught new skills, particularly interpersonal skills and how to work in teams. New organizational forms also require managers to carry out new tasks and roles. The informate phenomenon identified by Zuboff (1988) increasingly requires empowerment and wider responsibility for decision-making to be given to organization members.

Changing technology places additional strains on management. Education for new technology is important for two reasons: (i) strategically, to give a strategic view of IT; and (ii) organizationally – it is arguable that the chief contribution of managers to the competitive nature of organizations will be thinking creatively about organizational change.

Motorola spends $120 million every year on education, equivalent to 3.6 per cent of payroll. It calculates that every $1 it spends on training delivers $30 in productivity gains within three years. Since 1987, the company has cut costs by $3.3 billion – not by the normal expedient of firing workers, but by training them to simplify processes and reduce waste. For example, the purchasing department at the automotive and industrial electronics group set up a team called ET/VT = 1 because it wanted to ensure that all 'elapsed time' (the hours it took to handle a requisition) was 'value time' (the hours when an employee is doing something necessary and worthwhile). The team managed to cut from seventeen to six the number of steps in handling a requisition. Team members squeezed average elapsed time from thirty hours to three, enabling the purchasing department to handle 45 per cent more requests without adding workers (Henkoff, 1993).

Scott Morton (1991) contends that one of the challenges for an organization in the 1990s is understanding one's culture and knowing that an innovative culture is a key first step in a move towards an adaptive organization. Managers have a core set of beliefs and assumptions which are specific and relevant to the organization in which they work and are learned over time. The culture of the organization propagates many of the traditional assumptions which underlie organizations and also makes it extremely difficult to change. This is not something that is unique to organizations but is firmly based in a society which fosters individuality. Everyone tends to be pigeonholed from an early age and it is only to be expected that it be carried to working life. Management education itself promotes specialization by teaching functional courses.

Hirschhorn and Gilmore (1992) have identified four psychological boundaries which managers must pay attention to in flexible organizations: *authority* boundary, *task* boundary, *political* boundary, and *identity* boundary. Let us briefly explore each of these.

- *Authority.* In more flexible organizations, issuing and following orders is no longer good enough. The individual with formal authority is not necessarily the one with the most up-to-date information about a business problem or a customer need. Subordinates must challenge in order to follow while superiors must listen in order to lead.

- *Task*. In a team environment, people must focus not only on their own work, but also on what others do.
- *Political*. In an organization, interest groups sometimes conflict and managers must know how to negotiate productively.
- *Identity*. In a workplace where performance depends on commitment, organizations must connect with the values of their employees.

An innovative HR policy that supports organizational members as they learn to cope with a more complex and changing world is required. New criteria to measure performance are also needed. It is no use fostering cross-functional teams if evaluation and reward are based on individual criteria. Every manager, regardless of position or seniority, responds to the criteria by which he or she is evaluated, who conducts the review, and how it is conducted.

IS/IT development

The approach to IS/IT development needs to take cognizance of the business objective as described in the IS and organization strategies. Most of the perspectives discussed above depend on harnessing the power of IT to make it all possible. However, it is important that the overall business applications of which IT developments are part are owned by business management. This is because their key involvement in requirements definition, data conversion, new working practices, implementation and realizing the benefits.

IS/IT developments are not all the same and the approach adopted needs to be related to business objectives. Ward *et al.* (1990) propose the use of the applications portfolio which indicates appropriate management strategies, particularly in relation to financial justification, IS/IT management style, the use of packages, outsourcing, contractors and consultants. This portfolio approach makes more effective the use of the IT resource in relation to business requirements.

Delivering the IS strategy is traditionally seen as a purely technological issue. However, of key concern are the changes which accompany any IT implementation (Galliers, 1991). People issues are key reasons why many IT investments fail to realize benefits (Scott Morton, 1991). Involvement and ownership in the design and implementation are seen as critical for the success of any IT development. The training needs required for the new technology must be integrated when appropriate with the HR initiatives.

Conclusions

The traditional organization has been criticized by many writers on organization. Alternatives have been proposed but these merely represent a destination without a clear road map setting the direction rather than presenting a map and route to negotiate the obstacles to be encountered along the way.

In this chapter we have presented a framework to help organizations in planning and implementing their journey. This framework is constructed around the triumvirate of vision, planning and delivery with considerable iteration between all stages. This helps with the management of uncertainty and reconfirms the destination.

Crucial in the visioning stage are the critical success factors of the new organizational form which define the requirements of critical issues such as culture, teamwork, people, skills, structure, reward systems and information needs. This provided the basis for the gap analysis highlighting the nature of the journey to be undertaken and the subsequent delivery initiatives of HR, organization design and IS/IT. Central to our framework are the interactions between HR, organization design and IS/IT in a way that enables the delivery of the new organization form with its CSFs.

Fundamentally, we believe that managing the migration to the new organization form will require a significant amount of senior management time, energy and initiative. If this is not forthcoming because management is 'too busy', the likelihood of success is minimal. This must be the first paradigm to be broken.

References

Ansoff, H. I. (1979) *Strategic Management*, Macmillan, London.

Argyris, C. (1976) Single-loop and double-loop models in research on decision-making. *Admin. Sci. Quarterly*, **21**, 363–375.

Argyris, C. (1982) *Reasoning, Learning and Action: Individual and Organization*, Jossey-Bass, San Francisco.

Bartlett, C. A. and Ghoshal, S. (1990) Matrix management: not a structure, a frame of mind. *Harvard Bus. Rev.*, July–August, 138–145.

Bertalanfy, L. von (1956) General systems theory. *General Systems*, **I**, 1–10.

Bettis, R. A., Bradley, S. P. and Hamel, G. (1992) Outsourcing and industrial decline. *Acad. Manage. Exec.*, **6**(1) 7–16.

Burack, E. H. (1991) Changing the company culture – the role of human resource development. *Long Range Planning*, **24**(1), 88–95.

Burgelman, R. A. (1983) A process model of internal corporate venturing in a diversified major firm. *Admin. Sci. Quarterly*, **28**(2), 223–244.

Burns, T. and Stalker, G. M. (1961) *The Management of Innovation*, Tavistock Publications, London.

Business Week (1992) Learning from Japan. *Business Week*, 27 January, 38–44.

Butler Cox (1991) The role of information technology in transforming the business. *Research Report 79*, Butler Cox Foundation, January.

Chandler, A. D. (1962) *Strategy and Structure: Chapters in the History of the American Industrial Enterprise*, The MIT Press, Cambridge, MA.

Charan, R. (1991) How networks reshape organizations – for results. *Harvard Bus. Rev.*, September–October, 104–115.

Davenport, T. H. and Short, J. E. (1990) The new industrial engineering: information technology and business process redesign. *Sloan Manage. Rev.*, Summer, 11–27.

Dean, J. W. and Susman, G. I. (1989) Organizing for manufacturable design. *Harvard Bus. Rev.*, January–February, 28–36.

deGeus, A. P. (1988) Planning as learning. *Harvard Bus. Rev.*, March–April, 70–74.

Drucker, P. F. (1988) The coming of the new organization. *Harvard Bus. Rev.*, January–February, 45–53.

Dumaine, B. (1989) What the leaders of tomorrow see. *Fortune*, 3 July, 24–34.

Earl, M. J. (1989) *Management Strategies for Information Technology*, Prentice-Hall, Hemel Hempstead, UK.

Emerson, H. (1917) The twelve principles of efficiency. *Eng. Mag.*, xviii.

Ernst, D. and Bleeke, J. (eds) (1993) *Collaborating to Compete: Using Strategic Alliances and Acquisitions in the Global Marketplace*, John Wiley, New York.

Galliers, R. D. (1991) Strategic information systems planning: myths, reality and guidelines for successful implementation. *Europ. J. Inf. Sys.*, **1**(1), 55–64.

Garvin, D. A. (1993) Building a learning organisation. *Harvard Bus. Rev.*, July–August, 78–91.

Griffin, J., Beardsley, S. and Kugel, R. (1991) Commonality: marrying design with process. *The McKinsey Quarterly*, Summer, 56–70.

Hamel, G., Doz, Y. L. and Prahalad, C. K. (1989) Collaborate with your competitors and win. *Harvard Bus. Rev.*, January–February, 143–154.

Hammer, M. (1990) Reengineering work: don't automate, obliterate. *Harvard Bus. Rev.*, July–August, 104–112.

Hayes, R. H. and Jaikumar, R. (1988) Manufacturing's crisis: new technologies, obsolete organisations. *Harvard Bus. Rev.*, September–October, 77–85.

Hayes, R. H., Wheelwright, S. C. and Clark, K. B. (1988) *Dynamic Manufacturing: Creating the Learning Organization*, The Free Press, New York.

Hedberg, B. and Jonsson, S. (1978) Designing semi-confusing information systems for organizations in changing environments. *Accounting, Organizations, and Society*, **3**(1), 47–64.

Henderson, B. D. (1979) *Henderson on Corporate Strategy*, Abt Books, Cambridge, MA.

Henkoff, R. (1993) Companies that train best. *Fortune*, 22 March, 40–46.

Heygate, R. and Brebach, G. (1991) Corporate reengineering. *The McKinsey Quarterly*, Summer, 44–55.

Hirschhorn, L. and Gilmore, T. (1992) The new boundaries of the 'boundaryless' company. *Harvard Bus. Rev.*, May–June, 104–115.

Johnson, G. (1992) Managing strategic change – strategy, culture and action. *Long Range Planning*, **25**(1), 29–36.

Johnson, R. and Lawrence, P. R. (1988) Beyond vertical integration – the rise of the value-adding partnership. *Harvard Bus. Rev.*, July–August, 94–101.

Kaplan, R. B. and Murdock, L. (1991) Core process redesign. *The McKinsey Quarterly*, Summer, 27–43.

Katzenbach, J. R. and Smith, D. K. (1992) Why teams matter. *The McKinsey Quarterly*, Autumn, 3–27.

Kochan, T. A. and Useem, M. (eds) (1992) *Transforming Organizations*, Oxford University Press, New York.

Kotler, P. and Stonich, P. J. (1991) Turbo marketing through time compression. *J. Bus. Strategy*, September–October, 24–29.

Krachenberg, A. R., Henke, J. W. and Lyons, T. F. (1988) An organizational structure response to competition. In *Advances in Systems Research and Cybernetics* (ed. G. E. Lasker), International Institute for Advanced Studies in Systems Research and Cybernetics, University of Windsor, Windsor, Ontario, 320–326.

Lawrence, P. and Lorsch, J. (1970) *Studies in Organization Design*, Richard D. Irwin, Homewood, IL.

Lorenz, A. (1993) BT versus the world. *The Sunday Times*, 16 May.

Lyons, T. F. Krachenberg, A. R. and Henke, J. W. (1990) Mixed motive marriages: what's next for buyer – supplier relationships? *Sloan Manage. Rev.*, Spring, 29–36.

Macdonald, K. H. (1991) Strategic alignment process. In *The Corporation of the 1990s: Information Technology and Organisational Transformation* (ed. M. S. Scott Morton), Oxford University Press, New York.

Macdonald, K. H. (1993) Future alignment realities. Unpublished paper.

Maslow, A. H. (1943) A theory of human motivation. *Psychology Rev.*, **50**, 370–396.

Maslow, A. H. (1954) *Motivation and Personality*, Harper, New York.

Mason, R. O. and Mitroff, I. I. (1981) *Challenging Strategic Planning Assumptions: Theory, Cases and Techniques*, Wiley, New York.

Mayo, E. (1971) Hawthorne and the Western Electric Company. In *Organisation Theory* (ed. D. S. Pugh), Penguin, Middlesex.

McClelland, D. (1976) Power as the great motivator. *Harvard Bus. Rev.*, May–June, 100–110.

Miles, R. and Snow, C. (1978) *Organization Strategy, Structure, and Process*, McGraw-Hill, New York.

Miles, R. and Snow, C. (1987) Network organizations: new concepts for new forms. *California Manage. Rev.*, Spring.

Miller, D. (1986) Configuration of strategy and structure: towards a synthesis. *Strategic Manage. J.*, **7**, 233–249.

Miller, D. (1987) The genesis of configuration. *Acad. Manage. Rev.*, **12**(4), 686–701.

Miller, D. and Mintzberg, H. (1984) The case for configuration. In *Organizations: A Quantum View* (eds D. Miller and P. H. Friesen), Prentice-Hall, Englewood Cliffs, NJ.

Mintzberg, H. (1973) *The Nature of Managerial Work*, Harper and Row, New York.

Mintzberg, H. (1979) *The Structuring of Organizations*, Prentice-Hall, Englewood Cliffs, NJ.

Mintzberg, H. (1991) The effective organization: forces and forms. *Sloan Manage. Rev.*, Winter, 54–67.

Mitroff, I. I. and Linstone, A. (1993) *The Unbounded Mind: Breaking the Chains of Traditional Business Thinking*, Oxford University Press, New York.

Nakamoto, M. (1992) Plugging into each other's strengths. *Financial Times*, 27 March.

Ohmae, K. (1989) The global logic of strategic alliances. *Harvard Bus. Rev.*, March–April, 143–154.

Ostrof, F. and Smith, D. (1992) The horizontal organization. *The McKinsey Quarterly*, **1**, 149–168.

Peppard, J. W. and Steward, K. (1993) Managing change in IS/IT implementation. In *IT Strategy For Business* (ed. J. W. Peppard), Pitman, London, 269–291.

Peters, T. and Waterman, R. H. (1982) *In Search of Excellence*, Harper and Row, New York.

Porter, M. E. (1980) *Competitive Strategy*, Free Press, New York.

Porter, M. E. (1985) *Competitive Advantage*, Free Press, New York.

Poynter, T. A. and White, R. E. (1990) Making the horizontal organisation work. *Bus. Quarterly (Canada)*, Winter, 73–77.

Quinn Mills, D. and Friesen, B. (1992) The learning organization. *Europ. Manage. J.*, **10**(2), 146–156.

Reich, R. B. (1987) Entrepreneurship reconsidered: the team as hero. *Harvard Bus. Rev.*, May–June, 77–83.

Rockart, J. F. and Short, J. E. (1989) IT in the 1990s: managing organization interdependencies. *Sloan Manage. Rev.*, **30**(2), 7–17.

Schwenk, C. R. (1988) A cognitive perspective on strategic decision-making. *J. Manage. Studies*, **25**(1), 41–55.

Scott, W. G. (1961) Organization theory: an overview and an appraisal. *Acad. Manage. Rev.*, April, 7–26.

Scott Morton, M. S. (ed.) (1991) *The Corporation of the 1990s: Information Technology and Organization Transformation*, Oxford University Press, New York.

Senge, P. M. (1990a) *The Fifth Discipline: The Art and Practice of the Learning Organization*, Doubleday/Currency, New York.

Senge, P. M. (1990b) The leaders' new work: building learning organizations. *Sloan Manage. Rev.*, Fall, 7–23.

Senge, P. M. (1991) Team learning. *The McKinsey Quarterly*, Summer, 82–93.

Slevin, D. P. and Colvin, J. G. (1990) Juggling entrepreneurial style and organization structure: how to get your act together. *Sloan Manage. Rev.*, **31**(2), Winter, 43–53.

Smith, A. (1910) *The Wealth of Nations*, Dent, London.

Snow, C. C., Miles, R. E. and Coleman, H. J. Jr (1992) Managing 21st century network organizations. *Organization Dynamics*, Winter, 5–20.

Stalk, G. Jr (1988) Time – the next source of competitive advantage. *Harvard Bus. Rev.*, July–August, 41–51.

Stata, R. (1989) Organizational learning – the key to management innovation. *Sloan Manage. Rev.*, Spring, 63–73.

Taylor, F. W. (1911) *Scientific Management*, Harper, New York.

Thompson, V. (1961) *Modern Organizations*, Knopf, New York.

Venkatraman, N. (1991) IT-induced business reconfiguration. In *The Corporation of the 1990s: Information Technology and Organization Transformation* (ed. M. S. Scott Morton), Oxford University Press, New York, 122–158.

Ward, J., Griffiths, P. and Whitmore, P. (1990) *Strategic Planning for Information Systems*, John Wiley, Chichester, UK.

Weber, M. (1947) *The Theory of Social and Economic Organization*, Free Press, New York.

Zuboff, S. (1988) *In the Age of the Smart Machine: The Future of Work and Power*, Basic Books, New York.

Questions for discussion

1　How does the concept of organizational form differ from that of organizational strategy and structure as presented in Chapter 4?

2　There is much talk today of achieving 'dynamic' and 'flexible' organizations. What does it mean to be 'dynamic' and 'flexible'?

3　Consider the six organizational forms discussed by the authors:
   - has any emerged as the dominant paradigm in the late 1990s/early 2000s?
   - are the forms mutually exclusive? What are some variants?
   - highlight the role of IT in each of the forms: what specific technologies are necessary to make the forms effective?
   - what are the impediments to the effective functioning of the forms?
   - what might be the appropriate IS strategy for the different forms?

4　What might be the role of IT in the human resource initiatives, mentioned by the authors as critical to the change management process?

16 Information Technology and Organizational Decision Making

The effects of advanced information technologies on organizational design, intelligence and decision making

G. P. Huber

This chapter sets forth a theory of the effects that computer-assisted communication and decision-aiding technologies have on organizational design, intelligence, and decision making. Several components of the theory are controversial and in need of critical empirical investigation. The chapter focuses on those technology-prompted changes in organizational design that affect the quality and timeliness of intelligence and decision making, as contrasted with those that affect the production of goods and services.

Introduction

This chapter draws on the work of organizational researchers, communication researchers, and information systems researchers to set forth, in the form of a set of propositions, a theory concerning the effects that *advanced information technologies* have on organizational design, intelligence, and decision making. The motivations for such a chapter are four.

One motivation concerns the need to reinvestigate and possibly revise certain components of organization theory. A large part of what is known about the factors affecting organizational processes, structures, and performance was developed when the nature and mix of communication technologies were relatively constant, both across time and across organizations of the same general type. In contrast, the capabilities and forms of communication technologies have begun to vary, and they are likely to vary a great deal in the future. For example, communication technology (or communication medium) is now a variable whose traditionally relatively constant range (from face-to-face at one extreme to unaddressed broadcast documents at the other, cf. Daft and Lengel, 1984, 1986) is being expanded by organizations to include *computer-assisted communication technologies* (e.g. electronic mail, image transmission devices, computer conferencing, and videoconferencing) that facilitate access to people inside and outside the organization with an ease that previously was not possible. Also, more sophisticated and more user-friendly forms of *computer-assisted decision-aiding technologies* (e.g. expert systems, decision-support systems, on-line management information systems, and external information retrieval systems) are in the late stages of development or early stages of implementation. Consequently, as the uses, capabilities, and forms of communication and decision-aiding technologies increase in their range, researchers must reassess what is known about the effects of these technologies because what is known may change. 'That is, new media impacts may condition or falsify hypothesized relationships developed by past research' (Williams and Rice, 1983, p.208). Thus, one motivation for setting forth propositions concerning the impact of advanced information technologies is to encourage investigation and debate on what the nature of organizational design, intelligence, and decision making might be when these technologies become more sophisticated and more widely used.

The second motivation is to take a step toward creating a theory of the effects that advanced information technologies have on organizations. *Advanced information technologies* are devices (a) that transmit, manipulate, analyze, or exploit information; (b) in which a digital computer processes information integral to the user's communication or decision task; and (c) that have either made their appearance since 1970 or exist in a form that aids in communication or decision tasks to a significantly greater degree than did pre-1971 forms. (For expanded discussion of the term *advanced information technologies*, see Culnan and Markus, 1987; Gibson and Jackson, 1987; Johansen, 1988; Rice and Associates, 1984; and Strassman, 1985a.) The need for such a theory has been exemplified in a review by Culnan and Markus (1987) and in a special issue of *Communication Research* (Steinfield and Fulk, 1987). In that special issue, the guest editors noted that, although there are many empirical findings concerning the effects of advanced information technologies on organizations, 'there has been little synthesis, integration, and development of theoretical explanations [and] that it is time for theory development and theory-guided research' (Steinfield and Fulk, 1987, p.479).

Together, the propositions in this chapter comprise a theory such as that called for by Steinfield and Fulk, but like any theory, it is limited. It includes as dependent variables only (a) characteristics of organizational intelligence and decision making, such as timeliness, and (b) aspects of organization design associated with intelligence and decision making, such as the size of decision units. Further, within this still rather large set of dependent variables, the theory includes only those (a) that seem to be significantly affected by advanced information technology, (b) that are of interest to organization scientists or administrators, or (c) whose variance seems to have increased with the advent of advanced information technologies. The dependent variables included in the theory are shown in Table 16.1. Variables that are not included in the theory, but whose omission is briefly discussed, include horizontal integration, specialization, standardization, formalization, and the distribution of influence on organizational decisions.

As independent variables the theory includes only (a) the use of computer-assisted communication technologies and (b) the use of computer-assisted decision-aiding technologies. The theory does not encompass the use of computer-assisted production technologies or the use of transaction-enacting technologies such as computerized billing systems. (For ideas concerning the effects of advanced information technologies, broadly defined to include

Table 16.1 *Dependent variables included in the theory (and the numbers of the propositions related to them)*

Design variables (subunit level)	Design variables (organizational level)	Design variables (organizational memory)	Performance variables
Participation in decision making (1)	Centralization of decision making (4, 5)	Development and use of computer-resident data bases (8)	Effectiveness of environmental scanning (10)
Size and heterogeneity of decision units (2)	Number of organizational levels involved in authorization (6)	Development and use of computer-resident in-house expert systems (9)	Quality and timeliness of organizational intelligence (11)
Frequency and duration of meetings (3)	Number of nodes in the information-processing network (7)		Quality of decision (12)
			Speed of decision making (13, 14)

computer-assisted automation, on a broader set of organizational attributes, see Child, 1984, 1988; Gibson and Jackson, 1987; Strassman 1985a; Zuboff, 1984.) Finally, the theory does not explicitly address use of advanced information technologies for impression-management purposes such as those described by Sabatier (1978) and Feldman and March (1981).

The third motivation for integrating the work of organizational researchers, communication researchers, and information systems researchers is to help researchers in each of these fields become more aware of the existence, content, and relevance of the work done by researchers in other fields. Without such awareness, the efficiency of the research establishment is less, opportunities for synergy are lost, and progress in theory development is inhibited.

The fourth and last motivation is of practical, administrative importance. Advanced information technologies are becoming a pervasive aspect of organizations, but their relatively recent appearance and rapidly changing nature virtually guarantee that administrators and their advisors will not have experience as a guide in anticipating and planning for the impacts they may have. In the absence of experience, the value of theory is considerable.

It is important to note that the theory described here is not based on a great deal of directly applicable empirical research. There are two reasons for this. The first is that the components of organization theory that were drawn upon in developing the propositions were not validated under conditions in which decision and communication systems were computer assisted; consequently, they may not be valid for organizations that presently use a good deal of advanced information technology. The second reason is that many of the empirical studies that were drawn upon inductively in developing the propositions pertain to forms of technology that are not necessarily representative of the more sophisticated forms now in use or expected to be in use in the more distant future. (See Hofer, 1970; Pfeffer, 1978; Rice, 1980; Robey, 1977; Whisler, 1970, for brief reviews of some of these early studies, and Olson and Lucas, 1982, for some thoughtful speculations concerning the effects of advanced information technologies on a variety of organizational attributes and behaviors.) Thus, most propositions about the organization-level effects of advanced information technology must be viewed with some caution, whether derived from mature, but possibly outdated, organization theory or from recent, but perhaps soon-to-be outdated, empirical findings.

The above cautions notwithstanding, the propositions set forth are supportable to the degree necessary to be responsive to the motivations just noted, especially if the qualifications attendant to each proposition are seriously considered by users. In any case, these propositions can serve as a basis for the development of specific hypotheses.

Nature of advanced information technologies

What are the critical characteristics of advanced information technologies that might cause these technologies to have effects on organizational design, intelligence, and decision making different from the effects of more traditional technologies?

For purposes of discussion, characteristics of information technologies will be divided into two groups. *Basic characteristics* are related to data storage capacity, transmission capacity, and processing capacity. Advanced information technologies, largely as a result of their digital computer component, usually provide higher levels of these basic characteristics (Culnan and Markus, 1987, p.420; Rice and Associates, 1984, p.34). (No distinction is made in this definition or in this chapter between data (stimuli and symbols) and information (data conveying meaning as a result of reducing uncertainty).)

Characteristics of the second group I will call *properties*. Although the above basic dimensions are relevant to users, often it is the multidimensional configuration of the levels characterizing a particular technology that is most relevant for a particular task. Some authorities have considered these configurations when comparing advanced information technologies with traditional information technologies, and have made generalizations about the resultant properties of advanced information systems. Because these properties cause the use of advanced information systems to have effects such as those noted in this chapter, some of these generalizations are reviewed here. (See Culnan and Markus, 1987; Rice and Associates, 1984, especially chapter 2, for discussions of how these properties follow from the levels that the technologies attain on the basic dimensions.)

In the context of *communication*, these properties include those that facilitate the ability of the individual or organization (a) to communicate more easily and less expensively across time and geographic location (Rice and Bair, 1984), (b) to communicate more rapidly and with greater precision to targeted groups (e.g. Culnan and Markus, 1987; Sproull and Keisler, 1986), (c) to record and index more reliably and inexpensively the content and nature of communication events, and (d) to more selectively control access and participation in a communication event or network (Culnan and Markus, 1987; Rice, 1984).

In the context of *decision aiding*, the properties include those that facilitate the ability of the individual or organization (a) to store and retrieve large amounts of information more quickly and inexpensively; (b) to more rapidly and selectively access information created outside the organization; (c) to more rapidly and accurately combine and reconfigure information so as to create new information (as in the development of forecasting models or financial analyses); (d) to more compactly store and quickly use the judgment and decision models developed in the minds of experts, or in the mind of the decision maker, and stored as expert systems or decision models; and (e) to more reliably and inexpensively record and retrieve information about the content and nature of organizational transactions. (Discussions of these properties of computer-assisted decision-aiding technologies, richer in detail than space allows here, are contained in Sprague and McNurlin, 1986; Sprague and Watson, 1986; Zmud, 1983.)

Mistaken impressions

It may be helpful to draw upon the above discussion of the basic characteristics and properties of information technologies to dispel some occasionally held, but mistaken, impressions. One such mistaken impression is that advanced information technologies are universally inferior or superior to traditional technologies. This impression is erroneous because the properties just delineated may be less important than other properties possessed by a more traditional technology. In addition, particular uses of the advanced technologies may have undesirable side effects (cf. Culnan and Markus, 1987; Markus, 1984; Zuboff, 1984). Further, traditional technologies often score higher with respect to acceptability, ease of use, and richness (cf. Culnan and Markus, 1987; Fulk *et al.*, 1987; Trevino *et al.*, 1987), or have scores that overlap on these properties with the scores of advanced information technologies. For these reasons, use of advanced information technologies will not eliminate use of traditional technologies. However, when the properties of advanced information technologies are useful for enhancing individual or organizational effectiveness, and when retarding forces such as those just noted are not potent, it is reasonable to believe that organizations will use the advanced technologies.

The availability of the advanced information technologies increases the communicating or decision-aiding options for the potential user, and thus in the long run, unless the selected technology is inappropriately employed, the effect is to increase the quality (broadly defined) of the user's communication or decision-making processes. Presumably, through experience or observation, organizational members learn which communication or decision-aiding technology is most likely to achieve their purpose, and then adopt it. Field studies, which will be cited later, verify this belief.

In a related vein, it is a mistake to view advanced information technologies solely as substitutes for traditional technologies. To the contrary, advanced information technologies are frequently used more as supplements and complements to traditional technologies, rather than as substitutes. For example, electronic mail is often used to confirm with text what was said in a phone conversation or to set up face-to-face appointments, and image transmission devices are often used to make available drawings that will be discussed after all the parties have had a chance to study them. Of course, people do substitute computer-assisted media for traditional media when it seems efficacious to do so. Overall, the effect of availability of user-friendly computer-assisted communication technology is to increase the range of options for the communicator. Presumably, through experience or observation, organizational members learn to choose communication technologies wisely. Evidence, which will be cited, indicates that this presumption is correct. An analogous discussion applies to computer-assisted decision-aiding technologies, but limits of space force its omission.

A final mistaken impression is that, although advanced information technologies may lead to rational outcomes (such as information that is more accurate and comprehensive or decisions that are more timely) in organizations characterized by strong adherence to a norm of economic rationality, these outcomes are unlikely in more highly politicized or power-driven organizations. In the absence of scientific evidence with which to develop the required contingency theory, three observations are offered. The first is that the external environments of many organizations are sufficiently competitive that, in order to survive, the organizations must adopt and properly use rationality-enhancing communication and decision-aiding technologies. If organizational politics interferes with such adoption or use, the marketplace or parent organization intervenes until universal conformance is achieved. Thus, in their time, the telegraph became a pervasive technology in railroads, the calculator in brokerage houses, and the radio in armies. In the organizations that survived, those managers whose proprietary inclinations caused them not to use the technologies to further organizational goals (such as timely delivery of freight, accurate and comprehensive information for investors, or effective coordination in battle) were evidently converted or purged. In essence, superordinates or organizations require subordinates or subunits to help them compete effectively or otherwise satisfy environmental demands, and if rational use of technology is necessary, it occurs in the long run, whatever the proprietary inclinations of the subordinates or subunits.

The second observation is that highly politicized or power-driven organizations also have highly competitive internal environments, and in such environments it is necessary for managers to maximize their own competitive effectiveness by appearing to satisfy the goals of resource controllers on an issue-by-issue basis. In these environments, technical or financial analyses are widely used to persuade the resource controllers that the manager's proposals best satisfy the resource controller's goals (Burgelman, 1982; Kelley, 1976; Shukla, 1982). Thus, even in organizations where power plays a significant role in resource allocation, so also do 'the numbers' (cf. Gerwin, 1979; Pfeffer and Moore, 1980; Sabatier, 1978; Shukla, 1982). Managers who do not employ the most appropriate technologies in developing and selling analyses are at a competitive disadvantage; they must adapt or lose out.

The third observation is that, in almost all organizations, effective fulfillment of organizational responsibilities contributes to the development and maintenance of a manager's reputation. Thus, aside from whatever a manager might do to negatively or positively affect the quality or timeliness of the design, intelligence, or decision making of superordinate units, he or she is likely to employ any communication or decision-aiding technologies that can contribute to his or her personal effectiveness or the effectiveness of his or her own unit (cf. Daft *et al.*, 1987).

Together, these observations suggest that even though power and politics influence organizational design, intelligence, and decision making, so too do information technologies; *for advancement of their own interests, organizational participants will use advanced information technologies in ways that increase their effectiveness in fulfilling organizational goals.* This fundamental assumption underlies many of the propositions included in the theory and seems to be validated in the studies referenced.

The propositions

The propositions are grouped for expositional purposes into four sections. The propositions in the first three sections portray the effects of advanced information technologies on organizational design, that is, the effects on (a) subunit structure and process, (b) organizational structure and process, and (c) organizational memory. Although these effects will most often result from evolved practices rather than from prior managerial intentions, I expect that in the future, as administrators and their advisors learn about whatever functional effects of advanced information technologies on organizational design and performance may accrue, more and more of the effects will be the outcomes of intentions. In the short run, however, many managers will probably continue to introduce advanced information systems in order to reduce the number of personnel, to increase managerial efficiency, or to imitate other managers. After the systems are implemented for these purposes, these managers or other organizational participants will sometimes see that the systems can accomplish other purposes and will adjust the organization's design to facilitate accomplishment of these purposes (e.g. by extending the scope of responsibility of an organizational unit that now has easier access to a broader range of information).

The propositions of the fourth section set forth the effects of advanced information technology on organizational intelligence and decision making. Some of these effects are direct and some occur indirectly through changes in design. (Organizational intelligence is the output or product of an organization's efforts to acquire, process, and interpret information external to the organization (cf. Porter, 1980; Sammon *et al.*, 1984; Wilensky, 1967). It is an input to the organization's decision makers.)

Each of these four sections contains specific suggestions concerning research that would seem to be useful for examining the validity and domains of particular propositions. The last section of the chapter contains more general recommendations for researchers in the areas of organization science and information systems.

Effects at the subunit level

The focus in this section is on those aspects of organizational design that ultimately affect organizational intelligence and decision making. For example, aspects of structure that affect the accuracy of communications or the timeliness of decisions are considered. The first three propositions of the section deal with variables generally thought of in the context of organizational subunits. The remaining six propositions deal with variables more associated with the design of the organization as a whole. (This distinction is made solely for expository purposes – the categorizations are not intended to have theoretical merit.)

Participation in decision making

In many organizational decisions, technical and political considerations suggest that the development, evaluation, or selection of alternatives would benefit from exchanges of information among a moderate to large number of experts or partisans. But communicating takes time and effort, and so the variety and number of participants is often narrower than *post hoc* analyses determine to be appropriate. Assuming that the time and effort involved in communicating are critical determinants of the number of individuals who become involved, *what is the effect of computer-assisted communication technology on the breadth of participation in decision making?*

Because computer-assisted communication technologies can greatly reduce the effort required for those individuals who are separated in time or physical proximity to exchange information (cf. Hiltz and Turoff, 1978; Culnan and Markus, 1987; Special Report, 1988), it is probable that more people would serve as sources of information. Thus, we have the story where

> . . . a product developer sent a message to distribution lists that reach thousands of people asking for suggestions about how to add a particular new product feature. Within two weeks, he had received over 150 messages in reply, cutting across geographical, departmental, divisional, and hierarchical boundaries, almost all from people the product developer did not know. (Sproull and Keisler, 1986, p.1510)

And, of course, teleconferencing and other similar computer-assisted communication systems are useful for sharing information (Johansen, 1984, 1988; Rice, 1984).

In contrast, authorities have argued that computer-assisted communication technologies do not enable decision makers to obtain 'soft' information (Mintzberg, 1975), 'rich' information (Daft *et al.*, 1987), the 'meaning' of information (Weick, 1985), or information about sensitive matters. To the extent that this argument is correct, it would preclude the use of computer-assisted communication technologies where the need for such information is paramount. However, the circumstances where the arguments of these authorities are salient may be fewer than first thought. For example, the argument that computer-assisted technologies provide fewer cues than does face-to-face communication is valid, but it misses the fact that managers and other professionals usually choose the communication medium that fits the communication task (Daft *et al.*, 1987; Rice and Case, 1983; Trevino *et al.*, 1987). Thus, computer-assisted communication technology might still be used to exchange factual or technical information, whereas other media are used to elaborate on this information or to exchange other types of information.

The issue is not one of the technologies driving out the use of richer media, but rather of the technologies enabling communications that otherwise would be unlikely to occur. For example, Foster and Flynn (1984), Sproull and Keisler (1986), and others (Palme, 1981; Rice and Case, 1983) reported that the availability of electronic mail caused organizational participants to increase the overall amount of their communication; there was not a one-for-one trade-off between media. Overall, the preponderance of arguments and the available empirical evidence suggest that:

Proposition 1: Use of computer-assisted communication technologies leads to a larger number and variety of people participating as information sources in the making of a decision.

There will be exceptions to the relationship explicated in this and all propositions. A proposition states that across a large number of cases, *ceteris paribus*, there will be a tendency for the stated relationship to be observed. Extensive testing of hypotheses derived from the proposition will, eventually, identify any *systematic* exceptions to the relationship.

Further research is needed, of course, to determine (a) if the increase in participation is of practical significance; (b) if the increase in participation leads to higher quality decisions or better acceptance of decisions; (c) if the information includes 'hard' information, soft information, or both; and (d) if the decision process becomes more effective. (For reviews of the effects that computer-assisted communication technologies have on group behaviors, see Johansen, 1984, 1988; Rice, 1984. For a review of the behavioral effects of teleconferencing in particular, see Svenning and Ruchinskas, 1984.)

It is important to note that although organizational members tend to use the technologies that communicate their messages with timeliness and veracity (Trevino *et al.*, 1987), they also consider the social acceptance of the technology (Fulk *et al.*, 1987), the ease of use (Huber, 1982), and other attributes (Culnan and Markus, 1987).

Size and heterogeneity of decision units

In many situations, organizational subunits are responsible for developing, recommending, or selecting a proposal for action. Thus, aside from the many individuals who might participate in this process, there is usually one individual or one group of individuals who is formally accountable for the decision. Such an individual or group is referred to as a *decision unit* (Duncan, 1974).

What is the effect of computer-assisted communication technology on the size and heterogeneity of decision units? To answer this question, note that small groups provide more satisfying experiences for their members (Jewell and Reitz, 1981; Kowitz and Knutson, 1980), and that small groups are less costly in terms of human resources. Also note that homogeneous groups provide more satisfying experiences and, if they have the necessary expertise, accomplish decision-related tasks more quickly (Jewell and Reitz, 1981; Kowitz and Knutson, 1980). Finally, note that the discussion associated with Proposition 1 suggests that computer-assisted communication technologies can help decision units to become relatively smaller and more homogeneous by obtaining information beyond that obtainable using traditional communication media; both experts and constituency representatives can often make their knowledge and concerns available through electronic mail, teleconferencing, or videoconferencing. Cost considerations suggest that organizations will seek such efficiencies in their use of human capital. For example:

> You cannot afford to have an expert in very rare kidney disease on your team, just in case you might need him or her someday . . . The technology allows you to have experts available electronically. (Strassman, 1985b, pp. 22, 27)

What is the effect of computer-assisted decision-support technology, as contrasted with communication technology, on the size and heterogeneity of decision units? Sometimes experts can be replaced by expert systems and information keepers can be replaced by management information systems. To the extent that a decision unit can properly use the expert system for resolving some uncertainties, the expert need not be a member of the decision unit; therefore, the unit's size and heterogeneity will be decreased.

Research is needed, of course, to determine if these changes occur. They may not. For example, it may be that organizational aspirations will rise and information technologies will be used to acquire additional diverse information, information whose acquisition and interpretation will require approximately the same size face-to-face decision-group membership as is presently found. If the group's task involves less the acquisition of information than it does the routine processing of information, then the increase in the unit manager's span of control that is facilitated by increased internal communication capability may lead to an overall increase in unit size. It will be interesting to see if future studies can ascertain the net effect of the conflicting forces under various conditions. However, it seems that there are many situations where the increasing efficacy of the technologies and the need for efficient use of human resources will make valid the following:

Proposition 2: Use of computer-assisted communication and decision-support technologies leads to decreases in the number and variety of members comprising the traditional face-to-face decision unit.

Thus, although Proposition 1 suggests that the total number and variety of *participants serving as information sources* are likely to increase with use of computer-assisted communication technologies, Proposition 2 suggests that the number and variety of *members within the traditional face-to-face decision unit* will decrease with use of either computer-assisted communication or decision-support technologies.

It was noted earlier that people consider multiple criteria when selecting communication media. Similarly, it is important to recognize that even though organizational members tend to choose decision aids and decision procedures that facilitate the making of timely and technically satisfactory decisions (Lee *et al.*, 1988; Sabatier, 1978), they also consider other criteria when making this choice (Feldman and March, 1981; Sabatier, 1978).

Meetings

Research confirms the everyday observation that completing an organizational decision process often takes months or years (Mintzberg *et al.*, 1976; Witte, 1972). Meetings are often used to speed up decision processes by creating situations where rate of decision-related information exchange among the key participants is generally higher than that which occurs outside of meetings. Meetings, whether *ad hoc* processes or co-joined with more permanent structures, such as standing committees, are an important component of organizational decision processes and occupy a good deal of the time of managers and other professionals.

What is or what will be the effect of computer-assisted communication and decision-support technologies on the time absorbed by meetings? Some arguments and evidence suggest these technologies will result in fewer meetings with no loss of progress in the overall organizational decision-making effort. For example, many times discussion is halted and another meeting scheduled because needed information is missing. On-line management information systems or other query-answering technologies, including expert systems, may be able to provide the information, avoiding the need to schedule a subsequent meeting. Also, electronic mail and other computer-assisted communication media sometimes can be used to access soft information that can be obtained only by querying people. Further, decision-support systems can sometimes be used within meetings to conduct analyses that provide new information with which to resolve disagreements about the significance of effects of different assumptions, and thereby allow progress to continue rather than forcing adjournment until subsequent staff work can clarify the effects and another meeting can be scheduled.

Reflection suggests that each of the technologies just mentioned as facilitating the completion of meetings can sometimes lead to the cancellation of meetings. That is, with the added communication and computing capabilities, organizational members can occasionally accomplish the task of the meeting before the meeting takes place. Finally, it seems that because group-decision support systems enhance information exchange, they contribute to the effectiveness of the meeting and, thus, may enable groups to complete their tasks with fewer meetings (Benbasat and Konsynski, 1988; Johansen, 1988).

In contrast, if managers and others involved in making organizational decisions believe that use of the technologies will result in more effective meetings, the availability of the technologies may encourage them to have *more* decision-related meetings than they would otherwise. In addition, electronic mail, decision support systems, and other information-sharing and generating technologies may facilitate mini-meetings. This might preempt the need for the larger, formal meetings, but the result might be more meetings in total. The outcome of the increase in technologically supported mini-meetings versus the decrease in traditional meetings is a matter for future empirical investigation. However, because such mini-meetings are likely to be shorter, and in view of the several preceding arguments, it seems reasonable to believe that on balance and across time:

Proposition 3: Use of computer-assisted communication and decision support technologies results in less of the organization's time being absorbed by decision-related meetings.

It is important to note that, because computer-assisted communication technologies facilitate participation in meetings by persons remote in time or geography, more people may ultimately participate in a meeting (see Kerr and Hiltz, 1982, and the discussion surrounding Proposition 1). In contrast, the mini-meetings that sometimes preempt the larger, formal meetings will typically involve fewer people. Because the net effects of these two phenomena are likely to be highly variable, no proposition is offered with *person-hours* as the dependent variable.

Validation of Proposition 3 would be a significant step in documenting the effect that computer-assisted technology has on organizational processes. It would be desirable to test this proposition for each technology separately. This may not always be possible, however, because many technologically progressive organizations will have a variety of technologies in place. (For a review of the effects of advanced information technologies on the overhead costs and benefits of technologically supported meetings, such as document preparation and meeting summaries, see Rice and Bair, 1984.)

Effects at the organizational level

Centralization of decision making

By enabling top managers to obtain local information quickly and accurately, management information systems reduce ignorance and help the managers to make decisions that they, otherwise, may have been unwilling to make (Blau *et al.*, 1976; Child and Partridge, 1982; Dawson and McLoughlin, 1986). Motivations for top managers to make decisions that address local, lower level problems might include lack of confidence in subordinates (Vroom and Yetton, 1973), desire to reduce stress (Bourgeois *et al.*, 1978), need for achievement (Miller and Droge, 1986), or concern that information about the organization's overall situation or about its policies be appropriately utilized (Huber and McDaniel, 1986). Thus, it seems likely that, on occasion, management information systems would cause decisions to be made at hierarchically higher organizational levels than if these systems were not available (cf. Carter, 1984). The opportunity to obtain contextual clarification with electronic mail and other computer-assisted communication technologies would amplify this tendency.

Conversely, electronic bulletin boards enable lower- and middle-level managers to stay better informed about the organization's overall situation and about the nature of the organization's current problems, policies, and priorities (cf. Fulk and Dutton, 1984) and, consequently, permit decisions made by these managers to be more globally optimal, rather than more parochial and suboptimal, as observed by Dawson and McLoughlin (1986). Further, computer-assisted communication technologies allow lower-level units to clarify information in a more timely manner. Thus, on some occasions it seems that computer-assisted communication technologies would cause decisions to be made at organizational levels lower than if such technologies were not available. Motivations that lead top managers to permit this practice include the desire to decrease the time for organizational units to respond to problems or the desire to provide autonomy for subordinates. Some evidence suggests that this downward shift in decision making occurs – after observing the implementation of networked personal computers in the General Motors' Environmental Activities Staff, Foster and Flynn (1984, pp. 231–232) concluded that 'from the former hierarchy of position power there is developing instead a hierarchy of competency. . . . Power and resources now flow increasingly to the obvious centers of competence instead of to the traditional hierarchical loci.'

Therefore, *is the net effect of the use of computer-assisted communication and decision-support technologies to increase centralization or to decrease it?* Perhaps this is the wrong question. Together, the arguments in the previous two paragraphs suggest that computer-assisted and decision-support communication technologies, when used to provide most organizational levels with information that was formerly known to only one or a few levels, enable organizations to allow decision making to occur across a greater range of hierarchical levels without suffering as much of a loss in decision quality or timeliness, as would be the case if the technologies were not available. Which hierarchical level would actually make a particular decision would depend on the inclination and availability of the relevant decision makers at the various levels (Cohen *et al.*, 1972) or other idiosyncratic factors, as noted by Fayol (1949/1916) and Duncan (1973). Thus, given that the technologies can reduce the one-to-one correspondence between certain organizational levels and certain types of information, it is likely that:

> *Proposition 4: For a given organization, use of computer-assisted communication and decision-support technologies leads to a more uniform distribution, across organizational levels, of the probability that a particular organizational level will make a particular decision.*

Corollaries to Proposition 4 are:

> *Proposition 4a: For a highly centralized organization, use of computer-assisted communication and decision-support technologies leads to more decentralization.*

and

> *Proposition 4b: For a highly decentralized organization, use of computer-assisted communication and decision-support technologies leads to more centralization.*

Propositions 4, 4a, and 4b follow from the arguments presented, but are not directly based on empirical studies. It may be that the forces implied in the arguments are weak relative to those that influence traditional practices. For example, advanced information technologies enable centralized organizations to become even more centralized without incurring quite the loss in responsiveness that would occur without their presence. Similarly, they enable decentralized organizations to operate in an even more decentralized manner. I believe that, on balance, the arguments preceding Propositions 4, 4a, and 4b will be the more predictive, but empirical studies may prove this judgment to be incorrect. Certainly, the propositions require empirical study.

It is important to emphasize that by increasing the hierarchical range across which a particular type of decision may be made without a corresponding loss in decision quality or timeliness, computer-assisted communication and decision-support technologies allow other decision-location considerations to be applied without prohibitive costs. Such considerations include political matters; adherence to organizational traditions, norms, or culture; and the preferred style of top managers. Because the relative influence of these considerations will vary from organization to organization it seems that:

> *Proposition 5: For a population of organizations, broadened use of computer-assisted communication and decision-support technologies leads to a greater variation across organizations in the levels at which a particular type of decision is made.*

Number of organizational levels involved in authorization

Consider the common situation where at least some conclusions of lower-level units about what actions should be taken must be authorized by higher-level units before being acted upon, and these are forwarded upward as proposals. In their study of the approval process for a research and development budget, Shumway *et al.* (1975) found that the organizational design caused seven hierarchical levels to be involved in the proposal authorization process. Because each hierarchical level requires time to process a proposal in addition to the time required to render its judgments, the more levels involved, the longer the process takes. Each corresponding increment in the duration of the approval process can, in turn, adversely affect both the timeliness of the authorized action and the enthusiasm with which the proposers carry out the action once it is authorized.

Why then do organizations commonly involve several levels in authorizations? Frequently, the answer is that each level in the hierarchy has knowledge or decision-specific information that qualifies it to apply criteria or decision rules that less well-informed lower-level units cannot apply (cf. Meyer and Goes, 1988). For example, each higher level in an organization tends to know more about organizationwide issues, needs, and resources, and more about the nature of currently competing demands for resources, than does its subordinate units. The greater the amount of such information needed, the greater the number of hierarchical levels that will be involved in the authorization process. (In some respects this is the basis for vertical differentiation.)

What is the likely effect of communication and decision-support technologies on the number of hierarchical levels involved in authorizing a particular decision? It seems that the technologies will cause a decrease in the number of hierarchical levels involved in authorizing a proposal because technologies such as management information systems, expert systems, electronic mail, and electronic bulletin boards make information more widely available. In some cases organizational levels can obtain information that was previously unavailable and, thus, they can apply criteria or decision rules that they previously were not qualified to apply. Consequently, because the technologies facilitate the vertical distribution of information and knowledge (understanding about how to use information), there is more commonality (less extreme differentiation) of information and knowledge across organizational levels. Therefore, except when information technologies are allowed to create a problem of information overload, a given organizational level is more likely to be qualified to apply more criteria and decision rules than it could without the technologies. Assuming that use of the technologies does not somehow cause the number of decision rules to increase greatly, it follows that:

> *Proposition 6: Use of computer-assisted communication or decision-support technologies reduces the number of organizational levels involved in authorizing proposed organizational actions.*

Possible support for Proposition 6 is found in the observations of managers that use of information technology is associated with a decrease in the number of organizational levels (Special Report, 1983a, 1983b, 1984). The link between these observations and Proposition 6 is questionable, however, since the observed decreases could follow from decreases in the number of employees. Apparently few systematic studies have examined the relationship between the use of information technology and the number of organizational levels involved in decision authorization. This is unfortunate, because more sophisticated studies may find that the two variables (i.e. the increases in the use of advanced information technology and the reductions in the number of levels) are less causally related to each other than they are related to other variables (e.g. attempts to reduce direct labor costs). Thus, such studies may find that observed correlations between the use of advanced information technology and reduction in the number of middle-level managers or organizational levels have much less to do with the seeking of improved decision processes than they have to do with general reductions in the size of organizations when robots replace blue-collar workers and when computers replace clerical workers (cf. Child, 1984).

Number of nodes in the information-processing network

Decision-making individuals and units obtain much of the information used to identify and deal with decision situations through an information-processing network. The outer boundaries of the network are the sensor units that identify relevant information from either inside or outside the organization. (Examples of sensing units include market analysis, quality control personnel, radar operators, and accountants.) These units serve as information sources, and in many situations they pass on their observations in the form of messages to intermediate units closer to the ultimate user, the decision-making unit. Quite often these intermediate units are at hierarchical levels between the sensor unit and the decision-making unit.

The recipients of the sensor unit's message process the message and pass it on to a unit that is closer still to the decision-making unit. The information processing performed by such intermediate units ranges from straightforward relaying to elaborate interpreting. For a variety of reasons the number of such units – the number of nodes on the network path connecting the sensor unit to the decision unit – may be greater than warranted: 'Most managerial levels don't do anything. They are only relays' (Drucker, 1987, p.61).

Besides the unnecessary costs implied in Drucker's observation, each information-handling unit in the network path tends to contribute distortions and delays, as detailed by Huber (1982). For these reasons, top managers sometimes attempt to reduce the role and number of such units and to use computer-assisted technologies as alternative means for obtaining the information (Special Report, 1983a, 1983b, 1984). This reduces the workload used to justify the existence of these intermediate units and levels. Computers sometimes can be used to merge, summarize, filter, and even interpret information, thus eliminating clerical workers, managers, and the organizational units of which they are a part. These observations suggest that use of computer-assisted information processing and communication technologies would lead to the elimination of human nodes in the information processing network.

There is, however, a contrary argument. Elimination of intermediate nodes in the network results in an information overload on the decision unit. When the processing functions performed by intermediate information-processing units cannot be as efficiently or effectively performed with technology or changed practices, such as those suggested by Huber (1984) and Hiltz and Turoff (1985), the units will be retained. So, *do the aforementioned technologies actually decrease the number of nodes in the organization's information-processing network?*

Informal surveys (Special Report, 1983a, 1983b, 1984) have found correlations between the use of computer-assisted communication technology and decreases in the number of managers. However, as mentioned previously, these surveys did not determine the cause of the correlation, and it may be the result of concomitant reductions in the overall number of employees. Certainly, there is a need for more sophisticated, in-depth studies to determine the nature of the cause–effect links between the use of computer-assisted technology and the number of nodes in the information-processing network. On balance, however, it seems that in some instances reductions would take place. Thus,

Proposition 7: Use of computer-assisted information processing and communication technologies leads to fewer intermediate human nodes within the organizational information-processing network.

(Note that Proposition 7 deals with the number of intermediate nodes, Proposition 1 deals with the number of information sources, and Proposition 2 deals with the number of members in the traditional face-to-face unit.) If the network processes information across hierarchical levels, then a corollary of Proposition 7 is:

Proposition 7a: Use of computer-assisted information processing and communication technologies reduces the number of organizational levels involved in processing messages.

The last two propositions of this section deal with the design of the organization's memory. Designing the organization's memory is a novel idea to organizational scientists, but will become more familiar as organizational learning becomes a more mature area of study and as top management increases its emphasis on intellectual capital.

Effects on organizational memory

In their discussion of information search routines in organizational decision making, Mintzberg *et al.* (1976) distinguished between an organization's memory search and the active or passive search of its environment. *Memory search* refers to 'the scanning of the organization's existing memory, human or paper' (or, today, computer-resident) (Mintzberg *et al.*, 1976, p.255).

Everyday experience and some research suggest that the human components of organizational memories are less than satisfactory. For example, research shows that forecasts about the time necessary to complete organizational tasks are quite erroneous, even when such tasks have been carried out in the organization on many occasions. Kidd (1970), Abernathy (1971) and Souder (1972) studied the judgments of project completion times made by managers, and found them to be woefully inaccurate, even though the managers had a good deal of experience with similar projects. Given what is known about the many factors contributing to inaccurate learning and incomplete recall (Nisbett and Ross, 1980; Kahneman *et al.*, 1982) and to motivational distortions in sharing information (Huber, 1982), it is not at all surprising that the human components of organization memories are less than satisfactory.

The problem of poor memory is, however, much more complex than simple considerations of the deficiencies of humans as repositories of organizational information and knowledge might suggest. Everyday observations make clear (a) that personnel turnover creates great losses of the human components of an organization's memory; (b) that nonanticipation of future needs for certain information results in great amounts of information not being stored or if stored not being easily retrieved; and (c) that information is often not shared by organizational members. For at least these reasons, organizational information and knowledge frequently are less available to decision makers than they would wish.

What are the effects of computer-assisted communication and decision-support technologies on the nature and quality of organizational memory? One answer to this question follows from the fact that more and more organizational activities are conducted or monitored using computer-assisted technology. For instance, it is possible to obtain and maintain information about the times necessary to carry out many organizational activities just as readily as it is to obtain and maintain information about the financial expenditures necessary to carry out the activities (e.g. times necessary to fabricate certain products, to receive shipments, to recruit or train employees, or to deliver services). With sufficient foresight such information can be readily indexed and retrieved through computer technology (Johansen, 1988). Although much organizational knowledge is computer-resident at some point, its users often do not recognize its potential usefulness for future decision making.

Another type of useful computer-resident information is information that is exchanged across the organizational boundaries. In the future, smart indexing (cf. Johansen, 1988) or artificial intelligence will facilitate retrieval of this transaction information and will result in computer-resident organizational memories with certain properties, such as completeness, that are superior to the human components of organizational memories. Ongoing increases in the friendliness and capability of computer-based information retrieval systems suggest that today and even more so in the future:

> *Proposition 8: Availability of computer-based activity and transaction-monitoring technologies leads to more frequent development and use of computer-resident data bases as components of organizational memories.*

Research is needed to understand what incentives are necessary for those organizational members whose actions produce the data to share it or to maintain its quality.

Since much of what an organization learns through experience is stored in the minds of its members, many organizations nurture members who are expert with respect to an intellectual task such as (a) diagnosing quality problems or equipment malfunctions; (b) learning the identities of extra-organizational experts, influence peddlers, resource providers, or other useful nonmembers; and (c) locating information or resources that cannot be located using official, standard sources. As the processes for eliciting knowledge, building expert systems (Welbank, 1983), and validating information (O'Leary, 1988) become standardized, organizations are creating computer-based expert systems using the knowledge of their own experts (Rao and

Lingaraj, 1988; Rauch-Hindin, 1988; Waterman, 1986). These expert systems have properties such as accessibility, reliability, and 'own-ability', that are both superior to humans and useful as components of organizational memories. Thus, even though expert systems have properties that are inferior to human experts, it seems reasonable to believe that:

> *Proposition 9: Availability of more robust and user-friendly procedures for constructing expert systems leads to more frequent development and use of inhouse expert systems as components of organizational memories.*

How do experts react when asked to articulate knowledge and, perhaps, their secrets, so that these can be incorporated into software that might diminish their importance? How do local managers react in such a situation when their influence and status, which are derived from this information or knowledge, is lessened by giving others the ready access to expert systems possessing much of this local information or knowledge? What incentives are appropriate and effective for motivating experts to explicate their knowledge so that it can be used without their future involvement? These are questions in need of investigation.

Propositions 8 and 9 suggest that certain advanced information technologies increase the range of memory components for an organization, just as other advanced information technologies increase the range of media with which the organization can communicate its information and knowledge.

Effects on other design variables

Before leaving this discussion of organizational design variables, it seems useful to comment on the effects of advanced information technologies on some design variables that have not yet been explicitly mentioned: (a) horizontal integration, (b) formalization, (c) standardization, and (d) specialization. *Horizontal integration*, important as it is, requires little additional comment. Since it refers to the use of communication structures and processes for facilitating joint decision making among multiple units or individuals, the effects are the same as those discussed in Propositions 1, 2, and 3, and, as will be seen, in Proposition 14.

Formalization is used to ensure adherence to standards, especially when behavioral norms cannot be counted on to provide the desired behavior. Thus, early in the adoption of any new technology, because the required norms have not had time to develop and to take hold, the level of formalization is often high. (Of course, very early in adoption, standards might not exist, so control might not be exercised through either norms or formalization.) As the new technology becomes familiar and 'ages', it seems reasonable to believe that the degree of formalization associated with it approaches the degree of formalization associated with the technology being replaced. Consequently, the long-term effect of new technology on formalization might be nil. Although advanced information technology greatly facilitates the recording and retrieval of information about organizational events and activities and, thus, makes control of behaviors and processes through formalization more viable, the use of advanced information technology for closely controlling intelligence development and decision making has not been reported in the literature, to my knowledge. This may be due to the frequent need for initiative and non-routine activities by those engaged in these processes (cf. Wilensky, 1967). (For a discussion of the use of advanced information technology for controlling other behaviors and processes in organizations, see Zuboff, 1984.)

Standardization is the reduction of variability in organizational processes. As noted earlier, advanced information technologies have greatly increased the range of communication and decision procedures. If organizational members can use discretion when choosing which information technology to use (and such discretion seems commonplace), the variation of technologies will increase, and standardization will decrease: This is so apparent that no proposition is needed.

With regard to *specialization*, advanced information technology can either lead to the addition of job categories (e.g. computer programmer) or the deletion of job categories (e.g. bookkeeper), and, therefore, will affect the degree of specialization within the organization. However, such specialities support, make operational, or become part of technologies. The increase or decrease in the variety of support personnel has little or no impact on intelligence or decision making, independent of the technologies. For this reason, *specialization* was not discussed as a design variable that affects organizational intelligence and decision making.

Propositions 1 through 9 describe the effects that advanced information technologies have on those aspects of organizational design that, ultimately, influence organizational intelligence and decision making. The next section deals with more direct effects of the technologies on organizational intelligence and decision making and, ultimately, on organizational performance in these areas. Of course the development of organizational intelligence and the making of decisions are organizational processes inextricably intertwined with an organization's design. The present conceptual separation of these processes from design is primarily for expository purposes.

Effects on organizational intelligence and decision making

This section sets forth two propositions dealing with information acquisition and then three propositions concerned with decision making and decision authorization.

Environmental scanning and organizational intelligence

To some degree, all organizations scan their external and internal environments for information about problems or opportunities. Yet sometimes managers do not learn about problems or opportunities in time to act with maximum effectiveness. In many cases the alerting message is delayed as it moves through the sequential nodes in the communication network. In other instances incumbents of adjacent nodes in the communication network have difficulty connecting across time, as in 'telephone tag'. *What is the effect of advanced information technologies on these impediments? What is the effect on information acquisition overall?* With regard to these questions, recall that the reasoning surrounding Proposition 7 suggested that the use of computer-assisted information processing and communications technologies leads to rifle-shooting of messages and ultimately to fewer intermediary nodes in the information processing network. This idea, in combination with the fact that the probability and duration of message delay and the probability and extent of message distortion are both positively related to the number of sequential links in the communication chain connecting the receiver to the information source, suggests that use of computer-assisted information processing and communication technologies would facilitate rapid and accurate identification of problems and opportunities.

A contrary line of reasoning exists, however. Since an important role of many information network nodes is to screen, package, and interpret messages, the use of advanced information technologies and the consequent elimination of nodes can result in an overload of irrelevant, poorly packaged, or uninterpretable messages. One study indicated that this danger may not be as serious as it appears. Hiltz and Turoff (1985) found that social norms and management practices tend to develop to reduce the problem to a level below what might be imagined. It is likely that computer-assisted technologies will be used to enhance information retrieval, especially from lower organizational levels and outside sources. Thus, on balance:

Proposition 10: Use of computer-assisted information processing and communication technologies leads to more rapid and more accurate identification of problems and opportunities.

Use of these technologies can aid not only in the identification of problems and opportunities, but also in a wide variety of more focused probes and data acquisitions for the purpose of analysis. Recalling Mintzberg *et al.*'s (1976) *active search*, and Mintzberg's (1975) notion that managers require timely information, consider that computer-assisted information systems can bring facts to the organization's decision makers almost immediately after the facts occur (e.g. check-out scanners and commodities market data).

Together, technologically advanced systems for the acquisition of external information and the development of computer-enhanced organizational memories enable organizations to increase the range of information sources that the producers and users of organizational intelligence can draw upon. Thus, in summary:

Proposition 11: Use of computer-assisted information storage and acquisition technologies leads to organizational intelligence that is more accurate, comprehensive, timely, and available.

This proposition is based on the assumption that the external information sources are accurate, comprehensive, timely, and available. Otherwise, garbage in, garbage out.

A matter of some interest is how inclined information users are to employ accessible sources, rather than those with the highest quality information (cf. Culnan, 1983; O'Reilly, 1982). How computer-assisted communications and information acquisition systems affect the trade-off between perceived accessibility and perceived quality, and the resultant information-seeking behavior, is an issue much in need of investigation.

Decision making and decision authorization

It is reasonable to believe that the quality of an organizational decision is largely a consequence of both the quality of the organizational intelligence (as implied in Proposition 11) and the quality of the decision-making processes. Further, the discussion associated with Propositions 1 and 3 (and perhaps other of the propositions related to organizational design) strongly suggests that, by facilitating the sharing of information, computer-assisted communication technologies increase the quality of decision making, and that by aiding in the analysis of information within decision units, computer-assisted decision-aiding technologies increase the quality of decision making. Thus, in helping with Propositions 1, 3, and 11:

Proposition 12: Use of computer-assisted communication and decision-support technologies leads to higher quality decisions.

Because reducing the number of levels involved in authorizing an action will reduce the number of times the proposal must be handled (activities of a logistical, rather than a judgmental nature), it seems likely that:

Proposition 13: Use of computer-assisted communication and decision-support technologies reduces the time required to authorize proposed organizational actions.

Authorization as a particular step in the decision-making process has received little attention from organizational scientists (for exceptions, see Carter, 1971; Gerwin, 1979), and the time required for organizations to authorize action also has received little attention (for exceptions, see Mintzberg *et al.*, 1976; Shumway *et al.*, 1975). These topics are worthy candidates for study in general, and the potential effects of information technology seem to be especially in need of examination, given their probable importance and the total absence of systematic research on their effect on decision authorization.

Once a problem or opportunity has been identified, several types of activities are undertaken that might be more effective if undertaken using advanced information technology. For example, management information systems and electronic mail might enable decision makers to immediately obtain the information they seek when deciding what to do about problems and opportunities (see Proposition 11). Decision-support systems might enable decision makers or their assistants to analyze this information quickly (at least for some types of problems). Electronic mail and video- or teleconferencing might help decision makers obtain clarification and consensus without the delays imposed by the temporary nonavailability, in terms of physical presence, of key participants (see Proposition 1). Finally, forms of advanced information technology might reduce the time required to authorize proposed organizational actions (see Proposition 13). These facts suggest that:

> *Proposition 14: Use of computer-assisted communication and decision-support technologies reduces the time required to make decisions.*

Available evidence supports this proposition:

> For instance, managers in the Digital Equipment Corporation reported that electronic mail increased the speed of their decision making and saved them about seven hours a week (Crawford, 1982). Managers at Manufacturers Hanover Trust reported that electronic mail saved them about three hours a week, mostly by eliminating unreturned phone calls and internal correspondence (Nyce and Groppa, 1983). (Sproull and Keisler, 1986, p.1492)

However, studies employing casual self-report data need to be supplemented with more systematic studies, such as some of those noted by Rice and Bair (1984). Sophisticated studies may find that the actual reduction in time is marginal, and that the net benefit may be offset to some extent by the losses in decision quality that may follow from a reduction in the time spent cogitating, as noted by Weick (1985).

Toward a conceptual theory

Extensive organizational use of advanced information technologies is too new, and systematic investigation of their use is too limited, for a theory of their effects to have evolved and received general acceptance. As a result, the propositions set forth here were not derived from a generally accepted theory. Instead, they were pieced together from organizational communication and information systems research, extrapolating only when it seemed reasonable.

A *theory* may be defined as a set of related propositions that specify relationships among variables (cf. Blalock, 1969, p.2; Kerlinger, 1986, p.9). The set of propositions set forth in this chapter, related to one another (at the very least) through their possessing a common independent variable, advanced information technology, passes this definitional test of a theory. Yet, more is expected from a theory, such as a framework that integrates the propositions.

If other connecting relationships can be found to link them, perhaps the propositions of this chapter can serve as building blocks for the development of a less atomistic, more conceptual theory. The result would, of course, be quite tentative, in that the propositions require additional substantiation and in that any one author's connective framework must be subjected to review, critique, and discussion across an extended period before gaining general acceptance. As a step in the development of a conceptual theory of the effects of advanced information technologies, the following concepts and constructs are offered. The constructs summarize and the concepts connect ideas that were mentioned previously but served a different purpose at the time.

Concept 1: Advanced information technologies have properties different from more traditional information technologies. *Availability of advanced information technologies* (Construct A) extends the range of communication and decision-making options from which potential users can choose. On occasion a technology will be chosen for use, and when chosen wisely – such that the chosen technology's properties better fit the user's task – use of the technology leads to improved task performance. This reinforcement in turn leads to more frequent *use of advanced information technology* (Construct B).

Concept 2: Use of advanced information technologies (Construct B) leads to more available and more quickly retrieved information, including external information, internal information, and previously encountered information, and thus leads to *increased information accessibility* (Construct C). Concept 2 follows from Propositions 1, 4, and 7 through 11.

Concept 3: Increased information accessibility (Construct C) leads to the *changes in organizational design* (Construct D). Concept 3 follows from Propositions 1 through 7.

Concept 4: Increased information accessibility (Construct C), and those *changes in organizational design* (Construct D) that increase the speed and effectiveness with which information can be converted into intelligence or intelligence into decisions, lead to organizational intelligence being more accurate, comprehensive, timely, and available and to decisions being of higher quality and more timely, decisions that lead to improvements in *effectiveness of intelligence development and decision making* (Construct E). Concept 4 follows from Propositions 11 through 14.

These constructs and concepts are summarized in Figure 16.1.

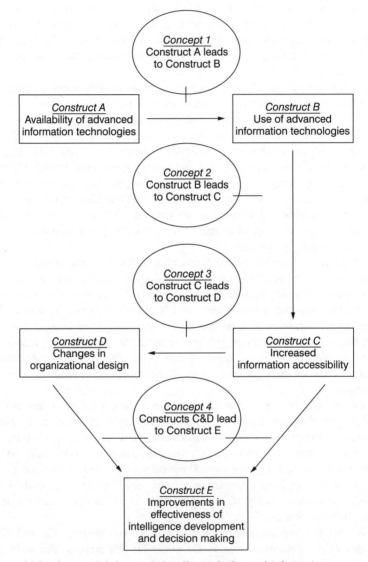

Figure 16.1 *Conceptual theory of the effects of advanced information technologies on organizational design, intelligence and decision making*

Summary and recommendations

In the form of propositions and their corollaries, this chapter sets forth a theory concerning the effects that computer-assisted communication and decision-aiding technologies have on organizational design, intelligence, and decision making. Subsequently, the propositions were connected with constructs and concepts, and from these a more conceptual theory was developed.

Some boundaries on the original theory (here called *the theory*) were delineated early in the chapter. The theory is, nevertheless, a candidate for elaboration and expansion. For example, it was not possible, within the space available, to extend the scope of the theory to include propositions having to do with the effects of advanced information technologies on the distribution of influence in organizational decision making (see Zmud, in press). Examination of some relevant literature makes clear that numerous propositions would be necessary because (a) the technologies may vary in their usefulness for generating the particular types of information used by decision participants having different sources of influence, (b) the technologies may vary in their usefulness for enhancing the image or status of participants having different organizational roles, and (c) the technologies may vary in their usefulness to different types of participants as aids in the building of decision-determining coalitions. Certainly, the theory is a candidate for elaboration and expansion, just as it is a candidate for empirical testing and consequent revision.

The process used to generate the propositions comprising the theory included drawing on components of established organization theory and on findings from communication and information systems research. Specific suggestions were made, with respect to many of the propositions, about matters in need of empirical investigation. In addition to these specific suggestions, three somewhat more global recommendations are in order. The first is directed to any researchers exploring the effects of advanced information technologies. In this chapter, different forms of advanced information technology were discussed by name (e.g. electronic mail) yet the propositions were stated in general terms. This latter fact should not obscure the need to specify more precisely the particular technology of interest when developing hypotheses to be tested empirically. As more is learned about the effects of computer-assisted communication and decision-support technologies, it may be found that even subtle differences count (cf. the discussion by Markus and Robey, 1988). Even if this is not so, as researchers communicate about these matters among themselves and with administrators, it behooves them to be clear and precise about what it is that they are discussing.

The second suggestion, directed to organizational researchers, is to believe (a) that information technology fits within the domain of organization theory and (b) that it will have a significant effect on organizational design, intelligence, and decision making. Organization researchers, in general (there are always welcome exceptions), may not believe that these technologies fit within the domain of organization theory. This would be an erroneous belief. Organization theory has always been concerned with the processes of communication, coordination, and control and, as is apparent from the research of communication and information systems researchers (Culnan and Markus, 1987; Rice and Associates, 1984), the nature and effectiveness of these processes are changed when advanced information technologies are employed. Organizational researchers also may not have recognized that organizational designs are, at any point in time, constrained by the capability of the available communication technologies. Two of the infrequent exceptions to this important observation are cited by Culnan and Markus (1987):

> Chandler (1977) for example, argues that the ability of the telegraph to facilitate coordination enabled the emergence of the large, centralized railroad firms that became the prototype of the modern industrial organization. Pool (1983) credits the telephone with the now traditional physical separation of management headquarters from field operations, and in particular with the development of the modern office skyscraper as the locus of administrative business activity. (p.421)

Also, Huber and McDaniel (1986) state that:

> Without telephones, corporations could not have become as large as they have; without radios, military units would be constrained to structures and tactics different from those they now use; without computers, the processes for managing airline travel would be different from what they are. Any significant advance in information technology seems to lead eventually to recognition and implementation of new organizational design options, options that were not previously feasible, perhaps not even envisioned. (p.221)

Since information technologies affect processes that are central to organization theory, and since they also affect the potential nature of organization design (a principal application of organization theory), a corollary of this second global recommendation is added: Organizational researchers should study advanced information technology as (a) an intervention or jolt in the life of an organization that may have unanticipated consequences with respect to evolved organizational design, (b) a variable that can be used to enhance the quality (broadly defined) and timeliness of organizational intelligence and decision making, and (c) a variable that enables organizations to be designed differently than has heretofore been possible. (A review of recent discussions of emerging organizational and interorganizational forms (Borys and Jemison, 1989; Luke *et al.*, 1989; Miles and Snow, 1986; Nadler and Tushman, 1987) suggests that use of computer-assisted communication technologies can enhance the usefulness of such designs, requiring, as many will, communication among dispersed parties.)

The third global research recommendation is directed toward information systems researchers. It is straightforward. As is easily inferred by observing organizational practices, much information technology is intended to increase directly the efficiency with which goods and services are produced, for example, by replacing workers with computers or robots. But organizational effectiveness and efficiency are greatly determined by the quality and timeliness of organizational intelligence and decision making, and these, in turn, are directly affected by computer-assisted communication and decision-aiding technologies and are also indirectly affected through the impact of the technologies on organizational design. Therefore, it is likely that administrators will ask information systems researchers to help anticipate the effects of the technologies. In addition, builders and users of computer-assisted communication and decision-aiding technologies generally do not explicitly consider the effects that the technologies might have on organizational design, intelligence, or decision making. Thus, information systems researchers should arm themselves with the appropriate knowledge by increasing the amount of their research directed toward studying the effects that advanced information technologies have on organizational design, intelligence, and decision processes and outcomes.

References

Abernathy, W. M. (1971) Subjective estimates and scheduling decisions. *Management Science*, **18**, 80–88.

Benbasat, I. and Konsynski, B. (1988) Introduction to special section on GDSS. *Management Information Systems Quarterly*, **12**, 588–590.

Blalock, H. M., Jr. (1969) *Theory Construction: From Verbal to Mathematical Formulations*, Prentice-Hall, Englewood Cliffs, NJ.

Blau, P. M., Falbe, C. M., McKinley, W. and Tracey, P. K. (1976) Technology and organization in manufacturing. *Administrative Science Quarterly*, **21**, 20–40.

Borys, B. and Jemison, D. (1989) Hybrid arrangements as strategic alliances: Theoretical issues in organizational combinations. *Academy of Management Review*, **14**, 234–249.

Bourgeois, L. J. III, McAllister, D. W. and Mitchell, T. R. (1978) The effects of different organizational environments upon decision and organizational structure. *Academy of Management Journal*, **21**, 508–514.

Burgelman, R. A. (1982) A process model of internal corporate venturing in the diversified major firm. *Administrative Science Quarterly*, **28**, 223–244.

Carter, E. E. (1971) The behavioral theory of the firm and top-level corporate decisions. *Administrative Science Quarterly*, **16**, 413–428.

Carter, N. M. (1984) Computerization as a predominate technology: its influence on the structure of newspaper organizations. *Academy of Management Journal*, **27**, 247–270.

Chandler, A. D., Jr. (1977) *The Visible Hand: The Managerial Revolution in American Business*, Harvard University Press, Cambridge, MA.

Child, J. (1984) New technology and developments in management organization. *OMEGA*, **12**, 211–223.

Child, J. (1988) Information technology, organization, and response to strategic challenges. *California Management Review*, **30**(1), 33–50.

Child, J., and Partridge, B. (1982) *Lost Managers: Supervisors in Industry and Society*, Cambridge University Press, Cambridge, MA.

Cohen, M. D., March, J. G. and Olsen, J. P. (1972) A garbage can model of organizational choice. *Administrative Science Quarterly*, **17**, 1–25.

Crawford, A. B., Jr. (1982) Corporate electronic mail – a communication-intensive application of information technology. *Management Information Systems Quarterly*, **6**, 1–14.

Culnan, M. J. (1983) Environmental scanning: the effects of task complexity and source accessibility on information gathering behavior. *Decision Sciences*, **14**, 194–206.

Culnan, M. J. and Markus, L. (1987) Information technologies: electronic media and intraorganizational communication. In *Handbook of Organizational Communication* (eds F. M. Jablin *et al.*), Sage, Beverly Hills, 420–444.

Daft, R. L. and Lengel, R. H. (1984) Information richness: a new approach to managerial information processing and organizational design. In *Research in Organizational Behavior* (eds B. M. Staw and L. L. Cummings), JAI Press, Greenwich, CT, 191–233.

Daft, R. L. and Lengel, R. H. (1986) Organizational information requirements, media richness, and structural design. *Management Science*, **32**, 554–571.

Daft, R. L., Lengel, R. H. and Trevino, L. K. (1987) Message equivocality, media selection and manager performance: implications for information systems. *Management Information Systems Quarterly*, **11**, 355–368.

Dawson, P. and McLaughlin, I. (1986) Computer technology and the redefinition of supervision. *Journal of Management Studies*, **23**, 116–132.

Drucker, P. (1987) Advice from the Dr. Spock of business. *Business Week*, 28 September, 61–65.

Duncan, R. B. (1973) Multiple decision-making structures in adapting to environmental uncertainly. *Human Relations*, **26**, 273–291.

Duncan, R. B. (1974) Modifications in decision structure in adapting to the environment: some implications for organizational learning. *Decision Sciences*, **5**, 705–725.

Fayol, H. (1949/1916) *General and Industrial Management* (Constance Storrs, trans.), Pitman, London.

Feldman, M. and March, J. (1981) Information in organizations as signal and symbol. *Administrative Science Quarterly*, **26**, 171–186.

Foster, L. W. and Flynn, D. M. (1984) Management information technology: its effects on organizational form and function. *Management Information Systems Quarterly*, **8**, 229–236.

Fulk, J. and Dutton, W. (1984) Videoconferencing as an organizational information system: assessing the role of electronic meetings. *System, Objectives, and Solutions*, **4**, 105–118.

Fulk, J., Steinfield, C. W., Schmitz, J. and Power, J. G. (1987) A social information processing model of media use in organizations. *Communication Research*, **14**, 529–552.

Gerwin, D. (1979) Towards a theory of public budgetary decision making. *Administrative Science Quarterly*, **14**, 33–46.

Gibson, C. F. and Jackson, B. B. (1987) *The Information Imperative*, Heath, Lexington, MA.

Hiltz, S. R. and Turoff, M. (1978) *The Network Nation: Human Communication via Computer*, Addison-Wesley, Reading, MA.

Hiltz, S. R. and Turoff, M. (1985) Structuring computer-mediated communication systems to avoid information overload. *Communications of the ACM*, **28**, 680–689.

Hofer, C. W. (1970) Emerging EDP patterns. *Harvard Business Review*, **48**(2), 16–31, 168–171.

Huber, G. (1982) Organizational information systems: determinants of their performance and behavior. *Management Science*, **28**, 135–155.

Huber, G. (1984) The nature and design of post-industrial organizations. *Management Science*, **30**, 928–951.

Huber, G. (1988) Effects of decision and communication technologies on organizational decision processes and structures. In *Organizational Decision Support Systems* (eds R. M. Lee et al.), North-Holland, Amsterdam, 317–333.

Huber, G. and McDaniel, R. (1986) Exploiting information technology to design more effective organizations. In *Managers, Micros, and Mainframes* (ed. M. Jarke), Wiley, New York, 221–236.

Jewell, L. N. and Reitz, H. J. (1981) *Group Effectiveness in Organizations*, Scott, Foresman, Glenview, IL.

Johansen, R. (1984) *Teleconferencing and Beyond*, McGraw-Hill, New York.

Johansen, R. (1988) *Groupwave: Computer Support for Business Teams*, Free Press, New York.

Kahneman, D., Slovic, P. and Tversky, A. (eds) (1982) *Judgment Under Uncertainty: Heuristics and Biases*. Cambridge University Press, Cambridge, UK.

Kelley, G. (1976) Seducing the elites: the politics of decision making and innovation in organizational networks. *Academy of Management Review*, **1**, 66–74.

Kerlinger, F. N. (1986) *Foundations of Behavioral Research*, Holt, Rinehart and Winston, New York.

Kerr, E. B. and Hiltz, S. R. (1982) *Computer-Mediated Communication Systems: Status and Evaluation*, Academic Press, New York.

Kidd, J. S. (1970) The utilization of subjective probabilities in production planning. *Acta Psychologica*, **34**, 338–347.

Kowitz, A. C. and Knutson, T. J. (1980) *Decision Making in Small Groups: The Search for Alternatives*, Allyn and Bacon, Boston, MA.

Lee, R. M., McCosh, A. and Migliarese, P. (1988) *Organizational Decision Support Systems*, North-Holland, Amsterdam.

Luke, R. D., Begun, J. W. and Pointer, D. D. (1989) Quasi firms: strategic interorganizational forms in the health care industry. *Academy of Management Review*, **14**, 9–19.

Markus, M. L. (1984) *Systems in Organizations: Bugs and Features*, Pitman, Marshfield, MA.

Markus, M. L. and Robey, D. (1988) Information technology and organizational change: conceptions of causality in theory and research. *Management Science*, **34**, 583–598.

Meyer, A. D. and Goes, J. B. (1988) Organizational assimilation of innovations: a multilevel contextual analysis. *Academy of Management Journal*, **31**, 897–923.

Miles, R. and Snow, C. (1986) Organizations: new concepts for new forms. *California Management Review*, **28**(3), 62–73.

Miller, D. and Droge, C. (1986) Psychological and traditional determinants of structure. *Administrative Science Quarterly*, **31**, 539–560.

Mintzberg, H. (1975) The manager's job: folklore and fact. *Harvard Business Review*, **53**(4), 49–61.

Mintzberg, H., Raisinghani, D. and Théorêt, A. (1976) The structure of 'unstructured' decision processes. *Administrative Science Quarterly*, **21**, 246–275.

Nadler, D. and Tushman, M. L. (1987) *Strategic Organization Design*, Scott, Foresman, Glenview, IL.

Nisbett, R. and Ross, L. (1980) *Human Inference: Strategies and Shortcomings of Social Judgment*, Prentice-Hall, Englewood Cliffs, NJ.

Nyce, H. E. and Groppa, R. (1983) Electronic mail at MHT. *Management Technology*, **1**, 65–72.

O'Leary, D. E. (1988) Methods of validating expert systems. *Interfaces*, **18**(6), 72–79.

Olson, M. and Lucas, H. C. (1982) The impact of office automation on the organization: some implications for research and practice. *Communications of the ACM*, **25**, 838–847.

O'Reilly, C. A. (1982) Variations in decision makers' use of information sources: the impact of quality and accessibility of information. *Academy of Management Journal*, **25**, 756–771.

Palme, J. (1981) *Experience with the Use of the COM Computerized Conferencing System*, Forsvarets Forskningsanstalt, Stockholm, Sweden.

Pfeffer, J. (1978) *Organizational Design*, AHM, Arlington Heights, IL.

Pfeffer, J. and Moore, W. L. (1980) Power in university budgeting: a replication and extension. *Administrative Science Quarterly*, **19**, 135–151.

Pool, I. de Sola (1983) *Forecasting the Telephone: A Retrospective Assessment*, Ablex, Norwood, NJ.

Porter, M. E. (1980) *Competitive Strategy: Techniques for Analyzing Industries and Competitors*, Free Press, New York.

Rao, H. R. and Lingaraj, B. P. (1988) Expert systems in production and operations management: classification and prospects. *Interfaces*, **18**(6), 80–91.

Rauch-Hindin, W. B. (1988) *A Guide to Commercial Artificial Intelligence*, Prentice-Hall, New York.

Rice, R. E. (1980) The impacts of computer-mediated organizational and interpersonnel communication. In *Annual Review of Information Science and Technology*, Vol. 15 (ed. M. Williams), Knowledge Industry Publications, White Plains, NY, 221–249.

Rice, R. E. (1984) Mediated group communication. In *The New Media* (eds R. E. Rice and Associates), Sage, Beverly Hills, CA, 129–154.

Rice, R. E. and Associates (1984) *The New Media*, Sage, Beverly Hills, CA.

Rice, R. E. and Bair, J. H. (1984) New organizational media and productivity. In *The New Media* (eds R. E. Rice and Associates), Sage, Beverly Hills, CA, 185–216.

Rice, R. E. and Case, D. (1983) Electronic message systems in the university: a description of use and utility. *Journal of Communication*, **33**, 131–152.

Robey, D. (1977) Computers and management structure. *Human Relations*, **30**, 963–976.

Sabatier, P. (1978) The acquisition and utilization of technical information by administrative agencies. *Administrative Science Quarterly*, **23**, 396–417.

Sammon, W. L., Kurland, M. A. and Spitalnic, R. (1984) *Business Competitor Intelligence: Methods for Collecting, Organizing, and Using Information*, Wiley, New York.

Shukla, R. K. (1982) Influence of power bases in organizational decision making: a contingency model. *Decision Sciences*, **13**, 450–470.

Shumway, C. R., Maher, P. M., Baker, M. R., Souder, W. E., Rubenstein, A. H. and Gallant, A. R. (1975) Diffuse decision making in hierarchical organizations: an empirical examination. *Management Science*, **21**, 697–707.

Souder, W. E. (1972) A scoring methodology for assessing the suitability of management science models. *Management Science*, **18**, B526–B543.

Special Report (1983a) A new era for management. *Business Week*, 25 April, 50–64.

Special Report (1983b) How computers remake the manager's job. *Business Week*, 25 April, 68–76.

Special Report (1984) Office automation. *Business Week*, 8 October, 118–142.

Special Report (1988) The portable executive. *Business Week*, 10 October, 102–112.

Sprague, R. H. and McNurlin, B. C. (1986) *Information Systems Management in Practice*, Prentice-Hall, Englewood Cliffs, NJ.

Sprague, R. H. and Watson, H. J. (1986) *Decision Support Systems: Putting Theory into Practice*, Prentice-Hall, Englewood Cliffs, NJ.

Sproull, L. and Keisler, S. (1986) Reducing social context cues: electronic mail in organizational communication. *Management Science*, **32**, 1492–1512.

Steinfield, C. W. and Fulk, J. (1987) On the role of theory in research on information technologies in organizations: an introduction to the special issue. *Communication Research*, **14**, 479–490.

Strassman, P. (1985a) *Information Payoff: The Transformation of Work in the Electronic Age*, Free Press, New York.

Strassman, P. (1985b) Conversation with Paul Strassman. *Organizational Dynamics*, **14**(2), 19–34.

Svenning, L. and Ruchinskas, J. (1984) Organizational teleconferencing. In *The New Media* (eds R. E. Rice and Associates), Sage, Beverly Hills, CA, 217–248.

Trevino, L. K., Lengel, R. and Daft, R. L. (1987) Media symbolism, media richness, and media choice in organization: a symbolic interactionist perspective. *Communication Research*, **14**, 553–574.

Vroom, V. H. and Yetton, P. W. (1973) *Leadership and Decision-making*, University of Pittsburgh, Pittsburgh, PA.

Waterman, D. A. (1986) *A Guide to Expert Systems*, Addison-Wesley, Reading, MA.

Weick, K. E. (1985) Cosmos vs. chaos: sense and nonsense in electronic contexts. *Organizational Dynamics*, **14**(2), 50–64.

Welbank, M. (1983) *A Review of Knowledge Acquisition Techniques for Expert Systems*, Martlesham Consultancy Services, Ipswich, UK.

Whisler, T. (1970) *Impact of Computers on Organizations*, Praeger, New York.

Wilensky, H. L. (1967) *Organizational Intelligence*, Basic Books, New York.

Williams, F. and Rice, R. E. (1983) Cummunication research and the new media technologies. In *Communication Yearbook 7* (ed. R. N. Bostrom), Sage, Beverly Hills, CA, 200–225.

Witte, E. (1972) Field research on complex decision-making processes – the phase theorem. *International Studies of Management and Organization*, **2**, 156–182.

Zmud, R. W. (1983) *Information Systems in Organizations*, Scott, Foresman, Glenview, IL.

Zmud, R. W. (in press) Opportunities for manipulating information through new technology. In *Perspectives on Organizations and New Information Technology* (eds J. Fulk and C. Steinfield), Sage, Beverly Hills, CA.

Zuboff, S. (1984) *In the Age of the Smart Machine*, Basic Books, New York.

Reproduced from Huber, G. P. (1990) A theory of the effects of advanced information technologies on organizational design, intelligence, and decision making. *Academy of Management Review*, **15**(1), 47–71. Reprinted with permission of the publishers, Academy of Management, Pace University, New York.

Questions for discussion

1   Consider the author's classification of technology into the basic characteristics of data storage, transmission, and processing capacity, and properties of communication and decision aiding. Would you add anything to this classification?

2   Consider your experience with electronic mail and compare this to the propositions. Does email increase participation? If yes, what are the results of such increased participation? Does email enable 'communication that otherwise would be unlikely to occur'. Does email increase 'information sources' but decrease the 'size of the decision unit'? Does email change the number of meetings held or the nature of meetings?

3   The author suggests that decision-aiding technologies will lead to greater centralization in companies that were decentralized and greater decentralization in centralized companies. Discuss how the opposite might occur. What have your experiences been?

4   The author states 'because the technologies facilitate the vertical distribution of information and knowledge, there is more commonality of information and knowledge across organizational levels'. What are some barriers to this?

5   The author considers the influence of IT on certain organization processes, what are some other organizational factors, beyond the scope of the current chapter, that IT has shaped?

6   If the propositions in the chapter are correct, what are the implications, if any, for organizational performance?

17 The Information Technology–Organizational Culture Relationship

Understanding information culture: integrating knowledge management systems into organizations

D. E. Leidner

Knowledge management initiatives to help organizations create and distribute internal knowledge have become important aspects to many organizations' strategy. The knowledge-based theory of the firm suggests that knowledge is the organizational asset that enables sustainable competitive advantage in hypercompetitive markets. Systems designed to facilitate knowledge management (knowledge management systems) are being implemented in an attempt to increase the quality and speed of knowledge creation and distribution in organizations. However, such systems are often seen to clash with corporate culture and, as a result, have limited impact. This chapter introduces a framework for assessing those aspects of organizational culture that are likely to be the source of implementation challenges. In so doing, it associates various organizational subunit cultures with different information cultures, and presents a series of propositions concerning the relationships among individual, organizational, and information cultures.

1 Introduction

When asked about why the organization was building a worldwide Intranet and knowledge management system, the Chief Knowledge Officer of a large multinational consulting firm replied: 'We have 80,000 people scattered around the world who need information to do their jobs effectively. The information they needed was too difficult to find and, even if they did find it, often inaccurate. Our Intranet is meant to solve this problem' (Leidner, 1998). Roughly a decade ago, case studies of organizations implementing executive information systems (EIS) suggested that a major reason behind these systems was a need for timely, accurate, and consistent information and to help managers cope with the problem of information overload (Rockart and DeLong, 1988; Houdeshel and Watson, 1987). And although a goal of management information systems (MIS) was to provide relevant information for managerial control and planning, MIS were unable to provide timely, complete, accurate, and readable data of the type executives needed for strategic decision making. Even earlier, in 1967, Ackoff notes that 'I do not deny that most managers lack a good deal of information that they should have, but I do deny that this is the most important information deficiency from which they suffer. It seems to me that they suffer from an overabundance of irrelevant information'. Interestingly, in 1997, Courtney *et al.* state that 'omitting the unimportant information [from corporate intranets] may be as important as concentrating on the important. The mere availability of "information" may have a distracting effect. . . .'. Is information systems' history repeating itself over and over again in a continuous cycle of providing more information in greater detail in a more timely manner in a more graphical format, yet forever doomed to be providing 'too much irrelevant' information while leaving the important information 'too hard to find'? Or, is it that each time progress is made on one front, new forms of barriers to the impact of IS are encountered? Alternatively, has the real culprit in IS's seeming failure to impact organizational effectiveness not yet been discovered?

Recommended approaches to helping ensure that information systems result in organizational improvements have included structuring information systems requirements analysis (Yourdan and Constantine, 1978), involving users in analysis (King and Rodriguez, 1981; Ives and Olson, 1984), attempting to link IT to the business strategy (Pyburn, 1983), and improving change agentry skills (Markus and Benjamin, 1996). The latter is reproduced in this collection as Chapter 5. All of the approaches merit consideration, as do contingency theories which would suggest that the success of information systems (IS) in an organization depends upon the proper fit of IT to the organization's structure and design. Yet despite the prescriptive advice, information-based systems still seem to fail to live up to expectations and often fail to provide the dramatic improvements in organizational effectiveness for which they are designed (Lyytinen and Hirschheim, 1987; Mowshowitz, 1976).* Moreover, there appears to be

---

* The term 'information-based' is meant to distinguish systems designed to provide managers with information from systems designed to improve communication (such as GSS and electronic mail) and systems designed to improve transactions (such as MRP and ERP).

almost a crisis in the image of IS in organizations, with such problems as high CIO turnover, executives not recognizing the strategic importance of IS, and declining top management commitment to large IS investments.

This chapter offers a new exegesis to the reasons why information-based systems appear to be encountering the same problems repeatedly despite significant advances in planning and implementation methodologies and theories, as well as in the technology itself: an incongruity with corporate culture. The chapter posits that information systems implementation efforts must take into account corporate culture when designing the plan for change; if not, such systems might produce results, some anticipated others not, but the systems will fall way short of providing the major improvements expected in most large systems implementation efforts.

This chapter first traces briefly information-based systems advancements and the dominant organizational paradigms used to investigate the organizational effects of IS, and will then examine current developments in information-based systems, namely knowledge management systems. It will show how these systems in particular call for a new paradigm of interpretation, that of organizational culture theory. It will introduce the notion of information culture in the context of knowledge management systems and will present a brief overview of the relevant work on organizational culture. The chapter offers the existence of information culture as a framework for assessing those aspects of organizational culture that are likely to be the source of implementation challenges. Propositions will be offered concerning the relationship between organizational subunit culture and information culture and these will be tied to managerial prescriptions on managing the implementation of knowledge management systems.

2 Advances in information systems

Information systems can be classified in several ways, including according to their broad function, to the organizational function they serve, to the underlying technologies, or to the organizational level at which they are used (Laudon and Laudon, 1997). Here, we will consider information systems by broad function since much of the IT literature focuses on particular systems classified in this manner, such as decision support systems, expert systems, and electronic mail. In particular, we are interested in systems designed to provide information to managers and professionals at any organizational level. Hence, we will focus primarily on MIS and EIS (as both systems aim to supply managerial information) and knowledge management systems (a new line of systems oriented to providing professionals and managers unstructured information).

2.1   MIS and the structuring of organizations

As noted in Somogyi and Galliers (1987) in Chapter 1, as firms began to computerize in the 1950s, the first applications were in the area of transaction processing. Transaction processing systems are computerized systems that perform and record the daily routine transactions necessary to the conduct of business such as payroll, sales order entry, shipping, order tracking, accounts payable, material movement control (Laudon and Laudon, 1997). These systems were designed to facilitate data collection and to improve the efficiencies of organizational transactions. Soon thereafter, with advances in programming languages, databases, and storage, systems oriented toward providing performance information to managers emerged (Somogyi and Galliers, 1987). MIS are computer-based information systems that provide managers with reports and, in some cases, with on-line access to the organization's current performance and historical records. MIS primarily serve the functions of planning, controlling, and decision making at the management level. Generally, they condense information obtained from transaction processing systems and present it to management in the form of routine summary and exception reports.

Simon (1977) predicted that computers, namely MIS, would recentralize decision making, shrink line organizational structures, decrease the number of management levels, and result in an increase in the number and size of staff departments. It was believed that information technology would enable greater centralization of authority, clearer accountability of subordinates, a sharper distinction between top management and staff, and the rest of the organization, and a transformation of the planning and innovating functions. The organizational theory used to evaluate the effect of MIS on organizations was contingency theory of organizational structure, technology, and the environment. Research prior to 1970 indicated that IT provided a means of collecting and processing large amounts of data and information, thus enabling a small number of persons effectively to control authority and decision making; hence, IT was said to facilitate centralization (Klatzky, 1970; Whisler, 1970; Stewart, 1971). Research after 1970 seemed to find that IT, by enabling organizations to gather and process information rapidly, facilitated decentralizing decision making (Carter, 1984; Foster and Flynn, 1984; Dawson and McLaughlin, 1986). For example, Carter (1984) felt that as the extent of computer utilization increased in subunit applications, the locus of decision-making authority would become more decentralized in the organization, and the division of labor as reflected by functional diversification, functional specialization and functional differentiation would increase. Carter found in her study of newspaper organizations that as computers become the predominant technology, upper management was released from the day-to-day encumbrances of centralized decision making, fostering a decentralized organizational structure. In other cases IT appeared to have had no effect when changes were expected (Franz *et al.*, 1986). Considering the weak relationships found when using technology as an independent variable, other researchers employed technology as a moderator variable between the environment and structure, or as a dependent variable. Robey (1977) found that IT supported an existing decentralized structure in organizations with uncertain environments but that in more stable environments, IT strengthened a centralized authority structure.

In summary, early research on the impact of IT, namely MIS, on organizations focused on the effect of IT on organizational structures. The results were highly mixed, leading to an emergent imperative which argued that the particular effects of IT were dependent on a given organization's context and, hence, were not predictable or systematic across organizations. An alternative perspective was that certain inherent limitations of MIS prevented predictable improvements to organizational effectiveness. Among the limitations of MIS are that they have highly limited analytical capabilities, they are oriented almost exclusively to internal, not environmental or external, events, and that the information content is fixed and not tailored to individual users (Laudon and Laudon, 1997).

2.2 DSS, EIS and organizational decision making

Decision support systems (DSS) and executive information systems (EIS) aimed to provide what MIS were unable to: specific online information relevant to decision makers in a flexible format. DSS are interactive modeloriented systems, and are used by managers and knowledge workers, analysts, and professionals whose primary job is handling information and making decisions (Keen and Scott Morton, 1982; Sprague and Carlson, 1982). DSS assist management decision making by combining data, sophisticated analytical models, and user-friendly software into a single powerful system that can support semi-structured or unstructured decision making (Keen and Scott Morton, 1982; Sprague and Carlson, 1982). DSS tend to be isolated from major organizational information systems and tend to be stand-alone systems developed by end-user divisions or groups not under central IS control (Hogue, 1987). EIS are computer-based information systems designed to provide managers access to information relevant to their management activities. Originally designed for senior managers, the systems quickly became popular for managers at all levels. Unlike DSS which are tied to specific decisions and which have a heavy emphasis on models, EIS focus on the retrieval of specific information, particularly daily operational information that is used for monitoring organizational perform-ance. Features distinguishing EIS from such systems as MIS and decision support systems include a non-keyboard interface, status-access to the organizational database, drill-down analysis capabilities (the incremental examination of data at different levels of detail), trend analysis capabilities (the examination of data across desired time intervals), exception reporting, extensive graphics, the providing of data from multiple sources, and the highlighting of the information an executive feels is critical (Kador, 1988; Mitchell, 1988). Whereas the traditional focus of MIS was on the storage and processing of large amounts of information, the focus of EIS is on the retrieval of specific information about the daily operational status of an organization's activities as well as specific information about competitors and the marketplace (Friend, 1986).

Huber (1990) advanced a theory of the effects of advanced decision- and information-providing technologies, such as DSS and EIS, on organizational decision making. While he also made propositions concerning the effect of such systems on organizational design and structure, the dominant paradigm for examining the organizational effects of information technology was turning towards decision making. Huber and McDaniel (1986) argued that decision making was the most critical management activity and that the effectiveness of IS rested more in facilitating organizational decision making than enabling structural responses to environmental uncertainty. A wide body of research emerged examining organizational decision making and the decision-making consequences of IS. However, most of the IS literature focused on the individual level of analysis, which was reasonable given that DSS were designed in most cases for individual decision makers, and most of the EIS research also supported individual rather than organizational improvements.*

While some of Huber's propositions have been substantiated (Leidner and Elam, 1995; Molloy and Schwenk, 1995), the organizational level effects have received little substantiation and have been overshadowed by the individual level effects (Elliott, 1992). Moreover, research on DSS showed that decision makers used the tools in such a manner as to reduce time, but not necessarily to increase quality (Todd and Benbasat, 1991), but in the cases where the systems did appear to increase quality, the decision makers seemed not to perceive subjectively this improvement (Le Blanc and Kozar, 1990). Empirical evidence has shown that EIS enable faster decision making, more rapid identification of problems, more analysis before decision making, and greater understanding of the business (Leidner and Elam, 1995; Elliott, 1992). Evidence also suggests that EIS allow single- and double-loop learning (Vandenbosch and Higgins, 1996). Other promises for EIS, which have not

---

* Group Decision Support System (GDSS) research examines the impact of GDSS on groups; however, GDSS are less about information provision than they are about providing tools for brainstorming and structuring group meetings. Hence, the term GSS (group support system) is commonly used to refer to IT designed to facilitate communication in groups.

been empirically substantiated, involved helping companies cope with reduced staff levels (Applegate, 1987; Applegate and Osborn, 1988), substantial monetary savings (Holub, 1988), power shifts and a change in business focus (Applegate and Osborn, 1988), and improving service (Holub, 1988; Mitchell, 1988; Kador, 1988). Interestingly, these promises sound reminiscent of the promises that were made for MIS and that are now being made for Intranets, as will be discussed later.

Among the most serious challenges to EIS implementation involved overcoming information problems, namely organizational subunits feeling ownership of information that was suddenly being accessed by senior managers who previously had relied on these subunits to summarize and analyze their own performance in periodic reports. Such ownership problems led to system failure in some cases, when subunits consciously and covertly altered data to be more favorable to the unit and thereby rendered the EIS inaccurate (Leidner, 1992). Other weaknesses of EIS are the difficulty of pulling information from multiple sources into a graphical PC-based interface, justifying the costs of the systems given the unclear payoff, and ensuring that the information remains relevant as the needs of managers changes (Leidner, 1992). In summary, DSS and EIS research adopted an organizational decision-making paradigm as a reference theory for determining the organizational impacts of these systems. While the systems have well-documented individual level benefits, the organizational level benefits have been less lucid.

2.3   Knowledge management systems and organizational culture

A new line of systems based on web technology has emerged which compensates for some of the limitations of EIS, namely the difficulty of integrating information across platforms. These systems return control for information content to organizational subunits, hence bypassing some of the informational problems encountered with EIS, yet also require active participation of users not only in the design process, but also in the process of information provision. Corporate intranets are private web-based networks, usually within a corporation's firewalls, that connect employees to vital corporate information. They let companies speed information and software to employees and business partners (Thyfault, 1996; Vidal *et al.*, 1998). The primary incentive is their ability to provide 'what computer and software makers have frequently promised but never actually delivered: the ability to pull all the computers, software, and databases that dot the corporate landscape into a single system that enables employees to find information wherever it resides' (Cortese, 1996). While there is a business case for the value of intranets, there is little proof of the economic value of such systems (Rooney, 1997).

Among the most lauded potential applications of intranets is the provision of tools for knowledge management. Knowledge includes the insights, understandings, and practical know-how that employees possess. Knowledge management is a method of systematically and actively managing ideas, information, and knowledge of employees. Knowledge management systems refer to the use of modern information technologies (e.g. the Internet, intranets, extranets, browsers, data warehouses, software filters and agents) to systematize, enhance, and expedite intra- and inter-firm knowledge management (Alavi and Leidner, 1998). Knowledge management systems (KMS) are intended to help organize, interpret, and make widely accessible the expertise of an organization's human capital to help the organization cope with turnover, rapid change, and downsizing. KMS are being built in part from increased pressure to maintain a well-informed, productive workforce.

The concept of systematically coding and transmitting knowledge in organizations is not new – training and employee development programs have served this function for years. The integration of such explicit knowledge involves few problems because of its inherent communicability (Grant, 1996). Explicit knowledge is that knowledge which is transmitted in formal systematic language (Nonaka, 1994). It is externally documented tacit knowledge (Brown and Duguid, 1991). It is declarative and procedural knowledge which can be divorced from the context in which it is originally created and transferred to various other contexts with little if any modification. Advances in information technology have greatly facilitated the integration of explicit knowledge through increasing the ease with which explicit knowledge can be codified, communicated, assimilated, stored, and retrieved (Huber, 1991). However, what has in the past proved elusive – that context-dependent knowledge obtained by professional workers (referred to as 'tacit knowledge' [Nonaka, 1994]) – is the focus of KMS. Figure 17.1

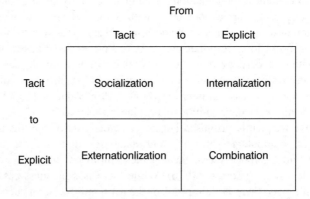

Figure 17.1   *The knowledge-creation process. (From Nonaka, 1994)*

classifies knowledge creation into tacit and explicit, based on Nonaka (1994).

Nonaka focused on knowledge creation, although the knowledge management process must give equal attention to knowledge storage, knowledge distribution, and knowledge integration in order to achieve significant organizational improvements (Alavi and Leidner, 1998). Indeed, the major challenge of tacit knowledge is less its creation than its integration (Grant, 1996; Davenport, 1997a); such knowledge is of limited organizational value if it is not shared. With KMS, it is not sufficient that users use the system, they must actively contribute their knowledge. This is a large departure from previous information systems where user involvement was needed primarily at the analysis and design phase, not the content provision phase. Moreover, such systems make information readily available at a low cost across functions and business units, hence implying the capacity for an integration of information even if the functions and units themselves remain unintegrated.

While there is not yet empirical evidence of the organizational impacts of KMS, preliminary descriptive research suggests that KMS may require a change in organizational culture and that the values and culture of an organization have a significant impact on the learning process and how effectively a company can adapt and change (Sata, 1989). Respondents in the Alavi and Leidner (1998) study suggested that the information and technology components of knowledge management constituted only 20 per cent of the challenge, whereas overcoming organizational cultural barriers accounted for the major part of effective knowledge management initiatives. Similarly, over half the respondents in Skyrme and Amidon (1997) recognize that corporate culture represents the biggest obstacle to knowledge transfer, and a similar proportion believe that changing people's behaviors represents the biggest challenge to its continuing management.

Junnarkar and Brown (1997) suggest that knowledge managers interested in the role of IT as an enabler of knowledge management should not simply focus on how to connect people with information but how to develop an organizational environment conducive to tacit knowledge sharing. Similarly, Newman (1997) sees information hoarding behavior resulting from perceptions of the strategic value of information. His modified Johari Window (see Figure 17.2) provides a view of when individuals are likely to cooperate and when they are unlikely to do so.

Poor communication between people can be a major barrier to learning. In many organizations, information and knowledge are not considered organizational resources to be shared, but individual competitive weapons to be kept private (Davenport, 1997b). Organizational members may share personal knowledge with a certain trepidation – the perceived threat that they are of less value if their knowledge is part of the organizational public domain. Research in organizational learning and knowledge management suggests that

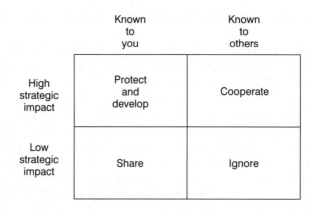

Figure 17.2   *The Johari Window. (From Newman, 1998)*

some facilitating conditions include trust, interest, and shared language (Hanssen-Bauer and Snow, 1996), fostering access to knowledgeable members (Brown and Duguid, 1991), and a culture marked by autonomy, redundancy, requisite variety, intention, and fluctuation (Nonaka, 1994).

Hence, in understanding the potential impact of KMS on organizations, it is first necessary to understand the cultural implications of such systems. We would argue that the division of knowledge creation into tacit versus explicit, while interesting, does little to advance our understanding of the users' view of the knowledge or information included in KMS. The Johari Window of knowledge sharing likewise does not explicitly deal with the users' view of their own knowledge (except to classify apparent knowledge as 'high or low in strategic value', although it is unclear if this is of value to the individual, organization, or both). If we consider the user as a contributor of information to the KMS, we can think of information as having a certain value to the user as an individual asset and a certain degree of value as a corporate asset. This is depicted in a simple matrix in Figure 17.3.

According to Figure 17.3, we would expect certain individuals to share knowledge willingly, others to hoard knowledge, others to be indifferent (labeled random sharing), and others to engage in selective sharing. Moreover, it should be noted that certain types of knowledge will be viewed differently than other types of knowledge. For example, explicit knowledge such as a company training manual is unlikely to be perceived as valuable as an individual asset. However, the very type of knowledge that KMS are designed to amalgamate – tacit knowledge such as lessons learned on a project – is likely to be the type of knowledge with the greatest potential for being viewed as an individual asset. One could try to classify various categories of knowledge into the four quadrants; for our propositions, we will consider the

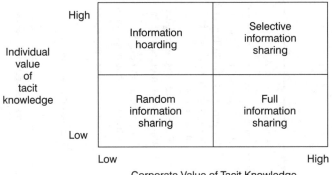

Figure 17.3 *Information culture matrix*

primary challenge of knowledge management to be that of fostering the sharing of tacit knowledge.

Based on the above discussion and Figure 17.3, we would venture the following propositions:

> *Proposition 1. Individuals perceiving their tacit knowledge to be high in individual value and high in corporate value will engage in selective sharing, sharing that knowledge which might bring recognition and reward to them but concealing that knowledge which might be successfully used by others with no reward for them.*
> *Proposition 2. Individuals perceiving their tacit knowledge to be high in individual value and low in corporate value will engage in information hoarding, choosing to avoid sharing their knowledge but attempting to learn as much as possible from others.*
> *Proposition 3. Individuals perceiving their tacit knowledge to be low in individual value and high in corporate value will engage in information sharing, sharing freely with others for the benefit of the organization.*
> *Proposition 4. Individuals perceiving their tacit knowledge to be low in individual value and low in corporate value will engage in random sharing, sharing freely when their knowledge is requested but not consciously sharing otherwise.*

In determining the factors that might influence information culture (i.e. the perceptions on the value of tacit knowledge to the individual and to the organization), an understanding of corporate culture is in order. This will be discussed in Section 3.

2.4 Summary

New classes of information systems for managers and professionals are continuing to emerge, yet the perennial problem of obtaining systematic

Table 17.1 *Summary of information-based systems*

	MIS	DSS	EIS	KMS
Purpose	Provide summarized performance reports to management	Provide tools, models, and data for aid in decision analysis	Provide online access to real-time financial and operational information	Provide online access to unstructured information and knowledge throughout the organization
Users	Managers at various levels	Analysts and middle managers	Senior and middle managers	Professionals and managers throughout an organization
Role of users	Participation in design	Participation as designer, active user	Participation in design, active user	Participation in design, active user, content provider
Information strategy	One-for-all	One-for-one	One-for-one	Anyone, anytime, anywhere
Interpretive framework	Organizational structure	Organizational decision making	Organizational decision making	Organizational culture

MIS = management information systems; DSS = design support systems; EIS = executive information systems; KMS = knowledge management systems.

benefits from such systems remains. IS researchers have attempted to explain the impact of IS on organizations by considering the effect of IS on organizational structure and decision making. The former line of research led to mixed findings and the latter, findings more at the individual than organizational level. With the changes in systems, summarized in Table 17.1, the role of the user has progressed from involvement in system design (MIS), to in many cases system designer (DSS), to interactive system user (EIS), to information content provider (KMS). This shift in the role of the user requires a concomitant shift in our conceptualization of information systems with less emphasis on the 'systems' aspect and more on the 'information' aspect, namely the users' view of information as an individual or corporate asset. Information has been classified according to its accuracy, timeliness, reliability, completeness, precision, conciseness, currency, format, accessibility, and perceived usefulness (Delone and McLean, 1992). Previous systems' design focused on these aspects as the foundation of information quality. What is missing is an understanding of the information culture issue. As we have seen, the latest class of systems requires far greater activity of users in not just information requirements processes, but in supplying information for the system.

Moreover, we seem to have moved from a 'one-for-all' to a 'one-for-one' to an 'anyone anytime anywhere' information provision strategy as we have advanced from MIS to DSS and EIS, to KMS. The latter strategy requires greater horizontal and vertical integration of information in an organization. It is arguable that the potential impact of systems is greater when a larger part of the organization is affected, such as with systems integrated organization-wide, or even across organizations. Yet the greater the required integration, the greater the potential implementation difficulties. As the degree of horizontal integration increases, we would expect structural constraints. For example, enterprise-wide systems are transaction-based systems which most effectively operate in environments with horizontal coordination. In organizations where little horizontal coordination existed, i.e. where units were highly decentralized, we would expect greater implementation challenges than in already centralized organizations. Likewise, vertical integration is expected to pose control challenges. In loosely formalized organizations, for example, email systems would not be expected to pose threats to power distributions (in that employees can easily communicate upward without hesitation), but in rigidly formalized organizations, the possibility of lower level employees by-passing individuals in the hierarchy via electronic communication might create difficulties. Systems requiring both vertical and horizontal integration will create the greatest cultural challenges for organizations (Figure 17.4). We will next examine organizational culture and its implication for KMS implementation.

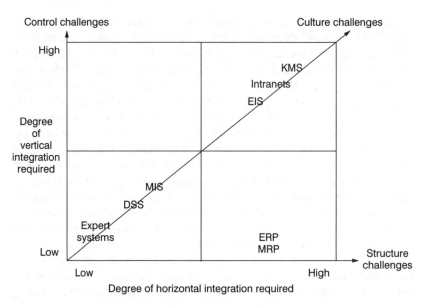

Figure 17.4   *Systems and organizational integration (KMS = knowledge management systems; EIS = executive information systems; MIS = management information systems; DSS = design support systems)*

3   Organizational culture and its implication for KMS

Schein (1985) defines organizational culture as 'the set of shared, taken-for-granted implicit assumptions that a group holds and that determine how it perceives, thinks about, and reacts to its various environments'. Burack (1991) defines culture as the 'organization's customary way of doing things and the philosophies and assumptions underlying these', and Johnson (1992), as 'the core set of beliefs and assumptions which fashion an organization's view of itself'. These are similar to Hofstede's (1980, 1991) definition of national culture as the 'collective programming of the mind that distinguishes one group of people from another'. Culture is hence viewed as a shared mental model which influences how individuals interpret behaviors and behave themselves, often without their being aware of the underlying assumptions. Schein (1985) states that the members of a culture are generally unaware of their own culture until they encounter a different one.

Culture is manifested in rituals and routines, stories and myths, symbols, power structures, organizational structures, and control systems (Johnson, 1992). Whereas a wealth of inconclusive contingency research examines the appropriate structure and technology in various environments to maximize organizational effectiveness, we are only now beginning to see research aimed at determining the contribution of organizational culture to organizational effectiveness. Part of the reason for this has been the difficulty of categorizing and measuring organizational cultures. Furthermore, there may have been an unstated view that cultures evolve and are beyond the control of organizational decision makers; hence, research focused on more malleable constructs such as structure, technology and decision making processes.

In the organizational culture literature, culture is examined either as a set of assumptions or as a set of behaviors. Behaviors, or norms, are a fairly visible manifestation of the mental assumptions, although some argue that the behaviors should be considered 'organizational climate' and the norms, as comprising organizational culture.* We will present a brief discussion of both the values and behavioral perspectives of culture.

3.1 The value view

Denison and Mishra (1995) studied the impact of organizational culture on organizational effectiveness and looked for a broad set of cultural traits that were linked to effectiveness in various environments. Denison and Mishra suggested that, from a values perspective, culture could be thought of as including degrees of external versus internal integration and tradeoffs of change and flexibility with stability and direction. They classified cultures as being adaptability oriented, involvement oriented, mission oriented, or consistency oriented. Their classification is drawn from Quinn and Rohrbaugh's (1983) value set which argued that organizations focus to various degrees internally or externally, and, in terms of structure preferences, have tradeoffs in stability and control versus flexibility and change.

Denison and Mishra found that in two of four organizations studied, organizational effectiveness appeared to be tied to consistency and mission, yet the cases also seemed to support the idea that involvement oriented cultures led to organizational effectiveness. In a survey, Denison and Mishra found that mission and consistency, traits of stability, predicted profitability, whereas involvement and adaptability, traits of flexibility, predicted sales growth.

Chatman and Jehn (1994) argue that organizational cultures within a given industry tend to deviate very little; in other words, they argue that the environment dictates to a certain extent cultures in organizations (at least for organizations that survive in the industry). A problem with Denison and Mishra's study is its inability to consider the effect of the environment on cultures, given that there was not sufficient industrial variation in the sample. Thus, we are unable to deduce if the environment might have influenced their findings.

---

* See Denison (1996) for a thorough review of the subtle differences between culture and climate.

Hofstede *et al.* (1990) examined culture both in terms of values and behaviors. In terms of value, they found that organizational culture was tied to the national culture dimensions identified by Hofstede (1980) and reflected preferences for centralized versus decentralized decision making (power distance), preferences for the degree of formalization of routines (uncertainty avoidance), degree of concern over money and career versus family and cooperation (masculinity/femininity dimension), and degree of identification with the company and preference for individual versus group reward systems (collectivistic/individualistic dimension). When the authors eliminated the effects due to nationality, the value differences between organizations were primarily dependent upon subunit characteristics rather than overall membership in the organization. Hence, the authors concluded that organizational subunits were the more appropriate level of analysis for organizational culture study. Moreover, they found that behaviors were a better means of distinguishing subunit cultures than were value systems.

3.2   The behavioral perspective

Although popular literature insists that shared values represent the core of organizational culture, the empirical data from Hofstede *et al.* (1990) showed that shared perceptions of daily practices formed the core of organizational subunit culture. The behavioral dimensions isolated by the authors were:

1   *Process vs. results oriented.* This dimension refers to a focus on improving the means by which organizational goals are achieved (process) as opposed to a focus on the attainment of goals.
2   *Employee vs. job oriented.* Employee orientation suggests a concern for people, whereas a job orientation refers to a concern over performing tasks effectively.
3   *Parochial vs. professional.* A parochial orientation suggests that individuals are loyal to their organization, whereas a professional orientation suggests that individuals are loyal to their profession.
4   *Open vs. closed system.* This dimension describes the communication climate in the subunit.
5   *Loose vs. tight control.* The control dimension reflects the degree of internal structuring, with loose organizations having few written or unwritten codes of behavior and tight organizations having strict unwritten and written policies.
6   *Normative vs. pragmatic.* Pragmatic units are market driven and customer oriented, whereas normative units are product oriented. Interestingly, some units were found to be pragmatic but not results oriented (i.e. a goal of improving customer service might not imply a goal of improving the bottom line).

The process/results, parochial/professional, loose/tight, and normative/pragmatic were found to relate partly to the industry, confirming Chatman and Jehn's (1994) conclusion that industry or environmental factors more generally affect organizational cultures, whereas the employee/job orientation and open/closed system were more determined by the philosophy of the founders and senior managers. These latter dimensions might therefore be more malleable.

In considering the possible influence of the behavioral dimensions of subunit culture on information culture, one dimension in particular appears more relevant to predicting the quality of the knowledge contributed to a system rather than to predicting the value placed on the knowledge. Specifically, loose versus tight control might influence whether individuals follow organizational rules and procedures about sharing knowledge but would not necessarily influence their beliefs about whether the knowledge was properly theirs or the organization's and, hence, might influence the quality of the knowledge they elected to contribute to a system but would not likely influence their attitude about the value of that knowledge to them or the organization. We therefore do not include this dimension in predictions about the influence of subunit culture on information culture. If we map the remaining dimensions into Figure 17.4 to form Figure 17.5, we might expect

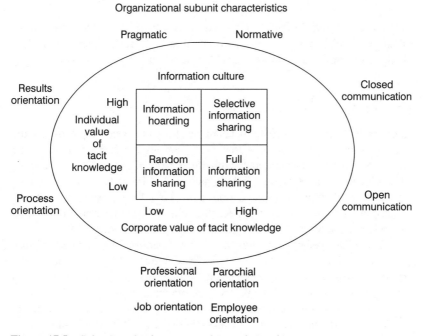

Figure 17.5 *Subunit and information culture relationship*

that certain of these subunit cultural behaviors would tend to foster the view of tacit knowledge as an individual asset, whereas others would encourage viewing tacit knowledge as a corporate asset.

> *Proposition 5. Individuals in subunits characterized by a results orientation will view tacit knowledge largely as an individual asset, whereas individuals in subunits characterized by a process orientation will view tacit information less as an individual asset.*
>
> *Proposition 6. Individuals in subunits characterized by a professional orientation will view tacit knowledge less as a corporate asset, whereas individuals in subunits characterized by a parochial orientation will view tacit knowledge more as a corporate asset.*
>
> *Proposition 7. Individuals in subunits characterized by an open communication culture will view tacit knowledge less as an individual asset, whereas individuals in subunits characterized by a closed communication climate will view tacit knowledge more as an individual asset.*
>
> *Proposition 8. Individuals in subunits characterized by a pragmatic culture will view tacit knowledge less as a corporate asset, whereas individuals in subunits characterized by a normative culture will view tacit knowledge more as a corporate asset.*
>
> *Proposition 9. Individuals in subunits characterized by an employee culture will view tacit knowledge more as a corporate asset, whereas individuals in subunits characterized by a job orientation will view tacit knowledge less as a corporate asset.*

The above propositions are intended to predict the possible influence of subunit cultural factors on information culture. A final consideration will be the dimension of culture at the individual level, as discussed next.

3.3   Individual cultures

Although Hofstede *et al.* (1990) discount the utility of considering culture at the individual level, others propose that individual level cultures interact either synchronously or disharmoniously with organizational culture (Patterson *et al.*, 1996; Chatman and Barsade, 1995). Chatman and Barsade (1995) examined individual level culture in organizations using the individualistic/collectivistic dimension of culture which has been the topic of extensive communication research at the individual level of analysis (Gudykunst *et al.*, 1996).

Individualism versus collectivism was first identified by Hofstede (1980) as a dimension distinguishing national cultures. Individualism is the preference for a loosely knit social framework in society in which individuals are supposed to take care of themselves and their immediate family as opposed to collectivism in which there is a larger in-group to which is given unquestioning loyalty (Hofstede, 1980). Individualism is related to a low-context communication style wherein individuals prefer information to be stated directly and exhibit a preference for quantifiable detail, whereas collectivism is related to a high-context communication style in which individuals prefer to draw inferences from non-explicit or implicit information (Hall, 1976; Gudykunst, 1997). In individualistic cultures, the needs, values, and goals of the individual take precedence over the needs, values, and goals of the ingroup. In collectivistic cultures, the needs, values, and goals of the in-group take precedence over the needs, values, and goals of the individual (Gudykunst, 1997; Hofstede, 1980). Research suggests that those who are associated with individualistic values tend to be less concerned with self-categorizing, are less influenced by group memberships, and have greater skills in entering and leaving new groups than individuals from collectivist cultures (Hofstede, 1980; Hall, 1976). Individualistic values are associated with preferences for individual rewards (or a norm of justice, meaning that an individual is rewarded according to his/her input rather than a norm of equality in which all individuals who work as a group are rewarded equally) (Gudykunst and Ting-Toomey, 1988).

Earley (1994) argued that organizations could also be thought of as being dominantly individualistic or collectivist. Organizations encouraging individuals to pursue and maximize their goals and rewarding performance based on individual achievement would be considered as having an individualistic culture, whereas organizations placing priority on collective goals and joint contributions and rewards for organizational accomplishments would be considered collectivist (Chatman and Barsade, 1995).

On an individual level, Chatman and Barsade (1995) propose that workplace cooperation – the willful contribution of employee effort to the successful completion of interdependent tasks – is as much dependent on individual culture as organizational culture. They suggest that individuals with cooperative dispositions place priority on working together with others towards a common purpose, while persons with a low cooperative disposition place priority on maximizing their own welfare irrespective of others. Cooperative persons are more motivated to understand and uphold group norms and expect others to cooperate, whereas individualistic people are more concerned with personal goals and expect others to behave in like manner. Chatman and Barsade (1995) proposed that people who have a high disposition to cooperate and who work in a collectivistic organizational culture will be the most cooperative, while people who have a low disposition to cooperate and who work in an individualistic culture will be the least cooperative. This may suggest that individualistic cultures are results oriented and tend to be closed, whereas cooperative cultures are process oriented and tend to be open. It might be that cooperative people in a cooperative culture could be more willing to share tacit knowledge than individualistic individuals in a cooperative culture or cooperative individuals in an individualistic

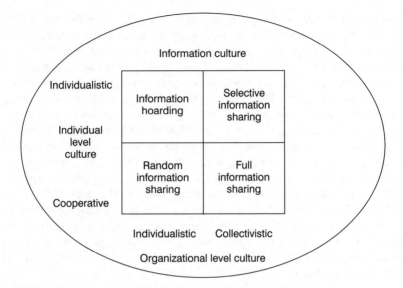

Figure 17.6   *Individual culture's relationship to information culture*

culture. When mapped into Figure 17.4, we would expect the following influence of individual culture on information culture (Figure 17.6).

If we consider the relationship between individual level culture, subunit culture, and information culture, we propose the following:

Proposition 10. Individualistic individuals in collectivistic organizational subunits will engage in selective sharing of tacit knowledge.
Proposition 11. Cooperative individuals in collectivistic organizational subunits will engage in full sharing of tacit knowledge.
Proposition 12. Individualistic individuals in individualistic organizational subunits will engage in hoarding of tacit knowledge.
Proposition 13. Cooperative individuals in individualistic organizational subunits will engage in random sharing of tacit knowledge.

3.4   Summary

This section has presented a brief summary of organizational subunit cultures and has made propositions concerning the relationship of subunit culture and individual culture with the information culture discussed in Section 2. The propositions, in abbreviated form, are summarized in Table 17.2.

The above propositions reflect an organizational imperative – that organizational factors, in this case organizational subunit and individual culture, influence the successful implementation and use of knowledge management systems. It is also conceivable that KMS will affect organiza-

Table 17.2 *Summary of propositions*

Nature of Proposition	Proposition number	Proposition (abbreviated)
Information culture	1	Individuals perceiving their tacit knowledge as high in individual and corporate value will engage in selective sharing of tacit knowledge.
	2	Individuals perceiving their tacit knowledge as high in individual and low in corporate value will engage in information hoarding.
	3	Individuals perceiving their tacit knowledge as low in individual and high in corporate value will engage in full sharing.
	4	Individuals perceiving their tacit knowledge as low in individual and corporate value will engage in random sharing.
Organizational subunit culture influence on information culture	5	Results, as opposed to process, oriented subunits will foster a view of tacit knowledge as an individual asset.
	6	Parochial, as opposed to professional, oriented cultures will foster a view of tacit knowledge as a corporate asset.
	7	Closed, as opposed to open, subunit communication climates will foster a view of tacit knowledge as an individual asset.
	8	Normative, as opposed to pragmatic, oriented cultures will foster a view of tacit knowledge as a corporate asset.
	9	Employee, as opposed to job, oriented cultures will foster a view of tacit knowledge as a corporate asset.
Individual and organizational culture influence on information culture	10	Individualistic individuals in collectivistic cultures will engage in selective sharing of tacit knowledge.
	11	Cooperative individuals in collectivistic cultures will engage in full sharing of tacit knowledge.
	12	Individualistic individuals in individualistic cultures will engage in hoarding of tacit knowledge.
	13	Cooperative individuals in individualistic cultures will engage in random sharing of tacit knowledge.

tional cultures (a technology imperative). There is evidence that as systems integrate information vertically and horizontally, organizational cultures are altered. For example, in the case of EIS, it has been found that by virtue of the fact that top managers are viewing detailed daily information previously viewed in monthly or weekly reports in a summarized fashion, all levels in the organization take notice of the information being tracked by the senior managers and alter their behavior in such a manner as to focus on the measures being examined by the top managers. In some cases, this was part of a planned attempt to help focus the attention of employees on the factors considered most critical by the top managers (Carlsson *et al.*, 1996). Over time, the underlying values might shift to be become consistent with the new behavior. KMS are being implemented in a time of increasing global competition and the need to be 'flexible'; as such, part of the implementation goal may be directed toward enabling a more flexible, adaptable culture. In this case, by implementing the system and inculcating desired sharing behaviors, over time the organizational culture may itself become more open, flexible, and employee oriented. However, this chapter purports to evaluate the constraints posed by organizational culture on the implementation of KMS, rather than the potential long-term consequences of KMS on organizational culture. The latter interesting question is left for future research.

4   Implications and conclusion

It can be argued that the first step in developing an implementation plan is understanding where barriers might be encountered and why. The above analysis is intended to help evaluate where and why such barriers might exist when implementing KMS. Several strategies for KMS implementation have been suggested: one strategy is to include information of high value such as corporate directories which make users comfortable with, and dependent upon, the corporate intranet. Another is education on the need and potential of such a system to improve individual productivity and customer service. Another commonly used strategy is providing rewards and incentives, such as bonuses, based on the amount and quality of knowledge one contributes. The strategy used to implement KMS should be tied to the organizational subunit culture. For example, individuals in reward-oriented subunits might respond well to incentive systems, whereas individuals in process-oriented subunits might require greater education and training on the benefits of such a system. Furthermore, changes in reward systems will do little to change the information culture; in which case, at most, we would expect that subunit cultures which foster a view of knowledge as a high individual asset (results-oriented, professional-oriented subunits) will be able to encourage selective information sharing but not the full sharing of the most valuable of tacit knowledge. To obtain full sharing in subunits that are results oriented, closed, professional oriented, and job oriented, the change management plan might need to focus first on changing the culture and only secondly, on implementing the system. It would be misleading to think that the system would encourage full sharing in organizations where the information culture ran contrary to such sharing, just as it has been found that electronic mail systems do not encourage greater communication among subunits with infrequent, irregular communication (Vandenbosch and Ginzberg, 1997). However, in organizations with cultures that foster the attitude of tacit knowledge as primarily a corporate asset, it would be expected that KMS could be implemented with little resistance.

This chapter has taken the view that organizational effectiveness in the highly competitive global environment will depend largely on an organization's capacity to manage individual employee knowledge. We have argued that knowledge management systems will be important computer-based information system components to such effectiveness, but that the success of these systems will depend on an appropriate match with organizational subunit and individual culture. We have offered propositions in an attempt to provide a framework for understanding where potential incongruity between these new IS and organizational culture might exist.

One way to consider the advances of information-based systems in organizations is to consider the dominant organizational theory underlying the assumptions of the need for information. The era of MIS can be thought to correspond to the organizational theory termed the 'information processing view of the organization'. This view posited that organizations process information to reduce uncertainty – the absence of information, and to reduce equivocality – the existence of multiple and conflicting interpretations about an organizational situation (Daft and Lengel, 1986). According to this view, information systems are needed to help organizations understand the environment and make appropriate plans in response. As DSS and EIS came into vogue, so was the information-processing view of the firm replaced with the decision-making view of the firm espoused by Huber and McDaniel (1986) wherein decision making was seen as the most critical managerial activity. This view placed the primary purpose of IS as supporting organizational decision makers by providing tools, timely information, and ready access to important operational and financial information. More recently, it is being argued that the most critical organizational activity is creating, sharing, and utilizing the knowledge that resides in employees (Nonaka, 1994). To understand the potential organizational effect of systems designed to harness knowledge, it is argued that the traditional paradigms of structure and decision making are insufficient, but a perspective incorporating organizational culture is needed.

The major intent of this chapter has been to encourage thinking about the important topic of current IS and its relationship to organizational culture, rather than to offer a complete set of guidelines on implementing KMS or evaluating the effectiveness of KMS in given organizational cultures. It is hoped that the reader leaves with a framework for assessing the potential conflicts resulting from cultural factors that may arise with the implementation of knowledge management systems, and can use the frameworks proposed herein to guide thinking on potential implementation strategies.

References

Ackoff, R. L. (1967) Management misinformation systems. *Management Science*, **14**(4), 147–156.

Alavi, M. and Leidner, D. (1998) Knowledge management systems: emerging views and practices from the field. Working paper, University of Maryland.

Applegate, L. M. (1987) Lockheed-Georgia Company: executive information systems. *Harvard Case (9–187–147)*, Harvard Business School, Boston, MA.

Applegate, L. M. and Osborn, C. S. (1988) Phillips 66 Company: executive information systems. *Harvard Case (9–189–006)*, Harvard Business School, Boston, MA.

Brown, J. S. and Duguid, P. (1991) Organizational learning and communities of-practice: toward a unified view of working, learning, and innovation. *Organization Science*, **2**(1), 40–57.

Burack, E. (1991) Changing the company culture – the role of human resource development. *Long Range Planning*, **24**(1), 88–95.

Carlsson, S., Leidner, D. E. and Elam, J. J. (1996) Individual and organizational effectiveness: perspectives on the impact of ESS in multinational organizations. In *Implementing Systems for Supporting Management Decisions* (eds P. Humphreys *et al.*), Chapman and Hall, London.

Carter, N. M. (1984) Computerization as a predominate technology: its influence on the structure of newspaper organizations. *Academy of Management Journal*, June, 247–270.

Chatman, J. A. and Barsade, S. G. (1995) Personality, organizational culture, and cooperation: evidence from business simulation. *Administrative Science Quarterly*, **40**, 423–443.

Chatman, J. and Jehn, K. (1994) Assessing the relationship between industry characteristics and organizational culture: how different can you be? *Academy of Management Journal*, **37**(3), 522–553.

Cortese, A. (1996) Here comes the Intranet. *Business Week*, 26 February, 76–84.

Courtney, J., Crosdell, D. and Paradice, D. (1997) Lockean inquiring organizations: guiding principles and design guidelines for learning organizations. *Proceedings of the 1997 Americas Conference on Information Systems*, http:hsb.baylor.edu/ramsower/ais.ac.97/papers/courtney.htm.

Daft, R. L. and Lengel, R. H. (1986) Organizational information requirements, media richness and structural design. *Management Science*, **32**(5), 554–571.

Davenport, T. H. (1997a) Knowledge management at Ernst and Young, 1997. URL: http:knowman.bus.utexas.edu/E&Y.htm.

Davenport, T. H. (1997b) Some principles of knowledge management. URL: http:knowman.bus.utexas.edu/kmprin.htm.

Dawson, P. and McLaughlin, I. (1986) Computer technology and the redefinition of supervision: a study of the effects of computerization on railway freight supervisors. *Journal of Management Studies*, **23**, 116–132.

Delone, W. H. and McLean, E. R. (1992) Information systems success: the quest for the dependent variable. *Information Systems Research*, March, 60–95.

Denison, D. (1996) What IS the difference between organizational culture and organizational climate? A native's point of view on a decade of paradigm wars. *Academy of Management Review*, **21**(3), 619–654.

Denison, D. and Mishra, A. (1995) Toward a theory of organizational culture and effectiveness. *Organization Science*, **6**(2), 204–223.

Earley, P. C. (1994) Self or group? Cultural effects of training on self-efficacy and performance. *Administrative Science Quarterly*, **39**, 89–117.

Elliott, D. (1992) Executive information systems: their impact on executive decision making. Doctoral dissertation, The University of Texas at Austin, May.

Foster, L. W. and Flynn, D. M. (1984) Management information technology: its effects on organizational form and function. *MIS Quarterly*, December, 229–236.

Franz, C., Robey, D. and Koeblitz, R. (1986) User response to an online IS: a field experiment. *MIS Quarterly*, **10**(1), 29–44.

Friend, D. (1986) Executive Information Systems: successes, failures, insights and misconceptions. *D55–86 Transactions* (ed. J. Fedorowicz), 35–40.

Galliers, R. D. and Baker, B. S. H. (eds.) (1994) *Strategic Information Management: challenges and strategies in managing information systems*, Butterworth-Heinemann, Oxford.

Galliers, R. D., Leidner, D. E. and Baker, B. S. H. (eds.) (1999) *Strategic Information Management: challenges and strategies in managing information systems*, 2nd edn, Butterworth-Heinemann, Oxford.

Grant, R. M. (1996) Prospering in dynamically-competitive environments: organizational capability as knowledge integration. *Organization Science*, **7**(4), 375–387.

Gudykunst, W. B. (1997) Cultural variability in communication. *Communication Research*, **24**(4), 327–348.

Gudykunst, W. B., Matsumoto, Y., Ting-Toomey, S., Nishida, T., Linda, K. S. and Heyman, S. (1996) The influence of cultural individualism-collectivism, self construals, and individual values on communication styles across cultures. *Human Communication Research*, **22**, 510–543.

Gudykunst, W. B. and Ting-Toomey, S. (1988) *Culture and Interpersonal Communication*, Sage, Newbury Park, CA.

Hall, E. T. (1976) *Beyond Culture*, Anchor Books/Doubleday, Garden City, NJ.

Hanssen-Bauer, J. and Snow, C. C. (1996) Responding to hypercompetition: the structure and processes of a regional learning network organization. *Organization Science*, **7**(4), 413–437.

Hofstede, G. (1980) *Culture's Consequences*, Sage, Beverly Hills, CA.

Hofstede, G. (1991) *Cultures and Organizations: Software of the Mind*, McGraw-Hill, London.

Hofstede, G., Neuijen, B., Ohayv, D. D. and Sanders, G. (1990) Measuring organizational cultures: a qualitative and quantitative study across twenty cases. *Administrative Science Quarterly*, **35**, 286–316.

Hogue, J. T. (1987) A framework for the examination of management involvement in decision support systems. *Journal of Management Information Systems*, **4**(1).

Holub, A. (1988) What happens when info regarding the quality of a bank's services becomes visible. *EIS Conference Report*, **1**(4), 1–2.

Houdeshel, G. and Watson, H. J. (1987) The MIDS system at Lockheed-Georgia. *MIS Quarterly*, **11**(1) March, 127–140.

Huber, G. P. (1990) A theory of the effects of advanced information technologies on organizational design, intelligence, and decision making. *Academy of Management Review*, **15**(1), 47–71.

Huber, G. (1991) Organizational learning: the contributing processes and the literatures. *Organization Science*, **2**(1), 88–115.

Huber, G. P. and McDaniel, R. R. (1986) The decision-making paradigm of organizational design. *Management Science*, **32**(5), 572–589.

Ives, B. and Olson, M. (1984) User involvement and MIS success: a review of research. *Management Science*, **30**(5), 586–603.

Johnson, G. (1992) Managing strategic change – Strategy, culture and action. *Long Range Planning*, **25**(1), 28–36.

Junnarkar, B. and Brown, C. V. (1997) Re-assessing the enabling role of IT in knowledge management. *Journal of Knowledge Management*, **1**(2), 142–148.

Kador, J. (1988) ESSs keep execs in control. *Planner*, **11**(2), 10–14.

Keen, P. G. W. and Scott Morton, M. S. (1982) *Decision Support Systems: An Organizational Perspective*, Addison-Wesley, Reading, MA.

King, W. and Rodriguez, J. (1981) Participative design of strategic DSS. *Management Science*, **27**(6), 717–726.

Klatzky, S. R. (1970) Automation, size, and the locus of decision making: the cascade effect. *Journal of Business*, **43**, 141–151.

Laudon, K. and Laudon, J. (1997) *Essentials of Management Information Systems*, 2nd edn, Prentice-Hall, Englewood Cliffs, NJ.

Le Blanc, L. A. and Kozar, K. A. (1990) An empirical investigation of the relationship between DSS usage and system performance: a case study of a navigation support system. *MIS Quarterly*, **14**, 263–277.

Leidner, D. E. (1992) Reasons for EIS failure: an analysis by phase of development. Working paper, Baylor University, TX.

Leidner, D. E. (1998) Personal interview.

Leidner, D. E. and Elam, J. J. (1995) The impact of executive information systems on organizational design, intelligence, and decision making. *Organization Science*, **6**(6), 645–665.

Lyytinen, K. and Hirschheim, R. (1987) Information systems failures – a survey and classification of the empirical literature. *Oxford Surveys in Information Technology*, **4**, 257–309.

Markus, M. L. and Benjamin, R. (1996) Change agentry – the next IS frontier. *MIS Quarterly*, **20**(4), 385–408.

Mitchell, P. (1988) An EIS is good for you. *EIS Conference Report*, **1**(4), 4.

Molloy, S. and Schwenk, C. (1995) The effects of IT on strategic decision making. *Journal of Management Studies*, **32**(5), 283–311.

Mowshowitz, A. (1976) *Information Processing in Human Affairs*, Addison-Wesley, Reading, MA.

Newman, V. (1997) Redefining knowledge management to deliver competitive advantage. *Journal of Knowledge Management*, **1**(2), 123–128.

Nonaka, I. (1994) A dynamic theory of organizational knowledge creation. *Organization Science*, **5**(1), 14–37.

Patterson, M., Payn, R. and West, M. (1996) Collective climates: a test of their sociopsychological significance. *Academy of Management Journal*, **28**(6), 1675–1691.

Pyburn, P. (1983) Linking the MIS plan with corporate strategy. *MIS Quarterly*, June, 1–14.

Quinn, R. E. and Rohrbaugh, J. (1983) A spatial model of effectiveness criteria: towards a competing values approach to organizational analysis. *Management Science*, **29**(3), 363–377.

Robey, D. (1977) Computers and management structure: some empirical findings re-examined. *Human Relations*, **30**, 963–976.

Rockart, J. and DeLong, D. (1988) *Executive Support Systems: The Emergence of Top Management Computer Use*, Dow-Jones-Irwin, Illinois.

Rooney, P. (1997) Imposing order from chaos. *INTRANETS*, **2**(8), Computerworld Supplement.

Sata, R. (1989) Organizational Learning – the key to management innovation. *Sloan Management Review*, Spring, 63–74.

Schein, E. (1985) *Organizational Culture and Leadership*, Jossey-Bass, San Francisco, CA.

Schein, E. (1996) Culture: the missing concept in organization studies. *Administrative Science Quarterly*, **41**, 229–240.

Simon, H. A. (1977) *The New Science of Management Decision*, Prentice-Hall, Englewood Cliffs, NJ.

Skyrme, D. J. and Amidon, D. (1997) *Creating the Knowledge-Based Business*, Business Intelligence Limited, London.

Somogyi, E. K. and Galliers, R. D. (1987) Applied information technology: from data processing to strategic information systems. *Journal of Information Technology*, **2**(1), 30–41. Reproduced in Galliers, R. D. and Baker, B. S. H. (eds.) (1994), *op cit.*, 9–27 and in Galliers, R. D., Leidner, D. E. and Baker, B. S. H. (eds.) (1999), *op cit.*, 1–20 under the title 'Information technology in business: from data processing to strategic information systems'.

Sprague, R. H. and Carlson, E. D. (1982) *Building Effective Decision Support Systems*, Prentice-Hall, Englewood Cliffs, NJ.

Stewart, R. (1971) *How Computers Affect Management*, MIT Press, Cambridge, MA.

Thyfault, M. E. (1996) The intranet rolls in. *Information Week*, **564**(15), 76–78.

Todd, P. and Benbasat, I. (1991) An experimental investigation of the impact of computer-based decision aids on decision making strategies. *Information Systems Research*, June, 87–115.

Vandenbosch, B. and Ginzberg, M. J. (1996/97) Lotus notes and collaboration: plus ça change. *Journal of Management Information Systems*, **13**(3), 65–82.

Vandenbosch, B. and Higgins, C. (1996) Information acquisition and mental models: an investigation into the relationship between behavior and learning *Information Systems Research*, June, 198–214.

Vidal, F., Saintoyant, P. Y. and Meilhaud, J. (1998) *Objectif Intranet: Enjeux et Applications*, Les Editions d'Organisation, Paris.

Whisler, T. L. (1970) *The Impact of Computers on Organizations*, Praeger Publishers, New York.

Yourdan, E. and Constantine, L. L. (1978) *Structured Design*, 2nd edn, Yourdan Press, New York.

Questions for discussion

1 Do you agree or disagree with the assumption that culture is an important impediment (or facilitator) of effective IT implementation? What are some situations you have experienced that confirm or disconfirm this assumption?

2 Consider the likely reaction of colleagues you have worked with to a system such as KMS. What type of reaction would you expect? What types of incentives would be necessary to encourage information sharing?

3 Consider the assumption that KMS will only be effective if full information sharing occurs. Do you agree or disagree with this assumption? What would be the characteristics of an effective KMS?

4 Consider the organizational culture of organizations where you have worked. How important was culture to your satisfaction, motivation, and job performance? Which aspects of culture were most important? Which aspects of culture would be most important toward ensuring the success of systems such as KMS?

18 Information Systems and Organizational Learning

The social epistemology of organizational knowledge systems

B. T. Pentland

Current literature on organizational learning tends to be theoretically fragmented, drawing on analogies to individual learning theory or simply using organizational learning as an umbrella concept for many different kinds of organizational change or adaptation. This chapter introduces a framework for the analysis of organizations as knowledge systems (Holzner and Marx, 1979) composed of a collection of knowledge processes: constructing, organizing, storing, distributing, and applying. The knowledge system framework draws heavily on the sociology of knowledge and emphasizes the social nature of each of these constitutive processes. The chapter uses the framework to analyze the case of a small engineering consulting company that implemented a new information system to automate one of its core business activities: energy audits of commercial buildings. Traditional approaches to organizational learning have emphasized the ways in which information systems can lower the costs and increase capacity for search, storage, and retrieval of information. The knowledge system framework suggests a deeper level of influence, whereby information systems can also affect the objects of knowledge and the criteria for knowledge construction.

Introduction

There is an intuitive connection between organizational learning and information systems. At each stage of a system's life cycle, there are processes that evoke the metaphor of learning. Adopting a new kind of information technology, for example, has been described as a learning process (Attewell, 1992). Developing a new information system typically entails an intensive effort at identifying requirements and codifying organizational procedures and practices. Implementation often requires changes in individual skills, cognitions, and expectations, as well as changes in formal roles and structures. Once in operation, information systems typically affect the information processing patterns and capacities of an organization, a critical element in traditional learning models. Finally, maintenance of existing systems reflects adaptation to changing requirements, yet another archetypial example of organizational learning.

Despite the intuitive appeal of these examples, it is difficult to construct a systematic framework within which they can be analyzed or interpreted. This situation is characteristic of the literature on organizational learning, where many different phenomena are routinely grouped together under this broad metaphor (Huber, 1991; Levitt and March, 1988). The need for an integrative framework can be seen in the frustration expressed by Huber (1991, p. 108), who bemoans the lack of cumulative theory and findings. I believe this problem can be attributed, in part, to a lack of attention to the fundamentals of the phenomenon in question: the socially constructed, distributed, and embedded nature of knowledge, and the process through which it changes.

The objective of this chapter is to articulate a systematic framework for analyzing the effects of information systems on organizational learning that is grounded in the sociology of knowledge (Berger and Luckman, 1967; Bloor, 1976; Gurvitch, 1971; Holzner and Marx, 1979; Latour, 1987; Schutz, 1962). This rich and well-articulated theoretical tradition maps closely onto the phenomenon we are attempting to understand. The basic idea is to view organizations as 'knowledge systems' composed of a collection of socially enacted 'knowledge processes' (Holzner and Marx, 1979) which may be augmented (or impaired) by the introduction of new information systems. This provides a systematic basis for analyzing the effects of information systems, including the traditional information processing effects and the other kinds of examples mentioned above. The critical point, of course, is to move beyond the anthropomorphic metaphor of organizations as individual cognizers and treat them as social collectives that construct, organize, store, distribute, and apply knowledge through primarily social means. Viewing an organization as a social knowledge system provides a more encompassing framework within which phenomena like organizational learning can be analyzed and interpreted.

After outlining the knowledge system framework, I will use it to analyze the relationship between information systems and organizational learning in the context of a small engineering consulting company. This case is interesting because it concerns the development of a system designed specifically to embody the knowledge required for the firm's core line of business: energy auditing of commercial buildings. The question here is, how did the development and implementation of this system affect the knowledge system of the small consulting company that developed it? The framework calls attention to aspects of the case that would be glossed over in more conventional approaches to organizational learning (for example, by altering the objects of knowledge within the organization and the criteria by which new knowledge is constructed). In this way, the knowledge system framework provides a deeper and more systematic approach to the analysis of information systems and organizational learning.

The organizational knowledge system: a framework for analysis

While organizational learning is a popular concept, it is rather difficult to pin down empirically. Weick (1991) argues that the traditional behaviorist definition of learning from individual psychology – same stimulus, different response – is problematic when applied to organizations. Not only is this sequence of events rare and difficult to observe, but explanations other than learning are difficult to rule out. Furthermore, many organizational systems seem geared to produce the same response to an increasing variety of stimulus (thus absorbing uncertainty and environmental variations). Fiol and Lyles (1985) also point to the difficulties involved in measuring learning, given that organizations may develop cognitive resources that are not reflected in behavior. In practice, most empirical studies treat organizational learning as synonymous with performance improvements of the kind that characterize learning curves (Argote, 1993; Epple, Argote, and Devedas, 1991). Weick (1991, p. 121) suggested two strategies in response to these difficulties: (a) to retain the traditional definition; or (b) replace it 'with a definition that is tied more closely to the properties of organizations.'

This chapter pursues the second strategy by emphasizing the social nature of knowledge in organizations. Knowledge is always embedded in some social collectivity and is subject to the cultural assumptions, practices, and power relations operating within that collectivity. Holzner and Marx (1979) offer an analysis at the societal level that draws heavily on the phenomenological tradition in sociology of knowledge (Berger and Luckman, 1967; Gurvitch, 1971; Schutz, 1962). Their framework seems particularly appropriate to the analysis of organizational knowledge and learning because it focuses on pragmatic knowledge that is intended to achieve a certain end within a certain time and space. Holzner and Marx (1979) identify a set of five 'knowledge processes:'

1　Construction – This is the process through which new material is added or replaced within the collective stock of knowledge. The material in question need not be 'socially new' (Machlup, 1980) in the sense of being new to all humanity; it need only be new to the collectivity in question. Thus, transfer between social collectivities, such as organizations, entails some measure of construction within the recipient or 'learning' organization. There are many specific ways in which knowledge can be constructed by the community and integrated into their daily practices. As we shall see, there are a wide variety of criteria that social collectives use to ratify experience as knowledge.

2   Organization – This is the process by which bodies of knowledge are related to each other, classified, or integrated. For example, it turns out that lighting fixtures have a significant influence on the heating and cooling of commercial buildings; even high-efficiency fluorescent lights give off heat. It is not sufficient to simply construct knowledge about lighting fixtures as a separate domain; knowledge of new kinds of lighting fixtures and their thermal characteristics must be integrated into the knowledge base on heating and cooling. Establishing and maintaining these relationships as newly constructed knowledge is added is also a social process, subject to the same kinds of cultural assumptions and criteria as the construction process itself.

3   Storage – Once a new observation or experience has passed the test and been socially ratified as knowledge, it must be stored somehow. Without storage, there is no possibility for 'memory' or application. Naturally, computer-based information systems have a significant role to play here, along with paper-based filing and documentation systems, and of course, individual human memory. The effectiveness of these mechanisms as storage is always mediated, however, by social processes (Walsh and Ungson, 1991).

4   Distribution – A critical issue in any organization is distributing knowledge to places where it is needed and can be applied. Again, computer-based information systems have an increasingly important role to play, along with paper-based systems and face-to-face social interaction. Because of their communicative function, distribution processes naturally have an important social component (Manning, 1992).

5   Application, – Unless knowledge is applied in practice, there is no possibility of obtaining the kind of performance improvement that is characteristic of our intuitive understanding of 'learning.' Application takes many forms, of course, but it is a necessary part of any organizational learning system. As Pentland (1992) argues, it would be difficult to make an attribution of knowledge or competence to an organization that did not produce knowledgeable or competent performances.

It should be readily apparent that these five processes are all essential parts of any effective learning process in a social collectivity. Construction, organization, storage, distribution, and application are like links in a chain; if any one of them fails, it would be difficult to make an attribution of learning. This framework emphasizes the socially constructed and embedded nature of organizational knowledge, and explicitly calls attention to its distribution. It also suggests that organizational learning need not be seen as a single, monolithic construct. Rather, it can be treated as a collection of simpler processes, each of which contributes to the overall effect. One could construe these processes as narrowly technical, lacking in social content, as would be the case if each process were somehow automated. But as Collins (1990) has argued, even the operation of simple devices like pocket calculators ultimately depends on the interpretive framework provided by the social context in which they are used. Each knowledge process entails, by necessity, some degree of social interaction, if only through the use of language.

The knowledge system framework is similar to the typology of processes described by Huber (1991) in some respects. For example, Huber's (1991) encyclopedic review of the literature identifies ('knowledge acquisition,' 'information distribution,' 'information interpretation,' and 'organizational memory' as the four high-level processes in his typology of learning processes. Each of these (except for information distribution) is further subdivided into sub-processes. While Huber (1991) does an excellent job of categorizing published contributions, his typology of processes does not add up to systematic framework for analysis of organizations, nor does it claim to be. It is more like a conceptual umbrella under which many diverse processes are sheltered. Huber's (1991) analysis also embodies the kind of objectivist epistemology that is common to much of the literature he reviews, where knowledge is treated as an objective good to be 'acquired' (Epple, Argote, and Devadas, 1991). As a result, the social nature of the underlying phenomena gets lost in the rhetoric information processing and managerial decision making. While some authors discuss problems of sense-making (Daft and Weick, 1984) or superstition (March and Olson, 1976), the bulk of the literature seems to adopt, implicitly or explicitly, a simple objectivist epistemology. With the exception of those works informed by theories of practice (e.g., Brown and Duguid, 1991), the details of knowledge construction as a social process are largely assumed away or taken for granted.

In contrast, this framework emphasizes the socially constructed nature of knowledge and the variety of epistemic criteria that may be in use. But social processes do not cease to operate after construction; each of the other four processes is enacted by organizational members, as well, and must also be treated as problematic. The processes used to organize, store, and distribute apparently objective information are equally subject to social influence. For example, in a detailed comparative ethnography, Manning (1988) analyzes the transformative effects of information technology on the emergency calls received by two police organizations, one in the U.S. and one in England. Each police department used advanced information and telecommunications systems, but as messages crossed organizational boundaries (e.g., from the switchboard operator to the dispatcher to the squad car), their significance changed systematically. These kinds of effects are generally overlooked when an objectivist epistemology is adopted.

It is important to remember that each of these constitutive processes is, within the confines of this chapter, merely a label for a broad range of specific practices that may be defined and enacted within particular organizational settings. Unfortunately, as Bourdieu (1990) points out, labeling a practice tends to objectify it as a lifeless abstraction. Thus, in an effort to reduce 'organizational learning' into a more manageable set of analytical categories, one runs the risk of engaging in a kind of shell game, whereby the phenomenon of interest is pushed farther from view by a series of facile moves. The way out of this infinite regress, of course, is to present concrete descriptions of practice in specific situations. As Wittgenstein (1958) argues, practice is a kind of bedrock against which explanations of social phenomena must ultimately rest. In the case study that follows, such descriptions will be provided.

The use of the term *process* is an important aspect of the perspective taken here. The idea is that knowledge is the product of an ongoing set of practices embedded in the social and physical structures of the organization. It is meant to convey the dynamic quality of the overall system. Once constructed, however, 'facts' and other modalities of knowledge take on a static, objective quality for organizational members (Berger and Luckmann, 1967; Latour, 1987). These cultural products may be embedded into tools and other artifacts, most notably computer software. When these tools break down (Winograd and Flores, 1986), the veil of knowledge may be peeled away to reveal the fuzzy features below. Deconstructionists have made a discipline out of such peep shows, but for organizational members themselves, facts are facts until proven otherwise. One may adopt a critical stance towards these cultural products, but organizational members generally do not, and the knowledge system framework does not. In this respect, it adopts an 'emic' or insider's stance, taking cultural products at the face value assigned by organizational members (Geertz, 1983; Headland, Pike, and Harris, 1990). For this reason, it is important to consider the ways in which members make this determination.

Social epistemology: knowledge in practice

The core of a sociologically informed approach to organizational learning must be the sociology of knowledge. Over the last two decades, our understanding of the process of knowledge formation has evolved from one that gave a privileged place to formal scientific method and 'nature' as the ultimate arbiter of truth (e.g., Goldman, 1987) to a more empirically driven understanding of knowledge formation as grounded in human practice and interaction (Latour, 1987; Lave, 1988). Bloor (1976) advocates what has come to be known as the 'strong programme,' whose followers have conducted detailed observational studies of scientists and engineers at work. The findings of these studies suggest that even in the realm of laboratory science, knowledge is best viewed as a social construction (Knorr-Cetina, 1981; Latour and Woolgar, 1982). The critical insight is that the practices and criteria that social collectives use to ratify experience as knowledge is an empirical question that cannot be decided by philosophical argument.

Latour (1987) provides a set of guidelines for the conduct of such inquiry. Latour argues that one must follow scientists and engineers through society so that one can observe their practices. Latour's argument is based on the observation that once experience becomes formalized as 'knowledge,' it is increasingly treated as a black box whose contents are taken for granted. Once this occurs, the social origins of a particular fact can be difficult to trace. Hence, one must see what goes inside the black box before the lid goes on. Latour draws on examples from science (e.g., the development of Watson and Crick's model of the double helix) and engineering (e.g., the design of Data General's MV8000 computer) to argue that '[t]he fate of facts and machines is later users' hands; their qualities are thus a consequence, not a cause, of a collective action' (1987, p. 259). In other words, facts are only facts if other people treat them that way. They gain and retain their status as facts based on subsequent social discourse, not based on their relationship to nature.

While some philosophers decry what they perceive as the debasement of knowledge through faulty epistemology (e.g., Goldman, 1987), sociologists have observed that there are, in practice, a variety of different criteria that social groups apply to form and test their beliefs in discourse and interaction. Holzner and Marx (1979) offer some examples of criteria that are often used, in practice, to justify knowledge claims.[1]

1   Ritual superstitious – Ritual criteria for truth are commonplace in daily life, and are even quite common in high technology settings. Barley (1988) identified a variety of problem-solving routines used by radiological technicians that appear to be purely ritualistic, reflecting a blind faith that a given action has a beneficial consequence (e.g., banging on a machine in a particular way). The efficacy of such procedures need not be demonstrated;

---

[1] My point in mentioning these categories is to call attention to their diversity, not their purity, and to emphasize that as an empirical matter, people use many kinds of justifications for their beliefs. One of the key findings of the strong program on sociology of scientific knowledge is that so-called scientific criteria are, as a practical matter, rife with pragmatic, authoritative and ritual criteria (Hacking, 1992; Woolgar, 1988). Turkle and Papert (1990) provide an alternative view of epistemological diversity.

they are part of the common stock of knowledge because they are simply 'what is done here.' Appropriate performance of the ritual may signal group membership, as much as anything else (Collins, 1981).

2 Authoritative – Authoritative criteria are also quite common, as in the example of religious beliefs. The justification for a great many beliefs in our society is simply that a trusted (or respected, or perhaps feared) individual says that it is so. Among children, that is a major source of knowledge. Authoritative sources are foundation upon which both public education and propaganda gain their power (Cialdini, 1988).

3 Pragmatic – Practical experience is, of course, a major source of knowledge in any social group. Success is the critical test for many kinds of knowledge. Engineering knowledge, for example, has traditionally been based on pragmatic criteria, as have many medical procedures. Mulkay (1984, p. 92) offers the example of a British surgeon using strips of paw-paw fruit to clear up a post-operative infection after a kidney transplant. The doctor could not explain *why* the tribal remedy worked, but he had seen it work before; his knowledge of this remedy was pragmatic.

4 Scientific – Scientific criteria for truth have a strong grip on the minds of many scholars and academics, as reflected in the dominance of successive paradigms of scientific inquiry. Particular standards of proof vary among fields, but the acceptable standard of rigor and reproducibility generally goes beyond a simple test of efficacy. One crucial difference between scientific criteria and 'merely' pragmatic is that scientific criteria are explicitly intended to be objective or value-free. The resulting 'truths' are believed to be independent of the particular interests or biases of the individuals involved in their production because they reflect 'nature' (Latour, 1987). Pragmatic criteria, in contrast, are explicitly subjective and value-laden. To say that something 'works' implies that it works well enough for the purpose at hand, which may vary from time to time and from observer to observer. Scientific truths, on the other hand, are believed to transcend time, space, and culture.

Epistemic criteria act as rhetorical resources for members of an epistemic community to debate each others' knowledge claims. Scientists conduct such debates through journals and professional meetings, while engineers conduct them through design reviews and acceptance tests. Regardless of the particular setting or mode of discourse, these debates take place in the context of the theories, hypotheses, technologies and practices that permeate the community (Hacking, 1992); in this respect, epistemic criteria are but one of many factors that influence the status of a knowledge claim. As Latour (1987) argues, the status of a particular piece of knowledge depends on the outcome of these debates over time. Depending on the community in which the debate takes place, certain criteria may be more persuasive to members than others. As the debate converges, however, the issue will become more or less settled and take on the character of a black box (Latour, 1987).

The heterogeneity of organizational cultures makes it difficult to assume a single criteria for all members (Martin, 1992; Schein, 1985). This is one of the key issues involved in translating Holzner and Marx's (1979) framework to the organizational level. While they assumed a relatively homogeneous community of professionals, in a complex organization, various occupational or functional groups will not necessarily share epistemic criteria (Van Maanen and Barley, 1984). For example, different occupational groups (e.g., engineering vs. marketing) may accept different sources as authoritative or engage in different rituals. In this situation, the knowledge distribution process might be impaired as constituencies question each other's criteria. Thus, a complex organization must be treated conceptually as a collection of overlapping knowledge systems, each of which may correspond to a larger epistemic community, or to some functional or geographic area.

In the case study that follows, we will see how the implementation of a new information system brings members of different occupational communities into the organization. The case provides the opportunity to examine each core knowledge process over time and to examine the ways in which those processes were shaped by the introduction of new technology. It also provides an opportunity to illustrate each of the processes with a concrete example. I will argue that information systems can affect the critical processes of knowledge construction and organization by changing the epistemic criteria used in knowledge construction and by changing the content of the material that emerges from the creation process. To the extent that this is true, the effects of information systems can be deeper and more pervasive than traditional models of learning would suggest.

Overview of the case

The case presented here is drawn from 10 years of experience working at (and later consulting to) a small engineering consulting company that I will call EnerSave (a pseudonym). My involvement at EnerSave started in 1981 when I was hired as an HVAC engineer[2] to perform energy audits of commercial buildings. The nature of this work will be described in more detail below. I was soon asked to help with a software development project that occupied my time for the next 3 years. During this time, I designed and wrote software. Since it was a small organization, I also became involved in documentation and end user training. I left EnerSave in 1984, but I periodically returned to help with software maintenance and the implementation of new features until 1991. Thus, in terms of level and duration of involvement, I have a considerable experience

---

[2] Heating, ventilating, and air conditioning (HVAC) is a common category of engineering specialization and employment.

base with this case, but because my role at the time was exclusively that of participant, I am an observer only in retrospect. I have notes and archival records from the time period in question, including design documents, notes from meetings, examples of audit reports, input forms, and other artifacts of the work process. Although they were not collected for the purposes of this research, these notes provide important reminders and have helped me to reconstruct the events I describe here. Knowing the limitations of my own memory, however, I have limited the scope of my assertions accordingly. Naturally, there are many aspects of the case where more systematic data could be used to deepen the analysis.

EnerSave was founded in the mid-1970s to provide a range of energy conservation related consulting services to commercial businesses, public utilities, and government. The energy audit business started to boom after the OPEC oil embargo and EnerSave was there to take advantage of this opportunity. Energy costs soared, and the United States federal government began to offer energy tax credits, suddenly making conservation into an attractive investment. During the 10-year period between 1981 and 1991, EnerSave grew from a 30-person engineering and consulting boutique with one office, to a 600-person organization with offices in several major cities across the United States.

A significant part of their initial growth can be attributed to the development of a knowledge-based software application, which I will call EnCAP (EnerSave Commercial Audit Program). This program 'encapsulated' their specialized engineering knowledge and helped them deliver it at low cost to a large number of customers. By substituting high-school educated technicians using this sophisticated software for college educated engineers, EnerSave could provide a high-quality engineering analysis that would formerly have cost many thousands of dollars for only hundreds of dollars. Later, they implemented a variety of other systems to help utilities deliver a wide range of energy conservation services to their customers.

From a practical and economic standpoint, the program was a success. It was used for over 10 years by EnerSave personnel and by utilities across the United States to complete tens of thousands of audits. The question that will concern us here is, how did the development and implementation of this system affect the knowledge system in this organization? How can we compare the knowledge processes at EnerSave before and after the introduction of EnCAP? What implications does this case have for the implementation of other kinds of systems in other contexts?

Manual energy auditing: The good old days

An energy audit is like a financial audit: it provides a detailed analysis of the inputs and outputs of a system. But instead of an accounting system, the object of inquiry is an energy system. To perform an audit, one collects detailed information about the existing condition of all major energy systems in the building: lighting, heating, cooling, hot water, and the building envelope (walls, windows, and doors). In addition, for many kinds of commercial facilities, there may be large electric motors, air compressors, drying ovens, and so on. An important objective of energy auditing is to identify opportunities for cost-effective conservation measures, such as high-efficiency lighting or improved insulation. Thus, while data is being collected, the energy auditor typically starts to formulate ideas about what kinds of improvements are possible. As the analysis of the facility proceeds, the auditor develops these ideas into detailed recommendations about how to improve the energy performance of the facility, including costs, benefits, and payback periods.

Formerly, this task required fully trained engineers. Typical audits required a few weeks of engineering time, plus word processing support to create the report, which was often over 100 pages, including figures. As a result, these reports cost a minimum of several thousand dollars, and $10–20,000 was common. At these prices, however, only rather large facilities with high energy costs would typically engage an engineering firm to audit their energy use and make recommendations.

The manual audit process was customized to the particular needs of each customer, but there were certain aspects of the firm's methodology that were typically applied to every audit. For example, the engineers performed an overall energy balance on the facility to determine which end uses (such as lighting, heating, cooling, etc.) consumed what fraction of the total energy bill. Likewise, certain kinds of recommendations (such as replacing incandescent lighting with fluorescent lighting) were very common. As a result, the engineers had accumulated a library of standard analyses and recommendations. The analyses were sometimes coded into small computer programs written in BASIC and run on a timesharing system (personal computers and spreadsheets were not available yet). The recommendations took the form of 'boilerplate' text stored in a WANG document processing system that could be modified to fit into the client's overall report. Even when an analysis had to be performed by hand, the 'working papers' and supporting calculations from prior audits served as templates that could be re-used in subsequent audits. In these ways, the engineers in the firm accumulated experience and improved the efficiency of their services.

Automated energy auditing: A brave new world

In the early 1980s, state regulatory boards started to realize that it was cheaper and better to conserve energy than to build new capacity. Electric and gas utilities across the United States were mandated to provide energy audits to their residential and commercial customers as a means of encouraging conservation. In some cases, the audits were offered at a very low cost, while in other cases, the utilities were allowed to incorporate the cost of these audits into their rate base. In either case, this regulatory action created a substantial demand for cheap, effective energy audits.

In response to this opportunity, the management at EnerSave conceived the idea of an 'automated audit.' Their objective was to replicate their current, largely manual process, so that it would take less time and could be performed by people with less training. Their initial idea was to take a collection of analysis programs they had developed in BASIC (e.g., for heat transfer, discounted cash flow, etc.) and combine them into one large program. The absurdity of this proposal soon became apparent. To begin with, the programs shared no common data structures or interfaces and could barely be maintained in their current form. The idea of basing a large application on such a shaky foundation was quickly dismissed.

When it became clear that a more coherent development approach would be required, several young engineers were enlisted to write a set of 'modules,' one for each major area to be addressed in the audit. They worked in conjunction with some of the more experienced auditors to encode the relevant knowledge about each building energy system, such as lighting, heating, and so on. Each module would read its input, perform the necessary computations, and then prepare an intermediary file for further processing by a text formatting program called Scribe™. The text formatting program allowed the developers to make extensive use of a library of several hundred customizable paragraphs with large numbers of textual 'fill-ins' that created the impression of a fully customized report. Indeed, the new reports were often 50–60 pages, very similar in outline and appearance to the hand-produced reports.

Differences in the knowledge system over time: Effects of a new information system

To interpret the changes in the knowledge system over time, it is useful to break the case into three distinct time periods: before, during, and after the implementation of the automated audit system. For each time period, it is instructive to consider each aspect of the knowledge system: the members of the various occupational communities represented within the organization, the object of knowledge, the epistemic criteria, and each of the five knowledge processes (constructing, organizing, storing, distributing, and applying). To highlight the effects of the system and its implementation, I will examine each of these categories over time. Table 18.1 provides an overview of the differences, each of which is described in more detail in the following sections.

Table 18.1 *Summary of changes in the knowledge system by time period*

	Manual auditing (1976–1981)	System development (1981–1983)	Automated auditing (1983–1993)
People involved	Engineers (10–20) Typists (3–4)	Engineer/Programmers (6)	Programmers/Engineer (2–3) Technicians (several hundred) Administrators (5–10)
Primary domain	Building energy systems: Lighting, heating, cooling, etc.	VAX/VMS and languages	Completed application (EnCAP)
Epistemic criteria	Authoritative (little feed-back about results)	Pragmatic (immediate feed-back about results)	Authoritative Ritual/superstitious
Knowledge processes			
Construct	Trade associations and vendors are an authoritative source of methods and specifications Individual engineers gain experience in specific situations	Algorithms invented to mimic simplified engineering analysis Naming: Data structures, control structures, files, programs, libraries, etc.	Technicians learn necessary workarounds Administrators identify new requirements Programmers rediscover how system works during maintenance
Organize	Informally organized; indexed by individual engineers and projects	Energy auditing divided up into 'modules' and 'forms'	Organized around application artifacts: 'forms' and 'reports'
Store	Worksheets kept by individual engineers Old reports in company library WANG 'boilerplate' for use by typists BASIC programs for use by engineers	Embed algorithms into design of forms, modules, and measures Systems adopted for code management, version control, testing, etc. Documentation written	New (or modified) algorithms coded into the application 'Gurus' develop 'tricks' to achieve desired results 'Setup' files used to store basic program parameters and output text
Distribute	Trade publications Direct sharing	Frequent informal meetings among programmers	Application used in-house and licensed to large public utilities – includes training and documentation New features made available to all
Apply	Engineers use knowledge for next audit	Programmers embed engineering algorithms in code	Technicians use tricks to get results

Changing epistemic communities

The implementation of the automated auditing system affected one of the key components of the organizational knowledge system: the epistemic communities represented in the organization. As outlined in Table 18.1, during the manual auditing period, the organization consisted mainly of engineers and typists. The engineers collected data, performed computations, and made recommendations, while the typists prepared the reports from the templates available on the WANG word processing system. During system implementation, a new kind of member was introduced to the organization: the programmer. These individuals (myself included) were mainly recruited from the existing pool of engineers; two were hired especially for the project. Later, as the system was completed and rolled into production, the community of programmers shrank, while the community of technicians using the program began to grow rapidly in locations all over the country. To supervise this workload, it was necessary to add administrative staff, as well. Thus, the implementation of the system changed the basic membership of the epistemic community to include individuals whose background and training was very different than the traditional engineers. As the participants changed, it created the possibility that their approach to knowledge construction (and the other knowledge processes) might change as well. This is an area where contemporaneously collected data could be especially valuable because it is difficult for me to assess the impact of these changes retrospectively.

Changing objects of knowledge

The literature on organizational learning generally assumes that objects about which knowledge is being accumulated are relatively constant. For example, organizations learn about 'the environment,' 'the competition,' or 'production processes' (Huber, 1991). The specifics change, but the domain of relevant knowledge is assumed to remain the same over time. In the implementation of EnCAP, this assumption is clearly incorrect. During the manual auditing phase, the objects of knowledge were basically building energy systems: lighting, heating, cooling etc. I remember conversations in the hallway outside my office, where people would discuss the relative benefits of different lighting systems, heat exchangers, and so on. Engineers took a great deal of pride in having a working knowledge of these systems.

During systems development, however, the new members of the organization, including myself, were overwhelmingly concerned with issues of software design and implementation. The objects of knowledge became VAX/VMS (the operating system for the host computer), the PL/1 programming language, as well as the data structures, file structures, and architectural features of the rapidly growing application. This was naturally a period of intensive learning, but there is little doubt that the subject matter was completely different than in the prior period. Finally, as the finished EnCAP application was rolled out, the focus of learning turned away from the internal features of the software and its construction and towards the external features of the software and its use. As Latour (1987) would predict, the system progressively became a black box and the new object of knowledge was the application itself: inputs, outputs, bugs, features, and workarounds.

Once the application was in use, members of the community learned about the software rather than learning about energy auditing per se. A great deal of knowledge that was created at EnerSave since the introduction of EnCAP concerned details of how to use the program: how to 'fool' it to get the recommendation you want, how to work around various bugs, and so on. While this knowledge was clearly necessary to accomplish audits under the new system, it was idiosyncratic to the EnCAP audit process. Thus, in addition to embedding existing knowledge about auditing and commercial buildings, the software required the construction of new knowledge about EnCAP itself.

Epistemic criteria

The literature on organizational learning generally assumes that the criteria for knowledge never change. A scientifically oriented community, for example, is assumed to stay scientifically oriented. Like the objects of knowledge, epistemic criteria are taken for granted as an unchanging feature of organizational learning. Once again, this case illustrates the weakness of this assumption. During the period of manual auditing, the key epistemic criteria were primarily authoritative. As engineers, the staff at EnerSave relied heavily on published sources of information concerning the performance of particular products (for example, the energy consumption of a particular kind of lighting fixture) as well as the appropriate equations for computing energy savings. These were treated as authoritative sources, and were sometimes cited in client reports or in supporting computations.[3] There was very little opportunity to confirm the accuracy of these computations, however, because clients were rarely interested in paying for follow-up studies. One could, in principle, have applied pragmatic or scientific criteria for knowledge, but given the constraints of the business and the interests of the customer base, that was not possible. Recommendations were based strictly on authoritative sources.

---

[3] Like financial auditors the engineers at EnerSave routinely prepared 'working papers' that contained the computations that supported their analysis and conclusions. These working papers would include citations to the manual or product specification guide, so that others could retrace their steps, should the need arise.

During system development, a very different kind of criteria came into force. While authoritative sources were often consulted (e.g., concerning the syntax of a particular command), the basic criteria was strictly pragmatic: does this work? As with many development projects, deadlines made pragmatic criteria particularly salient. The objective was to create code that worked, whether or not it was elegant or efficient. Also, we were often confronted with situations where it was unclear why something did or did not work. Trial and error was a common, pragmatic approach to resolving these difficulties.

Once the implementation was well under way and automated auditing was in use, the epistemic criteria underwent a second transformation. There was, to some extent, a swing back toward authoritative sources, but different sources than before. The translation between manual practice and automated procedure was, in many cases, quite radical. As a result, the engineers who were masters of the manual practice were often helpless to explain the automated results. When people wanted to know why an audit turned out the way it did (e.g., why turning down the thermostat didn't seem to save much money), they had to consult the software engineers or one of a number of individuals who understood the workings of the program. These 'EnCAP Gurus' (who were often software engineers or technicians with substantial automated auditing experience) became the authoritative experts, rather than published technical references or the mechanical engineers.

In addition ritual superstitious criteria became much more prominent. As with any complex product that is hastily developed, there was a tendency to 'forget' why things worked the way they did, and the documentation for EnCAP was often sketchy. Many of the algorithms were based on rules of thumb of engineers who no longer worked at EnerSave, so it was sometimes difficult to pin down exactly why things worked the way they did. In the absence of authoritative sources, it became natural to adopt conventional (ritual) understanding and practices concerning the use of the software.

Constructing. Changes in the membership of the epistemic community, the objects of their knowledge, and their epistemic criteria have enormous consequences for the process of knowledge construction. During the period of manual auditing, knowledge creation was largely accomplished external to the firm, through trade associations, vendors, and other authoritative sources of analysis methods and product specifications. These would then be imported into the organization as individual engineers gained experience in specific situations that required them to consult these authoritative sources.

During system development, of course, the process of knowledge construction was very different. A major effect was devoted to creating algorithms to perform simplified versions of engineering analysis (e.g., lighting design). A major problem in designing an automated audit was how to account for the enormous variety in HVAC, lighting, and other building energy systems and to do so in a simple, easy-to-input format. The process of cataloging and categorizing equipment was a crucial piece of knowledge construction for the design team. At the same time, there was also an ongoing effort to construct appropriate data structures, files, programs, and libraries, as well as a set of tools for debugging, testing, and managing the software development and maintenance process itself.

As mentioned above, automated auditing evoked yet another round of knowledge creation, but in a different domain. Technicians constructed workarounds necessary to achieve the results they wanted. There was a great deal of knowledge constructed concerning the everyday use of the program. "Gurus" developed "tricks" to achieve desired results, such as fudging certain input codes that they knew would not appear in the output, but that would influence the results of the computations in the direction they desired.

In addition, the program needed to be maintained and enhanced overtime. Administrators struggled to identify new requirements for clients and to translate those into specific program features. For example, cooling systems in Florida are very different than those in the Northeast, and the program needed to accommodate these differences before it could be used by public utilities in Florida. These kinds of changes necessitated the creation of similar kinds of knowledge as the original development. But the special problems of modifying an existing system and customizing it for various clients forced the programming staff to create new kinds of testing procedures and systems for releasing multiple versions of the "same" product.

Organizing. During the period of manual auditing, the organization of new knowledge was handled primarily through the trade manuals and new product documentation that arrived periodically at the office. There were walls lined with bookshelves containing reference material on furnaces, cooling systems, industrial equipment, and other technical reference material. In addition, each engineer had a small library of his or her own, with a similar collection of more frequently consulted references. Consistent with the arguments of Holzner and Mark (1979), the organization of knowledge within this occupational group was guided by the structure of the larger engineering community of which they were members.

During system development, this process was affected in two ways. First, a new occupational group (the programmers) entered the organization, bringing with them a whole new set of materials and concepts. The programmers group needed their own process for organizing knowledge about the domain of systems implementation. Second, and perhaps more important, the systems development process imposed a new organization on the traditional domain of building energy auditing. Energy auditing was divided up into 'modules' each of which had a 'form' for data collection and data entry. Data about buildings needed to be streamlined and structured so that it could be analyzed by standard algorithms. The performance parameters of heating and cooling equipment, lighting fixtures, and so on had to be distilled into a uniform set of parameters that could be entered into a 'setup' file. Similarly, data concerning the weather conditions for each location where the program was to be used needed to be collected and structured appropriately. The process of organizing the open-ended libraries of reference materials into specific forms, fields, parameters, and algorithms was essential to the operation of the program.

Once automated auditing became routine, these structures imposed by the software dictated a local organization of knowledge that was far narrower than in the field at large. New products could be added to the system only if they could be squeezed into an existing field. In rare instances, if a new client was adamant and willing to pay for the changes new fields could be added. But the structuring effect of the input forms (and the algorithms behind them) created a very specific set of possibilities for incorporating new knowledge about building energy systems.

Storing

Under the system of manual auditing, there were many mechanisms in use that stored knowledge of various kinds. For example, there were worksheets kept by individual engineers that outlined their computations on a particular audit, as well as old reports in company library. These reports were also available on the WANG word processing, and could be used to provide 'boilerplate' for the support staff to customize and include in new reports. On a more abstract level, there was also a collection of BASIC programs for and by engineers that had been written on a mainframe time-sharing system. These programs were usually written on an *ad hoc* basis as the need arose and anything new that came along was simply added to the library. By and large, these storage mechanisms were a natural by-product of the work. No special steps were needed to create these forms of memory.

During system development, there was the usual effort to embed this substantive knowledge into the design of forms, modules, and so on, as described above. These were stored then, within the growing body of PL/1 code and associated documentation. By contrast with the manual system, these storage processes required enormous amounts of highly specialized work. In a sense, the firm was explicitly investing in stored knowledge in the form of software. To keep track of the rapidly growing system, the developers instituted a set of procedures for code management, version control, testing, and release. These procedures embodied many of the details of how the system was configured, maintained, and administered. Thus, software was used to embody both substantive knowledge about auditing and operational knowledge about the system itself.

Automated auditing institutionalized the use of the software as a vehicle for storing knowledge. New (or modified) algorithms could be coded into the application as new kinds of energy conservation options became available, for example, 'Setup' files were used to store basic program parameters, such as weather conditions, and the library of 'boilerplate' text. Automated auditing also gave rise to the possibility of collecting a database of audit results. When audits were conducted manually, the results were simply stored on a sheet there was little motivation to collate them into a single source that could be processed efficiently. It is questionable whether such a distillation would have been meaningful, in any event, since the audit reports contained a wide variety of different and often creative recommendations from the engineers. But the automated audit program created, as a natural byproduct of its operation, a database record containing essentially all of the inputs and outputs. When the audit process was 'informated' (Zuboff, 1988), a new form of storage became both possible and necessary.

Distributing

Within the small group of engineers conducting manual audits, the system of knowledge distribution was largely through informal, face-to-face contact. The engineers shared office space, so it was very easy to ask questions. The kinds of moves that Pentland (1992) identified were also used within this group to get help on some problems and give away others. The engineering group could also access library materials directly, thereby sharing and distributing the materials they contained. During system development, the programmers used a very similar process for distributing information. Work spaces were close together, so face to face contact was simple.

Automated auditing, once it took hold, necessitated a very different kind of distribution process. The main reason was that the community of individuals involved was no longer housed together, and quickly grew far too large for face-to-face communication. Distribution of substantive knowledge about energy auditing had to take place via the EnCAP software and the associated training materials. Performance characteristics of new kinds of equipment, such as heat pumps, had to be encoded into the software before they could be shared. Previously, engineers could share techniques, worksheets, and rules of thumb directly. Under the automated system, this knowledge had to be translated into a specification, approved, prioritized, coded, tested, and distributed before it could be used. Furthermore, the knowledge could be distributed outside the boundaries of the EnerSave organization to its customers, the electric and gas utilities.

Applying

In manual auditing, the application of knowledge was accomplished as the engineers performed computations and prepared their recommendations. To do so, engineers drew upon the resources mentioned earlier (manuals, prior audits, and each other). Typists assembled the final document for the clients, who might or might not actually implement the recommendations. The responsibility for following through rested with the client.

During system development, knowledge application took a different form because the object of the activity was so different. Rather than producing energy audits directly, the programmers were responsible for producing software to produce energy audits. As mentioned above, the knowledge and artifacts necessary to accomplish this task were quite different than those needed to produce an energy audit. But perhaps more important, the criteria for successful application were different, as well, because the software had to produce reasonable results over a wide range of different input data, while a manual audit was specific to a given set of facts about a particular building. A successful implementation required, in some sense, a higher standard of performance than an individual audit because it had to handle a broader range of cases. As with manual audits, the responsibility for actually implementing conservation recommendations rested with building owners.

Automated auditing brought yet another regime of knowledge application. Applying the algorithms embodied in the EnCAP program required a different set of skills, as described above. Technicians needed to know how to identify equipment and possible improvements, and then the program would take over and complete the computations and the details of the recommendation. As mentioned above, technicians often used tricks to get results they wanted from a program they did not fully understand. The end result (a completed audit report) was similar in form and content to the manual audit reports, but the application of technical knowledge about commercial buildings occurred through a very different process. This difference was a natural product of using an automated tool rather than performing the computations and producing the audit report manually.

Discussion

To help the reader evaluate the strengths and weaknesses of the knowledge system framework, it is useful to compare it with some of the main themes in the large and growing literature on organizational learning. Rather than attempting to review and synthesize all of this literature here, it is more useful to extract certain key dimensions for purposes of comparison. Table 18.2 outlines four key themes in the organizational learning literature and their interpretation in the knowledge system framework. Each of these themes is discussed in more detail later.

Table 18.2   *Themes in Organizational Learning Literature*

Theme	Knowledge system interpretation
Locus: Individual or organization	Locus is social interaction; purely individual level is not very meaningful
Level: Operational or strategic (single- *or* double-loop)	'Level' of learning is a question of content; it is not a separate process
Source: Experience (internal) or example (external)	Parallels the distinction between knowledge construction and knowledge distribution
Persistence: Short or long term	Failures of long-term memory result from failures of storage of distribution, as well as changing relevance

Locus of learning: Individual versus organization

The literature on organizational learning generally distinguishes between individual and organizational learning (e.g., Argote, 1993; Carley, 1992; Fiol and Lyles, 1985; Hedberg, 1981; Levitt and March, 1988). Some authors (e.g., March and Olson, 1976; Nonaka, 1994) make the relationship between individual and organizational learning explicit, while others tend to focus on the organization as the unit of analysis (Lant and Mezias, 1992). In contrast, the knowledge system framework downplays the importance of individual learning in favor of an explicitly social conception of knowledge. What a single individual 'knows,' in short, is of little value to anyone until it has been socially ratified in some way. The position is similar to that of Attewell (1992, p. 6), who argues that: 'The organization learns only insofar as individual skills and insights become embodied in organizational routines, practices, and beliefs that outlast the presence of the originating individual.'

Certain individuals, such as higher level managers, may hold sufficient authority within the organization to dictate and enforce the legitimacy of their own beliefs. Legitimation and authority are obviously essential aspects of knowledge construction (Latour, 1987) and may be influential in the organizational learning effects associated with executive succession (Virany, Tushman, and Romanelli, 1992). This perspective helps call attention to the explicitly social dimension of knowledge distribution, as well. For example, Pentland's (1992) study of software support hot lines revealed that solving customer problems depended on the ability to distribute knowledge among the group (e.g., by getting help). Socially enacted knowledge distribution processes allowed members of the organization to collectively solve a stream of problems that no individual could have solved alone. It is reasonable to hypothesize that in situations where specialized knowledge is unevenly distributed, enhancing distribution processes (for example, via email) would be an effective means of improving organizational performance.

In the EnerSave case, before automation, there were many instances where a single engineer would learn about a new kind of system (for example, a new kind of boiler) and share it with others. Until shared, however, it is hard to imagine calling that engineer's learning organizational. After automation, individual learning had to be filtered through a software maintenance routine (designing a new feature, coding and testing) to make the new learning available to the organization. Although I cannot document it, I find it unlikely that field personnel outside the main office would have been able to initiate such learning. Thus, the locus or organizational learning that could enter the knowledge system was probably narrower by automation.

Levels of learning: Operational or strategic

The level or kind of learning is another key theme in the organizational learning literature. Argyris and Schon's (1978) influential distinction between single- and double-loop learning can also be thought of in terms of operational and strategic learning. Lant and Mezias (1992) make a similar distinction, labeling the levels 'first order' and 'second order.' Single-loop learning involves the adjustments necessary to meet a given operational objective, as in the way a thermostat cycles a furnace on and off to hold the temperature in the room. Double-loop learning, however, involves deciding what the temperature should be. It is conceived of as a higher, more strategic level of learning because it concerns the definition of goals. Argyris and Schon (1978) argue that so-called 'higher' levels of learning involve challenging assumptions and standard procedures.

In terms of the knowledge system framework, the main difference between these levels of learning is the content of the knowledge being constructed, organized, stored, and so on. One might hypothesize that these processes might take different forms for operational or strategic knowledge, but the framework itself is indifferent. In the EnerSave case, as I saw it, the learning was primarily operational. One can assume that there must have been a parallel change in strategic knowledge over time as the firm moved from one line of business to another, and one kind of client to another. But even within the domain of operational knowledge, the shift in content was striking.

Source of learning: Experience or example

Broadly speaking, the learning literature points to two distinct sources of learning: experience and example. Learning from experience reflects the usual strategies of trial and error, successive approximation, and so on. Following the analogy to individual learning, models of learning by experience are often built at the organizational level (e.g., Lant and Mezias, 1992). Researchers have also identified the ways in which organizations learn from very limited experience, where there is no opportunity to improve based on repeated trials (March, Sproull, and Tamuz, 1991). Often, this entails the use of vicarious experience, or stories about others' experiences. Alternatively, it may be the product of systematic transfer between subunits (Argote, Beckman, and Epple, 1990). While the distinction between experience and example can be formalized and estimated statistically (Epple, Argote, and Devadas, 1991), the distinction is less clear than it might seem because it depends on the definition of the organizational boundary. That is, examples generated within the boundary (which may be drawn socially, geographically, temporally, or in some other manner) are counted as 'experience,' while examples generated elsewhere are not.

Within the knowledge system framework, the distinction between learning by experience and learning by example closely parallels the distinction between knowledge construction and knowledge distribution. Members testing the value of their own experiences would be constructing knowledge, while members testing the value of others' examples could be seen as engaging in knowledge distribution. Given the potential subtlety of some of these distinctions, it seems like it might be difficult to sustain the analytical distinction between construction and distribution. Within a particular knowledge system, the process of knowledge construction can draw upon a variety of sources, including members' experiences and observations of others. Thus, in practice, it is not clear how important this distinction would really be. Construction and distribution have very similar effects: they make knowledge available where it previously was not.

At EnerSave, before and after automation, learning was primarily by experience. To my knowledge, they spent very little time assessing or analyzing how other organizations performed similar work. While there were many firms offering automated residential audits, there were very few firms capable of producing an automated audit for commercial buildings. Thus, with respect to their core operations, there were few examples to learn from.

Persistence of learning: Short or long term

Empirical studies of organizational learning (Argote, Beckman, and Epple, 1990; Darr, Argote, and Epple, forthcoming) have shown that while organizations learn, they also forget. A significant component in this loss of knowledge can be attributed to turnover in personnel (Carley, 1992; Darr *et al.*, forthcoming). These studies have also shown that recent experiences are more valuable than older ones. Part of this effect is due to the changing nature of the environment; old skills and information may not be equally useful in the face of changing conditions. Knowledge becomes obsolete. Hedberg (1981) postulated the existence of forgetting processes and the critical importance of replacing outdated knowledge. More generally, there has been an increased interest in organizational memory (Walsh and Ungson, 1991) and in mechanisms to enhance it (Ackerman, 1993).

Questions of persistence or memory have a natural interpretation within the knowledge system framework. The storage and distribution processes are critical in maintaining the availability of knowledge to members. Failures in either of those processes could be viewed as forms of forgetting. In effect, the organization either cannot store or cannot access relevant knowledge. The problem of changing relevance, however, could be viewed more as a failure in application. When old methods are tried and no longer work, then it is the final link in the chain of knowledge processes that has broken.

At EnerSave, the use of software for storage and distribution had predictable effects: persistence was excellent, but continuing relevance could not be guaranteed. Software is an excellent vehicle for storage and distribution (and thus for long-term memory), but it tends to suffer from the problem of changing relevance for just that reason. The basic engineering computations generally retained their validity, but many of the 'rules of thumb' depended on assumptions about standard construction techniques, typical system efficiencies, and so on. These factors differ from region to region, and they tend to change over time. Thus, as the context of use changed, these assumptions needed to be surfaced, examined and, if necessary, changed. In short, the software required maintenance.

Conclusion

The preceding analysis suggests that many of the theoretical issues developed in the literature on organizational learning could be investigated as a system of knowledge processes (constructing, organizing, storing, distributing, and applying). In addition, by placing special emphasis on the social nature of the construction and distribution processes, this framework highlights the uniquely social dimension of the phenomenon that is often missing from literature that draws too heavily on the individual learning metaphor. The advantage of this framework is that it decomposes the overall phenomenon into a set of smaller and more observable processes. Although these processes are distributed in time and space, they are readily identifiable and can be measured and monitored in various ways. Observability also gives rise to an important practical benefit: it lends itself to diagnosis of ineffective or dysfunctional systems. By breaking the overall phenomenon down into constituent parts, it should be easier to isolate problems and, hopefully, recommend practical improvements.

It would be a mistake, of course, to generalize too broadly from this example. The information system described here was specifically designed to embody technical knowledge and automate key aspects of a job that was generally performed by engineers. In many respects, the results reported here are understandable by-products of automating the work: the people doing the work were no longer in a position to fully comprehend or modify the tool they were using. Zuboff (1988) makes similar points concerning the work in the organizations she studied. In the extreme case, the very tool that was intended to encode the knowledge of the organization could have destroyed the organization's capacity to learn by interfering with various knowledge processes. As it turns out, in this particular case, EnerSave seems to have maintained a strong engineering base (by diversifying into other areas besides auditing), and has maintained a strong connection to the larger knowledge system concerning energy use in commercial buildings.

Nonetheless, this example illustrates clearly that introducing an information system can have more profound effects than merely altering the storage, or retrieval, or distribution, or richness, of information. These basic information processing enhancements are well known and should, in theory, affect organizational learning. But I would argue that information systems can also change the membership of an organization, the objects of its knowledge, and its criteria for truth. These are the basic elements of social epistemology; they are the core of any social knowledge system. They are held constant in most treatments of organizational learning, thus obscuring the possibility that information systems might change them. Whether or not all of these elements belong under the umbrella of 'organizational learning,' information systems can change them. In doing so, information systems change the fabric of social epistemology and the backdrop against which organizations construct, organize, store, distribute, and apply knowledge.

More broadly, the example suggests a kind of technological epistemology, where our ways of knowing are mediated through machines and their maintenance. Should we be satisfied with a knowledge system where debugging and finding workarounds are a dominant mode of learning? To the extent that we view the world through a technological lens (Barrett, 1979; Heidegger, 1962), this problem becomes increasingly important. Ironically, technology may dull our senses, taking away the direct involve-ment, social interaction, and reflective conversation that has traditionally given rise to understanding (Rorty, 1979). The very systems that are meant to increase our information processing capabilities, thereby increasing understanding, may have the opposite effect by restricting the range of our inquiry and experience, effectively putting us in a kind of epistemological box. Whether information systems enhance or dull our senses is a difficult question to answer, but it is clearly an important question to ask.

Acknowledgements

The author would like to thank Eric Darr, Elaine Yakura, Richard Boland, and the anonymous reviewers for their comments on this manuscript.

References

Ackerman, M. S. (1993) *Answer garden: A tool for growing organizational memory*. Unpublished PhD, Massachusetts Institute of Technology.

Argote, L. (1993) Group and organizational learning curves: Individual, system and environmental components. *British Journal of Social Psychology*, **32**, 31–51.

Argote, L., Beckman, S. and Epple, D. (1990) The persistence and transfer of learning in industrial settings. *Management Science*, **36**, 140–154.

Argyris, C. and Schon, D. A. (1978) *Organizational Learning: A theory of action perspective*. Reading, MA: Addison-Wesley.

Attewell, P. (1992) Technology diffusion and organizational learning: The case of business computing. *Organization Science*, **3**, 1–19.

Barley, S. R. (1988) The social construction of a machine: Ritual, superstition, magical thinking and other pragmatic responses to running a CT scanner. In M. Lock and D. R. Gordon (Eds.), *Biomedicine examined* (pp. 497–539). New York: Kluwer Academic Press.

Barrett, W. (1979) *The Illusion of Technique*, New York: Doubleday.

Berger, P. and Luckmann, T. (1967) *The Social Construction of Reality*. Garden City, NY: Doubleday.

Bloor, D. (1976) *Knowledge and Social Imagery*. London: Routledge & Kegan Paul.

Bourdieu, P. (1990) *The Logic of Practice* (Richard Nice, Trans.). Stanford: Stanford University Press.

Brown, J. S. and Duguid, P. (1991). Organizational learning and communities of practice: Toward a unified view of working, learning, and innovation. *Organization Science*, **2**, 40–58.

Carley, K. (1992) Organizational learning and personnel turnover. *Organization Science*, **3**, 20–46.

Cialdini, R. B. (1988) *Influence: Science and practice*. Boston: Scott, Foresman.

Collins, H. M. (1990) *Artificial Experts: Social knowledge and intelligent machines*. Cambridge, MA: MIT Press.

Collins, R. (1981) On the microfoundations of macrosociology. *American Journal of Sociology*, **86**, 984–1014.

Daft, R. L. and Weick, K. E. (1984) Toward a model of organizations as interpretation systems. *Academy of Management Review*, **9**, 284–295.

Darr, E. D., Argote, L. and Epple, D. (forthcoming). The acquisition, transfer and depreciation of knowledge in service organizations: Productivity in franchises. *Management Science.*

Epple, D., Argote, L. and Devadas, R. (1991). Organizational learning curves: A method for investigating intraplant transfer of knowledge acquired through learning by doing. *Organization Science*, **2**, 58–70.

Fiol, M. C. and Lyles, M. A. (1985). Organizational learning. *Academy of Management Review*, **10**, 803–813.

Geertz, C. (1983) *Local Knowledge: Further essays in interpretive anthropology.* New York: Basic Books.

Goldman, A. I. (1987) Foundations of social epistemology. *Synthese*, **73**, 109–144.

Gurvitch, G. (1971) *The Social Frameworks of Knowledge.* Oxford, England: Basil Blackwell.

Hacking, I. (1992) Self-vindication of the laboratory sciences. In A. Pickering (Ed.), *Science as Culture and Practice.* Chicago: University of Chicago Press.

Headland, T. N., Pike, K. L. and Harris, M. (Eds.), (1990). *Emics and Etics: The insider/outsider debate.* Newbury Park, CA: Sage.

Hedberg, B. L. (1981) How organizations learn and unlearn. In P. C. Nystrom and W. H. Starbuck (Eds.), *Handbook of Organizational Design, Volume 1.* New York: Oxford University Press.

Heidegger, M. (1962) *Being and Time.* New York: Harper and Row.

Holzner, B. and Marx, J. (1979). *Knowledge Application: The knowledge system in society.* Boston: Allyn-Bacon.

Huber, G. (1991) Organizational learning: The contributing processes and the literatures. *Organization Science*, **2**, 88–115.

Knorr-Cetina, K. D. (1981) *The Manufacture of Knowledge: An essay on the constructivist and contextual nature of science.* Oxford: Pergamon.

Lant, T. K. and Mezias, S. J. (1992). An organizational learning model of convergence and reorientation. *Organization Science*, **3**, 47–71.

Latour, B. (1987) *Science in Action: How to follow scientists and engineers through society.* Cambridge, MA: Harvard University Press.

Latour, B. and Woolgar, S. (1982). *Laboratory Life: The social construction of scientific facts*, Cambridge, MA: Harvard University Press.

Lave, J. (1988) *Cognition in Practice: Mind, mathematics, and culture in everyday life.* Cambridge: Cambridge University Press.

Levitt, B. and March, J. G. (1988). Organizational learning. In W. R. Scott (Ed.), *Annual Review of Sociology*, (Vol. 14, pp. 319–340). Palo Alto, CA: Annual Reviews.

Machlup, F. (1980) *Knowledge: Its creation, distribution, and economic significance, Volume 1.* Princeton, NJ: Princeton University Press.

Manning, P. K. (1988) *Symbolic Communication: Signifying calls and the police response.* Cambridge, MA: MIT Press.

Manning, P. K. (1992) *Organizational Communication.* New York: Aldine de Gruyter.

March, J. G. and Olsen, J. P. (1976) *Ambiguity and Choice in Organizations.* Bergen, Norway: Universitetsforlaget.

March, J. G., Sproull, L. S. and Tamuz, M. (1991) Learning from samples of one or fewer. *Organization Science,* **2**, 1–14.

Martin, J. (1992) *Cultures in Organizations: Three perspectives,* New York: Oxford University Press.

Mulkay, M. J. (1984) Knowledge and utility: Implications for the sociology of knoweldge. In N. Stehr and V. Meja (Eds.), *Society and Knowledge: Contemporary perspectives on the sociology of knowledge* (pp. 77–98). New Brunswick: Transaction Books.

Nonaka, I. (1994) A dynamic theory of organizational knowledge creation. *Organization Science,* **5**, 14–37.

Pentland, B. T. (1992) Organizing moves in software support hot lines, *Administrative Science Quarterly,* **37**, 527–548.

Rorty, R. (1979) *Philosophy and the Mirror of Nature.* Princeton, NJ: Princeton University Press.

Schein, E. H. (1985) *Organization Culture and Leadership.* San Francisco: Jossey-Bass.

Schutz, A. (1962) *Collected Papers, Volume 1.* The Hague: Nijhoff.

Turkle, S. and Papert, S. (1990) Epistemological pluralism: Styles and voices within the computer culture. *Signs,* **16**, 128–157.

Van Maanen, J. and Barley, S. R. (1984). Occupational communities: Culture and control in organizations. *Research in Organizational Behavior,* **6**, 287–365.

Virany, B., Tushman, M. L., and Romanelli, E. (1992). Executive succession and organization outcomes in turbulent environments: An organization learning approach. *Organization Science,* **3**, 72–91.

Walsh, J. P. and Ungson, G. R. (1991) Organizational memory. *Academy of Management Review,* **16**, 57–91.

Weick, K. E. (1991) The nontraditional quality of organizational learning. *Organization Science,* **2**, 116–124.

Winograd, T. and Flores, F. (1986) *Understanding Computers and Cognition.* Norwood, NJ: Ablex.

Wittgenstein, L. (1958) *Philosophical Investigations.* New York: Macmillan.

Woolgar, S. (1988) *Science: The very idea.* Chichester: Ellis Horwood.

Zuboff, S. (1988) *In the Age of the Smart Machine.* New York: Basic Books.

Questions for discussion

1 To what extent is the EnCAP system considered in this chapter a knowledge management system as opposed to a typical IT-based information system?

2 Compare and contrast the approaches adopted by Leidner in Chapter 17 and Pentland in this chapter. What do you conclude from this comparison?

3 Pentland refers to the work of Lave (1988) and Brown and Duguid (1991) on what the latter term 'communities of practice'. To what extent is it useful (or not) to consider IT professionals in an organization a homogeneous community of practice? Relate your discussion back to the material introduced in Chapter 10.

4 To what extent might so-called knowledge management systems *restrict* rather than enhance organizational learning? Draw on case examples introduced in this book and on your own experiences when discussing this question.

5 'Knowledge management systems are like "old wine in new bottles".' Discuss.

6 What ideas introduced thus far in the book and in this chapter in particular might aid organizational learning?

19 Information Technology and Customer Service

Redesigning the customer support process for the electronic economy: insights from storage dimensions

O. A. El Sawy and G. Bowles

This chapter provides insights for redesigning IT-enabled customer support processes to meet the demanding requirements of the emerging electronic economy in which fast response, shared knowledge creation, and inter-networked technologies are the dynamic enables of success. The chapter describes the implementation of the TechConnect support system at Storage Dimensions, a manufacturer of high-availability computer storage system products. TechConnect is a unique IT infrastructure for problem resolution that includes a customer support knowledge base whose structure is dynamically updated based on adaptive learning through customer inter-actions. The chapter assesses the impacts of TechConnect and its value in creating a learning organization. It then draws insights for redesigning knowledge-creating customer support processes for the business conditions of the electronic economy.

Effective customer support in the electronic economy

Effective customer support and service has become a strategic imperative. Whether a company is in manufacturing or in services, what is increasingly making a competitive difference is the customer support and service that is built into and around the product, rather than just the quality of the product (cf. Henkoff, 1994). Customer intimacy is becoming an increasingly acknowledged strategic posture (Treacy and Wiersema, 1995) and the traditional distinction between products and services is becoming increasingly irrelevant (Haeckel,

1994). Companies are moving closer to their customers, expending more effort in finding new ways to create value for their customers, and transforming the customer relationship into one of solution finding and partnering rather than one of selling and order taking. Customer support and service comprises the way that a product is delivered, bundled, explained, billed, installed, repaired, renewed – and redesigned. As a growing envelope that can manage and grow successful long-term customer relationships, customer support and service is becoming one of the most critical core business processes.

The emphasis on customer support and service needs are driving IS priorities more than ever before. There has been research work on measures of service quality for information system effectiveness (Pitt *et al.*, 1995). Furthermore, results of the annual surveys of critical issues of IS management conducted by systems integrator Computer Sciences Corporation show that 'connecting to customers and suppliers' has jumped from sixteenth place in 1994 to seventh place in 1995 and 1996 (Savola, 1996). The 1996 survey also revealed that the corporate goal with which IS is aligning itself most is learning about and fulfilling customer needs more effectively, and that applications to support customer service is the number one focus of current systems development efforts (60% of 350 IS executive respondents). Similarly, a 1995 survey by *Information Week* (Evans, 1996) to identify the top criteria by which organizations evaluate the performance of IS professionals showed that two of the top five criteria centered around customer support and service. The two criteria were the ability to use IT effectively to improve customer service (76% of respondents) and how well they deployed IT to meets the needs of customers outside the organization (67% of all respondents).

However, there is more to this than just bringing more IT to customer support and service. The increased focus on customer support is taking place in a business environment that is characterized by unprecedented speed, rapid knowledge creation, increasing complexity, and spreading electronic networks: we are experiencing the emergence of the electronic economy. This new business environment breeds many more complex products with shorter life-cycles, and these products are used in customer contexts that are also complex and fast-moving. Customer support in such environments is much more demanding – especially in business-to-business situations – and that requires:

- Much faster response to resolving customer queries and problems as the business tempo escalates
- Smarter and faster ways of creating, capturing, synthesizing, sharing, and accessing knowledge about complex products and services
- More dynamic support for – and faster learning about – products that are frequently morphed due to rapid product innovation and dramatically shorter product life-cycles

- More collaborative problem-solving with other (possibly competing) companies as products from multiple vendors increasingly have to work in concert
- Taking advantage of new electronic channels and open networks for communicating and collaborating with customers and
- More fail-safe customer support as it becomes most critical to the customer.

Given these stringent requirements, how can customer support processes be transformed and IT-enabled to be effective in this new electronic economy? That is the challenge this chapter addresses.

The evolution of customer support for complex products

Customer support traces its origins to the 1850s when the Singer Sewing Machine company set up a program that used trained women to teach buyers how to use the sewing machine (Lele and Sheth, 1987). Traditionally, customer support has referred to after-sales support, which consists of all the activities that help increase customer satisfaction after they have purchased a product and started to use it. The marketing literature (cf. Lele and Sheth, 1987) has differentiated between specific *support services* and *feedback* and *restitution*. Support services refer to activities such as parts and service, warranty claims, customer assistance and training, technician training, and occasionally trading-in of older equipment. Feedback and restitution refers to activities such as complaint handing, returns and refunds, and dispute resolution. As manufacturers started to compete by bundling services with products (cf. Chase and Garvin, 1989; Shostack, 1977) the scope of customer service and support for products has expanded cross-functionally to include expert help from the manufacturing, engineering, and R&D functions. More recently, as long term customer relationships and partnering with customers have become very important (cf. Henkoff, 1994) the notion of customer support has expanded beyond 'after-sales' and has colored the whole way that customer service is provided. While, the terms service and support are loosely used interchangeably in some contexts, they are not the same. Customer support has a long term partnering flavor that signifies that the supplier wants to help the customer do their job effectively, and in this age of interdependence and alliances it seems to be a more apt term for the bundle of activities that comprise it.

Customer support is more critical and difficult for high technology complex products, especially with the breakneck speed in new product development for those products. Many customer support innovations and strategies in the last decade have originated from the computer and telecommunications industry. These include automated help desks, toll-free hot-lines, computer bulletin board systems, 7×24 service, remote online troubleshooting, and, most recently, the use of the Internet. As organizations have become critically dependent on information technologies and telecommunication networks for the operations of their business, so has the criticality of response time in supporting those products and services – and it has risen to unprecedented levels. The cost of providing effective customer support has also risen more than proportionately. The high technology industry has sought solutions that may provide ideas for other industries.

In order to improve overall service levels and reduce overall costs, the information technology industry has adopted a hybrid model for customer support (Entex, 1994). This includes having personnel on-site at major customer accounts (what IBM has been traditionally known for), using third party resellers or other vendors who can provide localized customer support for smaller accounts and consumers, and providing high-tech long-distance remote support through a centralized pool of talent whether in-house or through an external service (very common in commodity and low margin items such as PC hardware and software). Each of these options has a different cost structure and service advantage. Direct on-site support is expensive but provides superior service. Going through resellers requires heavy investments in training and qualification to assure good service. Remote high-tech support is a challenge for complex products and can be very impersonal if not very carefully managed. Different vendors in different market segments have different hybrid blends depending on their support strategy.

These options are further challenged when products interact with other vendor products, response time is critical, and the stakes in downtime are very high. Figure 19.1 illustrates how the required customer support level rises very quickly when there is an increase in the combination of complexity and connectivity of the product and its criticality to customer operations. For high-end products that are in non-stop heterogeneous networked environments where down-time is prohibitively expensive for the customer, the requisite level of customer support rises exponentially. It requires very fast response time, highly skilled personnel, and an ability for customer support personnel to learn very quickly about product innovations and quirks in their own products and those of other vendors' (that their product interacts with). That quick learning requires a radical rethinking about how learning occurs during the customer support process. The challenge is to find a way to very quickly capture and disseminate new learning around the customer support process through all the participants that come into contact with it in a simple and cost effective way.

This challenge was examined in the context of the customer support process at Storage Dimensions, a manufacturer of high-availability computer storage system products. Moreover, we believe that the lessons of this experience provide insights for rethinking the customer support process in all industries

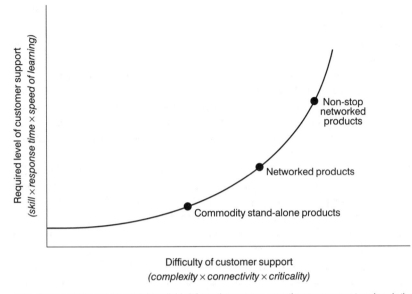

Difficulty of customer support
(complexity × connectivity × criticality)

Note: Our search through the publicly available information systems, operations management, and marketing literature did not uncover any models that captured this dynamic. The graph is meant to illustrate the magnitude of the challenge and what apparent factors appear to affect it rather than to be exhaustive.

Figure 19.1 *Rising customer support levels for complex products*

as the electronic economy makes such customer support levels more the rule than the exception.

The customer support challenge at Storage Dimensions

Storage Dimensions is a vendor of high-availability disk and tape storage for client/server environments. It was founded in 1985 in the heart of Silicon Valley in Milpitas, California, and went public in March 1997. Its 1996 sales were $72 million. The company designs, manufactures, markets, and support hardware/software products that provide open systems storage solutions for mission-critical enterprise applications. Its high-end storage solutions are targeted to organizations with enterprise-wide client/server networks that must keep mission-critical data protected and available 24 hours a day. The company's customer base is mainly Fortune 1000 companies in information-intensive industries that live and die by their data. These include airlines, banking, finance, insurance, retail, utilities, and government agencies. Storage Dimensions products are sold through distributors and resellers in the USA, Europe, and the Pacific Rim. The company also has a direct sales force to more effectively serve its key vertical market customers. More detailed information about the company and its products can be found at www.storagedimensions.com.

Storage Dimensions' products fall into three main categories: high-availability RAID disk storage systems, high capacity tape backup systems, and network storage management software for multi-server networks. RAID (Redundant Array of Independent Disks) is a fault-tolerant disk subsystem architecture that provides protection against data loss and system interruption and also provides improved data transfer/access rates for large databases. This protection ranges from simply mirroring data on duplicate drives to breaking data into pieces and 'striping' it across an array of three or more disks; if one drive goes down, the controller instantly reconstructs the lost data and rebuilds it on a spare drive. Other features include a combination of redundant hot-swap hot-spare power supplies, fans, and disk drive components to ensure non-stop operation and continuous access to data.

Following a 1992 buyout from Maxtor, company management refocused Storage Dimensions to become a higher-end and faster-response industry player. It was clear that exceptional customer support would be essential to success, and a customer-support-focused corporate strategy was put in place. The customer support process was reexamined and it was apparent that it was becoming inadequate for the growing customer base and expanding product line. Furthermore, with increased globalization the customers were dispersed geographically and in different time zones. The customer support process was too slow (as much as two to three hours to return a phone call in some circumstances), too haphazard (no organized online knowledge base for repeat problem solutions), too expensive (repeat problems frequently escalated to development engineers, long training periods), and very stressful to both support personnel (overloaded) and managers (little visibility for the what, who, why, when). Top management saw the need for a radical solution.

Given the mission-critical nature of its customers' network environments, the company expended much effort in providing exceptional customer support. It differentiated itself in the market by helping customers minimize their total life-cycle cost of ownership for network storage in the context of mission-critical applications. A storage system's total life-cycle cost-of-ownership is much more than the purchase price. Service, support, and downtime for RAID storage systems account for 80% of the total cost over the life of the system as per a Gartner Group study – and downtime is especially critical to customers. A Computer Reseller News/Gallup Organization 1994 study found that hourly losses due to network downtime in Fortune 1000 companies were $3,000 to $5,000 per hour (median), could often be $10,000, and sometimes $100,000 or more (6% of companies). Storage Dimensions instituted several customer support programs and innovations to enhance this lower total life-cycle cost-of-ownership customer support strategy. [For additional information on Storage Dimensions, see Chabrow, 1995.] One key element of that strategy was TechConnect, an online technical support system. The development of TechConnect is described in the next section.

The development of the TechConnect support system

As the customer support process was being reexamined in mid-1992, it became apparent to the management team that an IT-enabled solution with an artificial intelligence component had to be part of the remedy. They put their commitment behind it and a project was initiated. The core management team for the project consisted of the executive VP for marketing and customer service (who was also the project sponsor), the director of customer service and support, and the director of information systems (Figure 19.2 shows the organization chart). In addition, a cross-functional task force was formed consisting of three people: one from the customer support group, one from the IS group, and one from engineering. Together, and with input from both customers and others in the company, the management team and the task force came up with a list of the top operational objectives (see Table 19.1) and key technical usability requirements (see Table 19.2) for what they generically referred to then as the customer support management system. They then

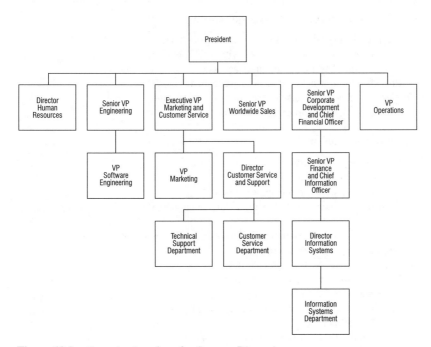

Figure 19.2 *Organization chart for Storage Dimensions*

Table 19.1 *Top 10 operational objectives of customer support management system in mid-1992*

1 Provide consistent, accurate responses to customer inquiries
2 Document and track all known problems and proven solutions
3 Create centralized sources of information about customers, known problems, solutions
4 Assist in developing solutions to new problems
5 Create a closed loop escalation process
6 Promote cross-training of support staff
7 Provide remote access for customers of problem solutions
8 Improve call tracking and problem reporting
9 Improve accountability and responsibility with clear audit trails
10 Improve productivity of customer support staff

Table 19.2 *Technical usability requirements of customer support management system in mid-1992*

IT Infrastructural/compatibility requirements

1 Multi-user, runs off current Ethernet network lines
2 Works under Microsoft Windows with a GUI interface
3 Dial-in capability for remote user access
4 Provides initial access for 25 users, expandable to 50 within one year
5 Must interface with cc:Mail for notification purposes
6 Must have data import/export capability

Usability Requirements

1 Call tracking capability
2 Problem/solution tracking capability
3 Keyword search for problems/solutions
4 Must have a method for assisting technical support staff with answering calls (AI or other)
5 Must have a report generator with user-definable reports without generating programming code or a script
6 Ability to create and define call queues
7 Have at least five user-definable fields
8 Have automated call escalation process
9 Must have a closed loop problem solving process
10 Provides call audit trail
11 Tracks and reports customer configuration data

searched the market for software packages that could help meet those requirements.

The search included various types of artificial intelligence shells, database managers, call management packages, and help desk software – most of which were not the least bit suitable and were quickly eliminated. Only four packages in the help desk software category came close, and these were evaluated in detail. These help desk software packages were not an off-the-shelf fit to the application context. First, the approaches of the packages and vendors were geared mostly to internal help desks rather than external customer support with different customer types. Second, the knowledge capture/update and keyword search capabilities (if any) were too primitive for complex products that changed quickly and had interactions with other vendors' products. Third, Storage Dimensions had a fairly sophisticated client/server network, and it wanted to link the customer support system to its e-mail and to its internal information systems and databases in other functional areas. As the help desk software vendors themselves acknowledged at the time, this would be a stretch.

The comparative analysis among the four help desk software packages was made based on how the software features fit the operational requirements. The Apriori GT help desk software from Answer Systems (since 1995 a part of Platinum Technology Inc.) was selected mainly based on its unique 'bubble-up' technique that could prioritize likely problem solutions (discussed in more detail later in this section), its good incident management capabilities, its good reporting capabilities, and its technical compatibility with Storage Dimensions' client/server network infrastructure and the Windows graphical user interface. Other Apriori GT capabilities at the time included call tracking, incident escalation, various search and retrieval features, custom notification and routing, e-mail and fax integration, accountability features, and tailorability for application integration.

While no programming changes would be made to the source code, there was much work to be done in structuring Apriori GT to fit the complexity of the Storage Dimensions environment and linking it (through Perl scripts and macros) to the internal information system infrastructure and e-mail. For the next 90 days the task force worked together with the software vendor to install, customize, script, and test the customer support application. Simultaneously, the customer support process and the way it was managed was being reengineered to take advantage of this new technology. Much input was sought and enthusiastically received at that stage from various parts of the company, and a pilot was run with selected customers. Fortunately, implementation was successful both technically and organizationally. Tech-Connect was online in late 1992.

The TechConnect system was set up on a Sun Sparc 670 MP server and cost $160,000 for hardware and software. It costs $15,000 to maintain per year.

The cost justification for TechConnect was not difficult based on out-of-pocket expenses. In the first year alone the reduced call-backs (due to higher problem resolution rate on first customer call) saved about $70,000 in long distance phone bills. In addition, the productivity gains obviated the need to hire more technical support engineers to handle the growing customer support load, saving another estimated $150,000.

The new IT-enabled customer support process

TechConnect enabled the redesign of the customer support process such that it could be more effective and better managed. Some key aspects of how this new online customer support process was managed follow.

- **Improved escalation paths for problem management:** A simplified diagram of the three-level escalation sequence is shown in Figure 19.3. After dispatch, the customer call goes to a level 1 technical support engineer. He/she tries to resolve the problem through an on-line TechConnect solution document. If it includes a request for material authorization, then an appropriate customer service representative is notified through TechConnect. If the problem is not resolved at level 1, it is automatically escalated and queued (path depends on the operating system used by the customer's client/server network hardware) to a level 2 applications engineer who is more skilled and who investigates it thoroughly. If the applications engineer is unable to resolve it, then it is

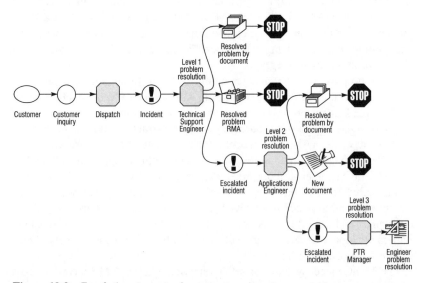

Figure 19.3 *Escalation sequence in customer support process*

automatically escalated to the problem tracking request (PTR) manager who verifies the problem and must decide whether to escalate it to a development engineer.

- **Closed loop problem resolution:** As the incident moves along the escalation path, both the caller and the customer support staff (and manager) always know who has the incident and what its status is. The process also ensures that the customer is informed in a timely manner. TechConnect keeps track of all the information related to the incident and stores it in the TechConnect database.

- **Analysis and reporting capabilities:** TechConnect provides a multitude of management and activity reports that help manage the customer support process and identify bottlenecks. It is possible to automatically flag unusual events and for customer support staff to spend more time on proactive rather than reactive customer support.

- **Automatic cross-triggering capabilities:** TechConnect is integrated into the Storage Dimensions network of information systems to automatically flag other business areas or information systems via e-mail based on problem incidents. This facilitates cross-functional coordination between customer support and other departments.

- **Amplified shared knowledge creation:** The intensity of shared knowledge creation through customer interactions around the customer support process is greatly amplified through TechConnect. The continuous production of online solution documents steadily creates a valuable knowledge base that is accessible to all: *everyone can be an expert, and everyone can contribute to the learning*. That transforms the way that the customer support process is carried out and managed, as does its knowledge-creating capacity. That critical aspect is discussed in more detail in the next section of the chapter.

With the use of the TechConnect system and a transformed customer support process, the customer support department has remained at the same size despite increasing sales volume. The group consists of eight technical support engineers, three applications engineers, and one manager. They work a basic 11-hour shift between them and also have a 24 hour on-call system.

TechConnect as an adaptive learning IT infrastructure

The TechConnect system is based on a knowledge base software architecture that adaptively learns through its interactions with users. It is based on a unique software-based problem resolution architecture (patented in 1995 by Answer Systems) that links problems, symptoms, and solutions in a document database. All problems or issues are analyzed through incident reports, and resolutions are fed back into the online knowledge base in the form of solution documents. The software is able to link one master solution or solution-in-progress with variants of multiple symptoms. This unique many-to-one relationship allows the help desk to update the solution in a single place in the knowledge base and communicate meaningful updates to users automatically.

The way that the TechConnect knowledge base learns is through the very well-structured dynamic feedback loops that are managed by the problem resolution architecture. As problems are analyzed and resolved by technical support specialists, development engineers, and customers, the results are integrated into the knowledge base as solution documents, and new knowledge is created and synthesized (see Figure 19.4). As a result, solutions are consistent and readily available to support specialists and customers alike. Solutions are 'fresh' (up-to-date), accurate, and based on the latest experience of customers (200 new data points per week). At this writing, support specialists and customers have access to information from over 35,000 relevant incidents. In total, 1,700 solution documents are currently available electronically. Because 80% of incoming calls are repeat problems, existing solution documents often provide resolutions within minutes.

Another key feature of the TechConnect system is the Bubble-Up solution management technology (see box below) that enables the TechConnect knowledge base to adaptively learn through its interaction with users. It automatically prioritizes solution documents based on 'usefulness/frequency

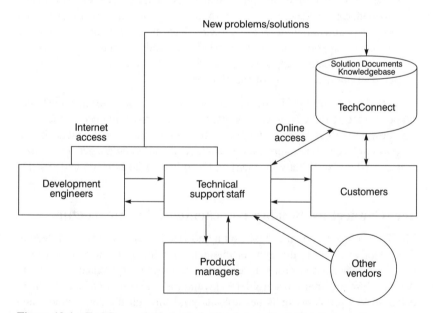

Figure 19.4   *TechConnect's dynamic feedback loop for knowledge creation*

of use' in resolving specific problems, and the higher priority ones rise to the top of the list. This helps less experienced inquirers to see the most useful solutions and speeds up problem resolution. The Bubble-Up process also adaptively changes the structure of the knowledge base and adapts it continuously to new knowledge.

In combination, the problem resolution architecture and the Bubble-Up software make it possible for the knowledge base to change its structure dynamically 'on-the-fly' as it gains new knowledge from those who interact with it. TechConnect can learn quickly from anyone who interacts with it: customer support specialists, development engineers, and customers. Furthermore, the knowledge is always fresh and usefully organized for rapid problem resolution for less-experienced users.

The TechConnect support system allows self-help by customers. It can be directly accessed by customers 24 hours a day through e-mail or through the Internet via the Storage Dimensions Website (http:storagedimensions/support/techsupport/). To access the knowledge base via the Internet self-help route or e-mail, customers complete a TechConnect search request form that includes symptom identifiers. Within two minutes, TechConnect automatically sends back a related list of solution documents from which to choose. Thus, through

---

What is Bubble-Up™?

Bubble-Up is a patented problem resolution technology that is embedded in the Apriori product. It enables an indexing scheme and intelligent filter that causes the most-used solution documents to rise to the surface of the volume of solution documents that are stored in a problem resolution knowledge base. The index structure of the knowledge base has multiple roots and is not strictly hierarchical. Moreover, it uses a proprietary algorithm to automatically modify the structure of the knowledge tree based on 'most-used' knowledge elements in the tree. 'Most-used' is based on a statistical weighting of both the actual usefulness and popularity of a solution document in solving a problem rather than just access (i.e., incorporates a voting heuristic). It can do this at any level of the index structure thus enabling selective filtering. A flowchart illustrating how the Bubble procedure works internally is shown in Figure 19.5. How it affects TechConnect from a user perspective is explained through an example in the next section of the chapter.

As new solution documents are created and/or their usefulness in solving problems changes (through user voting when accessed) the knowledge base is able to adaptively learn and automatically change its structure without any programming, and in a way that is transparent to the user. It is thus able to self-modify through use and learn as new problems, solutions-in-process, or solutions are added.

Bubble-Up was patented by Answer Systems in 1994. It won the 1995 Harold Short Jr. Innovations in Service Awards that recognizes tools and services that have a far reaching effect on service delivery.

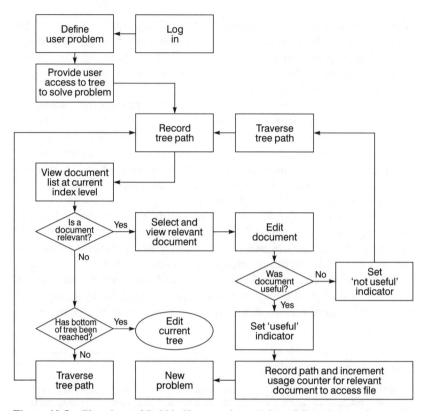

Figure 19.5   *Flowchart of Bubble-Up procedure. (Adapted from Answer Systems)*

an e-mail or web page request, TechConnect is able to search for solutions in the knowledge base, select and rank order them based on usefulness, and post them back to the web page. While technically possible, the structure of the knowledge base is not updated on-the-fly through the self-help route in order to protect the integrity of the database from spurious information. New knowledge from self-help incidents are first checked by technical support specialists before being submitted as updates.

The TechConnect knowledge base provides detailed information on installation, compatibility, troubleshooting, and support for Storage Dimensions' systems, as well as related products from other vendors (servers or operating systems or backup software). The customer support web page also has hot links to those vendors. Of course, for such a system to work effectively, it must be integrated into a very well-structured organizational customer support process that is well-managed. That was a crucial consideration in the redesign of the customer support process at Storage

Dimensions. The tightness of integration between the use of TechConnect and management of the customer support process is perhaps best shown through an example, presented in the next section.

How TechConnect drives the knowledge-creating customer support process

When a customer calls on the phone for support, a Storage Dimensions frontline technical support engineer sitting at a TechConnect screen asks questions about system configuration (enclosure type, operating system, type of drive, etc.) and an incident is created. Based on the customer's reported problem, the technical support engineer uses symptom words to search for an existing problem/solution document. Each solution document has symptom words associated with it that are assigned when the solution document is created or modified, and they are added to the master symptom list. On the TechConnect screen captured in Figure 19.6, the word 'hang' is selected (note asterisk next to it) from the master symptom list as one of the symptom words. An 'Auto Search' will look for any solution documents that are linked to the symptom words. A 'Manual Search' will do the same but will also prompt the

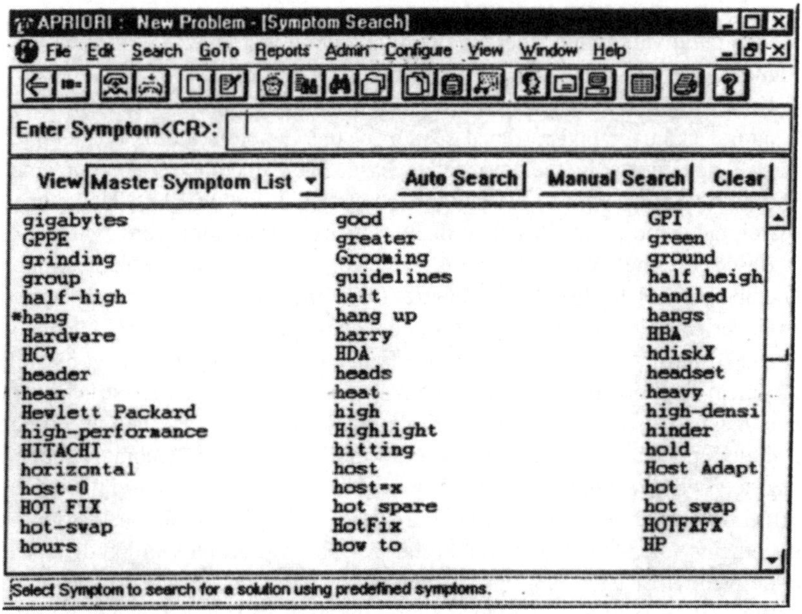

Figure 19.6   *TechConnect screen for symptom search*

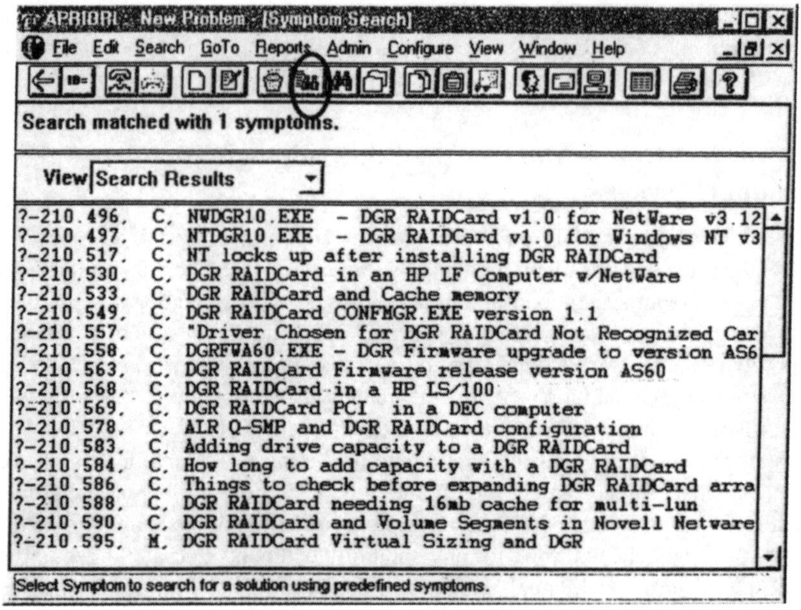

Figure 19.7   *TechConnect screen with list of possible problem/solution documents*

user to iteratively reduce the number of symptom words, if no documents are found in the initial search with all the symptom words.

If the simple indexed search does not locate any solution documents, then a natural language text retrieval search for the symptom words is attempted for all documents in the knowledge base, even documents not contained within the Apriori database (through icon circled in Figure 19.7). This type of search takes more machine time than an indexed symptom word search.

Based on the symptom words selected, a listing of problem/solution documents will be listed (see Figure 19.7) and then the technical support engineer can view them to see if any of them apply.

If a solution document cannot be found based on symptom words, the technical support engineer will then try to search the index structure of documents using TechConnect's Bubble-Up feature. By clicking on the Bubble-Up icon (circled under 'Reports' in Figure 19.8 the technical support engineer will see a hierarchical index structure as shown in the top half of the screen in Figure 19.8. The bottom half of the screen shows the top 12 solution documents for all of the available indexes based (and rank-ordered) on the effectiveness of each solution document. By clicking on any of the index buttons (BBS, Software, Hardware, etc.) the user drills down deeper into the index. For example, clicking on the 'Hardware' button will reveal the next index level (Computers, Drives, Tape Drives, etc.), and the top 12 documents for those index buttons will be listed. He/she can then start examining each solution document from the top of the list and clicking on the document they think is most relevant (this is a support system that supports the user's thinking, rather than replaces judgement).

As documents are read, the technical support engineer is prompted to vote on the usefulness of the document. They are requested to select between 'not useful,' 'useful,' and 'solved incident.' If either 'useful' or 'solved incident' is selected, then the document is moved up higher in the Bubble-Up list. If 'solved incident' is selected, then the customer's TechConnect account number becomes associated with the solution document so that any updates or modifications to the document will generate an automated notification to the customer.

If none of the documents provide a solution to the customer's issue, the technical support engineer will complete a 'new problem' report (by clicking on the 'new problem' icon circled under 'Go To' in Figure 19.8). The new problem report is generated whether the problem is resolved or not. If the problem was resolved, then the report will also describe the solution. If there is no resolution, then recommendations for a solution will be given (update manual, debug software, change hardware, etc.). If a specific index is not

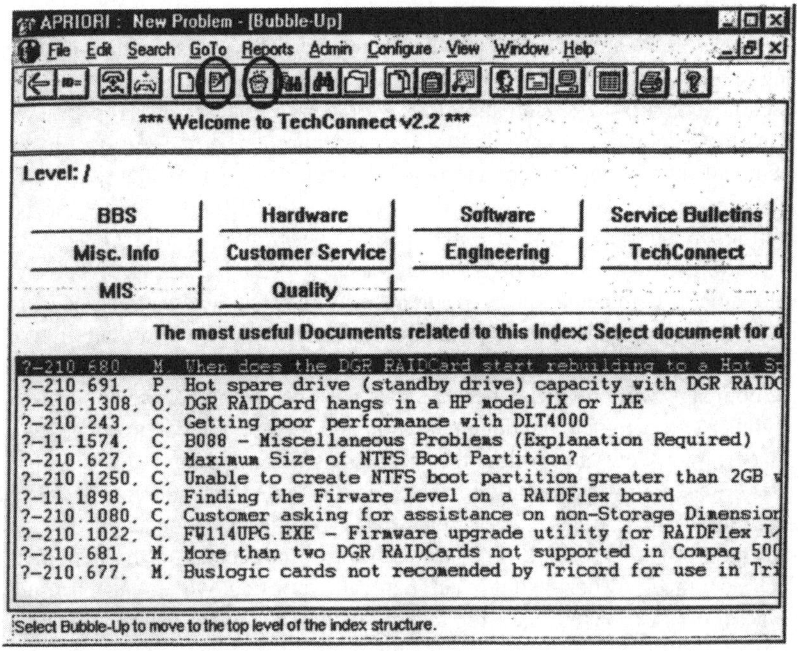

Figure 19.8 *TechConnect Bubble-Up solution document listing*

specified, then the new problem report will be assigned to the last index visited during the Bubble-Up search. The owner of that index (the applications engineer) will then be notified that a new problem has been submitted.

The applications engineer will then review the new problem and check that no problem/solution document or pending problem exists, that all information is present to replicate the issue if needed, and that all basic trouble shooting steps have been performed. If a solution was provided, the applications engineer will then verify the validity of the new problem report and edit it for clarity and effectiveness. It is at this time that the symptom words are assigned to the document. The document will then be marked with a status of 'marketing review' and the appropriate marketing product manager's e-mail address will be assigned to the document and they will be automatically notified that a new document has been created and is awaiting their review. Any comments or corrections are then forwarded back to the applications engineer to incorporate into the document. At that time, the document is set to the status of 'Closed.'

If no solution was included with the problem report, the applications engineer will then try to resolve the issue by interfacing with engineering, or other departments as needed, or by replicating the problem by duplicating the installation as close as possible. If the problem is resolved by the applications engineer, the document will be set to a status of 'marketing review' and follow the process explained above. If the applications engineer is unable to resolve the issue or is able to verify a hardware or software issue that requires engineering or another department's effort or resources to resolve, the document is set to a status of ('PTR (Open).' PTR stands for Problem Tracking Report and means that an issue was not able to be resolved by the technical support department and requires resources from another department in the company. After an appropriate person is identified to follow through with resolving the PTR, their e-mail address is assigned to the PTR and they are automatically notified on a weekly basis until the PTR is resolved. They can submit comments back to the submitting applications engineer for incorporation into the comments area of the document. The information in the comments area on PTR documents are compiled on a weekly basis and posted for company-wide review. Once the PTR has been resolved, the applications engineer will complete the documentation and then set the document status to 'marketing review' and follow that process as described above.

There is also a procedure for solution document update. If a technical support engineer finds a document that is incorrect or outdated, or new information is discovered, he or she can attach comments to the document. The document owner will be automatically notified via e-mail that new comments have been posted for that particular document. The applications engineer will then review the comments to see if they are appropriate to be included into the document. After the comments have been added, the document goes through the same 'marketing review' process as described earlier. After the comments have been posted, any customer or technical support person on that document's 'list' will be automatically notified via e-mail that the document has been updated.

Assessing the impacts and value of the TechConnect system

The TechConnect customer support system has paid for itself many times over. As mentioned before, it paid for itself in its first year by virtue of cost savings alone. More importantly, it has driven the transformation of the customer support process, has enabled the integration of valuable customer input into other areas of the business, and has revealed the enormous potential of an innovative type of IT infrastructure that enhances quick organizational learning as the environment changes. The TechConnect knowledge base and the process routes around it are now a growing part of Storage Dimensions' intellectual capital. It is not an overstatement to say that the TechConnect system has had strategic impacts on Storage Dimensions and has been instrumental in advantageously positioning the company for the electronic economy.

For purposes of exposition and assessment, the impacts have been divided into three categories: first order direct impacts on transforming the customer support process itself, second order impacts related to integrating customer input into other business areas, and third order indirect impacts related to building an IT infrastructure for the electronic economy.

First order direct impacts: transforming the customer support process

- **Faster customer response:** Average time to respond to a customer problem report is now 15 minutes, after being as much as two to three hours in some cases prior to TechConnect. Problem resolution time has dropped from an estimated four-hour average to a measured 50-minute average: 60% of all problems are resolved within 30 minutes and 70% within an hour. Also, about 20% of incidents are now handled by the self-help route through 7×24 Internet/e-mail with instant response to queries; 80% of these self-help incidents are resolved on the first try through online solution documents.
- **Accurate, consistent, and accountable problem resolution:** Due to the real-time currency of the TechConnect knowledge base and rank ordering of solution documents, repetitive problems are solved correctly and at the first level every time, no matter what the skill level of the technical support engineer. If escalation occurs on a difficult new problem, then both the customer and Storage Dimensions know the progress of the resolution at all times. It is impossible to be unaccountable.

- **Cost-effective problem resolution:** Due to orderly TechConnect escalation processes, valuable development engineer time is conserved. Currently, 67% of technical failure incidents are resolved at level 1, also conserving the time of application engineers. The remaining 33% are handled by level 2 applications engineers who thoroughly research the problem and solve it about 80% of the time. The remaining 20% (7% of the total) are escalated through the customer support manager to a development engineer. While a 33% escalation ratio may appear high in comparison to traditional internal help desks, it is actually low given the complexity of products and given that related server technology changes every 90 days (paced by Intel's synchronized 90-day release schedule for microprocessors).
- **Leadership in cross-vendor troubleshooting:** Most of the difficult technical problems in client/server environments are related to compatibility issues and integration across storage and server products made by different vendors. Storage Dimensions' capability for cross-vendor troubleshooting has been greatly amplified through TechConnect and has eliminated many hours of finger-pointing. There is no quantitative data, but there are anecdotes about how Storage Dimensions was able to provide a solution document to another vendor's compatibility problem and verify it before the other vendor's technical support person even arrived to the customer site. Such incidents have helped establish a reputation for the company as a customer support leader.
- **Vigilant and proactive management of customer support process:** TechConnect collects much data related to problem reports, activity levels, and customers. It easily provides ad hoc management reports for spotting process problems. It flags problems that require quick management attention and alerts of longer term capacity and service-level issues. The customer support process now has a greater proactive component based on such flagging. A telling (but unscientific) measure of this impact is the director of customer support's likening the discovery of TechConnect's management capabilities to uncovering the Holy Grail – even giving the system the nickname 'Galahad.'
- **More learningful customer support staff:** The word 'learningful' is concocted, but it aptly captures the spirit of what is being articulated. TechConnect enables staff to be more learningful in that they build on each other's knowledge and on that of more experienced senior colleagues and smart customers. Each and every customer support staff person has access to expert problem solutions through TechConnect – no matter what his or her current expertise level is. Similarly, each customer support person contributes to the knowledge base. The systematic structure through which TechConnect directs the problem resolution process has also sharpened problem solving skills and diagnostic logic. This has upped the general

skill level of the group as well as helped new hires ramp up their skills more quickly.

- **More learningful customer support process:** TechConnect has analysis capabilities that have enabled staff to uncover patterns and take proactive action for further prevention. This information is also fed back to other areas of the company depending on where the action is needed to be taken. It has ranged from changing a confusing paragraph on a page in an installation manual to a major redesign of a product component. Over three years, the number of incidents has dropped from 7,283 incidents per quarter in early 1993 to 1,715 incidents per quarter in early 1996 (see Figure 19.9). Even as a percentage of installed base, incidents have dropped from 1.45% to 0.49%.

In combination, these direct impacts and a qualitatively transformed customer support process translate to more satisfied customers. They also translate to more satisfied customer support staff. The staff (especially the junior staff) appreciate the positive feedback from being able to resolve problems quickly and the clear systematic guidance for the process that TechConnect provides. The turnover rate has dropped by about 50% in the last four years.

Second order impacts: integrating customer input into other business areas

The changes in the customer support process have also had impacts beyond its own confines in that customer input has been integrated into other business areas of the company. This has often been facilitated by TechConnect's 'trigger' feature that automatically triggers e-mail to other departments in the company depending on how questions are answered in a problem report. Examples of such second order impacts include:

- **Product improvements:** The number of incidents has decreased (see Figure 19.9) partly because of product improvements triggered through TechConnect. This has also provided valuable information to better track new products as they are introduced and on more than one occasion has helped to catch repetitive problems quickly. Proactive tracking of evaluation units at customer sites is now routinely done and the conversion rate (the conversion of a unit from evaluation to a sale) has increased by 30% since the use of TechConnect for that activity. This has fostered an appreciation of TechConnect by engineering.
- **Sales lead triggers and marketing support:** As TechConnect keeps a record of the nature of customer inquiries, through the 'trigger' feature it has become automatic to pass on any sale leads as well as provide new knowledge for marketing strategy.

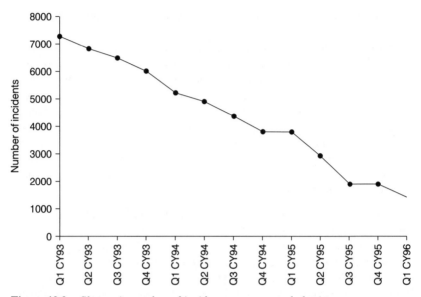

Figure 19.9   *Change in number of incidents on a quarterly basis*

- **Global expansion strategy support:** TechConnect allows customer support to be easily administered online from one centralized location in Milpitas. As Storage Dimensions continues its global expansion, that will make it possible for it to provide customer support in any remote location around the world without substantially increasing costs or sacrificing the level of support.
- **Discovering the potential of customer support as a revenue-generating business process:** The company has not yet fully examined how to convert their customer support savvy into a direct source of revenue, although their expertise with solving other vendors' compatibility problems is a source of know-how that could generate revenue. The challenge lies in taking advantage of it without jeopardizing the collaborative cross-vendor problem-solving that Storage Dimensions has sought to nurture.

Third order indirect impacts: building an IT infrastructure for the electronic economy

TechConnect has also had some broader indirect effects on the organizational vision of the company as a whole and its positioning for the emerging electronic economy. While perhaps more difficult to measure, these impacts may be the most profound for Storage Dimensions in the long run and are shaping the challenge that lies ahead.

- **Finding an IT infrastructure that learns quickly:** Somewhat serendipitously, Storage Dimensions has discovered an adaptive learning IT infrastructure that could be applied to the company as a whole. Management has now discovered a concrete, practical way to build a knowledge-creating company that learns quickly from its customers and partners. It is a somewhat unexpected revelation that perhaps a large portion of the 'fresh' intellectual capital of the company is being grown around and driven by the TechConnect support system. It is being extended to other parts of the company such as contracts and sales and some areas of engineering. It is becoming a possible foundation of an enterprise-wide IT platform suitable for the electronic economy where the capacity to learn faster, create knowledge quicker, and be nimbler is critical.
- **Shaping the vision for use of Internet platforms:** The TechConnect experience has illustrated early how useful the internet can be for self-help in customer support. Storage Dimensions is expanding internet use for tracking customer incidents in addition to telephone call tracking. It has also been developing software that monitors remote network storage at customer sites through the Internet (an extranet of sorts) and is tied to Storage Dimensions' VantagePoint product. VantagePoint software monitors the condition and performance of disk storage systems across a multi-server network, collects the performance data, and reports it to a single management console. It currently has alerting capabilities that are tied to both pagers and e-mail. The new Internet monitoring capability allows for global monitoring of customer network storage by Storage Dimensions. The performance characteristics transmitted through the Internet are matched through the software to a database with site configurations (host bus, type of network adapters, type of server, etc.). With the help of VantagePoint, it comes up with an error code that provides diagnosis and early warning to the customer support personnel through e-mail – allowing them to take pre-emptive action. The augmented database with its automatic and continuous performance data capture allows Storage Dimensions to have robust failure predictions based on learning from its own database and to take necessary corrective or preventive action earlier. This capability is expected to be fully available for customers in late 1997.
- **Developing customer-facing intranet applications:** The success of the Internet interface as a standard ubiquitous accessible way to communicate with customers has prompted Storage Dimensions to develop Internet applications for other functions that interact frequently with

customers. The company is currently implementing an intranet system with a standard browser coupled to a customized search engine for salespeople. Through this new application the approximately 25 Storage Dimensions salespeople will be able to gain access while on the road to the latest versions of sales-related documents (such as competitive information, benchmarking data, newsletters).

The challenge ahead

The project, like any successful IT-enabled organizational change effort, has had its share of typical technical, organizational, and managerial problems – and there were bumps and much learning along the way. However, none of those issues was major or unique enough to warrant the interest of readers. Nor can any advice be offered in that respect that is different from what is recommended in successful organizational change efforts that involve new information technologies. There are, however, some aspects related to the challenge ahead that are worth articulating.

First and foremost is the importance of realizing the imminence of the electronic economy and the business conditions that it progressively brings with it for fast response and shared knowledge creation. Second, when Storage Dimensions embarked on its customer-support-focused strategy in 1992, it started out with a passion for exceptional customer support, a strong belief that there had to be an IT-enabled solution, an understanding that this could only succeed if it was a company-wide effort, and an unwavering management commitment to make that happen. There is no functional management hero in this story, be it a customer service executive, or an IS executive, or a marketing executive. Rather, this is a company-wide cross-functional effort that required getting all the parts to work together in collaboration at all levels while continuously learning through customers. In the electronic economy, everyone fully participates in making IT-enabled solutions work and that will undoubtedly create new challenges and opportunities for the CIO and the IS function.

Third, we must point out that it is not just the TechConnect technology that has made the difference, but rather how the company has been able to stretch it, adapt it, and use it intelligently to better respond to the challenges of the present and simultaneously better prepare for the opportunities of the future. The customer support process has been transformed to be faster, smarter, cheaper, more learningful, and highly appreciated by its customers, partners, and industry – and even its competitors. What insights can be drawn that can be useful for others in redesigning IT-enabled knowledge-creating customer support processes that are suitable for the business conditions of the electronic economy?

Insights for redesign of knowledge-creating customer support processes in the electronic economy

Storage Dimensions is a small company with a grand total of 240 employees and limited resources. Many Fortune 1000 companies have more people than that solely in their IS departments. The company is also in the frenetically paced information technology Industry. Furthermore, because of the nature of Storage Dimensions customers' mission-critical applications and product complexity, the customer support requirements are extremely demanding. However, we strongly believe that the lessons learned and the insights gained from the Storage Dimensions experience are applicable in any industry to companies of any size that want to have effective customer support and service process in the electronic economy. It is just that the trying conditions in which Storage Dimensions operates have driven it to actively search for (and fortunately find) an innovative IT-enabled response to the customer support challenge earlier than other companies may have needed to. The future is already here; it is just unevenly distributed.

The insights gained and articulated below are based on four sets of inputs. First, and most influential, is the Storage Dimensions TechConnect experience. Second, our collective experience about customer support and service has been incorporated into technology-based companies. Third, we have drawn on the state-of-the-art in what is known about IT-enabled business process reengineering (cf. Bennis and Mische, 1996; Davenport, 1993; El Sawy, 1998). Fourth, we have attempted to integrate what practitioners and researchers of fast learning and knowledge management through problem resolution systems have reported and suggested (cf. Kirkbride and Deppe, 1995; Nonaka and Takeuchi, 1995). These four sets of inputs are synthesized to produce a generic set of insights for redesigning IT-enabled knowledge-creating customer support processes and the issues around them. Presented below are the top seven insights that 'bubbled up' at this stage of our learning.

Insight #1: IT's biggest leverage in knowledge-creating customer support processes is in enabling ubiquitous problem resolution, not in providing complex problem routing.

We have learned that it is better to use IT to make new knowledge accessible to everyone at the front line than to route different problems to different specialists. The biggest payoff from using IT in knowledge-creating customer support processes does not come from call tracking technologies for increasing the speed or automating the complexity by which customer inquiries are routed, queued, or escalated. The biggest payoff comes from IT-based problem resolution systems that enable front line employees to answer any known question consistently and accurately. The TechConnect system at

Storage Dimensions with its solution bubble-up feature enabled people without advanced expertise (whether a customer support person or a customer) to resolve any problem for which there was already an online solution. Using this philosophy had high payoff.

The nature of knowledge work is different from operational work and requires different reengineering strategies (cf. Davenport *et al.*, 1996). It requires ways of capturing relevant knowledge from everyone who interacts with the business process. It is aided by questioning that helps elicit tacit knowledge and converts it into explicit shareable knowledge that is synthesized such that it is usable by all (Nonaka and Takeuchi 1995). It also requires different coordination strategies (Rathnam *et al.* 1995). In high knowledge-creation customer support environments it is not as useful to focus on escalating the problem up to the expert or the right person. The high payoff challenge is to make sure that *everybody* is the right person.

Insight #2: Problem resolution technologies with adaptive learning capabilities are much more suitable than traditional expert systems as IT infrastructures for speeding, up learning and creating new knowledge around customer support processes in rapidly changing environments.

The TechConnect experience showed how an IT infrastructure based on adaptive learning problem resolution technology can help create new knowledge 'on the fly' through customer dialogues without lag time between discovery of a solution and its availability to all in an intelligently accessible form. Storage Dimensions considered an alternative IT infrastructure based on expert systems, but decided against it. Traditional expert systems, whether rule-based expert systems, case-based reasoning systems, or decision trees, do not work well in situations where conditions change rapidly and a large number of cases or rules must be maintained. They require much up-front development work to develop cases or rules, need skilled knowledge engineers to make changes, and are not suited to contexts that have fluid structures with solutions-in-progress.

As an example, Storage Dimensions has an almost endless number of product permutations because of the way storage systems must work with a variety of other products (something like 10 models × 5 to 10 storage capacities × 5 operating systems × 3 to 4 revision levels × ~100 configurations [memory, network interface card, peripherals]). The number of rules would be extraordinarily high. Furthermore, server technology changes every 90 days paced by Intel's microprocessor release schedule. Designing expert systems for creating knowledge in such a context would mean that by the time we finished redesigning it, its knowledge structure would have to be redesigned again. An excellent comparison of the robustness of adaptive learning systems as compared to traditional expert systems is available (Kirkbride and Deppe 1995). Key features of comparison are captured in Table 14.3

Table 19.3 *Key features of comparison*

	Traditional expert systems	*Adaptive learning systems*
Knowledge Capture	Time spent building workable rules and cases is prohibitive.	On-the-fly knowledge capture such that knowledge base learns quickly and easily.
Knowledge Retrieval	Unsuited to solutions-in-progress. Requires large number of cases to provide problem-solving accuracy.	Accommodates changing solutions and solutions that have fuzzy and incomplete knowledge.
Knowledge Base Maintenance	Very high effort to maintain changing rules with large numbers of cases.	Self-organizing adaptive knowledge structure.
Skill of Knowledge Engineer	Requires skilled knowledge engineers to translate knowledge to rules and develop expert system.	Problem/solution/symptom word structure is Intuitive and requires no special skill.

> **Insight #3: The World Wide Web's strength as a contact route to a knowledge-creating customer support process is that it can provide powerful remote computational functionality for casual users (customers) through a standardized familiar interface.**

The power of the World Wide Web for customer support is not in that it provides world wide e-mail, fancy multimedia, or brochure-ware capabilities. It is more than a pretty face: it provides a *standard customer interface* through web browsers that is ideal for capturing input from the *casual user*. In addition, it allows a user to submit a request for a complex computational task remotely and receive a response. For example, the TechConnect web access route allows a customer to submit problem symptoms to TechConnect that will then go search its knowledge base, make some computations that go beyond key-word search, and return with a list of probable solution documents. As Java-like capabilities are becoming more readily available, it is increasingly feasible to have more computational functionality for customer support interactions through the web. Already, we are beginning to see some vendors such as Netscape change the name of their browser software category from 'browser' to 'client' (cf. Muller, 1996 for an analysis of how help desk functionality is being expanded through the World Wide Web).

Insight #4: Use IT to enable as many different types of customer self-help routes as you can to a knowledge-creating customer support process, provided that you understand the prerequisite conditions for success.

In 1994, Storage Dimensions tried to give its resellers direct access to TechConnect from their remote computers by making it possible for them to appear to be a virtual TechConnect client complete with full GUI features. The technical implementation was superb, but they never used it. Apparently, for the casual user trying to play the role of technical support engineer, the functionality and richness of features of TechConnect were beyond what a casual user was willing to remember. On the other hand, the TechConnect e-mail and Internet connection are very successful, as previously discussed, and Storage Dimensions is steadily expanding the capabilities of those routes. The difference between the two situations is that Storage Dimensions has now understood the prerequisites for successful self-help routes. First, the route must fill a need that provides incentive for self-help (such as 24-hour access). Second, the functionality should not be more than a casual user can assimilate (currently TechConnect self-help does not allow direct knowledge base access). Third, there must be alternate routes with live customer support staff as self-help is not successful for all types of queries. Thus, self-help should only be attempted after a support staff is in place. Fourth, while the customer should be encouraged to provide new knowledge for the customer support knowledge base, care must be taken to protect its integrity.

Insight #5: There will be an increasing need in business organizations in the electronic economy to have a common interconnected 'fresh' knowledge warehouse that captures in near-real-time the knowledge created around all critical interdependent business processes, including the customer support process.

Data warehouses have become increasingly popular with business organizations in the last few years because businesses have become acutely aware of the criticality of joining data from the various interdependent parts of the organization and yet are able to serve each constituency in a customized way. There is a knowledge warehouse analogy to that for the electronic economy that would center around knowledge-in-action captured through various business processes (cf. Kalakota and Whinston, 1996). The key differences are inferred in Table 19.4.

It is envisaged that such knowledge warehouses would be built around knowledge creation processes rather than data, and there would be a much higher percentage of 'fresh' solutions-in-progress (or fuzzy data). A comparison of IT would probably have a higher percentage of inter-organizational knowledge-creating routes than today's warehouse has inter-organizational data feeds. As insight #7 suggests, the customer support

Table 19.4 *The shift to knowledge warehouses*

Data warehouse	Knowledge warehouse
Stable database structure	Emergent database structure
Does not learn from user access behavior	Learns from user access behavior
Passive; user retrieves information	Active; system may initiate discourse
Attribute search	Attribute search and pattern matching search
Scrubbed clean data	Fuzzy incomplete knowledge
Historical data	Fresh knowledge
Constrained interorganizational data feeds	Rich intranet/extranet knowledge-creation routes

process may be a promising space to start. However, it would also include knowledge created around other interdependent processes.

> **Insight #6: Methodologies for redesigning IT-enabled knowledge-creating customer support processes in the electronic economy will need to cater to both learning changes and process workflow changes.**

Business process reengineering methodologies for IT-enabled business processes have typically focused on changing the structure of workflow and the information around it. With customer support processes that have a large knowledge-creation component given the rapidly changing environment, there is an intimate interdependence between the mode of learning and knowledge creation (cf. Sampler and Short, 1994). Business process redesign methodologies will thus have to move to a higher order of analysis in which the way that the process learns (and becomes more learningful) is redesigned.

> **Insight #7: IT Infrastructures and knowledge bases built around adaptive learning problem resolution architectures linked to customer support processes can provide the first step toward building the faster-learning knowledge-creating organization of the electronic economy.**

The Storage Dimensions experience has shown that using problem resolution architectures based on adaptive learning is one of the most systematic and natural ways that one can structure the way we learn and create knowledge. It can have very well-defined dynamic feedback loops that, when utilized properly, can both speed up the learning process and amplify the shared knowledge creation capability of a network of people. It has built-in knowledge consistency checks through constant interaction. It minimizes the time between the creation of new knowledge and its incorporation into the knowledge base in intelligently accessible form. It accommodates different levels of expertise by assuring that novices are not penalized for their lack of expertise and that experts are not burdened by unnecessary steps. It is a very smart way of creating new knowledge around business processes in action and appears to be one of the most promising paradigms for building IT-based learning organizations. Perhaps, after more than 20 years of trying, artificial intelligence has finally produced an appropriately targeted paradigm that will be of critical and widespread business use.

Furthermore, the customer support process is an excellent context around which to do this knowledge creation because it is the natural meeting space around which the organization, its customers, its partners – and often its competitors – exchange dialogue about current issues of importance to all of them (cf. Savage, 1996). It is the swiftest and most obvious context around which to capture shared knowledge creation in action and systematically incorporate it into a corporate knowledge base. Furthermore, the usual lack of physical proximity among different participants and parties makes the use of IT network-mediated exchanges all the more natural.

There is evidence to believe, based on the TechConnect experience, that the combination of using adaptive learning problem resolution IT architectures and the customer support process context provides the most promising first step in building a faster-learning, knowledge-creating organization. It is a context and IT architecture in which the mode of combining both the exploration and exploitation aspects of organization learning (March, 1991) promises to be effective for both the short run and the long run. Other areas of the business can be more easily linked through the customer support process than any other critical business process we know of because of its simultaneous critical intersection with many knowledge sources and its built-in time pressures that can drive participants to augment learning quickly. It appears to be the best and fastest space from which to start building the structural intellectual capital of an organization (cf. Quinn, 1992; Stewart, 1994). It is an excellent arena for building a learning relationship with customers (Pine *et al.*, 1995).

Conclusion

This chapter began by showing how customer support and service needs are driving IS priorities more than they ever have before. It also pointed out that this is happening in the business environment of an emerging electronic economy in which fast response, shared knowledge creation, and inter-networked technologies are increasingly critical. The chapter has shown that there are new IT infrastructures and knowledge creation architectures that can make a difference and that perhaps the way that the customer support process is changing will trigger enterprise-wide change in redesigning IT-enabled knowledge-creating business processes. This also heralds new opportunities and new responsibilities for the ever-changing role of the CIO.

The number of business organizations that are fully participating in the electronic economy will soon reach a critical mass. Having robust internetworked IT-enabled knowledge-creating processes that learn quickly from customers (and employees, partners, and competitors) will not be a strategic choice: it will become a strategic necessity for success in the electronic economy. We hope that this chapter has provided a compelling example to show how that can be done and that it will stimulate both practitioners and academics to find new ways of using information technologies to expand the knowledge-creating capacity of business processes.

Acknowledgements

We would especially like to thank and acknowledge Bill Kirkwood, who was part of this. Todd Schakerl kindly provided detailed information about the TechConnect System. We would also like to thank Dick Chase, Ann Majchrzak, the reviewers, associate editor, SIM Paper Competition committee, and especially the Editor-in-Chief Bob Zmud for their helpful feedback and suggestions.

References

Bennis, W. and Mische, M. 'Reinventing through Reengineering: A Methodology for Enterprisewide Transformation,' *Information Systems Management* (13:3), Summer 1996, 58–65.

Chabrow, E. 'First Aid for Slipped Disks: RAID Vendor Storage Dimensions Builds the Virtual Help Desk,' *Information Week*, June 12, 1995, 54–56.

Chase, R. B. and Garvin, D. 'The Service Factory,' *Harvard Business Review*, July-August 1989, 61–69.

Child, J. 'Information Technology, Organizations, and the Response to Strategic Challenges,' *California Managment Review* (30:1), 33–50.

Davenport, T. *Process Innovation: Reengineering Work Through Information Technology*, Harvard Business School Press, Boston, 1993.

Davenport, T., Jarvenpaa, S., and Beers, M. 'Improving Knowledge Work Processes,' *Sloan Management Review*, Summer 1996, 53–65.

El Sawy, O. A. *Minding Your Own Business Processes: The BPR LearningBook*, McGraw-Hill, New York, forthcoming 1998.

Entex White Paper. 'Vendor Relationships: Trends, Options, Issues,' Entex Information Services, New York, 1994.

Evans, B. 'Numbering Success,' *Information Week*, 12 February 1996, 6.

Haeckel, S. 'Managing the Information-Intensive Firm of 2001,' in *The Marketing Information Revolution*, R. C. Blattberg, R. Glazer, and J. D. C. Little (eds.), Harvard Business School Press, Boston, 1994.

Henkoff, R. 'Service is Everybody's Business,' *Fortune* (132:26), 27 June 1994, 48–60.

Kalakota, R. and Whinston, A. *Frontiers of Electronic Commerce*, Addison-Wesley, Reading, MA, 1996.

Kirkbride, L. and Deppe, S. M. 'Evaluating Problem Resolution Technologies for the Help Desk,' White Paper, Answer Systems Inc, 1995.

Lele, M. and Sheth, J. *The Customer is Key*, Wiley Books, New York, 1987.

March, J. 'Exploration and Exploitation in Organizational Learning,' *Organization Science* (2:1), March 1991, 71–87.

Muller, N. J. 'Expanding the Help Desk Through the World Wide Web,' *Information Systems Management* (13:3), Summer 1996, 37–44.

Nonaka, I. and Takeuchi, H. *The Knowledge Creating Company*, Oxford University Press, New York, 1995.

Pine, III, J., Peppers, D. and Rogers, M. 'Do You Want to Keep Your Customers Forever? *Harvard Business Review* (73:2), March-April, 1995, 103–114.

Pitt, L., Watson, R. and Kavan, B. 'Service Quality: A Measure of Information Systems Effectiveness,' *MIS Quarterly* (19:2), June 1995, 173–187.

Quinn, J. B. *Intelligent Enterprise: A Knowledge and Service-Based Paradigm for Industry*, Free Press, New York, 1992.

Rathnam, S., Mahajan, V. and Whinston, A. 'Facilitating Coordination in Customer Support Teams: A Framework and its Implications for the Design of Information Technology,' *Management Science* (41:12), December 1995, 1900–1921.

Sampler, J. and Short, J. 'An Examination of Information Technology's Impact on the Value of Information and Expertise: Implications for Organizational Change,' *Journal of Management Information Systems* (11:2), Fall 1994, 59–73.

Savage, C. *5th Generation Management: Co-Creating Through Virtual Enterprising, Dynamic Teaming, and Knowledge Networking*, 2nd edn., Butterworth-Heinemann, Stoneham, MA, 1996.

Savoia, R. 'Custom Tailoring,' *CIO* (9:17), June 15, 1996, 12.

Shostack, L. 'Breaking Free from Product Marketing,' *Journal of Marketing* (41:4), April 1977, 73–80.

Stewart, T. 'Your Company's Most Valuable Asset: Intellectual Capital,' *Fortune* (133:7), October 3, 1994, 68–75.

Treacy, M. and Wiersema, F. *The Discipline of Market Leaders*, Addison-Wesley, Reading, MA, 1995.

Questions for discussion

1 Reconsider Question 6 at the end of Chapter 18 in the light of the Storage Dimensions case discussed in this chapter. How might the lessons to be drawn from the TechnConnect system be applied more generally?
2 Evaluate TechnConnect in the light of (i) Chapters 9 and 14, and (ii) Chapter 18. What recommendations would you make to Storage Dimensions as a result?
3 This chapter raises the important issue of improving customer support. What lessons do you take from this when considering information systems strategy and planning?
4 Relate the conclusions to be drawn from this chapter to those made by Porter in Chapter 13.
5 'Knowledge capture is one thing; knowledge creation is quite another.' Discuss this statement in the light of the Storage Dimensions case.

20 Information Technology and Organizational Performance

Beyond the IT productivity paradox

L. P. Willcocks and S. Lester

Despite the massive investments in Information Technology in the developed economies, the IT impact on productivity and business performance continues to be questioned. This chapter critically reviews this IT productivity paradox debate and finds that an important part, but by no means all, of the uncertainty about the IT payoff relates to weaknesses in measurement and evaluation practice. Based on extensive research by the authors and others, an integrated systems lifecycle approach is put forward as a long term way of improving evaluation practice in work organizations. The approach shows how to link business and IT/IS strategies with prioritizing investments in IT, and by setting up a set of interlinking measures, how IT costs and benefits may be evaluated and managed across the systems lifecycle, including consideration of potential uses of the external IT services market. An emphasis on a cultural change in evaluation from 'control through numbers' to a focus on quality improvement offers one of the better routes out of the productivity paradox. Improved evaluation practice serves to demystify the paradox, but also links with and helps to stimulate improved planning for management and use of IT, thus also reducing the paradox in practical terms – through the creation of greater business value.

Introduction

The history of numerous failed and disappointing Information Technology (IT) investments in work organizations has been richly documented. (Here IT refers to the convergence of computers, telecommunications and electronics, and the resulting technologies and techniques.) The 1993 abandonment of a five year project like Taurus in the UK London financial markets, in this case at a cost of £80 million to the Stock Exchange, and possibly £400 million to City institutions, provides only high profile endorsement of underlying disquiet on the issue. Earlier survey and case research by the present authors established IT investment as a high risk, hidden cost business, with a variety of factors, including size and complexity of the project, the 'newness' of the technology, the degree of 'structuredness' in the project, and major human, political and cultural factors compounding the risks (Willcocks and Griffiths, 1994; Willcocks and Lester, 1996). Alongside, indeed we would argue contributing to the performance issues surrounding IT, is accumulated evidence of problems in evaluation together with a history of general indifferent organizational practice in the area (Farbey *et al.*, 1992; Strassman, 1990). In this chapter we focus firstly on the relationship between IT performance and its evaluation as it is expressed in the debate around what has been called the 'IT productivity paradox'. A key finding is that assessment issues are not straightforward, and that some, though by no means all, of the confusion over IT performance can be removed if limitations in evaluation practice and measurement become better understood. From this base we then provide an overall conceptualization, with some detail, about how evaluation practice itself can be advanced, thus allowing some loosening of the Gordian knot represented by the IT productivity paradox.

'What gets measured gets managed' – the way forward?

The evaluation and management of IT investments is shot through with difficulties. Increasingly, as IT expenditure has risen and as the use of IT has penetrated to the core of organizations, the search has been directed towards not just improving evaluation techniques and processes, and searching for new ones, but also towards the management and 'flushing out' of benefits. But these evaluation and management efforts regularly run into difficulties of three generic types. First, many organizations find themselves in a Catch 22 situation. For competitive reasons they cannot afford not to invest in IT, but economically they cannot find sufficient justification, and evaluation practice cannot provide enough underpinning, for making the investment. Second, for many of the more advanced and intensive users of IT, as the IT infrastructure becomes an inextricable part of the organization's processes and structures, it becomes increasingly difficult to separate out the impact of IT from that of other assets and activities. Third, despite the high levels of expenditure, there is widespread lack of understanding of IT and Information Systems (IS – organizational applications, increasingly IT-based, that deliver on the information needs of the organization's stakeholders) as major capital assets.

While senior managers regularly give detailed attention to the annual expenditure on IT/IS, there is little awareness of the size of the capital asset that has been bought over the years (Keen, 1991; Willcocks, 1994). Failure to appreciate the size of this investment leads to IT/IS being under-managed, a lack of serious attention being given to IS evaluation and control, and also a lack of concern for discovering ways of utilizing this IS asset base to its full potential.

Solutions to these difficulties have most often been sought through variants on the mantra: 'what gets measured gets managed'. As a dominant guiding principle more – and more accurate – measurement has been advanced as the panacea to evaluation difficulties. In a large body of literature, while some consideration is given to the difficulties inherent in quantifying IT impacts, a range of other difficulties are downplayed, or even ignored. These include, for example:

- the fact that measurement systems are prone to decay
- the goal displacement effects of measurement
- the downside that only that which is measured gets managed
- the behavioural implications of measurement and related reward systems, and
- the politics inherent in any organizational evaluation activity.

In practice, counter evidence against a narrow focus on quantification for IT/IS evaluation has been gathering. Thus some recent studies point to how measurement can be improved, but also to the limitations of measurement, and areas where sets of measures may be needed because of the lack of a single reliable measure (Farbey *et al.*, 1995). They also point to the key role of stakeholder judgement throughout any IT/IS evaluation process. Furthermore some published research studies point to the political-rational as opposed to the straightforwardly rational aspects of IT measurement in organizations. For example Lacity and Hirschheim (1996) provide an important insight into how measurement, in this case benchmarking IT performance against external comparators, can be used in political ways to influence senior management judgement. Currie (1989) detailed the political uses of measurement in a paper entitled 'The art of justifying new technology to top management'. Additionally, there are signs that the problems with over-focusing on measurement are being recognized, albeit slowly, with moves toward emphasizing the demonstration of the value of IS/IT, not merely its measurement. Elsewhere we have argued for the need to move measurement itself from a focus on the price of IT to a concern for its value; and for a concomitant shift in emphasis in the measurement regime from control to quality improvement (Willcocks and Lester, 1996).

These difficulties and limitations in evaluation practice have become bound up in a widespread debate about what has been called the IT productivity paradox – the notion that despite large investments in IT over many years, it has been difficult to discover where the IT payoffs have occurred, if indeed there have been many. In this chapter we will address critically the overall sense that many have that despite huge investments in IS/IT so far, these have been producing disappointing returns. We will find that while much of the sense of disappointment may be justified, at the same time it is fed by limitations in evaluation techniques and processes, and by misunderstandings of the contribution IT can and does make to organizations, as much as by actual experience of poorly performing information systems. The focus then moves to how organizations may seek to improve their IT/IS evaluation procedures and processes. Taking into account the many limitations in evaluation practice continuing to be identified by a range of the more recent research studies, a high level framework is advanced for how evaluation can and needs to be applied across the systems lifecycle. The chapter also suggests that processes of evaluation, and the involvement of stakeholders, may be as, if not more, important than refining techniques and producing measurement of a greater, but possibly no less spurious, accuracy.

The IT 'productivity paradox' revisited

Alongside the seemingly inexorable rise of IS/IT investment in the last 15 years, there has been considerable uncertainty and concern about the productivity impact of IT being experienced in work organizations. This has been reinforced by several high profile studies at the levels of both the national economy and industrial sector suggesting in fact that if there has been an IS/IT payoff it has been minimal, and hardly justifies the vast financial outlays incurred. Two early influential studies embodying this theme were by Roach (1986) and Loveman (1988). A key, overarching point needs to be made immediately. It is clear from reviews of the many research studies conducted at national, sectoral and organization specific levels that the failure to identify IS/IT benefits and productivity says as much about the deficiencies in assessment methods and measurement, and the rigour with which they are applied, as about mismanagement of the development and use of information-based technologies. It is useful to chase this hare of 'the IT productivity paradox' further, because the issue goes to the heart of the subject of this chapter.

Interestingly, the IT productivity paradox is rarely related in the literature to manufacturing sectors for which, in fact, there are a number of studies from the early 1980s showing rising IT expenditure correlating with sectoral and firm-specific productivity rises (see Brynjolfsson and Hitt, 1993; Loveman, 1988). The high profile studies raising concern also tend to base their work mainly on statistics gathered in the US context. Their major focus, in fact, tends to be limited to the service sector in the US. Recently a number of studies question the data on which such studies were based, suggesting that the data is sufficiently flawed to make simple conclusions misleading (Brynjolfsson, 1993). It has been pointed out, for example that in the cases of Loveman (1988) and Roach (1986) neither personally collected the data that they analysed, thus their observations describe numbers rather than actual business experiences (Nievelt, 1992).

Still others argue that the productivity payoff may have been delayed but, by the mid-1990s, recession and global competition have forced companies to finally use the technologies they put in place over the last decade, with corresponding productivity leaps. Moreover, productivity figures always failed to measure the cost avoidance and savings on opportunity costs that IS/IT can help to achieve (Gillin, 1994).

Others also argue that the real payoffs occur when IS/IT development and use is linked with the business reengineering (BPR) efforts coming onstream in the 1990s (Hammer and Champy, 1993). However, recent UK evidence develops this debate by finding that few organizations were actually getting 'breakthrough' results through IT-enabled BPR. Organizations were 'aiming low and hitting low' and generally not going for the radical, high-risk reengineering approaches advocated by many commentators. Moreover there was no strong correlation between size of IT expenditure on reengineering projects, and resulting productivity impacts. In business process reengineering, as elsewhere (see below), it is the management of IT, and what it is used for, rather than the size of IT spend that counts (Willcocks, 1996b).

Bakos and Jager (1995) provide interesting further insight, as they argue that computers are not boosting productivity, but the fault lies not with the technology but with its management and how computer use is overseen. They question the reliability of the productivity studies, and, supporting the positive IT productivity findings in the study by Brynjolfsson and Hitt (1993), posit a new productivity paradox: 'how can computers be so productive?'

In the face of such disputation Brynjolfsson (1993) makes salutary reading. He suggests four explanations for the seeming IT productivity paradox. The first is measurement errors. In practice the measurement problems appear particularly acute in the service sector and with white collar worker productivity – the main areas investigated by those pointing to a minimal productivity impact from IT use in the 1980s and early 1990s. Brynjolfsson concludes from a close examination of the data behind the studies of IT performance at national and sectoral levels that mismeasurement is at the core of the IT productivity paradox. A second explanation is timing lags due to learning and adjustment. Benefits from IT can take several years to show through in significant financial terms, a point also made by Strassman (1990) in arguing for newer ways of evaluating IS/IT performance at the organizational level. While Brynjolfsson largely discounts this explanation, there is evidence to suggest he is somewhat over-optimistic about the ability of managers to account rationally for such lags and include them in their IS/IT evaluation system (Willcocks, 1996a).

A third possible explanation is that of redistribution. IT may be beneficial to individual firms but unproductive from the standpoint of the industry, or the economy, as a whole. IT rearranges the share of the pie, with the bigger share going to those heavily investing in IT, without making the pie bigger. Brynjolfsson suggests, however, that the redistribution hypothesis would not explain any shortfall in IT productivity at the firm level. To add to his analysis one can note that in several sectors, for example banking and financial services, firms seemingly compete by larger spending on IT-based systems that are, in practice, increasingly becoming minimum entry requirements for the sector, and commodities rather than differentiators of competitive performance. As a result in some sectors, for example the oil industry, organizations are increasingly seeking to reduce such IS/IT costs by accepting that some systems are industry standard and can be developed together.

A fourth explanation is that IS/IT is not really productive at the firm level. Brynjolfsson (1993) posits that despite the neoclassical view of the firm as a profit maximizer, it may well be that decision-makers are, for whatever reason, often not acting in the interests of the firm: 'instead they are increasing their slack, building inefficient systems, or simply using outdated criteria for decision-making' (p.75). The implication of Brynjolfsson's argument is that political interests and/or poor evaluation practice may contribute to failure to make real, observable gains from IS/IT investments. However, Brynjolfsson appears to discount these possibilities citing a lack of evidence either way, though here he seems to be restricting himself to the economics literature. Against his argument however, there are in fact frequent study findings showing patchy strategizing and implementation practice where IS is concerned (for an overview see Willcocks *et al.*, 1996). Furthermore, recent evidence in the IT evaluation literature suggests more evidence showing poor evaluation practice than Brynjolfsson has been willing to credit (see Ballantine *et al.*, 1996; Willcocks and Lester, 1996).

It is on this point that the real debate on the apparent 'IT productivity paradox' needs to hinge. Studies at the aggregate levels of the economy or industrial sector conceal important questions and data about variations in business experiences at the organizational and intra-organizational levels. In practice, organizations seem to vary greatly in their ability to harness IS/IT for organizational purpose. In an early study Cron and Sobol (1983) pointed to what has since been called the 'amplifier' effect of IT. Its use reinforces existing management approaches dividing firms into very high or very low performers. This analysis has been supported by later work by Strassman (1990), who also found no correlation between size of IT expenditure and firms' return on investment. Subsequently, a 1994 analysis of the information productivity of 782 US companies found that the top 10 spent a smaller percentage (1.3 per cent compared to 3 per cent for the bottom 100) of their revenue on IS, increased their IS budget more slowly (4.3 per cent in 1993–4 – the comparator was the bottom 110 averaging 10.2 per cent), thus leaving a greater amount of finance available for non-IS spending (Gillin, 1994).

Not only did the the top performers seem to spend less proportionately on their IT; they also tended to keep certain new investments as high as business conditions permitted while holding back on infrastructure growth. Thus, on average, hardware investments were only 15 per cent of the IS budget while new development took more than 50 per cent, with 41 per cent of systems development spending incurred on client/server investment (Sullivan-Trainor, 1994). Clearly the implication of this analysis is that top performers spend relatively less money on IS/IT, but focus their spending on areas where the expenditure will make more difference in terms of business value. An important aspect of their ability to do this must lie with their evaluation techniques and processes. Nievelt (1992) adds to this picture. Analysing database information on over 300 organizations he found empirically that IT as a coordinating, communicating and leveraging technology was capable of enhancing customer satisfaction, flattening organizational pyramids and supporting knowledge workers in the management arena. At the same time many organizations did not direct their IT expenditure into appropriate areas at the right time, partly because of inability to carry out evaluation of where they were with their IT expenditure and IT performance relative to business needs in a particular competitive and market context.

Following on from this, it is clear that significant aspects of the IT productivity paradox, as perceived and experienced at organizational level, can be addressed through developments in evaluation and management practice. In particular the distorting effects of poor evaluation methods and processes need close examination and profiling; alternative methods, and an assessment of their appropriateness for specific purposes and conditions need to be advanced; and how these methods can be integrated together and into management practice needs to be addressed.

Investing in information systems

In the rest of this chapter we will focus not on assessing IT/IS performance at national or industry levels, but on the conduct of IT/IS evaluation within work organizations. As already suggested, IT/IS expenditure in such organizations is high and rising. The United States leads the way, with government statistics suggesting that, by 1994, computers and other information technology made up nearly half of all business spending on equipment – not including the billions spent on software and programmers each year. Globally, computer and telecommunications investments now amount to a half or more of most large firms' annual capital expenditures. In an advanced industrialized economy like the United Kingdom, IS/IT expenditure by business and public sector organizations was estimated at £33.6 billion for 1995, and expected to rise at 8.2 per cent, 7 per cent and 6.5 per cent in subsequent years, representing an average of over 2 per cent of turnover, or in local and central government an average IT spend of £3546 per employee. Organizational IS/IT expenditure in developing economies is noticeably lower, nevertheless those economies may well leapfrog several stages of technology, with China, Russia, India and Brazil, for example, set to invest in telecommunications an estimated 53.3, 23.3, 13.7, and 10.2 billion dollars (US) respectively in the 1993–2000 period (Engardio, 1994).

There were many indications by 1995, of managerial concern to slow the growth in organizational IS/IT expenditure. Estimates of future expenditure based on respondent surveys in several countries tended to indicate this pattern (see for example Price Waterhouse, 1995). The emphasis seemed to fall on running the organization leaner, wringing more productivity out of IS/IT use, attempting to reap the benefits from changes in price/performance ratios, while at the same time recognizing the seemingly inexorable rise in information and IT intensity implied by the need to remain operational and competitive. In particular, there is wide recognition of the additional challenge of bringing new technologies into productive use. The main areas being targeted for new corporate investment seemed to be client/server computing, document image processing and groupware, together with 'here-and-now' technologies such as advanced telecom services available from 'intelligent networks', mobile voice and digital cellular systems (Taylor, 1995). It is in the context of these many concerns and technical developments that evaluation techniques and processes need to be positioned.

Evaluation: a systems lifecycle approach

At the heart of one way forward for organizations is the notion of an IT/IS evaluation and management cycle. A simplified diagrammatic representation of this is provided in Figure 20.1. Earlier research found that few organizations actually operated evaluation and management practice in an integrated manner across systems lifecycles (Willcocks, 1996a). The evaluation cycle attempts to bring together a rich and diverse set of ideas, methods, and practices that are to be found in the evaluation literature to date, and point them in the direction of an integrated approach across systems lifetime. Such an approach would consist of several interrelated activities:

1 Identifying net benefits through strategic alignment and prioritization.
2 Identifying types of generic benefit, and matching these to assessment techniques.
3 Developing a family of measures based on financial, service, delivery, learning and technical criteria.

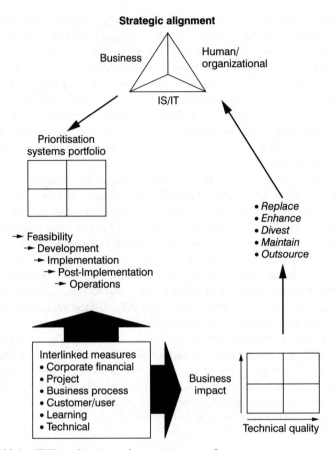

Figure 20.1 *IT/IS evaluation and management cycle*

4   Linking these measures to particular measures needed for development, implementation and post-implementation phases.

5   Ensuring each set of measures run from the strategic to the operational level.

6   Establishing responsibility for tracking these measures, and regularly reviewing results.

7   Regularly reviewing the existing portfolio, and relating this to business direction and performance objectives.

A key element in making the evaluation cycle dynamic and effective is the involvement of motivated, salient stakeholders in processes that operationalize – breathe life into, adapt over time, and act upon – the evaluation criteria and techniques. Let us look in more detail at the rationale for, and shape of such an approach. In an earlier review of front-end evaluation Willcocks (1994) pointed out how lack of *alignment* between business, information systems and human resource/organizational strategies inevitably compromised the value of all subsequent IS/IT evaluation effort, to the point of rendering it of marginal utility and, in some cases, even counter-productive. In this respect he reflected the concerns of many authors on the subject. A range of already available techniques were pointed to for establishing strategic alignment, and linking strategy with assessing the feasibility of any IS/IT investment, and these will not be repeated here (for a review see Willcocks, 1994). At the same time the importance of recognizing evaluation as a process imbued with inherent political character-istics and ramifications was emphasized, reflecting a common finding amongst empirical studies.

The notion of a systems portfolio implies that IT/IS investment can have a variety of objectives. The practical problem becomes one of *prioritization* – of resource allocation amongst the many objectives and projects that are put forward. Several classificatory schemes for achieving this appear in the extant literature. Thus Willcocks (1994) and others have suggested classifi-catory schemes that match business objectives with types of IS/IT project. Thus, on one schema, projects could be divided into six types – efficiency, effectiveness, must-do, architecture, competitive edge, and research and development. The type of project could then be matched to one of the more appropriate evaluation methods available, a critical factor being the degree of tangibility of the costs and benefits being assessed. Costs and benefits need to be sub-classified into 'for example' hard/soft, or tangible/intangible, or direct/ indirect/inferred, and the more appropriate assessment techniques for each type adopted (see Willcocks, 1994 for a detailed discussion). Norris (1996) has provided a useful categorization of types of investments and main aids to evaluation, and a summary is shown in Table 20.1.

After alignment and prioritization assessment, the *feasibility* of each IS/IT investment then needs to be examined. All the research studies show that the main weakness here have been the over-reliance on and/or misuse of traditional, finance-based cost-benefit analysis. The contingency approach outlined above and in Table 20.1 helps to deal with this, but such approaches need to be allied with active involvement of a wider group of stakeholders than those at the moment being identified in the research studies. A fundamental factor to remember at this stage is the importance of a business case being made for an IT/IS investment, rather than any strict following of specific sets of measures. As a matter of experience where detailed measurement has to be carried out to differentiate between specific proposals, it may well be that there is little advantage to be had not just between each, but from any. Measurement contributes to the business case for or against a specific investment but cannot substitute for a more

Table 20.1 *Types of investment and aids to evaluating IT*

Type of investment	*Business benefit*	*Main formal aids to investment evaluation*	*Importance of management judgement*	*Main aspects of management judgement*
Mandatory investments as a result of:				
Regulatory requirements	Satisfy minimum legal requirement	Analysis of costs	Low	Fitness of the system for the purpose
Organizational requirements	Facilitate business operations	Analysis of costs	Low	Fitness of the system for the purpose. Best option for variable organizational requirements
Competitive pressure	Keep up with the competition	Analysis of costs to achieve parity with the competition. Marginal cost to differentiate from the competition, providing the opportunity for competitive advantage	Crucial	Competitive need to introduce the system at all. Effect of introducing the system into the marketplace. Commercial risk. Ability to sustain competitive advantage
Investments to improve performance	Reduce costs	Cost/benefit analysis	Medium	Validity of the assumptions behind the case
	Increase revenues	Cost/benefit analyses. Assessment of hard-to-quantify benefits. Pilots for high risk investment	High	Validity of the assumptions behind the case. Real value of hard-to-quantify benefits. Risk involved
Investments to achieve competitive advantage	Achieve a competitive leap	Analysis of costs and risks	Crucial	Competitive aim of the system. Impact on the market and the organization. Risk involved
Infrastructure investment	Enable the benefits of other applications to be realized	Setting of performance standards. Analysis of costs	Crucial	Corporate need and benefit, both short and long term
Investment in research	Be prepared for the future	Setting objectives within cost limits	High	Long-term corporate benefit. Amount of money to be allocated

Source: Norris (1996).

fundamental managerial assessment as to whether the investment is strategic and critical for the business, or will merely result in yet another useful IT application.

Following this, Figure 20.1 suggests that evaluation needs to be conducted in a linked manner across systems development and into systems implementation and operational use. The evaluation cycle posits the development of a series of *interlinked measures* that reflect various aspects of IS/IT performance, and that are applied across systems lifetime. These are tied to processes and people responsible for monitoring performance, improving the evaluation system and also helping to 'flush out' and manage the benefits from the investment. Figure 20.1 suggests, in line with prevailing academic and practitioner thinking by the mid-1990s, that evaluation cannot be based solely or even mainly on technical efficiency criteria. For other criteria there may be debate on how they are to be measured, and this will depend on the specific organizational circumstances.

However there is no shortage of suggestions here. Taking one of the more difficult, Keen (1991) discusses measuring the cost avoidance impacts of IT/IS. For him these are best tracked in terms of business volumes increases compared to number of employees. The assumption here is that IT/IS can increase business volumes without increases in personnel. At the strategy level he also suggests that the most meaningful way of tracking IT/IS performance over time is in terms of business performance per employee, for example revenue per employee, profit per employee, or at a lower level, as one example – transactions per employee.

Kaplan and Norton (1992) were highly useful for popularizing the need for a number of perspectives on evaluation of business performance. Willcocks (1994) showed how the Kaplan and Norton balanced scorecard approach could be adapted fairly easily for the case of assessing IT/IS investments. To add to that picture, most recent research suggests the need for six sets of measures. These would cover the *corporate financial perspective* (e.g. profit per employee); the *systems project* (e.g. time, quality, cost); *business process* (e.g. purchase invoices per employee); the *customer/user* perspective (e.g. on-time delivery rate); an *innovation/learning* perspective (e.g. rate of cost reduction for IT services); and a *technical* perspective (e.g. development efficiency, capacity utilization). Each set of measures would run from strategic to operational levels, each measure being broken down into increasing detail as it is applied to actual organizational performance. For each set of measures the business objectives for IT/IS would be set. Each objective would then be broken down into more detailed measurable components, with a financial value assigned where practicable. An illustration of such a hierarchy, based on work by Norris (1996), is shown in Figure 20.2.

Responsibility for tracking these measures, together with regular reviews

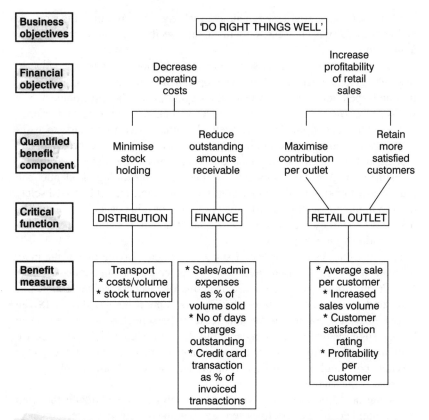

Figure 20.2 *Measurable components of business objectives for IT/IS. (Adapted from Norris, 1996)*

that relate performance to objectives and targets are highly important elements in delivering benefits from the various IS investments. It should be noted that such measures are seen as helping to inform stakeholder judgements, and not as a substitute for such judgements in the evaluation process.

Some detail can be provided on how to put metrics in place, monitor them and ensure benefits are delivered. The following schema is derived from work by Peters (1996) and Willcocks and Lester (1996). Projects were found to be managed well, and often over-performed their original appraisal, where a steering group was set up early in a project, was managed by a senior user manager, and represented the key operating functions impacted by the IT/IS. The steering group followed the project to a late stage of implementation with members frequently taking responsibility for delivering benefits from parts of

Benefits manager ＼ ＼ Performance variables	Sales manager	Purchasing manager	Accts payable supervisor	Warehouse manager	Production scheduler	Production supervisor
Orders/man day	E					
No. of suppliers		E				
Invoices/man day			E			
Finished inventory	S			E	S	
Stock out occurrence	S				E	
Slow movers leadtime	S					E

Figure 20.3 *Assigning responsibility for delivering benefits of IT/IS implementation (E = executive responsibility; S = support). (Based on Peters, 1996)*

the IT/IS implementation. Project benefits need to be incorporated into business area budgets, and individuals identified for monitoring performance and delivering benefits. Variables impacted by the IT/IS investment were identified and decomposed into a hierarchy based on key operating parameters necessary to deliver the benefit. A framework needs to be established for clearly identifying responsibilities for benefits (Figure 20.3). Peters (1996) suggests that the information on responsibilities should be published, and known to relevant parties, and that measures should be developed to monitor benefits at the lowest level of unit performance. We would add that links also need to be made between the individual's performance in the assessment role and his/her own appraisal and reward.

The steering group should regularly review the benefits gained, for example every three months, and also report less frequently to the IT/IS strategy steering group, with flushing out of IT/IS benefits seen as an essential extension of the strategic review process, not least in its capacity to facilitate more effective IT/IS implementation. What is clear in this scheme is that measurement that is business – not solely technical efficiency – focused plays an important part in evaluation but only in the context of appropriate processes in place operated by a wide range of motivated stakeholders.

Completing the cycle: existing and future investments

One all too often routinized phase of review is that of *post-implementation* (see Figure 20.1). Our own research suggests that this is one of the most neglected, yet one of the more important areas as far as IS evaluation is concerned. An advantage of the above schema, in practice, is that post-implementation evaluation arises naturally out of implementation assessment on an ongoing basis, with an already existing set of evaluators in place. This avoids the ritualistic, separated review that usually takes place in the name of post-implementation review (Kumar, 1990 – detailed discussion on how to perform an effective post-implementation review cannot be provided here, but see Norris, 1996).

There remains the matter of assessing the ongoing systems portfolio on a regular basis. Notoriously, when it comes to evaluating the existing IS investment, organizations are not good at drop decisions. There may be several related ramifications. The IT inheritance of 'legacy systems' can deter investment in new systems – it can, for example, be all too difficult to take on new work when IT/IS staff are awash in a rising tide of maintenance arising from the existing investment. Existing IT/IS-related activity can also devour the majority of the financial resources available for IS investment. All too often such failures derive from not having in place, or not operationalizing, a robust assessment approach that enables timely decisions on systems and service divestment, outsourcing, replacement, enhancement, and/or maintenance. Such decisions need to be based on at least two criteria – the technical quality of the system/service, and its business contribution – as well as being related back to the overall strategic direction and objectives of the organization (see Figure 20.1).

A further element in assessment of the ongoing systems portfolio is the relevance of external comparators. External benchmarking firms – for example RDC and Compass – have already been operating for several years, and offer a range of services that can be drawn upon, but mainly for technical aspects of IT performance. The assessment of data centre performance is now well established amongst the better benchmarking firms. Depending on the benchmarking database available, a data centre can be assessed against other firms in the same sector, or of the same generic size in computing terms, and also against outsourcing vendor performance. Benchmarking firms are continually attempting to extend their services, and can provide a useful assessment, if mainly only on the technical efficiency of existing systems. There is, however, a growing demand for extending external benchmarking services more widely to include business, and other, performance measures – many of which could include elements of IT contribution (see above). Indeed Strassman (1990) and Nievelt (1992) are but two of the more well known of a growing number of providers of diagnostic benchmarking methodologies that help to locate and reposition IT contribution relative to actual and required business performance. It is worth remarking that external IT benchmarking – like all measures – can serve a range of purposes within an organization. Lacity and Hirschheim (1996) detail from their research how benchmarking services were used to demonstrate to senior executives the usefulness of the IT department. In some cases external benchmarking subsequently led to the rejection of outsourcing proposals from external vendors.

This leads into the final point. An increasingly important part of assessing the existing and any future IT/IS investment is the degree to which the external IT services market can provide better business technical and economic options for an organization. In practice, recent survey and case research by the authors and others found few organizations taking a strategic approach to IT/IS sourcing decisions, though many derived economic and other benefits from incremental, selective, low risk, as opposed to high risk 'total' approaches to outsourcing (Lacity and Hirscheim, 1995). The Yankee Group estimated the 1994 global IT outsourcing market as exceeding $US49.5 billion with an annual 15 per cent growth rate. As at 1995 the US market was the biggest, estimated to exceed $18.2 billion. The UK remained the largest European market in 1994 exceeding £1 billion, with an annual growth rate exceeding 10 per cent on average across sectors. Over 50 per cent of UK organizations outsourced some aspect of IT in 1994, and outsourcing represented on average 24 per cent of their IT budgets (Lacity and Hirscheim, 1995; Willcocks and Fitzgerald, 1994).

Given these figures, it is clear that evaluation of IT/IS sourcing options, together with assessment of on-going vendor performance in any outsourced part of the IT/IS service, needs to be integrally imbedded into the systems lifecycle approach detailed above. Not least because an external vendor bid, if carefully analysed against one's own detailed in-house assessment of IT performance, can be a highly informative form of benchmarking. Figure 20.1 gives an indication of where sourcing assessments fit within the lifecycle approach, but recent research can give more detail on the criteria that govern successful and less successful sourcing decisions.

In case and survey research Willcocks and Fitzgerald (1994) found six key factors (see Figure 20.4). Three are essentially business related. Firstly, IT can contribute to *differentiating* a business from its competitors, thus providing competitive advantage. Alternatively an IT activity/service may be a commodity, not distinguishing the business from a competitor in business offering and performance terms.

Second, the IT may be *strategic* in underpinning the firm's achievement of goals, and critical to its present and future strategic direction, or merely useful. Third, the *degree of uncertainty about future business environment and needs* impacts upon longer term IT needs. High uncertainty suggests inhouse sourcing

	Tend to outsource		Tend not to outsource
Business:			
Are future business needs:	Certain	◄──────────►	Uncertain
Is the potential contribution of this IT service/activity to business positioning a:	Commodity	◄──────────►	Differentiator
Is the impact of this IT service/activity on the business strategy:	Useful	◄──────────►	Vital
Is the in-house cost for this IT service/activity compared to the market-place:	High	◄──────────►	Low
Technical			
Is this IT service/activity:	Discrete	◄──────────►	Integrated
Is the technological maturity:	High	◄──────────►	Low
Is the IT capability in-house compared to the market-place:	Low	◄──────────►	High

Figure 20.4   *Criteria for making sourcing decisions*

as a better option. As Figure 20.4 suggests the preferred option where possible, is to outsource useful commodities in conditions of certainty about business requirements across the length of the contract. Three technical considerations are also important. It is unwise for an organization to outsource in a situation of low *technology maturity*. This exists where a technology is new and unstable, and/or where there is an existing technology but being applied in a radically new way, and/or where there is little relevant in-house experience with the technology. Next, *the level of IT integration* must influence the sourcing decision. Generally we found it preferable not to outsource systems/activities that are highly integrated with other parts of the technical platform, and/or that interface in complex ways with many business users who will be impacted significantly by the service. Finally, *where inhouse capability is equivalent to or better than that available on the external market, there* would seem to be a less pressing need to outsource the IT service/activity.

Making sourcing decisions, in practice, involves making trade-offs among the preferences suggested by these factors. In addition, we note six reality checks that need to be borne in mind before deciding on a specific sourcing option:

- Does the decision make economic sense?
- How does the decision fit with the rate of technological change?

- Are there issues around ownership when transferring people and assets?
- Is a suitable vendor available?
- Does the organization have the management capability to deliver on the decision?

Will significant human resource issues arise – during the change process, and subsequently for in-house and vendor staff ?

Outsourcing is defined as the commissioning of third party management of IT assets/activities to required result. This does not exclude another way of using the market, of course, namely 'insourcing' – where external resources are utilized in an organization under in-house management. There is also an option to have long or short term contracts with suppliers. In situations of high business uncertainty and/or rapid technological change shorter term contract are to be preferred. We also found, together with Lacity and Hirschheim (1995), that selective rather than total outsourcing (80 per cent or more of IT budget spent on outsourcing), tended to be the lower risk, and more successful option to take.

In more detailed work, we found outsourcing requiring a considerable cultural change on evaluation. Before outsourcing any IT, the more successful organizations measured everything in a three to six month baseline period. This enabled them to compare more accurately the in-house performance against a vendor bid. It also prefigured the setting up of a tighter evaluation regime with more detailed and accurate performance measures and service level agreements. In cases where an in-house vendor bid won, we found that the threat of the vendor bid actually galvanized the in-house staff into identifying new ways of improving on IS/IT perform-ance, and into maintaining the improvement through putting in place, and acting on the output from, enhanced evaluation criteria and measures. This brings us full circle. Even where an organization does not outsource IT, our case evidence is that increasingly it is good practice to assess in-house performance against what a potential vendor bid might be, even if, as is increasingly the case, this means paying a vendor for the assessment. By the same token, benchmarking IT/IS performance against external comparators can also be highly useful, in providing insight not only into in-house IT/IS performance, but also into the efficacy of internal evaluation criteria, processes and the availability or otherwise of detailed, appropriate assess-ment information.

Conclusion

There are several ways out of the IT productivity paradox. Several of the more critical relate to improved ways of planning for, managing and using IT/IS. However, part of the IT productivity paradox has been configured out of difficulties and limitations in measuring and accounting for IT/IS performance. Bringing the so-called paradox into the more manageable and assessable organizational realm, it is clear that there is still, as at 1996, much indifferent IT/IS evaluation practice to be found in work organizations. In detailing an integrated lifecycle approach to IT/IS evaluation we have utilized the research findings of ourselves and others to suggest one way forward. The 'cradle to grave' framework is holistic and dynamic and relies on a judicious mixture of 'the business case', appropriate criteria and metrics, managerial and stakeholder judgement and processes, together with motivated evaluators. Above all it signals a move from 'control through numbers' assessment culture to one focused on quality improvement. This would seem to offer one of the better routes out of the productivity paradox, not least in its ability to link up evaluation to improving approaches to planning for, managing and using IT. As such it may also serve to begin to demystify the 'IT productivity paradox', and reveal that it is as much about human as technology issues – and better cast anyway as the IT-management productivity paradox, perhaps?

References

Bakos, Y. and Jager, P. de (1995) Are computers boosting productivity? *Computerworld*, 27 March, 128–130.

Ballantine, J., Galliers, R. D. and Stray, S. J. (1996) Information systems/ technology evaluation practices: evidence from UK organizations. *Journal of Information Technology* , **11**(2), 129–141.

Brynjolfsson, E. (1993) The productivity paradox of information technology. *Communications of the ACM*, **36**(12), 67–77.

Brynjolfsson, E. and Hitt, L. (1993) Is information systems spending productive? *Proceedings of the International Conference in Information Systems*, Orlando, December.

Cron, W. and Sobol, M. (1983) The relationship between computerization and performance: a strategy for maximizing the economic benefits of computerization. *Journal of Information Management*, **6**, 171–181.

Currie, W. (1989) The art of justifying new technology to top management. *Omega*, **17**(5), 409–418.

Engardio, P. (1994) Third World leapfrog. *Business Week*, 13 June, 46–47.

Farbey, B., Land, F. and Targett, D. (1992) Evaluating investments in IT. *Journal of Information Technology*, **7**(2), 100–112.

Farbey, B., Targett, D. and Land, F. (eds) (1995) *Hard Money, Soft Outcomes*, Alfred Waller/Unicom, Henley, UK.

Gillin, P. (ed.) (1994) The productivity payoff: the 100 most effective users of information technology. *Computerworld*, 19 September, 4–55.

Hammer, M. and Champy, J. (1993) *Reengineering The Corporation: A Manifesto For Business Revolution*, Nicholas Brealey, London.

Kaplan, R. and Norton, D. (1992) The balanced scorecard: measures that drive performance. *Harvard Business Review*, January–February, 71–79.

Keen, P. (1991) *Shaping the Future: Business Design Through Information Technology*, Harvard Business Press, Boston.

Kumar, K. (1990). Post-implementation evaluation of computer-based information systems: current practices. *Communications of the ACM*, **33**(2), 203–212.

Lacity, M. and Hirschheim, R. (1995) *Beyond the Information Systems Outsourcing Bandwagon*, Wiley, Chichester.

Lacity, M. and Hirschheim, R. (1996) The role of benchmarking in demonstrating IS performance. In *Investing in Information Systems: Evaluation and Management* (ed. L. Willcocks), Chapman and Hall, London.

Lacity, M. Willcocks, L. and Feeny, D. (1995) IT outsourcing: maximize flexibility and control. *Harvard Business Review*, May–June, 84–93.

Loveman, G. (1988) An assessment of the productivity impact of information technologies. MIT management in the nineties. *Working Paper 88–054.* Massachussetts Institute of Technology, Cambridge.

Nievelt, M. van (1992) Managing with information technology – a decade of wasted money? *Compact*, Summer, 15–24.

Norris, G. (1996) Post-investment appraisal. In *Investing in Information Systems: Evaluation and Management* (ed. L. Willcocks), Chapman and Hall, London.

Peters, G. (1996) From strategy to implementation: identifying and managing benefits of IT investments. In *Investing in Information Systems: Evaluation and Management* (ed. L. Willcocks), Chapman and Hall, London.

Price Waterhouse (1995) *Information Technology Review 1994/5*, Price Waterhouse, London.

Roach, S. (1986) *Macrorealities of the Information Economy*, National Academy of Sciences, New York.

Strassman, P. (1990) *The Business Value of Computers*, Information Economic Press, New Canaan, CT.

Sullivan-Trainor, M. (1994) Best of breed. In *The Productivity Payoff: The 100 Most Effective Users of Information Technology* (ed. P. Gillin), *Computerworld*, 19 September, 8–9.

Taylor, P. (1995) Business solutions on every side. Financial Times Review: *Information Technology*, 1 March, 1.

Willcocks, L. (ed.) (1994) *Information Management: Evaluation of Information Systems Investments*, Chapman and Hall, London.

Willcocks, L. (ed.) (1996a) *Investing in Information Systems: Evaluation and Management*, Chapman and Hall, London.

Willcocks, L. (1996b) Does IT-enabled BPR pay off? Recent findings on economics and impacts. In *Investing In Information Systems: Evaluation and Management*, Chapman and Hall, London.

Willcocks, L. and Fitzgerald, G. (1994) A business guide to IT outsourcing. *Business Intelligence*, London.
Willcocks, L. and Griffiths, C. (1994) Predicting risk of failure in large-scale information technology projects. *Technological Forecasting and Social Change*, **47**(2), 205–228.
Willcocks, L. and Lester, S. (1996) The evaluation and management of information systems investments: from feasibility to routine operations. In (1996). *Investing In Information Systems: Evaluation and Management* (ed. L. Willcocks), Chapman and Hall, London.
Willcocks, L., Currie, W. and Mason, D. (1996) *Information Systems at Work: People Politics and Technology*, McGraw-Hill, Maidenhead, UK.

Reproduced from Willcocks, L. and Lester, S. (1996) Beyond the IT productivity paradox. *European Management Journal*, **14**(3), June, 279–290. Reprinted by permission of Elsevier Science.

Questions for discussion

1 What is the IT productivity paradox? Does it actually exist in your view, and if so, to what extent is it sectorally based? Do you believe it will remain a problem in, say, 5 years' time?
2 Why is the evaluation and management of IT investment 'shot through with difficulties'? And what's wrong with the maxim 'what gets measured gets managed'?
3 Critically evaluate the IT/IS evaluation and management cycle introduced in this chapter. How might it be adapted so as to be integrated in an ongoing IS planning process?
4 Reflect on the question of the evolution and management of different types of IT investments mentioned in this chapter, and the 'stages of growth' concept introduced in Chapter 2. How might evaluation and management of IT evolve from one stage to another?
5 Managing benefits are highlighted as a critical success factor by the authors. Reflect on the differing roles an IT steering committee, individual executives and managers might take in dealing with stock-outs for example.
6 The authors introduce the issue of sourcing IT services. Why might outsourcing IT services require 'a considerable cultural change on evaluation'? Reflect on issues introduced in Chapter 16 when considering this question.

Author index

Subject index